Studies in Eighteenth-Century Culture

VOLUME 5

Studies in Eighteenth-Century Culture VOLUME 5

EDITED BY **Ronald C. Rosbottom**

Ohio State University

PUBLISHED for the

AMERICAN SOCIETY FOR EIGHTEENTH-CENTURY STUDIES

by THE UNIVERSITY OF WISCONSIN PRESS

Published 1976
The University of Wisconsin Press
Box 1379, Madison, Wisconsin 53701

The University of Wisconsin Press, Ltd.
70 Great Russell St., London

First printing

Printed in the United States of America

LC 74-25572
ISBN 0-299-06930-3

Editorial Committee for Volume Five

Contents

Preface   xi

RONALD C. ROSBOTTOM / Ohio State University

Probability and Improbability in Eighteenth-Century
Research (Presidential Address)   3

GEORGES MAY / Yale University

William Hogarth and London Theatrical Life   11

MARY F. KLINGER / California State University, Northridge

Francesco Guardi as an Apprentice in the Studio of
Giambattista Tiepolo   29

GEORGE KNOX / University of British Columbia

Hogarth and the Iconography of Time   41

SAMUEL L. MACEY / University of Victoria

Renovation of Form: Time as Hero in Blake's Major
Prophecies   55

MOLLYANNE MARKS / Oberlin College

Time, Sequence, and Plot in Restoration Literature   67

EARL MINER / Princeton University

Modes of Political and Historical Time in Early Eighteenth-
Century England   87

J. G. A. POCOCK / Washington University

Defoe's Women: Snares and Prey   103

PAULA BACKSCHEIDER / University of Rochester

Mary, Mary, Quite Contrary, Or, Mary Astell and Mary
Wollstonecraft Compared   121

REGINA JANES / University of Illinois, Chicago Circle

The Selling of Sex: Mandeville's Modest Defence of
Publick Stews   141
SAMUEL J. ROGAL / SUNY, College at Oswego
Condorcet, Feminism, and the Egalitarian Principle   151
DAVID WILLIAMS / McMaster University
Moratín's Circle of Friends: Intellectual Ferment in Spain,
1780–1800   165
JOHN DOWLING / University of Georgia
Concepts of the Grotesque before Goya   185
PAUL ILIE / University of Michigan
La Nouvelle Héloïse: La Répétition à la deuxième
puissance   203
GODELIEVE MERCKEN-SPAAS / Rutgers University
Justine, Or, The Vicious Circle   215
NANCY K. MILLER / Columbia University
Sensible Words: Linguistic Theory in Late Seventeenth-
Century England   229
MURRAY COHEN / University of California, Berkeley
Poetic Standards on the Early Augustan Battleground   253
HUGH ORMSBY-LENNON / University of Pennsylvania
Paris and Myth: One Vision of Horror   281
CATHERINE LAFARGE / Bryn Mawr College
A Slaughter of Innocents: Aspects of Child Health in the
Eighteenth-Century City   293
GEORGE ROSEN / Yale University
The Moment in Eighteenth-Century Art Criticism   317
FRANCIS H. DOWLEY / University of Chicago
The Education in Architecture of the Man of Taste   337
MICHAEL McCARTHY / University of Toronto
A Colonial Printer as Bookseller in Eighteenth-Century
Philadelphia: The Case of David Hall   355
ROBERT D. HARLAN / University of California, Berkeley
The Fortunes and Misfortunes of a Leading French
Bookseller-Printer: André-François Le Breton, Chief
Publisher of the Encyclopédie   371
FRANK A. KAFKER / University of Cincinnati

Small Profits Do Great Things: James Lackington and
Eighteenth-Century Bookselling   387
    RICHARD G. LANDON / University of Toronto
The "World" between Seigneur and Peasant   401
    ROBERT FORSTER / Johns Hopkins University
Rural Revolts and Protest Movements in France from 1675
to 1788   423
    EMMANUEL LE ROY LADURIE / Collège de France
The Irish on the Continent in the Eighteenth Century   453
    WILLIAM D. GRIFFIN / St. John's University
Daniel O'Connell and the Irish Eighteenth Century   475
    MAURICE R. O'CONNELL / Fordham University

Executive Board, 1975–76   496
Institutional Members   497
Index   499

Illustrations follow page 202

Preface

As editor of this collection of essays, I was charged to select those papers most representative of the heterogeneous nature of the American Society for Eighteenth-Century Studies from amongst all those presented in this country and Canada at regional and national meetings of the Society during the academic year 1973–1974. If my reader will pause a moment, and read quickly through the table of contents, he or she will discover that, in fact, heterogeneity predominates. During my editorial tenure, I have learned (one of many lessons) that it is our Society's very diversity which sustains it, and this diversity has accounted for the organization's encouraging success during the six or so years of its existence. As our President, Georges May, reveals to us in his apocryphal chapter of *Candide* (see the Presidential Address), isolated specialization is a form of "idiocy"—a danger which many of the great Enlighteners perceived, but one which is very difficult to obviate. The encyclopedic tendency of the Enlightenment was a response to such intellectual rigidification, and so was, concludes May, the decision to form academies. This tendency has continued into the twentieth century with the establishment of such societies as our own. We shall always be cursed with the spectre of Pangloss, but his form of "idiocy" can be attenuated within the context of an academy of learned and diverse critics and scholars.

The variety and richness of this collection of essays hamper any attempt to impose, in a preface, even the most superficial order.

Yet, every such collection, not unified by a central theme or method, must have a preface. The reader must be prepared for what he or she will find in the volume. Such is bibliographical etiquette; every student of the eighteenth century knows that prefaces were essential to the presentation of almost any book. Sometimes, authors apologized for prefaces, parodied prefaces, or dispensed with prefaces—but they always did so *in* prefaces! The preface was the first important contact between reader and writer, and the writers of the Enlightenment were learning that their readers not only bought and read, they helped create, and the preface pointed the way. So, having presented you with both sides of the argument, I shall try to do what probably cannot be done (structure this volume) and what must be done (prepare you for what follows).

Those who study the Enlightenment in Europe and America soon learn that there were no other periods in the history of Western culture which were more fascinated with all aspects of human communication, including the organization and presentation of knowledge, the creation of new ways to propagate the "truth," the mechanics of social interaction. The modern techniques of propaganda and other, less obvious forms of data transmission were developed during the eighteenth century. It can be called the first "book-centered" age of knowledge, that is, the period where the Book begins to fulfill all its potential functions, and where the scribal tradition irrevocably succeeds the oral as the primary means of transmitting and preserving cultural codes.

The study of communication is the study of relationships. Artistic communication presupposes interaction between the artist and his spectator, his reader, his "consumer." Communication also presupposes interaction between leader and follower, governor and governed, controller and controlled. All relationships which together form the contextual matrix known as "culture" or "society" are forms of communication. The eighteenth century was a period of new adventures in the verbal and non-verbal processes of communication, and, simultaneously, of a great mass of commentary on these processes. It is not a coincidence, for example, that first-person narration was the dominant narrative mode of the period. Both in the memoir-novel and the pre-eminent epistolary novel, writers sought to establish intimate contact, at first deceptive and later conspiratorial, with their readers. (In fact, it is this progression from duplicity to cooperation which marks the development of most prose fiction of the era.) What better way was there to convince a skeptical public to accept the frightening though obsessive urge toward self-discovery through self-examination? The presentation of the "self" (the "self" of tradition, of institutions, of class, as well as of the individual), and the concomitant understanding of the "other" (the teacher, the leader, the subject, the writer, one's peers) is not just one theme but a dominant cultural concern of the Enlightenment. And this was but one epistemological variant which helped in the revaluation and restructuring of the codes which were proving unsatisfactory to the Enlightenment's protectors and propagators.

The three essays in this volume which analyze different aspects of book-publishing and book-selling in America, England, and France (those of Harlan, Landon, and Kafker) all insist on the phenomenal "literary revolution" which preceded, and probably hastened, the Industrial Revolution. Men made fortunes selling, publishing, and trading in books, and these activities frightened governments into concerted efforts of censorship, the "natural" consequence of a vigorous and chaotic publishing industry in a repressive society. Another consequence of this "revolution" was a simultaneous development which would seem at first glance antithetical to the impulse I have just mentioned. Increasingly, writers of the Enlightenment were questioning the very matter of verbal art: words and their rhetorical use. In a century fascinated with masks, words soon came to be seen as masks, as impediments rather than aids to understanding and the efficacious description of truth. This linguistic self-consciousness, which was developing in the seventeenth century, would become of central philosophical concern by the time of the "high Enlightenment." The essays of Cohen and Ormsby-Lennon analyze two aspects of this phenomenon, as it was manifested during the period in England. Communication, its advantages and limitations, marked the musings of the Enlighteners, and all of its facets, from the most mundane to the most theoretical, are commanding increasing attention from contemporary scholars of the eighteenth century.

Those who have read the great historians of philosophy of the Enlightenment—writers such as Hazard, Cassirer, and Foucault—learn that the period was one of constant philosophical and epistemological restructuring. Nowhere is this more evident than in the period's conception of one of the essential dimensions of human experience: that of time. The concepts of relativity, of spatio-temporal relationships in philosophy and the arts, of the artificial re-creation of duration were all concerns of this era. The effect that time had on institutions, on traditions of culture, on art, and, perhaps most significantly for our own egocentric age, on self-knowledge and self-conception occupied the minds of many of the artists and thinkers of the century. It is again no coincidence that historiography, horological technology, and the artistic experimentation with time all reach advanced stages of development in the eighteenth century. The studies of Macey, Marks, Miner, and Pocock all examine aspects of time and its comprehension during this era.

The Enlightenment was a period very conscious of its place in history (it had in fact named itself) and of the role that historiography (the chronicling of time's passage) could play in maintaining and transmitting cultural patterns. Ernst Cassirer has taught us that the Enlightenment, beginning especially with the writings of the French exile Pierre Bayle, searched to discover *how* man perceived his place in time, not to list simply the stages through which temporal man had passed. The histories produced by these writers were, then, no longer annals of great events and great men, but subtle—and not-so-subtle—commentary on how these events should be perceived, and, once perceived, how these perceptions should be organized so they could have the greatest usefulness for men building new and better civilizations. History, as a philosophical entity, was examined, criticized, manipulated, and ultimately accepted as a valid conceptual mode by men as divergent in their definition and uses of it as Voltaire and Rousseau. The future was the essential temporal coordinate of the Enlightenment, and analyzing the past was seen as the surest way of controlling the future. This fascination with the future and man's place in history was much more complex than the hackneyed idea of "Progress" suggests. Or, perhaps, we have failed still to comprehend the complexity of the concept itself. Nevertheless, man and time, man and history, from the microcosm of a brief fictional epistolary exchange to the macrocosm of universal physical laws, concerned, intrigued, and eventually challenged the philosophers of the eighteenth century to produce some to the most influential historical treatises and commentaries ever written. As the writer of the Enlightenment formed his fictions, so he formed his histories, and so he formed the myth of the Enlightenment.

The largest number of essays in this volume of *Studies in Eighteenth-Century Culture* can be said to treat another aspect of the philosophical revaluation alluded to above: the growing and often eloquent demands of the "oppressed" of eighteenth-century European cultures for their rights. There are six papers on women (real and fictional), two on the French peasantry, and two on a little-known but significant minority, the Irish Catholic exiles and political activists. Those who have spent any time studying the literature and social institutions of the Enlightenment are aware of the feminine presence, and, at times, feminine dominance, in all matters of artistic, intellectual, and social life. A history of feminism in the European Enlightenment is still needed, and it would be a large undertaking. From the late seventeenth century, from the Quarrel of the Ancients and the Moderns ("les femmes sont nées modernes"), this presence was felt with increasing force. From Madame du Châtelet, Voltaire's brilliant friend, called the "female Newton," to Mary Wollstonecraft, the intellectual and political life of Europe was marked by the female mind. Some papers in this collection analyze this phenomenon as it expressed itself historically (especially those of Janes, Williams, Rogal) as well as in and through fiction (see those of Backscheider, Mercken-Spaas, and Miller). The emancipation of women did not advance very far during the Enlightenment, but it is during this era that the history of this emancipation should begin. The most subtle and vigorous minds of the period came back with astonishing regularity to this question, and feminine self-consciousness as well as male awareness of this self-consciousness began to coalesce then, artistically and philosophically, though it would still be a long while before the insidiousness of the anti-feminine bias would be completely understood. It is good that this volume of the Society's proceedings has a substantive number of essays on this subject; thereby do we join in an old and important debate, hopefully with felicitous results.

In their essays on the French peasantry of seventeenth- and eighteenth-century France, Professors Forster and Ladurie continue the revisionist trend of modern French historiography which seeks to explain the complexity of pre-Revolutionary society in socio-economic and politico-economic terms. The majority of the French populace did not form a homogeneous mass, but distinctive groups with well-defined areas of competence and performance. Also, the anti-governmental activities of the Third Estate, more often than not, resulted from cultural, fiscal and social traditions of specific geographical areas than from any strong urge to change the structure of the society of the Ancien Régime. The retrospective bias of most Revolutionary history continues to be undermined.

This group of papers on oppressed minorities and majorities (including the papers of Griffin and O'Connell on the Irish, of which the former leads us in the direction of cultural assimilation and maintenance) should remind the membership of the Society, and others who peruse this book, that most of the great doctrines of social and political liberation were born and successfully nurtured during the Age of Enlightenment. Their at times inchoate quality and their retrospectively incomplete application should not detract from the fact that a significant epistemological change occurred, as man began a quest, which is only now coming to an end, "to actualize the utopic."

An important aspect of this intellectual revolution was the

esthetic revaluation which accompanied it. The Enlightenment was a period of active invention, when new genres in all the arts were being experimented with, developed and discarded. Different media began to use and exploit characteristics of each other in order to effect fundamental artistic change. Music and painting and sculpture and drama and narrative prose all borrowed from each other. Fiction and non-fiction became confused, mostly inadvertently, often purposefully. Some of the articles in this volume of the *Studies* (including those of Dowley, Ilie, and Klinger) examine these esthetic relationships, and others, especially those of Knox and McCarthy, concentrate on the formation of artists, on their education and experience. The Enlightenment's desire to propagate the "truth" meant that new methods to convince the skeptics were needed, and this meant that different formal and thematic analogues were demanded by the creators. Their search for and experimentation with these analogues are constants of the intellectual history of the eighteenth century in Europe.

These are some of the major areas of research and speculation which volume five of *Studies in Eighteenth-Century Culture* covers. My brief remarks were meant, as I suggested at first, to show how they reflect the major considerations and conceptualizations of the period. Other papers treat urban life and the image of the city (those of Lafarge and Rosen) as well as the influence of establishment politics on a certain group of intellectuals in late eighteenth-century Spain (Dowling). All witness to the seemingly endless number of areas which demand the attention of scholars of the Enlightenment. I think that any reader of this volume, if he is ignorant of the purposes and scope of our Society, will be well educated in those purposes after having looked at it. This fifth volume, celebrating our fifth anniversary, hopefully presages well for the Society's institutional health. We are a heterogeneous membership in an increasingly homogeneous profession; we promise diversity and eclecticism, and should avoid conformity. And we hope that our efforts, modest as they may be, would still earn the admiration of those other scholars, organizers, and enlighteners whom we study and recognize in this collection.

A brief word should be inserted here on the volume's organization. All of these papers save one were presented at the Fifth Annual Meeting of the American Society for Eighteenth-Century Studies which was held in Philadelphia (under the auspices of the University of Pennsylvania), 24–27 April 1974. (Professor Rogal's paper was presented at the East-Central Regional Conference held in Virginia Beach in October 1974.) There are eleven sessions or sections of the national meeting represented in this collection. All papers given at the same session or section meeting were kept together to ensure some thematic coherence. The sessions which are represented are, in order of their appearance in the volume, Section F (Fine Arts), Section A (English and American Literature), Plenary Session IV (Women in Eighteenth-Century Culture), Section E (Philosophy, Religion, and the History of Ideas), Section B-5 (Spanish and Portuguese), Section B-2 (French Language and Literature), Section C-1 (Language, Rhetoric, and Style), Plenary Session VI (The City in the Eighteenth Century), Plenary Session IV (Taste and Arts in the Eighteenth Century), Section H-1 (Ancillary Disciplines: Bibliography, Biography, and the History of the Book), Plenary Session II (French Rural Society before the Revolution), and Section D (History, Economics, and Political Science). Finally, the winner of the annual prize awarded by the Society for the best article in eighteenth-century studies does not appear in this number, as is the custom. The reason is simple. The winner was Hayden V. White for his article "The Irrational and the Problem of Historical Knowledge in the Enlightenment," and it appeared first in *Studies in Eighteenth-Century Culture,* volume 2 (1972), 303–21.

This year, for the first time, there was an editorial committee to aid the editor, composed of scholars from all of the major disciplines of the Society. I extend my public thanks to these colleagues whose judicious and timely service made a difficult task much easier. I especially wish to thank Hoyt Trowbridge for his diligence and for his personal support in this enterprise. There were many others who helped a great deal, both tangibly and intangibly, in the preparation of this collection. My gratitude is offered to Paul

Korshin, Georges May, H. K. Miller, Harry Pagliaro, and Jean
Perkins for their confidence and valuable support; to the Department of Romance Languages of Ohio State University, and especially to its chairman, Robert Cottrell, for helping with the many
minor details which such an enterprise entails; to Hélène Konrath,
my forbearing student aide; and to all the following, who helped
me and the editorial committee in important ways: John Burn-
ham, Albert Kuhn, John McCarthy, Peter Machamer, Albert Man-
cini, David Miles, Maurice J. O'Sullivan, Gerald Prince, John Rule,
and Franklin Zimmerman. Finally, I would like to thank the
editorial staff of the University of Wisconsin Press for their expert
handling of the manuscript.

RONALD C. ROSBOTTOM

Columbus, Ohio
February 1975

Studies in Eighteenth-Century Culture

VOLUME 5

Probability and Improbability in Eighteenth-Century Research

GEORGES MAY

Two years ago, or, more precisely, two years minus one month ago, while this Society was holding its Third Annual Meeting in Los Angeles, I was enjoying a sabbatical year in Paris. I well remember the surprise and emotion which I felt when the telephone rang and the operator told me I had a long distance call from California. This was your Nominating Committee in the person of Alice Laborde. The purpose was to ask whether I would accept nomination as second vice president.

I just said I remember the surprise and the emotion: the emotion was of course one of intense pride, for I was not unaware of the probability of promotion in two steps from the second vice presidency to the presidency; but it was also one of awe at the enormous expenses incurred by the Nominating Committee in calling me from so far away. Indeed I was so awed that it inhibited me and caused me simply to assent passively to Madame Laborde's entreaties. I suspect this had been the strategy of the Nominating Committee all along. Only after I had hung up did I realize that I had not asked any question at all. I am sure Alice Laborde will do me the justice of corroborating this. I had not even inquired about the salary, let alone the other perquisites of office.

Yet perquisites there are, if not for the vice presidents, at least for the president. One in particular which very few people know about. Perhaps I should rather call it a symbol of office, for it is passed on from one president to the next. I am sure you can guess what it is: the Eighteenth Century being that of the Enlightenment, the symbol of office, appropriately enough, is a lamp . . . an antique lamp of knowledge. It was turned over to me last night in a private ceremony by Paul Korshin. I would have brought it with me this evening to display it, had I not discovered quite accidentally that it is much too valuable an object not to be locked up in a safe place. Therefore, it now rests in the safe of the Faculty Club.

After it had been given to me last night, I began to polish it, for the brass looked old and tarnished. I had no sooner begun to rub it than—lo and behold!— a genie appeared out of nowhere, clad in magnificent oriental garb, bowed ceremoniously to me and said: "O Master what wilt thou ask of thy humble servant?"

I was so taken aback that I could not think of the innumerable advantages both material and spiritual which I had long coveted,— such as an ability to digest the rich masterpieces of traditional French cuisine or to understand the heady masterpieces of modern French criticism. So I answered quite automatically, as I had Alice Laborde two years earlier, and, referring to the thing which was then uppermost in my consciousness, I said to the genie: "I have to give a speech tomorrow night to a very discriminating audience; it is on the subject of probability and improbability in eighteenth-century research; I have worked on it mightily, but I rather fear that it has been in vain; look at these notes and tell me."

The genie took my notes, bowed politely and disappeared. A few minutes later she reappeared—I say *she,* for I had forgotten to tell you that this is a female genie, as I could readily observe, eighteenth-century harem costumes being what they are. So she reappeared and said: "This is a very impressive speech, O Master. Seldom have I read anything so morally uplifting and so eloquently written; but, at the end of a banquet, even when it is called a delegates' dinner, one may fear that it would be wasted on an impatient or perhaps even slumbering audience. I have therefore taken the very great liberty, for which I beg forgiveness, to bring thee fresh material for a perhaps more appropriate speech, although surely less beautiful." Thereupon she pulled from her harem pants a scroll of ancient-looking paper, which she presented to me most respectfully, requesting that she be summoned again if the new material should prove disappointing.

It did not take me very long to discover what was on the scroll: it is a set of galley proof in French, and the text quite obviously is that of a hitherto unknown chapter of Voltaire's *Candide*. Of course the authenticity will have to be checked, but there is no doubt in my mind that the corrections are in Voltaire's own hand. And so, although I do not share at all the genie's opinion that my original speech was in any way deficient or inappropriate, I had to agree that no eighteenth-century scholar could ever dream of a better audience than the present one to unveil so important an *inédit* from so famous a writer. I therefore put away my original speech (I did not tear it up or burn it, for one never knows), and, out of deference to interdisciplinarity, I drafted a very hasty English translation of the text on those galley sheets. Although this text is not quite complete and presents a few lacunae caused by the poor condition in which the paper is, the context does make it clear that the discarded fragment was originally meant to belong between chapters 19 and 20 of *Candide*, as we know it.

You will recall that, at the end of chapter 19, Candide sails with Martin on a French vessel from Surinam for Bordeaux. It now appears, thanks to this variant, that the episode of the voyage in the New World was not meant originally by Voltaire to end so abruptly. From the context of the mutilated beginning of this unknown chapter, one can readily surmise that the ship first sailed, not a northeast, but a north to northwest course, for in the first lines we find our two heroes in a port city of the eastern seabord of north America, which derives its name from the dedication of its inhabitants to the ideal of brotherly love.

Here begins the newly discovered text, of which I shall now inflict upon you my inadequate translation:

In the inn where they had stopped Candide and Martin heard Philadelphians talk with pride of one of their fellow-citizens who had just left for England. The purpose of his voyage, they said, was to convey in person to their beloved King George the expression of the respect of his loyal subjects in the New World, along with a few modest complaints and urgent requests. The two foreigners asked who was this great man to whom so important a mission had been entrusted.

"His name is Mr. Franklin," the innkeeper said, "and he is the son of a Boston candle-maker."

"And what is Mr. Franklin's own profession?" asked Candide.

"He is a printer," answered the inkeeper. "But he is best known for having invented a new kind of eye-glasses, improved our mail system, and flown a kite with an iron spike attached to it. He has also founded a newspaper, a hospital, a library, and a fire insurance company. So we elected him to our Philadelphia Assembly and we sent him to England. No doubt King George will treat him well and grant all his wishes."

The innkeeper walked away from Candide and Martin to escort out of his establishment two gentlemen who had come there apparently to drown their sorrows. They looked sad and sick and the taller of the two appeared to have lost most of his hair and beard in a fire. While the innkeeper was so occupied, Candide asked his companion:

"What do you think, dear Martin, of a country still so primitive as to glorify a man like this Mr. Franklin, who has wasted his time and the talent he perhaps has acquiring a smattering of learning about matters as diverse as politics, physics, printing, economics, journalism, optics, and a few others, instead of becoming a true scholar in any one of them, as did my good master Pangloss, who is the greatest metaphysician in both the New and the Old World?"

"I think," answered Martin, "that your master is an idiot.

During the ten years that I worked for the book publishers of Amsterdam, I learned a little Greek, and I know that ἴδιος means 'particular, special,' and that a specialist is therefore properly speaking an idiot. Your master Pangloss has specialized in metaphysics to the point of neglecting all else; he is therefore an idiot. Moreover, since metaphysics is nothing but smoke, he is also ignorant; but that is of course far less serious."

The innkeeper, who had overheard the end of this conversation, after having escorted out of his tavern the two sad and sick-looking gentlemen, remarked:

"I do not know Doctor Pangloss, but, according to what Mr. Martin has just said, I suspect he is not unlike the two gentlemen who just left."

"Who are they?" asked Candide. "I noticed they did not look well or happy."

"Nor would they have any reason to," answered the innkeeper. "The shorter of the two is one of the best known physicians in Pennsylvania. A few weeks ago, he was summoned to attend a young girl, who had swallowed so much rat's bane that she was more dead than alive. He administered a massive dose of emetic in the nick of time, saved her life, and was lavishly rewarded by her grateful father. Alas! two weeks later the same girl jumped into the Delaware river, from which no amount of emetic could rescue her. She was buried yesterday. Her bereft and irate father is now suing the doctor, who, as you could see, is about to lose his mind with anguish."

"And so, the doctor is an idiot," declared Martin. "He is no doubt a specialist. All he knows is the body of his patients, whereas one cannot hope to cure the body without knowing something of the mind which is inside it. He deserves his misfortune and should be sentenced for malpractice."

"And who is," asked Candide, "the tall gentleman who was with him, and who looks as though the Holy Inquisition had half roasted him at an auto-da-fe?"

"He is a learned legal scholar," the innkeeper replied. "He received the finest of educations in the law schools of Germany and Italy. A tribe of Iroquois Indians from neighboring Ohio heard of his reputation and begged that he draw up for them a body of laws, that they may forever be ruled according to reason. The learned lawyer went to his books, and designed for his clients a fine constitution, entirely modelled after that of the Hebrews, who, as we know, enjoyed the best of all governments, for it had been given to them by the Almighty himself. The Iroquois, however, enjoy this superiority over the Hebrews that they worship not one, but twenty-three gods. And so, when put into effect, the new constitution generated immediate chaos and total anarchy. The only way to placate the wrath of the twenty-two neglected gods was to burn the lawgiving offender slowly at the stake, for it is well known on our continent as on yours that the smell of grilled human flesh is an infallible way to dispel divine anger. A most violent rainstorm put out the fire and saved the victim miraculously from total incineration; but, as you could see, not without much damage."

"And so," said Martin, "the lawyer too is an idiot. He failed to heed the sound observation of Président de Montesquieu that laws are but the reflection of all the customs of a people. He paid no attention to customs because he was solely interested in laws. He got only what he deserved. Indeed he was fortunate to escape with most of his skin left, and some of his hair."

"But, dear Martin," said Candide, "if you call an idiot anyone who has learned enough about anything to be an expert, how can one avoid being either idiotic or ignorant? We live in an age of progress and discovery. The accumulation of knowledge is so great and grows so fast, that it is no longer possible to be acquainted, as could our grandparents, with all areas of learning. Come what may, must we not choose, and therefore specialize, and therefore become idiots?"

"This is why," remarked Martin, "the books which sell best are encyclopedias. When I lived in Amsterdam, the publishers for whom I worked pirated at least one every year, to keep their children from starving."

"Our Mr. Franklin would quite agree with you," said the

innkeeper. "Compiling an encyclopedia is one of the very few things which he has not yet done; but, before leaving for England, he did create an Academy in this city, which is like a living encyclopedia, for it groups together learned men who are all specialists of one science or another, just as an encyclopedia lists in succession articles written by diverse specialists: '. . . Languages, History, Geography, Chronology, Logick and Rhetorick, Writing, Arithmetick, Algebra, the several Branches of the Mathematicks, Natural and Mechanick Philosophy, Drawing in Perspective, and every other useful Part of Learning and Knowledge . . .'."

"Ah!" said Candide, "I think I now understand how one can perhaps escape at the same time ignorance and idiocy. When I am back home in Westphalia, I shall marry Mademoiselle Cunégonde, and found a society to achieve this goal."

"And how will you do that?" asked Martin.

"I shall bring together many scholars, each of whom will be an expert in one thing, what you call an idiot. They will gather in small groups, talk to each other and read each other's works. There will be many diverse sections specializing in the various literatures of the world; others concentrating on history, religion, or philosophy; others again devoted to science and the fine arts; there may even be one for metaphysicians, headed by my good master Pangloss. Once in a while they will all meet together in one of the great cities of the world. Perhaps one day we will come back for this purpose to this city of brotherly love. Our noble goal will be to stamp out idiocy. No one will ever again have to jump into the Delaware River or be burnt at the stake. All will then be for the best in the best of all possible worlds, as my good master Pangloss always said."

"But," said Martin . . .

This is where the last galley sheet stops, and I do not know, therefore, how Voltaire proposed to conclude this chapter, but I do understand retrospectively why the genie suggested that these few pages contain material suitable for the occasion which brings us together tonight. Moreover I must confess she succeeded not only in respecting the title which I had announced three months ago to our Executive Secretary, but in illustrating it in a much more convincing way than I ever could without her assistance. Now of course it is up to you to decide what in all that I have said strikes you as probable—or improbable.

William Hogarth
and London Theatrical Life

MARY F. KLINGER

The vitality of eighteenth-century London theater audiences is known to us through the words of such sophisticated spectators as James Boswell, who records his elaborate intrigues in the Drury Lane pit, where he even lowed like a cow on one occasion.[1] His *London Journal* entry for 19 January 1763 describes a valiant but vain attempt to damn David Mallet's tragedy *Elvira*. After a dinner of juicy beefsteaks Boswell and two friends, Dempster and Erskine, "drank damnation to the play" and "eternal remorse" to the author. Then, Boswell continues:

> ...just as the doors opened at four o'clock, we sallied into the house, planted ourselves in the middle of the pit, and with oaken cudgels in our hands and shrill-sounding catcalls in our pockets, sat ready prepared .... As is usual on first nights, some of us called to the music to play *Roast Beef*. But they did not comply ... and we were not numerous enough to turn that request into a command, which in a London theatre is quite a different sort of public speech .... The prologue was politically stupid. We hissed it and had several to join us .... We did what we could during the first act, but found that the audience had lost their original fire and spirit and were disposed to let it pass.

Unable to rally more support, the three pit critics (who used borrowed names for the enterprise) were forced to lay aside, not without regrets, what Boswell deemed a "laudable undertaking."[2]

Even with such vivid verbal accounts, the lack of a pictorial chronicle for the eighteenth-century English stage generates interest in new or unexplored materials that can add to knowledge in this area.[3] William Hogarth's paintings and prints, without the precision of photography or film, do provide valuable visual clues to contemporary acting and theatrical practices. These graphic works are especially enlightening now that the calendar account in the volumes of *The London Stage, 1660–1800* points to a wider definition of theatrical conditions, certainly by mid-century. As G. W. Stone, Jr. notes, the "total impact" of an evening at Drury Lane or Covent Garden derived from the matrix of a "whole show," from preliminary music to the mainpiece and afterpiece, to entr'acte dancing, singing, and specialty acts.[4] Examining Hogarth's record extends our awareness of this drama in an age when parallels between verbal and visual were commonplace in art and literary criticism.

In this paper I wish to focus on the new dimension Hogarth's prints give to interrelationships operative in dramatic life (as defined by the *London Stage* calendar), specifically, to consider the quality of the evidence these visual structures contain for theater and literary history, and to evaluate what, if any, conclusions may be drawn from formal analogues. Of the Hogarth paintings, etchings, engravings and drawings I consider associated with drama and theater,[5] four will be examined here, together with selected writings of the artist.

The technique used to look at the portrayals draws on discussions by Robert Wark and Ronald Paulson of "reading" Hogarth, though it differs from them. For the paintings, Wark claims Hogarth's "narrative method" allows the spectator to accumulate "representational details" that are "read" in a rather helter-skelter way as signs and symbols telling the story.[6] For reading the plates, Paulson outlines at least two stages. Observing that the prints are "constructed on a tension between the linearity of the book and the simultaneity of the picture," he points to a booklike "initial linear pull" from left to right. This in turn is supplanted by a "rococo inner structure" leading the eye restlessly to pick out details and relationships.[7] My "reading" here is not subject to compositional directives in the prints themselves since it uses dramatic history to search for visual and theatrical correspondences.

Hogarth's involvement with theater as entertainment and drama as an art form shows in his own writings, the *Autobiographical Notes* and aesthetic treatise, *The Analysis of Beauty*, where he frequently draws analogies between his graphic words and the stage.[8] In a familiar passage from the *Autobiographical Notes*, Hogarth conceptualizes his role as an artist-dramatist: "my Picture was my Stage and men and women my actors who were by Mean[s] of certain Actions and express[ions] to Exhibit a dumb shew [*sic*]."[9] Another time he employs theatrical vocabulary of gesture and expression to describe the fusion of his "dumb" art with living drama: "The figure is the actor /./ The attitudes and his action together ⟨with which⟩ The face work[s] an expression and the words that must speak to the Eye and [make?] the Scene inteligible [*sic*]" (*Autobiographical Notes*, p. 203).

Close observation of stage form and content is very evident in the *Analysis* where for theoretical formulations, Hogarth relies on stage dancing to illustrate the serpentine "line of beauty," while incidents and characters from plays he has seen become prototypes of comic incongruity. Unpublished references in the notebooks to dramatic works and dances underscore frequent theater attendance.[10] In the *Analysis* itself the alert artist-spectator recommends the best seat in the house to see country dancing: "The lines which a number of people together form in country or figure dancing, makes a delightful play upon the eye, especially when the whole figure is to be seen at one view, as at the playhouse, from the gallery (pp. 159–160)." Other useful instances from evenings at the patent theaters to support the artist's theories of graphic humor range from burlesque routines in Rich's pantomime *Harlequin Doctor Faustus* to scenes from popular afterpieces and *Tom Thumb*. To exemplify humorous pictorial incongruities, he refers to the "Jumble or Junction of circumstances" of transformation and disguise in Nahum Tate's *Duke and No Duke* and Charles Coffey's *The Devil to Pay* (*Rejected Passages,* p. 180). Mock-heroic escapades of Fielding's diminutive protagonist in *The Tragedy of Tragedies* (one of which Hogarth illustrated) exhibit an "extravagant incompatibleness" that characterizes "drollery" for the artist (*Rejected Passages,* p. 186).

To move from the verbal to Hogarth's predominant medium, the visual, with a focus on theatrical elements therein, we find the extent to which his portrayals represent actual dramatic events has not been exhaustively surveyed,[11] and only recently have the six *Beggar's Opera* paintings been studied this way by Paulson in his biography of the artist.[12] Traditionally, a scholarly consensus discourages considering the prints as documents of theater history.[13] But conscientious assessment need not preclude Frederick Antal's claims for Hogarth as the first artist in England to represent scenes from actual plays, the first to interest himself in the offstage life of actors, and probably the first to show pit spectators watching a play.[14]

Thus *The Laughing Audience* of 1733 (fig. 1) goes beyond being merely a witty (and satiric) mosaic of the articulate London audience to give a lively sense of theatrical ambience in decor, spectators, vendors, and house musicians.[15] Hogarth advertised this subscription ticket (for the series *A Harlot's Progress*) as "a new etched Print, describing a pleased Audience at a Theatre."[16] This "mosaic," obviously not full of the attempted likenesses Hogarth often used nor of extreme distortions, falls more likely into the category Jean Hagstrum calls "portrait caricature" wherein the distorting line maintains a "realistic surface."[17]

For theatrical history, the wealth of detail found here corroborates information on audience composition and interior design in the patent theaters. This could be Drury Lane or Covent Garden. The fashionable stand in the boxes (two fops ignore the stage to flirt with ladies and orange girls), while in the pit sit gentlemen, some citizens and a sour-faced critic.[18] Up front, where "sitting at the spikes" denoted a first-row seat, the orchestra quieted assembling Londoners before curtain time with the "First, Second and Third Music" (*LS*, 5, I, lvi). They played in the "Music Room," segregated as a result of vigorous audiences who tried to get to the stage by climbing through the orchestra. To avoid such hazardous enthusiasm a row of iron spikes was constructed, placed at first on the stage and later around the orchestra, to separate musicians from the pit.

Hogarth's interest in theater audiences was not limited to this print of 1733. Fourteen years later he depicted more happy spectators in the twelfth and final plate of his cycle *Industry and Idleness* (fig. 2), where the London populace turns out for the Lord Mayor's Day pageant.

This topical scene exhibits striking parallels to the interior sketch, for here in the outdoors the artist conceives the crowds *as a theater audience*. In the teeming London panorama, parade watchers sit on scaffolding and a balcony—structural features analogous to the seating layout in the earlier view. On the upper balcony of the King's Head Tavern, in an arrangement very like the layout of royal boxes in the London theaters, a canopy of state separates Frederick, Prince of Wales, and his wife Augusta from the people beneath them. Paulson, who also notes the similarity here, remarks that the thematic contrast of inattention and attention between members of the royal party and the commoners below recalls *The Laughing Audience* (*HGW*, I, 202).

An even more technical parallel exists in the raked seats. In the street, the sloping is probably realistic, simply the result of an expedient mode of parade-watching from scaffolding in narrow London byways, while the interior view, smaller in plate size and subject shown, dictates a more severe but inaccurate sloping to collapse space. Moreover, this contraction for purposes of perspective bluntly underlines the fact that people in London theaters and streets *were* crowded. Another link through social fact to theatrical structure and dramatic theme appears in the Lord Mayor's

Parade itself, here emblematic of industry's rewards, but such pageants were dramatized and became popular productions on the London boards and in fair booths.

Ultimately street panorama and indoor audience need to be viewed as individuated artistic constructs, but one must remark visual and topical similarities cast in a theatrical dimension.

Yet another perspective of this world appears in Hogarth's 1738 engraving *Strolling Actresses Dressing in a Barn* (fig. 3), probably the premiere in English art of players rehearsing amidst the circumstances of their professional life.[19] It doubtless reports graphically a significant event in English theater history as strollers "dress" for a performance the 1737 Licensing Act makes their last. Furthermore, contrasts between acting roles as mythological deities and shabby surroundings are rightly deemed "mock-heroic."[20] But I think Hogarth's emphasis and comic vision forge an even broader base here, one that looks into the tiring room of drama and fuses formal elements with thematic Augustan juxtaposition. The print exposes with compelling immediacy universal materials of rehearsals such as last minute run-throughs, touch-up sewing, eating and painting. The structural realistic setting thus becomes one aspect of what Paulson calls Hogarth's indigenous mock-heroic allusions;[21] in this case, the occasional "dressing" in the print simultaneously exhibits referents of illusion and reality essential to the mock-heroic *and* the theater.

This backstage glimpse quite accurately depicts such properties as a clay candle ring (to light the performance), a rose-covered gateway, a flying machine drawn by dragons amid puffy clouds in the loft, and wave-rollers leaning on the left wall below. These tall waves provide a strong instance of the quality of Hogarth's pictorial reporting of stage mechanics in England and on the continent. The same kind of ocean waves exist today in usable condition at the Swedish Drottningholm Royal Court Theater of 1766. In this "most perfectly preserved eighteenth century court theatre in the world,"[22] the original Drottningholm "sea waves," which can still be manually operated, go to a length of about 6.5 meters.[23] Hogarth's strollers use wave rollers similar in size, shape and handles, though their supply is limited to two; a Drottningholm ocean requires five waves. Among these companies, where poverty was less often the exception than the rule, one troupe inventoried a "second-hand Dragon, wingless and clawless."[24] Hogarth's dragon, resting aloft, seems somewhat better equipped.

The artist's handling of these contemporary sets creates a scene rich in pictorial humor. Hogarth's green room projects the comic tensions of diminution and aggrandizement, attributes of the satiric mode employed by Pope, Swift, and Fielding. Hogarth casually blends properties of stage illusion with those of real life: a clothesline hangs before wings in need of brushwork, other laundry dries on a cloud, a chamber pot contains paint, farmyard strays perch on the almost perpendicular ocean waves, and a woman's aviary headdress distresses her hungry baby. The artist punctuates such contrasts when players articulate and gesticulate as gods and goddesses, efforts he would label droll in their "extravagant incompatibleness."

This print candidly views a special kind of actor—London players moonlighting as strollers off season—at a critical moment in their professional life. Atop a crown near a chamber pot lies a copy of the "Act against Strolling Players," a Licensing Act statute which restricted performances to the City and liberties of Westminster. The scene has been dated "around June 24, 1737," when the unlicensed theaters closed (*HGW*, I, 182).[25] The playbill on a small bed provides verbal exposition of the strollers' plight: "By a Company of Comedians from The Theatres at London at the GEORGE INN This Present Evening will be Presented THE DEVIL to Pay in HEAVEN Being the last time of Acting before y[e] Act Commences (*HGW*, I, 182)." Though the troupe will perform in the George Inn Yard, a locale often used by Bartholomew Fair booths, they rehearse in a leaky barn, where poorer itinerants were accommodated and played from time to time.[26] Their offering, complete with title and *dramatis personae*, is the invention of artist-playwright William Hogarth.

The hectic ambience of Thespian preparation communicates itself in stages of dress and undress as Hogarth's intent players unconsciously bare thighs, calves, ankles and arms. Structural and thematic patterns of process, of cover and exposure (evident even in the leering eavesdropper using the roof's aperture) seem to be centripetally drawn to the large figure of the half-nude goddess of chastity and the hunt. Commenting on the mock-heroic aspect here, Paulson remarks how Diana's traditional pose (one hand up ready to pull an arrow from the quiver and the other holding the bow) is rendered absurd since she has neither quiver nor bow. And, unlike her fastidious prototype, Hogarth's goddess smokes a pipe, drinks ale, lets her neckline plunge and exposes her thighs (*Life*, I, 397). This grooming inspired Georg C. Lichtenberg to observe: "As is well known, the Diana of antiquity is always represented with legs bare to above the knee, but otherwise carefully covered. Ours, on the other hand, appears almost completely naked except the legs to above the knee, which are even more carefully covered than is usual with the chaste sex."[27]

Another engraving attesting to Hogarth's interest in the exuberant variety of London's theatrical world is *Southwark Fair*, issued as the subscription ticket for *A Rake's Progress* and originally entitled "A Fair" (fig. 4). The print can be dated after August 23, 1733, when Theophilus Cibber's production of *Tamerlane* opened at Bartholomew Fair, where it played before moving to Southwark (*HGW*, I, 154). Here the artist's visual response puts forth a valuable account of how dramatic booths at the fairs operated. [28]

Evidence that Hogarth knew the London fairgrounds well appears in *The Analysis of Beauty* (1753). Fair shows were not only memorable, but proved useful as examples of humorous visual incongruities when he drafted the treatise. One instance can be traced from sketches and remarks in the notebooks (fig. 5) to their final form in the text and one engraving published to illustrate the *Analysis*. On the verso page of one draft, Hogarth's struck-through autograph appears to comment on the drawing below it thusly: "an incident in a Droll where a fat man [personates(?)] an infant crying for pap."[29] The longer note, also partially illegible, would seem to say:

which represents a fat mans
face with an infants cap on [illegible]
and so contriv'd with the [rest(?)]
of the child, plac'd under his chin
that it seems to belong to the face
this is a contrivance in a scene
of a Droll which
is the cause of excessive
laughter.

The figure to the right drawn from the back has a caption: "A childs [body?] with a mans wig and cap on."

Hogarth kept these visual and verbal notes in the *Analysis,* where the lengthier comment illustrates the thesis that laughter is excited when incongruities meet. In that work he writes: "For example, the figure refer'ed to . . . represents a fat grown face of a man, with an infant's cap on, and the rest of the child's dress stuff'd, and so well placed under his chin, as to seem to belong to that face. This is a contrivance I have seen at Bartholomew-fair, and always occasion'd a roar of laughter" (p. 48). Both may be more familiar from the engraving *Plate 1* of *The Analysis of Beauty,* where the baby is "No. 1" and the short child "No. 18". Differences between draft and print indicate Hogarth intensified pictorial "excesses"; the man-child's expression becomes more of an angry grimace, while the length and breadth of the child's wig increase and a more elaborate plumed headpiece is added. (Also the figure leaning on a cane or stick now stands with outstretched arms holding a scroll-like object in the left hand.) From sketch to print, increasing wig length but not changing truncated legs and especially exaggerating the man-baby's facial lines seem less like embellishments than conscious attempts to emphasize contrasting visual excesses.

Contrivances Hogarth observed at the fairs (besides drolls, plays and farces) included wax works, contortionists and tumblers, rope dancers and marionettes, as *Southwark Fair* demonstrates. Dramatic booths were managed by actors from the London companies, who seized the chance to earn extra money during late summer three-day runs at the fairs. Hogarth depicts most advertising media used by such actor-managers—railed platforms, costumed players, hawking drummers, and painted showcloths. Balconies or "parade platforms," the most characteristic feature of the booths, served to entice crowds to come inside a booth for the complete performance, as Hogarth's "parade" ticket hawks his cycle *A Rake's Progress*. But fair showcloths were the primary means of attracting paying customers, and functioned almost as do photographs outside theaters today. Painted with play scenes and titles in most cases, they distinguished one booth from another. [30]

On the ground the artist surveys a galaxy of keen competition from costumed actors to peep and even freak shows. And the focal figure here, an actress who drums up business for her troupe (one in Roman dress has just been arrested), becomes an emblem of the dramatic offerings throughout the fairgrounds. Aside from the commerce in this print, which is William Hogarth's offering, the variety and topicality here would seem to support a fresh approach to eighteenth-century plays, one that considers them as part of the wide spectrum of dramatic shows available to Londoners as recorded in the *London Stage* calendar.

One may argue with some plausibility that I am forcing a point in such crowded, contracted scenes (especially the Lord Mayor's Day Parade), seeing the stage in everything Hogarth draws (formally and thematically), and appropriating for the cause of theatrical influence what at face value seems to be a transcript from the raw material of life. But I think not. All Hogarth's art is selective. The *Autobiographical Notes*, the drafts and the *Analysis* clearly point to his constant concern with drama and theater as meaningful analogues for aesthetic postulates and creative method. They suggest that Hogarth perceived and utilized the advantage of form shared by artist and playwright over the writer—what Paulson describes as the ability to catch in "a single glance" the whole of a scene.[31]

Concentration of incidents and characters, and the sense of immediacy, are commonplace conventions of the boards and the canvas, the stage and the print. Yet I think it possible to discriminate among theatrical, literary, and social veins in the work of Hogarth in a manner that expands historical knowledge, opens up an approach to dramatic literature in this century, and even heightens biographical awareness.

Time limits a discussion of overlapping, but I believe the few samples herein exhibit parallels significant enough to extend knowledge of Hogarth's perceptions (and his applications of them) as a sensitive artist who was an observant theatergoer. These prints throw even more light on the dramatic prism of patent theaters, fairs, inns and provinces, for Hogarth adds to history in a period of rare and often dubious documentation. And if we accept the new definition of the London stage at the time as a matrix of cultural events from Shakespearean drama to pantomimic interludes, it is possible to see *Southwark Fair* as more of a transcript from theater history than merely a good illustration of social life at a London fair in 1733. Moreover, the reliance on Hogarth's graphic works by playwrights as sources for dramas in the eighteenth century indicates that the artist's contemporaries themselves responded to this potential in the plates.[32] Finally, success of the print sales points to subtle recognition of a relevant stage metaphor by Londoners who saw in the engravings and etchings not only selected highlights of their daily life but a graphic extension of what they were accustomed to evening after evening in the patent theaters, year after year at the fairs, and on occasion in the provinces.

The pervasiveness of the correspondences points to a new look at the interdisciplinary nature of the London stage and the work of William Hogarth, and possibly more sources in the art of the time for searching out such links. Aside from once again underscoring the value of examining parallels in visual and verbal structures, this "reading" generates insights into comparisons of acting and painting theory, studies of theatrical portrayals by other English artists, and explorations of the nature of theater in pictorial art. And for developing an aesthetic of dramatic literature in the eighteenth-century, sitting at the spikes with Hogarth and Boswell results in a sharper view of the complex elements involved.

A CHECKLIST
of William Hogarth's Portrayals Associated with Drama and Theater (Paintings, Engravings, Etchings and Drawings)

Dates for engravings and etchings indicate year of publication, not advertisement or subscription issue dates. This checklist follows for the most part Ronald Paulson's dating of engravings, etchings, three drawings ("The Beggar's Opera," "Falstaff Examining His Recruits," and "Hymen"), and most paintings mentioned in the "Catalogue" (Hogarth's Graphic Works, I, Revised Edition [New Haven and London: Yale University Press, 1970]), and Paulson's biography (Hogarth: His Life, Art, and Times, Vols. I–II [New Haven and London: Yale University Press, 1971]). However, R. B. Beckett's date for the painting The Enraged Musician: Hogarth [Boston: Boston Book and Art Shop, 1955]), and titles and dates for the two portraits of actresses questionably attributed to Hogarth, are included. I accept A. P. Oppé's date for "The Proportions of Garrick and Quin" (The Drawings of William Hogarth [London: Phaidon Press Ltd., 1948]). Preliminary sketches for Plate 1, The Analysis of Beauty ("The 'Old Baby', The Child in a Man's Wig, and The Ballet Dancer" and "A Roman General in a Perruque") appear in the British Museum manuscript drafts (Egerton MSS. 3011–3016) for the Analysis, and can probably be dated between 1745 and 1753, when Hogarth was working on the treatise he published in 1753. (See Paulson, Life, II, 154, and Joseph T. A. Burke, "Introduction," The Analysis of Beauty with the Rejected Passages from the Manuscript Drafts and Autobiographical Notes [Oxford: The Clarendon Press, 1955], p. xxix.)

Scenes from Plays

A Scene from The Tempest (Ptg. ca. 1735?)
The Beggar's Opera (Dr. ca. 1728; six paintings, 1728–ca. 1730)
A Scene from The Indian Emperor, or The Conquest of Mexico (Ptg. 1731)
Henry the Eighth and Anne Boleyn (E. and Engr. ca. 1728)
Falstaff Examining His Recruits (Dr. and Ptg. ca. 1728)

Benefit Tickets

Benefit Ticket for Spiller (E. 1720?)
Benefit Ticket for Milward (E. 1728)

Frontispieces to Dramatic Texts

*The Humours of Oxford (E. and Engr. 1730)
Perseus and Andromeda (E. 1729/30):

Perseus Slaying Medusa (Frontis.)
Perseus Rescuing Andromeda (facing p. 1)
*The Highland Fair (E. and Engr. 1730/1)
*The Tragedy of Tragedies (E. and Engr. 1730/1)
Select Comedies of Mr de Moliere (E. and Engr. 1732):
   *L'Avare
   *Sgnarelle ou le Cocu Imaginaire
**The Farmer's Return (E. 1762)

† *Portraits of Actors and Actresses*

David Garrick as Richard III (Ptg. 1745)
***Garrick in the Character of Richard III (E. and Engr. 1746)
David Garrick and his Wife (Ptg. 1757)
Mr. James Quin (Ptg. ca. 1740)
The Proportions of Garrick and Quin (Dr. 1746)
A Roman General in a Perruque (Dr.); Engr. as No. 19, Pl. 1, *The Analysis of Beauty*

Theatrical Dance

The Wedding Dance (The Dance, The Country Dance) (Ptg. ca. 1745); E. and
   Engr. as The Country Dance, Pl. 2, *The Analysis of Beauty* (E. and Engr.
   1753)

Audience

The Laughing Audience (E. 1733)

Everyday Life of Actors and Actresses

Strolling Actresses Dressing in a Barn (Ptg. 1737; E. and Engr. 1738)

Performances at the Fairs

Southwark Fair (Ptg. 1733; E. and Engr. 1733/4)
The 'Old Baby', The Child in a Man's Wig, and the Ballet Dancer (Dr.); Engr. as:
   Nos. 17, 18 and 20, Pl. 1, *The Analysis of Beauty*, 1753

Theatrical Satires

Masquerade Ticket (Engr. 1727)
Masquerades and Operas (E. and Engr. 1723/4)
A Just View of the British Stage (E. 1724)
The Charmers of the Age (E. 1741/2)
The Ballet Dancer (Dr.). See "Performances at the Fairs"

Theatrical Music

Frontispiece to Leveridge's Collection of Songs (E. and Engr. 1727)
The Gate of Calais, or O the Roast Beef of Old England (Ptg. 1748; Engr. 1748/9***
The Enraged Musician (Ptg. ca. 1740; E. and Engr. 1741)
A Chorus of Singers (E. 1732)
*Frontispiece to the Oratorio of Judith (E. and Engr. 1733)
The Laughing Audience. See "Audience"
Music Introduced to Apollo by Minerva (Engr. 1727)

Special Performances

Hymen and Cupid (Dr. ca. 1740; Engr. 1740)

*Hogarth Inv. G. Vandergucht Sc.
**Hogarth Inv. James Basire Sc.
***Hogarth Inv. Hogarth and C. Grignion, Sc.
****Hogarth Inv. Hogarth and Chas. Mosley, Sc.
†Two other portraits questionably attributed to Hogarth:
  Mrs. Margaret (Peg) Woffington (Ptg. ca. early 1740's)
  Lavinia Fenton, Duchess of Bolton (Ptg. ca. 1740)

NOTES

1 Boswell describes this incident in a note for 11–19 November 1773, *Journal of a Tour to the Hebrides with Samuel Johnson, L.L.D.*, ed. F. A. Pottle and C. H. Bennett (New York: McGraw-Hill, 1961), p. 387, where he relates that one night, sitting with Dr. Hugh Blair in the Drury Lane pit: "I entertained the audience prodigiously imitating the lowing of a cow. . . . I was so successful in this boyish frolic that the universal cry of the galleries was, 'Encore the cow! Encore the cow!' " Thomas Rowlandson's etching of the scene, published 20 June 1786, was entitled "Imitations at Drury Lane Theatre by the Journalist." Boswell's narration appears under the portrayal, one of Rowlandson's illustrations to the "Journal of a Tour in the Hebrides (sic)." See Joseph Grego, *Rowlandson the Caricaturist* (London: Chatto and Windus, 1880), I, 198, no. 10, and Metropolitan Museum of Art Print no. 17.3.888-345/c.
2 *Boswell's London Journal 1762–1763*, ed. F. A. Pottle (New York: McGraw-Hill, 1950), pp. 154–55.
3 Richard Southern speaks of the "present slight knowledge of early eighteenth century English theatre interiors," *The Seven Ages of the Theatre* (New York: Hill and Wang, 1961), p. 244, and Allan S. Jackson, "Little

Known Theatrical Prints of the Eighteenth Century," *Theatre Notebook,* 22 (Spring 1968), 113, notes that a "lack of pictorial material has always plagued students of theatre history."

4 *The London Stage, 1747–1776,* part 4, vol. I, p. xxiv. Stone posits that one cannot understand the "impact of eighteenth-century drama in the current of eighteenth-century life and ideas merely by reading the texts of the plays." Further references to the calendar account of *The London Stage, 1660–1880* (Carbondale, Illinois: Southern Illinois University Press, 1965–68) will be abbreviated as *LS,* 4, I, xxiv, in my text. I am indebted to Professor Stone for his valuable suggestions and comments on Hogarth and eighteenth-century theater and drama.

5 See Checklist at the end of this essay.

6 "Hogarth's Narrative Method in Practice and Theory," in *England in the Restoration and Early Eighteenth Century,* ed. H. T. Swedenberg, Jr. (Berkeley: University of California Press, 1972), p. 172.

7 "Hogarth and the English Garden," in *Encounters: Essays on Literature and the Visual Arts,* ed. John D. Hunt (New York: W. W. Norton & Company, 1971), p. 85. My debt to Ronald Paulson extends beyond the insights here to his helpful comments and pioneering work in Hogarth studies.

8 Paulson remarks Hogarth "thought of his pictures in terms of a stage representation—a succession of scenes, with lines spoken and gestures— rather than a book" (*"The Harlot's Progress* and the Tradition of History Painting," *Eighteenth-Century Studies,* 1 [Fall 1967], 85).

9 This fragment is among the manuscripts edited by Joseph T. A. Burke in *The Analysis of Beauty with the Rejected Passages from the Manuscript Drafts and Autobiographical Notes* (Oxford: The Clarendon Press, 1955), p. 209. Page references in my text cite this edition.

10 These unpublished references in the notebooks in the British Museum mention *The Rehearsal* (Egerton MS 3016 f 94b) and foreign stage dances.

11 Frederick Antal's Chapter 4, "Hogarth's Representations of the Theatre," in *Hogarth and His Place in European Art* (New York: Basic Books, 1962), pp. 58–75, is to my knowledge the most extensive examination of Hogarth and the drama and theater of his day.

12 *Hogarth: His Life, Art, and Times* (New Haven: Yale University Press, 1971), I, 290. He claims in particular that the "intimacy" (or "closeness and smallness of the stage") and "frequent changes of scene" of the English theater may have influenced the artist, an avid theatergoer. Paulson's discussion of the six versions painted between 1728 and 1730 considers the use of actual stage events and structure (*Life,* I, 183 ff.). Further references in my text to the biography appear as *Life* followed by volume and page number.

13 For instance, Richard Southern raises the question of authenticity in Hogarth's "illustrations" of stage incidents ("Hogarth: Prints of Scenes," *Theatre Notebook*, 8 [1953], 19), and with regard to eighteenth-century frontispieces, Bamber Gascoigne claims artists tended to "illustrate" the story of a play rather than depict the play in actual performance (*World Theatre* [Boston: Little, Brown and Co., 1968], p. 200). Allan Jackson acknowledges that eighteenth-century satirical prints give some idea of actual staging techniques, but concludes one can "never be sure" about their accuracy ("Little Known Theatrical Prints of the Eighteenth Century," 113 [above, n. 3]).

14 Antal, *Hogarth*, pp. 59, 71 and 65.

15 Gascoigne (above, n. 13), who feels Hogarth's intention was "satirical rather than realistic," notes that the "unruly air" of the "coarse spectators" is confirmed by a mass of evidence (p. 226). For links with theatrical music in this etched print, see my article "Music and Theater in Hogarth," *The Musical Quarterly*, 57 (July 1971), 422 and 425.

16 Ronald Paulson, *Hogarth's Graphic Works*, rev. ed. (New Haven: Yale University Press, 1970), I, p. 154. Further citations in my text to this catalogue will be abbreviated as *HGW*, I, 153.

17 "Verbal and Visual Caricature in the Age of Dryden, Swift, and Pope," in *England in the Restoration and Early Eighteenth Century*, ed. H. T. Swedenberg, Jr. (Berkeley: University of California Press, 1972), p. 178.

18 This arrangement fits Emmett Avery's outline of patent theater audiences (*LS*, 2, I, xlv).

19 Antal, *Hogarth*, p. 234.

20 Paulson, *HGW*, I, 182, and *Life*, I, 395–97. Antal, *Hogarth*, p. 73, notes that the "tragic-comic life of such a company, the incongruity between the miserable surroundings in which these poverty-stricken actors have to live and their roles as celestial figures, forms the main theme of the engraving."

21 "Hogarth and the English Garden," p. 86.

22 Philip L. Lorraine, *Drottningholm Court Theatre* (Stockholm: Föreningen Drottningholmsteaterns, Vänner, 1964), p. 3. The theater was built in 1754, destroyed by fire in 1762 and rebuilt in 1766. Thirty wing sets were found in good condition when the theater was rediscovered almost intact in 1921 (pp. 4, 6 and 12).

23 I am grateful to Mrs. Elsa Lindberg of Stockholm for this information.

24 Sybil Rosenfeld, *Strolling Players and Drama in the Provinces 1660–1765* (Cambridge: The University Press, 1939), p. 23.

25 Hogarth delayed publication of the portrayal one year (*Life*, I, 381).

26 Rosenfeld, *Strolling Players*, p. 28.

27 *The World of Hogarth: Lichtenberg's Commentaries on Hogarth's Engravings,* trans. I. and G. Herdan (London: The Chesset Press, 1966), p. 159.

28 Sybil Rosenfeld, *The Theatre of the London Fairs in the Eighteenth Century* (Cambridge: The University Press, 1960), p. 151. I have drawn on Chapter 9, "Theatres and Staging" (pp. 150–69), for information about fair showcloths and booths.

29 Egerton MS 3013 41b, British Museum. A. P. Oppé titles the sketch "The 'Old Baby', The Child in a Man's Wig, and The Ballet Dancer." See *The Drawings of William Hogarth* (London: Phaidon Press, 1948), plate 77, Catalogue no. 81(e), p. 51.

30 Rosenfeld, *Theatre of the London Fairs,* p. 155.

31 "Hogarth and the English Garden," p. 87.

32 For a brief discussion of such borrowings see my article "*The Rake's Progress:* A New Theatrical Version of William Hogarth's Prints," *Notes & Queries,* 19 (October 1972), 381–83.

Francesco Guardi as an Apprentice in the Studio of Giambattista Tiepolo

GEORGE KNOX

Some years ago Antonio Morassi published in *Master Drawings* a sheet showing a life class in a Venetian studio.[1] He attributed it to the young Giambattista Tiepolo, and he cautiously advanced the suggestion that it may have represented a life class in the studio of Piazzetta. It shows a reassuringly familiar scene, the diligent students grouped around the male model, and one would like to imagine that this was the way instruction continued in the Tiepolo studio, with successive generations of young aspirants receiving a sound basic education under the guidance of the master.

But however things may have been in the studio of Piazzetta, little attention seems to have been paid to life drawing in that of Tiepolo. Indeed, among the 6,000 extant drawings by Giambattista and his sons Domenico and Lorenzo, hardly more than a dozen can be counted which have some claim to be regarded as life drawings,[2] a fraction of one per cent, and we shall see that the instruction of the young artist, whom it would be perhaps more accurate to describe as the young apprentice, proceeded upon entirely different lines.

It seems that the number of apprentices in the Tiepolo studio were very few indeed. I believe that only six can be identified with certainty, and of these three were members of his own family. The six in order of appearance are his young brother-in-law Francesco Guardi and Giovanni Raggi of Bergamo, both born in 1712, Francesco Lorenzi of Verona, probably born in 1719,[3] Giustino Menescardi of Milan, perhaps born c. 1720, and his sons, Domenico and Lorenzo, born in 1727 and 1736 respectively. One may observe that the three who were not members of the family were also not Venetians, that we have no record of an apprentice in the studio prior to c. 1730, when Giambattista was thirty-four years old, and that once Domenico appears in the studio, I would say in the year 1743, no further apprentices or assistants from outside the family seem to have been engaged.

Documents relating to these apprentices or assistants barely exist, but the presence of Giovanni Raggi in the studio is established by two letters of 1734, and some attempt to establish his role in the studio, as illustrated in the drawings at least, was initiated at the time of the exhibition of Tiepolo drawings at the Fogg Art Museum in 1970.[4] The presence of Francesco Guardi in the studio is not attested by any document, and in spite of its inherent probability, I do not think that it has ever been explored as a possibility, much less demonstrated. And this is obviously a matter of some importance, for if Giovanni Raggi is a secondary figure and the definition of his role in the studio is a matter of some academic interest, which might lead to a more precise attribution of a few paintings and drawings, Francesco Guardi on the other hand is a major figure, and one moreover whose early development is entirely shrouded in mystery.

In the museum at Berlin-Dahlem there is a considerable volume of Tiepolo material which has been very little explored. Among it are two sketchbooks which have been briefly noticed. One of them, which need not concern us here, is filled with pen and wash drawings in a style which approximates to that of Giambattista c. 1740: so far as one can tell they are not copies but pastiches, and they may be attributed with some confidence to Giustino Menescardi of Milan, number four on the list above.[5]

The other sketchbook is much earlier in date. It consists of sixty-seven numbered sheets, which often have drawings on both sides, and already in 1927 Hadeln noted that several of the drawings are associated with the frescoes of the Archbishop's Palace at Udine, particularly with the frescoes of the Gallery, upon which Giambattista was engaged in or about 1726.[6] Thus Folio 8 recto (fig. 1) shows two figures: one stands in the foreground, holding a vase, and the other, further back, walks away bearing a vase on her head. The central fresco of the Gallery, which depicts the somewhat unusual story of *Rachel hiding the idols from Laban* (Genesis 31:17–35), shows a figure in the right part which corresponds pretty exactly to our drawing. The angle of the vase is slightly different: the woman wears a light turban on her head, and a child grasps her cloak. The second figure is nowhere to be seen.[7]

Another sheet, Folio 47 verso (fig. 2) shows the entire composition of another part of the decorations of the Gallery, which depicts the story of *The Meeting of Jacob and Esau* (Genesis 33), and here the drawing corresponds closely to the fresco, though certain details are omitted.[8]

When one compares these studies with the superb sheet by Giambattista at Chicago, depicting another Biblical story which is rarely found in art, *Moses Receiving the Offerings of the Princes* (Numbers 7),[9] a composition which is closely related to the *Rachel* fresco at Udine, and which could very easily have been a first proposal for the fresco in this central position, it is evident that they are far inferior in quality, and yet one can see clearly that they do strive to reproduce the characteristics of Giambattista's style as closely as possible. In short they are copies of Giambattista's studies for the Udine frescoes. This was evident to Hadeln, who noted the slight differences between the drawings and the frescoes, and who came to the entirely acceptable conclusion that "we have to consider the probability that the pupil copyist did not draw from the frescoes, but from obsolete preliminary designs," and he goes on to point out that "as reproductions of the latter, the copies are of historical value."[10]

The Berlin First Sketchbook is the earliest demonstration that we have of a practice which was to become standard in the Tiepolo studio, that is that the fundamental training of the student apprentice was to copy the drawings of the master. There is nothing very revolutionary about this, and the principle is set out in Algarotti's *Dialogue on Painting*. I quote from the London edition of 1764, chapter 1, "Of the first education of a painter," p. 6: "It is not a matter of so little importance, as some are, perhaps, apt to imagine, upon what drawings a pupil is first put to exercise his talents. Let the first profiles, the first hands, the first feet given him to copy, be of the best masters, so as to bring his eye and his hand early acquainted with the most elegant forms, and the most beautiful proportions. . . . A vessel will ever retain the scent which it has first contacted."

It would hardly be worth insisting upon this point were it not that hundreds of chalk drawings by Giambattista are still almost universally held to be copies, by other members of the studio, after details of his paintings and frescoes. All extant studio copies, which can be counted by the hundred, can be shown in most cases to be copies of original drawings by Giambattista.[11] How closely these copies conformed to the original model seems to be demonstrated by a second series of copies, also at Berlin, which are here held to be based upon the same set of originals.[12] If the sketchbook drawings are by copyist A, then the second set are by copyist B.

The copyist of the Berlin First Sketchbook was evidently quite young and relatively unskilled, but I submit that he learned fast. Among the loose drawings at Berlin are two sheets (figs. 3 and 4) which show the same composition. Berlin 11570 (fig. 3) is evidently a fine original study by Giambattista while Berlin 9956 (fig. 4) can be recognized as an extraordinarily free and vibrant copy. No longer does the copyist feel obliged to follow the model line by line, in fact his line now has a completely different and completely personal quality, more broken and angular. The wash too is applied boldly, with a full brush, and yet it observes the contours of the linear pattern exactly.

But copyist he is, for the original has numerous *pentimenti* which he ignores. Moreover the Berlin collection has a whole series of further examples by the same hand which are copies of drawings by Giambattista at Trieste, studies for the Villa Loschi at Biron of 1734 (figs. 5 and 6).[13] Curiously enough, we have a second series of copies of these Biron studies, not at Berlin but at Florence, and I would submit that just as the Berlin copies of the Trieste drawings show Copyist A in a more developed form, so the Florentine copies show Copyist B in a more developed form.[14]

I have never had much doubt about the identity of Copyist B. He appears to be Giovanni Raggi of Bergamo, who joined Giambattista when the latter was working in the Capella Colleoni at Bergamo in 1732–33. The characteristics of his style are clearly indicated in the series of drawings shown in the Fogg exhibition. One of these can now be shown to belong to the same series as those of Copyist B in Berlin, and both figures are recopied in the Berlin First Sketchbook by Copyist A.[15]

Raggi was undoubtedly an extremely skillful copyist of Giambattista's drawings, and in the absence of the original it is often extremely difficult to detect his hand. I myself was guilty of publishing a Raggi copy in *Master Drawings* as a Giambattista, only to have my gullibility demonstrated when the original emerged from total obscurity a few weeks later.[16] Moreover he seems to have continued to make these "facsimilies" throughout his years in the Tiepolo studio, long after his apprenticeship was over.[17] Unfortunately the total success of this aspect of his training did not save him from equally total obscurity and mediocrity once he left the Tiepolo studio.

But if Copyist B is Raggi, then who is copyist A? Let us consider a further pair of drawings showing *The Temptation of St. Anthony*. The original by Giambattista was formerly in the Boymans Museum, but it was lost during the Second World War. The copy is in the Wallraf collection. In a long article devoted to my shortcomings, Morassi went out of his way to publish the copy as a Menescardi, but I am sure he is mistaken, and that the copyist should be identified as the young Francesco Guardi. The problem is complicated by the fact that we have no securely dated drawing by Francesco prior to 1760, but I do not think that anyone has disagreed with Byam Shaw that the drawing in the British Museum, an *Allegory of Venice,* is an early Francesco Guardi, and I would say that the quality of the line and the mode of applying the wash are exactly the same as in the Berlin drawings of Copyist A.[18] Very similar characteristics may also be noted between the latter and the copies by Francesco Guardi after Pietro Longhi in the Correr Museum.[19]

Thus I would suggest that c. 1732–34 Francesco Guardi and Giovanni Raggi worked together in the Tiepolo studio, copying drawings by Giambattista: first a batch of drawings dating from the mid-twenties, which have vanished without a trace, and then a series of studies for the villa at Biron which still survive at Trieste. It is a curious twist of fate that has led to the survival of a substantial and representative series of copies of the latter by each apprentice. The merit, or demerit, of those by Raggi is that they are so close to the originals that they can easily be taken for drawings by Giambattista himself. The merit of those by Francesco Guardi is that, apart from their inherit excellence, they appear to throw some light on the very obscure beginnings of one of the least documented and most delightful painters of the Venetian *settecento.*[20]

Curiously enough, Tiepolo studies, and the pockets and even more the self-esteem of collectors of Tiepolo drawings, have not suffered unduly by mistaking studio copies for originals. It has been bedeviled rather by an excessive refinement of connoisseurship which has led to hundreds of original chalk drawings being condemned as studio copies, simply because they lacked the bravura of Giambattista's pen and wash drawings, having a completely different function.

Thus the superb album of original studies in the Hermitage for the celebrated frescoes of the Ca'Labia of c. 1744 is totally neglected, as a series of "copies after the frescoes" by Domenico (fig. 7). Perhaps this chorus of condemnation will abate now that an album of copies of those studies, either by Francesco Lorenzi or more probably by the young Domenico, has come to light (fig. 8).[21]

When Lorenzo Tiepolo entered the studio in his turn, during the Würzburg years (1751–53), at the age of fourteen and one half to sixteen and one half, he followed the tradition of the studio as it has been established for some twenty years, and copied the drawings of Giambattista, sometimes copying pen and wash drawings (figs. 11 and 12), and sometimes chalk drawings (figs. 9 and 10). The superb drawing in the Woodner collection (fig. 9) has never been doubted by anyone as an authentic Giambattista, save by those like Morassi who believe that he never made a chalk drawing in his life, but other copies from the same album as the one shown here (fig. 10) show that I was still infected with such doubts when I gave several drawings by Giambattista in the Fogg Museum to Domenico and Lorenzo.[22] Such are the benefits to be derived from considering the work of the apprentices in the Tiepolo studio.

One purpose of this article is to draw attention to the fact that over a long period, making copies of drawings by Giambattista was the basic training of the apprentice in the Tiepolo studio. It must be noted that it is drawings and not paintings which are so copied, and when paintings and other works of art are copied, they are those of artists other than Tiepolo. As a youth, Domenico made copies after Titian, Palma Vecchio and Bellini. In the same category are the studies by Giambattista himself after the bust of Palma Giovane by Vittoria,[23] after details of the Veronese *Family of Darius before Alexander,* now in the National Gallery in London,[24] and after the antique.[25]

The object of this training was to enable the apprentice to assimilate the "house-style" of the studio, and to acquire basic skills by a close study of the master's drawings. The enterprise would have no point if the models were not original drawings by Giambattista himself. Thus the copies do not only record many original drawings by Giambattista which are lost; they also authenticate many which survive.

NOTES

1 Antonio Morassi, "A 'Scuola del Nudo' by Tiepolo." *Master Drawings*, 9, no. 1 (1971), plate 19.

2 The main group is at Stuttgart; see exhibition catalogue *Drawings by Giambattista, Domenico & Lorenzo Tiepolo* . . . Stuttgart Staatsgalerie 1970, nos. 99–109.

3 The birth date of Francesco Lorenzi is generally given as 1723, but one source indicates 1719, and since we now have two drawings dated 1737 (exhibition catalogue *Le Dessin vénétien*, Paris/Venice 1971 [Cini 33], nos. 140, 141), the earliest date is more satisfactory. For further data on Lorenzi drawings, see exhibition catalogue *Tiepolo: A Bicentenary Exhibition* (Cambridge, Mass.: Fogg Art Museum, 1970), nos. 27–30; Agnes Mongan, "Some Drawings by Francesco Lorenzi," *Studi in onore di Antonio Morassi* (Venice: Alfieri, n.d. [c. 1971]), p. 347. Some of the important group of Lorenzi drawings in the Museo del Castelvecchio at Verona have now been published by Anna Maria Caiani, "Affreschi e disegni inediti di Francesco Lorenzi," *Arte Veneta*, 36 (1972), 154–66.

4 The letter from Tiepolo to Lodovico Feronati of Bergamo, preserved at the Accademia Carrara and dated April 1734, was published by Caversazzi in *Emporium* 1899, by Sack, *Tiepolo*, Hamburg 1910, p. 63, and by Fogolari in *Nuova Antologia*, 1, September 1942, p. 33. See also exhibition catalogue (Cambridge, 1970), nos. 22–26.

5 Inventory number 79 B 14a. Two leaves from this sketchbook are reproduced by Hadeln, *Handzeichnungen von G.B. Tiepolo* (Munich, 1927), plates 199, 200. Further material from this sketchbook is published in Knox, "Giambattista Tiepolo: Variations on the theme of 'Anthony and Cleopatra'." *Master Drawings*, 12, no. 4 (1974), figs. 4–8.

6 Inventory number 79 B 14. Modern, *Tiepolo* (Vienna 1902), p. 42, and Molmenti, *Tiepolo* (Milan: Hoepli, 1909), p. 237, note 13, regards it as the work of Giambattista himself. Molmenti publishes four leaves, 1909 ed., p. 213; 1911 ed. (Paris: Hachette), plate 175. Hadeln's comments are discussed below.

7 The best reproductions of the Udine frescoes are to be found in Aldo Rizzi, *Tiepolo: L'archivescovado di Udine* (Milan: Fabbri/Skira, 1969) in series "I grandi decoratori." For this figure see plate 29.

8 This is not properly reproduced anywhere, but see Rizzi, *Tiepolo*, plate 21.

9 Inventory number 58.554; exhibited Cambridge 1970, no. 3. I must agree with Morassi that the connection with the frescoes of the Gallery is undeniable. Muraro has argued that the frescoes of the Gallery represent a first phase of Tiepolo's activity at Udine which may go back to a period

as early as 1718: Muraro, "Ricerche su Tiepolo Giovane," *Accademia di Scienze, Lettere ed Arti di Udine* (Udine: Arti Grafiche Friulane, 1970).

10 Hadeln, *Handzeichnungen,* p. 4.

11 The issue was raised in the exhibition catalogue (Stuttgart, 1970), pp. 9, 10. It has since been discussed by Boeck, "Tiepolo Zeichnungen in Stuttgart," *Kunstchronik,* 34 (March 1971), 57–60; von Borries, "Bemerkungen zu den Kreidezeichnungen von Giambattista und Domenico Tiepolo," *Zeitschrift für Kunstgeschichte* (1971), pp. 135–46; Byam Shaw, "Tiepolo Celebrations: Three Catalogues," *Master Drawings,* 9, no. 3 (1971), 264–76; and Morassi, "Sui disegni del Tiepolo nelle recenti mostre di Cambridge, Mass., e di Stoccarda," *Arte Veneta,* 29 (1970), 294–304.

12 Inventory numbers 21919–46. All are in pen and grey wash; c. 390 x 265 mm. None have been published, but another specimen of the same series is now in the Art Museum at Princeton University. This is discussed below.

13 Inventory numbers 21954–59; the last records an original drawing by Giambattista which can no longer be traced (fig. 6). For the Trieste drawings, see Vigni, *Disegni del Tiepolo,* (Padua: Le Tre Venezie, 1942), nos. 8–22; 2d ed. (Trieste: La Editoriale Liberia, 1972), nos. 28–42.

14 The drawings in the Museo Bardini number fourteen, pen and wash on white paper; c. 260 x 170 mm. All are unpublished, but are photographed: negative numbers S.F.G. 44001–6; Gernsheim corpus 22,164–84.

15 Exhibition catalogue (Cambridge, 1970), nos. 22–26. No. 22, a drawing in the Art Museum at Princeton, shows two figures which are also copied on Folios 24 and 29 of the Berlin First Sketchbook. Morassi, *Arte Veneta,* 29 (1970), 297, doubts the attribution to Raggi on the grounds that, entering the studio in 1732–33, he would not have copied drawings which would have been already six years old. However, as has already been noted, we presently find him copying drawings of c. 1734 (see preceding note).

16 Knox, "A Group of Tiepolo Drawings Owned and Engraved by Pietro Monaco," *Master Drawings* 3, no. 4 (1965), 389–97, plate 29. Linda Boyer, letter in *Master Drawings,* 4 (1966), 169, plate 33.

17 An interesting example is offered by drawing sold, with an attribution to Raggi at my suggestion, at Sotheby's, 13 July 1972, lot 39, one of a group of four similar specimens, which is a line for line copy of a drawing by Giambattista in the Horne Museum, inventory number 6324; Hadeln, *Handzeichnungen,* plate 61, which is associated with the ceiling of the Palazzo Clerici of 1740. Another copy of this drawing, again by Raggi, passed through the Weinmuller sale, 13 October 1938, lot 661.

18 For the Boymans drawing, see Knox, "Group of Tiepolo Drawings," fig.
13; for the copy, see exhibition catalogue *Tiepolo et Guardi,* (Paris:
Galerie Cailleux, 1952), plate 2, and Morassi, *Arte Veneta,* 29 (1970), fig.
441. For the drawing in the British Museum, see Byam Shaw, *The
Drawings of Francesco Guardi* (London: Faber & Faber, 1951), plate 3.
Curiously enough this drawing was once attributed to Domenico Tiepolo,
as Byam Shaw points out.

19 Pallucchini, *Die Zeichnungen des Francesco Guardi im Museum Correr in
Venedig* (Florence: Sansoni, 1943), plates 2–5.

20 The question of early links between Gianantonio and Francesco Guardi
and their distinguished bother-in-law has been explored from time to
time. In 1933, Byam Shaw published two drawings in the Louvre as
copies by Francesco after two paintings now given to Domenico, now in
Barcelona (*Old Master Drawings,* 7 [March 1933], plates 56, 57). Two
contributions to the Convegno Guardi touched on the problem: Barry
Hannigan, "Tiepolo at the Mostra dei Guardi," and George Knox, "A
Group of Drawings Attributed to Giambattista Tiepolo," *Problemi
Guardeschi* (Venice: Alfieri, 1967), pp. 55, 62. The link between the
Guardi banner at Budapest and a Tiepolo drawing was pointed out by
Knox, "Tiepolo & Guardi: a new point of contact," *Burlington Magazine,*
110 (May 1968), 278, and further points were made by Alice Binion in a
letter in the *Burlington Magazine,* 110 (September 1968), 519. It may be
worth noting here that the verso of the *stendardo* recently published by
Francesco Valcanover, "Un nuovo stendardo di Francesco Guardi," *Studi
in Onore di Antonio Morassi,* 317, fig. 2, derives from the painting by
Domenico Tiepolo in the Albertini collection in Rome (Adriano Mariuz,
Domenico Tiepolo [Venice: Alfieri, 1971], plate 60). Other copies by
Guardi after drawings by Tiepolo are extant, but may be somewhat later:
see Morassi, "Antonio Guardi as a Draughtsman," *Master Drawings,* 6, no. 2
(1968), 132, plate 26. This is a natural development from the Berlin
drawings here given to Francesco Guardi, and I would propose an attribution to him rather than to Gianantonio. It is again a copy of a lost
drawing by Giambattista, a study for one of the "Scherzi di Fantasia"
which raises intricate and interesting problems: see Knox, "G.B. Tiepolo:
The Dating of the 'Scherzi di Fantasia' and the 'Capricci'," *Burlington
Magazine,* 114 (December 1972), 842.

21 A check-list of the Hermitage album is given in Dobroklonsky, *State
Hermitage Museum: Drawings of the Italian School of the 17th and 18th
Centuries* (Leningrad: Hermitage, 1961), nos. 1423–1694. The "Francesco Lorenzi Sketchbook," which is in a private collection in Europe, is
unpublished. A full account of these and other groups of similar material
will appear shortly: Knox, *Giambattista and Domenico Tiepolo: A Study*

and *Catalogue Raisonné of the Chalk Drawings,* to be published by the Clarendon Press.

22 Exhibition catalogue (Cambridge, 1970), nos. 63, 64. These are copied in the Würzburg Third Sketchbook, which went missing during the Second World War, and which has recently returned to the Martin von Wagner Museum at Würzburg, Folios 40 and 32. The drawing here reproduced (fig. 10), though recorded photographically, is not in the album now.

23 Maison, "The Tiepolo Drawings after the Portrait Bust of Palma Giovane by Alessandro Vittoria," *Master Drawings,* 6, no. 4 (1968), 392.

24 Exhibition catalogue (Cambridge, 1970), no. 32.

25 Knox, "Tiepolo Drawings from the Saint-Saphorin Collection," *Atti del Congresso . . . Tiepolo, Udine 1970* (Milan: Electa, 1970), figs. 4–8.

Hogarth and the Iconography of Time

SAMUEL L. MACEY

If, in Maynard Mack's terms, we think of the City in contra-distinction to the Garden, then Hogarth is clearly the artist of the City. As one might expect, both the denotation and the connotation in Hogarth's work reflect the radical changes taking place in London life. The most influential technological change was probably the achievement of mechanical timekeeping sufficiently accurate for the needs of modern urban man. Related to this were the batch production and division of labour methods then being introduced into the manufacture of clocks and watches. Some of the key dates are the use of the pendulum in clocks from 1657, and the use of the balance spring in watches from about 1674.

Until the third quarter of the seventeenth century, clocks and watches were expensive and decorative toys. The pendulum clock provided the first reasonably accurate method of mechanical time-keeping at a point in history ready for accelerated urbanization. *Britten's Old Clocks and Watches* introduces its chapter on the period as follows:

> The present chapter covers perhaps the most important period in horological history. In the space of a quarter of a century accurate timekeeping became a possibility and to a very large extent it

was actually achieved. In 1655 a clock did well to keep time to within five minutes a day; in 1675 its error might, under favourable circumstances, be only as many seconds. Similarly watches were brought from an almost entirely unpredictable performance to within two or three minutes' accuracy a day or even less with reasonable luck.[1]

Some clocks certainly could keep time "within five minutes a day"; for general purposes, Ward's statement that "clocks could not be relied on to keep time more closely than to about a quarter of an hour per day"[2] is probably a better reflection of the standard of technology before the advent of the pendulum clock. The revolutionary factor is that for the first time in man's history, it was possible to produce timekeepers accurate enough for any normal domestic purposes of urbanized man. The use of minute and second hands in clocks or watches—previously a rarity—now became common. The modern mechanical age had arrived and the techniques as well as the thoughts of men would never be quite the same again.

In 1675, Wycherley ridicules Sir Jasper Fidget, the City knight, when he is obliged to leave his wife in the home of Horner because his watch shows him that it is "a quarter and a half quarter of a minute past eleven," but the influence of watches and clocks was to permeate all areas of London life. Tompion, the father of English clockmaking, had produced no less than six thousand watches and five hundred clocks by the time that he died in 1713. (Both he and his successor, Graham, are buried in Westminster Abbey.) In the following year, the British Government offered by Act of Parliament the unprecedented prize of twenty thousand pounds for an accurate method of determining the longitude at sea. (The impetus for the greatest horological inventions came frequently from the needs of astronomy and navigation.) The Act set off a spate of invention not unlike our own advances in interplanetary technology that have recently pushed timekeeping to an accuracy of one second in thirty thousand years. It has been claimed—by Commander Waters and Bruton among others—that this prize "was in many ways responsible for the Industrial Revolution that followed."[3] Harrison's marine chronometer H3 was ready by 1760, and led to his ultimate receipt of the award. That was the year (shortly before the death of Hogarth) when our schoolbooks tell us that the Industrial Revolution began. Though steam power was ultimately essential to the Industrial Revolution, Lewis Mumford has claimed with some justification that "The clock, not the steam engine, is the key machine of the modern industrial age." As Carlo Cipolla puts it, "the construction of high precision timekeepers presupposed the solution of basic problems of mechanics that were at the very heart of the Scientific Revolution."[4] Insofar as the clock was concerned, the essential inventions belong to the "horological revolution" of 1660–1760.

This paper is not concerned with the many advances in metallurgy, mechanical invention, precision engineering, machine tools, and production methods that are directly attributable to the London centered "horological revolution." We should, however, be aware of the use of the clock analogy for the body, traceable from the "mechanistic" philosophy of Descartes through to Hartley and our modern behavioral sciences; the use of clock analogies during the horological revolution by such essentially different philosophers as Hobbes, Locke, Leibniz, Shaftesbury, and the early Berkeley; and the use of the clockmaker-clock analogy for God and his universe by such eminent scientists as Boyle and Newton.

It is the nature of language to explain difficult abstract concepts through an analogy with aspects of a topical concrete phenomenon readily understood by author and audience. During the horological revolution, clocks and watches frequently supplied this metaphor, but they were also of interest for their own intrinsic value. Defoe's *Moll Flanders* demonstrates remarkably well the importance of watches in the developing urban economy. It is worth noting that when his accomplice produced a gold watch taken during church from a lady's side, Defoe's Colonel Jack was "amaz'd at such a thing, as that in a Country Town." Yet, as Moll said of herself and her first fellow thief, before the latter was executed, "we had at one time one-and-twenty gold watches in our hands."

After 1675, men's watches disappeared into the waistcoat or the fob of the breeches, but ladies' watches were a most important piece of jewellery that hung from the waist, often with winding key, seal, and much else. Gulliver is made fast with "chains, like those that hang from a lady's watch in Europe, and almost as large." As Moll tells us more than once, "I had very good clothes on and a gold watch by my side, as like a lady as other folks." Hogarth's best example of a lady with her watch is his portrait of Miss Mary Edwards.[5] There are more equivocal and probably not unconnected examples in *Taste à la Mode* and *Marriage à la Mode,* Plate 4. Mother Needham in *Harlot's Progress,* Plate 1, and Young Squanderfield's mistress in *Marriage à la Mode,* Plate 3, demonstrate the use of the watch by low life aspiring above its station. Since Tompion's standard price was "£23 for an ordinary watch in a gold case" or "£70 for a gold repeating watch,"[6] and Moll was eventually caught by an unusually honest servant who earned three pounds annually, we can readily understand the temptation to "take a watch" reflected throughout the literature of the period.

For reasons that I am unable entirely to explain, the artist most directly concerned with the artifacts for measuring time was not a poet but a caricaturist and painter. The life of Hogarth (1697–1764) runs concurrently with the latter part of the horological revolution, and is almost exactly suited to the portrayal of its impact on society. The works of James Gillray (1757–1815) and Thomas Rowlandson (1757–1827), who took over the mantle of Hogarth, differ in nothing so much as the almost total absence from their works of clocks, watches, and sandglasses.[7] Much the same is true of Joseph Wright of Derby, "the first professional painter directly to express the spirit of the industrial revolution." In fact Klingender's valuable study, *Art and the Industrial Revolution,* finds no need either to mention or to portray clocks and watches. Steam engines and forges—whether as objects for pride or antagonism—provided a much more compelling metaphor through which to depict an industrial age. In a comparable manner, Sussman—though he has a whole chapter on Dickens in *Victorians and the Machine*—avoids horology. As he puts it: "machine technology did not truly engage the literary imagination until the coming of the railway."[8]

There had of course been illustrations of clocks and watches before the time of Hogarth. But these had been exceptional cases rather than themes found throughout the whole corpus of an artist's work. Of the earlier major artists, in any way comparable to Hogarth, one might have expected that Dürer would have treated symbolically the question of time. With one exception, there is a marked absence of clocks, watches, and sandglasses from Dürer's works. The hourglass is not only portrayed but it is essential to the symbolism of Dürer's three most famous copper engravings: *Knight, Death, and the Devil; St. Jerome in his Study;* and *Melancholia I.* (The hourglass after its invention early in the Renaissance was added to the iconography of Time and Death.)[9]

Like Dürer, Hogarth was trained as an engraver, but the nature of the times had added a new dimension to that trade. As George Vertue reported of Hogarth, he was "bred up to small gravings of plate work & watch workes."[10] Hogarth seems to have been conscious of the value of time for planning his own work. In his later portraits, he "sometimes painted little more than faces," and proposed to Wilson "to paint a Portrait in four sittings, allowing only a quarter of an hour to each." Hogarth extended his ingenious work-study methods to the sale as well as the paintings of pictures. Vertue reports on his auction of paintings—that included *A Harlot's Progress, A Rake's Progress,* and *The Four Times of the Day*—"by a new manner of sale . . . to bid Gold only by a Clock, set purposely by the minute hand—5 minutes each lott . . . and by this suble means. [*sic*] he sold about 20 pictures of his own paintings [*sic*] for near 450 pounds in an hour." When Hogarth is defending himself from the suggestion that he is vain, he turns to watchmaking for his exemplum. "Vanity," he maintains, "consists chiefly in fancying one doth better than one does"; but if a watchmaker claims that he can make a watch as good as any man, and demonstrates that he really can, "the watchmaker is not branded as infamous."[11]

It is in the nature of Hogarth's age that, unlike Dürer, he is generally concerned with mechanical timekeeping. A sermon glass is prominently displayed in *The Sleeping Congregation,* and a vertical sundial in the country scene of *Chairing the Member;* but these reflect the pulpit and the country in which such methods of timekeeping continued to prevail throughout the eighteenth century. In Hogarth's work, they are the exception rather than the rule. He is essentially an urban artist, a painter of the City. We have noted how the originals of *A Harlot's Progress* and *A Rake's Progress* were sold "by a Clock." Like Hogarth's other great progress, *Industry and Idleness,* they are both concerned, at one point, with the important "low life" occupation of "taking a watch." Ronald Paulson suggests that "It may have been *Moll Flanders* that first planted in Hogarth's mind the image of a harlot as one who, like Moll, simply wants to be a 'gentlewoman.' " Certainly, in Plate 3 we see Hogarth's harlot sitting on the edge of her bed with one breast exposed, and holding up a stolen watch. In Fielding's *Covent Garden Tragedy* "Plate 3 is alluded to when Stormandra reminds Bilkum 'Did I not pick a pocket of a watch, / A Pocket pick for thee?' "[12] In exactly the same structural position as the *Harlot's Progress* (the third plate out of six), the taking of a watch is once again the central motif for the *Rake's Progress.* In this case, the protagonist is the dupe who sits dallying with the inmates of a bordello. *Industry and Idleness* shows, in twelve plates, the very different progresses of two apprentices who start with equal opportunity. In much the same structural position as the *Harlot* and the *Rake,* the idle apprentice is disclosed in bed with "a common Prostitute"; she has stolen watches (complete with keys and seals) in front of her (Plate 7). The reverse side of life's coin is illustrated in Plate 8, "The Industrious 'Prentice grown rich, & Sheriff of London." This is in sharp contrast with Plate 9, "The Idle Prentice betray'd by his Whore, & taken in a Night Cellar with his Accomplice." They are caught red handed; the watches are between the men in the front center of the plate.

But Hogarth goes beyond Defoe; his horological allusions are not limited to the taking of a watch. In addition, he uses clocks for both denotation and connotation. In terms of denotation, *Four Times of the Day* indicate both morning and noon by means of the clock. In much the same way, *The Battle of the Pictures* uses a clock to denote the time of Hogarth's auction, to which reference has already been made. *The Battle of the Pictures*— whose theme is reminiscent of Swift's *Battle of the Books*—was to be used as the ticket of admission "on the last Day of Sale."[13]

In *Masquerade Ticket* (second state), the large clock at top center shows 1:30. Heidegger's face is so placed that the hour hand marked "Wit" looks like a riband over his left shoulder. But Impertinence on the minute hand and Nonsense on the pendulum dangle indecently beneath, flanked on each side by a pair of "Lecherometers" and the clearly suggestive notices "Supper below." On the left, as Paulson indicates, "masqueraders are killing 'Time' " at the altar of Priapus.[14]

The clock face in the top left corner of *The Times* (hanging outside the home of the Government) seems relatively innocuous in the scene of fire and chaos. But *The Times* takes on new connotations when one has "read" the engraving across to the bottom right hand corner. There a destitute child is playing with an almost identical clock. In the third of the four *Stages of Cruelty*, the gruesome murder of Ann Gill (who has become a thief for her seducer, Tom Nero) uses an iconography of stolen watches in the same climactic position as *Industry and Idleness*, *The Harlot*, and *The Rake*. The scene's graveyard atmosphere is emphasized by the clock. The woodcut (though not the engraving) shows a winged hourglass,[15] suggests the year 1750, and has enough lettering for one to decipher the message: "memento mori." It may be of significance that there is a full clock only in the engraving; it is cut in half by the outer edge of the woodcut. The same is true as between the clocks in the painting and engraving of Hogarth's *Morning*. In *Southwark Fair*, the clock in the clock-tower at the centre is also cut in half, this time by the large picture of the Trojan Horse.

Hogarth is, above all, a producer of character portraits; for this, too, he can make use of the watch. In *Analysis of Beauty*, Plate 2, the weakness of the apparently cuckolded husband, at the ball, is emphasized by the way that he points to his watch; in the drawing of *Thomas Morell,* the clock above the head of the protagonist serves a similar purpose to the hourglass above Jerome's head in Dürer's *St. Jerome in his Study.* The hourglass could be used as a general symbol of Temperance, Time, or Death. But the precise mechanical measurement of time and the widespread use of the minute hand began only in the second half of the seventeenth century. The extra possibilities for symbolism that the clock now offered provided Hogarth with a tool unavailable to his predecessors, and never fully exploited by subsequent artists.

The denotation and connotation of time that a clock could provide is perhaps exemplified as well as anywhere in Hogarth's delightful study in seduction, *The Lady's Last Stake.* The ornate clock on the mantlepiece is probably French, but it has an English-type dial and Hogarth has symbolically put Father Time's scythe into the hands of Cupid. At 4:55, with the moon rising through the window, the clock is about to show sunset, and there is very little time left for the lady to resolve the titillating dilemma. Hogarth describes the subject of the painting as "a virtuous married lady that had lost all at cards to a young officer, wavering at his suit whether she should part with her honour or no to regain the loss which was offered to her." The clock adds to the piquancy of the situation; Cupid with his scythe is mounted above it on a pedestal inscribed: "NUNC NUNC." Some seventeen years earlier, Hogarth had painted *The Graham Children* with Cupid and his scythe similarly (and perhaps even prophetically) placed. Here Hogarth depicts an English striking and probably also repeating clock of the type that is now very highly prized by collectors.

An even more ornate clock than the one in *The Lady's Last Stake* stands above the head of the dissipated husband in *Marriage à la Mode,* Plate 2. Even without considering the specific symbolism of the clock, in which fish and foliage are juxtaposed, one can readily observe how the over-dressed nobleman and the over-ornate clock emphasize each other's excesses. By way of contrast, in Plate 6, his City alderman father-in-law stands beneath a simple weight-driven clock that emphasizes frugality and punctuality.

In discussing the two states of *A Midnight Modern Conversation,* Paulson says: "By comparing these two pictures, it is easy to see how Hogarth moved from a portrait group, a 'conversation' in that sense, to a picture with moral overtones as well as portraits."[16] The same point is further stressed by the change in the position and nature of the clocks. The relatively small bracket clock on the right of the picture becomes a towering grandfather clock in the subsequent version. From the left hand rear corner of the room, it unmistakably points out the lateness of the hour to revellers and readers alike. Here, as elsewhere, there may be an intentional "pun" in the denotation of time. What at first seems to be twenty past midnight, appears on closer inspection to be three or four o'clock in the morning.

Not surprisingly, there is also a grandfather clock at the rear of Hogarth's Frontispiece for *Tristram Shandy.* This has a symbolic value of its own, but Sterne's clock (among other things) already symbolizes some of the negative qualities that came to be associated with the mechanical aspects of clockwork. Hogarth's own awareness of a negative quality in clockwork is demonstrated by his emphasis on the stiff and mechanical attributes of Vaucanson's duck, when he refers to this famous automaton in the *Analysis of Beauty* (1753).[17] Time is clearly involved in the complex and sinister symbolism of *The South Sea Scheme* (first state). There, Father Time has become the Devil himself. In his shop set up in the Guildhall, he uses his scythe to hack flesh from the golden haunches of the goddess Fortune (Hogarth has here reverted to the older iconography of Saturn-Time who consumed human flesh and was occasionally portrayed with Fortune and her wheel.)[18] Above Father Time, beside the clock, stands God or Magog. It is past 6:00 p.m. and the storm clouds are gathering. Just as the pillar at which Honour is being beaten is artistically related to the London Monument, so the wheel on which Honesty is being castigated is related to the South Sea merry-go-round and the clock.

In the same year as the Frontispiece for *Tristram Shandy*, Hogarth produced his provocative *The Cockpit* (1759). Paulson perceptively relates this to the influence of Dante and the circular structure of *Inferno*. But if it is a picture of hell and the apocalypse, it is one over the very center of which there falls the highly symbolic shadow of a condemned man holding up a watch. Klingender gives a valuable demonstration of the influence of contemporary iron mines, iron works, and railway tunnels on the haunting illustrations that John Martin made for the hell of *Paradise Lost* during the industrial revolution.[19] It is possible that Hogarth used the watch as a comparable metaphor for hell in his *Cockpit*. Certainly, he makes an ominous statement about time in the *Tailpiece*.

Hogarth used a complex symbolism of time for his last and perhaps most haunting work, *Tailpiece, or the Bathos* (1764). The title of the engraving, *The Bathos, or Manner of Sinking in Sublime Paintings* makes clear the debt to Pope's *Peri Bathous: or the Art of Sinking in Poetry* (1727). The subject cannot help but remind one of the end of *Dunciad* IV (1742–43), when the corruption in the arts has polluted all phases of existence: chaos is come again, "And Universal Darkness buries All."

But Hogarth's tailpiece, also produced at the end of his life, relies heavily on symbols of time. Father Time (so often and so variously represented in Hogarth's canon) rests on a broken column in the middle of the work. He had appeared three years earlier in *Time Smoking a Picture*. But now the word *Finis* is written in the smoke that comes from Time's mouth after he has removed his broken pipe. Among the debris lying around, are a broken palette, musket, crown, and bottle. The last page of a play shows the words *Exeunt Omnes;* a statute of bankruptcy—sealed with the rider on a white horse (from Revelation)—indicates that Nature is bankrupt; and a flame is just about to consume a picture entitled *The Times*. In the hand of Father Time, lies his last will and testament; he bequeaths his world, "all and every Atom thereof to [an erased lacuna] Chaos whom I appoint my sole Executor." The witnesses to the document are the three fates, Clotho,

Lachesis, and Atropos. Hogarth's message is further stressed by the broken building, the ruined tower, the gibetted man, the ominous gravestone, the sinking ship, and the falling inn sign that is entitled "The World's End" and shows an orb in flames.

All these are symbols indicating the passage of time. But there are also precise allusions to time reminiscent of the roles that the sun, the moon, the seasons, the bell, the hourglass, and the clock respectively had played in their contributions to time measurement. In Hogarth's great "Apocalypse," the sun chariot of Phaeton is falling from the sky, the moon is overcast, the autumnal scythe of time is broken, the great bell is cracked, the sand-glass is splintered, and the clock has no hands. In the original drawing, Time had been leaning against a much larger clock face which came between himself and the gravestone. Time's wing partly covered the clock, and the clock partly covered the skull and crossbones at the top of the gravestone.

Apart from the fact that he lived through London's horological revolution and was "bred up to small gravings of plate work and watch workes," it is difficult to suggest why Hogarth is the only plastic artist of the first rank to have demonstrated so wide an interest in mechanical clocks. One might argue that until the horological revolution clocks and watches were neither as numerous, as accurate, nor as readily marketable as Hogarth's symbolism required. The *De Horologiis in Arte* of Alfred Chapuis curiously illustrates nothing by Hogarth; Holbein and Jan Breughel are the two painters from whom he draws most examples.[20] But in these artists the iconography of time through clocks and watches is far less pervasive than in Hogarth. After the horological revolution, mechanical timekeeping probably lost some of its topical appeal. There is an almost total absence of clocks, watches, and sand-glasses in the works of James Gillray and Thomas Rowlandson who took over the mantle of Hogarth. As has also been previously noted, Klingender neither mentions nor illustrates clocks and watches in his standard work, *Art and the Industrial Revolution.* In addition, after the horological revolution, certain connotations—like "mechanical art" and "clockwork automations"—were to put a different emphasis on the clock than is generally evident in Hogarth.

It has, I think, been widely recognized that his City and his times are inextricably bound up in the denotation and connotation of Hogarth's work. My purpose has been to demonstrate how true this is in respect of clocks and watches that made so remarkable an impact on London life during the horological revolution of 1660–1760.

NOTES

1 G. H. Baillie and C. A. Ilbert, *Britten's Old Clocks and Watches and Their Makers,* 7th ed. (New York: Bonanza Books, 1956), p. 66.

2 F. A. B. Ward, *Time Measurement: Historical Review* (London: Science Museum, 1970), pp. 1, 17.

3 D. W. Waters, "Time, Ships and Civilization," *Antiquarian Horology,* 4 (June 1963), 85; and Eric Bruton, *Clocks and Watches* (Feltham: Hamlyn, 1968), p. 84.

4 Carlo M. Cipolla, *European Culture and Overseas Expansion* (Harmondsworth: Penguin, 1970), pp. 133, 135.

5 Ronald Paulson, *Hogarth: His Life, Art, and Times* (New Haven and London: Yale University Press, 1971), I, 336. I am indebted throughout this study both to the *Life* and to Paulson's other definitive work: *Hogarth's Graphic Works,* rev. ed. (New Haven: Yale University Press, 1970). All Hogarth references are to Paulson's *Life* and *Works* unless otherwise stated. The illustrations are from Rev. John Trusler's *Works of Hogarth* (London: E. T. Brain, n.d.). In 1766, Trusler was employed by Hogarth's wife, Jane, to write explanations of the prints.

6 R. W. Symonds, *Thomas Tompion: His Life and Works* (London: Spring Books, 1969), p. 232.

7 See Bernard Falk, *Thomas Rowlandson: His Life and Art* (New York: The Beechhurst Press, 1952), passim; and James Gillray, *Works* (London: Henry G. Bohn, 1851), passim. Gillray frequently alludes to opulence and loot, but he uses gold coins (in great profusion), and not watches.

8 Francis D. Klingender, *Art and the Industrial Revolution,* ed. Arthur Elton (London: Paladin, 1972), p. 46; and Herbert L. Sussman, *Victorians and the Machine: The Literary Response to Technology* (Cambridge, Mass.: Harvard University Press, 1968), pp. 9, 41.

9 Karl-Adolf Knappe, *Dürer: The Complete Engravings, Etchings and Woodcuts* (New York: Harry N. Abrams, n.d.), p. xliv and plates. See Erwin Panofsky's "Father Time," *Studies in Iconology* (New York: Harper & Row, 1962), pp. 71, 73, 80, 82, as well as the bibliographical references in this important article; and Soji Iwasaki's *The Sword and the Word: Shakespeare's Tragic Sense of Time* (Tokyo: Shinozaki Press, 1973), plates 21, 23, 24, 34, 46, 48, 51, 60, 61. Clocks and sundials were used less frequently. See Panofsky's plates 51 and 55 (Time appears here to be standing on the foliot of a clock rather than on a sundial as Panofsky seems to suggest on p. 80); and Iwasaki, plate 12.

10 Paulson, *Life*, I, 48, 513. See also pp. 50, 176, 514.

11 Ibid., II, 244; I, 494; and I, 433, 554.

12 Ibid., I, 251, 291.

13 Ibid., I, 492.

14 Heidegger's head was probably intended to move mechanically from side to side. Paulson suggests that Nonsense and Impertinence would be set in motion more frequently than Wit (*Works*, I, 133). See also references in Edward J. Wood, *Curiosities of Clocks and Watches* (1866; rpt. Wakefield: EP Publishing Ltd., 1973), pp. 127–28.

15 Panofsky, *Iconology*, p. 83n.

16 Paulson, *Life*, I, 234.

17 Ibid., II, 175.

18 Iwasaki, *Sword*, plates 5, 12, 28 (also pp. 21–32), and Panofsky, *Iconology*, plates 42, 46, 47, 56, 57, 60. Hogarth seems to have taken one step beyond Iwasaki's "Saturn-Time and Death" (pp. 32–44), and given some of Saturn's qualities to a fusion of Satan with Time.

19 Klingender, *Art*, plates 52 ff., and pp. 106, 109–10, 117, 128–29. See also Boswell's *London Journal*, December 15, 1762.

20 Alfred Chapuis, *De Horologiis in Arte* (Lausanne: Scriptar, 1954). Illustrations 55–64 (Holbein), 79–85 (Jan Breughel).

Renovation of Form: Time as Hero in Blake's Major Prophecies

MOLLYANNE MARKS

Because of his special sense of imagination, Blake had inevitably to abandon certain traditional ordering principles. Space, time, and even history itself are in his poetry subordinated to the human imagination. This is apparent dramatically in the mythic figure of Los, who represents imagination and time and whose struggles to overcome various opponents are central to the later poems; and it is evident also in the structure of the poetry itself. Indeed, the necessity for overcoming the limitations of time and space becomes the theme, the subject, and the informing principle of Blake's later poems. But there is perhaps a paradox here—a medium of imaginative expression that seeks to demonstrate the inadequacy of temporal and spatial forms can in its turn only create new forms. Blake signalled his awareness of this difficulty when he said, "I must create a system, or be enslaved by another man's." It is the evolution of Blake's "system," in which imagination labors to give a new and more human form to time and space, which I shall now consider, first moving quickly over the major tenets of Blake's theories of time and then discussing the specific way Blake attempts, in his later poems, to transcend the ordinary limits of form.

Critics have passed beyond the early notion that Blake was a mystic concerned only with the eternal to the realization that his ideas of time and space are particular, precise, and frequently innovative. Yet discussion has only begun on the more specific aesthetics of these ideas as they determine the form of Blake's art.[1]

In dealing with time and eternity, Blake endorses the Christian view of the Incarnation as the unique point in history which unites the human and the divine, but through his persistent redefinition of traditional concepts, he greatly alters its meaning. For Blake, it is Jesus who, "breaking thro' the Central Zones of Death & Hell/Opens Eternity in Time & Space;" (J. 3. 75:21–22; E. 229).[2] But Jesus, according to Blake, is the very embodiment of the Human Imagination: "All Things are comprehended in their Eternal Forms in the Divine [p. 70] body of the Saviour the True Vine of Eternity The Human Imagination" (V.L.J.; E. 545). Time and eternity are therefore reconciled whenever the divine and the human are one; in the fallen world human creativity remains subject to time until it has sufficiently transformed the universal consciousness to effect the apocalypse.

In the unfallen state, according to Blake, man is God and knows no distinction between reality and possibility. The Divine Humanity cannot conceive of anything without, by this very act, creating the thing itself. In his fallen state, man loses this ability; and those aspects of eternity, his former creations, which with his obfuscated senses he can still perceive, become time and space: "The Visions of Eternity, by reason of narrowed perceptions,/Are become weak Visions of Time & Space, fix'd into furrows of death;" (J. 2. 49:21–22; E. 196). It is imaginative death to believe that nothing exists beyond the limited reality we perceive:

> Many suppose that before [Adam] ⟨the Creation⟩ All was Solitude & Chaos This is the most pernicious Idea that can enter the Mind as it takes away all sublimity from the Bible & Limits All Existence to Creation & to Chaos To the Time & Space fixed by the Corporeal Vegetative Eye & leaves the Man who entertains such an Idea the habitation of Unbelieving Demons Eternity

Exists and All things in Eternity Independent of Creation which
was an act of Mercy (V.L.J.; E. 552–553)

Man's perceptions may be limited; yet reality is still the product
of a hobbled human creativity. It follows, then, that the shape an
artist gives his world reflects his imaginative state. More specifically, to Blake's way of thinking, the shape a man (or a nation)
gives to his conception of time indicates the extent of his vision
and reveals his spiritual state. By this standard Blake can pass
judgment on himself:

> ⟨The Greeks represent Chronos or Time as a very Aged Man this is
> Fable but the Real Vision of Time is in Eternal Youth I have
> ⟨however⟩ somewhat accomodated my Figure of Time to ⟨the⟩
> Common opinion as I myself am also infected with it & my
> Visions also infected & I see Time Aged alas too much so⟩ (V.L.J.;
> E. 553)

Blake no longer sees Time clearly as the youth of eternal
morning and reproaches himself for his own failure to perceive
Time (and the times) as clearly and vitally as he could. Blake's
struggle to overcome this failure of vision is portrayed in the later
poetry, especially *Jerusalem*. The hero of these poems, Los, who is
Blake's mythic representation of imagination, struggles continually
to transform the character of time from meaningless rehearsal of
the past to permanent instances of progress back towards man's
unfallen state. Interestingly, Los is also the figure representing
Time, and mortals viewing him with their limited vision participate
in Blake's confusion about the true nature of Time:

> But they depict him bald & aged who is in eternal
>   youth
> All powerful and his locks flourish like the brows
>   of morning
>   (M. I. 24:69–70; E. 120)

Los, like Blake's other mythological figures, is a projection of a
mode of consciousness, not a fully formed character. As a fragment of a more integrated Human Form Divine, he represents the

imaginative aspect of the mind, as well as the force of creativity working through history. Because Los is imagination, he is capable of remarkable development. As the vision embodied in Blake's work becomes clearer, Los approaches his true form, even as the poem's audience becomes better prepared to perceive him in his full strength. In the course of *Jerusalem*, for example, Los frees himself of encumbering garments, contorted postures, and the hovering menace of his Spectre, as well as from fear, selfhood, and self-doubt, to appear at last as a glorious naked human form, surrounded by a halo, free to rise infinitely and to create.

A progression in the illustrations emphasizes Los's development in the poem. On the Frontispiece he appears fully clothed, carrying with him his own limited source of illumination as he enters the dark door of the fallen Albion—the Human Form Divine. Plate 6 shows Los when he first confronts his selfhood. He is stripped here for action and appears with some of the tools of his craft. He holds his hammer, and his tongs are present. Yet his creativity is limited by a chain on his bellows and by the bat-like Spectre, his selfhood, who obscures his vision and to a large extent muffles the fires of his forge (See Figure 1.). Plate 37 anticipates the entire epic. The text or "story" recounts how Los offers to sacrifice himself for Albion, while Albion, harkening to his own Spectre, turns away. The two halves of the illustration describe these very different responses to the challenge of selfhood. Below, Albion's Spectre hovers over the prostrate form of Jerusalem, making her seem like death, because Albion has followed his Spectre who opposes creativity and change. Above Los chooses to fight his Spectre, sacrificing selfhood for a friend. He thereupon assumes the likeness of Jesus, helping the falling Albion to rise. The illustration in fact delineates a choice—two directions in which the same energy might go. It is the choice which of *Jerusalem* seeks to clarify for the reader. Finally, Plate 97 shows Los as he rises to his full strength and again takes a central role in Albion's life process. The contrast with the Frontspiece is pronounced, for here Los appears in a similar posture, but as a naked, muscular, human form. His lamp is now a major source of light, eclipsing the natural glow of the moon and the stars on the right.

Jerusalem works doggedly to confuse the reader's ordinary sense of time. The steady repetition of events with subtle variations, along with the contradictory assertions of various characters about which actions came first, virtually destroys our notions of cause and effect and effectively undercuts the narrative progress. The reader, after a time, cannot locate events in the poem in relation to one another or in relation to his own sense of lived time. Further complications are introduced by the illustrations, which often anticipate events in the written poem, thereby denying that a sequence of incidents narrated through time is at all necessary to convey meaning. The reader's sense of time as a fixed and external phenomenon is thus disturbed, and time itself is located where Blake thinks it properly must be, in the perceiving consciousness.

Time, as understood from a fallen perspective, is the agent of man's mortality, a consciousness of fall and failure. But the true meaning of time lies in its identity with the spirit of prophecy, for by speaking out, the prophet can reverse the cycles of history and make time an agent of mercy, rather than of destruction. Time has a saving potential for Blake, because it can be transformed into a semblance of eternity and thus bring about its own end: "Time is the mercy of Eternity; without Times swiftness/Which is the swiftest of all things: all were eternal torment:" (M. I. 24:72–73; E. 120).

The alternative to Los's redeeming view of time is embodied in his Spectre, whom Frye pertinently describes as "clock time."[3] Because the Spectre accepts the limits of man's fallen condition, he represents time as painfully short. Indeed, he lives in unremitting fear of the future, against which his only defense is pointless, frenetic activity. Los's struggle to subdue his Spectre is, then, an allegorical representation of the poet's attempt to achieve a more imaginative view of time.

For Blake, secular history, or natural history, merely repeats itself as civilizations rise and fall, and it is without significance except insofar as the transforming labors of the human imagination are manifest within its cycles. The creations of imagination endure forever and will one day again constitute man's entire universe, as in the beginning. Thus Los can say:

>   not one Moment
> Of Time is lost, nor one Event of Space unpermanent.
> But all remain: every fabric of Six Thousand Years
> Remains permanent: tho' on the Earth where Satan
> Fell, and was cut off all things vanish & are seen no more
> They vanish not from me & mine, we guard them first & last[.]
>   (M. I. 22:18–23; E. 116)

The creative act participates in eternity. Anyone who participates in this state—that is, who lives conformably with the prophetic imagination—can awake from the nightmare of fallen history, even before the return of the universal humanity to imagination, when history will cease for all of fallen creation.

All creative acts take place in a single, timeless moment:

> Every time less than a pulsation of the artery
> Is equal in its period & value to Six Thousand Years.
>
> For in this Period the Poets Work is Done: and all the Great
> Events of Time start forth & are concievd in such a Period
> Within a Moment: a Pulsation of the Artery.[4]
>   (M. I. 28:62–63; 29:1–3; E. 126)

The poetic act constitutes the only true history, and the six thousand years of fallen history are only a dream.

Time, then, is defined subjectively—it appears different from different perspectives and it is illusory from the perspective of eternity. Clearly this idea of time influences the composition of Blake's poetry. In the earlier prophetic books, particularly "The Book of Urizen," this is evident in Blake's abandonment of chronological narrative in favor of a structure which ironically emphasizes the essentially fallen nature of human perceptions even as it seeks to chronicle the descent from eternity into that fallen state. This poem, which is Blake's account of man's collapse and the consequent origin of his present world, is composed of a series of representations of the single moment of fall from eternity. The appearance of a progression in the poem turns out, upon close inspection, to be illusion, for all the events are the same event. Nor is the writing of the poem itself excepted; it, too, is an instance of the same fall. The need to isolate the different facets of the human fall in order to make it comprehensible is ironically yet another reflection of that fall, but also the necessary position from which Blake as poet must start on the way back to human integrity. In essence "Urizen" does no more than reveal, in its complexity, the dilemma Blake saw for the artist who, fallen himself, must nevertheless use the materials of a fallen world to build up a vision of an eternal life to which man might by that very act return. The problem is a traditional one, though Blake's presentation of it is not. But what seems to me special in Blake's work is the extent to which, in his later poems, dilemma and solution, form and content, are fused.

As in the earlier prophetic books, the structure of Blake's later epic poems is in considerable part determined by his notions of time. *Milton, Jerusalem,* and the unfinished "The Four Zoas" all present epic accounts of human fall and redemption. The real hero of these epic actions is Los, and his struggle to master himself, or his Selfhood, is the central epic action. As we have earlier observed, Los embodies time. Although Los is not an ordinary man, he is still a distinctly human faculty; and his characterization as time testifies to Blake's contention that time is essentially a human construct, as plastic as all human forms. Los's struggle to master himself is then also a struggle to subordinate time to imagination; and his success emphasizes that eternity is by no means discontinuous with human existence but rather that it is accessible to men through more imaginative ways of viewing time. Eternity is the world of imagination in which time has become fluid, capable of continual change and renewal in purely human forms.[5] This view of time is heralded in the later prophetic books by abrupt shifts in time sequences. Passages fixed firmly in England, 1804, abut directly on passages rooted in ancient Israel; these border in turn on passages whose locus is in a mythological universe altogether outside of time. Not only does Blake avoid transitions between such passages; the implication of the poetry is repeatedly that such passages, though temporally discrete, are still imaginatively continuous. Thus the poetry expresses in its form the increasingly flexible view of time that the reader is to acquire. Los himself is, of course, a constant reminder that our methods of perceiving time are, from Blake's point of view, susceptible to change. That Blake should locate the working out of his cosmic drama of ruin and salvation in the mind of man is not remarkable. What is remarkable, however, is Blake's peculiar form of allegory, in which figures are entirely the modes of consciousness they represent, and which itself embraces a self-conscious critique of art and a search for the appropriate means of transcending art's temporal and spatial limits.

Milton, for example, depends on the recognition of many selves within the same individual, of different times within the same moment, and of alternative forms all embraced within a single structure. The poem's narrative follows John Milton from an eternity which he inhabits through the power of his art, to the generative world in which he exhorts Blake to create, to the Hell in which he wrestles with the personification of his own imaginative errors. These actions appear consecutive, though the poem asserts that they are in fact simultaneous. The illustrations work even more directly to abrogate time, for they illuminate the moments of self-recognition which are the heart of the poem, and which discover the presence of one form within another. Plates 15 and 21, for example, depict Milton in attitudes of self-recognition. Plate 15 shows him confronting the Urizen within himself, and this confrontation, as the legend suggests, is the beginning of the annihilation of this form of the self. Plate 21 pictures a confrontation which, while it is projected as a meeting of distinct figures, yet is in reality a recognition of possibility within the self. In it Blake, kneeling, turns to find Los behind him in the path and discovers that they are twins. Blake need only rise to complete their identity. These two plates portray opposite theses of the poem's dialectic of self-recognition: one dramatizing the realization that restricting forces are within as well as outside the self; the other showing that creative strength waits within the self to be seen and embraced. Their effect is to emphasize through mirror images the simultaneity of different forms, one within the other, as well as to dissolve the gap between discrete recognitions by suggesting that these also can be identical. The recognition and casting out of selfhood is in fact tantamount to the release of imaginative power within the self, and this *Milton* exists to show.

There is background, digression, and repetition in *Jerusalem*, but the poem returns always to Los's struggle. The attempt of the imaginative faculty to consolidate and to clarify its vision is the constructive force in the poem and is opposed to the dream of fallen history which is Albion's deathlike sleep. Los's attempt to subdue his selfhood has many implications, but on one level it refers to Blake's own labors at composition and to his struggle against defeat and despair. A detailed allegory of the poet's inner life becomes, in *Jerusalem*, a universal myth of artistic process as in the figure of Los's selfhood, the Spectre, Blake gives form and voice to the despair with which he had seen other artists—like Cowper—whom he admired perish, both physically and imaginatively. This is the vision of the Spectre:

> Despair! I am Despair
> Created to be the great example of horror & agony: also my
> Prayer is vain I called for compassion: compassion mockd[,]
> Mercy & pity threw the grave stone over me & with lead
> And iron, bound it over me for ever: Life lives on my
> Consuming: & the Almighty hath made me his Contrary
> To be all evil, all reversed & for ever dead: knowing
> And seeing life, yet living not;
>
> (J. 1. 10:51–58; E. 152)

The closing plates of *Jerusalem* describe a complex conclusion to Los's labors. Succeeding at last in subduing the figure of his own selfhood by reshaping it on his anvil, Los rouses Albion, the representation of all fallen humanity, to do likewise. Los has become Blake's Jesus, the figure of the fully realized human imagination, exemplifying the act of self-sacrifice, an immolation undertaken so that all men might live eternally. Albion then espouses Los's example, surrendering himself to the appearance of eternal death in an act which is also, from another perspective, the resurrection of all men to eternal life. This moment of redemption is identical with the moment of Albion's full realization of Los's sacrifice of self, thus illustrating Blake's conviction that "Truth can never be told so as to be understood, and not be believ'd" (M.H.H. 10:69; E. 37).

Jerusalem moves toward the moment in its last plates when Los is free of his Spectre—free of the doubts and the limits of time and space. Los again becomes part of Albion and ends his separate existence. This reintegration may be expressed another way: as time merges into eternity, so loss, in both senses of the word, disappears. At the end of the poem Blake speaks of the four mythic figures representing the human faculties of emotion, reason, imagination, and instinctive unity as integrated once again:

> And They conversed together in Visionary forms dramatic which bright
> Redounded from their Tongues in thunderous majesty, in Visions
> In new Expanses, creating exemplars of Memory and of Intellect
> Creating Space, Creating Time according to the Wonders Divine
> of Human Imagination, . . .
>
> (J. 4. 98:28–32; E. 255)

"And I heard the Name of their Emanations they are named Jerusalem." These last are the concluding words of the poem. (See Figure 2.) Beneath them is an engraving showing Albion and the naked female figure of his emanation locked in a sexual embrace. They are surrounded by the flames of creative energy. The female form in this plate is Jerusalem, the woman who is the outward form of the creative energies of Albion, the Human Form Divine.[6] Their passionate embrace announces an end to the fallen state in which man, having lost control of the productions of his own creativity, allowed the natural world to come into being. But the figure is also that of the city Jerusalem, and her juncture with Albion is the climax of Los's efforts throughout the poem to reforge the connections between England the ancient Biblical lands. In the unfallen state there are no discrete intervals in space and time; Jerusalem and Albion's land are one because they are kindred centers of vision, and reality is only where imagination is. Finally, this Jerusalem is also *Jerusalem* the poem; as the last quoted passage states, the conversation of human faculties has become again an exchange of visionary forms dramatic. Literally these forms are mythic figures who have threshed out the problems of human creativity in the "action" of this poem. Through the medium of the poem itself they have again become sufficient means to communicate a vision of unity—the vision of the embrace. The passage goes on to tell of the ability of human faculties to create continually new forms of time and space. The meaning of these final plates, then, is that these faculties having returned to converse in visionary forms free of fixed time and space, the form of the poem *Jerusalem*, in which heretofore vision is fragmented into the appearance of narration that it might be comprehensible to a fallen understanding, is no longer necessary. The figures of Albion and Jerusalem embracing is now the full rendering of the poem's vision. The dialectic of form and meaning set up in this poem has led finally to the abandonment of the poem itself as a fixed narrative occupying space and time, even as, after *Jerusalem*, Blake largely abandoned the writing of poetry altogether.

Finally, it should be noted that *Jerusalem* makes special demands upon the reader. Since the poem dramatizes the subordination of clock time to imagination, it neither assumes the reality of an objective historical continuum nor itself depends on a narrative progression through time. For if the true history of life is but the sum of its creative moments, it follows that a vision of that life could be captured only in a work that broke with the rules of structure and with the restraints of a single art form to embody the artist's repeated attempts to clarify his essential moments of imaginative vision. Every aspect of *Jerusalem's* composition, from its metrical ordering and verbal structures through its direct identification of England and ancient Biblical lands, attempts to transcend spatial and temporal limits. One possibility is that the poem's reader might reenact for himself the saving experience that the poem describes, and so find his perceptions altered at the conclusion:

If the Spectator could enter into these Images in his Imagination approaching them on the Fiery Chariot of his Contemplative Thought . . . or could make a Friend & Companion of one of these Images of wonder which always intreats him to leave mortal things . . . then would he arise from his Grave then would he meet the Lord in the Air & then he would be happy (V.L.J.; E. 550)

NOTES

1 Ronald L. Grimes, "Time and Space in Blake's Major Prophecies," *Blake's Sublime Allegory,* ed. Stuart Curran and Joseph Wittreich, Jr. (Madison: University of Wisconsin Press, 1973), pp. 59–81, helpfully discusses Blake's ideas of time but largely leaves aside questions of how these ideas inform the poetry. F. B. Curtis, "Blake and the 'Moment of Time': An Eighteenth-Century Controversy in Mathematics," *Philological Quarterly,* 51 (1972), 460–70, suggests a possible source for some of Blake's ideas about time but does not deal with Blake's transformation of these concepts into art.

2 All quotations from Blake's poetry are from the text edited by David V. Erdman, *The Poetry and Prose of William Blake,* commentary by Harold Bloom (Garden City, N.Y.: Doubleday, 1965). For engraved poetry, line and plate numbers are specified. Page references to this edition (E.___) are given in all cases.

3 Northrop Frye, *Fearful Symmetry* (1947; rpt. Boston: Beacon Press, 1965), p. 298

4 This separation between orders of time is an important concept for Blake. It connects his thought with more traditional attitudes towards time, such as Milton's or Augustine's, and also indicates the distance his humanism has moved him in a new direction, because of his emphasis on imagination as the means of bridging the gap between these different orders.

5 In *Milton,* for example, the Sons of Los labor to restore the human character of Time:

> But others of the Sons of Los build Moments & Minutes & Hours
> And Days & Months & Years & Ages & Periods; wondrous buildings
> And every Moment has a Couch of gold for soft repose,
>
> (M. I. 28:44–46; E. 125)

6 For an interesting discussion of the allegory here, see E. J. Rose, "Blake's Fourfold Art," *Philological Quarterly,* 49 (1970), 420–23.

Time, Sequence, and Plot
in Restoration Literature

EARL MINER

Eve's love poem to Adam in *Paradise Lost* begins, "With thee conversing I forget all time . . ." She does, however, devote to him one of the two kinds of time they know in Eden, the diurnal. Without Adam, the wonders of the day from morning to evening are not sweet. The other kind of time known to them is retrospective and involves their memories, which do not extend far back. By the end of *Paradise Lost,* they do have far more to remember from direct or related experience. They also have less to enjoy, along with a third sense of time, the anticipatory. With Eve's poem, we discover past and especially present; subsequently we discover with her and Adam a sense of the future. And yet, her initial sense of time makes little post-lapsarian sense. She forgets all time, not that she has that much, in order to express heightened emotional experience. She seems unaware of the complex relations between sensation, memory, perception, cognition, anticipation, and expression—all those things that make concepts of time so difficult for us, all those faculties that we know to be dependent on time for development and exercise.

For all that, Eve's artistry gives another kind of sanction to her tribute. In praising Adam, she becomes a lyric poet, interested as lyric poets usually are, not in what Milton elsewhere calls the "tract of time," but in moments when feelings seem to displace time. As readers, we encounter that lyric in an epic, in a narrative already immense with an infernal and heavenly past to remember and portentous with a future to anticipate.

Eve's love poem seems different from most of the temporal world of *Paradise Lost*. Her kind of time represents in part a distinction between the Restoration and the first half of the century. In the earlier poetry, time had been fought by, or devoted to, the lyric (or the different larger tracts of drama). Narrative was admitted only as a sub-genre, and as such it competed with a dramatic sub-genre rather than with lyric. The gathering narrative energies of the 1640's and 1650's grew to such force by mid-century that the balance had shifted and the lyric depended as a sub-genre on narrative and drama with their larger, more complex temporal tracts. In a later poem such as Dryden's *Song for St. Cecilia's Day,* we find a true lyric, a true song, set to music and sung. But Dryden can write major lyrics such as this only when they are premised on time or history and narrative, only when they remember rather than forget all time. We also see this pattern of development in Milton's sonnets, which shift from an early lyric disregard of temporal tracts to a preoccupation with recent history.

We may regret with St. Augustine that we know what time is but cannot explain it. And we are certain that all literary experience has some degree of temporal duration. We also recall that time was a major theme with the Cavalier poets, who were obsessed by transience and the bad times. We remember and prize that other order of time, Eve's intense moment, a lyric time such as we value in Donne and Herbert. Donne's lovers in "The Sunne Rising" awake when the sun has the temerity to shoot a ray through a chink in their bed curtains. In badgering the sun as a busy old fool, in telling the sun that the two lovers govern him, Donne's speaker argues that man controls time by his own conception in a world in which, to the minds of the two lovers, "Nothing else is." Such intense lyric preoccupation is exactly the understanding of time offered by Eve, a conception allowing us to distinguish within Milton's epic narrative what is a song, a lyric.

Many narratives, most of them seldom read today, intervene between Donne and Milton. To my view, only two whole English narratives of importance appear before *Hudibras*: Cowley's *Civil War*, written sometime before 1656, and William Chamberlayne's madcap *Pharonnida*, which appeared in 1659. Before these poems, others had appeared that were unable to unite meaning and plot, and yet others that ended as fragments. We discover such failures in Henry More's fierce allegory, *The Song of the Soul*, and in Sir Francis Kynaston's highly readable froth, *Leoline and Sydanis*. Davenant's *Gondibert* and Cowley's *Davideis* bite off more than they can chew—or *vice versa*. It does seem that during the middle years of the century narrative was the genre struggling to be born, but that its delivery was painful, because after the earlier triumph of lyricism poets found it difficult to manage the large tracts of time required for narrative.

There is another matter. In the Restoration there emerge numerous forms of recognizable narrative, including such semi-narrative forms as satire. In all forms, however, the special characteristic is historical. Cowley discovered as much first in his *Civil War* and later in the last two books of his *Sex Libri Plantarum* (in English translation by others, *The Book of Plants*). Butler proved it conclusively and furiously in *Hudibras*. Dryden celebrated history in *Annus Mirabilis;* Milton universalized it in *Paradise Lost*. After that greatest of English poems appeared, numerous variations and manipulations appeared in *MacFlecknoe, Paradise Regained, Absalom and Achitophel,* and other poems. In *Paradise Regained,* for instance, we discover a single, forward-moving progression, unlike that sublime inversion requiring eight books in *Paradise Lost*. And yet in *Paradise Regained,* such so-called linear time is brought almost to a standstill by the relation of the events of a very few days and by a series of temptations that are essentially the same thing repeated until the last climax. We may say that in *Absalom and Achitophel* two historical tracts run in parallel, but also that their running involves little action. In *The Hind and the Panther,* the action, such as it is, transpires in talk from evening to dawn. That brief time allows Dryden somehow to introduce numerous narratives more detailed than the main one, in order to deal with what he believes to be timeless truth, and to develop by argument rather than by plot what amounts to a past, present, and future in the succession of his three talkative parts. The narratives of the Restoration seldom honor simple canons of story, but in all their variety they show that historical time is their ground of existence.

The Restoration reclaimed history for poetry and delighted in it for its own sake. One could make much of such differing histories as those by Stillingfleet, Clarendon, Aubrey, and the two Burnets, or of the diaries of Pepys and Evelyn. But it is enough to emphasize that with Dryden's poetry and criticism we have for the first time in England two essential historical concepts: the idea of an age or period, and the idea of change in the very nature of things. My present topic concerns the "Restoration," which is an entity that may be termed a historical fiction. We assume its existence so readily that we forget that Dryden gave us the idea of a literary period and that Rymer made it basic to his thought. As for Dryden's sense of historical process, I shall not repeat discussions already in print.[1] It will be enough to examine some major factors involved in Restoration ways of looking at history and narrative.

At a crucial point in *An Essay of Dramatick Poesie* Dryden's Crites echoes Sir Philip Sidney on the poet's creating almost a new nature. Sidney meant that the poet could invent things like chimeras and demigods that do not exist in nature. Crites and Dryden mean that in recent times men had discovered that the reality of nature to be imitated by poets had been discovered changeable, to have a historical dimension.[2] Views of literature could never be the same after that discovery, and the new understanding also had its effect on the kind of narrative written during the Restoration. The concepts of time and history that made possible Dryden's new critical conceptions also provided the grounds for the particular kinds of narrative practiced by Butler, Milton, and Dryden himself. In his "Account" prefixed to *Annus Mirabilis,* Dryden associates with the heroic not only the historical but also the panegyrical and, implicitly, the satirical. It is in such a wide sense of epic that his criticism and the finest poetry of the age is heroic. And it is the historical, panegyrical, and satirical that define the heroic, so setting the terms on which lyricism may enter: "With thee conversing I forget all time"; "From Harmony, from heav'nly Harmony, / This universal Frame began."

The historical, temporal character of the narrative that triumphs in the Restoration seems to me beyond question. But one must also understand that the new emphasis in narrative reflects a *need* for an understanding of time and history. Symptoms of the need emerge in the burst of millenarianism in the 1640's, for although the hoped-for event would have brought the end of time and history, the effect upon God's Englishmen was the conviction that their own times were fully historical. Even Marvell discovered that the times demanded that the forward youth must leave his garden to join the march of events, and that the poet of *carpe diem* had to seize a new day in which he had world too much and time. Butler begins as Spenser had not, with time rather than place, "When Civil Fury first grew high." He furiously argues with the times, with the history he has known, seeking in the spirit of the Rump Ballads to rhyme his rats to death.

Milton claimed at the end of his *Second Defence* that his prose had celebrated the epic of his countrymen in their time. That prose epic is instructive, because it undid itself into another, another, and another. The Long Parliament could not rule, nor could the Rump, nor the Barebones. Cromwell could rule, at the cost of sacrificing those very liberties that the revolution had been designed to secure. When Cromwell died and Tumbledown Dick Cromwell fell, Milton reacted in dismay, warning his countrymen not to choose a captain back to Egypt. We may say that from his insight and biblical comparison we gained *Paradise Lost* as well as *Absalom and Achitophel.* In order to be able to justify the ways of God to men, Milton had to reject his times and countrymen as subject, grappling instead with the largest tract of time imaginable by the human mind, total history bounded on either side by eternity.

Dryden did the same in the small lyric narrative of *A Song for St. Cecelia's Day*. He differs from Butler and Milton in numerous ways, but not in the new assumptions about narrative. One important difference is the optimism sustaining him until late in life, a happiness unknown to Butler and for Milton lying remote at the end of time. Dryden believed that his age would create new and lasting things, and he was right. The Puritans had shown that new systems of government could be introduced. From what is implied by such a discovery, Dryden postulated achievements in poetry, drama, architecture, science, music, and philosophy that in fact came about. As I have written recently, Dryden was animated by a heroic idea of his time.[3] That is to say he needed his epic conception and his idea of time's direction to write his poetry.

The great necessity for time and history found by no means the same expression among Restoration poets. Butler's pessimism vied with Dryden's hope, and Milton labored his way from the one to the other. Ironically, Butler despaired, although his side had at last won in the Restoration of Charles II. Milton had to found his hopes on the defeat of his good old cause, proving his argument on the basis of total history precisely because he could justify it on no smaller scale. It may seem strange that, conservative though Dryden was to the core over institutions, he was warmly liberal over the possibilities for individuals. In this he resembles in an odd way those revolutionary Presbyterians who had struggled for "a more thorough godly Reformation"—as well as for their property and liberties under the law. Like them, Dryden looked toward a bright and beckoning future that could only be understood by reference to the present. Butler—ever on the contrary—was caught up in fascination with a hideous, stupid past. Milton chose the ultimate past and the ultimate future as the bases of his hopes and his understanding of what we think of as history.

All three major Restoration poets derived the motives of their poetry from the sources usual to poets—the experience and thought crucial in their lifetimes. The Interregnum and Restoration offered definitions of human nature and history, whether for Butler's anger, Dryden's optimism, or Milton's universal epic. As their attitudes differed, so did their tracts of time. Butler could and did continue his historical tract into the Restoration, but he could not exorcise from the present the spectre of a terrible past. Milton could redeem the present only by stretching it humanly back to its origin in the fall or divinely to the creation, and then forward to the Second Coming. Dryden gazed on the present for its inheritance from the past and its potential for a heroic future. All three seem to inhabit a world long distant from those of Donne and Jonson. Donne's *Anniversaries* dissolve narrative into encomium and satire. Another mix of those ingredients dissolves the narrative of Jonson's *Famous Voyage* down the open sewer of London. They are disappointing as narrative poets, and we value them for lyrics and moral epistles.

In drawing this familiar generic history of the century with the colors of time, I have simplified some things and omitted some others. In what follows, I wish to discuss the last phase of Dryden's career in order to isolate other narrative possibilities and to theorize a bit about the nature of time in some kinds of narrative. We must consider Dryden in relation to 1688 and All That. By the time of the Glorious Revolution, the choleric Butler and the blind Milton were of course dead. Now turned fifty-seven, Dryden had to make sense of himself and his world in a revolutionary order. Like Milton in 1660, he discovered himself caught in a major constitutional shift invalidating his previous hopes and therefore putting at hazard those assumptions that sustained not just his earlier hopes but also his earlier kinds of narrative. In facing Milton's problem, Dryden may seem at first inspection to have reacted with Butler's anger. During what I shall loosely term the years of his *Satires,* from about 1689 to 1695, Dryden does indeed sometimes "snarl," as he once put it. The conclusion of *Eleonora,* the Preface to *Examen Poeticum,* the *Satires* themselves, and the poem to Kneller show fundamental dissatisfaction with his age. *Amphitryon* and *Don Sebastian*—to my mind his greatest plays—show how profoundly he had to question the human condition. His unhappiness with a new age rivals Milton's, although without verging on that alarming hysteria in some of Milton's late political prose.

By the last years of his century and his life, Dryden recovered as Milton had, leaving as monuments to a new epic effort his *Aeneis* and *Fables.* The changes Dryden makes in Virgil are too numerous in kind and number to detail, but this much deserves emphasis. His heart lies in the second half of the *Aeneid,* where the hero's great effort is tinged by tragedy. Books 8–10 are magnificently rendered, and the triumph of Aeneas, which is to say the death of Turnus, gets all the bleakness that classicists have recently found in Virgil's ending. A translation even of this magnitude does not permit many quick generalizations about the mind of its author. But in the context of his last plays and of the *Fables,* we can confidently presume that for Dryden the Virgilian *opus* and *labor* were mighty, and that humankind engaged in them with doubtful triumph, unquestioned suffering, and a fallibility that he found appealing under the species of eternity.

His *Fables Ancient and Modern* represents a further and last advance. I share the Romantics' high estimation of this work and regard it (with perhaps a year's violence to chronology) as the second greatest poetic achievement of the seventeenth century. Whatever our evaluation, we must agree that in the *Fables* Dryden turned to freer forms of narrative than he had practiced before. As stories or tales or fables, those taken from Ovid, Boccaccio, Chaucer, and Homer must be thought to behave far more like plain narrative than do *MacFlecknoe* or *The Hind and the Panther.* His remarkable discipline of mind and argument seems to ease in these poems. To free narrative yet further, he included in *Fables* poems like those to the Duchess of Ormonde and *Alexander's Feast,* whose status as narrative depends chiefly on their relation to other, purer versions of narrative and whose counternarrative elements qualify and control thematically the purer narratives.

My interpretation of the *Fables* as an integrated whole has found confirmation in the studies by Judith Sloman, and I think has won general agreement.[4] Assuming that interpretation to be true, then, the *Fables* represents in its integration the story of human struggle for the good life, with failure and success, in transactions between the heroic, the historical, the fabulous, and the comic. The search is itself an endearing one and is rewarded in fluctuations of success—and especially of failure when not sanctioned by religious and similar idealism. This larger narrative is made up of numerous discrete sub-narratives, or stories. The individual stories largely avoid the present and the historico-temporal orders of Dryden's earlier poems. There are, of course, allusions of a historical kind. But the stories taken from "ancient and modern" authors would seem very remote, were it not that those poems like *To My Honour'd Kinsman* function in the integrated whole to bring the remote into touch with present England and to work toward a generalizing of Dryden's predications about the human comedy. What particularly interests me are the temporal and narrative conditions of that integrated whole, a kind of large-scale story-telling whose chief radical differs from that of its individual fables like *Palamon and Arcite* in not possessing plot.

E. M. Forster once distinguished between story and plot by suggesting that a story satisfied our sense of "and then . . . and then . . . ," whereas plot satisfies our sense of contingency and cause. As example of story he gave: "The king died, and then the queen died." And of plot: "The king died, and the queen died thereafter of grief." We see his distinctions at once. But we also see through them, because both of his kinds are formally similar. They have a plot. I do not think that critics have had much success in defining what is meant by plot, and I shall not try. What I do wish to point to involves omitting a number of things crucial to plot: continuous causality, episodic division, and digression. Such large omission leaves us, however, with a succession involving continuity in such matters as location, characters, action, and morality—not all of which need continue but which in some continuing group enables us to understand and prize a plot.

Hudibras takes place on three days at half a dozen principal locations, from one to the other of which the characters shuffle, doing what they do with as much naturalness as is possible in that unnatural poem. *Annus Mirabilis* recounts a three-day sea battle and then the days of the Great Fire of London, with the King the central character in each episode. *Paradise Lost* and *The Hind and the Panther* clearly employ far more complex forms of plot, but the plots are still recognizable as such.

The point I am leading to is this. We can say of the action of *Annus Mirabilis* that it uses a single (that is, non-allegorical), clear story-plot that relates two principal national events in 1666. We can say no such thing about the larger narrative of *Fables*. Most individual poems in the collection do have a "clear story-plot," but if they do their plot does not concern principal national events. On the other hand, poems treating present history do not have clearly dominant plots or indeed any plot at all in the usual sense of the term. *To My Honour'd Kinsman* has long been thought Dryden's most Horatian poem, and for just such reason of its associative succession of topics, characters, and ideas without a plot. Within these two kinds of poems, or within our experience of reading them, we encounter two very different temporal orders. In the fables with plot, the temporal order defined by the plot is one remote from the poet and the reader alike. The poems without plots, on the other hand, generally treat of times and places close to Dryden—the England of *To the Dutchess of Ormond, To My Honour'd Kinsman,* and the "Fair Maiden Lady." Even the "Character of a Good Parson" out of Chaucer was thought by Dryden's contemporaries to describe Bishop Ken.

It will be observed that the distinction between plot-time and historical subjects is not necessarily in theory. *Annus Mirabilis, MacFlecknoe,* and other earlier poems may skimp on plot, but the plot and its time certainly work with the kind of historical time we find in *To My Honour'd Kinsman.* In other words, for the *Fables* Dryden has separated two elements that had once been one, writing on the one hand a freer narrative and on the other poems without plot. The distinction between plot-continuity and what I termed associative succession is necessary as an observation of Dryden's late practice. It tells us something about his ways of expressing his final understanding of himself in his world. And it will be of importance as we consider the fables as an entire narrative.

Most of the poems in the *Fables* are of the length of a novella, and all entail uses of time that involve, in Günther Müller's phrase, *Erzählzeit und erzählte Zeit,* the time involved in relation or reading and the time scheme set forth. The poem to the Duchess of Ormonde, for example, works constantly between a valued past and the fortunate present, as also between that present and a millenary future. That is the *erzählte Zeit,* rather than a plot of articulated, successively continuous series of events. The poem's related time involves a species of allusive, non-continuous time such as Dryden had also used in *Absalom and Achitophel,* but there with a simple basic plot that ordered allusion and action into a single experience.

As an entire narrative of integrated poems, Dryden's *Fables Ancient and Modern* works in a way contrary to *Absalom and Achitophel,* for in this last and greatest work of his life Dryden chose to use a radical of narrative other than plot for ordering the various plot actions and the unplotted poems into a single experience. As an integrated whole, then, the *Fables* is a narrative without plot as its radical. It does often use plots in individual poems, but these are not connected into a single plot, nor could they be. And they do not narrate Dryden's chief concern in *Fables.* That concern, as I have said, involves variant, repeated attempts by mankind to search for the good life in a human world, where alone it must be sought, but a search that can be fully rewarded only by attention to moral, philosophical, and religious values derived in one sense from God. In another sense, those values are derived more from the plot-less poems than from the fine stories taken from Ovid, Chaucer, and Boccaccio. More than that, Dryden cannot let alone even the original plots. He greatly amplifies and improves Theseus's philosophical speech at the end of *Palamon and Arcite*—thereby interrupting plot more extensively than had Chaucer. He does much the same with the problem of determinism and free will in *The Cock and the Fox*, at the end of which he adds a parabolic moral. Or, as with the last poem in *Fables, Cymon and Iphigenia*, he simply adds to its beginning a *Poëta loquitur* addressed to the Duchess of Ormonde. Beyond that, the thematic concerns I have been describing can best be exemplified by the incompatibility—as plots—of the plots of *Palamon and Arcite* and *The Cock and the Fox*. In brief, Dryden's thematic ends are well served by such variety, providing that he can find means to encompass and order it.

Dryden's ordering involves numerous techniques of linkage and of recurrent situations and motifs. I shall not discuss these, important as they are, because I have done so before and because I assume them in holding that the *Fables* is an integrated collection.[5] I shall add only a renewed emphasis that the ordering depends more upon the plot-less poems than on those with plot, in the sense that the poems without plot explicitly set forth those themes in the integrated whole that are less clear in the plot narratives. We are left with the presumption that our integrated collection has, as a collection, a narrative without a plot. We may well ask after the radical of plot-less narrative. And we shall wish to ask a subsidiary question about the nature of time in plot-less narrative.

I do not know that any term exists in English for the radical of plot-less narrative, or even that people think such a thing exists. Rather than search out some esoteric Greek word, I shall designate that radical as "sequence." I do so in the confidence that the history of Japanese literature provides examples very like Dryden's. The imperial collections beginning in A.D. 905 came more and more to integrate the five-line lyrics into collections forming unified wholes in ways anticipating George Herbert's collection, *The Temple*, or indeed Dryden's *Fables*. Since digression is one of the ancient principles of narrative, I shall take an excursus into Japanese literature.

The imperial anthologies are almost wholly organized by criteria at variance from our own. Poems do not appear clustered successively in terms of the chronology of successive authors, or of the chronology of a single author's canon. They appear instead ordered by the subjects they treat and by some sense of stage or fitness within the general subject category. In these collections, the two major sections include poems on the four seasons and on love. The seasonal poems begin with the new year and work progressively to the year's end. The love poems begin with the early stages of falling in love and progress through the vicissitudes of courtly love. Both seasonal and love poems use temporal progressions. Books on travel or the so-called "Miscellaneous" poems do not employ such a temporal progression as will be found in the love poems. In other words, temporal progression is a very significant factor, but it is neither necessary nor even wholly followed in the seasonal poems. Another ordering principle of great importance is association. Some connection in imagery or language or situation links one poem with the next. More than that, associations can make subsequences. For example a number of early spring poems may associate by reason of their imagery of remaining snow. Then the snow image can lead to another subsequence of poems on white plum blossoms that look like snow. From there, a further associational shift will lead to poems on the warbler singing among plum blossoms, and then to the warbler singing in the garden, etc. By such means, associations themselves can develop progressions, creating a narrative without a plot. Plot is not possible, because the identity of the speakers of the individual lyrics is constantly shifting. As the different speakers (men, women, priests, travelers, etc.) make their appearance, they may do so in quite different situations (in the capital, in the hills, in the mountains, at the sea shore, etc.). Such locations may be concatenated as a geographical progression and so provide some narrative force; or they may simply represent shifts in successive poems and so have no further discernible end.

The authors of the narrative sequences in the imperial collections are not the individual poets at all, but the compilers of the anthologies. It is this that allows for our presumption that the total collection gives a single experience. Of course we meet the individual speakers or poets as distinct, named or anonymous, poets. But we also meet the compilers as authors of a far larger integrated whole in which progression, association, and variance function to articulate and order a single large creation. Anyone interested in this subject may refer to one of the classic literary essays of our time, Jin'ichi Konishi's "Association and Progression: Principles of Integration in Anthologies and Sequences of Japanese Court Poetry, A.D. 900–1350."[6] And the subject could be followed through in terms of the poetic sequences by individual poets modeled on the imperial collections and by consideration of the various forms of linked verse practiced in Japan. In each instance we have forms of lyric narrative in which the radical is sequence rather than plot.

The practice of sequence narrative on a large and intelligible scale seems to require some kind of presence or signaling. We can think of the manifest ironies and parodies of Swift's *Tale of a Tub* or Sterne's *Tristam Shandy*. The Japanese imperial collections suggest the presence of their compiler-narrators with a Japanese preface and a Chinese postscript on the art of poetry, and the ordering of the books of poems follows traditional lines. Dryden goes farther. He stresses his role as translator-poet-arranger with a dedication and a long, very often personal, preface written in his finest prose style. He includes poems of his own along with the translations, placing them in conspicuous places, more or less at the beginning and end. In the first poem, *To the Dutchess of Ormond*, he begins by adopting the role of Chaucer to praise a new Emily in order to present the Duchess with his translation of *The Knight's Tale*. In *To My Honour'd Kinsman* he delivers, according to what he wrote in a letter to Montague, a memorial of his political principles to all posterity. Using these various devices, Dryden keeps himself and his role as shaper of the larger narrative very much before us. He does not adopt Ovid's strained pretense in the *Metamorphoses* that his sequence narrative is really a plot narrative, but he does also draw upon Ovid's techniques of sequential relation.

Unlike Swift and Sterne, Dryden does not write in prose. Unlike the Japanese collections, his individual fables are not lyrics—with a couple of exceptions. But there is no question that like all those other examples and Ovid's as well, his larger narrative is based on sequence rather than on plot. Sequential narrative does not imply continuity of characters, location, or actions, as does plot. On the contrary, it implies discontinuity, or rather finds continuity irrelevant. What it does imply is differing elements in succession that yet possess common concern—for example, Dryden's search for the good life, the sense of variability that is postulated by the Japanese love sequences, or the dominance of change and temporal flux in *The Metamorphoses.* And in the sequential succession we often find the gradual rise of parallelism and repeated motifs that are not themselves sequential with each other but that depend upon sequence for their emergence in that very narrative to which they give thematic emphasis. More simply, sequence implies some kind of related succession without a continuance of plot elements. For example, in *Fables* that related succession derives in a minor way from the linkings of poem to poem, and in a major way from treatments of a general theme, as also from its recurrent subjects: love, arms, retreat, philosophical reflection, historical implication, selfishness, and selflessness. The important fact about sequence is that it cannot be altered without fundamentally disturbing its meaning. Sequential narrative depends on its particular succession, rather than on the kind of continuousness of characters, causality, etc. so important to plot. The succession in sequential narrative determines its intelligibility and meaning.

It may be objected at this point that a particular succession is equally important to plot. I disagree. I wish to argue that plot and sequence are two distinct radicals of narrative; that there may be narrative without plot; but that there can be no narrative (in fact, no literature) without sequence. It is sequence as I have tried to define it that is the prime radical, or if one prefers, the simple, primitive radical of narrative. Once we understand this, we can surely appreciate anew the narrative power of *Hudibras,* mess that it is, and of those of Dryden's poems that seem to insist on being narratives although slighting plot. In addition, this distinction enables us to understand some essential things about Milton's art of narrative. Let us take the narrative of *Paradise Lost*. As everyone knows, the poem has an immense plot with a large number of characters and possible choices as to heroes. We also know that Milton's plot is the most conspicuously disarranged of any great epic. Whereas Virgil had spent three books in retrospection, Milton spends eight, an extraordinary feat. However, in every major particular, the plot of *Paradise Lost* would have been the same if he had begun at the beginning rather than there in Hell with the fallen angels. His plot remains what it would be in other orderings. But the sequence would differ with any other ordering. As *Paradise Lost* stands, only the last four books proceed according to so-called linear time, precisely because Milton wishes us to experience the *sequence* of hell, heaven, creation, war in heaven and all else so that by such a technique seemingly everything is made to bear on the decisive act in Book 9. His sequence is as original as his plot is familiar. Or again, in *Paradise Regained*, the plot consists of what is, at least for the Son of God, the same event repeated over and over again. He and the sympathetic reader have only a single faith with which to defeat Satan's various temptations. On the other hand, the sequence from the temptation to turn stones into bread to the climax on the pinnacle of the Temple is a rising one of great power.

The distinction between sequence and plot allows us to account for differing kinds of time in narrative. The *erzählte Zeit*, or better, the pluralistic times narrated, belong to the plot. As Milton shows, this order of time, this presumed historical chronology need not be that of the sequence narrative at all. Flashback and reminiscence are standard techniques, even in traditional narration. Today we have narrative collage and other techniques in the so-called anti-novel that disrupt or even abandon plot-time. But it is literally impossible to abandon sequence time. The attempt merely produces another sequence and its time. That other sequence and its time may be more or less interesting or beautiful. But it is impossible to narrate without sequence, and it is possible to narrate without plot.

I find it extraordinarily interesting that a wealth of variations in plot and sequence temporalities should have been discovered by Restoration poets. They belong to an age that also discovered the literary uses of historical events in what might be termed "public" time. It is worth saying again that discovery came from a need for such an understanding, but also the need was so important as to evoke narrative forms to represent and satisfy it. *Paradise Lost* and *Fables* are great narratives for many reasons. But I think that what we feel on other grounds is also testified to by their imaginative uses of temporalities to respond to the deepest challenges of their author's lives.

I shall end here, not seeking to go beyond 1700 or to proceed further in abstract discussion of time. But we may recall the lovely title of Emil Staiger's book, *Die Zeit als Einbildungskraft des Dichters.* I have difficulty with his thesis, that lyric uses the present, narrative the past, and drama the future. Nor do I think of time as one's imagination. But the two are deeply related in narrative and, as it happens, are crucial to the greatest Restoration poetry. Perhaps Staiger should have spoken rather of the imagination as creator of time, of the imagination as *Zeitbildungskraft.*

NOTES

1 My views are set forth in "Dryden and the Issue of Human Progress," *Philological Quarterly,* 40 (1961), 120–29, and in *Dryden's Poetry* (Bloomington: Indiana University Press, 1967), passim. Achsah Guiborry's excellent article—"Dryden's View of History," *Philological Quarterly,* 52 (1974), 187–204—is worth reading for itself and for her corrections of some of my statements in the article on Dryden's views of progress.

2 These three sentences reduce a much more complex argument presented in my "Renaissance Contexts of Dryden's Criticism," *Michigan Quarterly Review,* 12 (1973), 97–115.

3 See *The Restoration Mode from Milton to Dryden* (Princeton: Princeton University Press, 1974), ch. 6.

4 The argument is advanced in *Dryden's Poetry,* ch. 8, and in *The Restora-*

tion Mode, pp. 541–56. Between these two books there appeared Judith Sloman's excellent unpublished Minnesota dissertation, "The Structure of Dryden's Fables" (1968), and her article "Dryden's Originality in *Sigismunda and Guiscardo*," *Studies in English Literature*, 12 (1972), 445–57.
5 See the preceding note.
6 Konishi's long article appeared in the *Harvard Journal of Asiatic Studies*, 21 (1958), 67–127, and was translated by Robert H. Brower and myself. For convenience sake, the studies mentioned in these notes are entered under one or the other heading in the bibliographical note that follows.

BIBLIOGRAPHICAL NOTE
Time, Literature, and Integrated Collections

On Time, History, and Their Relation to Literature

Alkon, Paul. "The Historical Development of the Concept of Time," in *Biorhythms and Human Reproduction*, ed. Michel Ferin et al. (New York: John Wiley, 1974), ch. 1.
Augustine, St. *Confessions*, Books 11 and 12.
Bonaparte, Marie. "Time and the Unconscious," *International Journal of Psychoanalysis*, 21 (1940), 427–68.
Cassirer, Ernst. *The Philosophy of Symbolic Forms* (New Haven: Yale University Press, 1955).
Chen, Shih-hsiang. "The Genesis of Poetic Time," *The Tsing Hua Journal of Chinese Studies*, n.s., 10 (1974), 1–45.
De Man, Paul. "The Rhetoric of Temporality," in *Interpretation: Theory and Practice*, ed. Charles S. Singleton (Baltimore: Johns Hopkins University Press, 1960).
Guiborry, Achsah. "Dryden's View of History," *Philological Quarterly*, 52 (1974), 187–204.
Heidegger, Martin. *Being and Time*, tr. John McQuarrie and Edward Robinson (London: SCM Press, 1962).
Langer, Suzanne K. "The Image of Time," in *Feeling and Form* (New York: Scribner, 1953), pp. 104–19.
Man and Time (repr. from *Eranos Jahrbuch*; New York: Bollingen, 1957).
Miner, Earl. *The Cavalier Mode from Jonson to Cotton* (Princeton: Princeton University Press, 1971), ch. 3, "The Ruins and Remedies of Time."
Müller, Günther. "Erzählzeit und erzählte Zeit," in *Festschrift Paul Kluckhohn und Hermann Schneider* (Tübingen: Mohr, 1943), pp. 195–212.

Poulet, Georges. *Studies in Human Time,* tr. Elliott Coleman (Baltimore: Johns Hopkins University Press, 1956).

_____. *The Interior Distance,* tr. Elliott Coleman (Ann Arbor: University of Michigan Press, 1964).

Staiger, Emil. *Die Zeit als Einbildungskraft des Dichters* (Zurich: Niehans, ca. 1939).

Integrated Collection and Related Matters

Brower, Robert H., and Earl Miner. *Japanese Court Poetry* (Standford: Stanford University Press, 1961). See Index, *s.v.* "Sequences, poetic".

_____. *Fujiwara Teika's Superior Poems of Our Time* (Stanford: Stanford University Press, 1967).

Ellrodt, Robert. . . . *Les Poètes métaphysiques anglais,* 3 vols. (Paris: José Corti, 1960).

Iser, Wolfgang. *The Implied Reader* (Baltimore: John Hopkins University Press, 1974).

Konishi, Jin'ichi. "Association and Progression: Principles of Integration in Anthologies and Sequences of Japanese Court Poetry, A.D. 900–1350," tr. Robert H. Brower and Earl Miner, *Harvard Journal of Asiatic Studies,* 21 (1958), 67–127.

Martz, Louis L. *The Poetry of Meditation* (New Haven: Yale University Press, 1954), ch. 8, on Herbert.

Miner, Earl. *Dryden's Poetry* (Bloomington: Indiana University Press, 1967), ch. 8, on *Fables.*

_____. *The Metaphysical Mode from Donne to Cowley* (Princeton: Princeton University Press, 1969), ch. 5, on Herbert.

_____. *The Restoration Mode from Milton to Dryden* (Princeton: Princeton University Press, 1974), pp. 541–56, on *Fables.*

Otis, Brooks. *Ovid as an Epic Poet* [*The Metamorphoses*](Cambridge: Cambridge University Press, 1966).

Sloman, Judith. "The Structure of Dryden's *Fables*," Ph.D. dissertation, The University of Minnesota, 1968.

_____. "Dryden's Originality in *Sigismunda and Guiscardo,*" *Studies in English Literature,* 12 (1972), 445–57.

Modes of Political and Historical Time
in Early Eighteenth-Century England

J. G. A. POCOCK

History—in all but a few, rather esoteric, senses of the term—is public time. That is, it is time experienced by the individual as public being, conscious of a framework of public institutions in and through which events, processes and changes happen to the society of which he perceives himself to be part.

The public realm, unlike the social realm, must be thought of as institutionalized and formalized, since otherwise the distinction between public and private cannot be maintained; and the institutionalization of the public realm leads to the institutionalization of social experience and of modes of apprehending it, and consequently to the institutionalization and differentiation of apprehended time. To say that "history is public time," therefore, is to say that individuals who see themselves as public beings see society as organized into and by a number of frameworks, both institutional and conceptual, in and through which they apprehend things as happening to society and themselves, and which provide them with means of differentiating and organizing the things they apprehend as happening. This is why the archaic dictum that "history is past politics" has more to be said for it than we are disposed to recognize, and why the history of historiography is to so large an extent part of the history of political discourse.

There are a number of ways of classifying the conceptual frameworks by which people order their consciousness of public time. One may classify them professionally and institutionally, in such a way as to suggest that the law provides one ordering of time, the church another, parliament a third and so on; but in eighteenth-century England such orderings and their languages had drawn together to a point where it seems truer to say that time and history were ordered by consciousness of a public realm or political nation, which could itself be ordered and conceptualized in a number of different ways. A preferable mode of classification, therefore, may be one which enumerates different ways in which a political society may order consciousness of its existence in time and of time as the dimension of its existence. This classification can be arranged around two dominant notions, that of continuity and that of contingency. Under continuity we may see society describing itself as perpetuating its usages and practices, transmitting its different forms of authority and, in these and other ways, maintaining its legitimacy.[1] Society will be seen as a complex of institutions and as an institutionalized whole; and its continuity as a whole will be predominantly defined in terms of the modes of continuity characteristic of those institutions held to be peculiarly important to its structure. Under the heading of contingency, however, we become aware of other and less institutionalized phenomena. We are in the domain of fortune, as it used to be called: of the unpredictable contingencies and emergencies which challenge the human capacity to apprehend and to act, and which may appear either exterior or interior to the institutional structure of society.[2] In either case, however, what is institutionalized is now the capacity to act in response to contingency, and the institutional structure is now a continuous capacity for action rather than a continuous transmission of legitimacy—a change of emphasis which cannot but operate to diminish institutionality and render the institutional more of a short-term response to contingency than it was before.

When time is the dimension of continuity, the institutional structure is seen as successfully creating its own time—though if it is fully successful in doing so, this will by no means be the same as creating its own future, but rather ensuring that no future ever comes into existence. When time is the dimension of contingency, the structure is seen as striving to maintain itself in a time not created by it, but rather given to it by some agency, purposive or purposeless, not yet defined. It may succeed or fail in maintaining itself; and if it succeeds, this may mean that it succeeds in preserving its own existence in the midst of a history it does not otherwise modify, or that it succeeds in imposing itself on exterior time and re-creating the latter in the image of its own continuity—thus absorbing history into itself—or that it succeeds in adapting itself, together with its own continuities and their time-dimensions, to exterior contingencies and their histories, while at the same time imposing its changing continuities on exterior contingencies in such a way as to bring about a dialectical relationship between continuity and contingency, the political society and history. To the student of the patterns of historical consciousness that arise in these ways, the important question to determine is that of what the time-creating agencies are—institutional or extra-institutional, human or extra-human—and whether they act to perpetuate simple continuities, to perpetuate simple domains of contingency, or to create new futures.

As English political and historical thought—to which I propose to confine myself—passes from the seventeenth into the eighteenth century, we encounter some interesting and important case studies of this order. We seem—though it is possible to overstate this point—to be passing out of a period in which it was generally supposed that contingent time and its events were the creation of God, and that the history thus created was more than merely contingent, in the sense not only that faith in the goodness of providence entailed our believing that it had a pattern we did not know, but also that belief in the content of revealed prophecy gave us certain keys to the pattern of its eschatological climax. To seventeenth-century intellects, the fulfillment of types by antitypes, or the literal or symbolic fulfillment of specific prophecies, could be utilized, in expectation, to build up scenarios for sacred futures, in the movement towards which favored secular societies might realize their history as latter-day Israels. But in the wake of the Puritan failure England—though not New England—had opted for a less prophetic form of religion which made less demand for an Elect Nation;[3] and the millennial and messianic projections of the sacred future, which had formed so important a constituent of secular historical consciousness, seem to have survived mainly in the form described by Tuveson in *Millennium and Utopia*,[4] where the long-standing tendency to see the millennium as the resurrection of mankind's Adamic potential had led to its being described as the rational and even scientific perfection of human society in a future no less secular for being providential. This kind of religiose progressivism figures in eighteenth-century thought, but not as one of its major political rhetorics; one is tempted to call it the opium of the Unitarians, though the idea of a providentially ordained increase of rationality was not without its contribution to the formation of associationist utopias.

At the other end of the cosmic scale from that at which God created the phenomena of time from the standpoint of a *nuncstans* which knew no future, traditional thought had located the humblest and least rational or sacred—though far from the least important—of the time-creating agencies: that "custom" which was "recorded and registered nowhere but in the memory of the people."[5] Founded upon the individual's ability to recall and summarize his own experience and to presume its continuity with the experience transmitted to him as that of his ancestors, this conception had generated two distinct but closely-linked ideological patterns. The first of these was the ideology of the Ancient Constitution, properly so called: the elaborate set of historical arguments by which it was sought to show that the common law, and the constitution as it now stood, had been essentially the same since pre-Conquest times and—if the argument were pressed home—since time immemorial, or at least since an unrecorded beginning in the woods of Germany. The second, which could, though with difficulty, be expressed without reference to the first, was the more highly sophisticated philosophy of prescriptive conservatism outlined by Sir Matthew Hale after the Restoration and perfected by Burke a century and a quarter later. This emphasized that in a purely traditional system, where everything was known simply by the fact of its transmission, there was no more to be known concerning any institutional fact than that it must be presumed continuous with some antecedent fact or set of circumstances. Consequently, we could never locate a customary institution in any context, whether of universal laws or contingent circumstances, which might permit of its being evaluated or compared with what had been done under other circumstances—we might only accept it, on grounds which entailed acceptance of the whole complex of traditions or transmitting institutions from which it came.

These two ideological constructs, it should be noticed, entailed two images of public time, sharply opposed yet as intimately connected as the two faces of Janus. In the one, time appeared as pure transmission, the image and perpetuation of a past in which was contained, yet contained without a beginning, everything which was needed by way of an institutional complex—somewhat as Crusoe finds on the wreck everything he can want, without knowing how it got there. In the other, each moment in the creation and transmission of a custom could be depicted in such a way that the stress on the absence of beginnings made it possible to speak of each act as at once uniquely itself and perfectly continuous with all that had gone before it. The custom-creating people were now housed wholly within the continuity of their own transmission, and it became possible to speak of each act as uniquely theirs, performed in and out of their own historic individuality "as the silkworm spinneth all her web out of herself only."[6] It is the paradox of custom in Old Western thought that it deals with the wholly particular by making it appear wholly continuous, immemorial and self-creating; and part of the paradox is that the philosophy of custom has helped to generate the philosophy of historicism.

This way of thinking, however, while far from extinct and indeed formally triumphant at the beginning of the eighteenth century—and massively revived in a changed form by Edmund Burke at the end of it—had during the second half of the seventeenth undergone severe and damaging challenge from the resurgence of feudal studies, which had produced an image of the Norman-through-Plantagenet past as historically autonomous in the sense that it was founded upon a web of social relations which could be studied in detail and shown to be structurally unlike anything prevailing in either the antiquity which had preceded it or the modernity which had taken its place. The feudalization of the middle period of English and Western history—as it may be called—had produced two sharply differing ideological polemics, in the debate between which much of the significant historiographical activity of the eighteenth century goes on, and which may be compared in respect of the structures of institutionalized time to which each gave rise.

The first polemic—Tory at the time of its inception in the 1680s, but successfully taken over by the Whigs some twenty years later—was authoritarian in its implications and in due course gave rise to a kind of presentistic conservatism. (The ugliness of the former word is the result of our having no familiar or elegant term for thought which uses the uniqueness of the present as a source for political authority; "modernist," while slightly less abrasive, probably carries too many irrelevant connotations.) This line of argument emphasized that neither law nor parliament nor constitution was immemorial, and consequently that none could make claims against the sovereign authority on grounds of its supposed prior antiquity. Filmerian advocates of divinely appointed hereditary monarchy could of course go on to argue that if the constitution was not immemorial the kingship itself was, being rooted not in mere custom but in patriarchal and even Adamic antiquity and an original divine sanction. But after 1688 this argument—which had been widely but not monolithically adopted by Tories—became harder to maintain and the appeal to a feudal past was seen as carrying conservative implications of another and a less antiquarian kind. If the constitution constantly underwent historical change—from pre-feudal to feudal to post-feudal—it would follow that it contained no principles of antiquity on which claims either to or against authority might be based; and consequently the case for sovereignty became the case for some final, uncontrollable and in this sense absolute authority to which appeal might be made in fluctuating and lawless circumstances, and which was above the law for the simple reason that no law which might limit it could otherwise be found.[7] This was rather the case for sovereignty than the case for divine right; on grounds which were in their own way historicist it looked back to the *de facto* controversy of 1649 and after, to Hobbes, who was in some measure a participant in that debate,[8] and to those pioneer "bourgeois" and "liberal" theorists—these are not adjectives which I find specially illuminating—who had begun to argue that a sovereign was necessary because men in the pursuit of their natural freedom imposed bargains on one another to the limit of their power. This argument was presentist to the extent that it denied that any morally regulating principle was immanent in time, and saw nothing but the moment and its strategies as providing the context in which the effort to moralize and regulate must be made. There also seems to have been a fairly clear ideological association between the use of this argument and the tendency to see the economy as consisting in exchange rather than inheritance; the early economic individualists were all theorists of sovereignty, whether they believed that the sovereign should regulate the actors in the economy or should *les laisser aller*. It was in part on the question of commerce that presentist sovereignty, in its Whig phase, was to become the opponent of the second polemic, to which I now turn.

This second polemic founded on the feudalization of the past had a career even more complicated than the first. In party terms, it moved from Whig to a combination of Old Whig and Tory; in terms of content, it originated with the specialized brand of anti-Normanism—or more precisely anti-Gothicism—employed by James Harrington, under the Protectorate, to suggest that the

Ancient Constitution was feudal and outmoded, and therefore ripe for revolutionary transformation. For Harrington, there were no organizing principles immanent in the English past; what he called "ancient prudence" was Spartan and Roman, a commonwealth of armed freeholders which had been corrupted and feudalized by emperors and their Gothic mercenaries, but might now be restored to its true principle in England in consequence of the decay of military tenures.[9] This was to place England at a crucial point on an agrarian version of the Polybian cycle of constitutions, a vision of time more Hellenic than Christian, but to make that point a Machiavellian *occasione* at which there was opportunity to escape from history into the timeless stability of a true republic. By invoking cyclical imagery, Harrington invoked also the idea of a set of organizing principles, from which there could be only degeneration and to which there must be return; but he integrated English history into classic cycle, and by insisting that freedom must be rooted in individual autonomy, itself rooted in the individual's possession of land, he further kept alive the time-structure of the natural economy, in which property was better if inherited than if exchanged. His successors, the so-called neo-Harringtonians,[10] retained the essentials of his time-scheme, but reversed the pattern of his history; re-affirming in the conditions of the Restoration the orthodox ideology of the Ancient Constitution, they located the stable commonwealth of armed freeholders in a Gothic and parliamentary past, and imposed upon the present the burden of escaping corruption. The principles which must be preserved if corruption were to be avoided—the principles of republican balance—were now imputed to the English past, and the Ancient Constitution depicted as an equilibrium of king, lords and commons. To maintain the inheritance of immemorial custom now became the necessary means of escaping the *anakuklosis*.

We might term this a process of classicization. The principles—balance in the constitution, virtue and independence in the individual—on which the polity must rest were now represented as a stable and stabilizing structure, located in the past as a source of legitimacy, and any movement from them was represented as degeneration. The classical politics in Western thought included by this time the disturbing suggestion, made by Machiavelli, that since virtue was action, it must sooner or later alter the conditions on which it rested and so render itself impossible; but eighteenth-century classicism seldom conveyed Machiavellian ideas in their full dynamism and rigor, and intimations of political mortality usually took the form, first of hints that no system of virtue could hope to endure forever, and second of warnings that the process of corruption, once begun, was almost impossible to check, even by the one known cure of drastic return to the constitutions original principles. The stakes were high when the individual was engaged in the practice of civic virtue, for he must commit his entire moral personality to the preservation of a classic ideal amidst a history not inherently friendly to it. If the individual was to be virtuous, he must live in a virtuous city; in a corrupt city, the individual himself must be corrupted.

The historical scene was rendered far more precarious by the late seventeenth century's realization that the personal autonomy, necessary if the individual was to practice virtue in a republic, needed a material foundation in the form of property. If the function of property was to confer independence on the individual, it must involve him in as few as possible contingent relations with other individuals; and the ideal form of property thus came to appear the inheritable freehold or fee simple in land, on which the Roman or Gothic citizen warrior had based his capacity for self-defense and self-government. But this ideal existed in the past. By the closing decade of the seventeenth century English and Scottish social critics were increasingly disturbed by the rise of professional armies, in which the citizen alienated the vital function of self-defense to a hired and banausic specialist, and thus became in some measure corrupt; and it had already been perceived that what enabled him to take this fatal step was the increased circulation of goods and money, which enabled him to pay a substitute to defend him while he both enjoyed the benefits of an expanding culture and accumulated further riches as the means to further enjoyment. But what soon became known as "the progress of the arts" was an irreversible process, whether one thought of it as the expansion of culture or as the corruption of virtue; the uncomplicated Roman or Gothic world lay far in the past; and profound changes were beginning to occur in Western man's understanding of history, as a result of the perception that economic and cultural growth must be thought of as both progress and corruption. Culture and liberty, it began to appear, were ultimately incompatible; the Goths were both despicable as artists and admirable as freemen; and what raised man above the condition of the savage must ultimately sink him below the level of the citizen. Man's quarrel with his own history, that most characteristic feature of the modern mind, may be dated in England from about the foundation of the National Debt. And should anyone wish to challenge my use of the masculine gender, I will point out that the classical ideal in politics and history was still a profoundly masculine way of thinking, and that its perception of the feminine was part of the crisis in awareness which I am seeking to explore.

The National Debt was a device permitting English society to maintain and expand its government, army and trade by mortgaging its revenues in the future. This was sufficient to make it the paradigm of a society now living to an increasing degree by speculation and by credit: that is to say, by men's expectations of one another's capacity for future action and performance. Since a credit mechanism was an expansive and dynamic social device, the beliefs men had to form and maintain concerning one another were more than simple expectations of another's capacity to pay what he had borrowed, to perform what he had promised; they were boomtime beliefs, obliging men to credit one another with capacity to expand and grow and become what they were not. Far more than the practice of trade and profit, even at their most speculative, the growth of public credit obliged capitalist society to develop as an ideology something society had never possessed before, the image of a secular and historical future. Without belief in the progress of the arts, the investing mercantile society literally could not maintain itself.

But in what was belief in such a future to be rooted? Not in experience, since there is no way of experiencing a future; not in reason, since reason based on the perception of nature cannot well predict the exercise of capacities that have not yet been developed; not in Christian faith, since the most apocalyptic of prophecies is not concerned to reveal the future state of the market. There remained imagination, fantasy or passion; and Augustan social thought is visibly obsessed at times by the spectacle of a society advancing at high speed into a world it can only imagine as existing in the forms which it may desire. Not only must the speculative society maintain and govern itself by perpetually gambling on its own wish-fulfillments; a new dimension was added to that dependence of all men upon all men which thinkers in the classical tradition wished desperately to avoid—though Christian and Hobbesian thinkers alike rather welcomed it—by the imminence of a state of affairs in which not only was every man in debt to every other man, but every man was judged and governed, at every moment, by other men's opinion of the probability that not he alone, but generations yet unborn, would be able and willing to repay their debts at some future date which might never even arrive. Men, it seemed, were governed by opinion, and by opinion as to whether certain governing fantasies would ever become realized.[11]

If the speculative society constantly gave itself credit for attaining levels of wealth, power and satisfaction which it had not yet achieved, and so sought to advance towards them, it constantly sought to transform itself by actualizing the imaginable but not predictable. Now it is an evident fact in the history and sociology of inter-sexual perception that masculine minds constantly symbolize the changeable, the unpredictable and the imaginative as feminine, though why they do so I would rather be excused from explaining. The random and the recurrent, the lunar and the cyclical, were summarized by Roman and Renaissance minds in the figure of *Fortuna,* who symbolizes both the history in which the republic endeavors to maintain itself, and the contingent with which virtue—that obviously virile quality—contends. It frequently occurs, in that Augustan journalism concerned with evaluating the impact of public credit upon society, that Credit is symbolized as a goddess having the attributes of the Renaissance goddess Fortune, and even more than she equated with fantasy, passion and dynamic change.[12] She stands for that future which can only be sought passionately and inconstantly, and for the hysterical fluctuations of the urge towards it. There seems to be an important link between capitalism and romanticism in this renewed feminization of time and of the process of actualization of fantasies on which—though never quite completed—the speculative society depends.

The Augustan political journalists—Defoe, Steele, Addison, Mandeville—display an uneasy concern with the increasingly visible public role of women, and it would appear that this is connected with their increasing perception of the growth of credit finance. Defoe and Addison both employ a female figure to denote the idea that the credit mechanism has endowed society with an excessively hysterical nervous system, and both suggest solutions in terms of what Montesquieu was later to describe as the conversion of *crédit* into *confiance*.[13] That is, credit was no longer to fluctuate wildly with the hopes and fears of the investing public, but to acquire a stability based on continued experience of the real if mobile goods of society. Addison's famous parable of how the vaporish virgin Public Credit is cast into the depths of despair by one set of phantoms and raised to manic heights by another depicts only the beginnings of the process. Clearly, the lady was Danaë; she needed to be fertilized by a shower of gold; but was it continued experience that gave the gold its value, or only fantasy in another form? The conversion of paper into bullion, of *crédit* into *confiance,* was at best no more than the conversion of fantasy into opinion, and it did not appear that even that conversion could ever be quite completed. In the world of credit finance, government was founded on opinion and reason was the servant of the passions; and though Montesquieu had depicted a society which converted *crédit* into *confiance* by borrowing to expand its commercial and military power, even this mode of controlling and determining the future must remain dependent on the fears and fantasies of those who must continue to invest. If Credit was like Machiavelli's prophet in needing a sword in reserve in case the people should cease to believe, she needed it for the further reason that having once begun to prophesy, she could not stop. The secular future was open and indefinite, and society must go on advancing into it.

The frugal merchant appears at this point, as one whose willingness to invest in the future was the product of his confidence in the present. In a sense he was engaged in the process of reifying the exchange of fantasies, and thus creating an actual future; but what we earlier called presentist conservatism makes its return with him, because a present, no matter how solid in appearance, which consists in a series of steps towards an imagined future, can never be purged of fantasy and passion, or endowed with any set of principles more morally stable than the laws of the market. Bating an invisible hand—a concept whose presence even in Adam Smith can be overstated—there could be no moment in such a present at which human fantasies and passions were not less than perfectly self-disciplined, and the intervention of a sovereign, ultimate and uncontrollable power might not be called for. But the actions of sovereign and subject alike in such a scenario must remain imperfectly rational or moral, and the Machiavellian divorce between politics and morality retained its status as a decree *nisi*. But there was the other side of the Machiavellian formulation: if virtue was not absolute it was corrupt, and if it was corrupt must it not degenerate further? Neither David Hume nor Adam Smith denied that a society might be so heavily in debt to itself as to collapse altogether.[14]

There were in all this the makings of a historical dialectic, an ideology of self-transformation. But it is notorious that English culture, though it may produce great historians, does not produce philosophers of history; though there was a generation when Scotland produced the latter in some abundance, and the need to discover reliable laws of the market, inherent in the situation I have described, was among their motivations. But in England proper the dialectic between virtue and commerce did not reach a crisis. The Whig constitution, alleging its peculiar blend of classical balance and customary antiquity, worked too well. The American colonies broke away, proclaiming incorrectly the irredeemable corruption of the mother country,[15] and set up a republic of their own, on new principles which, as Gordon Wood has shown,[16] blended a new form of dynamism with the classical struggle to preserve virtue against change. But to Britons it seemed that either the repression or the surrender of the colonies would be worth while if it preserved the sovereign authority of parliament; and the writings of Josiah Tucker, perhaps the most authoritative presentation of the British theoretical response to the American crisis, form a classic of presentist conservatism.[17] They are overlaid, in our vision of the history of political thought about this time, by the fact that a few years later Edmund Burke, responding to Yorkshire radicals before he responded to French revolutionaries, began a re-statement of English conservatism along lines which display, in place of the realistic modernism of the commercial Whigs, dominant elements of the customary and traditional vision inherited from the seventeenth century. There were no original principles of the constitution, he declared, from which degeneration might occur or to which a return could be made; but this was not because a new world of commerce had come to replace that of Gothic agrarianism, but because, in a constitution whose every part was presumed to be immemorial, no such principles could be located.[18] Burke was effecting a return from presentist to traditionalist conservatism, though it should be remembered that in a properly articulated tradition, every moment is its own present; and he might well have assented to the interpretation, put forward by Hume before him and by Coleridge after him, of English history as an ongoing dialogue between conservators based on the land and innovators based upon commerce. The complexity of the institutions through which the dialogue was conducted helped guarantee its continuation.

A liberal interpretation of the constitution, of the relations between virtue and commerce, and of the relations between personality, polity and economy, ensured that England did not develop a dialectical historicism based on the need to maintain consciousness of a self being constantly transformed into its anti-thesis.[19] Nor did the younger Pitt's war finance produce, in the third cycle of major French wars, the sort of reaction against the alliance between the military and monied interests which Swift had launched against Marlborough and Godolphin. In 1776–a year whose significance in the history of political thought will be celebrated elsewhere–there appeared, among other notable documents, Adam Smith's *Wealth of Nations* and Jeremy Bentham's *Fragment on Government*, each signifying in its own way that the interaction between the ideas of balance and corruption, virtue and commerce, which had marked what I am tempted to call the first eighteenth century, was beginning to be played out. In the second eighteenth century, that of the democratic revolutions and the struggle against Napoleon, new perceptions of institutionalized time were to be generated by political discourse, at once less classical and–for all the convergence of Coleridgean and German thought–less dialectical. England, having done much to transform the historical self-perception of Europe, was now moving away from France and Germany along paths of her own, while at the same time English and American thought were to develop along sharply divergent lines.

NOTES

1 J. G. A. Pocock, *The Ancient Constitution and the Feudal Law* (Cambridge: Cambridge University Press, 1957; New York: W. W. Norton, 1967); "Time, Institutions and Action: An Essay on Traditions and their Understanding," in *Politics, Language and Time: Essays in Political Thought and History* (New York: Atheneum, 1972); "Modes of Action and their Pasts in Tudor and Stuart England," in Orest Ranum, *National Consciousness, History and Political Culture in Early Modern Europe* (Baltimore: Johns Hopkins University Press, 1975).

2 J. G. A. Pocock, *The Machiavellian Moment: Florentine Political Thought and the Atlantic Republican Tradition* (Princeton: Princeton University Press, 1975).

3 William Haller, *Foxe's Book of Martyrs and the Elect Nation* (New York: Columbia University Press, 1963); William M. Lamont, *Godly Rule: Politics and Religion, 1603–1660* (London: Macmillan and Co., 1969).

4 Ernest Tuveson, *Millennium and Utopia* (Berkeley and Los Angeles: University of California Press, 1949).

5 Sir John Davies, *Irish Reports* (London, 1674), preface dedicatory, unpaginated. See *The Ancient Constitution and the Feudal Law*, pp. 33–34, and for the antithesis between custom and the *nunc-stans*, *The Machiavellian Moment*, chs. 1–2.

6 Davies, *Irish Reports; Ancient Constitution*, pp. 33–34.

7 *The Machiavellian Moment*, chs. 13–14. This interpretation replaces that stated in the concluding chapter of *The Ancient Constitution and the Feudal Law*, where it was suggested that belief in the antiquity of the constitution reigned supreme after 1688. See also Isaac F. Kramnick, *Bolingbroke and His Circle: The Politics of Nostalgia in the Age of Walpole* (Cambridge, Mass: Harvard University Press, 1968).

8 Quentin Skinner, "Conquest and Consent: Thomas Hobbes and the Engagement Controversy," in G. E. Aylmer, ed., *The Interregnum: The Quest for a Settlement, 1646–1660* (Hamden, Conn.: Archon Books, 1972).

9 *Ancient Constitution*, ch. 6; *Politics, Language and Time*, ch. 4; *The Machiavellian Moment*, ch. 11.

10 *Politics, Language and Time*, chs. 3–4; *The Machiavellian Moment*, ch. 12.

11 For detail see *The Machiavellian Moment*, ch. 13.

12 Defoe, *Review*, III, nos. 5–7, 92, VII, nos. 55, 57–9, 116; Addison, *Spectator*, no. 3.

13 *De l'Esprit des lois*, book XIX, ch. 27.

14 Hume, *Essays Moral, Political and Literary*, "Of Public Credit"; Smith, *The Wealth of Nations*, book V, ch. 3, "Of Public Debts."

15 Bernard Bailyn, *The Ideological Origins of the American Revolution* (Cambridge, Mass.: The Belknap Press, 1967); *The Origins of American Politics* (New York: Knopf, 1968); Pocock, "Virtue and Commerce in the Eighteenth Century," *Journal of Interdisciplinary History*, 3 (1972).

16 Gordon S. Wood, *The Creation of the American Republic* (Chapel Hill: University of North Carolina Press, 1969).

17 There is no contemporary study of this weighty thinker, Dean of Gloucester Cathedral and protector of Loyalist exiles. See his deliberately anti-Lockean and anti-neo-Harringtonian *Treatise on Government* (1781).

18 See *Politics, Language and Time*, ch. 7, "Burke and the Ancient Constitution: A Problem in the History of Ideas."

19 Professor Marks's paper, printed elsewhere in this volume, suggests that Blake's Prophetic Books supply England with both a national apocalypse and a vision of self-transformation, expressed in terms including and transcending the national self.

Defoe's Women: Snares and Prey

PAULA BACKSCHEIDER

The women in Daniel Defoe's novels have traditionally been seen as resourceful, courageous, ingenious, ambitious, delightful, shrewd, practical, solitary—the list of adjectives goes on in this fashion. The single exception had been Roxana, but in recent years apologies for her have been found in social theories, her experiences, and Defoe's social purposes. Even scholars who are critical of Roxana and the other heroines are more likely to complain about Defoe's writing than about the characters of the women. Defoe's women are passionless, sexless, undeveloped, "primitive psychologically," morally "muddled," and wholly materialistic—all faults which might be attributed to their creator's ability.

In actuality, they are women entrapped by circumstances and by social codes hospitable only to married women. Because they are trapped, Defoe can present them sympathetically. Because they are strong women with a developed sense of self, they fight back against the social evils which victimize them. But in doing this, they become predators and for this Defoe judges them guilty. He would prefer that they act with more honor and prudence and wisdom and even believes that such action is possible. Defoe's women are not at all his idea of exemplary, commendable women

103

who achieve middle class status, nor are they botched products of a hasty, mediocre craftsman.

The difficulties of the Roxanas, Molls, Governesses, and Susans in eighteenth-century society were myriad. At the mercy of men throughout their lives, they entered a society in which they were commodities with less preparation than a hog has for market. Their education omitted such important topics as money management. As Moll's young mistresses note, it mattered not what advantages she or other young girls had, money was necessary for a good match.[1]

Marriage among the upper classes' sons and daughters was a commercial venture which could be ruthless. With power shifting away from inherited titles to land and with the rise of commerical, imperialistic England, marriage was often the easiest means to financial aggrandizement. Clarissa Harlowe is perhaps the best case study: the jealousy and greed unleashed by her "romantic" grandfather ordain her destruction. Soames is so attractive to her family because he is willing to reduce his family fortune and settle it on Clarissa or even on her family if they have no children. At one point, Lovelace seems to think Clarissa is holding out for a better settlement. Clarissa provides a battleground for the conflict between materialistic and romantic considerations. Every genre of the period provides corroboration for the economic nature of marriage: from Congreve's *The Way of the World:* "Love's but the frailty of the mind,/When 'tis not with ambition joined"; from Swift's "Strephon and Chloe": "[He] bravely drove his Rivals down/With Coach and Six, and House in Town./The bashful Nymph no more withstands./Because her dear Papa commands./The charming Couple now unites:/Proceed we to the Marriage Rites."

Defoe deplored the commercial motives for marriage. In *Conjugal Lewdness*, he says,

> Ask the Ladies why they marry, they tell you 'tis for a good Settlement; tho' they had their own Fortunes to settle on themselves before. Ask the Men why they marry, it is for the Money. How few Matches have any other Motive except such as I must

mention hereafter, and indeed will hardly bear any mention at all, for many known Reason. How little is regarded of that one essential and absolutely necessary Part of the Composition, called Love, without which the matrimonial state is, I think, hardly lawful, I am sure is not rational, and I think, can never be happy.[2]

Conversations between miserable, dissatisfied married couples confirm the unfortunate results which Defoe predicts. One husband says, ". . . I broke my Faith and Honour with the Angel I lov'd; for the curs'd Thirst of Money: My Father knew not what he did, when he persuaded me to it: But I must marry a Fortune!"[3]

Roxana's marriage is arranged to the brewer, the disastrous product of a convention that ignored both individuals and fixed eyes on the money involved. After the brewer leaves, she, like Moll, is left to cope with the life of a lone woman unaided. Both are fully aware that sobriety and modesty will get them nowhere, and they put on the armor of deceit. Society rewards deceit. Neither Moll nor Roxana is able to arrange a successful marriage with a man whose parents might be involved. They must settle for table scraps—the widowers, the divorced, the unfaithful, the opportunists. That they do as well as they do is evidence of their unusual good looks, pleasant personalities, and ingenuity.

Should a woman lose the male protection of father, uncle, brother, or husband, her lot was a sorry one. An unruly daughter in *The Family Instructor* is told, "if you once go out of your father's doors, take my word for it, your character is at everybody's mercy."[4] Few jobs were open to a woman: shop girl, maid, cook, seamstress, prostitute. A woman with money was fair game; Moll searches desperately for a financial advisor, even Roxana chooses her men with one eye toward their ability to help her manage her money. Once married, the woman could not retain or own property without a special legal proviso. There were no provisions for widows. Defoe was well aware of these problems, for he proposed insurance, pensions, or compensation for widows several times. A typical instance is in "Assurances: For Widows" in *An Essay Upon Projects*.

In a class oriented society, women were particularly at the mercy of what the men in their family or acquaintance did. Many heroines of popular novels were crushed by naiveté and withdrawal of male protection as Clarissa, Moll, and Roxana were. Women were well aware that they were fair game for "men [who] make no scruple to set themselves out as persons meriting a woman of fortune when they had really no fortune of their own." Once the trap is sprung, the women react with despair or grief. There is little surprise, anger, indignation, or complaint. Their society has demanded a passive part from them—things happen to them, not because of them. Roxana's passivity has been criticized, but Moll, too, is passive until she learns her lesson. They, and Defoe's other women characters, grow increasingly independent, resourceful, and unconventional; they learn new patterns of behavior, and, as "Men-women," survive and prosper.

Defoe, then, sets a trap for each woman. In a situation from which society provides no escape routes, they have been given a sip of the "good life"—Moll in the Colchester house, Roxana as a young girl, Susan in Roxana's London house. Ordinarily their "place" would be to go to service, but Defoe has allowed us to see they have been taken advantage of by society. The lack of provisions for orphans, the laws for property, the educational system, all denied them a legitimate chance to rise. Denied options, they became the prey of households looking for cheap labor, of men and women offering money to satisfy their avarice or lust, or of men hoping to gain a few dollars in a not too troublesome marriage.

The novels are full of snare images. *Moll Flanders* alone has at least seventeen. Jemmy's former mistress "laid so many Snares and took so many weary steps" to catch Moll. Moll says, "Poverty is, I believe, the worst of all Snares" and the Devil provided bait and "laid the Snare" which began her career as a thief. The child with the necklace is another "Snare in my way." When Moll goes back to the governess, she is invited to live there and gradually trained to be a master thief, supporting herself and the governess by her crimes. Roxana also says that the Devil was the "Snare at the bottom." Both are trapped by their poverty and the nature of the society which made it nearly impossible for a woman to function independently. Both perceive the Devil baiting situations so that they are caught and sin before they realize the full implications of their acts.

Affection was a particularly vicious snare. The youngest daughter in *Religious Courtship* says,

> Really, sister, I am afraid to go on any farther; for, I must confess, I begin to have a strange kindness for him: and if I go any further, I may love him better, affection be a snare to me, and I may be prevailed with to take him, without farther inquiry, which I shall have no peace in.[5]

Moll found this out most cruelly. She was burned by both of the two men she loved romantically. Roxana must always be cautious and politic with the Prince; although part of her fondness for him was ambition, she genuinely suffers because of him and never really forgets him. While she symbolically gains what he could have given her, wealth, titles, for instance, no other man keeps her as happy.

Defoe uses this aspect of English society to gain reader sympathy for his characters. Moll is the best case in point. Taken in by the Colchester family, she sees herself as superior to the daughters and has had no training to warn her against seduction. Almost any young girl would believe love prompted the man to come to her and to give her presents (money in this case is not illogical—the family would have noticed jewelry or other objects), and to believe the situation rather than inclination prompted his desire for secrecy. Even if she were not as naive as Moll, the desire to believe might overwhelm her caution. It is only after the older brother's callous behavior that Moll becomes cynical and self-seeking in her liaisons. She has learned well that money is all and that no one is disinterested in love. Her subsequent experiences reinforce this lesson and extend the list of pitfalls. Her second husband is a "gentle-man tradesman" whose naive, ridiculous pretensions match Moll's. They ride to Oxford in an ostentatious coach and have their servants call them "Countess" and "my lord." *The Complete English Gentlemen* makes clear Defoe's scorn for this "land-water" existence.[6] Jemmy and his confederate go to great lengths to deceive Moll. That Moll is doing the same thing is both ironic and sad. He is deceiving her to get her money, she is deceiving him to gain respectability and security. The society has forced her to deception while Jemmy has more options. Her encounters with the Bath gentleman, her half brother, and the old gentleman from Bartholomew Fair emphasize her lack of self-determination, and she turns and preys on them out of fear and insecurity.

Roxana presents much the same situation. When her fool husband wastes his fortune and hers, then deserts her, she is in a hopeless situation. Unlike Moll, she is not even trained to go to service. She sells what she has and sits among her rags, depleted possessions, and crying children, and argues with Amy over alternatives. A masterful literary technique, this dialogue allows Defoe to present the extent of Roxana's entrapment and, by having Roxana protest Amy's immoral suggestions, appear nearly uncensurable. If *she* relentlessly names the sin in terms harsher than the reader might use, her actions appear more necessary and more of an affliction. Amy periodically reminds us that Roxana is boxed in; she says, for example to Roxana's husband, "Alas! who will marry her, in the Poor Condition she is in?" The landlord, the prince, the jeweler become instruments of security. She is faithful to each.

Roxana is an extension of Moll's cynical reaction to her first love affair. Both realize they must be out for themselves; Roxana, however, carries this too far. She decides she must be a "man-woman" and fears marriage while Moll believes to the end that she can find happiness, security, and even romance in a respectable way. Moll cares about each husband's financial situation but only because of what it would allow her; Roxana is out for profit. Moll is a snare because of what she needs, Roxana because of what she desires. For this reason, Moll is the more attractive character. Yet Roxana is not the totally unsympathetic character that some scholars make her out to be. Her dilemma is very real, her alternatives non-existent, and her excesses psychologically logical. Moll understands her lack of prudence with the Colchester older brother, but Roxana was guiltless—her marriage had been arranged. Robin had been a good husband to Moll; Roxana had known only desperation and desertion. It is deplorable that she was not a stronger person, but it is worse that she was forced into a relationship that left her morally bankrupt. She lost hope, her sense of self-determination and personal worth and became amoral and miserable. Moll reaches this state only in Newgate. The extent of Roxana's misery does much to redeem her in the reader's eyes, for between every evil act she suffers deeply and writhes in her trap.

Furthermore, the characters draw our moral outrage away from their actions by their candor, their abhorrence of excuses, their situation, and their engaging personalities. Defoe habitually distinguished between act and actor,[7] and the more sympathetic the character the greater the distance between the two. For instance, Moll's horror and revulsion at the proposal that she marry Robin and Roxana's grim insistence that she is a whore tend to focus attention on the woman's predicament and self as opposed to her action. Their final acceptance of the situation comes by grim necessity.

Consistent with much of Defoe's narration, motive is not simple but additive. Roxana goes on beyond poverty and gratitude to vanity. Roxana is always more the woman than Moll. She is young and pretty and naturally longs to be "courted, caress'd, and embrac'd." She has sold things and dressed in rags for a long time—the affectionate tenderness that the jeweler accords her is thus more difficult to resist. Finally fear motivates her; should she renounce the gentleman she would "fall back into the same Misery." In a young person faced with her alternatives, her choice is obvious; Defoe sets up the first of many choices in which Roxana cannot be right.

So successful is he at this that the nature of the women as predators is nearly obscured. That Defoe considers the women predators cannot be overlooked, however. He had no intention for the reader to accept "necessity" as sufficient excuse for Moll's and Roxana's conduct. His "conduct books" such as *Conjugal Lewdness* and *Religious Courtship* as well as the novels themselves contain discourses on and models for different behavior in similar situations. Exemplary servants, sober women, and exempla occur frequently. A quick glance at publication dates argues the direct connection between conduct books and novels. *Moll Flanders, Col. Jacque,* and *Religious Courtship* were published in 1722; *Roxana* and *The Great Law of Subordination Consider'd* in 1724; *The Family Instructor* had been revised in 1718 and *Conjugal Lewdness* was published in 1727. Incidents tend to recur from book to book. For example, Defoe uses a story from Sir Roger L'Estrange's *Aesop* in *Conjugal Lewdness* which he had reworked for *Moll Flanders.* In each a widow says, "Well! I am undone, for want of a good, honest, understanding, sober Man, to look after my Affairs." And then a friend helps her find such a man.

The major female characters generally have been servants or have been in a position in which they considered being servants. Only Amy seems content in the role. Although Moll is reared to service, when actually faced with the situation, she becomes physically ill. When she does become "Mrs. Betty," her temper is never suited to her condition and she never really admits her position. Repeatedly she insists that she is superior to the girls of the house—her looks, her singing voice, her ability to learn, she says, are greater than theirs. Defoe's proud observation that in Colchester any child from five years up can make a living should come back to us. No need for a child to steal or beg in this country. Rather than accumulate money by honest labor as Col. Jacque and George in *Memoirs of a Cavalier* are satisfied to do, Moll is delighted with the money that Robin's brother gives her and dreams of the fine lady she will be when he marries her. After this, Moll, like Jacque, is driven to crime primarily because she has no way to make a living—at least no way acceptable in her opinion.

Being a servant was an honorable occupation and an educational experience for many of Defoe's major characters. Col. Jacque learned a trade and received religious training while an indentured servant in the colonies. In *Religious Courtship,* two servant girls carry on a lengthy, instructive discourse on the importance of piety and obedience. Mary is finally discharged as a bad influence. Defoe insists upon the importance of servants as influences on mistresses responsible for their servants' conduct and moral improvement. Not infrequently, servants bring their masters to repentance as William does in *Religious Courtship* or William Walters does in *Captain Singleton.* One servant's mocking behavior causes dissension in an otherwise happy home and ends family worship in *Religious Courtship.* Amy is frequently the temptress in *The Fortunate Mistress.* Her sophistical arguments rationalize Roxana's conduct in almost every new liaison. The servant, then, should be a responsible part of a household.

Moll's conduct becomes entirely censurable. Rather than conducting herself as Jacque, George, or William and letting her virtue motivate her rise, she learns behavior and tastes above her condition, airs like Susan's and those maids whom Defoe ridicules for dressing like their mistresses, and she learns to take advantage of her situation. In *The Great Law of Subordination Consider'd,* Defoe complains of

> . . . the gaiety, fine Cloaths, Laces, Hoops, etc., of the Maid. Servants, nay, even to Patches and Paint, are hardly to be describ'd; it would be a Satyr upon the Ladies, such as perhaps, they would not bear the reading of, should we go about to tell, how hard it is sometimes to know the Chamber-Maid from her Mistress. . . .[8]

Servants also scheme to get a good housekeeper discharged and to help a "ravisher" or "scoundrel" violate their ladies' honor. As a woman and as a servant, Moll was responsible for her own good behavior. Betty in *Religious Courtship* makes clear that sober behavior is part of the duty of a servant. The servant Margaret in *The Family Instructor* might be Moll's jury. She is from a good family but in adverse circumstances goes to service. She is such a sober, religious woman that she teaches the child in her keeping so effectively that he is the instrument of salvation for his whole family. She refuses to leave her mistress even when offered great advantage and double the money. Her reward is what Moll sought in other ways—marriage to an established, wealthy gentleman. If she and Jacque could rise from servant to gentility, couldn't Moll? The Quakeress in *The Fortunate Mistress* has fallen on hard times, too, but conducts herself prudently. She, like Roxana, takes in boarders, but with far different results.

Moll and Roxana are continually examining their souls—their distance from heaven (or, more appropriately, hell) is audited as often as their money. Perhaps their most painful discovery is that they are snares. Both are nearly continually in search of or preying on men. Both take great pains in laying their traps—Moll's elaborate deceptions in order to appear to be a rich widow and Roxana's to appeal to the prince are far from isolated examples. Without doubt, they see themselves as snares and feel varying degrees of pride and guilt in this role.

Many of Moll's infrequent metaphors define her as a snare. She says she "play'd with this Lover as an Angler does with a Trout: I found I had him [Jemmy] fast on the Hook." She is a snare to the linen draper and to the old gentleman she robs in the coach. This man and the Bath gentleman form a contrast which illustrates the hardening of Moll's character. Her attitude with each, her ambitions, and the amount of initiative and scheming on her part indicate she is a different woman in the Mint. Moll, the snare, is more prominent as the work progresses. With the banker she is especially coy, and her casuistical discussions of divorce with him again bring to mind the patient, wily angler. She puts him off and raises objections throughout her confinement and recovery. When she consents to marry him, her conscience overwhelms her anyway:

> I turn'd from him, for it fill'd my Eyes with Tears too; and I ask'd him leave to retire a little to my Chamber: If ever I had a Grain of true Repentance for a vicious and abominable Life for 24 Years past, it was then. O! what a felicity is it to Mankind, said I, to myself, that they cannot see into the hearts of one another! How happy had it been for me, if I had been Wife to a

Man of so much honesty, and so much Affection from the
Beginning?

Then it occurr'd to me what an abominable Creature am I! and
how is this innocent Gentleman going to be abus'd by me! How
little does he think, that having Divorc'd a Whore, he is throwing
himself into the Arms of another![9]

In typical fashion, she decides to make the best of the situation
and be a good wife, but she has felt the jaws of the trap and
realized that she has trapped another. Well aware of this part of
her nature, Moll reproaches herself and fears this will be one more
reason she stands in need of repentance. About the linen draper
she says, "I then reproached myself with the Liberties I had taken,
and how I have been a Snare to this Gentleman, and that indeed I
was principal in the Crime." In Newgate she cries vehemently and
wonders just how many sins are on her head: "How many poor
People have I made Miserable? How many desperate Wretches have
I sent to the Devil: This Gentleman's Misfortunes I plac'd all to
my own Account." Roxana, too, knows she has an account, a
debt, because of Amy, the Prince, the Dutch merchant, and even
the jeweler. When she discovers how virtuous the Princess is and
the grief she has caused, she reflects, "I confess it was a Circumstance that it might be reasonably expected should have wrought
something also upon me." She has tried to "manage the Point" to
keep the Prince with her and now she will surely lose him. Upon
reflection, Roxana realizes she should have learned from misfortune; poverty and necessity had no part in her motives, and,
therefore, the punishment was to be expected.

Whenever Defoe treats women, he scrutinizes the preying-prey
facet. Men get women drunk and take them to bed, and the
women reciprocate by getting the men drunk and marrying
them.[10] With such relationships, Defoe insisted upon the right,
necessity, in fact, of the woman making careful inquiries into the
man's character. A direct parallel between sections of *Religious
Courtship* and *Moll Flanders* exists. When Moll helps her friend
marry the man who would not let his character be examined, she
is following the model of the young lady in *Religious Courtship*

which was published in February of the year *Moll* was.[11] Defoe insists that a woman who believes a man will marry her and allows sexual liberties is a fool who "ought to expect" to be jilted. In *Conjugal Lewdness,* he says,

> It may be true, that Promise of Marriage is Marriage, but it is not marrying. Our Laws have therefore carefully provided that Marriages should not be esteemed fair and legal if not performed in a fair and open Manner, by a Person legally qualified to perform the Ceremony, and appointed to it by Office. . . .[12]

So insistent is Defoe upon the necessity for a woman's scruple that he defends himself against the charge of partiality:

> If the women seem to be favoured in this story, and have the better part of the staff put in their hands, it is because really the hazard is chiefly on their side, and they are generally the greatest sufferers in the success: but if it were otherwise, yet, if they are treated with more than ordinary regard, the author hopes they will not lay that sin to his charge.[13]

While the non-fiction sources extend the list of feminine disadvantages, they also provide damning testimony against the women. "Really the hazard is chiefly on their side" describes Roxana's experience with the brewer and Moll's with her first seducer and with Jemmy. That Moll made no inquiries and ignored all criteria but fortune makes her both foolish and censurable. Many a Defoe heroine has lamented biting for the money and being reeled in to unhappiness. Every speech, every incident in *Religious Courtship* insists upon the responsibility of the woman to investigate the principles of her suitors. A woman should even prefer going to service to marrying the wrong man. A two thousand pound a year estate will not "lessen the misery at all to a good woman; I am sure she had better go to service or marry a good religious shoemaker, and I would do it myself."[14] Again, domestic service is an honorable occupation.

In a 1704 *Review*, Defoe gave a "Caution to the Sex, in General." Comparing Roxana and Moll is instructive:

A Woman ought in Policy, tho' no such thing as Conscience was concern'd in it, never to admit a Man on the most Sacred promise in the World, for the following Reasons:

1. Because she is under his Lash for ever, and Subject to the insults of his Tongue.
2. He will always plead his Merit, and think her obliged to him.
3. He can never believe she will be Honest, because, once a Whore and always so.
4. She forfeits the Dignity of her Office, as Wife, and makes her Consent of Marriage, which should be esteemed a Favour obtain'd by her Husband, be a Bounty bestow'd upon her.[15]

Roxana's delay in marrying the Dutchman helps her in part, but perhaps Defoe had a lighter meaning at the end of Roxana! Perhaps she was a subjected wife nagged about her earlier lapses, a state she would have abhorred.

Moll and Roxana, Susan and Amy are condemned by nearly every case history in the conduct books. Susan is the haughty servant seen over and over. She dresses above herself, has unseemly pretentious habits, ignores advice and warning. Amy ignores her moral responsibilities. Her advice is usually licentious, immoral, or even criminal. Servants of sinful families were advised to quit or, at least, retain their autonomy. Amy allows Roxana to drag her into sin and finally commits murder. Roxana also violates the mistress-servant relationship. Defoe insisted that servants and apprentices were to be regarded as children needing religious instruction. Roxana, however, forces Amy into bed with the jeweler and perverts the relationship among them all. Amy is always her accomplice in deceit and manipulation. The conduct books condemn every period of the women's lives—they are not studious, serious children; they use money rather than piety as the measure of a man; they know nothing about a man's character before pursuing him;[16] they are unnatural mothers,[17] scattering nameless children over England, France, and America; they fail to instruct a single child in "who made them"; throughout middle and old age they behave recklessly and frivolously.

Defoe's women are good evidence that the non-fiction writer

always lurked in the novelist. The themes that Defoe insisted upon in newspapers and pamphlets are hammered upon in the novels. Women are, and are subject to special dangers, and special caution and behavior is demanded of them. The women in the novels are, as he insists, exempla: his readers could learn much from them. Just as he has case studies in *The Great Law of Subordination*, he has case studies in the novels. What are the penalties and rewards for certain courses of action? What excesses should be guarded against? How can middle class status be gained? Defoe meant what he said when he introduced his writings with

> Things seem to appear more lively to the Understanding, and to make a stronger Impression upon the Mind when they are insinuated under the cover of some Symbol or Allegory, especially where the moral is good, and the Application obvious and easy.[18]

and in recommending *Moll Flanders* "as a Work from every part of which something may be learned, and some just and religious Inference drawn, by which the Reader will have something of Instruction, if he pleases to make use of it."

Defoe presented the pitfalls of the feminine condition. Perhaps he wanted to reach those girls deaf to *Religious Courtship*—although "1000's of copies a year" were being sold one-hundred-thirty years after the original publication,[19] Defoe still would have desired a broader audience. Perennially concerned with society, he joined Fielding, Richardson, D'Urfey, Wycherley, and Butler in criticizing contemporary marriage customs and the destructive emphasis on economic marriage liaisons. From his early tracts to the end, he was sensitive to women's predicaments and limitations.

Nevertheless, Moll, Roxana, Susan and Amy are not heroic characters. Despite Defoe's identification with Moll, he still regards many of her actions with detached disapproval. As a young woman, Moll committed nearly every foolish, indiscreet act imaginable. Defoe's, and the reader's, sympathy grows for her as her predicament becomes less of her own making. Never, however, does Moll have Defoe's full approval.[20] The thief and prostitute are tawdry. Even the repentant Moll is not commendable. When she gives Humphrey the stolen watch, she appears miserly and hypocritical. When she deceives Jemmy, she appears greedy and insincere. Once again she is risking security and happiness for a few more pounds. Both she and Defoe make remarks that throw doubt on her continued religious consciousness.

The endings of the novels seem especially suited to Defoe's purposes and to his reader's tastes. Susan has been disposed of—she has been the ambitious, scheming servant, the trouble-maker, like the tale-bearing maid, also named Susan, in *The Behavior of Servants in England*. Amy has disappeared, apparently a friendless fugitive, for her perverted loyalty. Roxana is suffering, if not for her legal crimes, for her social sins. She missed her chance for an honorable marriage and her excesses have resulted in a titillatingly vague suffering. The punishment to fit her crimes remains necessarily vague—her sins, more interpersonal than crimi-nal or public, her desires made clear and poignant by her interlude with the Quakeress, Roxana might be more effectively punished by some discovery, some loss of respect and self-determination. A kind of poetic justice occurs here—Roxana has sacrificed her children, Amy, the Prince's happy marriage, and the Dutchman to her ambitions to be a "man-woman." Finally she is at the mercy of nearly everyone. Moll offers another kind of satisfying ending. She has made mistake after mistake, been punished or suffered disappointment, started over, and finally resolved the complica-tions. She is a servant who makes good, not through marriage to an elder son, by tricking a prosperous tradesman, or from the fruits of crime alone, but through marriage to a man of approxi-mately equal social status and ambitions and through colonization (a means to get ahead that Defoe frequently recommended). In Jemmy and Moll we very nearly find

> . . . the Felicity of a married Couple, engaged before Marriage, by a mutual, a sincere, and well-grounded Affection; who Love, and know why they do so; love upon the solid Foundation of real Merit, personal Virtue, similitude of Tempers, mutual Delights; that see good Sense, good Humour, Wit, and agreeable Temper in

one another, and know it when they see it, and how to judge of it; that make each the Object of a reciprocal Choice, and fix all the View of their future Felicity in the Possession of the Person so loved; whose Affection is founded in Honour and Virtue, their Intentions modest, their Desires chast, and their Designs equally sincere.[21]

The novel *Col. Jacque* demonstrates Defoe's consistency. Jacque has risen from transported felon to prosperous landowner "when the Devil laid a Snare" which he says almost ruined him ("There dwelt a Lady in the house opposite—"). Thus begins Jacque's career as a husband. This lady "ensnares" him, "draws him in," was a "Posture mistress," a chameleon. She has heard that he was a great Merchant and that she would live like a Queen.[22] She is an extravagant and bad-tempered wife and Jacque divorces her for adultery three years later. His second marriage is the result of a war-time drunk. She is discovered to be a whore. Jacque still desires a "settled family life" so he marries a widow a few months later with whom he enjoys six happy years before she begins to drink. Totally debauched, she dies, and Jacque promptly marries a middle-aged country woman, who, after the marriage, admits a "slip" in her youth; she dies two years later. Each one of these marriages presents the women as a snare, a variety of circumstances likely to lead to unhappy marriages, couples with poor motives and no investigation of the intended, and many examples of "matrimonial whoredom." The ending of *Col. Jacque* is similar to that of *Moll Flanders.* Jacque is reunited with his now repentant first wife in Virginia. Again, legally married equals are united in the colonies.

Defoe's readers were the readers of popular novels, the Bettys and Margies, the country people who bought their novels in installments from the local newspapermen, men and women who bought adventure books, romances, and borrowed books from coffee houses.[23] The readers of *Robinson Crusoe* would enjoy the novelty of women adventurers. The women's ingenuity in the newly money-oriented society and the compromising moral dilemmas related to casuistry columns[24] engaged another audience.

Furthermore, the novels are a kind of escape literature. Their adventures and dreams and final successes are common to popular novels of any time. Their most engaging quality, however, is the heroines' refusal to accept the life of an eighteenth-century servant. In the face of the realities of life for women, they are models of courage, ingenuity, and aspiration.

NOTES

1 ˙Spiro T. Peterson, "The Matrimonial Theme in *Roxana*," *PMLA*, 70 (1955), 183–90; Arnold Kettle, "In Defense of Moll Flanders," in John Butt, ed., *Of Books and Humankind* (London: Routledge and Kegan Paul, 1964), pp. 61 ff.; See also, P. F. Vernon, "Marriages of Convenience and the Moral Code of Restoration Comedy," *Essays in Criticism*, 12 (1962), 374–75:

> Obviously any writer who intended to deal with marriage and sexual relationships at all seriously in that age had first to recognize the overriding impact of current economic movements.
> The great problem for those interested in personal relationships lay not in the difficulty of dissolving marriage but in the original difficulty of arranging it on anything other than a commercial basis.

In Daniel Defoe's *The Family Instructor*, the family agrees with Moll's Colchester family; in speaking of Margaret, the sober, middle-aged servant: "Nay, captain, she wants nothing to make her a complete wife but money; for I assure you she come of a good family, and has been very well bred, though her parents are low; and yet I cannot advise you to it, for many reasons" (ii, 361).
2 Daniel Defoe, *Conjugal Lewdness* (Gainesville: Scholars' Facsimiles Reprints, 1967), pp. 27–28.
3 *Conjugal Lewdness*, p. 275.
4 *Family Instructor*, p. 84.
5 Daniel Defoe, *Religious Courtship* (Cincinnati: Applegate, 1853), p. 17.
6 For a detailed discussion, see Michael Shinagel, *Daniel Defoe and Middle Class Gentility* (Cambridge: Harvard University Press, 1968), pp. 151–53.
7 In discussing debtors he makes a distinction between those who run into debt "by innocent Mistake" and those who do it with forethought, and he suggests the penalties should be different for each type. *Review*, III, pp. 397–400, ed. A. W. Secord, Facsimile Text Society edition.
8 Daniel Defoe, *The Behavior of Servants in England Inquired Into* (London: H. Whittridge, 1724), pp. 14–15.

9 Daniel Defoe, *Moll Flanders* (New York: Crowell, 1970), p. 144.

10 *Behavior of Servants*, p. 68–69.

11 *Religious Courtship*, pp. 51, 60–61, 64, and 66, and *Moll Flanders*, pp. 57–62.

12 *Conjugal Lewdness*, pp. 273–74. See also *Review*, September 5, 1704.

13 *Religious Courtship*, p. 4.

14 *Religious Courtship*, p. 79.

15 *Review*, September 5, 1704.

16 The second daugher in *Religious Courtship* says, "It is no matter what the man is, if the estate be good," and provides a lesson for any who might think this way (p. 8).

17 Michael Shinagel, "The Maternal Theme in *Moll Flanders*," *CLJ* (1969), pp. 3–22. However, Moll is never free to be maternal until her reunion with Humphrey. It would appear that the evidence is inconclusive.

18 Daniel Defoe, *A Collection of Miscellaney Letters*, iv. p. 210.

19 American Preface to the 1855 edition of *Religious Courtship*.

20 Maximillian Novak says, "Moll is more guilty than Jacque because she makes no restitution for her crimes against other people" in "The Problem of Necessity in Defoe's Fiction," *Philological Quarterly*, 40 (1961), 522.

21 *Conjugal Lewdness*, p. 113.

22 Daniel Defoe, *Col. Jacque* (London: Oxford University Press, 1965), pp. 186–87.

23 Richard Altick, "The Emergence of Popular Reading and Scholarly Activity in the Eighteenth and Nineteenth Century," *Forum*, 7 (1969), 9–17; R. M. Wiles, "Middle Class Literacy in Eighteenth Century England," in *Studies in the Eighteenth Century*, ed. R. F. Brissenden (Toronto: University of Toronto Press, 1968), pp. 51–65.

24 G. A. Starr, *Defoe and Casuistry*, treats this in detail (Princeton: Princeton University Press, 1971).

Mary, Mary, Quite Contrary, Or, Mary Astell and Mary Wollstonecraft Compared

REGINA JANES

To speak of eighteenth-century feminism is to commit a vile anachronism, for there was no movement, no concerted demand for change in the political or economic sphere. What there was instead, was a widespread dissatisfaction with the condition of women that found various expression in satire and in sober counsel, in theoretical arguments, practical proposals, and practical action. Most writings on women are by men and fall into one of two large categories: the traditional satires with their familiar Juvenalian topics—feminine infidelity, luxury, vanity, pedantry, promiscuity, masculinity, and shrewishness; and the serious writings on education and marriage meant to fit women to be better companions to their husbands and mothers to their children.[1] Much of the serious advice is a simple obverse to the satire and reduces to avoiding the characteristics satirized in an expansion on Juvenal's opposition of the old-fashioned hard-working wife to the modern woman. The principal advance on Juvenal's analysis is the attribution of feminine deficiencies to education. The dissatisfac-

121

tion with what women are like implicit in both the satire and the advice, is directed at women of the middle classes and above, and is a dissatisfaction with women's performance of their duties towards men.

If we leave the vapors aside, there seem to be three possible channels for the expression by women of discontent with their sex or their situation: (1) an explicit demand for feminine activity outside of or beyond the conventional roles; (2) the insistence that the conventional roles be better fulfilled; (3) the simple expedient of activity without theory: if the role pinches, make a larger one by performing beyond its bounds. These alternatives are not mutually exclusive; all three appear in Wollstonecraft, the first and third in Astell, and the second and third are a very frequent combination.

The first is of course the rarest. Women active as the managers of households, of schools, of affairs of gallantry, minding their pens, their pies, their admirers, are not necessarily prey to discontent. Activity is an antidote to spleen; putting the Yahoo to work stops his wailing and his melancholy. But discontent does surface, although the discontent felt by women with the limitations of their situation is expressed infrequently and is usually confined to the subdued murmurings of momentary irritation in the privacy of correspondence. To demand that women perform beyond the conventional sphere requires that some ideal higher than the domestic ideal be available to provide a focus and give a shape to the felt dissatisfaction.

Both Astell and Wollstonecraft possessed such an ideal, and the difference between those ideals marks in one more form the profound changes in thinking about society that occurred in the eighteenth century. In spite of actual changes in the status of women,[2] it was possible to perceive the condition of women in much the same terms in 1790 as in 1690. What alters is the theoretical framework by means of which discontent is articulated.

Separated by almost a hundred years, Mary Astell and Mary Wollstonecraft give us a common portrait of the position of women in the world and a common sense of the limitations imposed upon the women of the relevant classes (middling and quality). No sketch could be more familiar than that they provide. By custom, women are not public, but private, characters, removed from the active world and suited for a retired, contemplative, and essentially domestic life, in part because of their exclusion from the public sphere, in part because of their maternal function. By habit, dressing is the "grand devourer" of their time and money; their conversation is froth, impertinence, censure, spiced by envy; and "like Machines [they] are condemned every day to repeat the impertinencies of the day before,"[3] if they do not descend from impertinence to vice. Prepared for marriage from the cradle, they neglect the friendship so superior to love and often find in marriage the only useful school they are ever put to, that of adversity: wakened by the neglect of their husbands from romantic reveries, they turn, perforce, to virtue.[4] Inconstant, unfixed of mind, they pursue facile admiration and evanescent pleasures, which "to want or to enjoy . . . is equally tormenting."[5] Kept from learning and all that is excellent by scornful opinion, they trifle away their capacities and neglect their duties in a round of unmeaning follies.[6]

All this uselessness and waste of life, so vehemently conveyed by both our authors and so precisely by Pope, is attributed to the education the world provides and the education it precludes. Kept by the force of opinion and custom from exercising their understanding and improving their reason, women are kept from true virtue, which has its root in reason.[7] Both contend that women, like men, possess powers or faculties capable of improvement, and that given the possession of a faculty capable of improvement, there exists a concomitant and necessary obligation to improve that faculty. The obvious corollary to the obligation of improvement is that women, at the present time, are not improved and are not putting themselves in the way of improvement. The immediate deficiency to be rectified is in women, not in the world or in men, and women are the first object of attack and persuasion.

There the similarities end. United in their common resistance to fashionable modes of behavior and in their attribution of women's defects to a cause external to the female character, Astell and Wollstonecraft constitute the political as well as the chronological extremes of eighteenth-century thinking about women. Their politics differ, their rhetoric differs, and so do the social assumptions that underlie both. All movements for reform require a theoretical framework for articulating the discontent that provides their energy, and Astell and Wollstonecraft found their models in different places, the one looking back towards monastic establishments and passive obedience to established authority both religious and secular; the other looking through the rights of man to the perfection of reason in the world and the progress of mankind in society. For Astell, "the Grand Business that Women as well as Men have to do in this World [is] to prepare for the next,"[8] while Wollstonecraft would have women "advance, instead of retarding, the progress of those glorious principles that give a substance to morality."[9] Both link the end of man with activity of mind: women are "to attend the great Business they came into the world about, the service of GOD and improvement of their own Minds" and are "human creatures, who, in common with men, are placed on this earth to unfold their faculties."[10] But Astell would have "all their Care and Industy to Centre" on preparation for the next world, while Wollstonecraft looks for change in this, though hoping little from "the present state of society."[11] The primary difference is that between a focus that is first and last religious and a focus fundamentally social, between a framework that justifies its demands for change in religious terms and one that justifies its demands in secular terms. The difference in focus coupled with the difference in social and political attitudes affects the nature of their proposals for women and the rhetoric with which they offer up those proposals.

From the beginning, Astell possessed a religious orientation that provided a framework for thinking about women in asexual terms, with the center of women's lives shifted from their biological and social functions in this world to that world to come in which distinctions of sex, it was hoped, disappear. Unlike Wollstonecraft, the frame of whose most vigorous work is permeated even to the title by a political idea new to her, the rights of humankind, Astell's work shows no new ideas or new ordering of thought consequent upon a new intellectual discovery. In her first work, the first part of *A Serious Proposal to the Ladies* (published in 1694), her religious convictions supply both the motive for the work and the substance of the proposal.

She suggests that a "Monastery, or Religious Retirement" without vows and with free egress for marriage be established in which ladies might serve God and improve their minds. The suggestion depends upon the conviction that the main design of our lives, our "true and greatest interest,"[12] as rational creatures, is religion; but while the desire for a monastery follows from religious conviction, it is not a necessary consequence: men and women have been devout without withdrawing from the world. The proposed withdrawal provides a declaration of independence from the world for women, without stating explicitly that it is doing so.

She calls the retirement "a Type and Antepast of Heav'n," Mother Eve's paradise without the serpent.[13] There the religious may perfect their minds and their virtue; they will be "careful to redeem their Time" in "prayers and Praises to God . . . in study in learning themselves or instructing others . . . in spiritual and corporal Works of Mercy."[14] The end is to combine the good works of an active life with the pleasure and serenity of the contemplative. But the description of the height of the contemplative life is hardly serene:

> And to compleat all, that *Acme* of delight which the devout Seraphic Soul enjoys, when dead to the World, she devotes her self entirely to the Contemplation and Fruition of her Beloved; when having disengag'd her self from all those Lets which hindred her from without, she moves in a direct and vigorous motion towards her true and only Good, whom now she embraces and acquiesces in with such an unspeakable pleasure, as is only intelligible to those who have tried and felt it, which we can no more describe to the dark and sensual part of Mankind, than we can the beauty of Colours and harmony of Sounds to the Blind and Deaf.[15]

The passionate exclusiveness of this religious affection combines with the withdrawn society of the religious to make up a world without familial or domestic relations. Women's customary ties to the great world are severed and replaced by a more satisfying communion with God that frees them from dependence on the "indifferency of a husband," that substitutes for unreliable man, a lover who is never indifferent,[16] and provides a locus for those feelings ordinarily lavished upon husbands and children, or lovers less worthy.

As a projector, Astell's rhetoric is persuasive, rather than exhortative or expressive, and the topics persuasion finds define the elegance of her audience. The audience is both wealthy and well born, and more value is placed upon birth than upon money.[17] She alludes to the lower orders only to mark the greater advantages and obligations of the fortunate.[18] Assuming that her audience shares certain preoccupations with physical beauty, dress, and the perquisites of material wealth, she employs a meliorative rhetoric that changes the object of conventional gallantries from the body to the mind in a multitude of variations on the theme, "Behold the first in Virtue as in Face."[19] The ladies' natural desire to excel one another, she would transform into a desire for excellence itself, for "to be ambitious of perfections is no fault."[20]

The proposal offered a socially acceptable channel for feminine excellence, and the seminary failing of establishment,[21] there emerges in the later works an acerbic resentment of the exclusion of women from all places of power and trust and of their prescriptive submission to men in will as in worldly power. In the midst of an argument upholding the subordination of women in marriage, she explicitly substitutes the other world as compensation for women's civil disabilities in this:

> She will freely leave him the quiet Dominion of this World whose Thoughts and Expectations are plac'd on the next. A Prospect of Heaven, and that only will cure that Ambition which all Generous Minds are fill'd with, not by taking it away, but by placing it on a right Object. She will discern a time when her Sex

shall be no bar to the best Employments, the highest Honor; a time when that distinction, now so much us'd to her Prejudice shall be no more. . . . This is a true, and indeed the only consolation, this makes her a sufficient compensation for all the neglect and contempt the ill-grounded Customs of the World throw on her.[22]

Elsewhere she observes that power and authority are not usually lodged in women's hands, but precedents, Anne, Deborah, Esther, show that it is neither just nor truly interested in men to withhold such power; and she levels an early attack on the practices of masculine historians:

Some good Examples are to be found in History, though generally the bad are ten for one; but how will this help our Conduct, or excite in us a generous Emulation? since the Men being the Historians, they seldom condescend to record the great and good Actions of Women; and when they take notice of them, 'tis with this wise Remark, That such Women *acted above their Sex*. By which one must suppose they wou'd have their Readers understand, That they were not Women who did those Great Actions, but that they were Men in Petticoats![23]

Nowhere does she suggest that the order of things should be altered or that women should write history, but the order is clearly unsatisfactory to her, and she rejoiced that Lady Mary Wortley Montagu's *Travels* demonstrated to how much better effect a woman travelled than the men.[24]

What Astell would change are not the external circumstances and restrictions to which she objects, but the internal relationship of women to those circumstances. As in the proposal for a seminary, her prescriptions resolve the conflict between her ambitions for women and the opportunities available to women in this world, by dropping out this world. The possibilities for action and her ideas about society afford no cure to the situation that produces the resentment.

In politics, Astell adhered to that highly vocal minority that maintained doctrines of passive obedience, distrusted all opposition to government, and, indeed, all politics and politicking. Yet she does not forbid political activity to women and uses her remarks on the subject to glance at men and male politicians:

> A little Practice of the World will convince us, That Ladies are as grand Politicians, and every whit as Intriguing as any Patriot of the Good-old-cause. . . . This made me think it not improper to take notice of the plain and genuine Sense of Christianity in this matter, That if Ladies will needs be Politicians they may not build upon a Rotten and Unchristian Foundation. . . . How busie looks and grand concern about that Bill and t'other promotion, how whispers and cabals, eternal disputes and restless solicitations, with all the equipage of Modern Politicians, become the Ladies, I have not skill to determine. But if there be any thing Ridiculous in it, I had rather leave the Observation to the Men, as being both more proper for their Wit, and more agreeable to their Inclinations.[25]

Similarly, she defends marriage as the institution of heaven, but she is still intent upon severing women's primary commitment to any worldly relation: "The Service she at any time becomes oblig'd to pay to a Man, is only a Business by the Bye. Just as it may be any Man's Business and Duty to keep Hogs; he was not Made for this, but if he hires himself out to such an Employment, he ought conscientiously to perform it."[26] The duty of a wife to her husband could have found an analogy less reductive of husbands, and also of wives. If husbands are hogs, a wife is no more than one who ministers to the comforts of pigs. In such passages, hostility is vented upon men instead of upon the society which is not to be altered, and the contagion begins to reach towards women as well.

The pressure of her conflicting ideas becomes most evident when in the body and virulent preface to the *Reflections upon Marriage* (1700; the preface was added to the third edition in 1706), she adopts for her own purposes the language of oppression and revolt. In the preface, she states that her purpose was to "retrieve, if possible, the Native Liberty, the Rights and Privileges of the Subject,"[27] and it is in this context only that she uses such terms without ironic import. The extent to which she is adopting cant language is evident in that her argument has nothing to do with "retrieval"—the discovery of a Norman yoke for women was reserved to a later age. In conformity with her other views, she does not confirm the right to resist, but points out that "in *fact* [Tyranny] provokes the Oppress'd to throw off even a Lawful Yoke that sits too heavy."[28] Comically and poignantly, the political metaphor finally turns against her own position. Speaking of the lack of recourse available to women should the "Matrimonial Yoke" gall, she observes that

> He who has Sovereign Power does not value the Provocations of a Rebellious Subject, but knows how to subdue him with ease, and will make himself obey'd; but Patience and Submission are the only Comforts that are left to a poor People who groan under Tyranny, unless they are Strong enough to break the Yoke, to Depose and Abdicate, which I doubt wou'd not be allow'd of here. For whatever may be said against Passive-Obedience in another case, I suppose ther's no Man but likes it very well in this; how much soever Arbitrary Power may be dislik'd on a Throne, not *Milton* himself wou'd cry up Liberty to poor Female Slaves, or plead for the Lawfulness of Resisting a Private Tyranny.[29]

Unwilling to draw the revolutionary conclusions that words like "tyranny" and "oppression" call for, she exploits the emotive weight of the terms to register an attitude rather than to propose an action.

The only liberty through rebellion that she advocates with complete conviction is the independence of women's minds in whatever circumstances they are placed. In the conclusion to the preface, she confronts the unwillingness of most women to strive for that independence and abandons them and her literary efforts on their behalf in the same moment:

> Women are not so well united as to form an Insurrection. They are for the most part Wise enough to Love their Chains, and to discern how very becomingly they set. . . . As to those Women who find themselves born for Slavery, and are so sensible of their own Meanness as to conclude it impossible to attain to any thing

excellent, since they are, or ought to be best acquainted with their own Strength and Genius, She's a Fool who wou'd attempt their Deliverance or Improvement. No, let them enjoy the great Honor and Felicity of their Tame, Submissive, and Depending Temper! . . . Let them enjoy the Glory of treading in the Footsteps of their Predecessors, and of having the Prudence to avoid that audacious attempt of soaring beyond their Sphere! Let them Huswife or Play, Dress and be entertaining Company! Or, which is better, relieve the Poor to ease their own Compassions, read Pious books, say their Prayers, and go to Church, because they have been Taught and Us'd to do so. . . . But let them not Judge of the Sex by their own Scantling. For the great Author of Nature and Fountain of all Perfection, never design'd that the Mean and Imperfect, but the most Compleat and Excellent of His Creatures in every Kind, shou'd be the Standard to the Rest.[30]

Here, in the last sentences of her last work written on behalf of women, Astell leaves those who will not "soar beyond their sphere" to their worldly occupations and turns to the Author of all Perfections to validate both her own endeavors and her dismissal of those who will not follow. With the failure of her persuasive efforts, the rhetorical identification with her audience has disappeared, and she directs her attack for the first time fully at women themselves.

In resigning her efforts for women, she consigns them to their conventional activities and roles while the ideal for women retains its sexlessness. It is the other-worldly bent of her thought that both permits the expression of so uncompromising a demand for feminine independence and collaborates with her social and political views to prevent a demand for social change in this world. She possessed more ambition for women than she could fully articulate and than most of her successors through the century were even to feel. Odd, idiosyncratic, aloof, Astell resolved the tension between the world's demands on women and her ambitions for them, not by redefining women's roles in the world, but by looking into the past and retrieving for women an ancient ascetic ideal. Resentful of women's disabilities in the world, she can propose nothing to improve that situation and so denigrates the world, locating women's rightful ambitions beyond it. When her sex fails her, she turns from them also, back to the constant center, that was there from the beginning and is there at the end.

For Mary Wollstonecraft, afflicted with the same dissatisfaction with women's opportunities and artificially induced limitations of character, the discovery of a solution to the problem with women took a very different form and much longer to find. While Astell's works begin with a *Proposal* and decline to *Reflections*, Wollstonecraft begins with desultory *Thoughts* and ends with a *Vindication*. The religious center that provided Astell with a focus from the beginning served Wollstonecraft only briefly, and in its place she put, when she had found them, the rights of man. For both authors, the problem with women is a problem with the world, but while Astell solves the problem through abandonment, Wollstonecraft seeks a solution closer to the terms in which the problem is felt.

To an indeterminate extent, the source of the difference is a consequence of different personal circumstances. Astell's indentification with the upper classes is evident in her title and her choice of audience as well as in what she advises. In addition, the lack of any visible means of support in what can be learned of her life [31] and the absence of any interest in how women are to earn livings or support themselves unmarried, indicates a level of economic and status security that facilitates identification with a class in whose life style she feels no urge to participate and which she rejects as inappropriate for thinking beings. Wollstonecraft's familiar and copious history portrays a typical case of status insecurity: the gentlemanly ambitions and economic failures of her father, the successive uprootings of the family and the discord within it, the need and determination to earn her own living and the difficulties she encountered in doing so, the humiliations of the life of a governess and the failure of her school.[32] While they do not explain, these dislocations almost certainly contributed to her sense of classlessness and the concern in the works and letters with day to day survival.

In the early and innocuous *Thoughts on the Education of*

Daughters (published 1787) Wollstonecraft gives us most of the topics and the main lines of the position that will be developed at more length and within a different structure five years later in the *Vindication of the Rights of Woman* (published in 1792). Her inaugural work differs from Astell's in that while Astell's purports to be a practical proposal, Wollstonecraft's is in fact a practical handbook offering miscellaneous advice on various topics from the suckling of children through the improvement of taste to the vacuity of the entertainment offered in public places. It differs from other practical handbooks in only two important respects. The advice concerning manners, behavior, and "exterior accomplishments" is not seconded by a constant recurrence to the "pleasingness" of such behavior to men; instead, the sanction for behavior is the improvement of the mind in virtue preparatory to "a state of purity and happiness."[33] Secondly, while she takes for granted that domestic duties are the province of women, she dedicates an evidently autobiographical chapter to "the unfortunate situation of females fashionably educated and left without a fortune" whose "modes of earning a subsistence" are few, "and those very humiliating."[34]

She describes at length the humiliations to which a gently educated governess is subject in her position between the servants and the people, moves through a series of melancholy exclamations on sensibility oppressed, and ends with an Astellian resolution that lacks the emotive force of Astell's version:

> It is impossible to enumerate the many hours of anguish such a person must spend. . . . The mind must then sink into meanness, and accomodate itself to its new state, or dare to be unhappy. . . .
> Yet if a young woman falls into it, she ought not to be discontented. . . . The main business of our lives is to learn to be virtuous; and He who is training us up for immortal bliss, knows what trials will contribute to make us so; and our resignation and improvement will render us respectable to ourselves, and to that Being whose approbation is of more value than life itself.[35]

Her remarks on the painful situation of such a young woman indicate a reservoir of resentment waiting for a rhetoric to displace it. While the means of escape from an intolerably limiting circumstance is still, as in Astell, to ignore the circumstance by focussing attention elsewhere, that Being here checks the effusions of sensibility instead of receiving them.

With her discovery of the rights of man, she acquires a vocabulary that supplements the consolations of religion by linking the social progress of reason and virtue with God's purpose for mankind. The new vocabulary does not obliterate the old: that Being retains his importance as the guarantor of immortality and of natural rights, but this world and that to come are seen as continuous rather than disjunctive. The vocabulary allows an antagonistic stance towards the social order responsible for a problem felt in social terms.

The combative stance that transforms the earlier complaints into active attacks is evident in her titles, *A Vindication of the Rights of Men* and *A Vindication of the Rights of Woman*, both of which imply an antagonist who would deny those rights. In the first, there does exist a named enemy, Edmund Burke, whose uncongenial *Reflections on the Revolution in France* afford a point of departure and a point of attack. In the *Rights of Woman*, however, the enemy is more diffuse. In the most general terms, the antagonist is "the present state of society," which is responsible for the particular evils to be extirpated. Since society is the enemy the speaker wants no part of, her identification is with no particular class or segment of that society, but with the position of the critic outside the established order. This identification, itself a political act, has two rhetorical consequences: the absence of a clearly defined audience to be persuaded and a lack of complicity with those whose rights she vindicates. The audience explicitly addressed constantly shifts, from Talleyrand to whom the work is dedicated,[36] through "ye foolish women," to "ye men of understanding." While Astell writes to "Ladies," Wollstonecraft objects that most instruction has been addressed to "ladies" and that she will write "with particular attention to those [women] in the middle class, because they appear to be in the most natural state."[37] While this extension of the audience evidences a democratization of concern, to describe a set of people as being in "the most natural state" is not, of course, to identify with them. It is to have surveyed them from the superior vantage of Johnson's narrator in the *Vanity of Human Wishes* and to have passed judgment upon them without that poem's closing acknowledgment of the identity of interests of speaker and audience.

That there should be no possibility of identification with those whose rights she argues for is a consequence of her attitude towards the female character. The sexual character of women, that idealization of feminine weakness and docility, was an opponent Astell did not have to confront, for it emerged as the dominant mode for talking about women only in the forties and fifties of the century. The criticisms Wollstonecraft levelled at feminine behavior in *Thoughts*, she now takes as a prime instance of the disorder of society. So sunk in her eyes is the feminine character that when she wishes to degrade another sector, in particular soldiers or the rich, she likens them to women.[38] Wollstonecraft has no use for Astell's device of translating women into "little, useless and impertinent Animals"[39] if they do not comply, for women already occupy the lowest place available. The rights that are vindicated are those of "woman," the idea of the sex as a whole, a noble abstraction composed at present of deficient particulars, "women."

The primary social model Wollstonecraft holds out for women is respectable motherhood. While Astell wants women to soar beyond their sphere, Wollstonecraft decrees that woman out of the maternal character is out of her sphere.[40] Astell would have neither men nor women meddle in politics, but is glad that some women have performed notably. Wollstonecraft deliberately refuses to avail herself of any instances of historical female excellence and makes much of the disasters wrought by foolish women effective behind the scenes in political affairs.[41] The ideal she preaches for women is the domestic ideal, and there is no necessary connection between the rights of man and the domestic ideal. What they have in common is the levelling tendency. The ideal society is one in which a constantly increasing mediocrity of virtue is diffused through all classes and in which there shall be no need for the great exertions of greater men: "I wish to see women neither heroines nor brutes; but reasonable creatures."[42] The properly equilibrated household in which husband and wife are rational companions to one another with their separate, complementary spheres of duty is a version in miniature of such a state. The analogy between family and state has become egalitarian with a division of labour, rather than hierarchical.

At the same time, there exists an unresolved conflict between the domestic ideal and her insistence on independence. Originally, the word signifies "*an* independence," "the grand blessing of life, the basis of every virtue . . . [which] I will ever secure by contracting my wants, though I were to live on a barren heath."[43] The complaint of the *Thoughts* that women's means of earning a subsistence are few and humiliating is transformed in the *Vindication* into an argument for the expansion of women's economic opportunities. She would like to see women practicing as physicians, managing farms and shops, to see the means of independence available to them. When she speaks of independence within the family, the definition changes to discharging the duties of one's station, and in some contexts the word becomes almost meaningless, a desirable quality without content: "It is vain to expect virtue from women till they are in some degree independent of men; nay, it is vain to expect that strength of natural affection which would make them good wives and mothers."[44] It is difficult to maintain the primarily economic meaning of "independence" when the household is ever more rapidly losing its economic functions, and the meaning of the word begins to approach Astell's notion of excellence. The difference of course is that independence is a social term in transit between an economic and a psychological referent, while excellence refers exclusively to the achievement of the solitary mind.

The ideal of independence and the ideal of domesticity manifest Wollstonecraft's concern for the activities of women within the world, outside and inside the house. The social duties on which she founds her argument for rights are the rock from which Astell's argument rebounds. Astell's solution, in which motherhood is only a martyrdom for the sake of raising up souls to heaven,[45] has the consistency of a closed system; Wollstonecraft's does not. The principal deficiency of Wollstonecraft's version is that she does not explicitly perceive the problem of the conflicting demands made upon women by the family and the desire for self-actualizaion (i.e., the need for independence within the family), but the alternatives are present in their modern form: confused and unresolved.

Without the theoretical framework of the rights of man, without the rhetorical force that system of ideas provided her, Wollstonecraft's work would have been no more than another treatise of female education, another Thoughts on the Education of Daughters. But the theoretical framework she found permitted the anger she shared with Astell and others to be directed outward, against society, past the hapless women, who, while they share responsibility through complicity, are in part also its victims. By having no audience with which she identifies, she obviates the necessity of agreement and can turn her argument at the last not against those whose reformation she desires, but against "ye men of understanding" who must allow women the privileges of ignorance if they deny the rights of reason, "or ye will be worse than Egyptian taskmasters, expecting virtue where nature has not given understanding!"[46] The language of rights provides her with something Astell did not want—an argument for change not only in women, but also in the world. Transferring the onus from the individual to society not only for the source but also for the solution to the problem, Wollstonecraft ends not with a repudiation but with a threat. Between her attack and Astell's withdrawal, there lies the difference between one whose allegiance is elsewhere, and one who must find her happiness in this world, or not at all.

NOTES

1 In the main, the satires and gallant defenses of women seem to belong to the earlier part of the century, while sober advice proliferates in the later.

2 The steadily increasing importance of women as consumers of literature has been frequently pointed out, and it has been estimated that a majority of the novels written in the eighteenth century were written by women. As striking is the transition from scandalous Behn to delicate Burney, prominence without notoriety.

3 [Mary Astell], *A Serious Proposal to the Ladies, for the Advancement of their True and Greatest Interest.* In Two Parts (London: R. Wilkin, 1697), Part I, pp. 64, 88, 73; Part II, p. 7. Parallel passages appear in Mary Wollstonecraft, *A Vindication of the Rights of Woman*, ed. Charles W. Hagelman, Jr. (New York: W. W. Norton and Co., 1967), pp. 201, 277, 278.

4 Wollstonecraft, *Rights of Woman*, p. 103; [Mary Astell], *Reflections upon Marriage*, 3rd. ed. (London: R. Wilkin, 1706), p. 57.

5 Astell, *A Serious Proposal*, Part I, p. 79; Wollstonecraft, *Rights of Woman*, p. 105.

6 Much of the surface similarity in these descriptions derives from Wollstonecraft's reading of the authors of Astell's period. To make points about the character of women, she quotes, among others, Milton, Dryden, and Pope. Milton she quarrels with; she uses Dryden and Pope, especially Pope, for proof.

7 Wollstonecraft, *Rights of Woman*, p. 39; Astell, *A Serious Proposal*, Part II, pp. 23–28.

8 Astell, *A Serious Proposal*, Part II, p. 203.

9 Wollstonecraft, "To M. Talleyrand-Perigord," *Rights of Woman*, [p. 5].

10 Astell, *A Serious Proposal*, Part I, p. 37; Wollstonecraft, *Rights of Woman*, p. 33.

11 Astell, *A Serious Proposal*, Part II, p. 203; Wollstonecraft, *Rights of Woman*, p. 39.

12 Astell, *A Serious Proposal*, Part I, pp. 34, 44.

13 Astell, *A Serious Proposal*, Part I, pp. 42, 40.

14 Astell, *A Serious Proposal*, Part I, pp. 53–54. In his attack on Astell in the *Tatler*, no. 63, Sept, 3, 1709, Swift makes much of the "pens, compasses, quadrants, books, manuscripts, Greek, Latin, and Hebrew" that are to occupy the ladies. Astell herself shows less interest in the ladies' erudition than in the their acquiring the ability to write clearly and to spell correctly.

15 Astell, *A Serious Proposal*, Part I, pp. 41–42.

16 Astell, *A Serious Proposal*, Part I, p. 10; [Mary Astell], *The Christian*

Religion, As Profess'd by a Daughter of the Church of England (London: R. Wilkin, 1705), p. 152.

17 Astell, *A Serious Proposal*, Part I, pp. 4, 90, 93. In *Workfellows in Social Progression* (New York: Sturgis & Walton Co., 1916), Kate Stephens incorrectly attributes to Astell "the democratic idea of education for many" (p. 127). The impoverished who are to be educated are the daughters of decayed gentlemen only.

18 Astell, *The Christian Religion*, p. 302; *A Serious Proposal*, Part I, p. 89; Part II, pp. 85–86.

19 Astell, *A Serious Proposal*, Part I, pp. 3–4, 58.

20 Astell, *A Serious Proposal*, Part I, pp. 20–22.

21 According to Ballard, a "prominent lady" thought of giving £10,000. to establish Astell's academy, but was dissuaded by a "celebrated bishop," whom Elizabeth Elstob identified as Bishop Burnet. The lady has been said to be both Lady Elizabeth Hastings and the Princess Anne, with more evidence pointing toward the latter. Burnet's ground for disapproving the academy was not opposition to the education of woman, but a "Romanist tendency" in the proposal. Florence Mary Smith, *Mary Astell* (New York: Columbia University Press, 1916), pp. 21–23.

22 Astell, *Reflections*, pp. 88–89.

23 Astell, *The Christian Religion*, pp. 292–93, 353.

24 [Mary Astell], Preface, *Letters of the Right Honourable Lady M—y W—y M—e: Written during her Travels in Europe, Asia, and Africa* (London: B. Dodd, 1776), p. vi. The preface is signed M. A. and dated 1724.

25 Astell, *The Christian Religion*, pp. 178–79.

26 Astell, Preface, *Reflections*, p. 5.

27 Astell, Preface, *Reflections*, p. 2.

28 Astell, *Reflections*, p. 95.

29 Astell, *Reflections*, p. 27.

30 Astell, Preface, *Reflections*, pp. 22–25.

31 Florence M. Smith's *Mary Astell* remains the most thorough biographical and critical treatment. Other essays on Astell appear in Kate Stephens, *Workfellows in Social Progression*, and Ada Wallas, *Before the Bluestockings* (London: G. Allan & Unwin, 1929).

32 Lives of Mary Wollstonecraft continue to multiply. The best interpretive biography was Ralph M. Wardle's *Mary Wollstonecraft: A Critical Biography* (Lawrence, Kansas: University of Kansas Press, 1951) until Claire Tomalin's brilliant *The Life and Death of Mary Wollstonecraft* (New York: Harcourt Brace Jovanovich, 1974) appeared. Eleanor Flexner's *Mary Wollstonecraft* (New York: Coward, McCann, and Geoghegan, 1972) provides some valuable new information on the Wollstonecraft

family finances and her correspondence with William Roscoe. One of the more valuable interpretive studies is Margaret George's *One Woman's "Situation": A Study of Mary Wollstonecraft* (Urbana, Illinois: University of Illinois Press, 1970).

33 Mary Wollstonecraft, *Thoughts on the Education of Daughters* (London: J. Johnson, 1787), p. 160.

34 Wollstonecraft, *Thoughts*, p. 69.

35 Wollstonecraft, *Thoughts*, pp. 70, 74, 78–79.

36 Appropriately, she dedicates her work to Talleyrand because he has failed to support national education for women.

37 Wollstonecraft, *Rights of Woman*, p. 33.

38 Wollstonecraft, *Rights of Woman*, pp. 45–46, 92, 97.

39 Astell, *Proposal*, Part I, pp. 43–44.

40 Wollstonecraft, *Rights of Woman*, p. 263.

41 Wollstonecraft, *Rights of Woman*, p. 127. The lists of illustrious women belong to the traditional defenses of women; Wollstonecraft's work is not a defense and belongs to the educational species.

42 Wollstonecraft, *Rights of Woman*, pp. 109, 127.

43 Wollstonecraft, Dedication, *Rights of Woman*, [p. 5].

44 Wollstonecraft, *Rights of Woman*, pp. 213, 218.

45 Astell, *Reflections*, p. 93.

46 Wollstonecraft, *Rights of Woman*, p. 287.

The Selling of Sex: Mandeville's Modest Defence of Publick Stews

SAMUEL J. ROGAL

The state of prostitution in London during the reigns of Anne and the first George can be described easily in a single term: *excessively healthy*! In fact, throughout the Restoration and eighteenth century, the ladies of the night (and day) were everywhere in evidence; "their business is so far from being considered as unlawful, that the list of those who are any way eminent in this profession is publicly cried about the streets: the list, which is very numerous, points out their places of abode, and gives ... the several qualifications for which they are remarkable. A new one is published every year, and sold under the piazza of Covent Garden, with the title of *The New Atlantis*."[1] By the end of the century, Patrick Colquhoun estimated the number of prostitutes within the capital to be 57,500, or approximately 4.5 per cent of the total population.[2] If this figure is reliable, a significant proportion of London males spent considerable periods of their time wandering through the vineyards of Venus and indiscriminately partaking of the various fruits; some, as young James Boswell, often wished they had plucked the berries less crudely.

However, in spite of their numbers and the benefits derived from free advertizing, the stewardesses of the stews found themselves under constant siege by over-zealous guardians of the public's morals. Since the early years of William III, the Society for the Reformation of Manners had been active against such vices as lewdness, gaming, profanations of the Lord's day, and drunkenness. For example, in 1730, the Society and its satellites successfully prosecuted 251 persons for lewd and disorderly practices, 30 for keeping bawdy houses, and 424 for exercising their trades and callings on the Sabbath.[3] To men of reason, as well as to those of pleasure, such militancy was hardly warranted. "The Chief Thing ... which Lawgivers and other wise Men, that have laboured for the Establishment of Society, have endeavour'd, has been to make the People they were to govern, believe, that it was more beneficial for every Body to conquer than indulge his Appetites, and much better to mind the Publick than what seem'd his private Interest. As this has always been a difficult Task, so no Wit or Eloquence has been left untried to compass it; and the Moralists and Philosophers of all Ages employed their utmost Skill to prove the Truth of so useful an Assertion."[4] So stated Bernard Mandeville in *An Enquiry Into the Origin of Moral Virtue*, appended to the 1714 edition of *The Fable of the Bees*. The comment really marks the beginning of the writer's participation in this particular conflict over the individual's right to function by and for himself, a struggle from which he emerged not as an exponent of immorality, but as a strong defender of a truly rational concept of virtue and social order.

According to Mandeville's reasoning, as set forth in "Remark (H.)" to *The Fable of the Bees* (1714), two basic qualities necessitated the promotion and success of lawful prostitution: first, the conscious yet uncontrollable appetites of men; second, the unconscious actions of virtuous women, which tended to inspire this appetite. He accepted the first quality as being perfectly natural; attempts to control it were simply the work of fools and hypocrites: "The Passions of some People are too violent to be curb'd by any Law or Precept; and it is Wisdom in all Governments to bear with lesser Inconveniences to prevent greater."[5] The second resulted from a combination of innocence and fashion; since virtuous action produced something of benefit, it, too, could not be controlled effectively. For, honorable and handsome women "have no Thoughts of Men in dressing Themselves, Poor Souls, and endeavour only to appear clean and decent, every one according to her Quality."[6] The problem, then was to preserve the spark but, at the same time, to protect it from excessive re-kindling.

Mandeville naturally cast his eye in the direction of the Continent—immediately upon his native Holland, and then on Italy and Spain, where he had been on tour prior to his arrival in London. In Amsterdam, the city fathers licensed, in the most disreputable sections, palaces of pleasure for the benefit of incoming seamen, staffed by contingents of para-professionals who spent their daylight hours hawking fruits and vegetables. The owners of these establishments, in an effort to suppress the noise brought on by the principal and peripheral activities within, provided organ music; this, according to Mandeville, served as an economical means for affecting a proper atmosphere and a strict sense of decorum. In Venice, Naples, Rome, and in the major cities of Spain, he noted that public stews not only stood as protective walls separating lewdness from virtue, but bestowed needed revenues upon various levels of government. All of the evidence cited by Mandeville tended, naturally, to support his thesis that government recognition and even sponsorship of public prostitution was the most logical means for identifying and then containing the distinct moral and economic divisions obviously apparent in early eighteenth-century society. In order to satisfy lust and to protect virtue, he recognized "a Necessity of sacrificing one part of Womankind to preserve the other, and prevent a Filthiness of a more heinous Nature. From whence I think I may justly conclude . . . that Chastity may be supported by Incontinence, and the best of Virtues want the Assistance of the worst of Vices."[7]

Not until 1723 did any formidable opposition to Mandeville's argument appear before the public. In this year Edmund Parker issued a second and enlarged edition of *The Fable of the Bees*, which, of course, included "Remark (H.)." On 11 July, the *Evening Post* printed the presentment of the Grand Jury for the

County of Middlesex, in which the jurors at the outset indicted "the many Books and Pamphlets that are almost every Week Published against the Sacred Articles of our *Holy Religion*" and that "have a Direct Tendency to *propagate Infidelity*, and consequently Corruption of all Morals."[8] However, by the time any reader had reached the fifth article of the document, there was little doubt about what or whom the Grand Jury had in mind: "... the very *Stews* themselves have had strained Apologies and forced Encomiums made in their Favour and produced in Print, with Design, we conceive, to debauch the Nation."[9] The presentment concluded with the identification of the two villains: *The Fable of the Bees* (2nd ed., 1723) and four numbers (16 March through 15 June 1723) from *The British Journal*. For Mandeville, the action of the Middlesex Grand Jury represented accurately the hypocrisy and stupidity to which he had alluded in the beginning of "Remark (H.)." He wasted little time preparing his rebuttal, issuing first, in 1723, a six-penny pamphlet entitled *A Vindication of the Book, from the Aspersions Contain'd in a Presentment of the Grand Jury of Middlesex*, followed in 1724 by *A Modest Defence of Publick Stews; or, an Essay upon Whoring, As it is now practis'd in these Kingdoms. Written by a Layman* (London: Printed by A. Moore near St. Paul's, M.DCC.XXIV).

The *Vindication* is a relatively calm document, intended simply to explicate the author's thesis for the benefit of jurymen, professional moralists, and the general readership. In replying to the charge that portions of the *Fable* contained "strained Apologies and forced Encomiums" in favor of the stews, Mandeville merely retraced the steps of his reasoning as set forth in "Remark (H.)," trusting that his opposition would at least recognize the dilemma created by the existence of two evils, both of which could not possibly be ignored or even eliminated. He concluded with an appeal to reason and understanding of what he had originally written, clinging to the overall purpose of the *Fable* as advanced in the title-page: "... *that private Vices by the dextrous Management of a skilful Politician, may be turn'd into publick Benefits.*"[10]

Considering the relatively short interim between the publication of the *Vindication* and that of *A Modest Defence*, the earlier effort must stand as a quick thrust temporarily intended to counter the immediate effect of the Grand Jury action and the publication of its presentment. *A Modest Defence*, on the other hand, was a full-scale offensive, a piece of satire mounted not only against the grand-jurors of Middlesex, but aimed even more in the direction of the moral societies, whose "great Pains and Diligence ... employ'd in the Defence of Modesty and Virtue, give You an undisputed Title to the Address of this Treatise. ..."[11] Mandeville's real purpose in this project is almost as ancient as the profession he appears to champion: the sheer absurdity of self-styled and self-appointed guardians of public morality attempting to eradicate permanent and natural human drives and conditions. As he reasons in his preface, "... as long as it is the Nature of Man ... to have a Salt Itch in the Breeches, the Brimstone under the Petticoat will be a necessary Remedy to lay it; and let him be ever so sly in the Application, it will be found out."[12] In other words, despite his own anger over the actions of grand juries and moral societies, Mandeville continued to remain firm within the confines of his old arguments, choosing once again to advance his case in behalf of transforming private vices into public benefits.

Reduced to the simplest of terms, *A Modest Defence* is an endeavor, through reason, to disarm the unreasonable attitudes and actions of those who would mold society in their own images. Thus, "Phil-Porney," the author of the treatise, inundates his readers with an avalanche of specific causes, results, and cures in his determination to promote the welfare and happiness of all of mankind. From the outset, he maintains that "publick Whoring is neither so criminal in itself, nor so detrimental to the *Society*, as private Whoring; and that the encouragement of publick Whoring, by erecting *Stews*, will not only prevent most of the ill Consequences of this Vice, but even lessen the Quantity of Whoring in general, and reduce it to the narrowest Bounds which it can possibly be contain'd in."[13] The ill-effects are the obvious ones carried over from former arguments: disease, filth, ruination of women and children, destruction of virtue, extravagance, murdering of bastard infants, and the rotting away of that most ancient of social institutions, the family. Porney asserts that the establishment of public stews will do away with these evils because of the government's power and ability to manage them; history has proven that the ill effects from private whoring will be plowed under in short order by the efficient machinery of civil regulation. The direction of the argument becomes lucid almost from the beginning: Porney is on the way toward creating an idealistic sub-city of Whoredom, where impoverished wenches may gain affluence, passion-ruled gentlemen may find both satisfaction and sanitation under a single roof. And, most important, beyond the gates of this commune, Virtue and Virginity stroll arm in arm, safe in the knowledge that violation can come to them only in their sometimes undisciplined imaginations.

Few details seemed to have escaped Mandeville's projector as he outlines the specifics of his grand scheme. For instance, he envisions the larger cities of Great Britain each capable of accommodating one hundred houses; every stew would be staffed by twenty women under the direction and supervision of a matron. Porney further proposes that the matrons stock these dwellings with sufficient quantity and variety of liquor—custom and excise free. In addition, the community would maintain one large dwelling as an infirmary, wherein two physicians and four surgeons might labor to insure the health of all concerned. Finally, as a means for promoting order and proper conduct, three commissioners would oversee the entire settlement. Demonstrating his skills in economics and social organization, Porney proposes to divide the twenty mistresses of each stew into four distinct classes: eight ladies would charge their patrons half a crown, six a crown, four a half-guinea, and two—operating obviously for the benefit of the wealthy—would charge a guinea. He further suggests that the government levy a moderate tax to defray some of the expenses necessitated by such a community: "For if the first Class pays but forty Shillings Yearly, and the rest in Proportion, it will amount to above ten thousand Pounds a Year, which will not only pay the

Commissioners Salaries, Surgeons Chests, and other Contingencies, but likewise establish a good Fund for the Maintenance of Bastard-Orphans and superannuated Courtezans."[14]

Undoubtedly a major problem for Mandeville's projector in setting forth the argument in favor of public stews was the disarming of the opposition, those who might recoil from the prospect of a nation that openly recognizes and even licenses such immoral activity. Phil-Porney, however, comes forward as no mere empty-headed schemer incapable of visualizing the benefits to be derived from his grand plan. Indeed, he emerges as a high-minded social reformer, a true advocate of a return to the Horatian Golden Mean. In his eyes, the public stews provide answers to a number of pressing problems; his carnal community becomes a benefit to the entire nation in that it furnishes the magic nostrum for all of its ills. Large numbers of lower-class women, who might otherwise have no alternatives in life but crime, street-walking, and eventual poverty, will find instant fame, respect, and prosperity within the confines of the pleasure palaces. That infectious disease known as "the French pox" will be contained by the surgeons and physicians of the stews' infirmaries; to these stations also will come a majority of the nation's bastard infants, who will find heretofore unknown means of preservation and maintenance. Men of business may now regulate their passions according to their abilities and the sizes of their purses, thus freeing the greater portions of their minds for concentration upon the conduct of the nation's economy. The stews will function as a recognized training-ground where young gentlemen anticipating marriage may learn from their tutors what to expect from the highest gratifications of love; thus, the lessons learned from the bawd can be applied to satisfying the bride. Young men not yet arrived at the peak of maturity, but nevertheless prime prospects for the evils from manufriction and from private intrigues, can circumvent the traps of youth and proceed directly to the grand climax of manhood. Honest women will be protected from the dangers of debauchery because the limits of whoring will be strictly regulated and defined. And, perhaps the most significant benefit of all, the public stews may prove to have no small effect upon certain aspects of Britain's relations with the major states of Europe. Porney suggests a statute for encouraging the importation of foreign women, which eventually would preserve almost totally the honor of English womanhood and curb the wanderlust of British males: ". . . whereas most of our estated Youth spend a great Part of their Time and Fortunes in travelling Abroad, for no other End, as it seems by most of them, but to be inform'd in the *French* and *Italian* Gallantry; they would then have an Opportunity of satisfying their Curiosities in foreign Amours, without stirring out of *London*." [15] Obviously, the projector does not take up the matter of the consequences of such legislation upon the stews of France and Italy, or upon the economies of these nations; such delicate matters as balance of payments, trade deficits, and tourism he leaves to the concern of future generations.

Few can read Mandeville's *Modest Defence* without directing their thoughts toward another document thinly veiled in modesty and presented to the world some five years later. Most certainly, similarities exist between Phil-Porney's tract on the stews and Swift's *Modest Proposal*. Both Swift and Mandeville set out to shock societies and their leaders into realizing that they have been handling serious social problems in an absurd and even hypocritical fashion. Both essayists hand over their arguments to apparently reasonable projectors, social statisticians and logicians who focus on the specifics of their proposals and extend them forward to seemingly ultimate conclusions. However, it is senseless to elaborate further on general points of comparison, for the differences between the two works become recognizable immediately. The reader of Swift's project reels in disgust at the prospect of murdering infants and feeding their flesh, cooked or otherwise, to an undernourished populace, while the establishment of licensed stew colonies—which to some may be an outright violation of moral law—may indeed be construed as a public benefit in the minds of a considerable segment of Britain's population. Anyone who fails to see the irony in Swift is, no doubt, a fool; one who misunderstands Mandeville's intentions can only be accused of wishful thinking. In the final paragraph of his proposal, Swift's projector maintains that he has "not the least personal Interest in endeavouring to promote this necessary Works. . . . I have no Children, by which I can propose to get a single Penny; the youngest being nine Years old, and my Wife past child-bearing."[16] Contrast this impersonal tone to the overall manner of Phil-Porney, who appears throughout the tract as a concerned defender of public morality and of womanhood, a social reformer, a physician who fears for the health and general well-being of his nation, an advocate of lawful love who would, in the end, have his readers "learn to prefer the Chaste Embraces of Innocence before the bought Smile of Harlots loveless, joyless, unindear'd casual Fruition."[17] Thus, Mandeville's *Defence* can never be viewed within the harsh context of Swift's *Proposal.* Swift, with his devastating force of irony, his almost totally destructive and negative effect, sets out to champion the image of man as savage beast. Mandeville, although he lacks Swift's ability to compress, at least holds fast to a lighter side of life, suggesting to his reader that if he finds the improvement of his virtues to be too arduous a task, why not have a go at his vices.

After the publication in 1724 of the first edition, *A Modest Defence* enjoyed modest success in England: another edition in 1725, two issued sometime between 1730 and 1739, and two more published in 1740. The French, seemingly more receptive to change and innovation, issued translations of Mandeville's tract in a steady stream between 1727 and 1881. Aside from a facsimile edition published recently by The Augustan Reprint Society, the work has received little or no attention either from scholars or literary historians. The reason may be too obvious: for, in the final analysis, *A Modest Defence of Publick Stews* exists primarily as an elaboration and explication of what its author had set forth ten years earlier. And, in spite of the essayist's wit and his attention to the strict principles of classical rhetoric, the result is perhaps too lengthy, made bulky by historical illustrations, anticipated counter-arguments, digressions and repetitions that—while they may serve to solidify and then substantiate Mandeville's thesis—never really cast any fresh light upon the problem. But the work does

have merit and it does deserve discussion in terms of the relationship between literature and society during the late Restoration and
early eighteenth century. Mandeville's *Defence of Publick Stews*
stands as an example of satire intended to offend only those who
would be offended by it, and to provide amusement for those who
would have preferred to frolic away their lives in a blissful state
somewhere between the oceans of Dissipation and the shores of
Heaven.

NOTES

1 Peter J. Grosley, *A Tour to London; or, New Observations on England
and Its Inhabitants*, trans. Thomas Nugent (London: printed for Lockyer
Davis, 1772), I, 55.

2 Patrick Colquhoun, *A Treatise on the Police of the Metropolis* (London:
C. Dilly, 1797), pp. vii–xi.

3 William Thomas Laprade, *Public Opinion and Politics in Eighteenth-
Century England. To the Fall of Walpole* (1936; rpt. Westport, Connecticut: Greenwood Press, 1971), p. 325.

4 Bernard Mandeville, *The Fable of the Bees*, ed. B. F. Kaye (Oxford: At
the Clarendon Press, 1924), I, 42.

5 *Fable*, I, 95.

6 *Fable*, I, 95.

7 *Fable*, I, 100.

8 *Fable*, I, 384.

9 *Fable*, I, 385.

10 *Fable*, I, 411–12.

11 Bernard Mandeville, *A Modest Defence of Publick Stews*, Introduction by
Richard I. Cook (Los Angeles: The Augustan Reprint Society, 1973), p. i.

12 *Modest Defence*, pp. xv–xvi.

13 *Modest Defence*, p. 2.

14 *Modest Defence*, p. 14.

15 *Modest Defence*, pp. 65–66.

16 *The Prose Works of Jonathan Swift*, ed. Temple Scott (London: George
Bell and Sons, 1905), VII, 216.

17 *Modest Defence*, p. 71.

Condorcet, Feminism, and the Egalitarian Principle

DAVID WILLIAMS

In the literature of feminism that forms a distinctive, if somewhat platitudinous, feature of dissident writing in eighteenth-century France, the work of the marquis de Condorcet still offers some challenging perspectives. Looking back upon the historical flow of ideas in this area, I would argue that Condorcet's attempts to create an issue of public conscience out of the melancholy position of the women of his time constitute a clear landmark in the evolution of European political-sexual attitudes.

With the Enlightenment, the sporadic and largely ineffective resistance of earlier periods to entrenched anti-egalitarian doctrines gradually became orchestrated as an apparently viable movement.[1] The question of woman's status tentatively extricated itself from the sterile but safe abstractions of theological and metaphysical nicety. During the reign of Louis XV a renewed political awareness had quickened the pulse of the French feminists by bringing into sharp focus the dazzling corollary of the debate around the irrationality of woman's status, namely the irrational, protean nature of all political structure and social artifice.

151

At the same time, the challenge of the eighteenth-century *philosophes* to the rationale of sexual inequality was by no means clearcut and uncompromising. The thirty-eighth letter of the *Lettres persanes* is not sufficient to exonerate Montesquieu from charges of ambivalence.[2] The *Encyclopédie*'s article on marriage is astonishingly conservative.[3] The period's greatest propagandist, Voltaire, is a distinct disappointment.[4] Rousseau, of course, is unmentionable, and thus much of the feminist momentum during the middle years of the century had to come from the pens of novelists, playwrights, journalists, pamphleteers, and secondary writers.[5]

Prior to Condorcet in the second half of the century, the vital thrust came from Diderot and d'Holbach amongst the *philosophes* of international reputation. Diderot's essay *Sur les femmes* (1772), and d'Holbach's work *Des femmes* (1773) can be seen in retrospect as the key documents which explored the interplay between political structures, legal codes, social customs and the cultural and physiological factors that conditioned women to their role. Diderot addressed himself specifically to the problems imposed upon women by the deceptions inherent in a monogamous culture with its peculiarly western notions of love and fidelity, exposed in all their emptiness by the hypocrisies of *galant* codes of sexual behavior, by the harsh legal implications of marriage, the burdens of motherhood, and the cruel neglect of old age. "On lui choisit un époux. Elle devient mère. L'état de grossesse est pénible presque pour toutes femmes. C'est dans les douleurs, au péril de leur vie, aux dépens de leurs charmes, et souvent au détriment de leur santé, qu'elles donnent naissance à des enfants . . . . L'Age avance, la beauté passe . . . arrivent les années de l'abandon."[6]

D'Holbach's essay, *Des femmes*, published in the third volume of *Le Système social, ou Principes naturels de la morale et de la politique, avec un examen de l'influence du gouvernement sur les mœurs*, expanded several of the themes touched upon by Diderot, and advanced the feminist case on a number of vital levels. Foreshadowing Condorcet, d'Holbach illuminated the deeply political nature of the subjugation of women, at the heart of which lay the educational question. *Des femmes* presents an impressive analysis of the pressures to which women were purposefully made vulnerable with a view to conditioning them to a passive acceptance of their role. As with Diderot, the feminist polemic merges with broader issues. The social system, with its legal, moral, political, religious and psychological apparatus, has poisoned at source the citizen's happiness. Marriage itself has contributed, through its inflexibility and indissolubility, to the atmosphere of moral decadence.[7] "L'on voit donc les usages, les loix, les institutions humaines, loin de chercher à rendre les citoyens plus sages et plus heureux, contribuent très souvent à les rendre insensés et misérables" (*Système*, III, 131). Even with Diderot and d'Holbach, however, the natural law argument, now stripped of some of its mystique and honed down to its biological nucleus, still intruded—particularly with Diderot. However, while the full implications of the egalitarian principle continued to cause a measure of intellectual discomfort, the logical direction of the debate had been indicated.

The breakthrough was to come in the following decade, and it was with Condorcet that natural law arguments were finally discarded. The substance of Condorcet's views on the status of women is to be found in the *Lettres d'un bourgeois de New-Haven à un citoyen de Virginie* (1788), in the *Essai sur la constitution et les fonctions des assemblées provinciales* (1788), *Sur l'admission des femmes au droit de cité*, written in 1790 for the Journal of the 1789 Society, in his notes on Voltaire, in his pedagogical treatise, *Sur l'instruction publique* (1791-92), and in his last and greatest work, the 1795 *Esquisse d'un tableau historique des progrès de l'esprit humain*.[8] It was in the second of the *Lettres d'un bourgeois de New-Haven*, and in the *Admission*, that Condorcet first formulated his demands for the granting of full legal and constitutional rights for women, closely anticipating the appearance in England of that more celebrated document of the period, Mary Wollstonecraft's *A Vindication of the Rights of Women*.

The *Admission*, in particular, represents a climactic moment in

Enlightenment feminist polemics, and its insight, though not its impact, is comparable to that of Mill's *On The Subjection of Women*, written some eight decades later. With Condorcet one can pinpoint that final convergence of French feminism with the mainstream of the period's political and moral radicalism. Condorcet pleaded the egalitarian principle first of all at the level of human nature itself, thereby colliding squarely with the 'tout est au mieux' biological objections of the anti-feminists. He argued that what men and women have in common as human characteristics is more relevant to a discussion about their respective rights and roles than their differences, and in the opening paragraphs of the *Admission* he confronted natural law with the overriding principle of natural rights. He observed that by invoking natural law slogans legislators and philosophers had calmly violated the natural rights of half of the human race by withholding from them the franchise, and here Condorcet underscored the recent historical irony that had allowed France to have a revolution in the name of equality for a few hundred men, but to forget the plight of twelve million women (X, 121). To justify what must otherwise be called tyranny, legislators must show that the natural rights of women are of a different order to those of men, and to do that, argued Condorcet, it would be necessary to demonstrate that the nature of the two sexes differed in ways that rendered women incapable of exercising their duties and privileges as co-equal citizens.

Responding to his own rhetoric, Condorcet insisted that men's rights crystallized in a functional relationship to certain natural qualities inherent in their human make-up. Men were "êtres sensibles", i.e., sensitive creatures, capable of formulating and rationalizing moral concepts. Since the humanity of women could be identified with precisely the same natural characteristics, it must necessarily follow that the natural rights of one sex could be legitimately claimed by the other. Either no member of the human race has natural rights, or they all have. The argument was clinched, to Condorcet's satisfaction at least, with a neat aphorism: He who opposed the rights of another human being because of religion, color or sex, abjures his own rights (X, 122).

Having established the moral fulcrum of his position, Condorcet then proceeded to examine and dismantle the main anti-egalitarian suppositions. From the outset he recognized physiology as the anchor theme of the natural law argument in the scientific age. Emulating Voltairean attack methods, Condorcet deflates and disarms with deceptively simple language, laced with occasional ironic stings and an abrasively naive candor, with the aim of exposing cogently, in readily understood terms, the hollowness of the premises upon which the doctrines of female destiny were based. Those who were susceptible to pregnancy and menstruation were as capable of fulfilling their duties as citizens as those who were susceptible to gout every winter and to colds throughout the year. If men enjoyed an apparent intellectual advantage, it was the consequence of unequal educational opportunities rather than the forces of physiological determinism. If the argument is accepted that no woman has ever made a significant scientific discovery, or every shown real genius in the arts, then it would be logical to limit the franchise only to geniuses, since the average male has clearly no more intellectual claim to a privileged franchise than the average female, and in many cases far less (X, 123).

Falling back on the example of history, like all good children of the Enlightenment, Condorcet pointed to the gifts of Elizabeth I, Maria Theresa, and the two Catherines, who all proved that the necessary qualities of leadership and political courage were not lacking in those women who were able, through the accident of birth, to wield power. Was it believable that Mrs. Macaulay could not have performed better in the House of Commons than many of the elected members? Could she not have defended the Revolution better than Burke, who could only oppose the cause of freedom with a revolting farrago of nonsense? Would she not have been able to debate such questions as liberty of conscience more sensibly than Pitt? Would Mme. de Lambert have authorized laws against Protestants, thieves and Negroes as ridiculous and barbaric as those enacted by the Guardian of the Seals? Would not Montaigne's daughter have defended civil liberties more effectively than Courtin, who openly believed in witches and the occult? "En jetant les yeux sur la liste de ceux qui les ont gouvernés, les hommes n'ont pas le droit d'être si fiers" (X, 123–24).

Emphasizing the copious evidence to the contrary, Condorcet acknowledged the amazing tenacity of the belief that women were governed by sentiment and impulse rather than by reason and logic, and were therefore unpredictable, unreliable and possibly dangerous if given political power:

> Les femmes sont supérieures aux hommes dans les vertus douces et domestiques; elles savent, commes les hommes, aimer la liberté, quoiqu'elles n'en partagent point tous les avantages; et, dans les républiques, on les a vues souvent se sacrifier pour elle; elles ont montré les vertus de citoyen toutes les fois que le hasard ou les troubles civils les ont amenées sur une scène dont l'orgueil et la tyrannie des hommes les ont écartées chez tous les peuples. On a dit que les femmes, malgré beaucoup d'esprit, de sagacité, et la faculté de raisonner portée au même degré que chez de subtils dialecticiens, n'étaient jamais conduites par ce qu'on appelle la raison. Cette observation est fausse; elles ne sont pas conduites, il est vrai, par la raison des hommes, mais elles le sont par la leur (X, 124–25).

He countered this argument by reverting to the educational issue. If women appeared to reason in a way that was different to that of men, then again this was a contingent consequence of their moral and social training, and symptomatic of their whole cultural predicament:

> On a dit que les femmes, quoique meilleures que les hommes, plus douces, plus sensibles, moins sujettes aux vices qui tiennent à l'égoïsme et à la dureté du coeur, n'avaient pas proprement le sentiment de la justice; qu'elles obéissaient plutôt à leur sentiment qu'à leur conscience. Cette observation est plus vraie, mais elle ne prouve rien: ce n'est pas la nature, c'est l'éducation, c'est l'existence sociale qui cause cette différence. Ni l'une ni l'autre n'ont accoutumé les femmes à l'idée de ce qui est juste, mais à

celle de ce qui est honnête. Eloignées des affaires, de tout ce qui
se décide d'après la justice rigoureuse, d'après des lois positives,
les choses dont elles s'occupent, sur lesquelles elles agissent, sont
précisément celles qui se règlent par l'honnêteté naturelle et par le
sentiment. Il est donc injuste d'alléguer, pour continuer de refuser
aux femmes la jouissance de leurs droits naturels, des motifs qui
n'ont une sorte de réalité que parce qu'elles ne jouissent pas de
ces droits (X, 125).

For Condorcet education was central to his feminism, and to his
whole program for economic progress and social improvement on
a mass scale.[9] Among the other freedoms, as is clear from *Sur
l'instruction publique*, enlightenment was also a natural right, and
indeed a political and social necessity; it was difficult to see why
one sex reserved for itself certain subjects of knowledge, and why
matters that are generally useful to every human being should not
be taught equally to both sexes:

> L'instruction publique, pour être digne de ce nom, doit s'étendre
> à la généralité des citoyens. . . . D'ailleurs, on ne pourrait l'établir
> pour les hommes seuls, sans introduire une inégalité marquée, non
> seulement entre le mari et la femme, mais entre le frère et la
> soeur, et même entre le fils et la mère. Or, rien ne serait plus
> contraire à la pureté et au bonheur des moeurs domestiques.
> L'égalité est partout, mais surtout dans les familles, le premier
> élément de la félicité, de la paix et des vertus (VII, 218–219).

To substantiate his argument that women could profit from a
scientific training, and could themselves make significant contributions to knowledge, Condorcet cited the cases of Professors Bassi
and Agnesi who, despite their sex, had occupied respectively the
chairs of anatomy and mathematics at the University of Bologna
with notable success,

> sans qu'il en soit résulté ni le moindre inconvénient, ni la
> moindre réclamation, ni même aucune plaisanterie dans un pays
> que cependant on ne peut guère regarder comme exempt de
> préjugés, et où il ne règne ni simplicité, ni pureté dans les moeurs
> (VII, 221).

It was ignorance that engendered inequality, and which corrupted the relationship between the sexes (VII, 223). Given the lack of proper educational facilities for women, and the inequitable laws, with their origins in force and their perpetuation in sophistry, women were compelled to live in a different social reality from that of men. They were confronted with a different order of problems, and their rationality was directed by a male-oriented society towards different ends (X, 126). This was not to say, however, that rationality did not exist.

Condorcet reduced the problem to that of a prejudice, masquerading as the 'public interest.' Here was the crux of the matter. Again it was, thought Condorcet, another argument of convenience without logical or moral merit, but possessing concrete political force and substance. It was in the name of "utilité" that French industry was groaning in chains, that the African Negro was enslaved, that the Bastille was full, that books were censored, that torture and secret trials were accepted (X, 126). He did not hesitate to raise the political temperature of the feminist issue in France by grafting on to it the most flagrant aspects of contemporary injustice and cruelty. A transformation in the status of women would not, he insisted, be against the public interest. Women would not be torn from their domestic duties. The enfranchized wife would not abandon her children, any more than the enfranchized farmer would abandon his plow, or the enfranchized shopkeeper his shop (X, 128). On the contrary, the fabric of society would be strengthened as women found political and intellectual fulfillment, and lost their burning sense of injustice (VIII, 141; IX, 14–15, 17–18).

Condorcet was just as concerned with the private as with the public world, and it was here that he revealed the most iconoclastic and anachronistic side of his feminism. The necessity to protect at all costs the institution of the family, the sanctity of marriage and its associated property laws, the primacy of the maternal role, were all major weapons in the armory of the conservatives, permitting the invocation of natural law, in its more modish physiological guise, to confirm *de facto* female dependence. Like

Sade in another context, Condorcet saw quite clearly the close relationship between sex and politics. Arguing that marriage should be a civil contract only, he pressed vigorously the case for divorce. The indissolubility of the marriage laws spawned grave social problems: adultery, prostitution, bastardy and promiscuity. He proposed, rather quaintly, that divorce should be granted upon the recommendation of an advisory council consisting of relatives of both parties, who would decide questions of alimony and custody of any children. Again, the legal structure stood behind the unhappiness of the citizen. Vicious and hypocritical sexual attitudes all stemmed from those laws which, while preventing divorce, upheld the harsh authority of parents to make unsuitable marriages of convenience on behalf of their daughters: "J'observerai ensuite que les désordres causés dans les familles ont pour origine presque unique la distinction des rangs, la grande inégalité des fortunes, les lois qui privent les enfants du droit de disposer d'eux sans le consentement de leurs parents; enfin de l'indissolubilité du mariage" (VI, 523).

In the 1795 *Esquisse*, Condorcet developed a forceful apology for birth control, and illuminated this issue in a way that took him well beyond the horizons of his age. Referring to the necessity to plan families prudently, and to the inalienable rights of women to control their pregnancies, he speculated boldly on the possibility of a future in which the prejudices of superstition had ceased to corrupt and degrade mankind. Man's obligation to future generations is not just to bring them into existence, but to assure them of happiness. Man's obligation is to the welfare of the species as a whole and not to the puerile concept of filling the earth with useless and unhappy creatures. The earth's resources are limited. If premature destruction of the race is to be avoided, there must be a limit to population growth:

> Mais, dans ces progrès de l'industrie et du bien-être, dont il résulte une proportion plus avantageuse entre les facultés de l'homme et ses besoins, chaque génération, soit par ces progrès, soit par la conservation des produits d'une industrie antérieure, est appelée à des jouissances plus étendues, et dès lors, par une suite de la

constitution physique de l'espèce humaine, à un accroissement dans le nombre des individus; alors ne doit-il pas arriver un terme où ces lois, également nécessaires, viendraient à se contrarier; où l'augmentation du nombre des hommes surpassent celle de leurs moyens, il en résulterait nécessairement, sinon une diminution continue de bien-être et de population, une marche vraiment rétrograde, du moins une sorte d'oscillation entre le bien et le mal? . . . Si on suppose qu'avant ce temps les progrès de la raison aient marché de pair avec ceux des sciences et des arts, que les ridicules préjugés de la superstition aient cessé de répandre sur la morale une austérité qui la corrompt et la dégrade au lieu de l'épurer et de l'élever, les hommes sauront alors que, s'ils ont des obligations à l'égard des êtres qui ne sont pas encore, elles ne consistent pas à leur donner l'existence, mais le bonheur; elles ont pour objet le bien-être général de l'espèce humaine ou de la société dans laquelle ils vivent; de la famille à laquelle ils sont attachés, et non la puérile idée de charger la terre d'êtres inutiles et malheureux. Il pourrait donc y avoir une limite à la masse possible des subsistances, et, par conséquent, à la plus grande population possible, sans qu'il en résultât cette destruction prématurée, si contraire à la nature et à la prospérité sociale d'une partie des êtres qui ont reçu la vie (VI, 256–57, 258).[10]

Elsewhere Condorcet advocated the establishment of special hospitals for unmarried pregnant girls to which they could go without incurring the usual penalties. He was concerned equally with the plight of their illegitimate children (VIII, 465–66). As with political freedom, women had the right to sexual freedom, and Condorcet saw the manipulation of sexual attitudes and fears historically as one of the root sources of power and the abuse of power. He took the view that women had been penalized for their sexuality by church and state alike, yet, he observed in his notes on Voltaire, the confessors of kings have done more damage to Europe than royal mistresses. Puritanical sexual codes were the surface manifestation of a brutalizing and decadent alliance between the temporal and the spiritual, producing always repressive political systems (IV, 212–18). No virtue was easier, or appeared easier, to practice than chastity; it was compatible with the absence of real virtue and the presence of every vice. From the moment that chastity was considered important, every scoundrel was sure of obtaining public esteem at little expense, and in countries which boasted high standards of sexual morality, every vice, every crime and debauchery were sure to be prevalent (IV, 218).

Condorcet's work reflects in fact a broad range of ideas and proposals that are still controversial. He dismissed the supposed evils of pornography—after all the satellites of Cromwell did not have to carry indecent books in their saddle-bags to inspire them to atrocities (IV, 89). He argued the case against police harassment of prostitutes (VIII, 469–70), and he denounced the barbarous laws against homosexuals (IV, 561).[11] Condorcet was not simply aiming to shock or titillate the bourgeois with shallow rhetorical posturing, and, as many an embarrassed biographer has hastened to assure us, he was himself no libertine.[12] He was, however, a rigorous logician; his arguments are untainted by emotional prejudice, and perhaps most refreshingly of all, are free from that peculiar brand of polemical fanaticism that some of the eighteenth-century *philosophes* and *idéologues* could not resist.

For Condorcet, the relationship between the sexes was central to mankind's political consciousness, yet because of the fears, prejudices and perversions that existed and were exploited within that relationship, reason had not been allowed to prevail. Behind the abstractions of philosophical argument, he was able to perceive individual men and women, and their problems, in a frank, practical and intensely human way. His feminism, his views on human nature, on mercantilism, on the slave trade, on political institutions are all interlinked aspects of his tightly argued revolutionary stance. To destroy the laws that militated against women's natural rights was part of a mosaic pattern of argument that attacked simultaneously the commercial doctrines that were strangling France's trading position, guild regulations that held the working man back from prosperity, censorship that suppressed free thought, sexual attitudes that debased human values, and served in the end only the interests of power groups.

In a century that had perfected the use of "galanterie" and

sentimentality to disguise with flowers the chains of an uncompromising subjugation, Condorcet was able to see woman as a free human personality, an "être sensible" capable of conducting herself as a three-dimensional individual with moral, intellectual and political extensions to her identity. In this Condorcet gave unique feminist expression to the communal dream of his time. He dreamed of man's progress and perfectibility; he shared that endearing, perhaps groundless, faith of the Enlightenment in man's potential ability to rationalize his world and eventually himself.

NOTES

1 See particularly L. Abensour's *La Femme et le féminisme avant la Révolution* (Paris: Leroux, 1932); A. Humphreys, "The 'Rights of Women' in the Age of Reason: 1. John Dunton to Catherine Macaulay," *Modern Language Review*, 41 (1946), 257; my "The Politics of Feminism in the French Enlightenment," *The Varied Pattern: Studies in the Eighteenth Century*, ed. Hughes and Williams (Toronto and Amsterdam: A. M. Hakkert, 1971), pp. 333–51.

2 See, for example, the case argued by R. F. O'Reilly, "Montesquieu: Anti-feminist," *Studies on Voltaire and the Eighteenth Century*, 102 (1973), 143–56.

3 The article "Femme" is equally conventional.

4 Voltaire's article "Femme" in the *Dictionnaire philosophique* has an anthropological rather than a sociological emphasis, and contains, in my view, little trace of feminist sympathies. In the article on "Homme" Voltaire saw positive moral advantages accruing to women as a result of their physical and social inferiority, and his initially sympathetic approach to women's position in the section *Mémoire pour les femmes* in the article "Adultère" is more than balanced by his comments on female infidelity in the first part of that article. There are Platonic comments on the wasted political potential of women in the section dealing with salic law in the *Essai sur les moeurs*, and in the *Dictionnaire* article "Loi salique." See also Voltaire's defense of the rights of women to an intellectual life in the dedicatory epistle to *Alzire*, dedicated to Mme. Du Châtelet—in which the case for intellectual parity is not quite stated. The correspondence is very reticent on the whole issue.

5 See my "Politics of Feminism in the French Enlightenment," pp. 339–43;

E. Sullerot, *Histoire de la presse féminine des origines à 1848* (Paris: A. Colin, 1966).

6 *Oeuvres complètes* (Paris: Garnier frères, 1875–77), II, 257.

7 *Système social* (London, 1773), III, 130. Subsequent references will appear in the text.

8 *Oeuvres complètes* (Paris, 1847–49; rpt. Stuttgart, 1968). All references to Condorcet's work will be to this edition, and will appear in the text.

9 See chapter 11 of J. S. Schapiro's *Condorcet and the Rise of Liberalism* (New York: Harcourt, Brace, 1963); F. Vial, *Condorcet et l'éducation démocratique* (Paris: Delaplane, 1903); G. Compayré, *Histoire critique des doctrines de l'éducation en France* (Paris: Hachette, 1885), II, 9–22.

10 Cf. A. Chamoux et C. Dauphin, "La Contraception avant la Révolution française," *Annales: E.S.C.*, 24 (1969), 662–84. There was of course no question at this time of a decline in population; see Sir Julian Huxley's "A Factor Overlooked by the Philosophes: The Population Explosion," *Studies on Voltaire and the Eighteenth Century*, 25 (1963), 862–63. P. Fryer's treatment of this aspect of the growth of the feminist conscience is interesting; see *The Birth-Controllers* (London: Secker, Warburg, 1965). Writing in 1778, Auget de Montyon could report that the use of birth control techniques was widespread, even amongst peasant women; see *Recherches et considérations sur la population de la France* (Paris: Moutard, 1778), II, 102.

11 These points are more fully covered by Schapiro, *Condorcet*, pp. 192–95.

12 The best biographical studies on Condorcet are listed, with critical comment by Schapiro, in *Condorcet*, p. 285. Even Schapiro feels obliged to "explain" Condorcet's feminist sympathies by repeating the old chestnut about Condorcet's "childhood experience in wearing girl's clothes" (p. 189). My own preference with regard to biographies is still L. Cahen's *Condorcet et la Révolution française* (Paris: Alcan, 1904).

Moratín's Circle of Friends: Intellectual Ferment in Spain, 1780–1800

JOHN DOWLING

Juan Antonio Melón, in some "disorderly notes" on the life of Leandro Fernández de Moratín, mentions how there developed around Moratín during the 1780's a coterie of half a dozen young men in their twenties. Besides Melón and Moratín, they were Pedro Estala and his fellow Piarist Padre Navarrete, León de Arroyal, and Juan Pablo Forner. The relation of Moratín, Melón, and Estala, especially in later years, has always been known; but the group as a whole has not been studied in literary or intellectual history. Moratín and Forner have been treated separately, but their relationship has not been clarified. León de Arroyal was, it would seem, intentionally assigned by government authorities in his own lifetime to an obscurity from which he has emerged only in the last decade. I myself must set aside Padre Navarrete. He has not been satisfactorily identified, and he seems not to have distinguished himself in the intellectual life of this time.[1]

The period 1780 to 1800 embraces the young manhood of these intellectuals. For Moratín it means the period from the age

165

of twenty to forty, and it was more or less the same age for the others. Juan Pablo Forner died at the age of forty-one, before the new century began. Historically, the period covers the final years of the reign of Carlos III; the new reign of Carlos IV and his consort María Luisa, who are known to us so well through the paintings of Goya; the trauma of the French Revolution; and the rise of Manuel Godoy, a man seven years younger than Moratín, to the pinnacle of his power.

Melón and León de Arroyal were walking one day in 1781 in the Calle de Alcalá near the point where it intersects the Paseo del Prado. There they encountered two young Piarists, Pedro Estala and Padre Navarrete, in the company of Leandro Fernández de Moratín. Estala had known Melón at Salamanca, and he introduced him to his friend Leandro. "I found Moratín taciturn and reserved," Melón recalled, "but I could tell that he took a liking to me. . . . Among all of us," he continued, "a friendship was established which lasted all our lives."[2]

At the time, Moratín was twenty-one years old. His father had died the previous year, and he was living at home with his mother and working as a jeweler at his uncle's shop in Madrid. He had published his narrative poem *La toma de Granada por los Reyes Católicos* (*The Capture of Granada by the Catholic Sovereigns*; 1779), which was printed at the expense of the Royal Spanish Academy because it was awarded the *accessit*, a sort of second or consolation prize, in a contest.

Pedro Estala was a Manchegan from the town of Daimiel between Manzanares and Ciudad Real. Two of his brothers became Dominicans, and he was a Piarist friar, an *escolapio* in Spanish. He was born in 1759 and hence was a year older than Moratín. We may suppose that he and Navarrete taught at the Escuelas Pías de San Fernando in the Calle de Lavapiés, although neither pious devotion nor teaching boys seems ever to have loomed large in Pedro Estala's life.

Juan Antonio Melón became Moratín's closest friend. If the age he gave the French police in 1827 was correct, he was born in 1763 and hence was three years younger than Leandro.[3]

Oldest of the group was Melón's friend León de Arroyal, who was about twenty-six when he met Moratín. Arroyal, who had also studied at Salamanca, had that year of 1781 published his first book, a devotional in Castilian verse translation of the short office of Our Lady according to the Roman Breviary.[4]

The sixth member did not join the coterie until the end of the following year 1782. He was Juan Pablo Forner. He was about the same age as Arroyal, and the two had been fellow students at Salamanca. Later, Arroyal married Rita Piquer, a cousin of Forner's mother. In 1782 Forner and Moratín entered the contest of the Royal Spanish Academy, and Forner won the prize while Moratín was awarded an *accessit* for the second time.[5] When Moratín expressed an interest in knowing his rival, his companions arranged a meeting from which a close friendship grew.

Estala and Navarrete, although Piarists, apparently lived at the convent of La Victoria, which belonged to the Minims. The convent, popularly known as La Soledad, because it contained the famous image of Our Lady of Solitude, was located in the very center of things, at the southeast corner of that irregular plaza, the Puerta del Sol. Moratín had been accustomed to visit the Piarists in Estala's cell, and Melón now joined him there. The four of them formed a close-knit group. Arroyal seems to have been on the periphery, perhaps because he only visited Madrid from his home at Vara del Rey, a Manchegan village thrity-six leagues (some two hundred kilometers) southeast of the court. When Moratín and Forner met, they became very close, as Forner testified using the pastoral names they assumed: "Aminta and Mirtilo are two youths in whom the similarity of their relationship, the coincidence of their inclinations, and especially their decided fondness for poetry have engendered the sincerest friendship. . . ."[6]

The group gathered frequently in the evenings and on holidays in Estala's cell, and they would remain until the convent doors closed for the night. On Sundays, if the weather was good, they used to meet at a fountain in the Buen Retiro near the pond. Moratín called it the Aganippe after the spring of the Muses at the foot of Mt. Helicon. Whether in Estala's cell or at the fountain,

Moratín was inspired in the presence of intimate friends, losing that reserve which characterized him. "He enlivened our conversation," Melón remembered, "with such mirth, such jests, such wit, such repartee that our group was convulsed with continuous laughter."[7]

The young men were full of plans. Some projects were for sport, such as a mocking heroic play done in collaboration. Others were serious: translations, a collection of books for women, editions of classical authors. Like most youthful projects, few got beyond the talking stage. The young men also devoted time and energy to satirizing their elders and attacking either privately or openly an out-of-favor man like Vicente García de la Huerta or an establishment writer like Tomás de Iriarte, who, with his brothers, enjoyed the approval of men who held high office in the government of Carlos III. My story tells how these young men—Moratín, Forner, Melón, Estala—moved from the limbo of outsiders to a favored position in the official intellectual life of Spain. One of them, however, was consigned to oblivion; León de Arroyal got out of step with the Spanish establishment.

This generation came of age at a critical period in the history of the Bourbon monarchy in Spain. The 1780's saw the culmination of the policies that Carlos III had brought with him from Naples after he became king of Spain in 1759. The decade preceding his death was one of apparent prosperity as the constructive zeal of Philip V and the stable peace of Fernando VI paid off. But the Spanish Bourbons, though more frugal than their French cousins, had overspent, and financial crisis loomed on the horizon in the 1780's. Then, six months to the day after the death of Carlos III, the storming of the Bastille occurred in Paris, and Spain was confronted with a whole new set of political problems.

Of the Moratín circle, Juan Pablo Forner was the most quarrelsome. His story is already well known. Before he met Moratín, when he was twenty-five, he launched his first attack on Tomás de Iriarte: he thought that Iriarte's eclogue, to which the Royal Spanish Academy had awarded a prize, was inferior to the one by Juan Meléndez Valdés. By 1785 he had been told he could publish nothing without the express permission of the monarch himself. Yet the king's minister, the Count of Floridablanca, had an eye on the difficult young subject. When Forner applied to the Council of Castilla in 1782 for permission to publish a book, an informant wrote: "People say he is a man of good habits, that he is melancholy and so retiring and devoted to his books that his attachment borders on vice. As a result few people in Madrid know him personally."[8]

Four years later the Count paid Forner 6,000 reales for his defense of the Spanish nation against its foreign detractors. Two questions had provoked a furor in Spain; they appeared in the volume devoted to geography in the new *Encyclopédie méthodique* (Paris, 1782), which grew out of the famous one by Diderot and D'Alembert. The author of the article on Spain was Nicholas Masson de Morvilliers. From the rarefied heights of the French enlightenment he asked with Gallic arrogance: "What do we owe to Spain? In two centuries, in four, in ten, what has she done for Europe?"

The first reply to Masson's insolent questions came from Don Antonio José de Cabanilles, an abbé and a botanist who was living in Paris as tutor to the children of the Duke of Infantado. His *Observations* (1784) were more of a catalogue than an essay, and his remarks on contemporary Spanish literature especially left him open to the barbs of even his own compatriots.

The Spanish government intervened in the affair. It protested to the French government in Paris, and it refused permission for the sale of the encyclopedia in Spain. The Royal Spanish Academy, at the end of 1784, offered a prize for the best "Apology or defense of the nation which should deal solely with its progress in the arts and sciences."[9] Probably in response to the announcement of this contest Forner wrote his *Oración apologética por la España y su mérito literario* (*Apology for Spain and its Literary Merit*). However, the Academy did not award a prize, and Forner's essay remained in manuscript.

Then on January 26, 1786, an Italian abbé from the Piemonte, Carlos Denina, was moved to deliver a *Réponse à la question "Que doit-on à l'Espagne?"* before the Academy of Sciences in Berlin. He was impelled more by Francophobia than Hispanofilia.

When Denina's defense appeared in print, Don Eugenio de Llaguno y Amírola, first clerk of the Secretariat of State (and editor in 1789 of the new edition of Luzán's *Poética*) commissioned Forner, through a former professor, Francisco Pérez de Lema, to do a translation. Instead of composing notes to the translation as had been requested, Forner used his *Oración apologética* as an introduction. He sent it to Llaguno on May 14, 1786, and Llaguno forwarded the material to Floridablanca with a note in which he wrote: "I have cut out things that might shock people."[10]

The Count's decision was to set aside Forner's translation and print Denina's work in the original French together with Forner's apology. The material went to the printer before the end of May. Apparently satisfied with the project, Floridablanca, with royal approval, authorized that Forner be paid 6,000 reales. This sum was more than his friend Moratín earned annually in wages at the jewelry shop, although Moratín made more in extra pay for special assignments than he did in wages. The payment was made months later, in November.

It is reasonable to suppose that the polemic and Forner's apology were discussed in the circle of friends. We may wonder, of course, to what extent the others shared Forner's ideas, and we may even question whether Forner expressed his own thoughts or whether, in the final redaction, he chose to state sentiments that he knew would please Floridablanca. It behooves us, nevertheless, to analyze what he says in the *Oración apologética,* a work which merited the approval of the establishment in 1786.

Julián Marías has done this in detail in his book *La España posible en tiempo de Carlos III* (Madrid, 1963). We must, to be sure, bear in mind that Forner's purpose, as he himself stated, "was to write more as an orator than as a critical historian." [11] Nevertheless, what concerns us is not so much the tone of his work as the assumptions, the hypotheses, on which his statements are based. Marías demonstrates that Forner has foregone impartiality, that he has abandoned the middle way, and that he has taken an extreme position with respect to the basic ideas of the nascent Spanish Enlightenment. He does so by employing the argument of sufficiency which gives him the outward appearance of moderation. Spaniards in his view have sufficient liberty; they have sufficient knowledge. If Spanish thought stops short of speculative philosophy, he is satisfied. Spain has a *Quijote*; Forner can do without Descartes' *Discours de la méthode*. In short, in Marías' view, Forner's position is retrograde vis-à-vis the decisive themes of the age: modern philosophy, modern science, and freedom.[12]

Forner's book evoked protests. Luis Cañuelo, editor of *El Censor*, devoted all of his Discourse 113 to Denina's and Forner's apologies, which he had received just hours before. His tone is ironic. "To believe that Spain possesses mathematicians, philosophers, theologians, jurisconsults, political scientists, economists, historians, critics, orators, or poets as excellent as those in any other nation in Europe is to believe nonsense. It is a loss of common sense. It is to be ignorant of what the arts and sciences are about. . . ."[13] Cañuelo admits that in Spain a certain type of science and a certain type of art have indeed flourished, and they have, in his view, kept the nation confined within its ignorance and its poverty.

In the ensuing controversy, more than a hundred articles, pamphlets, and books appeared before the Spanish government, frightened by the consequences of the French Revolution, prohibited all periodical publications on February 25, 1791. *El Censor* itself devoted Discourse 165 to the wonderfully ironic *Oración apologética por el Africa y su mérito literario*. The anonymous author of the *Cartas de un español residente en París a su hermano residente en Madrid* (*Letters from a Spaniard Living in Paris to His Brother Living in Madrid*) published his treatise in the Imprenta Real in 1788, the same press that had printed Forner's work. The fact is indicative of the equivocal posture of the Floridablanca government, once characterized by enlightened views and still willing to support opposing views in the polemic, for the writer's position on scientific investigation and philosophical inquiry, like Cañuelo's in *El Censor*, is critical of Spain in contrast to Forner's advocacy of sufficient knowledge.

In the same year, 1788, the author of another anonymous pamphlet, *Conversaciones de Perico y Marica* (*Conversations Between Pete and Mary*), reiterated the economic-social question that Cañuelo had injected into the debate by his insistence on poverty in Spain. Whatever we may conclude about Forner's views, we must credit his *Oración apologética* with provoking in Spain much thought and discussion at a time when Europe was on the verge of plunging into modern times.

I cannot leave Forner, however, without pointing to evidence which suggests that he was not so retrograde as Marías would have us believe. The *Exequias de la lengua castellana* (*Last Rites for the Castilian Tongue*) is devoted principally to literary problems and was written, I believe, about the same time as a work that it resembles in its intent, Moratín's *Derrota de los pedantes* (*Defeat of the Pedants*), which went on sale not long after Bastille Day, 1789. The composition of the two works, therefore, would fall in the period of the polemic over the *Oración apologética*. Forner's book, unlike Moratín's, did not get into print. Several years later, in 1794, at the request of Manuel Godoy, at the time Duke of Alcudia, the great Francisco Antonio de Lorenzana (1722–1804), then Cardinal Archbishop of Toledo and Primate of Spain, reviewed the manuscript for possible publication.

In his appraisal, which is dated March 2, 1795, Lorenzana cites passages from Forner's manuscript which led him to make a negative recommendation: "On page 88 verso he [Forner] says: 'Leave disputes about genealogy to those countries where the tradition of birth gives a fool or a knave the right to enjoy the broadest perquisites, distinctions, and powers; whilst virtue and wisdom, with anguished and sweaty brow, beg for support at the gates of an indifferent nobility.' " This statement, Lorenzana observes, is consonant with what is said in these verses on page 31: "How scant and stinted is the bliss of men/ who live in civil union's harsh confines./ A thousand workers toil from dawn to dusk/ that one vain fool may loll in opulence." This doctrine— Lorenzana continues—is substantially the basis of the arguments of the French Conventionists against hereditary monarchies and the nobility. It is the theme of all the perverse and seditious publications that everywhere incite and invite nations to shake off the yoke of their sovereigns and to despise the nobility. The authors do not realize that, as in France, many tyrants like Robespierre will rise to the surface as thieving and unjust as those whom Cicero accused as traitors to the Roman republic.[14]

In the person of Forner we observe the seeds of that ambivalence which became acute in the years ahead. The Francophobia that we discover in him may puzzle us if we try to reconcile it with our concept of what the Moratín group stood for. Is not Moratín the *afrancesado* in literature and politics that the defenders of traditional Spanish values have always said he was? And is not neoclassic poetics intimately associated with the admiration and imitation of everything French? Let us examine some documents.

The young men who met in Estala's cell or at the Aganippe fountain, like young men in other ages and other places, opposed the intellectual establishment until they became a part of it. In opposition to the Royal Spanish Academy they planned their own academy. The statutes were signed by Estala, Forner, Moratín, and a fourth person—he uses his pastoral name—who I suppose is either Melón or Navarrete. "The only oath that will be required of each member," reads a paragraph of the statutes, "will be to detest the semi-Gallic sect and defend by fire and sword true Castilian good taste both in prose and in verse. Therefore, the member obligates himself to promote a liking for our best writers of the sixteenth and seventeenth centuries, who will be his only rule and guide."[15]

This statement is entirely in consonance with the two poems of 1782 which brought Forner and Moratín together: the former's *Sátira contra los vicios introducidos en la poesía castellana (Satire on the Defects Introduced into Castilian Poetry)* and the latter's *Lección poética (Lesson in Poetry)*.[16] The two poems are both anti-baroque and anti-Gallic, and both recommend sixteenth-century Spanish poets, especially Garcilaso, as proper models for imitation. To be sure, Moratín used a quotation from Boileau to identify his poem ("On sera ridicule, et je n'oserai rire?" from Satire 9), and he later wrote that his poem served as the nearest Spanish equivalent of L'Art poétique until someone should produce a better one. Nevertheless, the contents of both poems as well as of La derrota de los pedantes and Exequias de la lengua castellana are consistent with what Russell Sebold has told us of Luzán's Poética: the authorities in Luzán's treatise are overwhelmingly classical and Italian in both the 1737 and 1789 editions, and in the 1789 edition Spanish authorities exceed the French by a significant degree.[17]

If we assess the literary ideas of this group in these years, we must conclude that they were opposed to the baroque, that they upheld neoclassic principles, and that they were nationalistic. "The Spanish comedy," Moratín wrote referring to one genre, "is to wear the basquine skirt and the mantilla."[18]

We may turn to a series of letters to determine Moratín's ideas on those subjects which interested enlightened men in these years. They are letters that he wrote in 1787 and early 1788 when he went to France as secretary to the financier Francisco de Cabarrús, founder of the Banco de San Carlos. They coincide with the polemic that followed the publication of the Oración apologética. We must use them with caution, for René Andioc has demonstrated that Moratín, following his custom with both his own and his father's works, later polished and even revised them.[19] Perhaps they better represent what he would like to have thought in 1787, but I suspect the polishing was more stylistic than substantive, as it was in the other cases for which we have clearer evidence.

Moratín admired what he saw in France in 1787, and he remarked on the ways that France was superior to his own country. As an enlightened young man writing to an enlightened older man, he told Jovellanos about the Languedoc canal. He had traveled on it from Toulouse to Narbonne and during the trip he could not help but think of the Campos canal, "which was begun," he commented, "as everything good in Spain is begun, never to be finished."[20] In a letter to the art historian Ceán Bermúdez, Moratín praises the medical school of the University of Montpellier, where all the sciences auxiliary to medicine were also taught. "If you want Alcalá de Henares to equal it," he sarcastically writes, "it will be necessary to get rid of everything that is there now beginning with the residential colleges. . . . In their place you will put excellent professors who teach useful things employing sound methods instead of filling youthful heads with nonsense. Then you will get good physicians and surgeons, good scientists and pharmacists. People will know chemistry, and you will have industry, factories, and the arts and all the other things that we don't have" (p. 43).

Moratín's admiration for the Paris theater is undisguised. At the Comédie Française he observed that "if everything is not perfect, it comes close to being so"(p. 83). There he learned lessons in the staging of comedy which he was to emulate in later years when he could supervise the rehearsals of his own plays.

Yet Moratín maintained his perspective. "I have not yet denied my own country," he wrote (p. 97). He saw that the Roussillon in France was well behind Cataluña in its agriculture, industry, and commerce (p. 42). But "I have seen other people, other customs, another country," he wrote to Jovellanos; "I have acquired new ideas, and I have either rectified or confirmed those that I had" (p. 97).

In summary, Forner and Moratín were enlightened young men who were determined to escape from the morass of baroque literature. They were receptive to a range of new ideas from abroad, but they were patriotic Spaniards. Forner, combative by disposition, made an exaggerated defense of Spanish values when a haughty Frenchman looked down his nose at Spain. Because of this response, which was more emotional than intellectual, traditionalists like Menéndez y Pelayo have laid claim to him. Forner, we must concede, is contradictory in his ideas. He represents one extreme within the group, but he is not so distant from Moratín as a reading of the *Oración apologética* alone would suggest.

For the 1780's, we have little to guide us regarding the ideas of

Estala and Melón. Both were interested in publishing or translating classical authors. Estala undertook such vast projects as translating Buffon's *Histoire Naturelle* and translating and continuing Joseph de Laporte's *Le Voyageur français*. He was also printing editions of Spanish poets, especially those of the sixteenth century that were favorites of the Neoclassics. Estala himself, however, in his manner and style, brings to mind baroque writers from earlier in the century: Torres Villarroel or Francisco Mariano Nifo. He is full of nonsensical ideas, and there is a note of hysteria in much that he wrote. Yet he was responsible for the staging in 1792 of Forner's *El filósofo enamorado (The Philosopher in Love)*, which people said was written "in the spirit of a Jacobin." Still he described himself as "inimical to all the horrors of France and its perverse doctrines."[21]

In the 1790's and continuing into the new century, Melón edited a weekly magazine on agriculture, one of those many enlightened efforts to improve the welfare of country people and thereby the national economy. His interest in the subject was stimulated by León de Arroyal, that member of the group who has seemed to be on the periphery.

If we make a spectrum of this coterie measuring their degree of enlightenment, we would place Forner and Estala to the right and Moratín and Melón in the center. To the left we would place León de Arroyal.

Arroyal was a religious man whose devotion was simple, private, and profound. Like Jovellanos and Bishop Tavira, he belonged to that strain of eighteenth-century Spanish Catholicism which has sometimes been designated "Jansenist," although without solid ideological justification. Arroyal translated the Psalms and the breviaries with the idea that the people should possess their religion. When he married Rita Piquer and drew up his will, at the age of thirty, he asked that he be buried outside the "temple."[22]

The evidence suggests that he can best be classified as a primitivist. He believed in the discipline and the simplicity of the first centuries of the Christian church. He was not an enemy of the church nor was this Spanish philosophe a Voltairean. In the *Cartas político-económicas* he was later to write: "Whatever brings us closer to the first centuries of Christianity is worthy of praise. Let it be by whatever route possible."[23]

In his poetry, which Forner disparaged and which no one since has esteemed, Arroyal expressed ideas that the nineteenth-century described as "disolventes," that is, subversive. When he wrote Epigrama XXXIX, addressed to a certain Don Juan, Arroyal compared the lot of farm workers, which he knew at first hand, with what he saw on his trips to Madrid. His negative reaction recalls the verses by Forner which Bishop Lorenzana spotted as subversive:

> When I observe your ostentatious show,
> and see you ride in fancy coaches, John,
> I'm rightly shocked, because I know for sure
> to pay for them you've cruelly bled the poor.[24]

There is a difference, however, in the tone of the two men. Forner wrote with bitter satire. Arroyal expresses his anguish. His attitude toward poverty coincides with that expressed in the anonymous pamphlet *Conversaciones de Perico y Marica*.

The full impact of Arroyal's ideas is to be found in two works which circulated anonymously and clandestinely: the *Cartas político-económicas al Conde de Lerena* (*Letters to the Count of Lerena on Politics and Economics*) and the *Oración apologética que en defensa del estado floreciente de España dixo en la Plaza de toros de Madrid D. . . .* (*Apology which Don . . . Made in the Madrid Bullring about the Prosperous State of Spain*). François López has written two superb articles on the attribution of these works, and we may now accept them definitively as belonging to Arroyal.[25] They create his significance as a writer of the Enlightenment. If we put this material together with other things that we are learning about Luis María García del Cañuelo, the editor of *El Censor*, about Santiago Felipe Puglia, and others, we may reassess our views of the Spanish Enlightenment.[26] We shall find it curious indeed that ideas so subversive of the *ancien régime* should have emerged precisely from the Moratín circle, which also produced what has come to be accepted as Forner's defense of traditional Spanish values.

The *Cartas político-económicas* deal mostly with taxation, a subject as critical in Spain as it was in France in the 1780's. Alfred Cobban said of Louis XIV: "The great king had endowed France with a modern system of government while retaining a semi-medieval system of financing it."[27] The Spanish Bourbons imported the French system of government; as Arroyal's letters show, they did nothing to improve the old Habsburg system of taxation. On the death of the Conde de Guasa, who had been finance minister since 1766, Carlos III appointed Pedro López de Lerena to the post. At the same time he and his ministers were eagerly accepting the ideas of Francisco de Cabarrús, the entre-preneur who came from France as a youth. Cabarrús established the system of *vales reales*, thus increasing enormously the circula-tion of currency, and he founded the Banco de San Carlos, which the Comte de Mirabeau attacked. Moratín became his secretary in 1787, and according to Melón wrote at least one pamphlet that was attributed to Cabarrús.[28] Moratín's job lasted until López de Lerena succeeded in jailing Cabarrús in 1790, so that the period coincided closely with the polemic over Forner's *Oración apolo-gética* and with Arroyal's *Cartas* to Lerena, which are dated from 1786 to 1790.

The *Cartas* themselves are impassioned but sedate. The prologue is by contrast expressive. Arroyal's picturesque language reminds us of Forner's invective. He calls Lerena's accountants, whom he names, "caga-tintas," a picturesque word for members of that odious profession that I am not bold enough to translate. He observes that the Count of Floridablanca "understood as much about economics as he did of castrating mice. . . ." (pp. 53–54).

In his analysis of the *Cartas político-económicas* François López points out that Arroyal's ideas are those of a *philosophe*. Writing from the Manchegan villages of Vara del Rey and San Clemente, Arroyal demonstrates sympathy for the farm workers, distrust of commerce and speculation, scorn for the parasites of the court. "When I see a thousand, two thousand, or three thousand duros spent on some amusement or on some trifle, I think of ten, twenty or thirty thousand unhappy laborers covered with the dust and sweat of their work in the fields. They take a whole day to earn what a courtier wastes in an hour" (pp. 141–42).

In his democratic ideas, his defense of laborers, his scorn of the nobility, and his severe views about luxury, he is in spirit revolutionary. In his other work he carried these ideas to their logical extreme. The pamphlet with the ironic title *Oración apologética . . . en defensa del estado floreciente de España . . .* was an outgrowth of the polemic that Forner caused by his *Oración apologética.* Arroyal's tract remained anonymous while it circulated in manuscript in the 1790's, at Salamanca, for example.[29] It became famous much later when it was first printed in 1812 under the title *Pan y toros (Bread and Bulls)* and was attributed to Jovellanos.

The work is a call to revolution, but the government, headed first by those aging statesmen of yesteryear, Floridablanca and Aranda, and then by the youthful lover of Queen María Luisa, Manuel Godoy, had already buried Arroyal in his provincial village. He lived on until 1813, but his voice and what he stood for faded into obscurity, silenced by an effective censorship.

Until the 1780's the initiative for the Enlightenment came from the Crown and from the king's ministers: Campomanes, Aranda, and Floridablanca himself. In the 1780's, however, these men were older, and at the same time they saw that progressive ideas in France were undermining the Bourbon monarchy there. Whereas Campomanes in the 1770's had had to deal with reactionary pamphleteers who attacked the reform-minded government, by the end of the 1780's the situation was inverted. Progressive-minded pamphleteers had moved out ahead of the government ministers and were a threat to the foundations of the *ancien régime.* The government tried to deal with its young radicals by drawing them into its sphere. Thus, Moratin's circle was absorbed into the official cultural life of Spain. The process began with Floridablanca's payment to Forner for the *Oración apologética.* The definitive step came about through a curious concatenation of circumstances. When Leandro was a youth, his family lived in the same house with Ignacio Bernascone, and Leandro even fell in love with his niece. Bernascone served in the Italian Company of the King's Guards. Through him Moratín met a younger member of the Guards named Francisco Bernabeu. Bernabeu, Moratín, and Forner used to go to dances together (*Epistolario*, p. 127). Bernabeu introduced Forner and Moratín to his companion in the Guards, Don Luis Godoy, who in turn presented them to his brother Don Manuel Godoy. This handsome Guardsman with the melodious voice, younger even than the writers in Moratín's circle, was to have a meteoric rise when he was spotted by Queen María Luisa. He found himself in a position to dispense favors to his intellectual friends. Moratín was awarded the church benefices that enabled him to go to Italy and was later given the lucrative government post of Secretary of the Interpretation of Languages. Forner was appointed prosecuting attorney first in Sevilla, later Madrid. Melón and Estala got government support for their publishing ventures, Melón for his agricultural journal and Estala for his travel books and his translation of Buffon.

In this way, a once enlightened government, grown frightened and conservative, seduced the bright young men of Moratín's circle through jobs, fellowships, and grants. In their twenties these men were rebellious; in their thirties and forties they joined the establishment. Only León de Arroyal remained outside the pale, isolated in his village on the Manchegan plain where an idealistic Don Quijote had once tilted at windmills.

NOTES

1 We do not know his first name. Aside from Melón's references to him, we find mention of him in Moratín's diary in 1797, 1798, and 1800: *Diario: mayo, 1780–marzo, 1808*, ed. René and Mireille Andioc (Madrid: Editorial Castalia, 1967), passim. I think he must not have been Martín Fernández de Navarrete (1765–1844), a naval man, and later the biographer of Cervantes and author of a book on Castilian orthography.

2 Leandro Fernández de Moratín, *La comedia nueva*, ed. John Dowling (Madrid: Editorial Castalia, 1970), pp. 23–25, which reproduces Biblioteca Nacional, Madrid, MSS. 18666, No. 24, and 18668, No. 3.

3 Archives Nationales, Paris, F⁷ 12065, Dossier 2461. Melón was the sort who might well have taken a few years off his age.

4 León de Arroyal, *Versión castellana del Oficio parvo de Nuestra Señora, según el Breviario romano* (Madrid: Joaquín Ibarra, 1781).

5 Leandro Fernández de Moratín, *La derrota de los pedantes. Lección poética*, ed. John Dowling (Barcelona: Editorial Labor, 1973), pp. 15–17.

6 Private archive of Don Juan Grinda. When I consulted it (1960), the sketch was in Leg. 4, leaves 14–15.

7 *La comedia nueva*, ed. John Dowling, p. 25.

8 Mary Fidelia Laughrin, *Juan Pablo Forner as a Critic* (Washington: The Catholic University of America Press, 1943), p. 4. Standard studies which deal with Forner and which are not cited elsewhere in these notes are: María Jiménez Salas, *Vida y obras de D. Juan Pablo Forner y Segarra* (Madrid: Consejo Superior de Investigaciones Científicas, Instituto "Nicolás Antonio," 1944); Jesús Alvarez Gómez, *Juan Pablo Forner (1756–1797), preceptista y filósofo de la historia* (Madrid: Editora Nacional, 1971); and the "Prólogo" to Juan Pablo Forner y Segarra, *Los gramáticos, historia chinesca*, Edición crítica por John H. R. Polt, University of California Publications in Modern Philology, 95 (Berkeley: University of California Press, 1970; simultaneouly published by Editorial Castalia, Madrid).

9 Emilio Cotarelo y Mori, *Iriarte y su época* (Madrid: Sucesores de Rivadeneyra, 1897), p. 314.

10 Archivo Histórico Nacional, Madrid, Sección de Estado, Leg. 3238, Exp. 15, No. 6. The documentation continues through Nos. 7 to 10.

11 Juan Pablo Forner, *Oración apologética por la España y su mérito literario para que sirva de exhortación al Discurso leído por el abate Denina en la Academia de Ciencias de Berlín, respondiendo a la cuestión: "¿Qué se debe a España?"* ed. Antonio Zamora Vicente (Badajoz: Imprenta de la Excma. Diputación, 1945), p. 7.

12 Julián Marías, *La España posible en tiempo de Carlos III* (Madrid: Sociedad de Estudios y Publicaciones, 1963), p. 73.

13 E. García-Pandavenes, ed., *El Censor (1781–1787)* (Barcelona: Editorial Labor, 1972), pp. 48–49.

14 Archivo Histórico Nacional, Madrid, Sección de Estado, Leg. 3238, Exp. 15, No. 24, dated March 2, 1795.

15 Leopoldo Augusto de Cueto, "Bosquejo histórico-crítico de la poesía castellana en el siglo XVIII," in *Poetas líricos del siglo XVIII*, Biblioteca de Autores Españoles, 61 (Madrid: Ediciones Atlas, 1952), I, cxlvi, n. 2.

16 Moratín, *La derrota de los pedantes. Lección poética*, ed. John Dowling, pp. 13–24.

17 Russell P. Sebold, "Análisis estadístico de las ideas poéticas de Luzán: sus orígenes y su naturaleza," in *El rapto de la mente* (Madrid: Editorial Prensa Española, 1970), pp. 57–97, especially pp. 70–75.

18 John Dowling, *Leandro Fernández de Moratín* (New York: Twayne Publishers, 1971), p. 25.

19 René Andioc, "Introducción" to Leandro Fernández de Moratín, *Epistolario* (Madrid: Editorial Castalia, 1973), pp. 22–32.

20 *Epistolario*, p. 100. Subsequent references are in parentheses.

21 Juan Pérez de Guzmán, "Veintiuna cartas inéditas de D. Pedro Estala dirigidas a D. Juan Pablo Forner, bajo el nombre arcádico Damón, para la historia literaria del último tercio del siglo XVIII," *Boletín de la Real Academia de la Historia*, 58 (1911), 7.

22 François López, "León de Arroyal: auteur des *Cartas político-económicas al Conde de Lerena*," *Bulletin Hispanique*, 69 (1967), 31–32.

23 León de Arroyal, *Cartas político-económicas al Conde de Lerena*, ed. Antonio Elorza (Madrid: Editorial Ciencia Nueva, 1968), p. 179.

24 León de Arroyal, *Los epigramas* (Madrid: Joaquín Ibarra, 1784), p. 21.

> Quando miro tus galas ostentosas,
> Juan; quando veo tus soberbios coches,
> con razón me horrorizo; pues conozco
> que todo ello es sangre de los pobres.

Iris Zavala has suggested to me privately the possibility that the Juan of Arroyal's epigram may be the intellectual Don Juan Antonio Picornell. She has written about him in "Picornell y la Revolución de San Blas: 1795," in *Historia ibérica: Economía y sociedad en los siglos XVIII y XIX*, No. 1 (Long Island City, N. Y.: Anaya/Las Américas, n.d.), 35–54.

25 Besides the article cited in note 22, François López is the author of "*Pan y toros*: Histoire d'un pamphlet. Essai d'attribution," *Bulletin Hispanique*, 71 (1969), 255–79.

26 Santiago Felipe Puglia (May 1, 1760–August 26, 1822) [Genoa (Italy)–Charleston, S. C.] was born the same year as Moratín. In his twenties, from about 1782 to 1787, when Carbarrús was founding the Banco de San Carlos, he was engaged in business in Cádiz. He went bankrupt, was jailed for eighteen months, and abandoned Spain in 1790 on a ship bound for Philadelphia. There, about the time that Arroyal's *Oración apologética* was circulating in manuscript in Salamanca, Puglia published *El desengaño del hombre* (Filadelfia: En la imprenta de Francisco Bailey, 1794). In it he translated a few pages of Thomas Paine's *The Rights of Man*. The

Spanish government feared that Puglia's book was intended for circulation and subversion in its American colonies and attempted to have it suppressed. For these details I am indebted to Professor Merle Simmons (Indiana University), whose manuscript I have seen: "Santiago F. Puglia, Early Philadelphia Propagandist for Spanish American Independence."

27 Quoted by Howard Mumford Jones, *Revolution and Romanticism* (Cambridge, Mass.: Harvard University Press, 1974), p. 14.

28 Moratín, *La comedia nueva,* ed. John Dowling, pp. 28–29.

29 Richard Herr, *The Eighteenth Century Revolution in Spain* (Princeton, N.J.: Princeton University Press, 1958), pp. 330–25.

Concepts of the Grotesque before Goya

PAUL ILIE

The cruel, dark fantasies of Goyesque satire, said Baudelaire, were modern in spirit, no longer jovial or gay as in Cervantes' time, but violent, full of the blank horrors of nature, and in love with the ungraspable.[1] We might add that the grotesque in Goya is more a point of departure for romantic deformations of reality than the culmination of an eighteenth-century grotesque. It is simple enough to recognize the similarities between the Goyesque nightmare and an earlier Spanish tradition. But this relationship was not what a romantic like Gautier had in mind when he compared the fury and gloom of the *caprichos* with Hoffmann's tales and Delacroix's illustrations for *Faust*. For us to regard Goya in this way as primarily a precursor of romanticism does not require us to ignore the aspects of moral satire bearing kinship to the satirical sketches of Cadalso, Isla, and Villarroel; and from the grotesque portraits in Villarroel to their antecedents in Gracián and Quevedo is but one short step. However, my assumption for this paper, and I think it is easily proven, is that what attracted Baudelaire and Gautier was the irrational and private vision in Goya. The major esthetic values of the eighteenth century may have been at work in Goya, but it was his fantastic cosmology, a world based on subjective symbols, which prompted Baudelaire to speak of "quelque chose de sombre." What enabled French romantics to distinguish the Goyesque from the Cervantesque, was this deeply irrational factor, rather than any of the subjective components of neo-Aristotelian and eighteenth-century artistic theory.

Nevertheless, Baudelaire did not address himself to the century and a half that separated Goya from Cervantes, nor did he ask what had happened to the grotesque esthetic during the Enlightenment and earlier. Yet in order to pose the question realistically, without overcomplicating a difficult problem, it is useful to exclude Goya's esthetics. Therefore I propose that we think of grotesque manifestations independently of Goya, as the function of earlier traditions, and as a mode involving techniques partly governed by taste and partly dictated by the themes themselves. My purpose is to identify the concepts behind that mode, concepts of the grotesque prior to Goya as they appear on the interface between literary practice and the theory of artistic expression in general.

This means dealing with material of a certain kind, while passing over other sorts of material, and since I have gathered a large amount of information on the grotesque in eighteenth-century Spain, I shall outline below what will be omitted. But first let me define what I mean by "grotesque." I use the term in the narrow sense to indicate a particular modality, an expressive manner whose techniques of deliberate distortion are employed for the purpose of creating incongruous configurations. This definition excludes but does not reject the additional implications of the grotesque arising from non-textual considerations. For instance, the psychological ramifications of viewer perception are interesting to reflect upon, and eventually we must join with scholars like Kayser and Clayborough, and ask such questions as whether distorted phenomena arouse a sense of the uncanny or the absurd or the ridiculous. But for the purpose of this essay I wish to present a limited approach that focuses on the imagistic phenomenology of deformation, and especially on those ideas that seem to encourage such deformation. Now here, two kinds of material are available in the eighteenth century. On the one hand we have theoretical discussions of beauty and ugliness, of verisimilitude and inverisimilitude, of the roles of imagination, caprice, and dream. On the other hand we have literary examples of the grotesque. In this second area the instances are too many to digest in an essay of this length. But it is useful to sketch in the range of existing grotesque phenomena in order to have a point of comparison with the concepts that either led to an awareness of distortion or else helped to create a climate of creative freedom.

There are four categories of activity which deviate from neoclassical norms by exhibiting pure deformation; and if they do not deform reality in the modern sense they constitute exaggerated elements that provoked commentators of the period to censure them with responses like "monstruoso," "extravagante," "delirante," "quimérico," "disparate," "demencia," "disonancia," and similar epithets of varying intensity. One category of grotesque contains the semi-folkloric creations of mass entertainment: the *gigantones* and *máscaras* of street parades whose literary counterpart in low comedy and burlesque ballads include *figurones*, harlequins, and satirical figures or phrases in such works as Luis Salazar y Castro's *Palacio de Momo*,[2] or Francisco Botello's *Historia de las cuevas de Salamanca*, or even some of the poems of Gerardo Lobo. This popular substratum eventually merged with more refined artistic levels, as occurred in Goya's case where he made use of masked figures. A good literary example is *La Serafina*, where the motif of the carnival retains the purity of its popular origins. The scene in this novel creates an atmosphere that exudes carefree gaiety. The motif contrasts with its counterpart in the romantic grotesque, where the carnival is exploited for its epistemological delusion, as happens in Espronceda, while in Bécquer the motif appears in the context of spiritual malaise and disillusion.

The second category of grotesque practices, more deformed than the first, concerns moralistic caricature, which also uses popular types for satirical purposes. The grotesque portraits of Torres Villarroel's *Visiones y visitas* feature character analyses that are meant to be ethical in content but in fact invite attention due to their representational aberrations.[3] Similar effects can be seen in Isla's vignettes, such as the one of Fray Gerundio's mother:

> Como la buena de la Catanla abría tanto la boca para pronunciar su *a*, y naturaleza liberal la había proveído de este órgano abundantemente, siendo mujer de un bocado se engullía una pera de donguindo hasta el pezón, quiso su desgracia que se la desencajó la mandíbula inferior tan descompasadamente, que se quedó hecha un mascarón de retablo, viéndosela toda la entrada del esófago y de la traquiarteria, con los conductos salivales, tan clara y distintamente, que el barbero dijo descubría hasta los vasos linfáticos, donde excretaba la respiración.[4]

Isla's extreme caricatures of the archpriest and the flagellant[5] illustrate what Fielding called the "burlesque" in his preface to *Joseph Andrews*: "an exhibition of what is monstrous and unnatural." Grotesque portraits even appear in moralist literature, where Calderón Altamirano condemns drunkenness by using the composite techniques of Arcimboldo.[6] In all of these caricatures the authors manipulate the plastic surface properties of their subjects while placing ethical or religious defects in a sociological dimension.[7]

Now for the third and fourth groupings of literary examples. In the third category are instances that concentrate within a word or a phrase the entire impact of the distortive process. This is done by the placement of strategic qualifications like "frenético," "monstruo horrendo," "hospital de locos," "mico," "enano," "bufón," "sombras, visiones, fantasmas"—these are some of the references appearing in the *Cartas marruecas*. By the deployment of these lexical devices the author achieves his inframimetic goal. The fourth and final category includes material which in itself is not grotesque but which manifests a sensibility running counter to the neoclassical values of moderation and order. Later I will have occasion to contrast the rational norms of Luzán's poetics with the grotesque implications of irrational creativity. The point to be made about the fourth category and its sensibility is that both show features of violence and antinatural phenomena. These features not only highlight their own exaggerated contours, but they rupture the unity of the work and become structural dissonances within the harmonic totality. The best illustrations are narrative epic poems like *El Alphonso* and *El Pelayo,* where both Botello and Solís utilize Virgilian episodes in combination with grotto elements, horrible beasts, and sinister magic. These fantastic components have their counterpart in prose fiction—the cave scene in Estrada Nava's *Vida del gran Thebandro español*—and in the preromantic sensibility of Meléndez Valdés, especially in his second *elegía moral* to Jovino, where the atmosphere of macabre, funereal horror culminates in the poet's escape from the ghosts that menace him.

The four categories of literary examples comprise a wide spectrum extending from pure grotesquerie to a mild romantic phantasmagoria. This range is one of the two major areas which I began by distinguishing in regard to grotesque material in the eighteenth century. The second major area is theoretical: the treatises that fix the rules and standards to be followed in composing literature or creating works in the visual arts. The examples of literary practice form a backdrop against which to place the treatises on literature and painting, a metaphorical horizon making visible whatever protrusions emerge from the artistic norms and ideals of the theorists. These norms of beauty, proportion, and verisimilitude are known and require little comment. They do place restraints on a capricious artist with a strong imagination. Let us recall Luzán's maxim that the basis of poetic beauty is truth, and that truth is beautiful because it is always uniform, regular, and proportioned. In contrast, said Luzán, "la falsedad ostenta siempre la fealdad y la descompostura de las partes que la componen, en las cuales todo es desunión, irregularidad y desproporción."[8] It follows therefore that "lo irregular, lo desordenado y desproporcionado no puede jamás ser agradable ni hermoso en el estado natural de las cosas . . . consistiendo su belleza en lo vario y uniforme, en lo regular, en lo bien ordenado y proporcionado de sus partes" (I, 118).

Another aspect of this rationalist formulation is its perfectionism, the degree to which it puts the artist under the obligation to press his invention into the service of idealization. As late as 1780 we find Antonio Mengs beginning his treatise with two assertions: first, that we apprehend the beautiful through an intellective act involving our understanding of perfection; and second, that an object is beautiful when it corresponds to the idea we have of its perfect state: "La belleza consiste en la perfección de la materia según nuestras ideas."[9] To aspire to and correspond with perfection is to fulfill the concept of conformity. And conversely, to disconform is to abandon the pursuit of perfection. But when all the parts of an object conform to our idea of a perfect whole, that object appears to be beautiful. Therefore to disconform is to fall from beauty to ugliness, from perfection to imperfection. The question is, what kind of imperfection? If beauty is perfection, it has the quality of proportion. And if an object is ugly, if it is imperfect, then it is disproportioned. But if proportion is congruity, a disproportioned object must be incongruous. Incongruity is that feature of ugliness which proceeds from disproportion. On this point Mengs bears us out by an unusual illustration: "Un niño será feo, si tiene cara de viejo: lo mismo sucederá al hombre que tenga cara de mujer; y la mujer con facciones de hombre no será ciertamente hermosa" (p. 8). The statement addresses itself not simply to ugliness or imperfection, but to the incongruous mixture of qualities. It is the neoclassical counterpart to the famous warning by Horace in the *Epistle to Pisos*, a warning against hybridization which in Mengs is more subdued because the incongruities are confined to the human species. Nevertheless, the transexual examples are striking, not to say Goyesque.

All of this is to say that while deformation kept appearing erratically in literary practice, the theorists legitimized its existence by recognizing it to be a subject of discussion. They did not sanction ugliness or incongruity, but they called attention to these errors with a consistency that will become apparent. Had they ignored the ugly or reduced its visibility, public awareness of deviant forms might have been weak. But theorists gave negative examples of the ideal by citing the defective. It is true that when

Luzán praised Virgil's perfect description of the grotesque Polifemo, his applause was not for the creature itself. Even so, in effect the appearance of Polifemo as a deformed subject was tolerated. From there it was a short step to Arteaga's assertion of the esthetic pleasure to be found in "esta metamorfosis admirable de feo en hermoso."[10]

Linked to the mythical giant was another horrendous myth from antiquity: Laocoon and the writhing contortions of the serpent. Arteaga was joined in his enthusiasm by Mengs and by Rejón de Silva, who advised young painters to study the sculpted group. Nevertheless, even Arteaga was detained from embracing the full implications of a universal grotesque for all media. Again citing the Polifemo, he noted that while the subject suited poetry, no one could stomach a painting or statue of the giant crushing the bones of Ulysses' companions between his teeth, "ni dejaría de horrorizarse viendo la hedionda y descomunal boca de aquel gigante con un hombre atravesado en medio de ella, y la sanguaza que le ensuciaba" (p. 43). This statement was made prior to Goya's painting of Saturn devouring his child.

The retentive strength of neoclassical values held these grotesque impulses in check. Where such impulses broke free they produced cracks in the stronghold of ideal beauty, the fortress built upon the foundations of geometrical proportion, rational order, good taste, and the sublime. Compared to the full range of grotesque examples I outlined earlier, preceptual statements like Luzán's and Arteaga's can hardly be said to represent invitations to distort and deform. On the other hand, there is no treatise or manifesto before the twentieth century which invites artists to cultivate incongruity. The fact that a grotesque current runs more strongly through eighteenth-century literature than seventeenth can be ascribed in good measure to the erosion of theoretical authority among the neoclassical treatise writers. Their very legislation of values such as symmetry and proportion, or the balance of imitation and invention, led to increasing space devoted to the sublimation of ugly qualities by means of the esthetic process. Even while Spaniards thus defended ideal beauty, they increased their awareness of distortive elements which might subvert that ideal.

One of the best indicators of this progressively wider consciousness is the semantic evolution of the word "grotesco" in Spanish usage. At the beginning of the century, lexicographers barely recognized that "grotesco" had currency. In 1705 Francisco Sobrino defined it in his *Diccionario nuevo de las lenguas española y francesa*, but he gave only the French usage. Under the listing "grotesque" are the synonyms "ridicule," "bizarre," and "extravagant" ("extravagante," "ridículo"). Yet under the Spanish counterpart we find a reference to look elsewhere: "grutesco, ve redículo," and under "redículo" the word "grutesco" does not appear. Even this cross-reference disappears in 1734, when the *Diccionario de Autoridades* reverts to the old Covarrubias definitions involving painting and architecture. These areas now draw more attention than before, and both adjective and noun are listed separately, with related meanings: "imitación de cosas toscas, e incultas, como breñas y grutas . . . especie de adorno . . . compuesto de varias hojas, peñascos y otras cosas, como caracoles y otros insectos." Note that value judgments are not implied in these terms, nor any suggestion of the kind of creative activity underlying "imitación." The word "grotesco" is not a concept but a strictly limited category of visual elements compounded artificially but patterned on the natural world.

By the middle of the eighteenth century, "grutesco" becomes associated with the creative act. In 1753 Miravel translates Moreri's *Gran diccionario histórico*, which modifies the information known to Spaniards from Covarrubias by adding a new note: "pequeñas figuras de hombres y animales, que se representan mezcladas de ornatos chiméricos y ridículos." This restores the lost valuation of "ridiculous," while the previous suggestion of imitation is now supplemented by the fantastic quality—chimerical—which is addressed antithetically to the idea of representation. Implicitly the Moreri definition recognizes inverisimilitude to be an acceptable norm of ornamentation for a genre of this kind. The outlines of a concept begin to emerge, but we must not forget that the historical dictionary translated by Miravel is destined for an elite readership, and in any event does not reflect the linguistic reality of the Spanish vocabulary. We may conclude from this that the awareness of the grotesque in the late eighteenth century alternates with a certain indifference to it. In 1780 the abridged one-volume Academy dictionary assumes a conservative role by perpetuating the 1734 definition; that is, it merely repeats the details of insects and snails in painting and architecture. In 1782, however, Forner uses the term "literatura grotesca" without regard to specific ornamentation when he attacks bombastic and ridiculous writing in his *Exequias de la lengua castellana*. Forner's valuative usage combines with the generic meaning in a listing by Terreros y Pando in the 1787 *Diccionario castellano . . . de ciencias y artes:* "lo que pertenece a gruta, y en la Pintura, Talladura, y Escultura se llama grutesco aquello que trae consigo una especie de fantasía y capricho . . . También . . . lo que es extravagante y ridículo." One year later Rejón de Silva places an entry in his *Diccionario de las nobles artes:* "grutesco o brutesco: Véase Follage."[11] And under "Follage" Rejón writes: "Adorno de cogollos, hojas harapadas, sátiros, bichas y otras sabandijas. Llámanse Grutescos, por haberse hallado esta moda en las grutas y subterráneas de Roma; como también Brutescos, por los animales brutos que en él se introducen." The preoccupation with zoomorphic elements, which increases here with the mention of satyrs, finds full expression in 1790 when Isidro Bosarte quotes Horace's *Epistle to Pisos* condemning "los monstruos biformes, de dos naturalezas incompatibles, en las figuras de los adornos."[12] It was an impossible artistic hypothesis, said Bosarte: "semejante grutesco ni lo había en Roma, ni en Grecia" (p. 15).

And so we have a philological diachrony in which the ornamentational constant unifies grotesque motifs in the public mind throughout the century. But as semantic changes lead to shifts in emphasis, the grotesque achieves immediacy by its increased repertoire of animalesque forms—even satyrs. And the same philological evolution amplifies the merely descriptive "imitación" into a more conceptual framework of creative processes: "una especie de fantasía y capricho"—whatever these activities may be.

This brings us logically to a discussion of the terms *capricho* and *fantasía,* two topics broad enough to inspire separate papers. [13] The issues they raise—problems related to the creative process and the perception of reality—are complicated by still another faculty—the dream. I've already dealt to some degree with the *sueño* in Villarroel (note 3), and this need not be repeated. If space allowed me to present all the evidence related to dream, *capricho,* and imagination or *fantasía,* the conclusions that could be drawn might be summarized as follows. All three concepts refer to the phenomenology of irrational expression. They gain prominence in eighteenth-century treatises, after a century of casual references, because their psychological mechanisms pose difficulties for mimetic or neoclassical rationalism. For example, the hostility to *capricho* can be found as late as 1792, when Valzania deplores the lack of planning in modern buildings, and attacks construction "cuando así la colocación como la expresión depende de un capricho sin fundamento." [14] Even Jovellanos can be shown to be ambivalent about *capricho,* for he makes statements both in support of and against the anti-mimetic quality of caprice in architecture. [15] Examples aside, what arises is a conflict between preceptual respectability and esthetic modality. Capricious and grotesque practices may not have been respectable according to seventeenth- and eighteenth-century rules, but practiced it was, and in fact esteemed, if the continued popularity of Bosch and Quevedo is any proof. [16] The use of distortion is an esthetic countermode, the undercurrent which gains prestige as concepts of imagination liberate the artist and his subjective impulse to create without regard to rational precepts. Hence the *capricho,* the *disparate,* and the *sueño* which, for example, is sanctioned at the end of Forner's *Exequias.* All these are phenomena in the world of art, although in the world of ordinary discourse they remain just words with a pejorative connotation.

We witness, then, degrees of rational disintegration. Neoclassical beauty is the norm, and deviation is described by value judgments: *extravagancia, monstruo.* These terms may not themselves represent anything grotesque, but they identify the forbidden area of creativity. As Eximeno pointed out in regard to music, "las circunstancias que pueden en nuestra imaginativa alterar la naturaleza de un objeto, son infinitas."[17] For Eximeno it was bad taste which encouraged the imagination to indulge in the infinite capacity for distortion: "el mal gusto consiste en la extravagancia o en la desconformidad de los objetos inventados con los naturales." Disconformity varied, of course: there were degrees of extravagance. For Luzán, as we have seen, the range was limited, whereas for Iriarte the game consisted of irrationalizing the rational to the extent that symmetry itself could begin in burlesque and end in caprice.[18]

Nor does the disintegration of rational values follow a comprehensible chronology. Cracks in the fortress of ideal beauty appear in 1702 in the *entremeses* of Francisco de Castro.[19] In 1717 Palomino dedicates one chapter of *El museo pictórico y escala óptica* to the freakish and marvellous aspects of nature and calls it "Prodigios de naturaleza en abono de la pintura" (I, 12). In 1789 Preciado de la Vega publishes a treatise on painting in a format whose central metaphor is stated in the title: *Arcadia pictórica en sueño: Alegoría o poema prosaico*. Yet these same periods produce important formulations on behalf of artistic orthodoxy. Mengs treats the grotesque mode in terms of bad taste while ignoring its historical origins: "se hacían cosas necias, inverisímiles y falsas; y así nació el gusto que llamamos grotesco."[20] Yet even Mengs recognized the esthetic beauty of mythological creatures: satyrs, fauns, centaurs, tritons (ibid., p. 386). True, he did not classify them among grotesques, but Palomino did just that by grouping them historically as one stylistic occurence among many rather than considering them in terms of good taste: "los grutescos de varios cogollos, hojas, tallos, y cartelas, artificiosa y galanamente compuestas, y otros diferentes adornos, con grifos, sátiros, faunos, silvanos, centauros, bichas y otras varias y exquisitas sabandijas, cuya semejanza no hay *in rerum Natura,* sino solamente en la idea del artífice."[21]

The relationship between good taste and imagination presents itself as one key issue, and I will conclude by dealing briefly with the question of whether artists felt obliged to rule their private fancy with the yoke of collective good taste. Was it true, as Capmany suggested, that the abuse of imagination made the artist unable to "distinguir lo miserable de lo suntuoso, lo disforme de lo bello, lo monstruoso de lo regular"?[22] If so, then a paradox seems to have passed unnoticed, for when good taste was neglected, the work "se inunda de extravagancias *ingeniosamente monstruosas*" (p. 12, italics mine). Capmany's complaint was not against imaginative activity altogether, only against the failure to distinguish between "la bella imaginación siempre natural" and "la falsa, la que amontona cosas incompatibles" (p. 20). So-called false imagination was termed "la fantástica, la que pinta objetos que no tienen analogía ni verosimilitud" (p. 20). [23]

Capmany's position recognized the grotesque mode and rejected it, and he was joined by theoreticians in other media: music, architecture, painting. In tracts like the 1780 *Reglas generales para que una composición de música sea perfecta* by Pedro Aranaz y Vives,[24] and the 1783 *Arquitectura civil* by Benito Bails, the instinctive quality of individual taste was understood. Bails wrote of modern building design that "ni el capricho ni el acaso deben influir en este gusto" (p. 625). As for music, Aranaz allowed for innovation provided that no incongruity entered to create "ridiculez y extravagancia." Bails argued that mixture was monstrosity, and that it caused "disparidad, y quita(r) la unidad tan esencial en la decoración de los edificios. Mucho mayor monstruosidad será todavía, si, conforme se ve en algunas obras modernas, se juntaren el orden dórico y jónico con el toscano" (p. 748). Unless the architect avoided "todos los atavíos que fuesen obras del capricho," unless he followed "la debida proporción" and the principle of unity, he would undermine "el buen gusto" whose "principal guía es la razón" (pp. 614, 625). But what about taste itself? Was it not already and inherently subjective? Bails understood the instinctive character of taste without dismissing it. Because individual taste had irrational origins, it could disfigure art. To imitate was one matter, to imitate capriciously was quite another. Yet if the steady hand of reasoned intelligence controlled private taste, then the true and difficult beauty of nature could be captured:

"cuanto es difícil imitar la bella naturaleza, tan fácil es desfigu-
rarla; es más fácil pintar ballenas gigantes, que no héroes" (p. 625).
The regulation of taste, therefore, was not isolated. It partici-
pated in the activities of imitation, and to imitate was to hold
certain models of reality above patterns of taste. In other words,
mimesis preceded individual preference and sometimes the
mimetic impulse even aspired to universal representationalism. A
particular manifestation of reality could be improved and raised to
a higher and universal or ideal level. For example, Mayans insisted
that the artist's duty was to correct the defects found in the model
chosen from nature: "si hay hombres tuertos, como el Rey Anti-
gono, la pintura hermosamente ideal los representa con ojos vivos
y sanos."[25] Horrible elements were of no interest; in fact, duty
required their elimination. Yet Mayans viewed the spectacle of a
horrible object in art within the context of esthetic pleasure. That
is, at least sometimes he conceded esthetic experience to be more
positive than the contemplation of a horrible object in its uncor-
rected form. Did this mean that Mayans was attracted by the
grotesque in an ambiguous way? At the least, his chapter on
"invención" deals kindly with Bosch's paintings. The prestige of
Bosch had been established early in the century when Palomino
praised his "exquisitos y extravagantes sueños."[26] Mayans sub-
scribed to that position while adding the qualification that "si en
algo mereció ser culpado, fue en ser demasiadamente ingenioso, y
fecundo en amontonar representaciones simbólicas y de raras
figuras." These excesses appear beyond reproach, perhaps because
Bosch is welcomed for the religious content of his paintings.
Whatever the reason, he is defended as a unique if bizarre painter.
Among the nonrational categories of invention, only his finds
acceptance, and it contrasts with the inferior work of another
painter, Eustrapio, whose "invención" is "ridículamente caprichosa." That is, Bosch's invention is "extravagantemente ingeniosa
y maravillosa." His "disparate" "se compone de partes en sí
perfectas al parecer, amontonadas disparatadamente, pero en real-
idad inventadas, y con relación al intento de la pintura seriamente
ingeniosa." Even so, the grotesque representation and the idiosyn-

cratic taste are exceptions for Mayans, not examples to be followed. Elsewhere his treatise places the subject of imitation and "imaginación interior" under a strong rationalistic idealization. Orthodoxy still dominates, yet an outstanding proponent of grotesque vision survives.

The following conclusions may be derived from my discussion: that the forms of distorted invention could be seen as alternatives to rational art; that these distortions arose from an extravagant use of imagination in the absence of rational controls; and that such practices were undesirable because they sprang from individual capriciousness rather than from collectively approved rules of taste and imitation. Those grotesque practices did exist nevertheless; they were widespread throughout the century; and on occasion they were combatted ambiguously by the very treatises that aimed at purging them. The grotesque before Goya not only existed in spite of its antagonists, but it survived in part by virtue of the attention paid to it.

NOTES

1 "Les Espagnols sont très-bien doués en fait de comique. Ils arrivent vite au cruel, et leurs fantaisies les plus grotesques contiennent souvent quelque chose de sombre" ("De l'essence du rire," *Oeuvres complètes,* éd. Y-G Le Dantec et Claude Pichois [Tours: Bibliothèque de la Pléiade, 1961], p. 988). On Goya: "Il unit à la gaieté, à la jovialité, à la satire espagnole du bon temps de Cervantes, un esprit beaucoup plus moderne, ou du moins qui a été beaucoup plus cherché dans le temps modernes, l'amour de l'insaissable, le sentiment des contrastes violents, des épouvantements de la nature et des physionomies humaines étrangement animalisées par les circonstances" ("Quelques caricaturistes étrangers," ibid., p. 1018).

2 Swift refers in this sense to Momus as the god of mockery: "What *Momus* was of old to *Jove,*/ The same a Harlequin is now;/ The former was *buffoon* above / The latter is a *Punch* below" ("The Puppet-Show," *Works* [London, 1766], XIV, 239). The context of Salazar y Castro includes a moralist background: ". . . se llama monstruo cualquier cosa en la naturaleza deforme, que exceda o falte a lo natural . . . desviándose de

la ley de la naturaleza el hombre en el entender, y obrar, despreciando la razón que la misma naturaleza inspira, es *monstruo*. La naturaleza es arte de Dios en las cosas criadas: (eso en lo físico) es orden de Dios, que ilumina comunicado a la razón, que produce la luz natural: (esto en lo moral) quien se aparta de este orden es monstruo; porque es la ley de la naturaleza, ordenada de su Autor. Esta manda, que del conocimiento del hombre nazca la adoración a sólo Dios, y el amor, el culto, y la obediencia que se le debe; siempre que a esto falta, contraviene a la ley de la naturaleza, y es monstruo moral de sí proprio: desconforma la apariencia con la verdad, parece que forma otra especie de animal sin razón, o su locura . . ." (*Palacio de Momo* [León de Francia (Madrid) 1714], p. 117).

3 See my article "Grotesque Portraits in Torres Villarroel," *Bulletin of Hispanic Studies*, 45 (1968), 16–37.

4 José Francisco de Isla, *Fray Gerundio de Campazas*, ed. Russell P. Sebold (Madrid: Espasa-Calpe, 1960), I, 117.

5 Ibid., IV, 121–22; I, 82–83.

6 The portrait begins: "Satirizar al ebrioso: La cabellera es de pámpanos: la frente una calabaza: las cejas dos corbillos: los ojos dos uvas gruesas coloradas: las narices espitas, las mejillas adormideras, la boca de tinaja, la barba de azadón, el cuello de cauce, el talle de cuba, las manos como cardos, los pies de pardal, el movimiento de un navío un poco lastre, el cuerpo de botejón, el alma de bota . . . Tiene la cabeza de pámpanos porque sus pensamientos son racimos. Es la frente una calabaza porque sólo para especies de vino se sirve esta vasija. Ser las cejas corbillos es porque así se llaman los instrumentos que usan los viñaderos," etc. *Opúsculos de oro, virtudes morales cristianas* (Madrid, 1707), pp. 502–3.

7 Add to these the portraits of men and women in *discursos* 49 and 119 of *El Censor (1781–1787)*, ed. E. García Pandavenes (Barcelona: Labor, 1972), pp. 99–100, 217; those by Juan Pablo Forner in *Los gramáticos*, ed. J. Jurado (Madrid, 1970), pp. 73–74, 113–14; and to some extent the sketch of the *proyectista* in José Cadalso's *Cartas marruecas, carta* 34.

8 *La poética*, ed. L. de Filippo (Barcelona: Selecciones bibliófilas, 1956), I, 120.

9 *Obras de Don Antonio Rafael Mengs*, ed. J. N. de Azara (Madrid, 1780), p. 8.

10 *La belleza ideal*, ed. M. Batllori (Madrid: Espasa-Calpe, 1955), p. 50. At one moment, Arteaga exclaims with relish: "¿Qué cosa, por ejemplo, más asquerosa que la imagen de Polifemo . . . cuando, después de haberse atracado de trozos de carne humana y vaciado en su vientre dos o tres zaques de vino, se tumba boca arriba en medio de la cueva?" (pp. 35–36).

11 The same cross-listing occurs in Palomino's *Indice de los términos privativos del arte de la pintura, y sus definiciones* of 1724.

12 *Observaciones sobre las bellas artes* (Madrid, 1790), I, 15–16.

13 See my article "*Capricho/caprichoso*: A Glossary of Eighteenth-Century Usages" in a forthcoming issue of *Hispanic Review*.

14 *Instituciones de arquitectura* (Madrid, 1792), pp. 118–19.

15 During the same period (1801–8), Jovellanos opposes *capricho* in painting while approving it in architecture: "Porque no debiendo haber en el arte lo que no pueda haber en la naturaleza, los volantes y colgantes de los paños, hechos a capricho, son defectuosos, y siéndolo, no se pueden autorizar con el ejemplo de otros pintores, y menos los movimientos y ondulaciones del dibujo en las figuras, cuya simplicidad es siempre preferible, no tanto porque la buscaron los griegos, cuanto por ser más conforme con la razón del arte, y con la naturaleza, que es su tipo" (*Obras* [Madrid, 1952], II, 158b). "Así es como el artista quiso representar estas bóvedas péndulas en el aire, y es fácil concebir cuán extraña y graciosa será su apariencia, y cuánto gusto y pericia supone la simétrica degradación de estos arcos, que enlazándose por todas partes y en todos sentidos entre tan desiguales muros, producen la más elegante y caprichosa forma" (*Obras,* I [Madrid, 1963], 394a). Jovellanos here changes his mind from the statement of 1785 about the Moorish style in twelfth- and thirteenth-century architecture: "hasta qué punto puede extraviarse el genio, abandonado a las inspiraciones del capricho" (I, 371b).

16 Bosch is praised by Palomino for "el dibujo intencional, o quimérico . . . *cuyo ser objetivo sólo está en el entendimiento;* esto es, que no tiene existencia física, y real . . . tales son los grutescos . . . cuya semejanza no hay *in rerum Natura,* sino solamente en la idea del artífice, que hace un conjunto de varias naturalezas, para formar un compuesto, cuya existencia repugna; en que fue extremadísimo el Bosco, en sus exquisitos y extravagantes sueños" (*El museo pictórico y escala óptica* [Madrid: Aguilar, 1947], p. 72).

A description of festivities during the War of the Spanish Succession tells of Philip V's return to Madrid after victories at Brihuega and Villaviciosa in 1710: "una célebre, hermosa, y vistosa máscara, con tanta variedad de invenciones que pudiera el Bosco tomar modelos para sus imaginarias ideas, pues era tan raro lo extraño de las orejas que se vieron." Pablo de Montestruich Fernández de Ronderos, *Viaje real del rey . . . Phelipe Quinto* (Madrid, 1712), p. 227.

Francisco de los Santos is impressed with Bosch's moral, not esthetic, value, and describes the Capilla del Colegio in the Escorial: "Encima de la cornija, sobre la del Entierro de Cristo, está una original de Gerónimo Bosco, el que fundando en aquel lugar de Isaías, que dice: toda carne es heno, y toda su gloria, como flor del campo; pinta un carro de heno, y sobre el heno, los deleites de la carne, y la Fama y ostentación de su gloria y alteza figurado en unas mujercillas tañendo y la Fama de demonio, con alas y trompeta, que publica su grandeza y regalos. Tiran este carro siete bestias fieras, símbolos de los vicios capitales, y alrededor van siguiéndole los hombres . . . y al fin todo el anhelo es por alcanzar del heno. Yo confieso que se lee más en esta tabla en un instante para la enseñanza y desengaño que en otros libros en muchos días" (Antonio Palomino y Francisco de los Santos, *Las ciudades, iglesias y conventos en España* [Londres, 1746], pp. 104–5).

The same painting is described in detail among others by Gregorio Mayans in the *Arte de pintar* of 1774 (Valencia, 1854), pp. 71–73, in a chapter titled "De la invención" which deals primarily with Bosch. See further footnote 26 and the next to last paragraph of this article.

17 *Del origen y reglas de la música* (Madrid, 1796), p. 193.

18 "Los juguetes festivos y graciosos, / Compuestos de pasages caprichosos / En el estilo cómico, parlante, / Con un compás simétrico y saltante, / Propio de la burlesca pantomima, /Que al buen humor, y aun a la risa anima" (*La música* [Madrid 1779], p. 37).

19 Cf. *Alegría cómica*, 3 vols. (Zaragoza, 1702), especially *Los gigantones, Los burlados de carnestolendas, La fantasma*. The collection *Cómico festejo*, 2 vols. (Madrid, 1742) contains the aforementioned plus *Las brujas, Los locos* and *Hombre mujer*.

20 "Reflexiones . . . sobre la belleza y gusto en la pintura," *Obras* (Madrid, 1780), p. 23; see too pp. 253–54. Mengs's disdain is attributed by his biographer Azara to his noble character. Highmindedness made Mengs averse to plebeian art forms: "No podía sufrir la música bufa, ni las bambochadas, y mucho menos los ridículos grotescos o arabescos" of such depraved standards (p. xxvii).

21 *El museo pictórico* . . . , p. 72.

22 *Filosofía de la elocuencia* (Madrid, 1777), p. 10.

23 Capmany's attack was aimed at rhetorical as well as pictorial grotesque ornamentation: "¡Qué profusión! ¡qué prodigalidad de . . . hipérboles colosales, de alegorías monstruosas . . . de frases afiligranadas . . . y de otros mil rasgos y follajes que no tienen nombre ni número" (pp. 12–13).

24 First published by Mariano Soriano Fuertes in *Historia de la música española* (Madrid: Martin y Salazar, 1856), III, 237, 238, 241.

25 Mayans, *Arte de pintar*, p. 17.

26 See above, note 16. The next quotations are from Mengs, *Obras*, pp. 73 and 69.

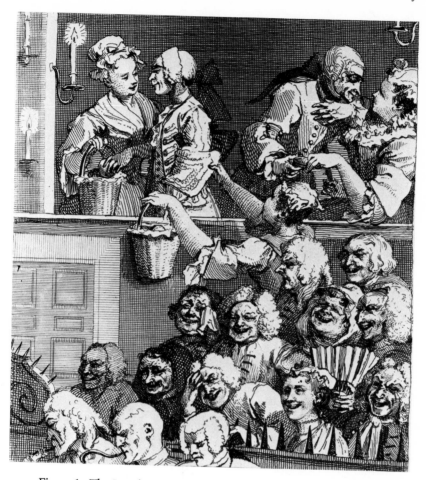

Figure 1: *The Laughing Audience*. Courtesy of Richard A. Vogler.

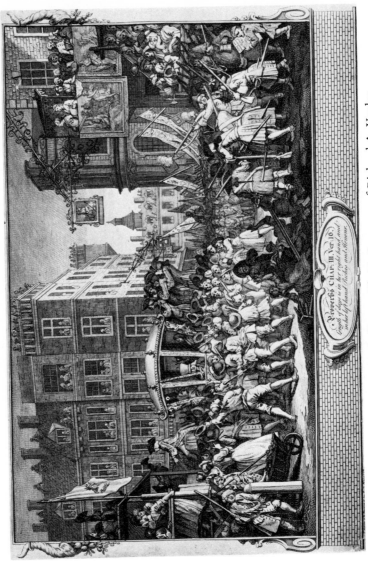

Figure 2: *Industry and Idleness, Pl. 12.* Courtesy of Richard A. Vogler.

Figure 3: *Strolling Actresses Dressing in a Barn.*
Courtesy of Richard A. Vogler.

Figure 4: *Southwark Fair*. Courtesy of the Huntington Library, San Marino, California.

Figure 5: Egerton MS 3013 41b. Courtesy of the British Museum.

Figure 1: Francesco Guardi(?), *Two Women Carrying Vases*. Copy of lost studies by Giambattista Tiepolo for the frescoes of the Gallery of the Archbishop's Palace at Udine, c. 1726. Berlin First Sketchbook, Folio 8 recto. Pen and wash; 324 × 224 mm. Berlin-Dahlem, Staatliche Museen Preussischer Kulturbesitz, Kupferstichkabinett, 79 B 14.

Figure 2: Francesco Guardi(?), *The Meeting of Jacob and Esau*. Copy of a lost study by Giambattista Tiepolo for a fresco of the Gallery of the Archbishop's Palace at Udine, c. 1726. Berlin First Sketchbook, Folio 47 verso. Pen and wash; 324 × 224 mm. Berlin-Dahlem, Staatliche Museen Preussischer Kulturbesitz, Kupferstichkabinett, 79 B 14.

Figure 3: Giambattista Tiepolo, *Minerva, Nobility, and Cupid*. Here identified as a study for the ceiling of the Villa Loschi, near Vicenza, 1734. Pen and wash over pencil; 290 X 435 mm. Berlin-Dahlem, Staatliche Museen Preussischer Kulturbesitz, Kupferstichkabinett, 11570-343-1920.

Figure 4: Francesco Guardi, *Minerva, Nobility, and Cupid.* Copy of a study by Giambattista Tiepolo for the ceiling of the Villa Loschi near Vicenza, c. 1734 (cf. Fig. 3). Pen and wash; 236 × 366 mm. Berlin-Dahlem, Staatliche Museen Preussischer Kulturbesitz, Kupferstichkabinett, 9956.

Figure 5: Francesco Guardi, *Giudice*. Copy of a study by Giambattista
Tiepolo for the frescoes of the Villa Loschi near Vicenze, 1734. Pen and
wash; 283 X 188 mm. Berlin-Dahlem, Staatliche Museen Preussischer
Kulturbesitz, Kupferstichkabinett, 21957.

Figure 6: Francesco Guardi, *A Standing Man*. Copy of a lost study by
Giambattista Tiepolo for the frescoes of the Villa Loschi near Vicenze,
c. 1734. Pen and wash; 283 × 188 mm. Berlin-Dahlem, Staatliche Museen
Preussischer Kulturbesitz, Kupferstichkabinett, 21959.

Figure 7: Giambattista Tiepolo, *The Head of Anthony*. Study for the
Banquet fresco of the Palazzo Labia in Venice, c. 1744. Black and white
chalk on blue paper; 440 × 300 mm. Leningrad, State Hermitage Museum 35278.

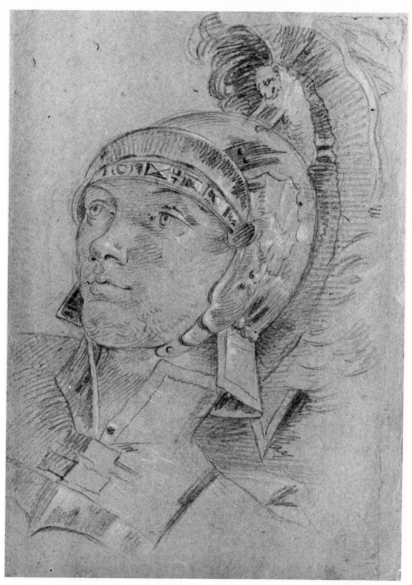

Figure 8: Domenico Tiepolo (or possibly Francesco Lorenzi), copy of
the study by Giambattista Tiepolo for the frescoes of the Palazzo Labia
in Venice, c. 1744 (cf. Fig. 7). Black and white chalk on blue paper;
300 × 210 mm. Private collection.

Figure 9: Giambattista Tiepolo, study for the head of a page, c. 1751—53.
Red and white chalk on blue paper; 250 X 170 mm. New York, Ian Woodner.

Figure 10: Lorenzo Tiepolo, a copy of the study by Giambattista Tiepolo
for the head of a page, c. 1753 (cf. Fig. 9). Red and white chalk on
blue paper; 325 × 200 mm. Würzburg, Martin von Wagner Museum (formerly).

Figure 11: Giambattista Tiepolo, *The Head of an Old Man*,
from the Owen-Savile Album, c. 1755. Pen and wash; 240 X 175 mm.
Saint-Brice-sous-Fôret, M. le Duc de Talleyrand.

Figure 12: Lorenzo Tiepolo, copy of a study by Giambattista, c. 1755
(cf. fig. 11). Red, black, and white chalk on blue paper; 309 × 217 mm.
Weimar, Schlossmuseum 1424.

Figure 1: *The Masquerade Ticket.*

Figure 2: *The Times.*

Figure 3: *The South Sea Scheme.*

Plate 4: *The Bathos, or Manner of Sinking in Sublime Paintings.*

Figure 1: Plate 37 *Jerusalem*. From the collection of Mr. and Mrs. Paul Mellon.

Figure 2: Plate 99 *Jerusalem*. From the collection of Mr. and Mrs. Paul Mellon.

Figure 1: Carlo Maratti, *Apollo and Daphne*. Brussels, Musée royale des beaux arts.

Figure 2: Paolo de Matteis, *Choice of Hercules*. Temple Newsam, near Leeds.

Figure 3: Nicolas Poussin, *The Death of Germanicus.*
Minneapolis, the Institute of Arts.

Figure 4: Nicolas Bernard Lépicié, *The Disembarkation of William the Conqueror in England.* Caen, Lycée Malherbe.

Figure 5: Rubens, *Quos Ego*—, sketch. Cambridge, Mass., Fogg Art Museum.

Figure 6: Poussin, *Coriolanus*. Les Andelys, Hôtel de Ville. Courtesy of Agraci.

La Nouvelle Héloïse:

La Répétition à la Deuxième Puissance

GODELIEVE MERCKEN-SPAAS

Réexaminer un roman comme *La Nouvelle Héloïse* n'est pas une tâche téméraire, même si la critique qui lui a déjà été consacrée semble avoir presque tari les sources de nouvelles analyses.[1] Il est axiomatique de dire que le nombre d'interprétations possibles d'une oeuvre d'art est inépuisable. Une re-lecture de chaque oeuvre à la lumière des progrès de la critique littéraire et de la pensée en général s'impose dès lors d'une façon permanente.

Le procédé narratif qui forme l'objet de cette étude est celui de la répétition. Tzvetan Todorov et Oswald Ducrot définissent la répétition comme un procédé rhétorique qui désigne "la reprise du même mot ou du même groupe de mots."[2] Pour Michael Riffaterre, la répétition entre dans la catégorie des procédés stylistiques qui supposent "une combinaison de valeur phonique et sémantique."[3] Selon Julia Kristeva, la répétition est essentiellement "une figure syntaxique."[4]

Si les auteurs mentionnés soulignent surtout l'aspect fonctionnel du procédé de répétition, Gilles Deleuze, dans son oeuvre *Différence et répétition*, examine le champ conceptuel du mot. Deleuze distingue deux espèces de répétitions: ". . . l'une d'exacti-

203

tude et de mécanisme, l'autre de sélection et de liberté."[5] "La première," écrit-il, "est une répétition nue, la dernière une répétition vêtue dont les masques, les déplacements sont les premiers, les derniers et les seuls éléments."[6]

Une étude du procédé de la répétition est particulièrement souhaitable pour *La Nouvelle Héloïse* qui, comme le titre l'indique, est gouvernée par ce principe. Les variations répétitives du motif d'Héloïse tout au long du récit ont été étudiées par David Anderson.[7] En plus de ces variations, la narration est tissée de doubles occurrences de certains processus ou thèmes, de reproductions de certaines actions ou idées. Les répétitions formées par ces doubles occurrences se composent de deux unités narratives ayant des éléments communs. Nous appelons "répétition" l'ensemble de ces deux occurrences dont la première est l'antécédent, la deuxième le conséquent.

Le présent travail se propose d'examiner la répétition à la lumière des développements récents du concept. Un tel examen se fait nécessairement selon deux perspectives, l'une sémantique, l'autre syntaxique. L'étude sera sémantique dans l'analyse des ressemblances, des différences et des oppositions entre les unités narratives. Elle sera syntaxique dans l'exploration des moyens d'enchaînement employés pour les relier.

Les répétitions qui forment le corps essentiel de cette étude sont celles qui se rapportent au couple central, Julie et Saint-Preux, les deux amants qui doivent renoncer à leurs amours. Les répétitions qui se rapportent à l'un des deux ou aux autres personnages, à Wolmar, mari de Julie, au père de Julie, à Edouard, ami de ce dernier, et à la servante Fanchon, seront étudiées en fonction des répétitions principales.

Donnons, à présent, un petit aperçu des répétitions les plus importantes du roman. Saint-Preux assumera par deux fois le rôle de précepteur, une première fois de Claire et de sa cousine Julie, dont il devient l'amant, une seconde fois de leurs enfants. Wolmar oblige Saint-Preux et Julie, devenue sa femme, à renouveler leur premier baiser en sa présence et au même endroit que jadis. Saint-Preux conduit son ancienne amante à la Meillerie, endroit où autrefois il donnait libre cours à sa passion. Il y a deux unions sexuelles. Il y a également deux unions symboliques, la première lors de l'inoculation volontaire de Saint-Preux quand Julie est atteinte de la petite vérole, la deuxième au moment de la mort de Julie par la confession d'amour de cette dernière. A deux occasions Fanchon et son ami Claude Anet ont besoin de l'intercession de Julie pour assurer leur union. La tâche d'intermédiaire est assumée deux fois, d'abord par Edouard qui essaie d'intervenir auprès du père en faveur des deux amants, ensuite par Wolmar, qui après la mort de Julie remet à Saint-Preux la confession d'amour de celle-ci. Et enfin, la scène de la mort de Julie est également sujette à répétition: "Il fallait que [Julie] ressuscitât," écrit Wolmar, "pour me donner l'horreur de la perdre une seconde fois" (p. 560). Si Wolmar doit passer deux fois par l'horreur de perdre Julie, Saint-Preux, lui, dans la deuxième union sexuelle, passe deux fois par l'espoir de la posséder, car Saint-Preux voit son espoir déçu lorsque la première tentative d'union échoue.

Pour la plupart des répétitions mentionnées, les deux occurrences sont très distantes l'une de l'autre. L'antécédent se trouve dans la première partie du livre, avant le départ de Saint-Preux, le conséquent dans la deuxième, après le retour de ce dernier. Deux répétitions font exception à cette répartition symétrique: les deux unions sexuelles et la double mort de Julie. Ces répétitions se trouvent respectivement au début et à la fin du roman. Elles forment deux pôles sémantiques qui ouvrent et ferment le récit: le pôle de la vie représenté par la seconde union sexuelle, qui a pour but de procréer, et le pôle de la mort indiqué par la double mort de Julie.

Les répétitions principales étudiées dans ce travail sont celles du baiser, de la scène à la Meillerie, des unions sexuelles et symboliques.

Afin de discerner le système qui gouverne cet ensemble, il est nécessaire d'examiner la transformation à l'oeuvre entre les deux termes de la répétition. Cette transformation peut être soit négative, soit positive. Elle est négative quand le conséquent représente un déclin, une dégradation de l'antécédent. Elle est positive quand le conséquent consiste en une amélioration de l'antécédent.

La répétition du baiser et celle de la scène à la Meillerie subissent une transformation négative. Dans l'antécédent de la première répétition, le baiser échangé dans le bosquet déclenche un désir si passionné que Julie se voit obligée d'éloigner d'elle Saint-Preux; dans le conséquent de cette même répétition, le baiser donné pour la deuxième fois "n'eut plus rien," écrit Julie, "de celui qui m'avait rendu le bosquet redoutable." De même, en ce qui concerne la double scène de la Meillerie, le conséquent est inférieur à l'antécédent. En effet, Saint-Preux évoque avec nostalgie la première occurrence où l'image seule de Julie faisait son bonheur. Par contre, quand la scène est répétée, et bien que Julie soit alors présente, Saint-Preux ne sent que l'interdit qui pèse sur son amour. Dans ces deux répétitions, le conséquent appauvrit donc l'antécédent. Pour cette raison, nous les appellerons des répétitions stériles.

Dans les répétitions que nous appellerons fécondes, la transformation qui a lieu dans le conséquent est positive. C'est ce qui se présente dans les deux unions sexuelles et les deux unions symboliques. La première union sexuelle est considérée par Julie comme une chute, elle a cédé à Saint-Preux par faiblesse. La deuxième union sexuelle représente un engagement de sa part, Julie cherche à réparer sa faute et à forcer le destin en s'unissant à Saint-Preux dans le but de devenir enceinte et de rendre leur union durable.

Une transformation semblable s'effectue pour la double union symbolique. Le première, celle de l'inoculation volontaire de Saint-Preux, est marquée par la temporalité et par l'interdit qui pèse sur l'amour; la deuxième, par contre, se caractérise par l'abolition de cette temporalité et de cet interdit, et par la certitude d'une union mystique et éternelle. De chacune de ces unions, Saint-Preux conserve le témoignage concret de l'amour: les marques de la petite vérole et la lettre écrite par Julie. Le conséquent dans les répétitions fécondes, contrairement à celui des répétitions stériles, apporte une amélioration de l'antécédent.

Examinons à présent selon quel procédé les unités narratives des répétitions stériles et fécondes s'enchaînent. Les deux éléments de la répétition stérile sont liés par une reprise de signifiants, de signes extérieurs derrière lesquels le signifié de l'antécédent ne peut guère être reconstitué. Le baiser est répété au même endroit, mais le sens en est perdu. Au cours de la scène à la Meillerie, Saint-Preux s'efforce d'évoquer les détails de ses premières visites: le chiffre gravé dans le rocher, la pierre où il s'asseyait pour contempler l'autre rive, mais tous ces indices ne sont que les débris d'un amour que Saint-Preux ne parvient plus à reconstituer. Alors que pendant la première visite à la Meillerie la nature était morne, mais l'amour heureux, à la deuxième visite, bien que tout soit en fleur, l'amour est interdit. Quoique transformés, les mêmes éléments restent présents lors des deux prises de conscience à la Meillerie, de même qu'un fond commun sert de cadre aux deux baisers. La continuité entre antécédent et conséquent est donc assurée par la reprise des relations externes de contiguïté.

Dans les répétitions fécondes, la continuité entre antécédent et conséquent n'est point fondée sur le principe de contiguïté, mais sur les principes de substitution et de ressemblance. Chaque union est construite selon la structure de l'échange: Saint-Preux, actant sujet dans les deux antécédents, devient actant objet dans les deux conséquents, tandis que Julie, actant objet dans les antécédents, devient actant sujet dans les conséquents. La première union sexuelle s'accomplit sur injonction de Saint-Preux, la deuxième sur invitation de Julie. Dans la première union symbolique, Saint-Preux déclare son amour en s'inoculant volontairement, dans la deuxième, Julie exprime son amour en écrivant la lettre. Chaque terme de la répétition ne représente donc qu'un moment du processus de l'échange qui ne sera complet qu'après permutation des rôles.

Le lien entre l'antécédent et le conséquent est également assuré par des rapports de ressemblance. Ceci est particulièrement frappant dans la double union symbolique. Le rapport qui unit les deux éléments de la première union, la petite vérole et les traces que celle-ci laisse sur le visage de Saint-Preux, est analogue au rapport qui existe entre les éléments de la deuxième, la mort de Julie et la lettre écrite par cette dernière. Il en est de même des aspects latents de ces unions: la première se caractérise par la temporalité et par une transcendance du moment esthétique vers un moment moral, la deuxième par l'espoir de l'éternité et par la transcendance du moment moral vers un moment mystique. Le rapport entre éléments est identique:

Première union			*Deuxième union*		
Traces	:	Maladie	::	Lettre	:	Mort
Transcendance morale	:	Temporalité	::	Transcendance mystique	:	Eternité

Les répétitions fécondes sont donc agencées soit selon un moyen de substitution interne, soit selon des rapports de ressemblance, tandis que les répétitions stériles sont ordonnées par la reproduction des relations externes de contiguïté.

Une telle distinction a été étudiée par Roman Jakobson dans le langage.[8] Selon Jakobson un sujet en amène un autre, soit par contiguïté, soit par ressemblance. Dans le premier cas nous pouvons parler de procédé métonymique, dans le deuxième de procédé métaphorique. Il est autorisé, comme dit Roland Barthes, de transposer la distinction de Jakobson à "d'autres systèmes de signification."[9] Si nous transposons cette distinction dans l'étude de la répétition, nous pouvons dire que l'enchaînement dans la répétition stérile se fait selon le mode métonymique, celui de la répétition féconde selon le mode métaphorique.

L'agencement des répétitions exprimé en termes des figures stylistiques métonymie et métaphore nous aide à mieux comprendre le système formé par l'ensemble des répétitions. Le rapport métonymique des répétitions stériles révèle une structure linéaire ou syntagmatique, c'est à dire une structure comme celle de la disposition d'un mot *après* l'autre dans la chaîne parlée ou écrite, tandis que le rapport métaphorique des répétitions fécondes révèle une structure paradigmatique, c'est à dire une structure comme celle de la substitution d'un mot *pour* l'autre. Les premières répétitions sont caractérisées par un aspect successif, les dernières par un aspect sélectif. Ce sont les répétitions fécondes qui représentent, d'après Deleuze, les vraies répétitions, car ce n'est qu'au niveau du paradigme que la sélection est possible.[10] La sélection représente l'essence d'une vraie répétition.

La distinction entre procédés métonymique et métaphorique souligne le mode d'agencement qui régit chacune des deux formes essentielles de la répétition, mais ceci ne revient pas à dire que la contiguïté est absente dans les répétitions fécondes ou la ressemblance dans les répétitions stériles. Les signifiants représentent le lien essentiel entre les unités de la répétition stérile, les signifiés entre celles de la répétition féconde. Dans ces dernières les détails extérieurs, quoique présents, n'assurent pas la continuité entre les occurrences d'une même répétition, mais ces détails relient une répétition à l'autre. C'est ainsi que la deuxième union sexuelle est reliée à la première union symbolique par la répétition des mêmes détails spatiaux et temporels: quand Saint-Preux entre dans la chambre de Julie atteinte de la petite vérole, il se souvient de leur deuxième union sexuelle: "Je traverse les mêmes lieux à la même heure." Par cet enchaînement le passage de l'union sexuelle à l'union symbolique est assurée. Ce même passage ressort de la position des répétitions secondaires qui se juxtaposent aux répétitions fécondes. La deuxième union sexuelle et la deuxième union symbolique sont toutes deux précédées par une demande d'intercession de la servante Fanchon et de Claude Anet. Elles sont toutes deux suivies d'une tentative de médiation: après la deuxième union sexuelle Edouard intervient auprès du père en faveur des deux amants; après la deuxième union symbolique Wolmar devient intermédiaire entre Julie et Saint-Preux. De même, l'absence du père se manifeste lors de la tentative d'union sexuelle et lors de la deuxième union symbolique. Il faut remarquer en outre que ces deux conséquents ont une même structure répétitive. Chacune s'accomplit pour ainsi dire en deux temps: la deuxième union sexuelle est différée, comme l'est l'acceptation de la mort de Julie.

Les répétitions fécondes s'emboîtent donc l'une dans l'autre grâce à des répétitions secondaires qui s'intercalent entre les termes de la répétition féconde. L'ensemble des répétitions fécondes forme ainsi un réseau complexe dont les éléments s'entrelacent. Cet agencement diffère considérablement de la structuration des répétitions stériles. Les conséquents de ces dernières se suivent l'un l'autre, comme l'ont fait leurs antécédents. Elles se juxtaposent donc d'une façon parallèle, structure stérile par excellence. Les répétitions fécondes, elles, s'entrecroisent de telle façon que les termes de l'union symbolique reprennent les termes de l'union sexuelle tout en les transposant à un niveau supérieur. La double union sexuelle est reprise par une double union symbolique et nous obtenons ainsi la répétition d'une répétition, c'est à dire une répétition à la deuxième puissance.

Cette double répétition n'est pas une reprise "d'éléments ou de parties extérieures successives, mais de totalités coexistant à différents niveaux ou degrés."[11] Dans la répétition féconde, les totalités internes sont reproduites et transformées; dans la répétition stérile, les détails externes sont répétés et les répétitions elles-mêmes juxtaposées. Utilisant une analogie tirée du domaine mathématique, nous pourrions dire que les répétitions stériles forment une série arithmétique où tous les éléments se suivent linéairement, et que les répétitions fécondes forment une série géométrique où les éléments sont élévés à une puissance; on n'ajoute pas chaque fois une nouvelle occurrence, mais on porte, comme dit Deleuze, "la première . . . à la nième puissance."[12]

La présence de ces deux structures différentes, ou, pour reprendre la distinction jakobsonnienne, la présence des deux procédés stylistiques de métonymie et de métaphore dans un même roman, crée une tension dramatique. L'opposition des deux procédés peut se relier à la présence de deux modes de pensée relevés fréquemment par les critiques, le rationalisme du dix-huitième siècle (Wolmar) et le romantisme qui s'annonce (Saint-Preux). Le premier mode correspondrait au procédé métonymique, aux répétitions stériles, le dernier au procédé métaphorique, aux répétitions fécondes.

Il y a dans le roman, non seulement co-existence des deux systèmes, mais également conflit entre ces systèmes. Ce conflit est concrétisé dans une des scènes finales du livre. Wolmar fait habiller Henriette, nièce de Julie, à l'image de cette dernière et la laisse imiter sa tante. Mais Wolmar lui-même offre la possibilité de la répétition féconde en mettant fin à ce mimétisme stérile.

Si nous réexaminons à présent les deux pôles sémantiques vie et mort qui, comme nous l'avons mentionné au début, délimitent l'espace des répétitions, il devient clair qu'au niveau de la structure profonde du récit on trouve un renversement de ces pôles. Le récit progresse apparemment du principe de vie (double union sexuelle) vers le principe de mort (mort de Julie). Mais le système de répétitions révèle une progression à partir de la stérilité vers la fécondité. Deux faits narratifs, parmi d'autres, concrétisent ce renversement: la deuxième union sexuelle entre Julie et Saint-Preux, symbole de vie, est suivie de la perte du fruit conçu de cette union. La double mort de Julie, au contraire, est suivie du don symbolique des enfants de Julie à Saint-Preux: "En vous laissant mes enfants," écrit-elle, "je m'en sépare avec moins de peine" (p. 566). La paternité qui a été reniée à Saint-Preux lui est maintenant donnée symboliquement.

En étudiant l'ensemble des répétitions stériles et fécondes dans le mouvement général du récit, nous pouvons faire ressortir une certaine dialectique de la répétition. Les trois phases de l'évolution de Julie correspondent à la progression de la répétition. Dans un premier moment dialectique, le moment esthétique de la jouissance, les unités narratives sont posées et contiennent une virtualité de répétition. Dans le moment dialectique de la moralité, la phase par laquelle Julie passe après son mariage, la répétition ne peut se réaliser et reste donc stérile. Dans le moment mystique, elle est non seulement possible, mais l'antécédent se voit transformé et transcendé, la répétition devient dès lors féconde.[13] Mais cette répétition n'est pas limitée aux procédés de la narration. La transposition de l'union sexuelle en union symbolique engendre une répétition à la deuxième puissance. La dimension nouvelle d'une transformation de cette double union en union mystique au-delà du récit crée une possibilité d'élévation à une puissance supérieure. D'autres répétitions dépassent les limites du récit: Saint-Preux, précepteur au départ, redeviendra précepteur dans un avenir immédiat, mais postérieur au roman.

Si la répétition s'inscrit dans un au-delà du récit, elle trouve aussi une origine antérieure au texte. Julie, la nouvelle Héloïse, reprend un thème qui se situe en dehors de la narration, dans la tradition littéraire: le thème d'Héloïse et Abélard. Le thème sera répété à nouveau par Henriette dont l'association avec Julie a déjà été soulignée. Henriette sera la nouvelle Julie, la nouvelle nouvelle Héloïse. La répétition féconde s'inscrit donc dans une série de termes dont le premier et le dernier se situent dans le passé et dans l'avenir.

Il devrait être clair à présent que la répétition dans *La Nouvelle Héloïse* est un procédé au moyen duquel un système de significations est créé. Les répétitions ne forment pas simplement une chaîne de syntagmes narratifs, mais créent aussi un réseau paradigmatique grâce à la substitution sélective s'opérant dans les conséquents. Elles sont agencées, soit selon un procédé métonymique, soit selon un procédé métaphorique. Les unes se succèdent, les autres s'entrelacent. En faisant converger ces deux modes de pensée dans une seule oeuvre littéraire, l'auteur concrétise l'effort de l'être humain pour vaincre sa stérilité. Le texte narratif devient ainsi lui-même une répétition féconde de cet effort humain et universel en le transposant dans un univers littéraire.[14]

NOTES

1 Jean-Jacques Rousseau, *Julie ou la Nouvelle Héloïse* (Paris: Garnier-Flammarion, 1967). Les numéros de page sans indication de source renvoient à cette édition.

2 Oswald Ducrot et Tzvetan Todorov, *Dictionnaire encyclopédique des sciences du langage* (Paris: Seuil, 1972), p. 354.

3 Michael Riffaterre, *Essais de stylistique structurale* (Paris: Flammarion, 1971), p. 60.

4 Julia Kristeva, Σημειωτική: *Recherches pour une sémanalyse* (Paris: Seuil, 1969), p. 230.

5 Gilles Deleuze, *Différence et répétition* (Paris: Presses universitaires de France, 1968), p. 368.

6 Deleuze, p. 368.

7 David L. Anderson, "Aspects of Motif in *La Nouvelle Héloïse,*" *Studies on Voltaire and the Eighteenth Century*, 44 (1972), 25–72.

8 Roman Jakobson, "Deux aspects du langage et deux types d'aphasie," *Les Temps modernes*, 17 (1962), 853–80.

9 Roland Barthes, "Éléments de sémiologie," *Communications*, 4 (1964), 116.

10 Deleuze, p. 368.

11 Deleuze, p. 367.

12 Deleuze, p. 8.

13 Cf. Søren Kierkegaard, *La Répétition.*

14 La distinction métaphore/métonymie ou fécondité/stérilité peut être retrouvée au niveau stylistique. Cette hypothèse forme le sujet d'une recherche en cours.

Justine, *Or, The Vicious Circle*

NANCY K. MILLER

I don't know whether we must burn Sade; I do know that it is difficult to approach his work without getting burned: any literary analysis runs the risk of betraying Sadian *écriture,* of neutralizing what is meant to be violation, of bridging the gap where there is meant to be *rupture.* The difficulty, of course, lies in the coincidence of sex and text: inevitably turned on or turned off, analysts, in the main, tend to treat one *problématique* at the expense of the other.[1] Aware of the danger, and without seeking to put out the fire, I would like to propose a reading of one of Sade's novels, confronting simultaneously sexuality and textuality.

I have chosen *Justine, ou les malheurs de la vertu,*[2] neither the original nor the ultimate version, but the second variant which has provoked both extreme distaste: "C'est une sorte de conte philosophique dans lequel l'héroïne est caricaturée franchement, et franchement invraisemblable;"[3] "Sade a écrit là sa plus mauvaise oeuvre, la seule vulgaire;"[4] and boundless admiration: "L'oeuvre de Sade sans doute la plus complète et la plus parfaite, parce qu'en allant jusqu'au bout de sa conviction et de son génie, le philosophe-poète y reste maître de son imagination, de son coeur, mais d'abord de son art."[5] This polarized reaction (a perfect homology to Sade's own *esprit de contradiction)* is symptomatic of the

215

double and very literary bind in which Justine II places her readers. Leaving to one side the problem of esthetic *value*, however, but respecting both the protocol of consumption encoded in the text and its status as the product of a genre, I shall try to expose the *text* of the dilemma, the reader's—and the critic's—trap.

Justine apparently obeys the conventions of fictional organization as they prevail in the eighteenth-century novel: a first-person account of suffering virtue. And not any virtue, but that eminently popular and vulnerable commodity, exemplary femininity via the metonymy of virginity. From the beginning, however, the reader can anticipate not only *Perversion* with a capital "P" as Sollers defines it, "la pensée théorique elle-même,"[6] but a concretization of the phenomenon by a *conversion*[7] of establishment values, where positivity is marked with a negative sign, and negativity with a positive one.

The title itself serves as the first "signpost" directing the calvary to come; and the English translation, *Justine or Good Conduct Well Chastised,* points even more clearly to the reversal of canonical and positive itineraries, the sagas of virtue well rewarded. The dedication explicitly states the author's preference for literary revalorization: "Le dessein de ce roman (pas si roman que l'on croirait) est nouveau sans doute; l'ascendant de la Vertu sur le Vice, la récompense du bien, la punition du mal, voilà la marche ordinaire de tous les ouvrages de cette espèce; ne devrait-on pas en être rebattu?"[8]

However, if the byway down which the reader is then invited to travel is characterized as "une route peu frayée jusqu'à présent,"[9] there is familiar and comforting compensation promised for any hardships incurred along the way: "l'une des plus sublimes leçons de morale que l'homme ait encore reçues."[10] The dedication thus *officially* salutes the reigning ideology while preparing the reader for a renewal of its dominant cliché. This double stance which involves co-opting a structure designed to support other values, is the key to this version of *Justine.* As *Shamela* mocks *Pamela, Justine* subverts every quest for happiness undertaken by a virginal heroine in the fictional universe of the eighteenth-century novel, although it is a parody that elicits no laughter.

The novel opens with the all-purpose eighteenth-century celebration of the truth as guiding light, and the reader's indulgence is requested for the exposure of the "situations quelquefois un peu fortes,"[11] that love for truth requires. Yet it is not difficult to predict that verisimilitude, as Genette has defined it, "le principe formel de respect de la norme, c'est-à-dire l'existence d'un rapport d'implication entre la conduite particulière attribuée à tel personnage, et telle maxime générale implicite et reçue,"[12] will suffer in the process of illumination. It is a rule of thumb that authenticity serves as license to mutilate the maxim, to promulgate the implausible and/or unacceptable. In the eighteenth-century novel, "fact" is often stranger than fiction.

The opposition of Vice to Virtue is first concretized in the characters of Justine and Juliette; as the title of the novel indicates, it is Justine's destiny that has been granted primacy. Nonetheless, Juliette's function is crucial to the structure of the novel; not merely as the dark-haired vicious foil to Justine's blond virtue, but as a point of narrative suture: Juliette solicits Justine's tale of woe. Juliette's dizzying rise, the author informs us, begins with the successive and successful exchange of her "pristine fruits." [13] Hyperbolic courtesan, she sleeps her way to the top. Justine, on the other hand, like the virtuous heroine of the sentimental novel, is mortified by and rejects the prospect of such prosperity attained at the cost of purity. It is her misfortune that poverty does not guarantee integrity: it is difficult to remain poor and honest, Pamela notwithstanding.

It has been said that in eighteenth-century fiction, chastity attracts rape as the sacred invites sacrilege.[14] And what figure is more vulnerable to sexual catastrophe than a destitute, friendless, virginal and virtuous orphan? Justine is indeed marked for disaster: "Elle n'avait qu'une ingénuité, une candeur qui devaient la faire tomber dans bien des pièges."[15] Like Candide, that other innocent abroad, Justine's physiognomy matches her soul. She looks the part she is to play: "un air de vierge,"[16] corroborated by the appropriate material complements—the most beautiful blond hair, big blue eyes and the loveliest complexion. Every detail of the portrait is a cliché, which means that Justine is introduced to the reader as a type of feminine perfection. Moreover, if the accumulation of superlative attributes is a sure sign of type-casting, the presence of an extra-textual model is confirmed by the pictorial code that concludes the portrait: "Voilà l'esquisse de cette cadette charmante, dont les grâces naïves et les traits délicats sont au-dessus de nos pinceaux."[17] Justine defies depiction and the completion of the sketch is left to the reader's imagination.

Similarly, Voltaire, in a more blatant acknowledgement of the titillating powers of the artist's brush, withdraws at the last moment in his portrait of Agnès Sorel in La Pucelle: "Mais la vertu qu'on nomme bienséance/Vient arrêter mes pinceaux trop hardis."[18] But Voltaire's heroines belong to another type of femininity; they have attributes of availability corresponding to what we might call the code of woman as fruit. Candide's beloved Cunégonde is "haute en couleur, fraîche, grasse, appétissante,"[19] the Pucelle herself, equally healthy, shares those tasty qualities, although they are metonymically assigned to her mouth: "Vive en sa couleur/Appétissante et fraîche par merveille."[20]

Justine's source of attraction comes, on the contrary, not from her ripeness (after all she is only twelve years old at the start) but from her greenness. Or to choose a less gustatory metaphor from the catalogue of descriptive clichés of femininity, she is the bud and not the rose. Her fragility, her delicacy, the essence of positive femininity in the eighteenth-century novel, provide the measure of her potential for suffering: she is not robust enough for comedy. The occasion of Justine's first trial, the one with which her narrative opens, clearly establishes the pathetic-erotic pattern of her trials to come. Confronted with the sexual imperative, Justine adopts the position of the victim and pleads for mercy on her knees, seeking generosity from her tormentor: "Soyez assez généreux pour me secourir sans exiger de moi ce qui me coûte assez pour vous offrir plutôt ma vie que de m'y soumettre."[21] Like the sentimental heroine, Justine prefers death to dishonor. Such is not her destiny, however; consistently she is condemned to that fate worse than death.

In this first round, Justine is saved from the fatal sacrifice and is left technically pure, but the significance of the initiation is not lost on her: "Il semblait que l'Etre suprême voulût, dans cette première circonstance de ma vie, imprimer à jamais en moi toute l'horreur que je devais avoir pour un genre de crime d'où devait naître l'affluence des maux dont j'étais menacée."[22] Within the first scene of sexual confrontation, the fundamental paradigm is established: as a victim, Justine's unique means of self-defense consists of a posture of supplication; the supervising agent of her destiny is in heaven, and all is not right with the world.

From the beginning, Justine is concerned with assuring the reader as to the authenticity of her suffering and alienation: "J'étais loin de vouloir agir, c'était beaucoup de me prêter: mes remords n'en sont pas éteints. . . ."[23] Thus, in conformity with the role of the victim, Justine submits, protests and regrets. Yet there are those who find complicity, or at least an index of ambiguity in her claims to pure disgust. Another case of the lady protesting too much. While this may be true of Cunégonde, who, it has been noted,[24] admires the skintone of her very own Bulgarian captain, thus casting some doubt on the resonance of her lamentations, Justine is less oblique. She in fact admits, early in her history, to an overwhelming attraction for the Comte de Bressac: "Rien au monde ne pouvait éteindre cette passion naissante, et si le comte m'eût demandé ma vie, je la lui aurais sacrifiée mille fois."[25] These irresistible feelings constitute the one and only error in her accounting: "la seule faute involontaire que j'aie à me reprocher."[26] But "triste rebut de la nature entière," Justine's love remains unrequited; her sex, for once, is a deterrent.

The problem posed by Justine's version of the facts, it seems to me, is less a function of psychological reliability than narrational liability. As subject and object of a scatalogical destiny, Justine must account for the repertory of sexual experiments and experiences in which she is a reluctant participant. Moreover, since the

Sadian erotic involves at least as much sexual discourse as sexual intercourse, Justine's role as narrator compels her to relay and relate to the reader the text of her oppression—the libertine's credo. This results in what some consider an insurmountable implausibility: "Les arguments philosophiques du sadisme, beaucoup plus développés que dans la première version sont sans vraisemblance dans la bouche de la victime qui les retranscrit."[27]

Adopting an intertextual perspective, I would suggest that this aspect of verisimilitude is part of a larger problem, and one that afflicts the first-person narrators of what are essentially briefs designed to elicit both sympathy and salvation. A case in point is that victim with impeccable credentials, Diderot's *religieuse,* Suzanne Simonin. Condemned to a "life-style" fundamentally abhorrent to her sense of self, in order to authenticate her victim status, to reinscribe her martyrdom, Suzanne relates in glowing detail both the words and deeds responsible for her misery. On any page taken at random, the reader finds the "je" representing her voice at the service of the oppressive "on."

Moreover, in order for the reader's compassion to be sustained in the face of what is essentially the same old story, pathos-producing devices must be varied. Therefore, to balance self-pity, self-congratulatory remarks, tinged with complacency, sporadically punctuate these texts. They serve to revalorize the victim in the reader's eye (the "I was meant for better things" syndrome) and should not be interpreted as a sign of complicity. For example, while Justine is working as Gernande's medical assistant, she boasts about her tactics: "Cependant j'avais trouvé le secret de me mettre on ne saurait mieux dans l'esprit de cet homme: il avouait naturellement que peu de femmes lui avaient tant plu. J'acquis de là des droits à sa confiance, dont je ne profitai que pour servir ma maîtresse."[28] The rationale for ingratiation is assigned to the laudable motive of rescuing a fellow victim; and through the use of indirect discourse the burden of self-aggrandizement is displaced onto another.

Still, Justine does admit to knowledge of the dynamics of feminine wiles which she generally claims to ignore or despise:

indeed, the very confident "naturellement" is a dead giveaway that she understands the dialectic of seduction. Yet does that make her less of a victim and more to the point, does it undermine her credibility as reporter at the scene of the crime? We might consider Suzanne's last words as she wonders whether *her* M. de Corville will think that she has addressed herself to his vice rather than to his charity: "Cette réflexion m'inquiète. En vérité il aurait bien tort de m'imputer personellement un instinct propre à tout mon sexe. Je suis une femme, peut-être un peu coquette, que sais-je? Mais c'est naturellement et sans artifice."[29] It is my feeling that a measure of ambiguity is always encoded in the discourse of a virtuous and female narrator, as though sexual availability were always lurking just beneath the pristine surface. It is a *topos* in the representation of femininity and thus not a pertinent sign.

The sexual reliability of narrative voice, however, is only one area of critical attack on Justine's believability as a character. Justine has often been accused of mental and physical retardation: "Whatever befalls her, Justine is unprepared for it, experience teaches her nothing, her soul remains ignorant, her body more ignorant still."[30] But this sort of criticism proceeds from the assumption that Justine is a character with the potential for development associated with the traditional psychological novel, where according to the famous Jamesian formulation, character determines incident and incident illustrates character in an interlocking system of exchange. Justine above all must carry the weight of the author's counter-demonstration as articulated in the dedication. From the title she is presented as suffering virtue itself. Like Candide whose name is given as an equivalent to optimism, and whose trials and tribulations serve to deliver a message, rather than to motivate a "rounded" character, Justine's suffering is designed not to enhance her, but to support the system in which she circulates.

However, even Candide as character and tale is narrated by a voice that can comfortably arrange the events of the narrative to support his case. So to return to a point made earlier in another perspective, the problem in Sade's text is to close the credibility gap between subject and object of narration, to justify the *instance* of narration. By this I mean that a situation must be created from which this kind of narration could plausibly be generated. Thus for Justine to speak for herself, and at length, a captive is granted an audience. Motivated by the extraordinary posture in which she finds herself, Justine, like Scheherazade, is given one night to tell her story. My comparison with that story-teller is no less motivated.

I suggest that Sade's novel belongs to that form of literary production defined by Todorov in his essay "Les hommes-récits."[31] In this kind of literature (exemplified by the *A Thousand and One Nights)*, action is privileged at the expense of character, what counts is the verb and not the subject (or in our case, the object) of the verb. In such an a-psychological mode, a character is no more than his own story, an "homme-récit," he is what happens. As a result, tautology replaces causality[32] : thus, Justine is a victim because she is victimized; she is victimized because she is a victim. If to understand a character, one adopts Genette's formulation, "comprendre la conduite d'un personnage, c'est pouvoir la référer à une maxime admise,"[33] then there is only one maxim possible that can account for Justine in etiological terms, and it is a uniquely Sadian one: "Le devoir d'une victime est de se prêter."[34]

But the added dimension to Justine's suffering as the exemplary victim in a universe where eros is inseparable from logos, is that she must also record and play-back. In this sense, more like Scheherazade than Suzanne, Justine's life is defined and measured solely by what she tells—as a "femme-récit," her life ends when there is nothing more to tell. Nevertheless, despite the potential for the infinite prolongation of the process of narration that characterizes a mode of production where "le récit égale la vie; l'absence de récit la mort,"[35] at some point there is an ending.

Indeed, although Justine is denied the satisfaction of even a superficial linear progression—she goes in circles despite her desire to reach the south of France, and at the end of practically every adventure finds herself back where she started with the only and minimal difference that time has passed and things are worse—the fiction of her wanderings is at last brought to a close. And to my mind, the final installment of the trials of suffering virtue crystallizes the problems of narrativity and credibility in the text as I have sketched them out until this point. My hypothesis is that at the end of the novel, the disparity between the code and the message, the mimesis of the quest and its subversion, is unequivocally confirmed.

It is Saint-Florent, Justine's first violator, who orchestrates Justine's last torture, her final incarnation as hyperbolic victim. Justine warns her listeners that this experience represents the summit in the hierarchy of horror: "Oh! madame, jamais rien de pareil n'avait encore souillé ma vue, et quelles que soient mes descriptions antérieures, ceci surpassait tout ce que j'ai pu peindre, comme l'aigle impérieux l'emporte sur la colombe."[36] The neoclassical comparison and the cliché of narration as depiction mark the discrepancy between Justine subject of discourse and Thérèse object of violation. Moreover, the temporary pause in transmission, the acknowledged shifting of gears, so to speak, serves as a signal to the reader to be on the alert, and creates a sense of progress in Justine's unhappy pilgrimage.

The scene begins with the familiar permutations of postures available to four libertine men and one female victim; nothing unusual for Justine. What is new is the preparation for immolation that she must undergo to satisfy Saint-Florent, whose specialty consists in deflowering virgins. He requires that Justine be altered to reproduce the measurements of her virginal dimensions. She is to be sewn up. Despite her vast experience, Justine is puzzled, confused by the obscurity of the message: "Je n'entendais pas cette expression: une cruelle expérience m'en découvrit bientôt le sens."[37]

This particular variant of torture has elicited critical attention: for Roland Barthes,[38] sewing represents a secondary castration and a desexualization; for Michael Riffaterre, reading Sade with Barthes, sewing, in this context, is a "purely verbal scandal."[39] It seems to me, beyond the merits of either analysis, that this extraordinary needlework confirms the fundamental circularity of the text. What I am suggesting is that the fact of Justine's being sewn up, restored to her virginal space, just as previously her wounds were healed to leave no traces, means that her story as *souffre-douleur* is potentially endless, despite the conclusion of the novel, beyond the terminus of the printed page. Curiously, this also means that in the final analysis, Justine's virginity can be reproduced as artificially as Juliette's was at the beginning of her career—which undermines, once again, the sanctity of virginity— and to return to another point of departure, the reader may recall that Justine's first venture on the job-market was to approach her mother's seamstress.

In any event, after the relation of this final torture, Justine is recognized and rescued by Juliette and M. de Corville. In the comfort of home, through tender loving care, Justine is nursed back to health and restored to her edenic before. All traces of former misery are erased. Justine, however, is not made for happiness; though more fortunate than Cunégonde in that her suffering is not engraved on her face, she lacks the strength to cultivate a garden. But before she has time to pine away, lightning strikes, in a final impalement. Horror-stricken, Juliette interprets Justine's death as a divine warning, and promptly embarks on a career of compensatory piety. Like Cécile at the end of the *Liaisons dangereuses,* she enters a Carmelite order, and like the Princesse de Clèves, she becomes a legend in her own time.

Finally, the very last paragraph of the novel takes up the terms of the dedication, evoking the tears shed over the misfortunes of virtue, apologizing again for the "heavy brushstrokes,"[40] and praising the mysteries of divine providence and its ultimate rewards. The novel stops having come full circle. But then the obvious question: what kind of circle has been described? Which brings me at last to my title and conclusion, the circle of my own text.

While the vicious circle is an expression of common parlance, a glance at the dictionary is still informative. One finds three definitions in Webster's Third New International; all three pertain to different aspects of the novel. The first, "a chain of circumstances constituting a situation in which the process of solving one difficulty creates a new problem involving increased difficulty in the original situation," applies to the automatic conversion process that controls Justine's interaction: she asks for help and is betrayed by her protector, she extends a helping hand and is victimized by her beneficiary—whatever she does, she makes matters worse. The third, "a chain of abnormal processes in which a primary disorder leads to a second which in turn aggravates the first one," characterizes the chain reaction of disasters set in motion by her first sexual encounter (we might recall here Justine's evaluation of that abnormality: "un genre de crime *d'où devait naître* l'affluence des maux dont j'étais menacée.")[41] The second, "an argument or definition that is valueless because it overtly or covertly assumes as true something which is to be proved or defined," describes the author's discourse as demonstrated by the identity of his assumptions and conclusions.

Indeed, when as readers we arrive at the end of the road, and we measure the distance traveled, we realize that like Justine we have gone around in circles.[42] The narrative has ended; there seems to have been a story with a beginning, a middle and an end, an innocent heroine, villains, an unfortunate destiny and a moral—in other words structural conformity with the eighteenth century's house of fiction. And the end of the novel is a model of literary construction: just as the beginning of Justine's suffering is marked by the separation of the two sisters, an end to suffering is brought about by their reunion. Moreover, the apparent reversal of the relation of their trajectories in which Justine's descent had been opposed to Juliette's rise, provides the novel with the moral ending as promised: Justine's death engenders Juliette's conversion.

However, if a disfiguring death blow dealt by a divine hand, or the nunnery, as the consequences of contact with illicit sexuality, are narrative clichés perfectly consistent with the verisimilitude of the eighteenth-century novel, mimesis is subverted by *conversion:* Justine is given the punishment the ideology of the period would have visited on Juliette, and Juliette is given the privilege of a retreat from the world that would have suited Justine. To return to the English title, it is indeed a case of good conduct well chastised.

Thus if it is true, as Todorov points out,[43] that we weep when we read *Manon Lescaut,* but not *A Thousand and One Nights,* by the same token, despite the author's confidence that we have shed tears upon hearing of virtue's miseries, we have not. And of course, we are not meant to. Despite the intertextual connections between Justine and related victims of suffering virtue cited earlier, there is a founding difference at work. As a result, one cannot take Justine's response to the extended rape that constitutes her life span with the seriousness, say, of Clarissa's. On the other hand, if the reader smiles when Agnès Sorel sighs, "C'est donc en vain que l'on fait ce qu'on peut/N'est pas toujours femme de bien qui veut,"[44] or smirks when Cunégonde repeats her leitmotif of violation, Justine's lamentations do not provoke laughter. Unlike Cunégonde and Agnès Sorel, sisters in serial violation, Justine is resolutely closed to humor. Ultimately Justine is neither a comic nor a tragic heroine; she is the object of a verb used to trap the reader and lure him into Sade's world.

Under the Sadian sign of perversion, the linear logic of before/ after, now/then, why/because, the logic of memoir as history, proves to be vicious. What Justine as narrator registered as chronology was in fact stasis and progression repetition. Justine's text is but a pretext for a sexual combinatory whose permutations are infinite.[45] It is not surprising, then, that Justine and Juliette should be revived for a final version a few years later. Vicious circle where circle of virtue spirals into circle of vice, there is no way or reason to stop until the author or his reader is exhausted.

N O T E S

1 Michael Riffaterre takes a similar point of departure in his article "Sade, or Text as Fantasy," *Diacritics,* 2 (1972), 2–9; concluding, however, that since Sade's "writing differs in no way from *poetic* language" (9; emphasis added), linguistic analysis provides the only pertinent metalanguage.

2 All references to this text are drawn from the Union Générale d'Éditions (Paris, 1969) edition.

3 Henri Coulet, "La Vie intérieure dans *Justine*," in the Acts of the Aix Colloquium on Sade, ed. Jean Fabre, *Le Marquis de Sade* (Paris: Armand Colin, 1968), p. 92.

4 Henri Coulet, *Le Roman jusqu'à la Révolution* (New York: McGraw-Hill–Armand Colin, 1967), p. 488.

5 Jean Fabre, "Sade et le roman noir," in *Le Marquis de Sade*, p. 273.

6 Philippe Sollers, "Sade dans le texte," *L'Ecriture et l'expérience des limites* (Paris: Seuil, 1968), p. 52.

7 Sollers speaks of a "reversal" performed upon our definitions of madness and sanity, ibid., pp. 52–53.

8 *Justine*, p. 7.

9 Ibid., p. 10.

10 Ibid.

11 Ibid., p. 14.

12 Gerard Genette, "Vraisemblance et motivation," *Figures II* (Paris: Seuil, 1969), p. 74.

13 *Justine, or Good Conduct Well Chastised*, trans. Richard Seaver and Austryn Wainhouse (New York: Grove Press, 1966), p. 464.

14 Pierre Fauchery, *La Destinée féminine dans le roman européen du dix-huitième siècle* (Paris: Armand Colin, 1972), p. 317.

15 *Justine*, p. 15.

16 Ibid., p. 16.

17 Ibid. For a theoretical discussion of the pictorial code, see Roland Barthes "Le Modèle de la peinture," in *S/Z* (Paris: Seuil, 1970), pp. 61–62.

18 In *Oeuvres complètes,* vol. IX (Paris, 1819), p. 19.

19 *Candide*, in *Romans et contes* (Paris: Garnier-Flammarion, 1966), p. 179. Cited by Jean Sareil in his *Essai sur Candide* (Geneva: Droz, 1967), with the comment that this purely physical description "explique son funeste pouvoir d'attraction" (p. 72).

20 *La Pucelle*, p. 3l.

21 *Justine*, p. 30.

22 Ibid., p. 31.

23 Ibid.

24 Sareil, *Essai sur Candide*, p. 73.

25 *Justine*, p. 71.

26 Ibid.

27 Henri Coulet, *Le Roman jusqu'à la Révolution*, p. 488.

28 *Justine*, p. 213.

29 *La Religieuse* (Paris: Armand Colin, 1961), p. 178.

30 Jean Paulhan, "The Marquis de Sade and His Accomplice," in *The Marquis de Sade* (New York: Grove Press, 1965), p. 13.

31 Tzvetan Todorov, "Les Hommes-récits," *Poétique de la prose* (Paris: Seuil, 1971), pp. 78–91.

32 "Un trait de caractère n'est pas simplement la cause d'une action, ni simplement son effet: il est les deux à la fois, tout comme l'action. X tue sa femme parce qu'il est cruel; mais il est cruel parce qu'il tue sa femme" (pp. 80–81).

33 "Vraisemblance et motivation," p. 75.

34 *Juliette* (Paris: Pauvert, 1969), V, 79, cited by Jean Biou, in "Deux oeuvres complémentaires: *Les Liaisons dangereuses* et *Juliette*," Fabre, ed., *Le Marquis de Sade*, pp. 103–14.

35 Todorov, "Les Hommes-récits," p. 86.

36 *Justine*, p. 302.

37 Ibid., p. 305. I have discussed at length the implications of this scene in my unpublished doctoral dissertation, "Gender and Genre: An Analysis of Literary Femininity," Columbia University, 1974.

38 *Sade, Fourier, Loyola* (Paris: Seuil, 1971), pp. 172–73.

39 "Sade, or text as fantasy," p. 5.

40 *Justine, or Good Conduct Well Chastised*, p. 743.

41 *Justine*, p. 31, emphasis added.

42 For a discussion of spatial circularity in Sade, I refer the reader to Jean-Jacques Brochier's excellent article "La Circularité de l'espace," Fabre, ed., *Le Marquis de Sade*, pp. 717–84.

43 Todorov, "Les Hommes-récits," p. 80.

44 *La Pucelle*, p. 173.

45 Curiously, although Mario Praz defends the opposite point of view ("The cycle of possible chemical disaggregations which constitute . . . [the libertine's] . . . tortures is soon exhausted, because as Proust remarks, nothing is more limited than pleasure and vice."), he is seduced nonetheless by the metaphor of the vicious circle: "and—to make a play on words—it may be said that the vicious man moves always in the same vicious circle" (*The Romantic Agony* [Cleveland: Meridian Books, 1968], p. 105).

Sensible Words: Linguistic Theory in Late Seventeenth-Century England

MURRAY COHEN

It is a truth critically acknowledged that every literary work is "about language." What this has come to mean is that words themselves are the literary essence, that form is meaningful and style is character. But when Restoration and eighteenth-century authors write about language, they are as interested in elementary linguistic features as they are in such literary qualities as form and style. When Dryden promotes an English language which has a "certain measure" or when he recommends rhyme, first, for the "help it brings to the memory" and, second, for its ability to "bound and circumscribe the fancy . . . and bring forth the richest and clearest thoughts,"[1] he is claiming that literary language must be systematic and that its system determines how and what the mind thinks. When, in *A Tale of a Tub*, Peter obeys the letter of his father's will by picking at its actual letters or when Walter Shandy "mends" Erasmus by using his penknife to "mar" a letter, what is being satirized is the submission of otherwise uncon- strained will to the physical elements, the literally visible parts, of written authority. When Pope's Belinda confuses her public and her pubic hairs, because she exaggerates a metaphoric analogy into a necessary identity, then the reader is alerted to what linguistic events—like metaphor, rhyme, punning—do to the mind. Restoration and eighteenth-century literature abounds in such linguistic-based events—in personified tautology, dialect, convention, and allusion; in language projects and epistles—yet the obvious sources of this literary interest in linguistics, the linguistic texts of the period, have neither been adequately collected nor interpreted in a literary context.

If Restoration and eighteenth-century literature is, in important ways, "about linguistics," then we need to know the kinds and assumptions of contemporary linguistic texts. In this paper, I survey the types and trends of linguistic work in the second half of the seventeenth century and give special emphasis to the most popular and familiar of those texts, that is, to books for the grammar schools.

Some of the texts have been cited in surveys by both historical linguists interested in grammatical categories, pronunciation, rhetoric, or universal languages, and intellectual historians arguing for a dominant and controlling principle—anti-Ciceronianism, scientific method, or utilitarianism.[2] Although we are likely to be more familiar with the historians of ideas since they, like most of us, are "literary" types, I want to emphasize that both groups tend to be equally, though differently, provincial in their studies. The historical linguists too often accept categories which aren't real. They write "whole" books on a part of a system, and such vertical views of history inevitably sacrifice writers and their works to progressive principles. For example, Ian Michael's important work, *English Grammatical Categories,* does not get close enough to the texts he studies because of his self-imposed method of organizing his material. He dismisses the inconsistencies within individual grammars by choosing "to follow one consistent practice [that is, his own descriptive outline] rather than to attempt in each case a judgment about the author's intentions" (202). Michael claims that English grammarians, unlike their French counterparts, were not deeply interested in the philosophy of language. In fact, their essential interests were the theological origins and theoretical implications of their proposals, and the inconsistencies within their systems indicate the complexity of the issues they accepted as relevant to grammar. The place of linguistic texts in the works of the intellectual historians is equally narrow. In the works of Croll, Williamson, Jones, and Adolph, linguistic texts are used as sources of evidence supporting grander theoretical constructs. Such a method tends to turn particular writers into witnesses and deprives them of a coherent identity independent of the particular trial being conducted. Once we elevate "minor" texts from footnotes and lists, we see that much of what is important in each linguistic text emerges from looking at the sequence of its argument and its printed presentation.

If we avoid the methodological constraints of intellectual history and historical linguistics, we immediately recognize two important qualities of seventeenth-century linguistic texts. First, by not automatically giving a linguistic work an ideological, categorical, or institutional referent, we see that one of the most important linguistic issues of the period is the nature of signification itself. What education tracts, discussions of sermon style, proposals for universal language, tables of possible sounds, and word lists share is concern for the interrelatedness of words, objects, and minds. Second, we more readily recognize the variety of interests represented in every text and the significant diversity of works by individual linguists. We repeatedly find combined in single texts or in works by a single writer presentations of grammar, pronunciation, characters, shorthand systems, dictionaries, general sign systems, and rhetoric.

In addition to the theoretical emphasis and practical inclusiveness in these texts and authors, there is pride and ambition. Terms like "Royal," "Universal," "New," and "Real," which appear frequently in the title pages of these works, advertize their originality, openness, and presumption.[3] Although many of the writers are grammar school masters, provincial scholars who boldly offer the idea of a lifetime or compile the lessons of a life's work, they all agree that linguistics touches on every pertinent issue. In their texts they try to represent characters and sounds as the clear and distinct sources of meaning and to arrange words to reveal the structure of mind and the structure of reality. Those goals aren't all: if the physical elements of words and their orderly arrangement allow us to know not only what the world is but how we know it, then the English language will, like other languages, correspond to other ideas of order. Once the language is thus exalted it can compete politically and culturally with other languages and, perhaps, redeem the curse of Babel.

To destroy the Tower of Babel, God dispersed the builders and confounded their speech; to "make a new name for themselves," English grammarians collected the parts of their language and systematized their speech. God's triumph had been so complete, particularly in England, that the grammarians were forced to treat English as if it were a foreign language. This is a striking quality of both grammars which try to make English conform to Latin and grammars which offer another more universal model. In either case, their goal is organization and clarification of a "new" language. Every element of language is explained—the shapes of letters, the number and kinds of sounds, the formation of the plural, the use of interjections. In effect, the grammarians discover English as a language and go to work on its materials, origins, forms, and functions. Disagreements among the grammarians have to do principally with systems of the parts of speech; but examples of their inconsistency, incompleteness, instability, and diversity indicate a lively struggle with the structure of language, or, more precisely, with the relationship between reality and language.[4] And the relationship between language and reality, they agree, must be sought in the physical parts of writing and speech, that is, in letters and sounds.

Whether seventeenth-century English grammars are explicitly organized according to the materials of language—letters, syllables, words, and sentences—or to its processes—orthography, pronunciation, etymology, syntax, and prosody—practically all of them give initial and extensive attention to the materials, specifically to the shapes and sounds of letters.[5] Equally important are the ways in which this interest is represented on the printed page. For instance, Joseph Aickin, whose *English Grammar* (1693) is a representative grammar of the late seventeenth century, begins with a section on orthography. However, since right spelling cannot be imposed, Aickin offers a system of English letters strictly conformable to sounds. To prove this conformation, Aickin provides a physical description of sounds, lists of symbolical letters, riddles, pictures, and phonetic descriptions ("What's like the half-moon? c C c see"), and, subsequently, lengthy tables of syllables. The combination of these techniques for visually displaying the organization of sounds and letters—the lists, columns, tables, diagrams, and illustrations—is a distinctive characteristic of seventeenth-century linguistic texts.[6]

Reducing language to physical properties visually organized on the page justifies operating on words as objects. If the written and spoken language can be touched, tabulated, and visualized, then it can be secured, improved, perfected, and rationally taught. Aickin's grammar typically moves easily between its modest function as "An English Grammar for the English School" and his claim for his method: it is "a work wherein the pictures of all creatures, beasts, fishes, fowls, trades and occupations, and whatsoever is visible to the eye might be evidently presented to the sense" (66). For Aickin meaning is evident in language, and the distinctive features of linguistics, words, are all the evidence needed to prove any proposition, assuming words are written "with proper and fit letters."

Conceiving the minimal components of language to be the vocalization and visualization of letters is a habit not only of grammars of English in the period, but it is also characteristic of anti-Lily Latin grammars in English. John Bird's *Grounds for Grammar* (1639), for instance, sets out to correct "our old Grammar" (A3ᵛ) by starting with the rudiments—letters, syllables, words. Since, for Bird, English and Latin are quite distinct and since a word is "a perfect voice or sound, made of one or more syllables" (8), then he must supply a literal and complete system for English. By starting with letters, Bird, like his contemporary grammarians, assumes that words consist of parts, that words are analogous to matter, and as with other objects, relationships between the parts can be sensed and visually represented.

In an anonymous grammar of 1688, *The Compendious School-master,* the author begins with orthography, as is common, but dwells on it to an unusual, and revealing, degree. He delivers his "Words not by Tale, but by Weight, reducing them in due Place and Order into . . . regular Squadrons, and proper Divisions" (A6ᵛ). His ideas of order are completely letter-based. After carefully drawing and listing the letters, he divides his own prose into syllables "be-cause long Words are ea-si-ly read, when right-ly di-vi-ded" (57). And he adds "Pithy Proverbial Sayings" in what is, for him, a moral order, that is, "Alphabetically digested" (78).[7] Walter Shandy would have been impressed to find this earlier comprehensive pedagogue emphasizing the importance of proper Christian names so that children "might be stirred up to ve-ri-fie the va-ri-ous sig-ni-fi-ca-tions of their Names" (61). Such Shandean nonsense points precisely to what is implied by these grammars which develop language from letters: the physical materials of language are the elements out of which meanings are made.[8]

Interest in pronunciation, which is usually closely associated in seventeenth-century grammars with orthography, points to a similar collection of assumptions: that English must be studied as if for the first time, that the steps of any study begin with the basic parts of which any language is constituted, that whatever is distinctive about English will appear in the classification of these constituent parts, and that meaning derives from the basic parts of language. Interest in pronunciation takes an important turn in the seventeenth century—toward phonetic specificity and visual descriptions. Early in the century, in the work of Robert Robinson, *Art of Pronunciation* (1617), the elements and parts of the voice are discussed in physical terms and every simple sound is given a letter. But it is with John Wallis' *Grammatica* (1653) that the physical elements of speech are presented as the basis of a complete linguistic description of existence. The first third of the *Grammatica* consists of a treatise subsequently published independently, *De Loquela,* and a summary of this opens the next section, on English grammar. The *Tractatus de Loquela* systematically describes the articulation of sounds and even provides a modest tabulated synopsis, but more important, Wallis argues, throughout the *Grammatica,* that the distinctive features of the English language are its sounds which are the bases for letters from which one can construct words and sentences. In sounds, as in letters, there is meaning: not only are there sounds signifying qualities, dimunition, and power, but a correspondence between sounds and meaning ("st" suggests strength, "sp," dissipation, and so on). Sounds also have a physical, visualized basis; thus we have Owen Price illustrating, in *The Vocal Organ* (1665), the physiology of sounds and John Wilkins picturing a system of articulated sounds in his *Essay Towards a Real Character and a Philosophical Language* (1668). All this, of course, is in the service of making language, whether spoken or written, representable and systematic. As Elisha Coles insists in *The Compleat English Schoolmaster* (1674): "All words must be spell'd, as they are afterwards to be pronounc'd" (B2^r). For Coles, the agreement between sound and letters is the basic form of more elaborate relationships between words and images and one language and another. The term he is fondest of is "Syncrisis," a principle "as Ancient as Nature it self."[9] Syncrisis justifies his combination grammar-emblem book: *Nolens Volens: or You Shall make Latin Whether you will or no . . . Together with The Youth's Visible Bible: Being An Alphabetical Collection . . . of such General Heads as were judg'd most capable of Hieroglyphicks* (1675). The related terms in that title—letters, grammar, pictures, truth—capture the integrated linguistic inquiry I am describing.

A more sensible example is Christopher Cooper's *The English Teacher* (1687). Cooper is another provincial schoolmaster, "Master of the Grammar School of Bishop-Stortford in Hartfordshire," who associates his work with both a century-long tradition of attempts to bring English "to Rule" (A3^v) and more recent efforts to understand "the Philosophy of Sounds . . . the Nature of Characters" by "a clear, distinct, and particular explication of the Fundamentals, which must be as Rules" (A3^v). A more elaborate tabulation of sounds than appears in Wallis places letters "according to their Nature: 1. In respect of the Organs by which they are framed. 2. Of their sound. . . . 3. The several degrees of Apertion or closure." Cooper uses this descriptive "ground-work of reading and writing . . . according to the true power of the letters" (29) to reduce language to rule, visually to lists of syllables—of beginning and ending consonants, of vowels, of alphabetized words illustrating the sounds of each letter. Alphabetizing is such an independently important principle that, in spite of Cooper's detailed descriptions of physcial sounds, he alphabetizes words in which the "w" is silent (73–74). *The English Teacher* concludes with alphabetized lists of words: 1) with the same pronunciation but different significations, 2) with different sounds but the same spelling, 3) with the same sounds but different spellings, and so on. But all this—the sections on phonology and phonetics—precedes a grammar which Cooper leaves untranslated from his *Grammatica Linguae Anglicanae* of 1685. His sense of priorities, of making as prerequisite to using, matches the working principles of seventeenth-century pedagogy: to make the method of teaching, the sequence of learning, and the structure of language compatible with the order of things.

Cooper lays the groundwork; he reduces learning and language to the rule of a philosophy of sounds; he finds the possibilities of language in the "powers" of characters; he trusts that the stages of linguistic inquiry correlate with the process of learning; and he argues that all languages share the same principles. All these qualities show how closely aligned Cooper's work is with the various grammars, rhetorics, universal language theories, spelling and pronunciation guides, word lists, and education tracts in the period.

Common to all this linguistic activity is an assurance that language, spoken and written, can be visually represented. Sounds, letters, and meaning are parallel systems of different elements of language. Therefore, we not only see the repeated use of tables, lists, and illustrations, but we find a burgeoning interest in shorthand and sign language systems and in the origin and nature of characters. Proponents of shorthand systems in the seventeenth century exhibit the same diversity and rivalry evident in the grammatical battles. The competitiveness is often amusing but it also indicates an intensity of commitment which can best be accounted for by the involvement of these shorthand systems with the liveliest and richest linguistic issues of the period. As early as Timothy Bright's *Characterie* in 1588, we find a lengthy table of English words reduced in number and to order by a "Table of characterie" based on the assumption that Chinese characters were ideographs. In John Willis' oft-reprinted *Art of Stenographie* (1602), we find the quite explicit intention to connect the marks of the shorthand system and a theory of signification. The growing number and increasing assertiveness of shorthand systems during the century are quite noticeable.[10] Some, like John Willis', are explicitly phonetic, others rely on other natural systems, but all agree that ideas can be visually represented, contained in the contours of lines on a page or evoked by the distribution of agreed upon marks. Willis' figures "hath some agreement with the Signification of the word" (B4ᵛ), and the philosophical context of his abbreviated characters is quite explicitly stated in his *The Art of Memory* (1621). Since an idea is "a visible representation, bestowed by the Imagination in one of the places of a Repositorie, by the remembrance whereof we call to mind that which was therby signified" (12), then a shorthand, like any other character system, is an example of the transformation of propositions into pictures.[11] Although most of the shorthand systems in the century are not similarly tied to sophisticated tracts, they all assume responsibility for convincing the world to accept a shorter, easier, plainer, and more precise system of representing meaning. They all give significant attention to the layout of their systems on the printed page.

Makers of shorthand systems seek physical, visual, and precise representation of language—its forms and meanings; and in their intentions and assumptions they are quite close to another effort of seventeenth-century linguistics—sign systems for the deaf and dumb. Among these "reformers," as among all the groups of linguists we have noted, what is most striking is the recurrence of names and sources, their competitiveness, and the comprehensiveness of their intentions.[12] Just as each grammar intends to provide, at last, a complete analysis of language and, therefore, a basis for training a nation, so inventors of sign systems refer their catalogued gestures to a similar philosophic basis and claim for them similar educational effectiveness. George Dalgarno, in his *Didascalocophus, or the Deaf and Dumb Mans Tutor* (1680), reflects back on his earlier universal grammar, the *Ars Signorum* (1661), claiming that attempt to "remedy the difficulties and absurdities" of all languages should have been called "Sematology" (A2v). Sematology is "a general name for all interpretation by arbitrary signs," that is, it is the "art of impressing the conceits of the mind upon sensible and material objects" and thus the basis for any sign system whatsoever. Even accepting the "equally arbitrary and *ex institutio*" nature of all written and vocal signs, there must be a real basis for the effectiveness and coherence of sign systems, and that basis is the collection of rules found in "a Natural and Universal Grammar" (18). Beneath the diversity of sign systems, he maintains, there is a rational and realistic connection between kinds of signifiers and the natural significations, and it is that connection which Dalgarno pursues in his own universal grammar and in his sign system. The context in which he offers his handbook for the deaf and dumb is indicated by his citations to Seth Ward, John Wilkins, and John Wallis, whose various roles as preachers, pedagogues, and projectors are evocatively caught by the ambiguous "or's" in Dalgarno's description of his goal as "that primitive and Divine, or purely rational Sematology, taught by Almighty God or invented by Adam before the Fall."[13] Every linguist and each linguistic work pursues the same philosophical terms and claims equally wide importance. Dalgarno traces the development of his own diverse linguistic inquiries from a study of Hebrew which excited him "to do something for improving the art of Short-hand; that drove me before I was aware upon a Real Character; that again, after a little consideration, resolved itself into an Effable language" (*Works*, 163).[14]

John Wallis, to whose works on grammar and phonology I have already drawn attention, also figures importantly, and somewhat notoriously, in the case of one Alexander Popham, deaf and dumb. William Holder presented evidence of the success he had in teaching Popham to speak to the Royal Society in 1669 and followed this with his *Elements of Speech: An Essay of Inquiry into the Natural Production of Letters* (1669). Wallis answered, claiming his own success in teaching a Mr. Whaly, also deaf and dumb, to speak was actually the precedent for all such cases (*A Defense of the Royal Society*, 1678). Holder's claims, in *The Elements of Speech*, are quite like those of Wallis, Ward, and Wilkins; that is, he seeks a "Natural Alphabet . . . to prepare a more easie and expedite way to instruct such as are Deaf and Dumb . . . to be able to pronounce all Letters, and Syllables, and Words, and in a good measure to discern them by the Eye" (15), by consulting "Nature at hand" (21). Like Wallis, Holder organizes the "store-house" (18) of sounds and uses a tabulated system of these as the groundwork for letters, syllables, words, and syntax. The debate between Holder and Wallis may have been motivated by a sense of injured pride, but, as with the many examples of linguistic rivalry in the period, it is carried on at an impressively substantive level: each party competes by providing a phonic-grammatic-pedagogic-semiotic system.[15]

All the works and interrelated kinds of linguistic inquiry I have mentioned emphasize peadgogical techniques, most commonly a plan for some variety of visual mnemonics. The presentation of linguistics in visually convenient ways is motivated by theoretical assumptions and confirms, by the predicted success of the method, the truth of those assumptions. The student, in the process of acquiring the language, discovers the system which the linguist has made; and their final compatibility assumes a correlation between the tools of expression and the determinants of what is expressible. How students acquire language determines how and what men think, and how and what men think characterizes their moral natures, and upon their moral natures depends national worth (literary and otherwise). Although the nearest philosophical source

of the importance of the relationship between the linguistic nature
of thinking and the content of thought is Bacon, the critical figure
in the specific alliance between linguistics and learning is Comenius. Comenius, a contemporary of Bishop Wilkins, and, also like
Wilkins, the center of a pre-Royal Society group eager to institu-
tionalize a new systematic methodology, stands out because of his
confidence that the proper acquisition of language must logically
lead to the conversion of the world. Institutionalization of his
syllabus precedes conversion because revelation is the consequence
of using language correctly. For Comenius, language learning leads
to brotherhood, grammar to God. Once "the multitude, the variety, the confusion of languages" is overcome by means of "language absolutely new, absolutely easy, absolutely rational," [16]
then the progress to universal books to universal schools to a
universal college to universal love will be easy and necessary. The
necessary first step is to establish the connection between the
structure of language and "the course of things" (183); and this is
accomplished in grammars and phonologies "by constantly expressing the nature of things with which [language] deals by the
very sounds which it uses" (184).

Comenius pursues his goal in the ways with which we should
now be familiar: by "containing all things which are necessary to
be Knoune . . . with an exact Index"; [17] by providing the key to
knowledge in and as a book; by offering an "epitome" of language
as prerequisite to the grammar of any particular language; by
printing word lists so as to represent the "prime and fundamental
notions of all learning, manners and piety"; [18] by compiling a
visual grammar and "encyclopedia" to prove "there is nothing in
the understanding which was not before in the sense." [19] Comenius' *Visible World*, a translation of his *Orbis Sensualium Pictus*
(1659), was presented by Charles Hoole, Teacher of a Private
Grammar-School in Lothbury, London, recommended by Heze-
kiah Woodward, "an eminent Schoolmaster in London," and
proved a popular school text throughout the seventeenth century. [20] The *Orbis* begins, typically, with a rough phonology,
associating letters with animal sounds, and then provides a picture

book of an ordered and well-defined universe originating in Deus-God and continuing through the sequence of created things and actions. Separate columns of English and Latin descriptions on the right-hand page are keyed by numbers to pictures on the left-hand page. Importantly, the verbal columns not only denote objects, professions, and actions, they also give syntactic connections between the substantives. Moreover, these connectives are printed in a different type face from the substantives, so that there are four type faces on the page, two in each column.

The eyes instruct the mind: we see, writes Comenius, a "little Encyclopadia of things subject to the senses" (A5ᵛ), and we see that the things of the world and the names of those things exist in connected systems. The eyes see more that Comenius intends, however. In representing Patience, for instance, Comenius illustrates a brief essay rather than simply picture a list of qualities. He shows someone kneeling with an arm resting on an anchor which is attached to a ship being buffeted by winds and rain from dark clouds which also release lightning which strikes someone who wails while his dog howls. The dramatic unity of the illustration corresponds to the integrated discourse of the enumerating narrative and to the syntactic relations revealed by the different type faces. One of Comenius' definitions of what he intends in the *Orbis* indirectly refers to this aspect of the work: the *Orbis* is "a Picture and Nomenclature of all the chief things in the World, and of mens Actions in their way of living" (A3ᵛ). Comenius' emphasis, like that of all his contemporaries, is on the significance of the elements of language, as if meaning existed, naturally or rationally, in their systematic representation. But, as the integrated actions and connected speeches illustrated in the *Orbis* show, there is more to language than its lexical elements. Comenius' illustrations are designed principally to represent words, but they also indicate the importance of the relationship between words, that is, of syntax.

What is distinctive about the seventeenth-century visual grammars is that they attempt to perfect a visual representation of linguistic performance, but, in the later part of the century, there is a noticeable and new emphasis on sentences rather than words, on words more as parts of speech than as bits of reality. An instructive, if peculiar, expression of this new tendency is Bassett Jones' *Herm'aelogium, or an Essay at the Rationality of the Art of Speaking* (1659). He offers it as a "Supplement to Lillie's Grammar, Philosophically, Mythologically, and Emblematically" (A3ʳ). He begins, typically, by "analogizing words with things," and he discovers just three parts of speech: words of being, words of motion, and words of quality. These are syntactic universals, or "gradual emanations of the same Naturing Nature" (7). The differences between the world's languages, he writes, are simply variations in "vocality" and climate; in "point of syntax" (A6ᵛ) they all agree. This distinction proves "the product of words to be more from nature; as of sentences from reason." On the basis of his syntactic universals he draws "Philosophical and Pedagogical . . . Emblems" (A4ʳ) which show how the parts of speech connect, how nature coheres, how God operates, how children learn, and how we know that all these activities are alike. Jones' emblems are unreasonably ingenious, but his arguments and methods are repeated in more appropriate pedagogic forms throughout the rest of the century.

In the last quarter of the seventeenth century, a number of language texts, many of them attempting to represent grammatically Comenius' pictorial discourses, indicate a shift in emphasis from lexical symbolization to rational syntax. Mark Lewis, following Comenius, contributed a number of school texts in order to bring "down the Rudiments of Grammar to the Sense of Seeing."[21] He shares Elisha Coles' fondness for the term "syncrisis," which becomes, in Lewis' *Vestibulum Technicum* (1675), a printer's cue: "Each Part of Speech is distinguished by the Character it is Printed in, (a Method never used before) and sufficient Grammar is brought down to the sense of Seeing, in regard of the thing signified" (A1ʳ).[22] Lewis' reliance on a visual key fits his reasons for reforming Lily. Lily erred by beginning his grammar with catalogues of general rules, by relying on the moral weight of examples drawn from classical authors, and by building a vocabulary word by word. Such submission to authority and to isolated lexical bits and pieces violates Lewis' sense of the proper pedagogy which, by beginning with the sense of seeing, uses the same methodology to "learn things Natural, Artificial, Moral, and Divine" (13). His method imitates his epistemology:

> ... whatever is in the world is matter and motion; thoughts are the Picture of this matter and motion, words are the Copy of our thoughts; as is the thing, so is the Picture. As is the Picture, so is the Copy; therefore every sentence must consist of a Substantive, thing or matter, called the Nominative Case; and the verb or motion of it, with so many more Substantives as do depend upon these; these cannot exist without qualities, which we express by Adjectives. Prepositions and Conjunctions are a kind of cement. (A4^v)

In passages like this one, appearing throughout his work, Lewis connects the stages of the true epistemology (and, thus, the proper pedagogy) to the nature of existing things, so that learning properly and writing correctly reconstitute reality.

Lewis repeatedly refers to language as a body—with substantives as the bones, adjectives the flesh, nominatives the cranium, accusatives the body—because Lewis wants language, however arbitrary the specific relationship between *a* signifier and *a* signified, to represent naturally and completely "what God works by nature" (*Vestibulum*, p. 16). Lewis has an equally operational sense of language and of God—both are to be interpreted as functioning systems, not simply as static collections of emblems. *How* God works is also how language works; therefore, the right method for acquiring language, that is, "from the Senses to the Understanding, and from thence to the Memory" (*Essay*, 1), cannot help but train minds which would be, ideally, universally compatible and unproblematically orthodox. Since the "end of words and common things is divine knowledge" (*Apologie*, 37), the systematic visual representation of language has as much religious power as it has scholastic influence. The competitiveness among linguists reveals their sense of their own importance; they scurry as if the proper patronage were a patent for universal brotherhood in the name of

the most successful grammarian. Their interest in students and
other linguistically and, therefore, spiritually handicapped people
(like the deaf and dumb) logically leads to spiritual promises, the
most common of which is the determination to redeem the curse
of Babel.[23]

The epigraph Comenius chooses for his *Orbis* is Genesis 2:19–
20, the traditional source for discussions of Adamic naming.
Adamic naming is, traditionally, only *naming*, but the inventors
and proponents of natural and visual grammars and universal
languages interpret Adam's linguistic talent as Adamic *speech*, that
is, the possibility of universal communication by virtue of a shared
sense of the operations, not necessarily the atoms, of speech.
Comenius uses conventional characters and familiar Latin and
English vocabularies as the elements of his universal language; his
linguistic reformation does not depend on new linguistic features
but on seeing existing languages differently. Since God "implanted
everyone its nature, that is, a vertue to observe the place, manner,
and kind assigned unto it" (*Porta*, p. 4), then an analysis of
language in terms of the place, manner, and kinds of its parts of
speech would represent the functions of a language as compatible
with God's creation.[24] Indeed, since God has permanently provided a model for how to do things with words, the common
assertion of seventeenth-century linguists to repair, redeem, or
cure the curse of Babel should not surprise us if we are willing to
accept the possibility of visualizable speech acts, of language as
systematic, progressive performance. In fact, linguistic texts in the
seventeenth century are laid out to show that there is a divinity
that shapes our speech, a spirit revealed by pictures of vocal
organs, of animals vocalizing, of letters "speaking," of objects; by
lists of sounds, syllables, related words; by parallel columns of
words.[25]

A revealing linguistic subtype in the period is the catechistical
grammar, in which the general emphasis on systematic language
acquisition leads to divine speech by way of a dialogue.[26] Most
agreeable of these is Samuel Shaw's *Words Made Visible: or
Grammar and Rhetorick Accommodated to the Lives and Manners*

of Men (1679). Shaw, self-advertised as a "Philosophical Priscian" (A1ᵛ) for his times, presents the court of King Syntaxis, King of the Grammar Commonwealth. The dialogue is often witty, the dramatic situations even amusing, but the important claim Shaw makes is that "the most illiterate people in their most ordinary communication, do Retoricate by Instinct. . . . But that's not all; for men live Tropes and figures as well as speak them" (99). His elaborately orchestrated representation of the parts of speech operates in every mind: "every individual man is a system" of rhetoric. Such a complete, clear, distinct, and systematic sense of linguistic performance signifies, as directly as any "real" character, man's place in God's creation, for Shaw assumes that the proper development of man's linguistic competence imitates God's self-representation in everyday life.[27] When a work like Shaw's *Words Made Visible* is read in the context I have outlined in this paper, one comes closer to understanding the theoretical assumptions and practical implications of seventeenth-century linguistic texts than has been possible given the prevailing conventions of intellectual and linguistic history.

I have deliberately avoided dwelling on the universal and philosophical grammars, the real characters and the like associated with the origins of the Royal Society because the very familiarity of the Bacon-Beck-Ward-Wilkins and the Hartlib-Comenius-Turnbull lines has helped isolate their works from the common principles of seventeenth-century linguistics. Bishop Wilkins' *Real Character*, for instance, should seem less odd and less a dead end when considered in the terms I have suggested. The overwhelming evidence of the many and diverse linguistic texts of the period gathers under five shared principles which, as I will show in subsequent essays, also operate in the development of a particular literary language in the latter part of the seventeenth century.

First, the evidence from the prefaces, practice, and printed format of these texts shows determined *systematization*. They use indices, lists, columns, pictures, tables, type faces, and personifications to name, describe, classify, and even dramatize. Proposals for an English Academy are only a surface symptom of a much deeper, and more important, desire to bring language to order and rule. Restoration attempts to specify a literary language are versions of this taxonomic approach to language generally. For Dryden, for instance, the couplet is the basic unit of poetry, the guide to how we read, and the goal of an ordered art. The techniques of couplet art—paralellism, crossing, enjambment, inversion—are visible variations on the systematic features of literary language.

Second, all the linguists share a sense of the importance of *sequence* in the system. The sequence must represent the order in which language developed; it must match the progressive steps of epistemology; it must be adapted to the training of students; and it must reflect the combinational and relational operations of language use. Sequence reflects and combines historical, psychological, pedagogical, and philosophical principles. The importance of sequence for the development of literary language in the Restoration is suggested by Dryden when he defines the order of a fable as the relation of the parts to the whole "like the links of a curious chain";[28] when he popularizes Aristotle's idea of action; and when he accepts and promotes as the model of a literary career the succession of pastoral, georgic, and epic languages.

Third, the most important step in the system's sequence is the first—the *materials* of language, the distinctive features of speaking and writing. Here, too, Dryden, as he organizes and defines a literary language, typically draws attention to the origins, sounds, and poetic appropriateness of specific words and lexical groups.

Fourth, these basic physical components, like later steps in the sequence, can be represented *visually*. Consider, in terms of Restoration discussions of literary and sermon language, definitions of regularity and irregularity in poetry which involve the shapes of stanzas as indices of the nature of the poetic mind; or the development of the distinctive genres of late seventeenth-century poetry—topographic poems, building and city poems, and physico-theological poems which correlate visual analogies and linguistic associations with proofs of God's presence.

Fifth, the attention to system, sequence, materials, and visualization comes to characterize equally the nature of mind, reality, language, and God, so that epistemology, ontology, syntax, and divine presence tend to be represented in *operational* terms. Language, for example, is a sign system the functioning of which is analogous to the structure of nature. The thoroughness of this active or operational structure of language is evident in works ranging from Wilkins' *Real Character* to Edward Somerset's *A Century of the Names and Scantlings of Such Inventions as at present I can call to mind to have tried and perfected* (London, (1663). Somerset's little work is his "summum Bonum,"[29] as well. It lists what and how to do things with words, including a "cypher and character so contrived, that one line, without returns and circumflexes, stands for each and every of the 24 letters" (5), "seals contrived to tell whatever owners want to know," and "systems for holding discourse without noise or notice even at night. He also offers methods for writing with needle and thread, knotted silk string, and fringes of a glove, as well as the means of communicating by jangling bells, smells, tastes, touches, and holes in a sieve. Language, here, is not a collection of symbols referring to discrete conceptions but a system of signs functionally expressing the reality of man's participation in a similarly constituted world. The first consequence of any sign theory is that signs draw attention to themselves as simultaneously the agents and ends of communication. The effect of this operational or sign theory principle on the literature of the period needs separate study, but its importance can be suggested by the prominence of literary signs (i.e., the texts themselves and the characterization of topics within the texts) which draw simultaneous attention to what is signified and to the signifying function itself—and this while a literary language is self-consciously being developed. The dual nature of linguistic and literary signs lies behind discussions of literary rules in the Restoration—the unities, for instance, and the preference for specific poetic forms, techniques, and styles.

These five principles of seventeenth-century English linguistics operate throughout an impressive variety of works ranging from competing provincial school texts to projects of the Royal Society, from language texts which begin with psycholinguistic definitions and move to theological ends to theological treatises which, from linguistic descriptions, progress to a vision of the redeemed society of man. And it is in the context of this integration, in linguistic theory and practice, of language, psychology, society, and belief that we ought to reconsider the development of a literary language and of literary forms in late seventeenth-century England.

NOTES

1 John Dryden, "To the Right Honourable Roger, Earl of Orrery" (prefixed to *The Rival Ladies*, 1664), in James Kinsley and George Parfitt, eds., *John Dryden: Selected Criticism* (Oxford: Oxford University Press, 1970), p. 5.

2 See, for examples, Ian Michael, *English Grammatical Categories and the Tradition to 1800* (Cambridge: Cambridge University Press, 1970); E. J. Dobson, *English Pronunciation 1500–1700* (Oxford: Clarendon Press, 1957), particularly vol. I: *Survey of the Sources*; W. S. Howell, *Logic and Rhetoric in England: 1500–1700* (Princeton: Princeton University Press, 1956); and, for summaries of the universal language projects, Michael, *English Grammatical Categories*, pp. 162–83, Vivian Salmon, "Language Planning in Seventeenth-Century England," in C. A. Bezell et al., eds., *In Memory of J. R. Firth* (London, 1966), pp. 370–97, and Jonathan Cohen, "On the Project of a Universal Character," *Mind*, 63 (1954), 49–63. The principal intellectual historians are, of course, Morris Croll, whose major essays are available in J. Max Patrick et al., eds., *Style, Rhetoric, and Rhythm* (Princeton: Princeton University Press, 1966); George Williamson, *Senecan Amble* (Chicago, 1951); R. F. Jones, whose relevant essays are collected in two volumes, *The Triumph of the English Language* (Stanford: Stanford University Press, 1953), and *The Seventeenth Century* (Stanford: Stanford University Press, 1956); and Robert Adolph, *The Rise of Modern Prose Style* (Cambridge, Mass.: M.I.T. Press, 1968). See, also, two important reviews of this second group of historians: Jackson Cope, "Modes of Modernity in Seventeenth-Century Prose," *Modern Language Quarterly*, 31 (1970), 92–111; and Stanley Fish, *Self-Consuming Artifacts: The Experience of Seventeenth-Century Literature* (Berkeley: University of California Press, 1972), particularly "Epilogue: The Plain Style Question," pp. 374–82.

3 John Twells, in his *Grammatica Reformata* (London, 1683), claims that there were no new grammars between 1551 and 1636 (this is only mildly inaccurate), but "since then New Grammars have been ever and anon coming forth ('tis to be concluded somewhat is amiss in the Old, why else should the Learned Authors of them spend their pains in the compositions of New?)" (18).

4 Timothy Baker, *Reflections upon Learning* (London, 1700), observes many of the same qualities as Ian Michael—the inconveniences, variations, and mutability of language; the cumbersomeness of dictionaries and the failure of academies—and accounts for them, not by ignoring the question of intention, but by comparing the goals of competing linguistic systems. For Baker the inconsistencies are morally significant.

5 The earliest grammars I have seen which set out to model their method on nature and in print are Alexander Gill, *Logonomia Anglica* (London, 1619), and Joseph Webbe, *An Appeale to Truth* (London, 1622).

6 The reliance of grammarians on visual schemes which can only be made with the help of printers is a dramatic effect of what Walter J. Ong has described, in a number of books and articles, as the aural-to-visual shift which marks the transition from the ancient world to the Renaissance. Ong's most important work documenting this development remains his *Ramus, Method, and the Decay of Dialogue* (Cambridge, Mass., 1958). He has commented briefly on the effect of the new typographical culture on seventeenth-century schools in "System, Space, and Intellect in Renaissance Symbolism," reprinted in *The Barbarian Within* (New York, 1962); and on typographical schemes in "From Allegory to Diagram in the Renaissance Mind," *Journal of Aesthetics and Art Criticism*, 17 (1959), 423—40.

7 The alphabet itself is recognized as a conceptual tool by seventeenth-century linguists. Thomas Urquhart, in his *Logopandecteision* (London, 1653), traces variations in living languages to the absence of an alphabetical consistency which he plans to correct, as a "Grammatical Arithmetician" (13), by a "Trissotetrial trigonometry, for facility of calculation by representatives of letters and syllables" (15). Lines from a prefatory poem to Thomas Blount's *Glossographia; or a Dictionary Interpreting all . . . Hard Words* (London, 1656) suggest the importance of the alphabet:

> Our Tongue, grown Labyrinth and Monster too.
> Confusion, in this Book, in Order's set,
> An Heap is form'd into an Alphabet:
> Old Babels ruins this in part repairs
> And in an handsom Work the Rubbish rears . . . (A8^r)

8 Henry Rose's *A Philosophicall Essay for the Reunion of the Languages* (Oxford, 1675), a translation of Pierre Besnier, *La Réunion des langues* (Paris, 1674), argues that the first step toward a universally accepted language would be to study the vocal organs to find the "precise number of all the simple sounds" (46). An analysis of the original corporeal nature of all words would lead to an original language, "Naked and intirely dispoil'd of all that trompery that disguis'd them" (60). Rose indicates the importance of the project by trusting that the projector will "receive the same favour that persons . . . granted Copernicus" (79). Equally ambitious are Louis Gerard de Cordemoy, *A Philosophicall Discourse Concerning Speech* (London, 1668); Matthew Hale, *The Primitive Origination of Mankind* (London, 1677); and Seth Ward, *Vindicae Academiarum* (Oxford, 1654).

9 Elisha Coles, *Syncrisis, or, the Most Natural and Easie Method of Learning Latin* (London, 1675), A2^r. Probably preceding Coles' use of the term syncrisis is Mark Lewis' in *An Essay to Facilitate the Education of Youth by bringing down the Rudiments of Grammar to the Sense of Seeing* (London, 1674). Lewis' work also derives, as he readily admits, from Ramus and Comenius.

10 R. C. Alston, *A Bibliography of the English Language*, vol. VIII: *Treatises on Shorthand* (Leeds: E. J. Arnold and Son, 1966), lists twenty-eight separate titles before 1659. Alston includes many facsimile pages which show the persistent, often peculiar, effort of shorthand inventors to provide helpful and ingenious visualizations of the systems.

11 Frances Yates, in *The Art of Memory* (Chicago: The University of Chicago Press, 1966), discusses Willis' work briefly (pp. 324–26), but the connection between the development of linguistic schemes and the fate of memory systems in the seventeenth century has not been explored. Since both projects deal with the relationship of the mind to the world, it would be interesting to compare what scholars have suggested about the representation of the mind in the seventeenth century and the efforts of linguists to shape minds with linguistic tools. See, also, Yates' *Theatre of the World* (Chicago: University of Chicago Press, 1969), and Richard Bernheimer, "Theatrum Mundi," *Art Bulletin*, 38 (1956), 225–47.

12 If we are to characterize seventeenth-century linguistics accurately, we must acknowledge the interconnections between various linguistic interests which recur. Francis Lodowyck, for example, claims in *A Common Writing* (1646) the invention of "a kind of hieroglyphical representation of words" (A2^r) which leads not only to a phonetic shorthand but also to a philosophical language based on "radicall Characters" (A2^v) and a universal primer. William Petty, in *The Advice of W. P. to Mr. Samuel Hartlib* (London, 1647), summarizes the goals of the Hartlib group by

associating the advancement of learning, an art of double writing, and the reformation of style. He emphasizes in this tract suggestions for educating children to "not onely . . . write according to our Common Way, but also to write Swiftly and in Reall Characters" (5). Also, see John Webster, *Academiarum Examen* (London, 1653).

13 George Dalgarno, *Works* (Edinburgh, 1834), p. 164. See Vivian Salmon, "The Evolution of Dalgarno's *Ars Signorum*," in *Studies in Language and Literature in Honor of Margaret Schlauch* (Warsaw: Polish Scientific Publishers, 1966), pp. 353–71, and J. R. Knowlson, "The Idea of Gesture as a Universal Language in the XVIIth and XVIIIth Centuries," *Journal of the History of Ideas*, 26 (1945), 495–508.

14 The literal and physical connection between characters and meaning occurs commonly in discussion of real characters and, as with Dalgarno, in commentaries on Hebrew, Chinese, and Egyptian characters. See D. C. Allen, "Some Theories of the Growth and Origin of Language in Milton's Age," *Philological Quarterly*, 28 (1949), 5–16.

15 The mid-century debate over the integrity of the academy between John Webster and Seth Ward shows the variety of impulses which led to quite similar linguistic approaches. Webster's objections to the philosophical indifference of the universities and Ward's ill-humored defense of experimental science, although mutually antagonistic, exhibit the same theory of language and meaning. Both agree that a clear and distinct linguistics would fully represent the God-given order of nature. For a view which emphasizes the contrasting origins of the two positions see Allen G. Debus, *Science and Education in the Seventeenth Century: The Webster-Ward Debate* (New York: American Elsevier, 1970).

16 John Amos Comenius, *The Way of Light*, trans. E. T. Campagnac (London: Hadder and Stoughton, 1938), p. 8.

17 John Amos Comenius, *A Patterne of Universal Knowledge* (Notthampton, 1651), p. 4.

18 Jan A. Comenius, *The Gate of Tongues Unlocked and Opened* (London, 1633), trans. Th. Horn, A3ᵛ. See also Wye Saltonstall, *Clavis ad Portam* (Oxford, 1634). Saltonstall's key is an alphabetized list of words with page reference to Comenius' *Porta Linguarium* (London, 1631).

19 John Amos Comenius, *Orbis Sensualium Pictus*, ed. John E. Sadler (London: Oxford University Press, 1968).

20 James Bowen, "Introduction" to Comenius' *Orbis Sensualium Pictus* (Sydney: Sydney University Press, 1967). Bowen notes ten editions in the first decade after its appearance (in 1658) and claims that the work is the "first illustrated school text" (26).

21 Mark Lewis, *An Essay to Facilitate the Education of Youth* (London, 1675?), p. 16.

22 Mark Lewis, *Vestibulum Technicum, or An Artificial Vestibulum* (London, 1675), A1[r]. Lewis takes his title from Comenius' *Vestibulum Linguarium* (London, 1667). Lewis cites Comenius and Ramus; the latter reference is suggestive for it is Ramus' logic which is the starting point for the interest in the visual representability of language, logic, and meaning.

23 References to the repair of Babel are surprisingly common even among churchmen. In the frontispiece to John Becheri's *Character* (Frankfurt, 1661), most strikingly, men point admiringly to a tower inscribed with the universal characters Becheri introduces in his book, and each of the prefatory poems to Cave Beck's *The Universal Character* (London, 1657) refers to redeeming the curse as does the dedicatory epistle to Wilkins' *Essay*.

24 The relationship between the system of speech and the order of the world raises the question of style to theological levels, which is where we find most discussions of style in the period—in sermons and among divines. Further, the common assumption that language is the key to creation subsumes apparent disagreements about particular linguistic features or about the specific nature of God (see note 15).

25 Henry Edmundson, *Lingua Linguarum; The Natural Language of Languages* (London, 1658), invents more opportunities for alphabetized word lists than any other work I saw. This note by way of delayed praise.

26 See Jean de Graue, *The Pathway to the Gate of Tongues* (London, 1633), another Comenius disciple (as Edmundson, above), and William Hickes, *Grammatical Drollery* (London, 1682), for a comic dialogue. The "achievement" of Wilkins' *Real Character* is the Lord's Prayer in the new characters which concludes his massive work.

27 Robert Adolph, in *The Rise of Modern Prose Style*, bases his argument on a distinction between an old plain style in which words represent ideas or images and a new plain style in which words refer to things outside the mind. This is not a functional distinction in seventeenth-century linguistics. What is operative throughout the period is a repeated series of methodological approaches to the representation of the ordered connection between minds, speech, and creation.

28 Dryden, *Selected Criticism* ("Heads of an Answer to Rymer"), p. 147.

29 Edward Somerset, *A Century of Names* (London, 1663), A3[v].

Poetic Standards
on the Early Augustan Battleground

HUGH ORMSBY-LENNON

In 1656, after announcing his premature divorce from poetry, Abraham Cowley remarked that "a warlike, various and tragical age is best to *write of*, but worst to *write in*."[1] Just why this should be the case would not have been evident to his Renaissance predecessors; in their battle lines Mars was joined by the Muses. "Poetrie," Sir Philip Sidney declared, "is the companion of the Campes."[2] In the early 1640's Cavaliers like Lovelace toyed with their newly acquired military roles as self-consciously as did Rupert Brooke with his. But hereafter the poets bear, for us, a greater resemblance to one of Spenser's ubiquitous "raskall routes" than they do to Sidney at Zutphen or to Castiglione outside the walls of Mirandola: well-bred Hortulan saints and noseless heroic poets close ranks with ballad-mongers and political journalists on the run.

When Humphrey Moseley, the most notable publisher of poetry at the time, presented Milton to the reading public in 1645, it seemed to him that "*the slightest Pamphlet is now adayes more vendible then the Works of learnedest men.*"[3] At the other end of

the social and intellectual ladder, Samuel Sheppard, the self-styled
successor to Francis Quarles, grumbled that

> Apollo, grieves to see the Times
> So pester'd with Mechannicks lavish Rimes.[4]

Yet verse was only a statistical drop in the buckets of polemical
ink so freely spilled by those "Word-peckers, paper-rats, book-
scorpions,"[5] whom Marvell so briskly dismisses; of the fourteen
thousand works published between 1641 and 1660 only six per
cent can be termed poetry, and it is within these eight hundred or
so volumes that we may expect to find just a few of the stylistic
changes generally observed in the period.[6]

II

Literary historians have often marshalled documentary evidence
from such familiar works as Thomas Sprat's *History of the Royal
Society*, John Wilkins' *Essay towards a Real Character*, or Joseph
Glanvill's *Essays* in their attempts to confirm and illustrate the
development of a poetic style in which they generally see the
decay of the metaphysical mode. Parallels between a "poetry of
statement" and the non-metaphoric prose of laboratory and pulpit
can indeed be drawn with a deceptive (and convincing) ease. By no
means, however, is a simple unanimity to be found in the camp of
the experimental scientists and their Latitudinarian allies: Tillotson toned down the language of Barrow when he prepared his
sermons for the press; Robert Boyle, not himself notable for
practicing what some in the Royal Society preached, defended the
use of "*a stile more Fashionable than That of meer Scholars is
wont to be.*"[7] "*To keep a due decorum in the Discourses*" of *The
Sceptical Chymist* he argued, "*it was fit that in a book written by
a Gentleman, and wherein only Gentlemen are introduc'd as
speakers, the language should be more smooth and the Expression
more Civil than is usual in the more Scholastick way of writing.*"[8]

In his reference to decorum, Boyle clearly stressed a significant element that can too easily be overlooked by modern scholars. Rhetorical strategies were carefully tailored to the author's requisite ends; different contexts of discourse—in natural philosophy itself—generated different stylistic approaches. More pertinently, it should be remembered that we ourselves cannot apply to one universe of discourse the stylistic criteria which govern another without the danger of distortion or oversimplification. "When we read the representative Restoration critics," William H. Youngren reminds us (though not without some exaggeration), "we do not find them demanding that poetry become like Royal Society prose; in fact they are often interested in enumerating and celebrating the qualities which they assume make it unlike prose—qualities like strength, sensuous immediacy, energy and concentration—and they are at their most eloquent when doing so."[9]

While such care about unwarranted trespass across stylistic boundaries is salutary, it avoids consideration of the deeper relationships between the different strata of language—that is, the way in which the poetry and prose of any era reflect basic assumptions about the nature and function of words. From this inclusive perspective we may well observe a greater congruity of attitude and approach among different contemporary practitioners of language than could be evident from a survey of the landscape above. Throughout the ensuing discussion I shall make use of the tools developed by the Prague structural linguists in their discussion of the aesthetic function of language. These discussions are marked by a non-prescriptive flexibility and a sensitivity to the poetic use of language, both of which are often missing from stricter and more linguistically rigid analyses of poetic discourse. For example, Jan Mukařovský refrains from fencing off the structured aesthetic of poetry from other types of linguistic functions; indeed he insists upon "the interpenetration of the esthetic and the communicative attitudes":

> The esthetic in language must likewise be looked for in *all* kinds
> of verbal responses, not only where it predominates, such as in

poetry; and on the other hand, neither may the observer of poetry lose sight of the various shadings of the communicative function and its significance for the poetic structure.[10]

Such hesitancy before the omnipresent and well-baited trap of categorization is surely commendable.

It is, nonetheless, the tactical distinctions between "standard" and "poetic" language actually drawn by the Prague linguists which are most significant for this inquiry. Such distinctions, of course, may ultimately emerge as chimerical, for "ordinary" and "deviant" discourse have a disconcerting propensity for chasing their own tails in any logical argument where the one is defined in terms of the other.[11] (Mukařovský and his colleagues, to their credit, are more interested in the color-blocks than in the dividing lines upon the map of language.) The social use of language in all the genres of poetry and prose should instead be considered as a continuum in which we can discern innumerable contexts and situations, all with their appropriate rhetorical strategies and linguistic registers. Future discussions will surely be better served by recourse to the ethnography of communication rather than to "simple linguistics" (which are hardly simple).[12] Yet from the Prague School distinction between the "poetic" and the "standard" use of language we can, on this occasion, derive a helpful heuristic way of examining the developing relationship of poetry and prose in the seventeenth century.

Bohuslav Havránek has offered the fullest definition of the "standard language"; to it he assigns primarily the areas of both workaday technical and scientific technical communication. Unlike folk speech which is "usually limited to oral communication and private conversation" standard language is, moreover, "usually made to serve for various kinds of public utterances and written communication."[13] The standard language approaches its fullest realization in advanced technical and scientific discourse where tenor rather than vehicle is of prime concern; the desired transparency of meaning is attained by "intellectualization" and "automatization."

"Intellectualization" entails the use of unequivocal words, precise distinctions, and abstract summarizing terms in "statements which reflect the rigor of objective (scientific) thinking in which the terms approximate concepts and the sentences approach logical judgements."[14] We remember Sprat's familiar ideal of a "return back to the primitive purity, and shortness, when men deliver'd so many *things*, almost in an equal number of *words*."[15] The Royal Society exacted from its members "a close, naked, natural way of speaking; positive expressions; clear senses; a native easiness: bringing all things as near the Mathematical plainness, as they can."[16] Glanvill wished to see "the *Notion* of *Faith*" stated "plainly and clearly" and stripped "out of its *Chymerical* clothing" so that "Religion could be restored to its native *plainness* and *simplicity*" by a "sober, rational, experimental method of action."[17]

"Automatization"—"such a use of the devices of the language . . . that the expression itself does not attract any attention"[18] — also furthered the attainment of these twin Latitudinarian objectives: "specious *tropes* and *Figures*" and "the *gayness* of *metaphors*, or *prettiness* of *similitudes*" are to be banished from the standard languages of natural philosophy and of religion.[19]

The program for Restoration standard languages was ill-defined, however. Bishop Wilkins, in the purest distillation of the many projects and catechetical handbooks, hoped that his universal character could be used in "*facilitating mutual* Commerce, *amongst the several Nations of the World and the improving of all* Natural Knowledge . . . *the spreading of the knowledge of* Religion"; yet simultaneously he intended the philosophical language on which it was based to "*prove the shortest and plainest way to the attainment of real* Knowledge, *that hath yet been offered to the World*."[20] "It was clearly a mistake," comments Jonathan Cohen, "to think that the same language could serve adequately both as an unspecialized international auxiliary and also as a scientific terminology."[21] The standard languages of Sprat and Glanvill betrayed a similar lack of clarity in their conception. Despite his straining after "intellectualization" and "automatization," Glanvill also wished to avoid the scholastic precision of *"needless words* of *Art,* or *subtile distinctions"* and, like Sprat, sought the "common" and "familiar" words in "the language of Artizans, Countrymen, and Merchants."[22] The resulting ideal was a hybrid that uncomfortably straddled a desire for the common sense discourse of empirical observation and the necessary possession of the abstract and rational language of logical deduction. Resolving this linguistic tension could promptly lead us into a discussion of the clash between Baconianism and Cartesianism in the early years of the Royal Society—or into consideration of the relationship between practical religion and dogmatic theology in the late seventeenth century; but for our present stylistic purposes we need simply note the premium that was set upon the denotative and "prosaic" dimension of prose.

In complete contrast to the austere function of "intellectualization" and "automatization" in the standard is the expressive role of "foregrounding" in language. While "foregrounding" invigorates everyday discourse—for example, in the racy colloquialisms of the folk dialect or in the variations played upon the standard language of communication by journalism—its mode of operation is essentially unstructured; it is only in poetry that it attains its fullest realization:

> The function of poetic language consists in the maximum of foregrounding of the utterance. Foregrounding is the opposite of automatization, that is, the deautomatization of an act; the more an act is automatized, the less it is consciously executed; the more it is foregrounded, the more completely conscious does it become. . . . The standard language in its purest form, as the language of science with formulation as its objective, avoids foregrounding.[23]

While the Restoration exponents of standard language did not underrate the necessity of conscious rhetorical selection, they clearly hoped the appropriate lexical and syntactic choices would become "natural"—programmed responses; poetic style, by stressing metaphoric surprise, phonetic and semantic contrasts, and structural repetition, obviously works in contrary fashion. Whereas the languages of science and practical communication emphasize accuracy of communal observation and probabilistic prediction, poetry accentuates personal imaginative distinctions and plays with the expectations of its readers: "automatization schematizes an event; foregrounding means the violation of the scheme."[24] Nevertheless, "the regular foundation of *poetic language* is the standard,"[25] since

> for poetry, the standard language is the background against which is reflected the esthetically intentional distortion of the linguistic components of the work, in other words, the intentional violation of the norm of the standard. . . . [This] systematic violation is what makes possible the poetic utilization of language; without this possibility there would be no poetry.[26]

The drive towards a (nominally) meticulous codification of the standard by the linguistic reformers of the 1660's might initially seem to provide the poets with more effective ground on which to display the novelty and versatility of their mode of "foregrounding," their figures of thought and speech. While scientists like Robert Boyle and John Ray attempted to tidy up reality, and theorists like Wilkins strove to equip them with the necessary denotative linguistic tools, the poets *might* have grasped the contemporary "disenchantment of the world"[27] and of its languages as an auspicious moment for the exercise of their own imaginations. Mukařovský demonstrates the way in which such a situation can occur: "The more the norm of the standard is stabilized in a given language, the more varied can be its violation, and therefore the more possibilities for poetry in that language."[28]

Instead, the leading poets actually cooperated with the reformers in the task of pruning imagistic excess and verbal excrescence. Dryden and Waller were members of the Royal Society's "committee for improving the English language"[29] and, although the Great Plague and the Second Dutch War quickly put an end to the committee's formal activities, the poets shared common goals of a purified poetic diction and regularized form and meter with other contemporaries such as Cowley and Denham. Dryden summed up the desired achievement in his *Of Dramatic Poesy: An Essay*: "every one was willing to acknowledge how much our poesy is improved by the happiness of some writers yet living, who first taught us to mould our thoughts into easy and significant words, to retrench the superfluities of expression, and to make our rhyme so properly a part of the verse that it should never mislead the sense, but itself be led and governed by it."[30] These poets were attempting to replace what Mukařovský calls "the traditional esthetic canon"; this canon is the second dimension of "automatization" that lies behind a poem—"the set of firm and stable norms into which the structure of a preceding school of poetry has dissolved by automatization."[31] This dead hand from whose grip, even before the Restoration, the stylistic innovators fought to free themselves—despite their own varied indebtedness to it—was incorporated in the remains of a metaphysical (and allegorical) style, the decay of which the Civil Wars only speeded.

The pre-Restoration mode had deteriorated not into bland homogeneity but rather into a murky alphabet soup of anagrams, mixed metaphors, and cabalistic number-letter transformations. The influential poets writing after 1660 wished to establish novel criteria for "foregrounding" that would serve to differentiate their style more from the preceding aesthetic canon than from the new standard language of religion and science; while they did join linguistic reformers in the concerted effort to leave "hard words" and extravagant metaphors in the smoky past of Civil War and Interregnum, where such excesses belonged, the poets managed to develop new modes of "foregrounding" as well. Cowley used his "libertine way of rendring foreign Authors" to notable effect in his imitations of Pindar which fell "from one thing into another, after his *Enthysiastical* manner . . .";[32] it was, interestingly enough, to classical precedent (this time Horace) that Dryden turned for his stress upon "choice of words, and heightening of their natural signification."[33]

Such conscious strategies were, however, subverted by one of Michel Foucault's "epistemic shifts";[34] concerned as they were with the possibilities of poetic articulation inherent in the range of words their society offered, Cowley and Dryden could hardly be fully aware of the reordering of the underlying linguistic strata. It is only when we juxtapose the oddly unprocreative diction of Cowley's lyrics and odes or the "expansion" of Dryden's metaphors with, say, the writings of Hobbes or the sermons of Tillotson that we sense, albeit obscurely, a change in the repertoire of language *available* for choice as much as in the explicit or conscious choices of the writers themselves.

III

The Renaissance belief in the triune relationships of reality, language, and literature, genetrix of allegory and finally of the metaphysical poem and sermon, was very different from the linguistic conventionalism espoused by the "official" reformers of the Restoration. Names, commented Wilkins, are "such arbitrary *sounds* or *words* as Nations of men have agreed upon, either casually or designedly, to express their mental notions of [objects]."[35] As in Ferdinand de Saussure's *Cours de linguistique générale,* the linguistic sign is characterized by the arbitrariness of the conjunction of *signifiant* and *signifié.*[36] For many theorists of the sixteenth century there was, by contrast, a necessary, often magical, connection between concepts, words, and the world signified; thus language was "motivated." Cassirer succinctly describes such a situation: "the world of things and the world of names form a single undifferentiated chain of causality and hence a single reality. The same form of substantiality and the same form of causality prevail in both, linking them into one self-enclosed whole."[37]

Poet and scientist approached God's book of creation through the same avenues: metaphor, etymology, anagram, and number-letter transformations were not merely treated as the sport of a willful fancy but as licit means of interpreting the hieroglyphic construction of the natural world *via* language, within which glimmered the remnants of Eden's perfect semiology.[38]

Nonetheless, technologists like Agricola attacked the redoubtably individualistic uses of such *arcana* in the alchemical sciences where they wrought havoc with the possible development of a true standard language in which different scientists could communicate intelligibly. The German metallurgist's complaint that the alchemists "use strange names, which do not properly belong to the metals . . . [which] enjoy now one name and now another, invented by themselves"[39] was prophetic of the far more turbulent situation compressed into the mid-seventeenth century. Agricola's espousal of an "unmotivated" standard language anticipates Bacon's rejection of linguistic theories which "by curious inquiry, or rather by apt feigning [claim] to have derived imposition of names from reason and intendment."[40] Bacon's argument that words have "force only by contract or acceptation"[41] was in turn the theory on which Wilkins was to base the ideal denotation of his standard language.

Agricola also pointed to the semantic propinquity of alchemy and poetry, thereby anticipating (even as he modifies) Marjorie Nicolson's remark that "The language of poetry and of science was one when the world was one."[42] The gradual emergence of an "automatized" (technical) language of science and the slow demise of the "foregrounded" (enigmatic) language of science certainly complicated that "foregrounding" to which poetry aspired. Much verse sided with alchemy and the sublime sciences in their task of unhusking and activating the magical potentialities in words. Thus Sidney and his chemistry teacher John Dee each took the brazen language of everyday discourse and delivered a golden, which made things "either better then Nature bringeth forth, or, quite a newe, formes such as never were in Nature, as the *Heroes, Demigods, Cyclops, Chimeras, Furies*, and such like."[43] The nonaccidental relationship posited between words and events was also appropriated by the Tudor and Jacobean propagandists, notably in verse panegyrics and the symbolism of joyous entries and masques. The poets were instrumental in this development of the mythology of royal power. Hence in that majestic celebration of the English *imperium, The Faerie Queene,* Spenser becomes a dazzling *bricoleur,* pressing Isidorean ingenuity and folk etymologies into national service alongside Christian apocalypticism; even the hardheaded Ben Jonson, elsewhere a doubtful friend of natural magic, employs the anagram CHARLES JAMES STUART/CLAIMES ARTHURS SEAT as significant patriotic prophecy on several occasions in his masques.[44] Metaphysical wit and the *concetto predicabile* emerge from this world of hierarchic correspondence, and do their "best to hold the elaborate structure together, extending it through unexpected and daring lines of thought or reinforcing it in surprising ways by noticing unfamiliar correlations between familiar things."[45] But, with their new dimension of more personal eccentricity, they are heralds of the disintegration of a multifaceted world order in which brilliantly imaginative personal exegesis had been sanctioned by an (admittedly extravagant) shared hermeneutic system.

The magical mode survived, more fantastically caparisoned than ever, in the lavish unreality of the Caroline masque and in such strange maverick volumes as Henry Reynolds' *Mythomystes* or Robert Fludd's vast compendia, notably the *Utriusque Cosmi Historia.* But their sustaining infrastructure in the "motivated" Renaissance conception of language, now fragmenting under the various assaults of Baconian empiricism and Cartesian rationalism, went into the melting pot, along with so much else, in the 1640's; and it was in those seething waters that Dryden and his peers witnessed the consequences of metaphysical poetry and its conceptual precursors.

A vertiginous linguistic relativism characterizes the period between 1640 and 1660. What Edward Benlowes called the "vast Librarie"[46] of the heavens, hitherto the preserve of the educated or the well-born, was now open for public consultation. The collapse of effective press censorship precipitated the translation and diffusion of what had previously been forbidden or inaccessibly learned works, consequently delivering the tools of Renaissance hermeneutics (those former endorsements of hierarchy) into the hands of the "base Mechanicks and the Rout."[47] Not only were the prismatic Renaissance connexions between language and reality shattered by the quixotic variety of contemporary interpretations so quickly hurried into print—discussions of the Rosicrucian "*Angelical* and *Paradisical* language" or of Jacob Boehme's man, "the Hieroglyphick of Eternity and Time";[48] but the disparate linguistic styles and registers in which the authors embodied their discoveries contributed to the widespread belief in a breakdown in the communicative function of language:

> Nay homebred heads unsocially did strive
> T'estrange themselves and SHIBBOLETHS contrive;
> *Tradesmen* affected uncoth words to cant,
> And blunder in terms non-significant;
> Each *Company* would be thought a little Nation
> And coyn a Dialect in their own fashion.[49]

The pullulation of "*Babylonish* dialects"[50] ("dialect," like "shibboleth," was a term which enjoyed an especial currency) largely destroyed the possibility of any automatization in folk language, while the Helmontian and Paracelsian scientific ideologies failed to encourage the development of a standard language; indeed denotation was often eschewed in the drive to encompass as various a spiritual meaning as possible. Verbicide and semantic ambiguity were rampant.

IV

In such a context how was poetry to achieve the necessary foregrounding—from the proliferation of folk dialects (the foregrounded potentialities of which, previously limited to speech, had now achieved the dignity and fixity of print), from an increasingly confused aesthetic canon, from the fractured standard language in which Robert Fludd and Francis Bacon met in gay abandon? In their dependence upon the statuary of the classical pantheon and the conventional strategies of breathlessly hyperbolic wit, the uneducated poets, "who when / They stuffe their page with Godds, write worse than Men,"[51] not only failed to distinguish themselves from the figurative and exaggerated expression of much non-literary discourse but compounded, for their social and intellectual betters, the problem of choosing a suitably fore-grounded lexicon, syntax, and image-bank. "Almost every author, Royalist or Puritan, highbrow or popular, thought of himself as 'literary'," comments Joseph Frank. "Thus controversial verse, addressed to the presumably largest public, is frequently almost as full of classical allusions, self-conscious rhetoric, and fancy diction as a philosophical poem by, say, Edward Benlowes. . . . Whether one is reading a bit of contrived juvenalia or the 'outcry' of an oppressed workman, he is likely to encounter Olympian gods, inherited similes, stock diction and rhymes, convoluted syn-tax."[52] We are witnessing the creation of an "automatized poetic canon": "The outward manifestation of this automatization is the ease with which creation is possible in terms of this canon, the proliferation of epigones, the liking for obsolescent poetry in circles not close to literature."[53]

Faced by this situation, John Cleveland decided to indulge his own university taste for poetic grotesquerie in a policy of strategic parody, but although his badger-fanged lines wrought havoc with the Puritan perversions which characterized "the Language of the dayes,"[54] they also perpetuated the unforegrounded style by exemplifying it so brilliantly—in addition to falling foul of the imitative fallacy: by the mimicry of a world-upside-down, they helped to prolong its literary existence.

Other poets decided to withdraw into more private worlds of their own wit, where a dedication to an abstruse vocabulary and philosophy, any refraction of contemporary debate notwithstand-ing, would ensure the necessary foregrounding. Marvell's success in his unpublished poems was singular; the failure of those epigones of the metaphysical style—Mildmay Fane or Edward Benlowes—was more typical. The latter thrust his florid *Theophila* into the world only to contribute to the general linguistic deterioration. In the midst of this jawbreaking foray into possible human imitations of "The THEANTHROPIC WORD" Benlowes formulated an extraordinarily absolutist theory of "foregrounding."[55] "Poets," he proclaimed, "have *Legislative Pow'r* of making *Words*."[56] God and his poet-servant are both verbidextrous alchemists:

> . . . Nature's chang'd alone
> By GRACE; THAT is the *Chymick-stone*
> And thy all pow'rful *WORD* is pure *Projection*.[57]

For Sidney, the alchemical connection between the human and divine uses of language had been imaginatively central to his age as well as to *An Apologie for Poetrie*; seventy years later it is, at best, eccentric; at worst, it veers toward schizophrenia: the Paracelsian movement was more than politically radical—with its "wild and whirling words" (a vocabulary that was increasingly non-referential), it flirted with the semantic solipsism of private languages.[58]

Thus Samuel Butler's acid comparison of Prynne and Benlowes penetrates beneath the poet's explicit Royalism and Anglicanism to develop the deeper congruence between poetic and religious extremism:

> There was one that lined a Hat-Case with a Paper of *Benlowse's* Poetry—*Prynne* bought it by Chance, and put a new Demi-Castor into it. The first Time he wore it he felt only a singing in his Head, which within two Days turned to a vertigo. He was let Blood in the Ear by one of the State-Physicians, and recovered; but before he went abroad he writ a Poem of Rocks and Seas, in a stile so proper and natural, that it was hard to determine, which was ruggeder.[59]

Butler then notes the unmistakable affinity between Benlowes' unduly distorted poetic language and the zanily mysterious plates chosen for *Theophila*;[60] in these the theurgic word and cosmic emblem, of Renaissance provenance, have reached a suitably complementary state of lunatic deterioration:

There is no Feat of Activity, nor Gambol of Wit, that was ever performed by Man from him that vaults on *Pegasus*, to him that Tumbles through the Hoops of an Anagram, but *Benlows* has got the Mastery in it, whether it be high-rope Wit or low-rope Wit. He has all sorts of *Echoes, Rebus's, Chronograms* &c. besides *Carwitchets, Clenches, and Quibbles*—as for *Altars* and *Pyramids* in Poetry, he has out-done all Men in that way; for he has made a *Gridiron*, and a *Frying-Pan* in Verse, that, beside the Likeness in Shape, the very Tone and Sound of the Words did perfectly represent the Noise that is made by those Utensils . . ."[61]

Despite its verbal and visual excess, Benlowes' poetry suffers from insufficient foregrounding in the context of its time; in trying to raise himself too much above the mundane, Benlowes simply joined the ranks of the mad. He shares his tumidity of style with wild writers like Thomas Vaughan and John Webster and in his supposedly significant juggling of letters and numbers he is at one with the crazed prophets, Arise Evans and Eleanor Davies.[62]

Differences in specific prediction and of political affiliation do not destroy the similarity of exegetical method that links these writers. Thus the Restoration was, like Swift, ready to dismiss any manifestation of "the Dialect of those *Fanatick Times*,"[63] regardless of the opinions of the author; poets like Benlowes and Cleveland were treated no better than the old and unwanted Cavaliers who thronged Whitehall in 1660. Benlowes died while waiting for admission to an almshouse; his *Theophila*, a vanity publication to end all vanity publications, sank like a stone with his literary reputation, which has only surfaced once—in the dragnet of Pope's footnotes to *The Dunciad*.[64] Despite the widespread popularity of the "Clevelandism" and the steadily growing number of attributions in each new edition, Cleveland's style was rejected by the fashioners of the emergent aesthetic norm; Dryden condemns his predecessor's scholastical harshness and allegorical opacity in a scornfully compact image: "he gives us many times a hard nut to break our teeth, without a kernel for our pains."[65]

A number of mid-century poets endeavored to pour the oil of smoother poetic measures upon what Hobbes called "the windy blisters of a troubled water," the language of the period.[66] Yet the literary achievement of the early 1600's was itself overwhelmed by the turbulent billows of a muddled standard language and apocalyptic linguistic theorizing: thus fabulous romances, strong lines, and even Shakespeare's fracture of decorum all seemed prophetic of the confused national situation with its Babylonish dialects. The citadels of authority swarmed with men who confused romance and reality; sanctioned interpretive ingenuity had ebbed "*downe dry to pebble*-Anagrams" in the vaporings of Fane or Benlowes, not to mention those of the fringe fanatics; it seemed to new readers that Shakespeare's "trunk-hose-Wit" had done little more than amuse the "unjudging Rout":

> Brave Shakespeare *flow'd, yet had his Ebbings too,*
> *Often above himselfe, sometimes below.*[67]

The Prague School approach to such different stylistic perspectives is characteristically illuminating; its emphasis upon moving currents of language frees both literary and linguistic analysis from the log-jam of mere synchronicity: "Even in the synchronic approach . . . we must take into account the dynamic character of language. Of course, synchronic description is not a motion picture, it is only a snapshot; but we must try to find out the synchronic projection of the movements, the changes in the language."[68] Jan Mukařovský and Felix Vodička, who approach the development of poetic diction and syntax with just such a sense of their mobility, are thus aware of the intersection of the contemporaneous plane of language by its gestation in history. Hence Mukařovský can see how literary perceptions are distorted when older poetry is projected onto a novel standard ground:

> The condition of the norm of the standard language is not without its significance to poetry, since the norm of the standard is precisely the background against which the structure of the work of poetry is projected, and in regard to which it is perceived as a distortion; the structure of a work of poetry can change completely from its origin if it is, after a certain time, projected

against the background of a norm of the standard which has since changed.[69]

Such a theory helps to explain the Royalists' incapacity to understand fully the literary achievements of their predecessors; their unwillingness to appreciate it is clarified by Vodička's introduction of a sociological dimension constituted by such "heteronomous elements" as "the publisher, the book market, advertising . . . sudden turns in political life, or political pressures."[70] When he describes how older works of literature are judged in these situations Vodička (somewhat optimistically) approaches the issue from its positive rather than its negative angle, but his analysis of the change still holds good for literary metamorphoses of the mid-seventeenth century:

> As soon as the work is perceived on the basis of the integration into another context (a changed linguistic state of affairs, other literary requirements, a changed social structure, a new set of spiritual and practical values), then precisely those qualities of the work can be perceived as esthetically effective which previously were not perceived as esthetically effective, so that a positive evaluation may be based on entirely opposite reasons.[71]

In such periods of literary revaluation, adds Vodička, "not all that pretends to be a real norm is one."[72] Cleveland's ironic and Benlowes' unintentional inversions masqueraded as one norm; other Royalists, however, were determined to exercise control of a literary world that was right side up, in which "all their Order and their Place maintain."[73] In the novel vision of concord, with which Cowley praised the return of Lord Falkland from his Scottish campaigns early in the 1640's, metaphoric transformations (whether in the real or an imaginative world) were impossible:

> So thousand diverse *Species* fill the aire,
> Yet neither crowd nor mix confus'dly there,
> Beasts, Houses, Trees and Men together lie,
> Yet enter *undisturb'd* into the Eye.[74]

To ensure precedents for the newly acceptable mode of "fore-grounding," Royalists turned to the non-metaphoric chastity of Ben Jonson's lyric verse or the "cleare," "free and cleane" expression, "ever brim full," of those gentlemen dramatists Beaumont and Fletcher.[75] The more immediate precursor of the new "fore-grounding" was the aesthetic canon that had been embraced pre-war by members of the Great Tew Circle, such as Waller and Lord Falkland, who eschewed metaphysical ruggedness or undue conceptual complexity in the subdued conceits or mellifluous meter of their own lines.[76] The perspicuous currents of the new verse were calmly distinguished from the "mutinous waves"[77] of civil strife and hard words:

> Though deep, yet clear, though gentle yet not dull,
> Strong without rage, without one-flowing full.[78]

In the gestation of *Cooper's Hill* we see mid-century topsy turvy-dom stood upon its head.

V

What Benlowes praised in the "enucle'ate Mysteries" of metaphor[79] —the capacity of the mind to synthesize different orders of reality by the interpenetration of their verbal signs—was also being jettisoned by poet and scientist alike in their determined reaction against linguistically veiled epistemological confusion and in their rejection of Renaissance mythography and allegorical technique. Clarity of vision, unclouded by figurative language, was the new *desideratum*. The mind of Man, affirmed Sprat, "is no *Magical Glass*, like that with which *Astrologers* use to deceive the Ignorant; by making them believe, that therein they may behold the Image of any *Place*, or *Person* in the World, though never so farr remov'd from it."[80] The space and time travel of Fancy in the chariot of metaphor—"Up presently to the *Primum Mobile*, and the trepidation of the Firmament. Dive into the Bowels and hid treasures of the Earth: Dispatch forthwith for Peru and Jamaica"[81] —was considered highly dangerous for it disrupts the slow examination of reality's surfaces, religious or scientific, which the mind necessarily conducts in the standard language. That great Christian virtuoso Boyle punctuated his brilliant rebuttal of the occult in chemistry with denunciations of the "Mystical Termes, and Ambiguous Phrases" and the "Canting way of delivering the Principles of Nature" which marked the style of the spiritual chemists of the Revolution.[82]

After railing in almost enthusiastic fashion against the radical resuscitation of the *prisca theologia*, with its "Emblems, Fables, Symbols, Parables, heaps of Metaphors, Allegories," Samuel Parker herds the philosophical "Poets and Romancers" out of the terrain of the standard language which their metaphoric armies had invaded.[83] Unfortunately, the landscape of literary romance was itself no longer available for occupation since more progressive poets like Davenant had eliminated the supernatural dimension. The House of Astragon supplanted the Garden of Adonis; the House of Sidrophel replaced the Cave of Merlin. Cowley, though an ardent admirer of Spenser, praised Davenant thus:

> Methinks *Heroick Poesie* till now
> Like some fantastick *Fairy Land* did show,
> *Gods, Devils, Nymphs, Witches* and *Gyants Race*,
> And all but *Man* in *Man's chief work* had place.
> Thou like some worthy *Knight* with sacred *Arms*
> Doth drive the *Monsters* thence and end the *Charms*.[84]

"Savage Metaphors (things rudely great)" were no more acceptable in the foregrounded verbal ordering of poetry than were "impenetrable Armors, Inchanted Castles, invulnerable bodies, Iron men, flying Horses" in the world which they described.[85] "To bring your *Tropes* and *Figures* here," writes Cowley from Jersey:

> Strange as to bring *Camels* and *Ele'phants* were,
> And *Metaphore* is so unknown a thing,
> 'Twould need the *Preface* of, *God save the King*.[86]

Has our low-lying path through this literary undergrowth of verse epistles and dedicatory poems blinded us to the stateliness of the overarching forest—to *Davideis, Hudibras,* or *Pharonnida,* for example? Possibly; but Vodička observes that "we should not imagine the literature of a given period merely as the set of existing literary works but also, and equally, as the set of existing literary values."[87] Nothwithstanding, the literary values which are explicitly canvassed in the minor works only attain full significance when life is lent them by the appearance of a major work, for while "the commonplace may be understood as a reduction of the exceptional . . . the exceptional cannot be understood by amplifying the commonplace."[88]

The relationship of linguistic theory to the contemporary state of language resembles, in part, such connections between literary values and achievement: reflection and realization are simultaneously (and symbiotically) active. George Dalgarno's *Ars Signorum* and John Wilkins' *Essay towards a Real Character* were not full polemical blows struck for the exponents of denotation and logical clarity in their frequent skirmishes with the defenders of mystical ambiguity and Rosicrucian linguistics;[89] even so, the treatises bear the unmistakable print of their historical moment while betraying, as well, traces of the "epistemic shift" far below. Ironically, Wilkins' whole enterprise has been seen as emerging from "the memory tradition on its occult side. The seventeenth century universal language enthusiasts are translating into rational terms efforts such as those of Giordano Bruno to found universal memory systems on magic images which he thought of as directly in contact with reality."[90] As in Hooke's transformation of Trithemius' "telephone system" of angelic magic into a *mechanically* instantaneous form of communication,[91] the terms of the whole equation, its epistemic configurations, have been changed.

Thus, linguistic speculation cannot escape from the ideological context of its time; to underline this truth Vladimír Skalička took issue with Louis Hjelmslev's interpretation of the Saussurian image of language as chess game, "a play and nothing more." Skalička argues that it is "against this conception of play that we have to object," showing how and why "play" can only be understood within the value system of its particular context:

> The play of chess is not just identical with those few rules that can be easily learned by a schoolboy of ten. The sense of the game of chess only emerges from another kind of rules which are very difficult to fix and are found to be always changing, rules to be observed if the game is to be brought to a successful conclusion . . . The game of chess assumes various aspects according as it is a pastime of a handful of people or a mass phenomenon etc. And this dependence on social implementation must be valid in language even more so.[92]

Wilkins' elaborate division of reality into ranked taxonomies, each with its cognate linguistic signifiers, should be seen in such a light; by defining the limits of the empirical world (and its contents) as well as of its semantic space, he hoped (with paradoxical idealism) to sever the hydra-headed solipsisms of the previous twenty years—to render them literally inconceivable. While it took the naive mind of Samuel Parker to squeeze out most of the implications of Wilkins' theories for thought-and-word control,[93] the *Essay* itself is instinct with just such considerations: the urgency of contemporary issues presses in upon the chess game (or, for Wilkins, dice or card game)[94] of linguistic theory at every juncture.

Now "foregrounded" from a degenerate aesthetic canon, from the folk dialects, and from the standard languages (such as they were!) of the mid-century, respectable poetic diction began to succumb to similar ideological pressures—in this case, the first infusions of "the rules." Its relationship to the new language of science did not preclude such novel methods of "foregrounding," as Cowley's "*Pindarical* falling from one thing into another" or Dryden's "heightened signification" of words; yet the semantic space in which these were deployed was significantly more circumscribed than the linguistic universe in which metaphysical wit had made its spectacular grasshopper leaps. In the closer approximation of words to things, the excess of *signifié* over *signifiant* in the metaphysical conceit was greatly reduced and the resulting conversion of the energies of literary language from field force to binary flow prepared the way for Swift. Mukařovský shows why classicism is obliged to clamp so severely the connotations of its words, and indicates, implicitly, how its aesthetic energy is harnessed to the further definition of this perspicuity:

> The word as an element of style is thus subject to strict discipline by classicism: the more unexpected and individual it is, the more it is feared, because classicism limits the freedom of naming severely. It considers particularly dangerous metaphorical designations which attract attention to themselves and threaten the architectonic order of the sentence structure by the ungovernable associations which they provoke and by the unpredictable relations into which they enter with neighboring words; it is well known to what extent a poetic image can color a broad surrounding context. Therefore the stylistic legislation of classicism takes great care to render imagery harmless . . .[95]

VI

"In a work of poetry of any genre," argues Mukařovský, "there is no fixed border, nor, in a certain sense, any essential difference between the language and the subject matter."[96] After the mid-century pillaging of the Orphic mysteries by the sects and the depredations upon Parnassus by the levellers in rhyme, Sprat and Cowley felt compelled to repudiate the "confused antiquated *Dreams* of senseless *Fables* and *Metamorphoses*"[97] of the classical past:

> The *Wit* of the *Fables* and *Religions* of the *Ancient World* is well nigh consum'd: They have already serv'd the *Poets* long enough; and it is now high time to dismiss them: especially seeing they have this peculiar *imperfection*, that they were only *Fictions* at first: whereas *Truth* is never so well express'd or amplify'd, as by those Ornaments which are *Tru* and *Real* in themselves.[98]

Consequently, they rejected a central Renaissance paradigm of "foregrounding" that had been realized simultaneously in style and subject matter. With sharp insight they appreciated that "Foregrounding brings to the surface and before the eyes of the observer even such linguistic phenomena as remain quite covert in communicative speech, although they are important factors in language."[99] Sprat and Cowley strove to destroy a mode of "foregrounding" (which we have seen advocated by Sidney) not only because of what it said but of what it implied about a tradition of language and the world which that language described. Sprat derived this fresh conception of the poetic canon from Cowley's concluding remarks in the "Preface" to *Poems, 1656*: "Does not," the poet asks, excitably:

> the passage of *Moses* and the *Israelites* into the Holy Land yield incomparably more Poetical variety, then the voyages of *Ulysses* or *Aeneas*? Are the obsolete threadbare tales of *Thebes* and *Troy*, half so stored with great, heroical, and supernatural actions (since *Verse* will needs *finde* or *make* such) as the wars of *Joshua*, of the *Judges*, of David, and divers others?[100]

A decade later the scientist replied—and enunciated a new ideal of "foregrounding" which we have already encountered, at the outset of our discussion, in its standard language form—the practical piety of Joseph Glanvill:

> The *Wit* that may be borrow'd from the *Bible* is magnificent, and as all the other Treasures of *Knowledge* it contains, inexhaustible. This may be us'd and allow'd without any danger of prophaness ...What irreligion can there be in applying some *Scripture-expressions* to *Natural things*?[101]

This program was brilliantly, and imaginatively, realized in a poem which did, however, make use of all the Renaissance tools of "foregrounding" even as it dismissed their vanity: the poem is the joker in our pack, the exception which disproves the standard: *Paradise Lost*.

NOTES

1 Abraham Cowley, *Poems 1656* (London, 1656). "The Preface," sig. (a)2^v.

2 Sir Philip Sidney, *An Apologie for Poetrie*, in *Elizabethan Critical Essays*, ed. G. Gregory Smith (Oxford: Oxford University Press, 1964), I, 188.

3 John Milton, *Poems* (London, 1645), "The Stationer to the Reader," sig. A3^r.

4 Samuel Sheppard, *The Times Displayed* (London, 1646), title page.

5 Andrew Marvell, "To his Noble Friend Mr. Richard Lovelace, upon his Poems," in *Andrew Marvell: The Complete Poems*, ed. E. S. Donno (Harmondsworth, Middlesex: Penguin, 1972), p. 33.

6 These statistics are given by Joseph Frank in *Hobbled Pegasus: A Descriptive Bibliography of Minor English Poetry 1641–1660* (Albuquerque: University of New Mexico Press, 1968), p. 5.

7 Robert Boyle, *The Sceptical Chymist*, 2nd ed. (Oxford, 1680). sig. A7^r.

8 Boyle, *Sceptical Chymist*, sig. A7^r.

9 William H. Youngren, "Generality, Science and Poetic Language in the Restoration," *English Literary History*, 35 (1968), 162.

10 Jan Mukařovský, "The Esthetics of Language," in *A Prague School Reader on Esthetics, Literary Structure, and Style*, trans. and ed. Paul L. Garvin (Washington: Georgetown University Press, 1964), p. 33.

11 See, for example, the recent overview of the problem by Stanley Fish, "How Ordinary is Ordinary Language?" *New Literary History*, 5 (1973), 41–54.

12 See Dell H. Hymes, *Foundations in Sociolinguistics* (Philadelphia: University of Pennsylvania Press, 1974).

13 Bohuslav Havránek, "The Functional Differentiation of the Standard Language," in Garvin, op. cit., p. 4.

14 Ibid., p. 6.

15 Thomas Sprat, *The History of the Royal Society* (London, 1667; facsimile rpt., ed. Jackson I. Cope and Harold Whitmore Jones, St. Louis, Missouri: Washington University Press, 1958), p. 113.

16 Ibid.

17 Joseph Glanvill, "Anti-fanatical Religion and Free Philosophy In a Continuation of the New Atlantis," *Essays on Several Important Subjects in Philosophy and Religion* (London, 1676), pp. 22, 31, 45.

18 Havránek, "Functional Differentiation," p. 9.

19 Sprat, *History*, p. 112; Glanvill, "Anti-fanatical Religion," p. 44.

20 John Wilkins, *An Essay Towards a Real Character and a Philosophical Language* (London, 1668), sigs. b1^{r-v}.

21 Jonathan Cohen, "On the Project of a Universal Character," *Mind*, 63 (1954), 61.

22 Glanvill, "Anti-fanatical Religion," pp. 42–43; Sprat, *History*, p. 113.

23 Jan Mukařovský, "Standard Language and Poetic Language," in Garvin, *Prague School Reader*, p. 19.

24 Ibid.

25 Havránek, "Functional Differentiation," p. 3.

26 Mukařovský, "Standard Language," p. 18.

27 For the competing world-views of the middle and late seventeenth century, see, for example, Keith Thomas, *Religion and the Decline of Magic* (London: Weidenfield and Nicolson, 1971). "The disenchantment of the world" is a phrase borrowed from Lawrence Stone's discussion of Thomas' work in the *New York Review of Books*, Dec. 2, 1971, pp. 17–25.

28 Mukařovský, "Standard Language," p. 18.

29 Thomas Birch, *The History of the Royal Society of London* (London, 1756; facsimile rpt. Bruxelles: Culture et Civilisation, 1968), I, 499–500.

30 John Dryden, "Of Dramatic Poesie: An Essay," In Geoge, *Of Dramatic Poesy and other Critical Essays*, ed. George Watson (London: Everyman's Library, 1962), I, 24–25.

31 Mukařovský, "Standard Language," p. 21.

32 Cowley, *Poems 1656*, sigs. Aaa2^{r-v}; p. 22.

33 Dryden, "Defence of the Epilogue," in Watson, op. cit., I, 177.

34 See Michel Foucault, *Les Mots et les choses* (Paris: Gallimard, 1966).

35 Wilkins, *Essay Towards a Real Chracter*, p. 20.

36 Ferdinand de Saussure, *Cours de linguistique générale*, ed. Charles Bally and Albert Sechehaye (Paris: Payot, 1968), esp. pp. 100–102, 157.

37 Ernst Cassirer, *The Philosophy of Symbolic Forms*, trans. Ralph Manheim (New Haven and London: Yale University Press, 1964), I, 118.

38 See, for example, D. P. Walker, *The Ancient Theology* (Ithaca, New York: Cornell University Press, 1972), pp. 25, 100–104.

39 Paolo Rossi, *Philosophy, Technology and the Arts in the Early Modern Era*, trans. Salvator Attansio (New York, Evanston and London: Harper Torchbooks, 1970), pp. 51–53.

40 Francis Bacon, *The Advancement of Learning*, ed. G. W. Kitchin (London: Everyman's Library, 1954), p. 138.

41 Ibid., p. 137.

42 Marjorie Hope Nicolson, *The Breaking of the Circle* (Evanston, Illinois: Northwestern University Press, 1950), p. 106.

43 Sidney, *An Apologie for Poetrie*, p. 156. On the occult dimensions of Sidney's thought, see Peter J. French, *John Dee: The World of an Elizabethan Magus* (London: Routledge and Kegan Paul, 1972), ch. VI.

44 Ben Jonson, *The Complete Masques*, ed. Stephen Orgel (New Haven and London: Yale University Press, 1969), pp. 143, 168, 290. Jonson may

have borrowed the anagram from his old schoolmaster, for it appears in William Camden's *Remaines of a Greater Worke* . . . (London, 1605), p. 153.

45 Robert M. Adams, *Strains of Discord: Studies in Literary Openness* (Ithaca, New York: Cornell University Press, 1958), pp. 107–8.

46 Edward Benlowes, "On Divine Poets," *Theophila* (London, 1652), sig. C6^v.

47 Abraham Cowley, *The Civil War*, ed. Allan Pritchard (Toronto: University of Toronto Press, 1973), Book III, line 41.

48 John Webster, *Academiarum Examen* (London, 1653), p. 27 (facsimile in Allen G. Debus, *Science and Education in the Seventeenth Century: The Webster Ward Debate* [London: Macdonald and New York: American Elsevier, 1970]); "The Preface of the Translator to the Reader," Jacob Behmen, *Signatura Rerum*, trans. J. Ellistone (London, 1651), sig. A2^r.

49 J. S., "To his Honored Friend Mr T. B. Upon his Glossographia," in Thomas Blount, *Glossographia* (London, 1656).

50 Samuel Butler, *Hudibras*, ed. John Wilders (Oxford: Oxford University Press, 1967), Part I, Canto I, line 97.

51 Sir John Berkenhead, "On the happy Collection of Master Fletcher's Works, never before Printed," in *Comedies and Tragedies Written by Francis Beaumont and John Fletcher Gentlemen* (London, 1647), sig. E2^r.

52 Frank, *Hobbled Pegasus*, pp. 22–23.

53 Mukařovský, "Standard Language," p. 22.

54 John Cleveland, "To P. Rupert," in *The Poems of John Cleveland*, ed. Brian Morris and Eleanor Withington (Oxford: Clarendon Press, 1967), p. 33.

55 Benlowes, *Theophila*, Canto I, "The Prelibation," st. LXXVIII.

56 Benlowes, *Theophila*, Canto III, "The Restauration," st. XLV.

57 Benlowes, *Theophila*, Canto I, "The Prelibation," st. XC.

58 On the radical dimension of Paracelsianism in mid-seventeenth-century England, see P. M. Rattansi, "Paracelsus and the Puritan Revolution," *Ambix*, 11 (1963), 23–32.

59 Samuel Butler, "A Small Poet," in *The Genuine Remains in Verse and Prose*, ed. R. Thyer (London, 1759), II, 119.

60 On the gestation, language, and engravings of *Theophila*, see Harold Jenkins, *Edward Benlowes (1602–1676): Biography of a Minor Poet* (Cambridge, Mass.: Harvard University Press, 1952), chs. XVI–XX, appendix IV; Maren-Sofie Røstvig, among others, has discussed the numerological structure of the poem: *The Happy Man: Studies in the Metamorphosis of a Classical Ideal*, 2nd ed. (New York: Humanities Press, 1962), I, 141–42.

61 Samuel Butler, "A Small Poet," p. 120.
62 On the mad Welshman and the crazed widow of Sir John Davies, see Christopher Hill, *The World Turned Upside Down* (New York: Viking Press, 1972), pp. 223–24.
63 Jonathan Swift, *A Proposal for Correcting, Improving and Ascertaining the English Tongue*, in *The Prose Works of Jonathan Swift*, ed. Herbert Davis (Oxford: Basil Blackwell, 1957), IV, 10.
64 Alexander Pope, *The Dunciad in Four Books*, III, 21.
65 Dryden, "Of Dramatic Poesy: An Essay," in Watson, ed. cit., I, 40.
66 Thomas Hobbes, "The Answer of Mr Hobbes to Sir Will D'Avenant's Preface before Gondibert," in *Sir William Davenant's Gondifert*, ed. David F. Gladish (Oxford: Clarendon Press, 1971), p. 52.
67 Berkenhead, "On the happy Collection," sigs. E1^v–E2^r.
68 František Daneš, "One Instance of the Prague School Methodology: Functional Analysis of Utterance and Text," in *Method and Theory in Linguistics*, ed. Paul L. Garvin (The Hague: Mouton, 1970) p. 144.
69 Mukařovský, "Standard Language," p. 27.
70 Vodička, "The History of the Echo of Literary Works," in Garvin, *Prague School Reader,* p. 78.
71 Ibid. p. 79.
72 Ibid., p. 78.
73 Cowley, "To the Lord Falkland. For his safe Return from the Northern Expedition against the Scots," *Poems 1656*, p. 4.
74 Ibid.
75 Berkenhead, "On the happy Collection," sigs. E2^r–E2^v.
76 See the discussion by Ruth Wallerstein, "The Development of the Rhetoric and Metre of the Heroic Couplet Especially in 1625–1645," *PMLA*, 50 (1935), 166–209.
77 Cowley, *The Civil War*, Book I, line 187.
78 Sir John Denham, *Cooper's Hill* (1655) in Brendan O'Hehir, *Expans'd Hieroglyphicks* (Berkeley and Los Angeles: University of California Press, 1969), p. 151.
79 Benlowes, "To my Fancie Upon Theophila," *Theophila*, sig. B3^r.
80 Sprat, *History*, p. 97.
81 Lawrence Eachard, *The Grounds and Occasions of the Contempt of the Clergy and Religion*, 9th ed. (London, 1685), p. 64.
82 Boyle, *Sceptical Chymist*, pp. 206–7.
83 Samuel Parker, *A Free and Impartial Censure of the Platonick Philosophie* (Oxford, 1666), pp. 68, 74.
84 Cowley, "To Sir William Davenant Upon his two First Books of Gondibert, finished before his voyage to America," *Poems 1656*, p. 24.

85 Berkenhead, "On the happy Collection," sig. E2^v; Hobbes, "Answer," p. 51.

86 Cowley, "An Answer to a Copy of Verses sent me to Jersey," *Poems 1656*, p. 26.

87 Vodička, "History of the Echo," p. 73.

88 Edgar Wind, *Pagan Mysteries in the Renaissance* (New York: Norton, 1968), p. 238.

89 See Vivian Salmon, "Language Planning in Seventeenth Century England: Its Context and Aims," in *In Memory of J. R. Firth*, ed. C. E. Bazell et al. (London: Longmans, 1966), pp. 370–97.

90 Frances A. Yates, *The Art of Memory* (Harmondsworth, Middlesex: Penguin, 1969), p. 364.

91 W. Derham, *Philosophical Experiments and Observations of the late Eminent Dr Robert Hooke* (London, 1726), pp. 142–50.

92 Vladimír Skalička, "The Copenhagen Structuralism and the Prague School," cited in Josef Vachek, *The Linguistic School of Prague* (Bloomington and London: Indiana University Press, 1966), p. 23.

93 Samuel Parker, *A Discourse of Ecclesiastical Politie* (London, 1670), pp. 108–9.

94 Wilkins, *Essay Towards a Real Character*, p. 442.

95 Mukařovský, "Esthetics of Language," p. 61.

96 Mukařovský, "Standard Language," p. 22.

97 Cowley, "Preface," *Poems 1656*, sig. (b)2^r.

98 Sprat, *History*, p. 414.

99 Mukařovský, "Standard Language," p. 29.

100 Cowley, "Preface," *Poems 1656*, sig. (b)3^r.

101 Sprat, *History*, pp. 414–15.

Paris and Myth: One Vision of Horror

CATHERINE LAFARGE

In the beginning of the eighteenth century Paris became in the eyes of the world a source of great interest and even of fascination. This phenomenon was brought about by a convergence of various historical, financial, intellectual and artistic forces. Paris exercised a powerful attraction on non-Parisians, both French and non-French, and inspired many types of writings—letters, diaries, memoirs, novels and pamphlets. Out of these works comes the representation of a city nurtured by the imagination of authors which bears little resemblance to reality, for Paris both attracted and escaped these writers. It is opened for exploration and yet remains secretive and mysterious. It is an elusive and multi-faceted world of contrasts. For some it offers retreat, it is the source of life, the guarantee of freedom, the center of the universe, an idealized world. For others it is a caldron of vice, a city to rival Sodom and Gomorrah, a new Babylon.

Although it is beyond the scope of this paper to go into a full discussion of these many aspects of Paris, I would like to give a few examples of varied visions before looking at one work in detail. Both Bernardin de Saint-Pierre in the *Etudes de la Nature* and Louis-Sébastien Mercier in the *Tableau de Paris* see the capital as an asylum, a place where one can live obscure and free. In his

281

Memoirs Goldoni confesses that he has been enchained by Paris, and Galiani, when back in Naples, feels the most disconsolate exile. He writes: "My kingdom is Paris . . . Paris or life it's all the same. . . When they tore me away from Paris, they tore my heart out."[1] Karamzin sighs with joy on his arrival in Paris, but notes the shocking mixture of wealth and poverty and adds that "it is the most magnificent and the most foul, the most perfumed and the most stinking of cities."[2] A less-balanced opinion is to be found in the chevalier de Mouhy's *Paysanne parvenue*; there Paris is seen as hell.[3] For Fonvizin Paris evokes Sodom and Gomorrah.[4] As for Alfieri, he loses his illusions as he enters the capital for the first time and wonders what has led him to this cesspool.[5] On a second trip in the spring of 1789 he has but one haste to leave "this fetid hospital . . . this awful Babylon."[6] And there was Fougeret de Monbron who called his last book *La Capitale des Gaules ou la Nouvelle Babylone.*[7]

To most, the work of Fougeret de Monbron is little known and seldom read. Nevertheless, it deserves attention on several grounds. First, in a few pages Fougeret impresses the reader as a skilled satirist whose caustic style brings to life the seamy side of the capital. Second, never losing sight of his aim—the destruction of a glorified and unreal Paris—he takes on different garbs and systematically proceeds to show the evils of the city as would an economist, a moralist, a social reformer, an artist, and a caricaturist.

Before analyzing what emerges from perhaps his most important work, and showing the place it occupies in the birth of a myth, I would like first to present a few facts about the author's life and suggest some ties to better-known authors and writings of the eighteenth and nineteenth centuries.

Fougeret de Monbron, born in 1706, was the son of a well-to-do member of the bourgeoisie who lived in the northern town of Péronne. During most of his life it was his father's wealth which enable Fougeret to lead the life of an idler. In Paris, where he came to live in his late twenties, he was an habitué of cafés, theaters, gambling-houses and brothels. He was indeed familiar with the sordid side of the capital, and when he describes it first in a pornographic novel *Margot la Ravaudeuse* and later in *La Capitale des Gaules*, it can be presumed that his information was first hand.[8] It happened, to his misfortune, that when *Margot* was still in manuscript form Fougeret was careless enough to give several readings of it. For this possible flight of ego he spent a month in prison at Fort-l'Evêque; the remainder of the sentence required that he remove himself to a distance no less than fifty leagues from Paris. He first went to London and then travelled to Turkey, Italy, Russia, Prussia and Holland. It seems reasonable to say that Fougeret became a compulsive traveller in an attempt to drown his boredom with life. He tells us of his restlessness in an autobiographical work, *Le Cosmopolite*, first published in 1750. It was in that same year that he actually published *Margot*, adding a particularly insulting dedication to Berryer, the lieutenant-general of police who had been mainly responsible for his arrest and imprisonment at Fort-l'Evêque. The French authorities not only found the publication intolerable but had also become highly suspicious of his travels. They thought he might well be acting as a spy, and a warrant for his arrest was issued. There followed a game of hide and seek through parts of Europe which lasted several years, and Fougeret was finally arrested in Toulouse and imprisoned in the Bastille where he spent five months in 1755. After his release he spent a few months in his home town and then moved to Paris where he lived until his death in 1760 at the age of 53.[9]

Diderot has left us a colorful anecdote in his first satire, *La Satire sur les Caractères et les Mots de Caractère, de Profession, etc.*, which tells us something of Fougeret. They attended the Opera together and had just heard a particularly beautiful and moving piece. Diderot turned to his companion and expressed his enthusiasm. Fougeret responded that he shared none of this feeling because as he put it he had "a hairy heart." Diderot shuddered and moved away from this "two-legged tiger."[10] There is little doubt that Fougeret was one of the sources for Lui, the cynic of Diderot's second satire *Le Neveu de Rameau*.[11] We also know that Fougeret had a knack for quarreling with persons of rank in the countries he visited and thus found himself, perhaps with some satisfaction, *persona non grata* in Prussia and Russia. A contemporary said of him that he was a bilious character and a twentieth-century critic wrote that he had the "soul of a scorpion."[12] On the whole one is left with the impression that Fougeret was a bitter man, a consummate misanthrope.

As for his literary influence, critics have convincingly shown what Voltaire's *Candide* owes to Fougeret's *Cosmopolite* and that Voltaire's character Paquette derives much from Fougeret's heroine Margot la Ravaudeuse.[13] Moreover it has been asserted that Lord Byron was inspired by the *Cosmopolite* when he wrote *Childe Harold.*[14]

Part I of *La Capitale des Gaules*, Fougeret's last published work, appeared in the first months of 1759, and part II, in which Fougeret addresses his critics and develops anew the ideas already expressed in part I, came out at the end of the year (the year before his death).[15] The work, written in two parts, is a short, scathing attack on Paris in which the author gives the lie to the idealized view of the capital. He sets up a counterpart to the myth of the ideal city. To many, writes Fougeret in the opening paragraph, Paris because it offers all the pleasures and conveniences of life is an "earthly paradise." But he points out that to those too poor to enjoy the amenities it has to offer, the capital is a "place of torture."[16] The juxtaposition of "earthly paradise" and "place of torture" is at the heart of this pamphlet. As one reads the text it becomes obvious that for Fougeret the "earthly paradise" does not exist anymore, though it had perhaps at some earlier time or even might exist somewhere else. There are two webs of reference in Fougeret's treatment of Paris: the first is the Paris of his ancestors and the second is places outside of Paris (either somewhere else in France or a foreign land and more often the provinces in general).

Fougeret is the creator of a lively evocation of Paris. Gambling-houses are death-traps where dupes and crooks come head on, cafés are refuges for the idle, public walks and gardens are favorite gathering places for *nouvellistes* who pass judgments on princes, ministers and generals and for prostitutes who show off their gold and jewels. Fougeret's Paris is seething with opportunists, not to mention loitering priests and servants. It is an anthill of shady characters. And he can become an apt caricaturist when sketching one of these types or outlining the qualities desirable in the "fashionable" man. The attitude and the tone adopted by Fougeret in his descriptions bring to mind pages of Diderot's *Neveu de Rameau*, Rétif's *Nuits de Paris* and Mercier's *Tableau de Paris* and *Nouveau Paris*.

The city, Fougeret tells us, is run and ruled by three estates: the financiers, the innumerable courtesans, and the schemers. They are the ones that set the tone and are considered good company. So whereas in "the old days" an honest man was a man of modest and decent demeanor who behaved well and was virtuous, the fashionable man now was quite different. He can easily be recognized by the way he spends his money or by the jewels or lace he wears. To Fougeret the fashionable man may well be a thief, undoubtedly in debt, likely responsible for the ruin of many families, and one who speaks on every subject without rhyme and reason.[17]

On marriage things are no better. Fougeret recalls that "in our fathers' days" a marriage was founded on virtue and honesty whereas now marriages were solely questions of vested interest, a time when spouses were haggled over like pieces of furniture. Furthermore there were no more honest women to be found; all had plunged into libertinism and debauchery. He notes that Boileau in his tenth *Satire* counted three honest women in Paris and asks how many could be found in 1759.[18]

By this time and with this recitation of Fougeret's views one may well say: "Enough, I have placed him on the liberal-conservative spectrum." Or one may say: "This was a troubled man and further detail becomes repetitious." But it is appropriate to touch on a few additional points he makes because my attempt here is to show how far he carried the assault on the myth of Paris as a place of culture and enlightenment. In these specific references we will see variations of the attack and some of the almost bizarre inconsistencies in it.

Fougeret was preoccupied with the unfortunate change wrought on Parisian life with the emerging vogue for cafés. For him they were hotbeds for idlers who, instead of being useful to the country, wasted their talents away. He spoke of how an earlier generation gathered in taverns where friendship was nourished with good food, wine and song. Fougeret assures us that there are no better people than drinkers and by replacing taverns with cafés, and thus replacing drinking with idle talk, an innocent golden age had indeed been lost.[19]

He also looks outside of Paris and writes of Brittany and honor. In Brittany when a nobleman has no money he works and forgets his nobility; in Paris he finds illegal means to live well. And though perhaps such a person may deserve to be hanged, nobody minds and soon all is forgotten, for "a reputation grows back like fingernails."[20]

He writes of Toulouse and gambling. Gambling he points out is a source of income for those who have no income and are incapable of earning one—the example of Prévost's hero, Des Grieux, comes to mind. In gambling-houses respectable rogues fleece young men and foreigners. In Toulouse, however, Fougeret saw that kind of thief arrested, whipped, marked and sent to the galleys for six years for tricks that Parisians would call trifles.[21]

Fougeret's most scathing attack in this work, however, is aimed at luxury and its various ramifications. To underline how much luxury is an essential component in his Paris—"the place of torture"—Fougeret uses both foils: the "before" and the "elsewhere," the latter being represented by the provinces. First he tells us that though earlier generations possessed less cash than his, they had less needs and were wealthy by virtue of their limited cravings. Similarly they had no use for the types of workers and artists whose livelihood depended upon the courtesans. Earlier the country swarmed with people, the lands were cultivated, farmers were happy and enjoyed the fruits of their work, and their children contributed to their wealth. Presently, on the contrary, agriculture was a low and degraded profession, farmers were harassed and the countryside was deserted.[22]

By defending agriculture Fougeret sides with the Physiocrats, the new economists of the day. He pronounces luxury gangrenous to all political bodies for it progresses imperceptibly, and when one is aware of it, it is too late; there is no remedy. Paris draws its riches and splendor from the famine and exhaustion of the provinces. How many have come to the capital and squandered away their inheritance? Paris is a dangerous Babylon in which many have lost their innocence, a place where reputations and fortunes have been wiped out.[23] This, of course, sets him apart from such supporters of luxury as Mandeville, Melon, Voltaire and Diderot, yet has him joining Rousseau where the attack had been given a masterly development in the *Lettre à d'Alembert sur les spectacles*, published a year before *La Capitale des Gaules*.[24]

Paris breeds not only luxury but also libertinism and a state of corruption which owe their origin to the establishment of the theater. "Comedy is a Pandora's box which inundates us with vices."[25] Fougeret includes a tirade against the evils of the theater inspired by Rousseau's *Lettre à d'Alembert*. He elaborates further on luxury. Public walks and gardens, originally created to decorate the city and to be used by all citizens for relaxation after work, have become places where laziness, indolence and luxury bring people together from all walks of life. Fougeret singles out the Palais-Royal as being a place where debauchery reigns. But the ramparts are also scenes of scandalous displays of luxury which he regrets bitterly because of their influence on young men and women.[26]

Here we have perhaps enough detail to see how black is his outlook. Fougeret, libertine turned moralist and social satirist, does not spare the city, its inhabitants or their cutoms. Everything is depraved and whatever was good at one time or in some other place in Paris turns sour; man's immoral and greedy instincts have taken over. Fougeret is an embittered supermoralist who on the one hand seems to believe in the perfectibility of man and yet in his own frustration with and hostility toward his immediate environment sees nothing but darkness. At the beginning of part II of *La Capitale des Gaules*, while answering one of his critics, the *abbé* de la Porte, Fougeret compares the *abbé*'s optimistic view on human nature to that of Voltaire's character Pangloss and his own pessimistic outlook to that of Martin.[27] We should note that *Candide* was published in the same year as *La Capitale des Gaules.* One can recall that when Candide and Martin land in France, Candide asks Martin to tell him about Paris. Martin responds that Paris is a chaos and that on his last stay in the capital he was robbed of all his worldly possessions and ended in prison. And indeed Voltaire sets out to prove Martin right. We know Candide is also robbed and thrown in prison so that when he finally is released and is about to sail to England instead of Venice where he really wants to go, he finds some comfort in the idea that at least he has been delivered from hell. Voltaire's hell corresponds to Fougeret's "place of torture." It is interesting to speculate what influence the writings of these two men may have had on each other.[28]

We are now prompted to ask was there more to this man than the compulsion to attack, to defame and to be cynically hostile? There are elements in Fougeret which can be read as the prescriptions of a constructive social reformer. Though one may disagree with some of his objects for change, he did have prescriptions and one should not leave this element out of a discussion of the man's work. He recommended closing the theaters and the cafés, razing the gambling-houses, opening the public gardens—but only on holidays. He wanted to rid Paris of many superfluous people. He felt the innumerable flunkies should be sent back to the provinces and enlisted as soldiers and farmers much needed by the nation. If Paris was draining the kingdom of its citizens, a way of correcting this imbalance would be to require that all administrators live in the places where their responsibilities lay and that all abbots should dwell in their parishes and all officers should stay close to their regiments.[29] Moreover, showing some deeper social insight, he regretted the discovery of the new world, for he warned that the blood of all the unfortunate people slaughtered in America would fall on the consciences of all Europeans and that they might well be cursed for it.[30]

Yet the balance sheet is mixed. His respect for the hierarchy is clear. He would be viewed in terms we use today as a clear-cut conservative. He thought it was all right for the nobility to have carriages and create traffic jams, but not so for other classes. He favored legislation that would distinguish between a nobleman or a magistrate and an ordinary person. He approved of ladies of the aristocracy wearing jewels, if only to differentiate them from the wives of merchants and tradesmen; he felt it not decent for middle-class women to defy persons whom they should honor and respect. He felt it perfectly proper for persons of rank to have a retinue, for he acknowledged that they were superior. And finally, an additional objection he had to the fashion for cafés was that in their midst might blow winds of independence and anarchy and that the air of freedom could bring republicanism.[31]

Among the many concepts of the eighteenth century, none is perhaps more important than the antithetic coupling of shadow and light. The ultimate goal of the greatest writers was to bring about by their writings a new age, that of reason. Their ways to enlighten the world were varied and too famous and too many, of course, to note here. But we know that shadow and light did coexist during the whole century, and shadow we find was represented not only by the state, the church, and the social order, but also by the work of writers such as Fougeret, as well as the better-known group who harassed the Encyclopedists.[32]

Reality is rarely described, the city is either idealized or vilified. This dialectic can be witnessed both within and outside of literature. The city can be seen as a gathering place of enlightened men, a drawing force, on the road to progress. The less perfect aspects—reality—were often left aside and forgotten. Others, including Fougeret, find the sordid reality of the city so overpowering and nightmarish that their spirits cannot escape it, they are enchained by it, and are surrounded by its darkness.

Fougeret belongs to the eighteenth century. His economic, moral and political ideas as well as the genre he chose are deeply rooted in tradition. It may be said that he added a particular picture of the city. Proceeding from the word Babylon, which he used in his title, and though building on exaggerations and giving a distorted and monstrous view of the capital, he nevertheless supplemented the writings of his contemporaries and elaborated on Paris as "the place of torture." In *La Capitale des Gaules* his reader is convinced that behind the Paris he knows hides another one, depraved and horrifying. Fougeret thus can be said to have anticipated what would be the setting-in-place of a particular myth of the city whose one-sided imagery would be used and elaborated on by subsequent writers.

NOTES

1 Ferdinand Galiani in his letters to Madame d'Epinay from 1769 to 1780.
2 Nikolai M. Karamzin, *Voyage en France* (Paris: Hachette, 1885), p. 88.
3 Chevalier de Mouhy, *La Paysanne parvenue* (Paris: Prault, 1756), IV, 179.
4 Denis I. Fonvizin, *Letters From My Second Journey Abroad (1777–1778)*, included in Harold B. Segel, ed., *The Literature of Eighteenth-Century Russia* (New York: E. P. Dutton, 1967), p. 328.
5 In August, 1767. Victor Alfieri, *Mémoires* (Paris: Firmin-Didot, 1862), p. 96.
6 Ibid., pp. 251–52.
7 *Le Cosmopolite ou le Citoyen du Monde* suivi de *La Capitale des Gaules ou la Nouvelle Babylone* (Bordeaux: Editions Ducros, 1970) (hereafter cited as *La Capitale des Gaules*).
8 *Margot la Ravaudeuse* (Hamburg, 1750).
9 For a more detailed description of Fougeret's life, see J. H. Broome, " 'L'homme au coeur velu': The Turbulent Career of Fougeret de Monbron," *Studies on Voltaire and the Eighteenth Century*, 23 (1963), 179–213.
10 Ibid., p. 179, where Broome makes reference to this account by Diderot; also see the Assézat-Tourneux edition of Diderot's works (Paris: Garnier Frères, 1875–77), VI, 304.
11 See R. Desné's introduction to *Le Neveu de Rameau* (Paris: Editions sociales, 1972), p. 44.
12 The abbé de la Porte in *L'Observateur littéraire* (Année 1759), II, p. 117, and R. Trousson in his introduction of *La Capitale des Gaules*, p. 12.
13 See A. Morize's critical edition of *Candide* (Paris: Hachette, 1913), and J. H. Broome, "Voltaire and Fougeret de Monbron," *Modern Language Review*, 55 (1960), 511–18.

14 See J. H. Broome, "Byron et Fougeret de Monbron," *Revue de littérature comparée*, 34 (1960), 337–53.

15 Critics of this work were: the *abbé* de la Porte, *L'Observateur littéraire* (Amsterdam, 1759), II, 117–21; Elie-Catherine Fréron, *L'Année littéraire* (Paris, 1759), III, 157–61; Pierre Rousseau, *Le Journal encyclopédique* (Paris, 1759), IV, 120–23, and Ange Goudar, *L'Anti-Babylone, ou Réponse à l'auteur de la Nouvelle Babylone* (London, 1759).

16 Fougeret de Monbron, *La Capitale des Gaules*, p. 133.

17 Ibid., pp. 134–35.

18 Ibid., p. 141.

19 Ibid., pp. 163–64.

20 Ibid., pp. 136–37.

21 Ibid., p. 139.

22 Ibid., pp. 142, 181–82.

23 Ibid., pp. 142–44.

24 See M. R. de Labriolle-Rutherford, "L'Evolution de la notion du luxe depuis Mandeville jusqu'à la Révolution," *Studies on Voltaire and the Eighteenth Century*, 26 (1963), 1025–36.

25 *La Capitale des Gaules*, p. 145.

26 Ibid., pp. 166, 169–71.

27 Ibid., p. 155.

28 Voltaire, *Candide*, chapters XXI and XXII. It should be added that Fougeret wrote two pieces on Voltaire: *La Henriade, travestie en vers burlesques* (Berlin [Paris], 1745), and *Epître à M. F. de Voltaire pendant son séjour à Mayence au retour de Berlin* (s.l., 1753).

29 *La Capitale des Gaules*, pp. 148–49, 194–95.

30 Ibid., p. 190.

31 Ibid., pp. 192, 150–51, 149, 161.

32 See F. Venturi, "Fougeret de Monbron," in *Europe des Lumières* (Paris-La Haye: Mouton, 1971), ch. 4, pp. 111–13.

A Slaughter of Innocents:
Aspects of Child Health
in the Eighteenth-Century City

GEORGE ROSEN

In 1767, the Scottish economist Sir James Steuart observed that "The principal objections against great cities are, that health there is not so good, that marriages are not so frequent as in the country, that debauchery prevails, and that abuses are multiplied." Moreover, referring to Paris and London, he added, "It is further urged that the number of deaths exceeds the number of births in great cities; consequently smaller towns, and even the country, is stripped of its inhabitants, in order to recruit these capitals."[1] The points listed by Steuart derive from views widely held at the time. That same year, for example, a Lutheran clergyman, Johann Brückner (1726–1804) noted that population was clearly hindered from increasing in large cities, because the poor who were the majority lived crowded together in miserable quarters and as a result died in large numbers.[2] Two years later, in 1769, the Italian economist and jurist Cesare Beccaria (1738–1794) published his *Elementi di Economia Pubblica* in which he discussed the causes that checked the increase or led to a decline of population. Among these Beccaria included the growth of cities at the expense of rural districts which led to an increase of vice, misery and disease, and consequently to a much higher urban mortality.[3]

Though these views do not apply in all respects and in the same degree to eighteenth-century cities and towns, yet they do reflect urban conditions in various parts of Europe, and are supported by contemporary evidence. There was no dominant German city comparable to London or Paris, where political, economic and cultural power was concentrated, but no matter whether one turns to a *Residenzstadt* such as Berlin or a commercial center like Frankfurt am Main, the health experience of the respective populations is not very different. According to the Prussian military chaplain and demographer, Johann Peter Süssmilch (1707–1767), from 1720 to 1744 in Berlin the number of baptisms was almost as large as the number of deaths, and in some years was greater, but on balance there was no internal growth. During the same period there was also a considerable excess of deaths over births in Vienna, and most other German cities had a similar experience in the course of the century.[4] In Frankfurt a. M. there were consistently more deaths than births throughout the period from 1710 to 1800.[5] In some years or places the births were higher than the deaths, as in Braunschweig, Coburg, Erlangen and Schweinfurt during 1755–56, and in Danzig, Hamburg and Altona in 1780.[6]

Although the statistics for the German cities are quite defective and must be pieced together from a number of different sources there can be no doubt about the main trends. On the whole deaths exceeded births in the towns and yet the urban centers continued to grow, some more rapidly, some more slowly. They depended for growth chiefly on the increase of the rural population and the influx of migrants from the countryside. This trend in the German states is linked to a characteristic of this period, namely, the rapid increase of population which began about the middle of the century. The population which until then had been practically stationary began to grow rapidly. From 1748 to 1800, for example, the population of Prussia almost doubled, while that of Berlin increased about fivefold from 1700 to 1797.[7]

The experience of England and London is similar in some respects. Around the middle of the century a marked and continuing increase in population was set in motion in England which carried through to the nineteenth century. In London, as in Berlin, deaths exceeded births during the first half of the century, but the situation began to change after 1750. Nevertheless, it was not until the final decade of the century that an excess of births began to occur regularly. Throughout the entire period the growth of London was due for the most part to a continuous flow of new people from rural areas. Indeed, about one out of ten Englishmen lived in the capital during the eighteenth century.[8] Urban growth was not limited to London. The population of Leeds, for example, had been about 6,000 in 1690 but by 1775 was around 17,000, and this rise continued into the nineteenth century.[9] Liverpool exhibited a phenomenal increase of population paralleling its growth as a port. Between 1710 and 1750 the increase was approximately threefold; thereafter it doubled about every thirty years. Other cities such as Manchester did not experience a population explosion until the later decades of the century, but once started, growth was rapid.[10]

The French experience was not dissimilar. Although the population of Paris did not increase appreciably during the eighteenth century, it attracted many from the countryside surrounding the city as well as from other parts of France and other countries. In *La Méprise*, Marivaux has one of his characters say "Paris is the world," and when Candide and Martin, his Dutch companion, landed at Bordeaux, they heard all the passengers saying "We are going to Paris."[11] Lyon also attracted people from its environs and even on occasion from more distant parts. Recent research has shown that more than half the inhabitants were not native to the city.[12] Except for Paris and Lyon there were no large cities with more than 100,000 inhabitants, but Bordeaux and Nantes approached this level in the course of the century. Despite a number of inadequacies in the sources, the available statistical information indicates that smaller towns also experienced population increase, though the magnitude of the change varied from one country to another. Thus Lille had 55,000 inhabitants in 1698 and 61,400 in 1811. During the same period the population of Strasbourg increased from 23,000 to 47,000, and that of Colmar from 7,140 to 14,400.[13]

The wave of urban expansion extended as far east as the Russia of the Empress Catherine. At the beginning of her reign she appointed a commission to plan for the building of new cities and the renovation of existing ones. Though her objectives were never fully achieved, the overall urban population nearly doubled between 1769 and 1792, though as a percentage of the total population it remained minute. A considerable portion of the urban population fluctuated seasonally, since various social elements came and went for a variety of reasons.[14]

The expanding cities like London, Paris, Lyon and Vienna were regarded by contemporaries as devouring Molochs, and no group of their population was consumed more voraciously than infants and young children. A rapidly expanding population means a world of new-born infants, and in the eighteenth century this world was menaced by an appalling infant mortality which was high in all classes, but particularly so among the children of the poor and those born out of wedlock. Joseph Addison and Edward Gibbon vividly depicted the situation. In his essay "The Vision of Mirza," Addison described the bridge of life and the fate of those passing over it. At each end of the bridge he saw a black cloud, and "As I looked more attentively, I saw several of the passengers dropping through the bridge, . . . and upon further examination, perceived there were innumerable trap doors that lay concealed in the bridge which the passengers no sooner trod upon, but they fell through them into the tide and immediately disappeared. These hidden pitfalls were set very thick at the entrance of the bridge, so that throngs of people no sooner broke through the cloud, that many fell into them."[15] The problem of infant mortality is made more explicit and is given a more personal note by Gibbon in his autobiography. "The death of a new-born child before that of its parents," he wrote, "may seem an unnatural, but it is strictly a probable event: since of any given number the greater part are

extinguished before their ninth year . . . Without accusing the pro-
fuse waste or imperfect workmanship of Nature, I shall only
observe, that this unfavorable chance was multiplied against my
infant existence. So feeble was my constitution, so precarious my
life, that, in the baptism of my brothers my father's prudence
successively repeated my Christian name of Edward, that, in case
of the departure of the eldest son, this patronymic appellation
might still be perpetuated in the family."[16] Since five brothers
and one sister died in infancy, the action of Gibbon's father was
not unfounded.

Neither the deaths of Gibbon's siblings nor the deaths in early
infancy of Queen Anne's eighteen children were misfortunes peculiar to these families. That they were commonplace is supported
by statistical and other evidence. According to Süssmilch, "The
primary cause for the higher mortality in cities is the greater
frailty of city children." Thus "in populous cities generally, of
10,000 deaths, 3,000 are those of children who died during the
first year of life." And he emphasized that "The force of mortality
is 3 to 4 times greater in the first year [of life] than in the
second."[17] Concern over the excessive mortality among infants
and young children under five was expressed by William Cadogan
(1711–1797), physician to the Foundling Hospital of London, in
his *Essay upon Nursing and the Management of Children* of 1748.
"But let anyone, who would be fully convinced of this matter,
look over the Bills of Mortality," he wrote, "there he may observe,
that almost half the number of those who fill up the black List,
die under five Years of Age: So that Half the People that come
into the World, go out of it again before they become of the least
Use to it, or themselves. To me, this seems to deserve serious
Consideration."[18]

These statements are not simply rhetorical; they are supported
by eighteenth-century statistics and by modern analysis of such
data. According to figures collected by Süssmilch, 45.3 percent of
all deaths in London during the years 1753–57 occurred among
infants and children under five. For Berlin during the period
1752–55, the corresponding rate was 49.1 percent, and for Paris,

45.9 percent (but no specific period is given). In his medical topography of Berlin published in 1796, Ludwig Formey noted that from 1779 to 1794, on the average, more than half of all deaths occurred in childhood, and "that half of those born were buried during the first year of life." In 1788, Christian Gottfried Gruner reported that of the 12,666 recorded deaths in Vienna that year, 5,396 (42.5 percent) were infants under one year of age. A modern analysis of the Viennese records for the years 1752–54 leads to the conclusion that 40.4 percent of all deaths occurred under one year of age, 16.2 percent between one and four years, and 4.8 percent between five and nine.[19] One point must be noted, however, that is, the variability of the death rates, particularly those of children. On the basis of ingenious calculations, the British medical statistician John Brownlee concluded that in the area of London covered by the Bills of Mortality, "From 1730 to the end of the century there is a steady decline in the number of deaths of children under two years, the death-rate at the end of the century being only 60 percent of what it was in 1730–40, so that a very remarkable fall in infantile mortality took place preceding the introduction of vaccination, the death-rate under two years of age per thousand births of children falling from 438 to 240." In addition, Brownlee calculated that the mortality under one year in the last decade of the eighteenth century in London was approximately 180 per 1,000 live births, not very much higher than in the decade 1861–70.[20] The conclusion that a decline occurred is undoubtedly correct, yet this change must be seen in perspective.[21] One must remember that infant mortality remained high throughout most of the nineteenth century, fluctuating around 150 per 1,000 live births. When compared with the rate of 94 for New York City in 1915, it is clear that even by the end of the eighteenth century there was still an enormous wastage of life in infancy and childhood.

Mortality of infants and young children is a sensitive indicator of community health, because it reflects the influences exerted by a number of societal factors. It is particularly sensitive to environmental conditions such as housing, sanitation, water and food.

Housing is important because overcrowding favors the spread of respiratory infections and other conditions communicated by airborne droplets, while lack of adequate washing facilities increases the likelihood of gastro-intestinal infection. Mortality in this age group is also affected by the level of knowledge of the physiology and pathology of infancy and childhood and the availability of medical care. These factors are intimately linked to the socioeconomic position of the family. On the one hand poverty and its attendant evils generally compounded the effect of these factors; on the other, wealth and position exposed infants and young children to deleterious influences because of prejudicial attitudes and social relations.

That branch of medicine known today as pediatrics was largely terra incognita in the eighteenth century. In 1689, Walter Harris (1647–1732), an English physician published a small book entitled *De morbis acutis infantum*. Although in no sense original, this work became very popular and in the subsequent fifty years passed through eighteen editions in various languages, the last English edition appearing in 1742. In his introduction Harris observed, "I know very well in how unbeaten and almost unknown a Path I am treading; for sick Children, and especially Infants, give no other Light into the Knowledge of their Disease, than what we are able to discover from their uneasy Cries, and the uncertain Tokens of their Crossness; for which Reason, several Physicians of the first Rank have openly declared to me, that they go very unwillingly to take care of the Diseases of Children, especially of such as are newly born, as if they were to unravel some strange Mystery, or cure some incurable Distemper."[22]

Apparently the situation had not improved very much by 1783, to judge from the remarks of George Armstrong (ca. 1712–ca. 1783), the physician who in 1769 opened the first Dispensary for the Infant Poor in Red Lion Square in London. In the fourth edition of his book on the diseases of infants and children (1783), he said, "I know there are some of the physical tribe who are not fond of practising among infants; and I have heard an eminent physician say, that he never wished to be called in to a young child; because he was really at a loss to know what to order for it. Nay, I am told, there are physicians of note here, who make no scruple to assert that there is nothing to be done for children when they are ill."[23]

The ignorance of many physicians and their reluctance to treat infants were abetted by social practices and attitudes. Most women were delivered by midwives, and so-called men-midwives were rarely involved except in cases of difficult labor requiring special manipulations, caesarian section or other operative procedures. When Mary Wollstonecraft was delivered of her daughter Mary, she was attended by a midwife. When the latter informed William Godwin of her inability to remove the afterbirth because it was adherent to the uterus, Dr. Poignand, a physician attached to the Westminster Hospital, was summoned. He removed the placenta piecemeal, causing severe hemorrhage and subsequently a fatal puerperal infection.[24] Since the first case of the newborn was generally the responsibility of the midwife, physicians rarely had an opportunity to study and to observe infants. Usually they were called in when an infant or young child was seriously ill. This situation improved somewhat in the later eighteenth century as hospitals and despensaries were established where children could be treated.

Another practice which contributed to the high mortality among infants and young children derived from the view prevalent throughout a good part of the eighteenth century that the tasks of nursing and caring for babies was too debilitating and coarse for women of fashion and social prominence. Among families of means it was customary to send infants away soon after birth to be suckled and looked after by some peasant woman for pay. [25] The practice prevailed in cities and towns in England, France and the German states, though there are indications that it was not as widespread there. In any case, contemporary observers agreed that where the custom existed the consequences were disastrous. At the end of the seventeenth century, in 1689, Walter Harris had already reported the appalling effects of this system. "The Rector of a Parish twelve miles from London, with great grief of mind told me that his Parish, which was not small either in its Bounds or Number of Inhabitants and was situated in a very Wholesome Air, was, when he first came to it, filled with sucking Infants, and yet in the space of one Year there he had buried them all, except two and one of his own which being weak he had happily committed to my Care from his very Birth, and that the same Number of Infants being soon twice supplied, according to the usual Custom of hireling Nurses, from the very great and almost inexhaustible City, he had committed them all to their parent Earth in the very same Year."[26] This was the practice also within the city. Infants were "often sent to be nursed even in London; sometimes too in a part much worse than [the parents] themselves live in; perhaps where noxious Effluvia are continually surrounding it; or in some narrow Lane or close Alley."[27] The similarity of the situation in France is evident from the comments of the Paris physician Jean Charles Desessartz in his *Traité de l'éducation corporelle des enfans en bas-âge,* published in 1760. Discussing the high mortality of infants, he noted that villages within ten to twenty leagues of Paris were filled with infants sent from the city to wet-nurses, but that scarcely one-twentieth of them lived long enough to return.[28] The fate of infants put out to nurse in cities such as Paris and Lyon was just as poor. Recent studies have shown that the death rate was above 50 percent.[29] German sources provide variations on such themes. According to J. A. Behrend's account of health conditions in Frankfurt a. M., published in 1771, mothers turned their babies over to wet-nurses because they were frail or for the sake of convenience. Since the wet-nurses were not infrequently filthy and suffered from skin conditions and syphilis (*Grind und Franzosen*), with which they infected their charges, many children died. As a result, a surgeon was appointed to examine women who offered their services as wet-nurses, but since it was not always possible in a brief examination to detect a communicable disease, Behrends strongly urged mothers to nurse their infants themselves.[30]

As regards nursing, the children of the poor were possibly in a somewhat better situation, since their mothers generally suckled them. But large families were an economic burden, so that weak or ailing children were not of much concern, and their death a relief. According to George Armstong, who practiced among the London poor, "children while in their infancy, especially if the young family is numerous, and the parents in straitened circumstances, are not thought of sufficient consequence to be much attended to, unless some sudden or violent illness happens to give an alarm. This Secret has sometimes come out in my hearing, even by persons who were not reckoned poor."[31]

Worst of all was the situation of children abandoned because of economic circumstances or because they were born out of wedlock. A striking feature of the urban scene in the eighteenth century is the very large number of foundlings, most of them illegitimate. Some of them may have been the offspring of unwed, pregnant country girls who came to the city to have their babies, hoping thereby to escape the social stigma and punishment which would otherwise have been their lot. What this meant is exemplified in *Tom Jones* by Mrs. Deborah urging Mr. Allworthy to issue a warrant for the arrest of the foundling's mother, "(for she must be one of the neighborhood) and I should be glad to see her committed to Bridewell, and whipt at the carttail. Indeed, such sluts cannot be too severely punished." The majority, however, were probably the children of the numerous serving women to be found in cities and towns at this time. In 1779, for example, the County of Mansfeld in north-central Germany had an urban population of 89,148, of which some 6 percent (5216) comprised female servants (*Mägde*). In Berlin, during the years 1793 to 1795, out of a civilian population ranging from 126,604 to 130,487, approximately 8 percent were serving women. According to a census of 1725, the population of Grenoble was 22,622. Of this total, 1406, a little over 6 percent, were female domestics.[32] For a number of reasons (not all of which can be discussed here), this was the single group most prone to out of wedlock pregnancy. Migration from rural to urban society may have been one important factor in the rise in illegitimacy which began in the early 1700s and rose sharply after 1750 in every city on the continent and Great Britain. A number of these women were undoubtedly exploited by their masters or other male members of the household or enterprise where they were employed, a situation which became increasingly common toward the end of the century and in the nineteenth century.[33]

Several avenues were open to women with unwanted children. These were to abandon the infant in the street at some secluded spot where it would starve or die of exposure, to leave it to be cared for by the parish authorities, or to "drop" it at the door of some wealthy family, hoping that it would be cared for. The frequency of these practices in London and elsewhere is attested by a broad spectrum of evidence ranging from Hogarth's design for the subscription roll of the Foundling Hospital to novels such as *Tom Jones* or to notices in periodicals and newspapers.[34] How common and how widespread the exposure of unwanted children was may be judged as well from a remark by Louis Sébastien Mercier that in a single year 900 abandoned infants died in Metz. In Dublin, deserted infants were frequently left on banks of a canal adjoining the Foundling Hospital, so that many fell in and were drowned, or died of exposure.[35] Nor were these practices limited to infants born out of wedlock; sheer poverty or despair of being able to cope with a large family led poor mothers to abandon their children. According to Mercier, the foundling hospital in Paris annually admitted seven to eight thousand infants, legitimate and illegitimate, and the number rose year by year. Viewing poverty as the basic cause of this situation, he asked, "How can one even think of feeding children when the mother who has just been delivered is poverty-stricken and from her bed sees only dilapidated walls?" Whether or not the parents benefited from the actions, certainly the children did not. Mercier describes the foundling hospital as an abyss from which hardly one-tenth of those who fall in can be retrieved, an opinion supported in part by recent investigators who have calculated a mortality rate of 80 percent among the abandoned children of Paris, of which three-quarters is attributable to the foundling hospital. The baneful consequences of placing infants in foundling institutions was

noted as well in other cities and by various individuals. From 1772
to 1784 the death-rate in the St. Petersburg foundling home was
85 percent. Between 1784 and 1796, out of 25,352 children
admitted to the Dublin Foundling Hospital, more than two-thirds
died.[36] In 1790, Johann Peter Frank (1745–1821), the outstanding exponent of eighteenth-century public health, delivered an
academic address to the medical graduates of the University of
Pavia, taking as his subject "The People's Misery: Mother of
Diseases." Discussing the consequences of poverty for the health
of children, he said, "Parents afflicted with misery are by no
means greatly upset by the death of their children. This is evidenced by the rather sad experience that the greatest part of all
children turned over to foundling asylumes have been exposed by
legitimate parents."[37] At the end of the century, in 1798, Malthus
was hardly exaggerating when he suggested that if someone
wanted to inhibit the increase of population and was not too
concerned about the means, he could offer no more effective
measure than the erection of a suitable number of foundling
asylums.[38] Interestingly enough, at about the same time, in 1796,
Ludwig Formey contrasted the gloomy experience of other cities
with that of Berlin, noting that it had no foundling asylums and
that exposure of infants was very rare there.[39]

A comment by Mercier points up an irony of the situation.
After noting the fate of children admitted to the asylum in Paris,
he observes that the creation of this institution prevented "a
thousand secret crimes: infanticide is as rare now as it was common formerly," since now unmarried pregnant girls are not
tempted to dispose of their unwanted babies by secretly murdering them. They abandon them to the foundling hospital. That
infanticide was a problem is evidenced by executions for the
murder of newborns which occurred fairly frequently in Britain,
the German states, France and other countries. Indications of
contemporary concern and interest are also present in the literature of the period, for example in two plays by Friedrich Schiller
and Heinrich Leopold Wagner, both entitled *Die Kinds-mörderin,*
and in G. A. Bürger's *Tochter des Pfarrherrn von Taubenheim.*

Probably more cases occurred than were discovered. In England they could be concealed as accidents under the diagnosis "Overlaid," a legal cause of death. Awareness that infanticide could be arranged as a legal cover is revealed when Pamela writes about Mr. B: "He is very kind: and Billy not being well when he came in, my grief passed off without blame. He had said many tender things to me; but added, that if I gave myself so much uneasiness every time the child ailed anything, he would hire the nurse to overlay him."[40]

At this point, one may wonder how any infants survived the first year, but enough children did survive to encounter the perils of other causes of ill health. Those who had not succumbed to convulsions, tetanus, "teething," diarrhea, "gripes," marasmus, atrophy, infantile scurvy, pneumonia or whooping cough were then exposed to various communicable diseases such as diphtheria, smallpox, scarlet fever, measles, tuberculosis and epidemic meningitis, or to nutritional disorders, of which the most important was rickets. Though a detailed account of these diseases is not appropriate here, some indication of their relation to the health of urban children is in order.[41]

By the beginning of the eighteenth century, smallpox was endemic in British cities and towns, and was a leading cause of death. Throughout the century, the disease was a continuing threat to the public health on the Continent as well as in Great Britain. It smoldered endemically in city and town, flaring up recurrently into epidemic outbreaks. The impact of the disease is reflected in various statements and estimates concerning smallpox mortality and its effects on the population. In 1723, James Jurin (1684–1750), first physician to Guy's Hospital and secretary of the Royal Society, published in the *Philosophical Transactions* "A comparison between the mortality of the natural smallpox and that given by inoculation." From a study of the London bills of mortality he showed that one-fourteenth of the population in or near London had died of smallpox during the preceding forty-two years. According to William Douglass, writing in 1760, smallpox was a chief cause of the high infant mortality in Europe. What this meant may be seen from Rosen von Rosenstein's statement in 1765 that "the smallpox carries off yearly the tenth part of Swedish children." In Berlin from 1758 to 1774 there were 6,705 deaths from smallpox. Of these, 5,876 were in the first five years of life. The London bills of mortality show that 50 percent of all deaths occurred among children under the age of five.[42]

London suffered severe epidemics in 1710, 1714, and 1720; and public opinion was strongly sensitive to the need for some method of dealing with smallpox. In the light of this situation it was no accident that when a practical possibility of preventing smallpox was suggested it was tried. It had been known for centuries that an attack of smallpox almost always conferred immunity to subsequent infections. Based on this principle, an effective prophylactic procedure against smallpox had been developed and had long been used in various parts of the world, especially in the East. In this method smallpox matter from a mild case was inoculated into a healthy individual so that a mild attack would occur; this would then provide protection against any future attack. The practice was first brought to the attention of English physicians in 1714 by Emanuel Timoni (d. 1718), a Greek of Constantinople. However, it was not until after Lady Mary Wortley Montagu had had her son inoculated in 1721, and the children of Caroline, Princess of Wales, had received the same protection in 1722, that the practice began to spread.[43]

Despite Voltaire's ardent agitation in favor of inoculation, it did not become general in France until after 1750. In 1767, Razoux, physician to the Hôtel-Dieu of Nîmes, reported that 86 children, most of them between one to ten years of age, had been inoculated in the city from 1757 to 1764.[44] Because of its close relations with England, the method was introduced early into Hanover, where the first inoculation was carried out in 1722. However, it was not introduced into the other German states until later in the century. In Braunschweig, for example, the introduction of smallpox inoculation followed a severe epidemic in 1766 when 619 people died. From 1768 to 1787 some 600 inoculations were performed. Though the practice was relatively effective, it did not completely prevent smallpox, since numerous individuals were not protected. Thus, Braunschweig had an outbreak in 1769 with 173 deaths and another in 1772 with 231 deaths.[45] The reason was that the method could not easily be applied on a mass basis, and only the rich could go to special isolation hospitals where precautions could be taken to prevent the disease from spreading, since patients with virulent smallpox were being used. As a result, smallpox persisted throughout the eighteenth century, and children were infected and many died. In 1798, Edward Jenner published his revolutionary discovery of vaccination, but the effect was to be felt in the following century.

Another important disease was tuberculosis. John Bunyan had already characterized consumption as "the captain of all these men of death," and it was an equally if not more lethal disease in the eighteenth century. In its insidious way, tuberculosis was without question a highly effective killer of large numbers of people, including children. However, any attempt to specify precisely the incidence and prevalence of tuberculosis in the eighteenth-century city confronts serious problems. The first is diagnosis. No doubt many other wasting diseases involving the lungs were confused with tuberculosis. The second problem concerns records and numerical data, which are sparse and fragmentary. Nonetheless, from such evidence as is available, one may infer that there was a great deal of pulmonary tuberculosis in London, Berlin, Paris and other European and American cities.

The evidence is clinical, individual, and based on community observation. Several forms of tuberculosis were described in the eighteenth century. In 1768, the first description of tuberculous meningitis in children appeared in the posthumously published *Observations on the Dropsy in the Brain* by Robert Whytt of Edinburgh. The same year the English physician John Fothergill also published an account of this condition, of which he saw about one or two cases annually. These observations indicate a wide prevalence of tuberculosis, since in areas with a high incidence of the disease, tuberculous meningitis occurs most commonly in young children early in their infection. A further indication of the widespread prevalence of tuberculosis and its effect on children is the publication in the same year, 1779, of descriptions by Percival Pott, surgeon of London, and Jean-Pierre David, a French surgeon, of the gibbous spine, the deformity caused by tuberculous caries of the vertebrae, and its sequelae. These descriptions did not link the condition to tuberculosis (consumption), even though this connection had been surmised in antiquity and was revived in 1744 by Johann Zacharias Platner, a German surgeon.[46]

Evidence of the prevalence of tuberculosis in cities and its effect on children is provided by William Heberden, a leading London pracitioner, whom Samuel Johnson called "ultimus romanorum, the last of our learned physicians," and who attended Johnson in his last illness. In 1782, Heberden noted that "A consumption appears by the London bills of mortality to be in that city most destructive of all maladies to adults; one in four of those that grow up to manhood being reported to be carried off by this distemper." Commenting on susceptibility to this disorder, he pointed out that "The persons most subject to a pulmonary phthisis are those who are born of consumptive parents, and those in whom, during their infancy, or childhood, the mesenteric glands, or the lymphatic glands of the neck and jaw were swelled, and scirrhous, and especially if they have suppurated." What Heberden described was the condition called scrofula, struma, or the "evil," which he defined as "that habit of body . . . in which the lymphatic glands are swelled with little or no pain. This happens most commonly in the neck, or armpits, more rarely in the groin." And he emphasized that "infants and children are particularly subject to strumous disorders, and more especially the weakly with very fair skins.."[47] In view of Heberden's relation to Samuel Johnson, it is worth noting that as a child the latter suffered from scrofula, for which he was touched by Queen Anne in 1712, one of the last to receive this therapy.

Further evidence on urban tuberculosis and its relation to child health is provided by continental physicians, particularly in medical topographies of specific cities and towns.[48] A survey of the St. Sulpice hospital of Paris in 1785 revealed that a large number of patients with tuberculosis were girls just entering adolescence. In his medical topography of Paris, published in the Yar II (1793–94), Audin-Rouvière reported that phthisis was one of the most common chronic diseases in the city. Furthermore, he wrote, though scrofula and rickets were not endemic, they did affect many children during the first years of life and led to the death of a large number. At the end of the eighteenth century Berlin was reputed to have a high mortality from consumption. Ludwig Formey, in 1796, agreed that this illness caused many deaths and calculated that over a ten-year period on the average over 1,000 people died every year from consumption, out of a total population somewhat more than 150,000. Formey also refers to scrofula as a significant illness among children, particularly in orphan asylums, though it is not as common as in England, but he does not link scrofula to consumption. However, in discussing the etiology of consumption Formey stresses a congenital predisposition, transmissible from parents to children, to which he attributes the increasing spread of the disease. On the other hand, he doubted that consumption was infectious and could be transmitted from one person to another, a position not shared by a number of his contemporaries. In 1780, Johann Ernst Wichmann strongly asserted the contagious nature of phthisis. "I have seen," he wrote, "entire households including children and servants slowly die off, because the sick person clearly communicated a true phthisis to unwitting healthy people."[49] He also noted that in families where the sick person slept apart from other members of the household the danger of transmission was diminished. Consequently he urged that such a person not share a bed with a healthy individual, for example in the case of husband and wife, or of siblings.[50]

Wichmann had grasped an important point in the epidemiology of pulmonary tuberculosis. A primary factor in the spread of the disease is the presence, in close proximity to those who may be susceptible, of an individual with an open case of the disease, who introduces tubercle bacilli into the environment by coughing and spitting. Close, regular contact for weeks or months is likely to lead to infection, especially among those with low resistance or lacking previous exposure to the tubercle bacillus. Conditions favoring such spread were quite common in the eighteenth-century city.

Voltaire savored the luxury, the refinement and the sensuality of the city of his time, but he conveniently overlooked its seamy side.[51] The cities and towns of the eighteenth century were to a considerable degree insanitary, dirty and pervaded by nauseating smells, because household refuse and sewage were often flung out of doors and windows, and because streets and alleys were poorly cleaned and remained befouled. In Rome the dirtiness of the streets in certain quarters and their pestilential atmosphere was aggravated by the absence of public toilets and of private facilities in houses. As a result, people relieved themselves without embarrassment, as a porter told Goethe, *da per tutto dove vuol.* When Rousseau came to Paris for the first time in 1731, he entered the city by the Faubourg St. Marceau through narrow filthy, stinking streets filled with dark, ugly houses. It was an environment marked by dirt and poverty, crowded with beggars, carters, vendors of used clothes, and dispensers of cheap refreshments, all shouting and demanding the attention of the passers-by. But conditions within the houses where these people lived were in many cases much worse.

During his stay in Turin in 1728, Rousseau lodged with the wife of a soldier, who provided a bed for one *sol* a night. She was young and newly married, but she already had five or six children. The other lodgers were mostly unemployed domestics. All slept in one room, mother, children and guests; and this remained the situation as long as Rousseau stayed there.

The conditions which Formey described in Berlin at the end of the century were as poor if not worse. In his view, the miserable dwellings inhabited by the ordinary people of Berlin contributed greatly to the illnesses of this class. Owing to a shortage of housing for the poorer people, families crowded together in one room, where the father not only carried on his occupation, but where the entire family also lived and slept. Owing to the high price of wood for heating, in winter all windows and doors were closed as tightly as possible to conserve heat, with the result that any stranger entering such a room felt threatened with suffocation. Formey emphasized the degree to which the poverty and the living conditions of this class influenced the mortality of children, and noted the effect as well on the development of those who survived. Not only were small children neglected in large families, but the lack of space, healthful air, clean clothes and proper food weakened them and stunted their growth. Obviously, in such a household, if children or adults were attacked by smallpox, diphtheria, scarlet fever, tuberculosis or other diseases, not only was the misery which ensued indescribable, but very often death was inevitable. Outbreaks of diphtheria, scarlet fever and other diseases of childhood prevailed through the eighteenth century in European and American cities and towns, claiming hundreds of victims.[52]

Without pursuing any further aspects of child health in the eighteenth-century city, it is clear from the preceding discussion that there was a great wastage of infant and child life. The city truly devoured its children, and for most of the century had to import replacements to make up the deficit in its bookkeeping of life and death.

NOTES

1 James Steuart, *An Inquiry into the Principles of Political Economy,* 2 vols. (1767; Edinburgh and London: Oliver and Boyd, 1966), I, 62.

2 C. E. Stangeland, *Pre-Malthusian Doctrines of Population: A Study in the History of Economic Theory* (New York: Columbia University Press, 1904), pp. 233–36 (see esp. p. 234).

3 Cesare Beccaria, *Opere,* 2 vols. (Florence: Sansoni, 1958), pp. 407, 418.

4 Johann Peter Süssmilch, *Die göttliche Ordnung in den Veränderungen des Geschlechts, aus der Geburt, dem Tode und der Fortpflanzung desselben erwiesen,* Dritte verbesserte Ausgabe, 2 vols. (Berlin, 1765), I, 235–72; also tables VIII and IX in the supplemental *Sammlung zur Betrachtung der Ordnung Gottes gehörigen Tabellen,* pp. 22–27.

5 W. Hanauer, "Geschichte der Sterblichkeit und der öffentlichen Gesund-

heitspflege in Frankfurt a. M." *Deutsche Vierteljahresschrift für öffentliche Gesundheits-pflege,* 40 (1908), 651–78 (see esp. p. 664).

6 J. G. Fritze, ed., *Medizinische Annalen für Ärzte und Gesundheitsliebende* (Leipzig, 1781), I, 404 and table; Alfons Fischer, *Geschichte des deutschen Gesundheitswesens,* 2 vols. (Berlin: F. A. Herbig, 1933) II, 168.

7 Otto Behre, *Geschichte der Statistik in Brandenburg und Preussen* (Berlin, 1905), p. 462; Ludwig Formey, *Versuch einer medizinischen Topographie von Berlin* (Berlin, 1796), p. 66.

8 M. Dorothy George, *London Life in the Eighteenth Century* (London, 1925; 1951), pp. 24, 329–30.

9 S. T. Anning, *The General Infirmary at Leeds,* vol. I, *The First Hundred Years 1767–1869* (Edinburgh & London: E. & S. Livingstone, 1963), p. 2.

10 François Vigier, *Change and Apathy: Liverpool and Manchester during the Industrial Revolution* (Cambridge, Mass.: M.I.T. Press, 1970), pp. 38–40, 92–96.

11 Marivaux, *La Méprise* (Scene 13); Voltaire, *Romans et Contes,* Pléiade edition (Paris: Gallimard, 1961), p. 205; Louis Chevalier, *Classes laborieuses et classes dangereuses à Paris pendant la première moitié du XIXᵉ siècle* (Paris: Librairie Plon, 1958), pp. 263–64.

12 Pierre Goubert, "Historical Demography and the Reinterpretation of Early Modern French History: A Research Review," in *The Family in History: Interdisciplinary Essays,* Theodore K. Rabb and Robert I. Rotberg, eds. (New York: Harper & Row, 1971), pp. 16–27.

13 Marcel Reinhard, "La Population des villes. Sa Mesure sous la Révolution et l'Empire," *Population,* 9 (1954), 279–88.

14 James H. Billington, *The Icon and the Axe: An Interpretative History of Russian Culture* (New York: Alfred A. Knopf, 1966), p. 227.

15 Joseph Addison, *Essays,* ed. H. R. Green (London: The Macmillan Co., 1892), p. 175.

16 Edward Gibbon, *Autobiography . . . as originally edited by Lord Sheffield* (London: Oxford University Press, 1935), pp. 20–21.

17 Süssmilch, "Göttliche Ordnung," 103; II, 318.

18 William Cadogan, *An Essay upon Nursing and the Management of Children from Their Birth to Three Years of Age* (London, 1784), p. 6. The first two editions were ascribed to an "Anonymous Physician." Not until the third edition did Cadogan publicly acknowledge his authorship.

19 Süssmilch, "Göttliche Ordnung," II, 314 ff.; Formey, *Topographie von Berlin,* p. 132; C. G. Gruner, *Almanach für Ärzte und Nichtärzte auf das Jahr 1788,* pp. 11 ff., cited by Fischer, *Gesundheitswesen,* p. 171; S. Peller, "Zur Kenntnis der städtischen Mortalität im 18. Jahrhundert mit besonderer Berücksichtigung der Säuglings- und Tuberkulosensterblich-

keit (Wien zur Zeit der ersten Volkszählung)," *Zeitschrift für Hygiene und Infektionskrankheiten,* 90 (1920), 227–62.

20 John Brownlee, "The Health of London in the Eighteenth Century," *Proc. Roy. Soc. Med.* (Section of Epidemiology), 18 (1924–25), 73–84. See p. 76.

21 M. D. George, "Some Causes of the Increase of Population in the Eighteenth Century as Illustrated by London," *Economic Journal,* 32 (1922), 346–47.

22 Walter Harris, *Treatise of the Acute Diseases of Infants,* trans. John Martyn (London: Astley, 1742).

23 George Armstrong, *An Account of the Diseases Most Incident to Children from Their Birth Till the Age of Puberty* . . . . (London: Cadell, 1783), p. 3.

24 Eleanor Flexner, *Mary Wollstonecraft: A Biography* (Baltimore: Penguin Books, 1973), pp. 251–53.

25 D. Hunt, *Parents and Children in History: The Psychology of Family Life in Early Modern France* (New York: 1970), pp. 100–109; R. Mercier, *L'Enfant dans la société du XVIIIe siècle (avant "l'Émile")* (Dakar, 1961), pp. 31–37.

26 G. F. Still, *The History of Paediatrics* (London: Oxford University Press, 1931), p. 381.

27 J. Nelson, *An Essay on the Government of Children under Three General Heads, viz., Health, Manners, and Education,* 3rd ed. (London: R. & J. Dodsley, 1763), p. 93. The first edition appeared in 1753.

28 Still, *History of Paediatrics,* p. 406.

29 Goubert, "Historical Demography," p. 21.

30 Fischer, *Gesundheitswesens,* p. 238

31 Armstrong, *Diseases,* p. 6

32 Formey, *Topographie von Berlin,* p. 66; Edmond Esmonin, *Études sur la France des XVIIe et XVIIIe siècles* (Paris: Presses Universitaires de France, 1964), pp. 442–43, 445; Carl Ludwig Oesfeld, *Topographische Beschreibung des Herzogthums Magdeburg und der Grafschaft Mansfeld* (Berlin, 1780) p. 81, cited in Fischer, *Gesundheitswesens,* p. 178.

33 Jacques Solé, "Passion charnelle et societé urbaine de l'Ancien Régime: Amour vénal, amour libre et amour fou à Grenoble au milieu du règne de Louis XIV," *Villes de l'Europe méditerranéene et de l'Europe occidentale du Moyen Age au XIXe siècle* (Actes de Colloque de Nice, 27–28 Mars 1969) (Paris, 1970), pp. 211–32; Abel Chatelain, "Migrations et domesticité feminine urbaine en France, XVIIIe–XXe siècles," *Revue d'histoire économique et sociale,* 44 (1969), 506–28; F. G. Dreyfus, *Sociétés et mentalités à Mayence dans la seconde moitié du XVIIIe siècle* (Paris, 1968), p. 254; Othmar Spann, "Die geschlechtlichsittlichen Verhältnisse

in Dienstboten- und Arbeiterinnenstande," *Zeitschrift für Socialwissenschaft*, 7 (1904), 287–303; Edward Shorter, "Illegitimacy, Sexual Revolution and Social Change in Europe, 1750–1900," *Journal of Interdisciplinary History*, 2 (1971), 237–72.

34 Ronald Paulson, *Hogarth: His Life, Art, and Times*, 2 vols. (New Haven: Yale University Press, 1971), II, 38, 45. The "Angel of Mercy" deals with the theme of child abandonment in a more "elevated" manner. For some notices in periodicals see Ernest Caulfield, *The Infant Welfare Movement in the Eighteenth Century* (New York: Paul B. Hoeber, 1931), pp. 32–34.

35 M. Hayden, "Charity Children in 18th-Century Dublin," *Dublin Historical Record*, (March–May 1943), pp. 92–107.

36 [Louis-Sébastien Mercier], *Tableau de Paris* (Hamburg and Neuchatel, 1781), pp. 367–71; Goubert, "Historical Demography," p. 21; A. Peiper, *Chronik der Kinderheilkunde*, 2. Aufl. (Leipzig, 1955), p. 129; Constantia Maxwell, *Dublin Under the Georges, 1714–1830* (London: Harrap, 1946), p. 133.

37 Johann Peter Frank, "The People's Misery: Mother of Diseases." An Address, delivered in 1790, translated from the Latin, with an introduction by Henry E. Sigerist, in *Bulletin of the History of Medicine*, 9 (1941), 81–100.

38 T. R. Malthus, *Essay on the Principle of Population, as it Affects the Future Improvement of Society* . . . (London, 1798). It should be noted, however, that Malthus emphatically encouraged a reduction of mortality in children, asserting that the "best criterion of happiness and good government" was the "smallness of the proportion dying under the age of puberty." *Essay* . . . , 3rd ed. (London, 1806), II, 513–14.

39 Formey, *Topographie von Berlin*, p. 124.

40 Samuel Richardson, *Pamela*, 2 vols. (London: J. M. Dent, 1929) I, 296.

41 For a full account of the acute communicable diseases chiefly affecting children see George Rosen, "Acute Communicable Diseases," in *The History and Conquest of Common Diseases*, ed. Walter R. Bett (Norman: University of Oklahoma Press, 1954), pp. 3–70.

42 S. Wilkes and G. T. Bettany, *A Biographical History of Guy's Hospital* (London: Ward, Lock, Bowden and Co., 1892), pp. 99–104; John Duffy, *Epidemics in Colonial America* (Baton Rouge: Louisiana State University Press, 1953), p. 20; A. Fischer, *Geschichte des deutschen Gesundheitswesens*, II, 266; Still, *History of Paediatrics*, p. 20.

43 Genevieve Miller, *The Adoption of Inoculation for Smallpox in England and France* (Philadelphia: University of Pennsylvania Press, 1957). See also Rosen, "Acute Communicable Diseases," references to smallpox.

44 Razoux, *Tables nosologiques & météorologiques très-étenduës dressées à*

l'Hôtel-Dieu de Nîmes depuis le 1ᵉʳ juin 1757 jusques au 1ᵉʳ janv. 1762 (Basle: Jean Rodolphe Im-Hof, 1767), pp. 312–47.

45 Walter Artelt, "Das medizinische Braunschweig um 1770. Aus dem Alltag einer kleinen Residenzstadt," *Medizinhistorisches Journal,* 1 (1966), 240–59.

46 R. Hingston Fox, *Dr. John Fothergill and His Friends: Chapters in Eighteenth Century Life* (London: Macmillan and Co., 1919), pp. 57–58, 65–67; John Fothergill, "Remarks on the Hydrocephalus Internus," *Medical Observations and Inquiries by a Society of Physicians in London,* 4 (1771), 40–57; R. Whytt, *Observations on the Dropsy in the Brain* (Edinburgh, 1768), pp. 27–31; Percival Pott, *Remarks on That Kind of Palsy of the Lower Limbs Which is Frequently Found to Accompany a Curvature of the Spine, and Is Supposed to Be Caused by It* (London, 1779); Jean-Pierre David, *Dissertation sur les effets du mouvement et du repos dans les maladies chirurgicales* (Paris, 1779).

47 William Heberden, *Commentaries on the History and Cure of Diseases* (London: T. Payne, 1802), pp. 370, 374, 418–19.

48 "Réflexions sur le genre de vie des malades que sont reçus à l'hospice S. Sulpice, & sur les maladies auxquelles ils sont le plus fréquemment exposés," *Journal de médecine, chirurgie, pharmacie,* 63 (1785), 25–38; Audin-Rouvière, *Essai sur la topographie-physique et médicale de Paris* (Paris, An II), pp. 25–26; Formey, *Topographie von Berlin,* pp. 179–82.

49 Johann Ernst Wichmann, "Die Schwindsucht. Eine Polizey-Angelegenhiet," *Hannoversches Magazin,* Stück 51 (1780), reprinted in Wichmann's *Kleine medicinische Schriften* (Hannover: Helwingsche Hofbuchhandlung, 1799), pp. 145–61. Wichmann was the first in Germany to urge specific governmental action to combat consumption.

50 Wichmann was not alone in his views. French authors also accepted the communicable character of consumption and urged separation of the affected person from others. See, for example, M. Emale, "Sur l'usage du lait de femme dans les phthisies pulmonaires," *Journal de médecine, chirurgie, pharmacie,* 63 (1785) 484–91; "Lettre de M. de Saint-Martin . . . à M. Evers," *Journal de médecine, chirurgie, pharmacie,* 64 (1785), 590–96.

51 Voltaire, *"Le Mondain et la Défense du Mondain,"* in *Mélanges,* Pléiade ed. (Paris: Gallimard, 1961), pp. 203–10; Maurice Andrieux, *La Vie quotidienne dans la Rome pontificale au XVIIIᵉ siècle* (Paris: Hachette, 1962), pp. 12–13; Jean-Jacques Rousseau, *Oeuvres complètes,* 4 vols., Pléiade ed. (Paris: Gallimard, 1959), I, 71, 159.

52 Rosen, "Acute Communicable Diseases," pp. 6–38; Formey, *Topographie von Berlin,* pp. 86–87. According to Mr. Stuart Lefkowich, one of my

students, who has studied Newcastle-on-Tyne, the housing and living conditions in the town during the later eighteenth century were quite similar.

BIBLIOGRAPHICAL NOTE

The present essay is not intended to be exhaustive, but rather to offer a picture of aspects of child health in the eighteenth-century city, with some emphasis on the urban centers of Central Europe. It is a part of a larger study, *Health in the City, 1700–1950*, now in preparation and of which several sections have already been published. For those who may be interested in pursuing this topic, the following references may be useful.

1 Philippe Dollinger and Philippe Wolff. *Bibliographie d'histoire des villes de France.* Paris: C. Klincksieck, 1967.

2 François Lebrun. *Les Hommes et la mort en Anjou au 17e et 18e siècles.* Paris-La Haye: Mouton, 1971. See particularly pp. 180–98, 261–66.

3 B. Saint-Jours. *La Population de Bordeaux depuis le XVIe siècle.* 1911.

4 Charles Higounet, ed. *Histoire de Bordeaux.* Fédération historique du Sud-Ouest, 1962–74. A multivolume work in which volume V, 1968, deals with the eighteenth century.

5 Mohamed El Kordi. *Bayeux aux XVIIe et XVIIIe siècles: Contribution à l'histoire urbaine de la France.* Paris: Mouton, 1970.

6 Marcel Lachiver. *La Population de Meulan du XVIIe au XIXe siècle (vers 1600–1870).* Paris: S.E.V.P.E.N., 1969.

7 Marie-Hélène Jouan. "Les Originalités démographiques d'un bourg artisanal normand au XVIIIe siècle: Villedieu-les-Poëles (17,11–90)." *Annales de démographie historique* (1969), 87–124.

8 Etienne Hélin. *La Démographie de Liège aux XVIIe et XVIIIe siècles.* Brussels: Académie royale de Belgique, collection in-8°, 2 ser., Imprimerie J. Duculot S.A. Gemboux, 1963.

9 A. M. van der Woude and G. J. Mentink. "La Population de Rotterdam au XVIIe et au XVIIIe siècles," *Population,* 21 (1966), 1180.

10 Nicole Arnaud-Duc. "L'Entretien des enfants abandonnés en Provence sous l'Ancien Régime," *Revue historique du Droit français et étranger,* 4e sér., 47 (1969), 29–65.

11 Léon Buias. *Les Enfants trouvés en Angoumois avant 1789.* Bulletin et mémoires de la Société historique . . . de la Charente, 1941.

12 Otto K. Roller, ed., *Die Einwohnerschaft der Stadt Durlach im 18. Jahrhundert.* Karlsruhe i.b.: Druck und Verlag der G. Braunschen Hofbuchdruckerei, 1907.

The Moment in Eighteenth-Century Art Criticism

FRANCIS H. DOWLEY

The doctrine of *ut pictura poesis*, reestablished and widely accepted during the Renaissance, continued to have a prevailing influence in the seventeenth century, and we find poets like Giovanni Battista Marino asserting that there is no difference between poetry and painting except that one imitates with words and the other with colors.[1] Likewise, the painter and commentator Charles Alphonse Dufresnoy, in *De Arte Graphica* of 1673, declared the two sister arts to be so close as to be interchangeable.[2] Acceptance of this theory was not of course universal, since Castelvetro for one had given more weight to the differences than to the similarities between the arts.[3] In the seventeenth century, however, commentators earlier than Dufresnoy had shifted attention to a kind of dissimiliarity that had not been previously much in focus, namely, the limitations of *ut pictura poesis* that became evident when tested in relation to time and temporal succession. In 1637 Franciscus Junius stressed in his *De pictura veterum* a fundamental dichotomy between poetry and painting, by contrasting the poet or historian who can readily follow the order of time from the origins of a narrative continuously to its conclusion, with

317

the painter who must seize its most crucial point in the midst of the narrative, "where it most concerneth him."[4] Only from such a central vantage point can a painter refer back to events in the past or forward to those in the future. However, Junius' adumbration of the problem of the dichotomy is not accompanied by specific applications.

Granting that a painter cannot represent motion or succession in time as a poet can, the question arises why it was no longer acceptable, as it had been in the Trecento and earlier, for an artist to introduce into the same composition and with the same proportions different actions at different times and in different locations. The development of one-point perspective put a premium on unity of space into which the insertion of diverse times and actions would have produced intolerable inconsistency. Was the unity of perspective space a cause or an effect of the trend to a stringent unity that soon reduced action and time to a single moment? The problem cannot be examined here. But the triple unity of space, time and action seems to have been implicitly assumed by painters long before they explicitly formulated it late in the seventeenth century. A member of the French academy of painting, Henri Testelin, clearly defined in 1675 the three unities of painting, consciously borrowing them from the drama, where of course they had been the center of controversy both in Italy and France since the days of Giraldo Cinthio, Robortello and many others.[5] Testelin states quite definitely that in painting it is necessary to distinguish times and actions according to the maxim of the three unities.[6] These unities would consist of a single time or moment; a single action occurring in that time; and the location of that action, which must be comprehensible within a single glance.

Although applicable to most subjects in painting, the unities were primarily intended for serious actions of moral import drawn from classical history, religion, or mythology. Consideration of such events as subjects for painting would always be within the hierarchy of kinds of painting through which a general parallel could be drawn between levels of painting and levels of poetry.

Paintings of moral action, or to use a better known term, paintings of history, were on the highest level of the hierarchy and corresponded to tragedy and serious drama on the highest level of literature. One need only recall the famous preface of Félibien to the *Conférences* on particular paintings in the royal collection, held in 1667.[7] On that exalted level painting should show the creative imagination, the psychological penetration, the moral example, that the highest poetry shows. But how is painting to rise to such a level, if it is bound to the imitation of nature at a given moment? How can painting offer sufficient scope to the free activity of an artist's mind, one both learned and imaginative, if it is so narrowly circumscribed by the limitations of the medium? How can painters reach beyond the confines of the moment and the restriction to a single space, so they can approximate the range of poetry and drama on the one hand, and yet develop the distinctive potentialities of painting on the other?

This was the crucial question. The solution was in the significant moment. If restriction to the moment put limits on the similarities formulated by *ut pictura poesis*, the concept or device of the significant moment attempted to reextend, as it were, those limits and restore some similarity of range between the two arts, though without losing the impact of the visual moment. But in specific cases, given a text as subject matter, how is the painter first to transform the literary narrative into a composition so that successive but diverse moments are reduced to a single moment? Still further, if the artist is not to be a mere illustrator of the text, he must improve upon it, or at least transform it into something different and distinctive.

The problem was posed and three solutions offered over half a century before Lessing formulated his theory of the moment in the *Laocoon*. Published in Berlin in 1766 the *Laocoon* had little influence in France before the end of the century, although known to both Falconet and Fuseli. No French translation appeared before 1802, and no English before 1836; nor do we find it applied to salon criticism much before Guizot in 1810. Besides, Lessing was more concerned with the superiority of beauty over expression than with distinctive qualities of painting in comparison with those of poetry.

Giovanni Pietro Bellori, the foremost Roman critic of the late seventeenth century, stresses the last factor in his key comparison of the treatment of the theme of Apollo and Daphne in poetry by Ovid, and in painting (fig. I) by the contemporary artist Carlo Maratti.[8] As a framework for this comparison, Bellori agrees that the aims of poetry and painting are the same, but the means of their attainment are different.[9] Given a text like the *Metamorphoses*, the painter must know how to convert the poetry of words into the poetry of colors, to use his expression. Rather than being a mere translator from one medium to another, he should know how to make the transformation an invention of his own. [10] He must make a single pivotal moment signify the essential development of the action with more immediate impact than the original poetry itself.

Taking the *Apollo and Daphne* as a specific example, Bellori shows how Maratti refers back to the prior incident in which Apollo, having just destroyed the python, taunts Cupid, the son of Venus, for playing with the arms of warriors. According to Ovid,[11] to take revenge at this slight, Cupid shoots the son of Jupiter with an arrow of gold, so he will fall in love with Daphne, the chaste nymph of Diana; but he aims at her an arrow of lead so she will remain indifferent to the advances of the god. Maratti expresses these preliminary actions by placing Cupid with his arrows hovering above the fleeing Daphne, who is desperately imploring her divine protectress just as Apollo is about to overtake her. But her transformation into a laurel is already beginning, Apollo has failed, and Cupid is triumphant. At the same time, her aged father, Peneus, throws out his arms as if to save her by an embrace, only to realize he too will lose her. The presence in the picture of tributary river gods and water nymphs is an anticipation of Ovid's epilogue when they gather to console the helpless Peneus, who has withdrawn to a subterranean cave to mourn his loss. Bellori calls their attendance, at the climactic moment when Daphne is still alive, an *ingegnoso anacronismo* on the part of

Maratti,[12] as there is nothing awkward or illogical about their witnessing the moment of metamorphosis.

Bellori analyzes how Maratti attempted to gather into a single moment the three major events in Ovid's narrative. The painter tries to sum up in one momentary scene the story that the poet deploys over a series of incidents. Choosing a moment with three converging currents, Daphne's escape, Apollo's frustration and Peneus' loss, Maratti surrounds the central action with figures referring to events leading up to it, like Cupid with his arrows, and to events flowing from it, like the river divinities who gather to console Daphne's father. These figures on the periphery of the action do not distract the spectator from its focal effect, and indeed their significance might be overlooked, if one did not know the text.

The attention given by Bellori to Maratti's organization of the moment and the significance he attaches to it, underlines *the differences* to be drawn between poetry and painting, with the consequent limitations of the doctrine of *ut pictura poesis*. Not that Bellori minimizes the latter, but he does not lend the similarities an overriding importance, balancing instead the differences against them.

In his endeavor to set up an equivalent for narrative, Maratti did not in a subject like Apollo and Daphne confront a serious problem in choosing a moment that could be significant. It is, on the contrary, the problem of the range of choice which is a principal concern of Shaftesbury in constructing his ideal composition for the *Judgement of Hercules*, first published in November 1712.[13] The problem would be posed more directly to a humanist like Shaftesbury who was himself engaged in programming in detail the conceptual structure of a projected picture (fig. 2), rather than to a critic analyzing a picture already designed and executed by another hand.[14] Taking Prodicus' allegory from the text of Xenophon, Shaftesbury examines it for the possible moments a painter could select in order to represent Hercules' choice between the way of virtue personified by Minerva and the way of vice personified by Venus.[15] Shaftesbury finds in the famous encounter four possible moments from which an artist seeking the most significant one could choose. The first is the actual meeting when the two goddesses accost Hercules seated in solitary contemplation. Shaftesbury rejects this moment because the action has not yet begun. Hercules is merely surprised, though lost in admiration. The second moment covers the dispute between the two goddesses in which each presents her case for the young hero's deliberation. In the second moment we become more aware that the struggle is two-fold: a) externally between the two goddesses; and b) internally between opposing tendencies within Hercules himself. But, though the struggle is engaged, it has as yet no firm direction, and Hercules vacillates, divided in doubt. What then are Shaftesbury's criteria for choosing the most significant moment? He was less interested than Bellori's in a moment that summed up all other moments, encompassing the entire plot. The final moment of victory, although culminating after long travail, or more concretely the fourth moment when Minerva had won, would not be suitable because the struggle would be over, and Hercules would embody only a monolithic attitude of resolute determination, but nothing more varied or imaginative. In the final moment there would be no opportunity to express the internal struggle in all its agitation, which creates the principal action, according to Shaftesbury. Two important criteria emerge then for selecting the key moment: a) it should be a moment of directed, but not final, action; and b) it should be internal and psychological, not external and physical, as Bellori's tended to be. The moment fitting these criteria best is the third, because it is in that moment that the struggle reaches a crisis and one side begins to gain on the other, as Hercules half turns towards Minerva. Unlike the second moment, the third does have a direction, and does point to the conclusion of the struggle. On the other hand, the struggle continues, and vice is not yet conquered. Shaftesbury regards the third moment as the real climax in making the judgement, for it expresses better than the other three "the agony and the conflict," to quote his phrase. This means that the essential action is internal and conflict psychological, for the will contends with the sensual passions, and the intellect weighs the alternative careers. The locus of action has been transferred from the extroverted world of Maratti's *Apollo and Daphne* to the internal world of decision making where Hercules must act within himself.[16]

Since the judgement is not complete in the third moment, it becomes an anticipation of the fourth, when the contest has been finally resolved. This sense of anticipation and the internal status of the action are fundamental for Shaftesbury's selection of the significant moment. For the third moment both refers backward by its emergence from the earlier stages of the struggle and points forward to the moment of victory by the gesture of Hercules turning towards Minerva.

But the process of transition needs further analysis. On the one hand, Shaftesbury insists on the integral unity of the moment, by which he means that once the artist has definitely chosen a possible moment, he is debarred from introducing into the same composition any other action occurring at another time or place. For once the unity of the moment is broken even for a short successsion, Shaftesbury says, it might as well be broken for years.[17] But such a unity would seem to result in such an isolation of the moment that it would be sealed off from any other moment, and so references to past or future times, or any sense of continuity, would become practically impossible. Besides, it would be artificial to conceive of the internecine struggle of the emotions, or of them with the will, as occurring within a series of discrete atomic units, as if they were Humian impressions. To resolve the problem of maintaining together both unity and continuity, Shaftesbury studied the fluctuation of emotional states. He applied within the framework of the moment their rise and fall and simultaneous occurrence at different rates of intensity. At a given moment, a crosscurrent of two emotions may supervene, one growing dominant for the future, the other diminishing from the past, and so of themselves they lead backward or forward, to past or future moments. The ebb and flow of simultaneous emotions can, therefore, occur within any single moment without destroying its integral unity, and so convey a sense of a succession of moments without passing out of the present into another time. The third moment of Hercules' process of decision has, therefore, both the unique status of a critical turn of direction, and of a transitional movement arising from the preliminary phase of indecision towards the final phase of definitive choice and resolution.

A contemporary, much influenced by Shaftesbury's theory of the moment, was the well-known critic and connoisseur Jonathan Richardson the Elder. He also approaches the problem of choosing the best moment by examining the range of possible alternatives available to a painter in a given text or subject. A more difficult case than the *Choice of Hercules* is Poussin's *Death of Germanicus*, which Richardson analyzes in his account of his travels in Italy, first published in 1722.[18] The classic source was Tacitus, who gives to the dying general and putative rival of the Emperor Tiberius a long speech made before expiring to his faithful friends, and to his wife, Agrippina, and their children. His last words, according to Tacitus, "entreated his friends to excite the people to compassion and revenge by the sight of his widow and children."[19] This is the moment chosen by Poussin for his famous painting datable in 1628,[20] and very influential in the seventeenth and eighteenth centuries (fig. 3).

Richardson examines the problem of choosing the moment from a somewhat different point of view from Shaftesbury. Poussin's treatment of the moment chosen is not self-explanatory, in fact, not entirely clear to Richardson taking the point of view of the spectator. Without sufficient knowledge of Tacitus, he thinks the spectator might confuse the meaning of the scene and "read" it (to use Poussin's term), not as Germanicus' plea for compassion and revenge, but as a more commonplace entreaty, which merely recommends his family to the care of his friends, as any dying man might do. The question arises whether Poussin could perhaps have used some device to avoid this possible ambiguity for those not very conversant with Tacitus' text. In other words, could the significance of the moment have been made clearer?

Independently of Richardson, another critic, the abbé Du Bos, surmised in his *Réflexions critiques* (first edition 1719) what the effect would have been had Poussin introduced a statue of Tiberius into the composition to which the dying warrior could have been pointing as the real source of the poison that was causing his fatal illness.[21] But the *abbé* doubts if even this gesture would be clear enough. Besides, such a device might have seemed forced and a little blatant, overemphasizing the thirst for revenge and neglecting the compassion due his widow and children. But of course Poussin might have suppressed the humane emotion and chosen a strongly accented attitude for Germanicus without introducing the statue. He would then have concentrated solely on the expression of vengeful indignation. But Richardson thought this alternative rather unworthy, even if clearer in import.

Poussin could have chosen another moment, as Richardson realizes, such as focussing on a solemn oath to seek revenge which his followers would be shown taking with all due ritual. But such alternatives Richardson thinks would have been wanting in the sense of nobility to be felt in the one Poussin actually did choose. However, he does not point out that a major cause for this susceptibility to divergent interpretations consists in the complex nature of Germanicus' reactions, if Tacitus' account is accepted as the principal text. The desire for both revenge and compassion would not be easy to express, in any case, whether or not the spectator had any knowledge of classical literature. Poussin's attempt to convey an individual's emotional crosscurrents raises once more the unresolved question how far painting can hope to emulate poetry in conveying even by indirect symbols what lies beyond the screen of the visual. Poussin's concern with the problem may be detected in his having Germanicus' friends at the death bed raise their arms as if pledging to heed their leader's last plea, or as if pointing upward to remind him of the tutelary gods. But is this enough to make the moment self-explanatory without a knowledge of Tacitus? If the clarity of the moment depends on the learning of the spectator, how much should the artist assume?

Henry Fuseli, in his third lecture before the Royal Academy in 1801, also discusses Poussin's *Death of Germanicus*, regarding it primarily as a real moment in history. If Poussin chose a particular historical moment, Fuseli maintains, he should treat it as an individual example of "a Roman dying among Romans . . . with all the real modifications of time and place which may serve unequivocally to discriminate that moment of grief from all others."[22] That means that the specific character of Germanicus' friends must be indicated so that, for example, Caius, Vitellius, the legates and centurions of Antioch, and so forth, can be identified in the picture. Fuseli seems to imply that Poussin has not been too specific in characterizing the participants, and so has not succeeded in giving the moment its unique place in Roman history. Such a criterion would not be alien to, though perhaps more exacting than, Poussin's own ideal of history painting.[23] But even if Poussin had been more explicit in his characterizations, would that have made any clearer the dual nature of the plea of Germanicus? Fuseli was not as concerned as Richardson with the problems of psychological communication.

Turning to France, we find Diderot under Shaftesbury's influence introducing further nuances in his analysis of the Choice of Hercules.[24] He stretches out the dispute of the goddesses to two moments, and then inserts another moment of complete uncertainty on the part of Hercules, which would come just prior to Shaftesbury's third moment, and just after the goddesses had finished speaking. Like Shaftesbury, Diderot selects the moment in which Hercules definitely begins to show his preference, but by inserting a preliminary moment of vacillation and uncertainty, Diderot heightens the suspense and the toll it takes on the hero. By making the drama more cumulative, Diderot further stresses the sense of anticipation, so essential a feature of Shaftesbury's third moment. It should be noted, however, that a moment of suspense or balancing of aims had in fact been selected by certain famous artists like Annibale Carracci[25] and Pompeo Batoni[26] in their own paintings of the subject. Rubens,[27] on the contrary, had shown Hercules looking at Venus, instead of Minerva, but without evident conviction. But Otto Van Veen, unlike almost everyone else, had chosen the fourth or final moment.[28]

Diderot applies the moment of anticipation to other great

compositions, notably Poussin's *Winter*[29] or the *Deluge* in his *Four Seasons* (1660–1664). This is a moment of anticipation prior to the final catastrophe in which all mankind outside the ark is lost. But unlike that moment of anticipation when Hercules is making his choice, this moment just a little before extinction, Diderot says, has the calmness and subdued atmosphere that occurs just before a tempest.[30] Diderot admires Poussin for choosing such a moment of imminence and introducing only a few figures—the last survivors—instead of a motley horde desperately struggling. Speaking as a dramatist, Diderot claims that it is much more difficult to express calmness, especially of an ominous sort, than excitement and passionate declamation. He presents another example of anticipation with more psychological impact in the ritual preliminaries before Iphigenia is sacrificed,[31] whether in Euripides' drama or Timanthes' lost painting. The spectator shivers when the attendant brings out the platter which will catch the blood of Iphigenia waiting for the high priest's sacrificial knife to descend. But the approach of the attendant is calm and routine compared to the agonizing conflict in Agamemnon's mind, present at the ceremony he has himself ordered to appease Diana so that he could proceed to the destruction of Troy. Here external and internal significance are combined in one moment.

Diderot was one of the first to use the moment as a standard of criticism in his famous reviews, beginning in 1759, of the official salon exhibitions. Numerous artists he would criticize for choosing the wrong moment in painting a given subject. For example, he found Doyen choosing a moment too much charged with one kind of emotion, in his *Combat of Diomedes and Aeneas*, exhibited at the Salon of 1761.[32] Or he blames the elder La Grenée for choosing a moment too close to the final catastrophe in his interpretation of the Sacrifice of Jeptha, exhibited at the Salon of 1765.[33] However, Diderot does not always confine himself to advocating the anticipatory moment in criticizing an artist's choice of what is significant.

At the same salon, he takes to task Nicolas Bernard Lépicié for his treatment of a then rather unusual subject, *The Landing of*

William the Conqueror in England.[34] According to an early account repeated in the entry of the salon catalogue,[35] as soon as the Duke of Normandy's troops were disembarked on the English coast, he had the invasion fleet burnt, and while the flames were consuming the ships, he summoned his soldiers about him, and commanded them to conquer, since they could no longer retreat. Diderot admired the duke's tactic to force his troops to conquer or die, both in itself and as a subject for painting.[36] But then he adds, provided the painter is not Lépicié! He has both chosen the wrong moment and treated it in a dull, cold, heavy-handed manner (fig. 4). The preferred moment, Diderot thinks, should be that when the Conqueror is announcing to his troops the terrifying alternative, while not far off the conflagration is consuming the ships and its glare on their faces illuminates all the variety of reaction, whether resolution, alarm, submission, dejection, faltering courage, and so forth. This is a moment of contrast between eloquence and consternation, but more than that, of the impact of an urgent need that was self-imposed.

Looking at Lépicié's rendering, the effect is anything but eloquent. Selecting a subsequent moment, he shows the Norman troops plodding inland, the fires burnt low, a gross lumbering procession of horses and men without any sense of vigilance, of an unknown terrain, or of approaching peril. This subsequent moment could have been made into something dramatic, Diderot thinks, by a Rubens, a Carracci, or a Lesueur, because for a genius there are no really recalcitrant moments. But such a comment only makes Lépicié look all the more inept, whether he is judged by baroque, classical or historical standards. On the other hand, he is an artist of considerable talent in other genres, notably scenes of everyday life.[37]

But Diderot raises another problem which brings us back to the vexed question of the relationship between the moment and *ut pictura poesis*. The pictorial imagination is not always compatible with the poetic imagination, so that an attempt to translate literally a poetic image into a pictorial image could in many cases lead to effects that were exaggerated, obscure or even ridiculous.

An hypothetical example Diderot finds in any pictorial rendering that would attempt to translate too literally and too exactly Virgil's *Quos ego*—in the first book of the Aeneid.[38] Neptune rises from the sea to banish the winds Juno has released to shipwreck Aeneas. Virgil's image of the god merely lifting his head above the waves Diderot claims would make a very awkward effect in painting. A head sticking out of the water would look like a head cut off, and the god would be deprived of the majesty of form so vividly evoked by Virgil's verses. Or if the rest of the god's body were seen beneath the water, it would have a filmy, dissolving appearance most inappropriate to the power of Neptune. To avoid such unconvincing visual results a later moment would have to be chosen in which the god would be shown in his chariot already fully emerged from the surface of the sea. Rubens,[39] Pietro da Cortona,[40] and Perino dal Vaga[41] all make this choice (fig. 5).

It might be objected, however, that Diderot assumes too realistic a point of view on the one hand, and too literal-minded an application of *ut pictura poesis* on the other. No doubt, much could be said for his criticism that to show merely the head above the surface of the water would seem almost ridiculously inadequate for so epic an occasion. And Diderot could not of course be expected to anticipate a more romantic and imaginative style of painting like that Turner used to conjure up the misty outline of Polyphemus when he depicts Odysseus deriding him in the well-known painting exhibited in 1829.[42] One cannot be certain, then, in the light of subsequent developments in painting, that it would be impossible to transfer Virgil's image to canvas without appearing paltry or ridiculous. The limitations of painting, like those of any other art, cannot be permanently defined or delimited in advance.

It is pertinent to recall at this point Bellori's dictum that the artist should not merely seek the closest equivalent in painting for his poetic source, but should endeavor to improve the translation by some invention of his own. Diderot seems somewhat to miss the central issue by emphasizing, albeit with some truth, that what is effective in poetry might lose its potency when transferred to painting. For a great painter would not merely aim at imitating Virgil's poetic effect, but would attempt some original invention, even if it required the choice of another moment. Rubens' and Perino's introduction of a chariot to lend the god more would have to be judged for their success in measuring up to this kind of significant invention.

The relation of the moment to invention can, however, be considered from a reverse point of view, and we find Henry Fuseli defining invention in terms of the moment. Without even attempting to glance at the complicated history of the concept of invention in painting, I will merely recall that the Abbé Laugier had preceded Fuseli in defining invention as consisting in the choice of the most interesting moment—invention itself being, he says, purely an affair of genius.[43] Invention stimulated by genius was generally regarded as the artist's most essential faculty. But Fuseli develops Laugier's definition much further. In the lecture mentioned above, Fuseli gives a preliminary definition of invention as "the combination of the most important moment of a fact with the most varied effects of the reigning passion on the characters introduced."[44] By "fact" he seems to mean an event that offers a choice of moment to the artist. The concept of the "reigning passion," or the prevailing tone which all participants express in varying degrees, whether negative or positive, is traceable in painting at least to Poussin and the commentators of the French Royal Academy of Painting and Sculpture like Félibien and Testelin.[45] But much more than they, Fuseli stresses the pregnant moment— "the moment of transition, the crisis big with the past and pregnant with the future"—and yet above all the moment with its own distinctive character.

Although claiming the moment to be best used when the subject is an historical event treated without allegory or emblem, Fuseli does not rigidly exclude personifications when their presence can heighten the significance of a moment by lending it a larger meaning.[46] Thus Poussin introduced a personification of Rome in his painting (fig. 6) representing Coriolanus faced with the pleas of his mother, who had sought him out in the hostile

Volscian camp.[47] Poussin has the goddess *Roma* appear while she and the other matrons are kneeling in desperation at the obdurate refusal of Coriolanus to heed them. But the sight of the goddess makes him sheathe the sword he has drawn against his native city. What makes the moment significant is her embodiment of the Rome whose future destiny is threatened by the attack he and the Volscians are about to launch. The presence of the goddess not only lends the moment significance, but serves to make it distinctive, instead of being just an ordinary example of a mother pleading with her son.

Checking Poussin's source in the second book of Livy reveals that the moment of Roma's appearance is the French painter's invention, and not simply a borrowing from the text.[48] It is indeed the kind of invention which shows the inadequacy of *ut pictura poesis* when that doctrine is interpreted as a one-to-one parallelism and which further shows the independence of the painter's invention, when a great artist knows how to make imaginative use of what a subject has to offer him.

However, a more famous example of the relationship of invention and the moment is David's *Oath of the Horatii*, exhibited at the Salon of 1785.[49] Although the motif of the oath could have been adapted by David from analogous subjects, or indirectly from the English theatre, it seems more probable that the moment of the oath is an invention of David himself.[50] In any case, it is not to be found in standard literary versions of the Horatii, whether ancient or modern. But even though the motif of the oath had been recently used for subjects like *The Oath of Brutus*, it is not only the swearing of the oath by the three Horatii brothers which make the moment distinctive and original, but also the presence of their sister, Camilla, whose mourning pose contrasts so strikingly with the martial attitude of her brothers on the opposite side. For she was beloved by one of the Curatii, the very enemies of Rome, whom her brothers were taking an oath to destroy. Her appearance in the scene is of great significance because it embodies a prediction of the ensuing double tragedy. Not only will two of her brothers and her lover be killed in the approaching combat, but she herself will lose her life when her surviving brother discovers that she has loved an enemy of Rome.

From these examples we realize that invention can no longer be defined as the choice of the moment, if the range of moments offered by various available texts or pictorial precedents is inadequate. Where none of the given alternatives offers satisfactory opportunities or vehicles for what the artist is groping to express, he must rely on his own internal resources for invention. Roger de Piles had defined invention in terms of a seeking for objects which the artist needed for painting a given subject.[51] But, instead of the seeking being conceived of statically in terms of objects out of which to build a subject, it was later in the eighteenth century conceived of as a searching for a new action, or a new moment of action, as in the case of the Horatii, whose oath is only one component factor in a new situation, where other seemingly accessory figures will later be subjects of future dramatic reactions.

David himself analyzed another of his famous compositions in terms of the significant moment. In 1802 when planning his *Leonidas at Thermopylae*,[52] he discussed alternative treatments of the subjects with one of his students, Delécluze, whom he had asked to make a sketch. Contrasting Delécluze's choice of moment with his own, he regarded them both as two kinds of anticipatory moment: one animated and resolute, the other calm and reflective—like the Lacedemonians themselves.[53] Then David adds that he always wants to imitate artists of antiquity in choosing only moments before or after a great crisis, not the crisis itself, a remark that recalls Lessing, but also Bernini.[54]

I mention this studio discussion less to analyze it than to point out the persistence of the idea of the significant moment beyond the Revolution, though how far it remained influential in the nineteenth century is a question yet to be studied. Indeed, this paper merely touches on a few high points in the history of an idea that emerges in mid-seventeenth century and develops amidst Roman classicism, the late baroque, eighteenth-century neo-classicism, with key applications by commentators like Shaftesbury, Diderot and Fuseli, who are better characterized as marking the confluence of different movements than as single-minded advocates of particular doctrines.

NOTES

1 *Dicerie sacre del Cavlier Marino*, 1st ed. (Turin, 1614), essay I, part ii; trans. Jean Hagstrum, *The Sister Arts* (Chicago: University of Chicago Press, 1958), p. 94.

2 Charles Alphonse Dufresnoy, *De Arte Graphica*, 3d ed. (2d ed. with French trans. and notes by Roger de Piles, Paris, 1673; 3d ed., 1684), p. 3.

3 Bernard Weinberg, "Castelvetro's Theory of Poetics," *Critics and Criticism*, ed. Ronald S. Crane (Chicago: University of Chicago Press, 1952), pp. 368–69.

4 Franciscus Junius, *De pictura veterum*, English trans. (London, 1638), p. 311.

5 Joel E. Spingarn, *A History of Literary Criticism in the Renaissance* (New York: Columbia University Press, 1899), pp. 91–101.

6 Henri Testelin, "L'Expression générale et particulière," in Henri Jouin, *Conférences de l'Académie royale de peinture et de sculpture* (Paris: A. Quantin, 1883), pp. 154–55.

7 André Félibien, *Conférences de l'Académie royale de peinture et de sculpture pendant l'année 1667* (Paris, 1669), preface, pages unnumbered.

8 Giovanni Pietro Bellori, "Dafne trasformata in Lauro," published with his *Vita di Carlo Maratti Pittore* in the 1732 Rome edition. Carlo Maratti's "Apollo and Daphne" was commissioned by Louis XIV in 1679, and is now in the Musée royale des beaux-arts in Brussels. The Administration of the Museum has graciously given me permission to publish the accompanying photograph of the painting.

9 Bellori, "Dafne trasformata," p. 120.

10 Ibid.

11 *Metamorphoses*, Book I, lines 452–567.

12 Bellori, "Dafne trasformata," p. 122.

13 Ashley Cooper, third Earl of Shaftesbury, *Second Characters*, ed. Benjamin Rand (Cambridge: Cambridge University Press, 1914). "The Tablature of the Judgement of Hercules" was first published, as Rand points out, in French in the *Journal des Savants* for November 1712. Shaftes-

bury died in Naples, where he had gone for his health, on Feb. 15, 1713. See Rand's Introduction, esp. p. xii.

14 The painting was executed by Paolo de Matteis, and is signed and dated 1712. It is now in the Museum at Temple Newsam, outside of Leeds. I am most grateful to the Administration of the Leeds Art Gallery for kind permission to publish this work and the accompanying photograph. For Shaftesbury and the Neapolitan painter Paolo de Matteis, follower of Luca Giordano, see W. Wells, "Shaftesbury and Paolo de Matteis," *Leeds Art Quarterly*, 2 (Spring 1950), 23–28.

15 Shaftesbury, *Second Characters*, pp. 34 ff.

16 It remains unknown whether Shaftesbury was inspired by, or even knew, Poussin's *Choice of Hercules* (ca. 1637), which represents the young hero turning towards Minerva. At Stourhead, Wiltshire.

17 Shaftesbury, *Second Characters*, pp. 35–36.

18 Jonathan Richardson the Elder, *An Account of Some of the Statues, Bas-reliefs, Drawings and Pictures in Italy with Remarks by Mr. Richardson Senior and Junior* (London, 1722), pp. 159–62.

19 Tacitus, *Annales*, Book II, lines 71.1 to 73.1. As translated in Richardson's text.

20 Minneapolis Institute of Arts, Minneapolis. For documentation in 1628, see Anthony Blunt, *The Paintings of Nicolas Poussin: A Critical Catalogue* (London: Phaidon, 1966), no. 156. I am much indebted to the Administration of the Minneapolis Institute of Arts for kind permission to publish this painting and the accompanying photograph.

21 Abbé Jean Baptiste Du Bos, *Réflexions critiques sur la Poésie et sur la Peinture*, 4th ed. in 3 vols. (Paris, 1740), vol. I, sec. XIII, p. 81.

22 Henry Fuseli, "Lecture III, Invention," in R. N. Wornum, ed., *Lectures on Painting* (London: Bohn, 1848), p. 430.

23 Most succinctly expressed perhaps in the letter dated April 28, 1639, in which Poussin writes, "lisez l'histoire et le tableau, afin de connaître si chaque chose est appropriée au sujet." *Correspondance de Nicolas Poussin*, ed. Chas. Jouanny (1911; rpt. Paris: F. De Nobele, 1968), pp. 20 ff. It is here that Poussin uses the term *reading a picture*.

24 Diderot, "Composition," *Dictionnaire encyclopédique*, ed. Assézat-Tourneux (ca. 1753; Paris: Garnier, 1876), XIV, 199.

25 Annibale Carracci's dates from 1596 and was the central piece in a larger allegory. It was practically canonical, as a composition. Pinacoteca Nazionale.

26 Pompeo Batoni's rendering deviates a little from symmetry. Signed and dated 1742 (Uffizi, Florence), it was probably unknown to Diderot.

27 Rubens' workshop, Uffizi, Florence. See E. Panofsky, *Hercules am Scheidewege* (Leipzig: Teubner, 1930), p. 113, plate XLI.

28 But his is a special case. Hercules is Alexander Farnese, and Minerva the

Church, whom he will defend. See J. M. Hofstede, "Rubens' St. Georg und seine frühen Reiterbildnisse," *Zeitschrift fur Kunstgeschichte*, 28 (1965), 97.

29 Louvre.

30 Diderot, "Salon de 1765," *Oeuvres complètes*, ed. Assézat-Tourneux (Paris: Garnier, 1876), X, 388–89. Under *Lépicié*.

31 Diderot, "Composition," XIV, 198–99.

32 Diderot, "Salon de 1761," X, 138–41.

33 Diderot, "Salon de 1765," X, 276–77.

34 Diderot, "Salon de 1765," X, 387–89. This very large painting (26 x 12 feet) seems to be still in the refectory of the Lycée at Caen. Profound gratitude is extended to the Municipal Administration of Caen for use of the photograph.

35 Although this very hazardous act has no basis in fact, it is traceable back to an early chronicle, "The Chronicle of New Battel Abbey." See Wace, *Chronicles of the Norman Conquest*, ed. Edgar Taylor (London: Pickering, 1837), pp. 130–31. The legend is mentioned, albeit with reserve, by the best French writer of English history whom the earlier eighteenth century produced, namely Rapin de Thoyras. See his *History of England* (Dublin, 1726 ed.), II, 106. In a footnote, Rapin de Thoyras attributes the legend to William Camden, who indeed repeats it in his *Britannia*, English trans. (1586; London, 1753), I, ccxiv.

36 Diderot, "Salon de 1765," X, 387.

37 The best account of Lépicié is still the *Catalogue raisonné de Nicolas-Bernard Lépicié* by Philippe Gaston-Dreyfus, published by La Société de l'histoire de l'art français (Paris: A. Colin, 1923), Introduction.

38 Diderot first uses this example when discussing the problem in his "Lettre sur les Sourds et Muets" (1751), ed. Assézat-Tourneux, I, 385–89; and then reverts to it at the "Salon de 1767," XI, 72–73. See also, *Aeneid*, Book I, lines 124–56, esp. 126–28.

39 Rubens' final painting of the *Quos Ego* is in Dresden, the oil sketch in the Fogg Museum at Harvard. The latter, dating from 1634, is here illustrated. Rubens' composition is an allegory, referring to the Archduke Cardinal Infante Ferdinand's successful journey from Spain to Italy in spite of a great storm. The painting was part of a much larger decoration designed by Rubens for the entrance of Ferdinand into Antwerp to assume the governorship of Flanders in April 1635. I am much indebted to the Administration of the Fogg Museum, and to Mr. Daniel Robins in particular, for kind permission to publish this sketch.

40 One of the scenes from the *Aeneid* on the vault of the gallery in the Palazzo Doria Pamphili a Piazza Navona, Roma. Cortona painted them from 1651 to 1654.

41 Perino depicts it in three known drawings (at Windsor, the Louvre, and

the Ashmolean at Oxford), all of which may be studies for a lost painting in the Palazzo Doria at Genoa, executed around 1535.

42 National Gallery, London.

43 Abbé Marc Antoine Laugier, *Manière de bien juger des ouvrages de peinture* (Paris, 1771), p. 100.

44 Fuseli, "Lecture I, Ancient Art," etc., p. 367.

45 See especially Poussin's famous letter on the "modes," addressed to Chantelou, from Rome, Nov. 24, 1647, *Correspondance*, pp. 370–75.

46 Fuseli, "Lecture IV, Invention (continued)," etc., pp. 440–41.

47 Dating from the later 1640s, this painting is in the Hôtel de Ville at Les Andelys. I am indebted to the Administration of Les Andelys for gracious permission to publish this painting.

48 The pertinent passages in Livy's *History of Rome* are in Book II, sections 39 to 41.

49 Louvre.

50 For one of the best recent discussions of this picture, see Robert Rosenblum, *Transformations in Late Eighteenth-Century Art* (Princeton: Princeton University Press, 1967), pp. 68–74.

51 Roger de Piles, *L'Idée de peintre parfait* (Paris, 1699), pp. 23–27; *Dialogue sur le coloris*, 2nd ed. (1673; Paris, 1699), p. 134; or in *Recueil de divers ouvrages sur la peinture et le coloris* (Paris, 1775 ed.), p. 257.

52 Louvre. Begun in 1802, but only finished after a long interruption, in 1814. Also has allegorical reference to contemporary events, notably young generals of Napoleon who died on the field of battle.

53 Etienne J. Delécluze, *Louis David, son école et son temps* (Paris: Didier, 1855), pp. 225–27.

54 While doing the bust of Louis XIV, Bernini said that the best time one can choose for the mouth is when one has just spoken or when one is going to speak—not the pronouncement of the words themselves. See M. de Chantelou, *Journal du voyage du Cav. Bernini en France*, ed. L. Lalanne, (Paris: Gazette des Beaux-Arts, 1885), p. 133 (September 4, 1665).

The Education in Architecture
of the Man of Taste

MICHAEL McCARTHY

The Swiss traveller Rouquet wrote an account of the arts in England during the middle of the eighteenth century, and remarked: "In England, more than in any other country, every man would fain be his own architect".[1] It is not the purpose of this paper to illustrate the truth of Rouquet's observation, but to point to some reasons why taste in England at that date should have been so concerned with the art of architecture, and to examine the avenues of education in taste that were available to those who sought to acquire and demonstrate good taste in their architectural undertakings.

The study of architecture was not something new to England in the eighteenth century. Writers on education had from time to time asserted the desirability of including architecture among the subjects of study for young men. Milton and Locke are examples from the previous century,[2] and in the early eighteenth century these prescriptions derived greater apparent validity from two new trends of thought. The first was the beginning of the theory of the sublime. Joseph Addison explicitly related this category of aesthetic experience to architecture in the *Spectator* issues devoted to the subject in 1712.[3] The second reason was the growth of national self-consciousness, a conviction of the greatness of England, and of the need to assert that greatness in the buildings of the country as much as in the literary arts.[4] Both political parties, Whig and Tory, professed the keenest patriotism, which encompassed all aspects of national life, including architecture. This has been demonstrated by Professor Kliger, who related gothic taste in architecture to the Whigs, and classical taste to the Tories.[5] However, there is too much that is contradictory in the evidence to support a tidy alignment of architectural taste along party lines. A. T. Bolton, for example, in contradiction of the tendency noted by Kliger, pointed to Jacobite feeling in Oxford as a possible source of the Gothic Revival.[6] These suggestions point to the importance of architecture in the eighteenth century. Clearly, the man of parts, whose hereditary position or personal talents led him to aspire to an active participation in the political life of his country, was well advised to be knowledgeable about architecture, and to display good taste as well as knowledge.

He had to achieve this aim by personal endeavor, mainly. Apart from the Office of His Majesty's Works, which had become the subject of political patronage, there was no mechanism for the training of an architect in England.[7] Art training of any sort in eighteenth-century England was "disgraceful," to quote the late Professor Wittkower's paper on the subject;[8] and the results of this indifference to professionalism were frequently deplored by architectural writers. One quotation from the author of *London and Westminster Improved*, published in 1766, must suffice: "In Great Britain, the designing and superintendency of works originally intended to be magnificent and elegant, is generally given to persons utterly unacquainted with the meaning of the word; how is it possible then that any work of that kind should be produced among us? If a magnificent edifice is to be erected, a common builder, little if anything superior to a carpenter or bricklayer, in point of taste or knowledge, is consulted instead of a regular architect."[9] In the light of this quotation, the satire written by James Bramston thirty years earlier, *The Man of Taste*, takes on more point:

Building so happily I understand,
That for one house, I'd mortgage all my land.
Doric, Ionic, shall not there be found,
But it shall cost me threescore thousand pound.
From out my honest workmen I'll select
A bricklay'r and proclaim him architect.[10]

The bricklayer, or at least the master builder, frequently did proclaim himself an architect without having undergone any specific training for the title. John Gwynn, the most authoritative voice among the architects of the mid-century, recognized this as an inevitable evil, and pleaded that exercises in draftsmanship be provided for the members of the building trades. "If they can form no designs of their own," he argued, "they are constantly obliged to copy those of better artists."[11] There is nothing to indicate that his pleas had any practical effect, and complaints of the inadequacies of draftsmanship among the builders of the eighteenth century are frequent. Sanderson Miller, for example, wrote to his colleague Thomas Prowse concerning designs for the new Shire Hall at Warwick, which they planned jointly: "I can always see more faults in my own performances than I love to think of, and I would never draw a line more if I did not see much worse in the shocking designs of common workmen."[12] William Kent also made this complaint, in a typically garrulous letter to Lady Huntingdon: "Let me tell you, your country workmen should never build anything for me of any consequence, because I can have work done otherways better and at least a third part less than anything you have done."[13] Even such well-trained and well-established artists as James Lovell occasionally produced designs which their patrons found totally inadequate for their needs in style and scale.[14]

We can gain some insight into the low standards of invention and draftsmanship among the London builders from an unpublished manuscript in the Beinecke Library, Yale University.[15] It was written by John Shrimpton and is dated 1734, but was evidently in progress for some years, since the date 1753 is inscribed on the drawing of an elevation for an unidentified and undistinguished house. It consists of 114 folio pages, of which 22 are blank, and there are a further 15 leaves inserted. The drawings in this book illustrate that striving for novelty of effect against which architectural writers of the mid-century constantly inveighed. One drawing shows a pseudo-gothic rose window framed with mannerist strapwork on the first story, with a travesty of a Borrominian panel above. Mannerism achieves an unforgettable level of the ridiculous in the icicled rusticated gateway of a second; and two further drawings show would-be Borrominian ornamental features making nonsense of the structural pretensions of these variations upon the theme of a single-storyed arch surmounted by an attic. Mr. Howard Colvin, in a letter written to the library in 1952 and now inserted in the manuscript, suggests the probability that this is an office reference book, to which Shrimpton and his assistants would turn for guidance. He has further identified the drawings as copies of those in a French book of architecture published in 1622, which had an English translation, carrying identical plates, in 1669. This is only one instance of outdated copying by London builders. Sir John Summerson has pointed to another, William Halfpenny's *Magnum in Parvo or the Marrow of Architecture*, 1722, which was a plagiarization of a book originally published in 1682.[16]

Halfpenny was one of the first of a new breed of authors in the eighteenth century, the compilers of pattern books, who sought to supply the deficiencies of architectural training by providing builders with ready-made solutions to any foreseeable problems. The most prolific of these was Batty Langley, who was held in such popular esteem that his designs were occasionally copied by other compilers. In the Mellon Collection for example, there is a manuscript titled *The Vitruvian Principles of Architecture Practically Demonstrated*, by W. Salmon Jnr., written in 1737, but apparently never published. The Preface to this work promises to give examples of designs from "Palladio, Sebastian Serlio, Sebastian Le Clerc, Inigo Jones, Mr. Gibbs, Mr. B. Langley"—distinguished company indeed for the most reviled of eighteenth-century architects! It fulfills its promise in Plates 6 and 47, the latter accompanied by a note which explains its appeal to carpenters of

Colchester and everywhere else: "This is a window of the second magnitude rusticated, by Mr. B. Langley, and is so plain by inspection as to stand in need of no explanation."[17]

Horace Walpole's justified criticism of Batty Langley's attempts at Gothic Revival design may well obscure for us the important service he rendered in providing a course of instruction in the language of architectural drafting. But clearly such pattern books were destructive of true architectural training by their encouragement of copying. Nor was this the only reason for their condemnation. They were criticized with some justice as the perpetuators of the taste and design which was considered decidedly bad in the eighteenth century. The writers of the time associated this taste largely with the great architects of the Roman Baroque, Bernini and Borromini, and were unsparing in their denunciations of these architects. Stephen Riou may stand as an example. Writing in 1760, he quoted Pompei's strictures of 1735, and continued: "These two artists did not introduce their unwarrantable novelties ignorantly, but through a ridiculous affectation of singularity.—And the worst is, that their characters were of consequence enough to give sanction to their follies.—The infection has totally spread through most countries of Europe.—It has at last reached this island with the additional mixture of Chinese, Gothic, French etc.—Even the designs of Inigo have yielded to the caprices of the times. Could one be reasonably blamed to wish for a return to the uncultivated rudeness of barbarous ages? La rozezza de de' barbari secoli?"[18]

Riou's reference to "the designs of Inigo" points to the eighteenth century's remedy for bad taste in architecture. In Inigo Jones lay the salvation of English architecture, and he had a powerful champion and propagandist in Richard Boyle, Earl of Burlington, who acquired as many of Jones's drawings as possible alone with those of Jones's mentor in good taste, Andrea Palladio, and had them published with a view to the reformation of taste in architecture. Analysis of Burlington's achievements must await the posthumous publication of studies by Professor Wittkower, but it is clear that his deep commitment to architecture was of the utmost importance in stimulating a concern for good taste among his compatriots and contemporaries. John Gwynn spoke for his generation when in 1766 he wrote of Burlington: "In short it may be said that he not only encouraged architects, but that it is entirely owing to him that architecture has any existence amongst us."[19]

But Burlington not only gave his age the model and standard of taste appropriate to it in proposing a return to the practice of Inigo Jones. In his own person he followed the same method of training in architecture that Inigo Jones had adopted, and thus set the pattern for architectural studies of the future. Despite the criticism of the redoubtable Lord Chesterfield,[20] Burlington studied the skills of draftsmanship and practiced them; he studied the designs of other architects in their published forms; and he travelled through Europe to study their buildings at first hand. The founding fathers of the architectural profession at the beginning of the nineteenth century were to adopt the same pattern of training.

The initiatory exercises in architectural draftsmanship were stated as follows by the most prolific author on the subject, Batty Langley: "The first work to be done in order thereto, is perfectly to understand the Five Orders of Columns, which I have placed precedent to the Designs for that purpose; and which I peremptorily admonish be well understood, before any Proceeding be made to attempt the Art of Designing."[21] The application of this precept was evidently consistent, for in many collections we find student exercises on the orders, notably among the drawings of King George III, Thomas Worsley of Hovingham Hall, Yorkshire, and Sir Roger Newdigate of Arbury Hall, Warwickshire. Most frequently these are pencil sketches made with the aid of a ruler and compass as the manuals directed. But occasionally they are heightened with wash and Indian ink, as in the drawing by Newdigate of a composite capital, which survives at Arbury Hall.[22] There cannot be any certainty that this is a student exercise, but the drawing of a capital and base of a column in the Worsley Collection at Hovingham Hall is signed and dated *T. W. Etonensis 1728*, so the future Surveyor of the King's Works certainly had his first lessons in architecture while at school. John Chute, who was to be the architect of Strawberry Hill in future years, attended Eton College also and may have begun his architectural studies there.[23] We know that his cousin, the future Lord Dacre of Belhus, Essex, had the opportunity while at school in Harrow to learn surveying and drawing on the half-holidays.[24]

Those who did not have the opportunity to learn something of architectural drafting at school could take advantage of the books published on the subject, of which the most important was James Gibbs's *Rules for Drawing the Several Parts of Architecture*. This had the decided advantage, for those who were weak at mathematics, of demonstrating the skill, "in a more exact and easy manner than has been heretofore practised, by which all fractions, in dividing the principal members and their parts are avoided."[25] First published in 1733, with a second edition five years later, and a third in 1758, this is the most handsome of the manuals of the age, and the basis of many of the smaller works on the same subject. A short address to the reader prefaces forty pages of text, well printed in large type on excellent paper, 11¼ inches by 18. Sixty-four plates, many with more than one design, follow the text, and each of the designs is accompanied by a brief explanatory paragraph. It is a seductive volume, which makes architectural drawing look very easy, and one can understand how William Shenstone, who owned and used several books on architecture, could write to Lady Luxborough on November 13, 1749: "I conceive the mechanic part of architecture to be a science easily acquired; and that a tolerable good *native* taste is generally what gives the distinction."[26]

Shenstone was busy constantly in these years about improvements to his property, The Leasowes, and Lady Luxborough's nearby property, Barrels. They maintained a correspondence which makes frequent reference to their use of architectural books, and it was to the cheaper and more popular builders' manuals that they turned for help. At first they were more ambitious. Shenstone wrote on April 18, 1748, of making fireplaces and niches from *Designs of Inigo Jones*, which he had borrowed from Lady Luxborough.[27] But the following year he wrote to his friend Richard Jago fo a book which a neighboring student, Sanderson Miller of Radway, was using: "Did you not tell me of a treatise your Mr. Miller had, where the author endeavors to vindicate and establish Gothic architecture? And does not the same man explain it also by draughts on copper plates? That very book, or rather the title and the author's name, I want.—I shall never, I believe, be entirely partial to Goths or Vandals either. But I think, by the assistance of some such treatise, I could sketch out some charming Gothic temples and Gothic benches for garden seats.—I do esteem it extremely ridiculous to permit another person to design *for* you, when by sketching out your own plans, you *appropriate* the merit of all you build, and feel a double pleasure from any praises which it receives".[28]

Letters published by Mrs. Williams reveal that Shenstone did in fact acquire Batty Langley's book, and later the same year, his *Builders' Jewel.*[29] What use he made of them does not appear specifically. He was known to be a passable draftsman, who had been in the habit of making presents of his drawings to appreciative young ladies since 1736.[30] His designs for urns are said to have been used by Birmingham manufacturers.[31] We know that he sent Lady Luxborough a pen drawing of Sanderson Miller's newly-erected castle at Hagley Park in 1748.[32] However, no drawings by Shenstone seem to have survived. He found the 1728 *Book of Architecture* by James Gibbs to be unhelpful because it "consists entirely of plans and supposes some previous knowledge."[33] Lady Luxborough helped him out by sending him a copy of the treatise of Vincenzo Scammozzi, which was, she declared, "the only one I have that teaches the rudiments of that science."[34] This was another favorite treatise of the age, found again, along with the works of Batty Langley, in the library of John Chute at The Vyne in Hampshire. His loving perusal of these volumes, and the practical effects of their teaching, are demonstrated graphically on the end papers, where he sketched proposals for architectural ventures, sometimes imaginary, sometimes quite practical, as in the sketches for the new library of Horace Walpole at Strawberry Hill.

Because of the lack of training for builders and architects in eighteenth-century England, the landed gentry were well advised to acquire some expertise in draftsmanship for the sake of their investments in buildings. Indeed, the spokesman for conscientious architects of the period, John Gwynn, encouraged gentlemen to be conversant with the art for very practical reasons. "Though it is not expected," he wrote, "that every person of great Fortune should be a practical Surveyor and actually plan his own Estate and draw the Ichnography and Elevation of his own Mansion; yet to be able to do this, and to examine, by his proper skill, such particulars as create in his mind either Doubt or Disgust, must contribute greatly to his Satisfaction and Delight, and sometimes even to his Profit."[35] Clearly there was no question, at this date, of architects objecting to "interference" by their patrons. Indeed several instances are known where interference by the local builder, often a self-styled architect, was the greater danger. Architectural studies were not just a fashionable pursuit of the leisured class in the eighteenth century; they were a necessary accomplishment for the good management of their estates.

Sir Thomas Robinson's experience with the strange character Mr. Lightfoot, in the rebuilding of Claydon Hall for Lord Verney, is a well-documented instance.[36] In the correspondence relating to that project, Sir Thomas cites the fate of a design for Sir William Strickland by Lord Burlington: "Lord Burlington gave him a beautiful design, with a Palladian roof and an Attick Story, instead of garrets and the old wretched and ugly roof of our Gothic ancestors—when the house was completed, Sir William went down, pleasing himself that he had improved the bad taste of his county, and should be the object of the envy of his neighbours, when alas he found the old-fashioned roof, and many other material alterations from the plan—he was not of a very passive disposition and said everything that rage and disappointment could utter—at last the undertaker of the Building was allowed to make his defense—which was in few words, that he took it for granted the Architect had made a mistake, therefore he put on the sort of roof etc. of all seats of the neighbourhood; no reply of Sir William's could however alter the mistakes, and it was a constant mortification to him while he lived."[37] This might be dismissed as a provincial builder's inability to comprehend the latest style of the capital. But in the case of Matthew Brettingham the Elder, we have a London architect of some stature. Sir Richard Lyttelton sent Brettingham the plan for his new house in Piccadilly, which had been designed by himself and his nephew Thomas Pitt while in Genoa. When the latter returned from Italy, he found to his consternation that Brettingham had erected a facade which bore little resemblance to that approved by Sir Richard, and was totally unacceptable.[38]

As we have seen, some of the landed gentry had the opportunity to study the fundamentals of architecture during their school years. For others, the impetus to acquire taste in architecture may have come during their university careers. In Oxford, Dean Henry Aldrich (d. 1710)[39] and George Clarke (d. 1736)[40] had established the respectability of a lively and active interest in architecture. Amateurs such as Sanderson Miller, Sir Roger Newdigate, and Sir Edward Turner studied in that stimulating atmosphere, though there is no evidence of their having received any architectural lessons while they were there. The strong tradition established by Aldrich and Clarke continued through the next generation, however, when Newdigate designed alterations for University College,[41] and Miller for All Souls.[42] The building of the Radcliffe Library from 1737 to 1749 provoked designs by another amateur architect and Fellow of All Souls as George Clarke had been, Robert Hampden Trevor, later Lord Hampden.[43]

In Cambridge Sir James Burroughs of Gonville and Caius was the acknowledged overseer of building alterations in the university,[44] and the tradition he established also continued in the following generation, as we can see from the letter addressed to Lord Grantham of Newby Park, Yorkshire, by his son Francis on June 25, 1766: "My brother will be surprised, but I hope not jealous when he hears, that I as an architect am consulted and am to have the superintendency of a publick building in the University. the case is this the Vice Chancellor has appointed some Doctors, Mr. Whisson (?) and myself, a Committee, or as we call it a Syndicate, for putting into execution a legacy of Sir James Burroughs which he left for the building of the Senate. It will never give me any trouble, and I fancy was meant as a compliment, it is however a feather in my cap."[45] Clearly Francis Robinson had had the opportunity to demonstrate some expertise and taste in architecture in the course of his undergraduate studies, though the precise nature of the demonstration does not appear from the family papers.

During these years Thomas Gray was in Cambridge, busily preparing the *Architectura Gothica*.[46] He maintained close contact with the friends he had made on his Grand Tour, Horace Walpole and John Chute, and through them he made the acquaintance of the brilliant, though erratic, designer Richard Bentley, formerly of Trinity.[47] So he was very conversant with thought and activity in architectural circles. It is clear from his letters that he encouraged his students to take the most lively interest in architecture. He persuaded the young Lord Strathmore, for example, to accompany Thomas Pitt to Portugal and Spain to study Moresque art and architecture.[48] He waited anxiously for Pitt's return two years later, because, as he explained to Joseph Wharton, "from him I hope to get much information concerning Spain, which nobody has seen: he is no bad observer."[49]

Private tutoring in architecture was a further means of study, and undoubtedly the most influential example of this was the tutoring of the Prince of Wales. William Chambers became his architectural tutor in 1757, after John Gwynn had declined the post.[50] This lent invaluable status to the study of architecture in a general sense, but it had a more practical result too. This was the publication in 1759 of Chambers's *Treatise on the Decorative Parts of Civil Architecture*, which was to replace the works of foreign authors and the pattern-books of builders and carpenters, to become, in the words of Dr. Eileen Harris, "The Englishman's Palladio and Vignola."[51] The correspondence of many of the architectural exercises which the future King George III drew out after patterns drawn mainly by John Yenn in the office of Chambers, with the designs in the *Civil Architecture*, makes it clear that the Prince of Wales was the sounding-board for the concepts embodied in the treatise.[52] It became the standard textbook for students of architecture in the following century.

Chambers was not the first tutor of the Prince. The author of an influential textbook on perspective drawing, John Joshua Kirby, had instructed the royal pupil from 1755 to 1757, and like Chambers later, he was proud to exhibit publicly the work of his student.[53] Nor did Kirby confine his classes to royalty. George Grenville was taught by him at the expense of his uncle Lord Temple in 1766. The course consisted of thirteen lessons, for which Kirby charged 5/3 per lesson and 1/6 for Indian ink. He was superseded the following year by the French artist Bonneau, who was even more expensive, charging 7/10½ per lesson, and extra for use of materials.[54]

The Grand Tour completed the education of the man of taste in the eighteenth century, and it provided further opportunities for instruction in architectural draftsmanship, as well as in the history and appreciation of the art.[55] The subject, however, is far too vast to be entered upon in this paper, and it is probably better that in the brief space remaining I point to a less well known and less adequately documented source of instruction in good taste in architecture, namely, the buildings of England.[56] Most gentlemen profited by the increasing ease of travel in England to visit the houses of the aristocracy and make detailed observations of their architectural features, which they then shared with friends in conversation and correspondence. An instance is the letter written by Sanderson Miller to Dean Charles Lyttelton on September 16, 1750, describing a tour which took him through the eastern counties. He comments first upon Horton House, Northamptonshire, then in the process of rebuilding, and then upon Wimpole Hall, Cambridgeshire, for the rebuilding of which he had himself supplied a design. From there he went on to Audley End, which he describes as: "a melancholy instance of the Folly of Human Grandure. I never saw anything half so magnificent. The Gallery is

226ft. 6in. long, 32 wide, besides the window recesses, and 24 high."[57] This letter is written from Gosfield Hall, and bears the frank of Robert Nugent, later Lord Clare.[58] Nugent and Miller were just then involved in building an additional wing to Gosfield Hall, so one may be sure that they enjoyed a very stimulating architectural discussion as a consequence of Miller's inspection of the country houses en route.

Another patron of Sanderson Miller, the poet and statesman George Lyttelton, wrote to him after a tour of Norfolk on July 30, 1754: "I have much discourse for you upon the fine things I saw there. You must take an opportunity of seeing them too; for to a man of your Taste no part of England is so well worth a visit, at least none that I have seen. Ld. Leicester's alone [Holkham Hall] would pay you the trouble and expence of your journey. The only danger is that it should put you out of conceit with your Gothic Architecture; but you are a man of too large ideas to be confined to One Taste."[59] Sanderson Miller sometimes took advantage of his journeys to make sketches of the architectural features seen, as in the measured ground-plan *Ld. Fitzwalter's at Moulsham by Leoni*, which appears on the back of a letter written to him by Robert Nugent on October 1, 1753.[60]

Miller's sometime colleague in architecture, Sir Roger Newdigate, travelled to Yorkshire in 1764 and made equally precise notes of the buildings he visited. The following extract is perhaps the most interesting since it details the work of the amateur architect Sir Thomas Robinson, who has already been mentioned. It is in reference to Castle Howard: "On the left as you look from the hall a new wing building upon a design of Sir T. Robinson, not unlike in stile, but in plan wholly different from the other contains some grand rooms not finished—a gallery 160ft. long contains an octagon in the middle of 36ft. diameter and two wings of 60ft. each and 4ft. wide—a dining [hall] of 80ft. long divided with Corinthian pillars with faces instead of volutes in the capitals of the beautiful white stone of the country, 38ft. between the columns 30ft. wide and high and a drawing room 60ft. by 30."[61] There are other undated accounts of journeys into Scotland and into Devonshire, and the existence of a map of Plymouth in Sir Roger's hand, which accompanies the latter, shows that he used his pencils as readily in England as when travelling in Italy.[62]

Instances such as these could be multiplied from unpublished sources, and are also known from such published sources as Horace Walpole's accounts of his travels through England.[63] The revolution in taste in architecture effected by Lord Burlington had borne such rapid fruit that the architect James Paine in 1767 could justifiably draw a parallel between the Augustan and Georgian ages in the following words of the introduction to his works: "The rapid progress of architecture in Great Britain within the last thirty years is perhaps without example in any age or country since the Romans."[64] Three years later, Horace Walpole felt it proper to qualify the comparison in England's favor: "She found more, and what Rome could not boast, men of the first rank who contributed to embellish their country by buildings of their own design in the purest style of antique composition."[65] By modern standards, the education in architecture of the man of taste in the eighteenth century, which has here been outlined, will appear haphazard at best. But posterity has endorsed the contemporary judgment of its effectiveness.

NOTES

1 J. Rouquet, *The Present State of the Arts in England* (London, 1755), pp. 96–97.

2 J. Milton, *Tractate on Education*, ed. A. Browning (Cambridge, 1897), p. 12; J. Locke, *Some Thoughts Concerning Education* (London, 1693), pp. 191–92.

3 June 21–July 3, 1712, nos. 411–21. For discussion see S. H. Monk, *The Sublime* (Ann Arbor: University of Michigan Press, 1960), p. 58, and W. J. Hipple, *The Beautiful, the Sublime and the Picturesque* (Carbondale: Southern Illinois University Press, 1957), ch. 1.

4 The multiplicity of schemes for an appropriate royal residence in London bears eloquent testimony to this concern in the eighteenth century. See H. Colvin, *Royal Buildings* (London, 1968), pp. 10–14.

5 S. Kliger, "Whig Aesthetics: A Phase of Eighteenth-Century Taste," *ELH, A Journal of English Literary History*, 16 (1949), 135–50.

6 *Journal of the Royal Institute of British Architects*, 3rd. series, 31 (1924), 343.

7 H. M. Colvin, *Biographical Dictionary of English Architects, 1660–1840* (London: J. Murray, 1954), pp. 13–14.

8 R. Wittkower, "The Artist," in J. L. Clifford, ed., *Man Versus Society in Eighteenth-Century Britain* (London, 1968), pp. 70–84.

9 J. Gwynn, *London and Westminster Improved* (London, 1766), p. 61.

10 J. Bramston, *The Man of Taste* (London, 1735).

11 J. Gwynn, *Essay on Design* (London, 1749), pp. 69–70.

12 L. Dickins and M. Stanton, *An Eighteenth-Century Correspondence* (London: J. Murray, 1910), p. 315.

13 ALS unpublished in the Department of Manuscripts of the Henry E. Huntington Library and Art Gallery, San Marino, California, quoted by kind permission of the Trustees.

14 M. McCarthy, "James Lovell and His Sculptures at Stowe," *Burlington Magazine*, 115, no. 841 (1973), 220–32.

15 Titled *Book of Architecture*, and marked *MS Vault Shelves*, quoted by kind permission of the Trustees of the Beinecke Library, Yale University, New Haven, Connecticut.

16 J. Summerson, *Architecture in Britain, 1530–1830* (London, 1969), p. 215. See now R. Wittkower, *Palladio and English Palladianism* (London: Thames and Hudson, 1974), pp. 95–114.

17 Quoted by kind permission of Mr. and Mrs. Paul Mellon.

18 S. Riou, *Short Principles for the Architecture of Stone Bridges* (London, 1760). For similar sentiments see S. Riou, *The Grecian Orders of Architecture* (London, 1768), p. 5; R. Morris, *An Essay in Defence of Ancient Architecture* (London, 1728), pp. 11–13; R. Morris, *Rural Architecture* (London, 1750), Preface.

19 J. Gwynn, *London and Westminster Improved* (London, 1766), p. 47.

20 Lord Chesterfield, *An Essay on Design* (London, 1749), pp. 62–63.

21 B. Langley, *The Art of Designing and Working the Ornamental Parts of Buildings* (London, 1745), Introduction.

22 Quoted by kind permission of F. H. Fitzroy-Newdegate.

23 W. H. Smith, *Originals Abroad* (New Haven: Yale University Press, 1953), p. 193.

24 T. Barrett-Lennard, *An Account of the Families of Lennard and Barrett* (privately printed 1908), p. 582.

25 J. Gibbs, *Rules for Drawing the Several Parts of Architecture* (London, 1733), "To The Reader."

26 M. Williams, *Letters of William Shenstone* (London, 1939), p. 230.

27 Ibid., p. 136. From other correspondence it is clear that the reference is to the volume by Isaac Ware, published first, probably, in 1735, with a second edition in 1743. See J. Hodgetts, *Letters of Lady Luxborough to William Shenstone* (London, 1775), p. 85.

28 Ibid., p. 204. The book has been identified as B. Langley, *Gothic Architecture Improved* (London, 1742), by William Hawkes.

29 Ibid., p. 193 and p. 230. *The Builders' Jewel, or the Youth's Instructor and Workman's Remembrancer* was first published in 1746.

30 T. Hull, *Select Letters* (London, 1778), pp. 5, 34, 39.

31 R. Graves, *Recollections of Shenstone* (London, 1788), p. 177.

32 Williams, *Letters*, p. 147.

33 Ibid., p. 219.

34 Ibid., p. 226.

35 J. Gwynn, *An Essay on Design* (London, 1749), p. 62.

36 Lady Verney and P. Abercrombie, "Letters of an Eighteenth-Century Architect," *The Architectural Review*, 59 (1926), 259–63; 60 (1926), 1–3, 50–53, and 92–93.

37 Ibid., p. 51.

38 ALS unpublished among the Lyttelton Manuscripts at Hagley Hall, Worcestershire, quoted by kind permission of Lord Cobham. For Thomas Pitt see M. McCarthy, "The Rebuilding of Stowe House, 1770–1777," *Huntington Library Quarterly*, 36, no. 3 (1973), 267–98.

39 For Aldrich see Colvin, *Biographical Dictionary*, pp. 37–38.

40 For Clarke see ibid., pp. 141–42, and the same author's introduction to *Catalogue of the Architectural Drawings of the 18th and 19th Centuries in the Libraries of Worcester College, Oxford* (Oxford, 1964).

41 M. McCarthy, "Sir Roger Newdigate: Drawings for Copt Hall, Essex, and Arbury Hall, Warwickshire," *Architectural History*, 16 (1973), 26–36.

42 Colvin, *Biographical Dictionary*, p. 389.

43 *Bibliotheca Radcliviana* (Oxford, 1949), pl. 10.

44 Colvin, *Biographical Dictionary*, pp. 108–9.

45 Leeds City Libraries, Archives Department, Newby Hall Papers, NH 2840/8, quoted by kind permission of Mr. Robin Compton of Newby Hall.

46 T. J. Matthias, *The Works of Thomas Gray* (London, 1814), II, 98–103 and 600–603.

47 P. Toynbee and L. Whibley, eds., *The Correspondence of Thomas Gray*, 3 vols. (Oxford: Clarendon Press, 1935), passim.

48 Ibid., p. 659.

49 Ibid., p. 771.

50 J. Harris, *Sir William Chambers* (London: A. Zwemmer, 1970), pp. 8–9.

51 Ibid., p. 128.

52 John Harris has identified Yenn's as the principal hand in the drawings from the office of Chambers which are in the Royal Library at Windsor Castle among the drawings of King George III.

53 For Kirby see Colvin, *Biographical Dictionary*, pp. 348–49. For Chambers see J. Fleming, *Robert Adam and His Circle* (London, 1961), p. 249.

54 Department of Manuscripts, the Henry E. Huntington Library and Art Gallery, San Marino, California, Stowe Papers, box marked "Personal Accounts 1767–1799" and "T3 NN4." Quoted by kind permission of the Trustees.

55 For one instance see M. McCarthy, "Sir Roger Newdigate and Piranesi," *Burlington Magazine*, 144, no. 832 (1972), 666–72.

56 For the background see E. Moir, *The Discovery of Britain* (London: Routledge and Kegan Paul, 1964).

57 British Museum, Stowe MSS., 753, ff. 145–47.

58 For Robert Nugent see C. Nugent, *Memoirs of Earl Nugent* (London, 1898).

59 Warwick County Record Office, Sanderson Miller Papers, 125B/645.

60 Warwick CRO 125B/168.

61 Warwick CRO, Newdegate Papers, 136B/4108, quoted by kind permission of F. H. Fitzroy-Newdegate of Arbury Hall.

62 Warwick CRO 136B/4583.

63 *The Walpole Society*, vol. 16 (Oxford, 1928).

64 James Paine, *Plans, Elevations and Sections* (London, 1767), p. 1.

65 H. Walpole, *Anecdotes of Painting in England*, ed. R. Wornum (London, 1888), III, 47.

A Colonial Printer as Bookseller in Eighteenth-Century Philadelphia: The Case of David Hall

ROBERT D. HARLAN

In 1743 Benjamin Franklin agreed to provide one year's trial employment for David Hall, a young Scottish printer who wished to try his luck in the New World. The following year Hall left the London shop of William Strahan for Philadelphia. This was the second exodus in his career, for a few years earlier he had made the shorter and less perilous journey from Edinburgh to London. Franklin also pledged to help defray the cost of Hall's return passage to London if either party should become dissatisfied. But Hall remained in America, was promoted to a printing partnership with Franklin, and, independently of this business, established an extensive booktrade which served Philadelphia, its environs, and even more distant points. Hall dealt mainly in imported books, as did most substantial colonial booksellers. His chief book agent was his former employer, William Strahan.

Hall is known primarily as Franklin's partner and as a printer, and he would probably have affirmed the modern judgment of the primacy of printing in his career. The trade in which he had been trained and certified was printing. It was his skill as a printer that had enabled him to emigrate to America and there in a short time to advance to the lucrative partnership with Franklin. But if his other tradesman's activities were secondary, they were nevertheless central aspects of his diversified enterprises.

When Hall first arrived in Philadelphia he must have been impressed and perhaps amazed at the "general store" appearance of Franklin's shop. For there, under one roof, books were printed and sold, a newspaper was published, and a wide assortment of goods, many of which had no relation to the trade, were offered. The shop also served as the post office and was very much "in the public Way."

Hall came from a different tradition, both in Edinburgh where he served his apprenticeship and in London where the rigid hierarchy of the trade kept most printers in an inferior and circumscribed position. Printers worked for other persons. A fortunate few possessed printing privileges and patents which could provide good profits; some were printer-proprieters of newspapers, but printers seldom owned literary property or copyshares, and if they sold books at all it was on a small scale.

Hall's hopes for wider opportunities in Philadelphia were fulfilled. In 1747 Franklin, so pleased with Hall's performance that he decided not to send him to establish a printing partnership in the West Indies, turned over the bookshop to his ambitious assistant. Hall's early bookselling career can be traced in the advertisements he placed in the *Pennsylvania Gazette* (referred to hereafter as the *Gazette*). Modest at first, these became within a year extensive lists of books offered in his shop. A substantial career was launched which was to span twenty-five years until Hall's death in 1772.

Hall enjoyed three main advantages in this new business: his association with Franklin, his access to the *Gazette*, and his choice of William Strahan as his chief London book import agent.

The continued connection of Franklin's name with the shop was, on the whole, a decided advantage. Franklin held no interest in the bookshop, but it occupied the same quarters as the printing establishment which bore his name, and to the public the separate establishments must have seemed as one. Hall was able, therefore, to enjoy the advantage of continuing an established firm rather than having to start a new one. Only once before the expiration of the partnership in 1766 was Franklin a source of financial discomfort to Hall. This was during the Stamp Act crisis when resentment over Franklin's seemingly conciliatory stand on the Act caused a sharp decline in the number of subscriptions to the *Gazette*.

The *Gazette* was a major source of support in Hall's bookselling business, for it provided a frequent, regular, inexpensive, and, as the most widely read newspaper in America, an effective advertising outlet. Hall issued handlists and catalogs of his book stock, from time to time, but the *Gazette* was his chief advertising medium. Whether Hall paid the printing partnership for these advertisements I do not know, but if he did, the cost would have been on the best terms. One of Hall's strongest objections to the Stamp Act was its threat to this comfortable arrangement, for if enforced the Act would have placed a two shilling tax on each advertisement each time it was printed.

The flow of books from the Old World to Hall's shop had its primary source in London, where William Strahan served as his book agent. The association was mutually beneficial, resulting in substantial profits for both men. Strahan's standing with the trade insured prompt and efficient attention to Hall's orders and, according to Strahan, on the best terms. Strahan used the profitable export market which Hall provided to further his own business interests at home. These considerations and his personal inclination to serve his friend "Davie" made him an unusually solicitous agent.

Strahan was in a better position than other book agents Hall might have employed to execute his orders. Yet Strahan never owned a bookshop (although he held silent partnerships with such important booksellers as Thomas Durham and Thomas Cadell) and did not sell books directly to the public. Some of Hall's customers wondered how it could happen that a bookseller did not have a bookshop. "The keeping of a Shop is of no importance," Strahan replied. "What constitutes a Bookseller is having Property in Copies . . . [and] of this Property I have more than nine parts in ten have, as may be seen by looking into the Title Pages of Books in General."[1] Strahan was not exaggerating. There were few contemporary English and Scottish authors of importance whose works he did not publish.

Holding copyshares in many titles, and several in conjunction with other booksellers, Strahan maintained wide contacts with the wholesale trade. He knew who was a likely source for Hall's requests when he could not supply them himself. And because he printed as well as sold books he had other booksellers at a disadvantage: ". . . as in my way of Business, most of the Whole Sale Printing Booksellers are in my Debt, they are always most ready to give me what Books I want on the lowest Terms, which . . . they will be more ready to part with than *ready Money itself*."[2]

Strahan's case is convincing, even though, from time to time, competitors for the American export market offered books at lower rates. This apparent contradiction between Strahan's pronouncements and his performance did not escape the notice of Hall or some of his customers. While retaining Strahan as his chief agent, Hall did inform Strahan of instances of competitors' lower prices. Strahan's explanations provide interesting insight into the state of the trade in Great Britain. For example, on the prices quoted by Gavin Hamilton and John Balfour of Edinburgh: "I don't wonder they charge what they send you cheap; for both printing and binding are cheaper in Scotland, and they pay no Copy Money for what they print. And in truth, as far as their Stock goes, they can sell on much better Terms than you can have them from London."[3] On a competitor's lower quotation for a copy of a standard law treatise: "This may easily be accounted for, as Tho[s] Osborne of Gray's Inn, whose sole Property it is, sells them sometimes cheaper, sometimes dearer, just as he happens to want Money, and often just as the Whim takes him."[4] A competitor showed Hall the invoice for a shipment of books which he had received from Richard Neave and Son of London. Hall itemized for Strahan's edification the differences in prices charged by the two London agents: "6 Dozen of Plays charged to him at 4/6 [a dozen] and I am charged 5/ for 500. Prices' Carpentry he is charged 6/6, mine from you not a bitt [sic] better 7/. Barclay's Apology 3/6 mine 4/6. Watts's Supplements 3/6 mine 4/6 . . . Lilly's Grammar 12/6 a Dozen, mine 15/. For five Dozen of Dilworth's Spelling Books he is charged 8/ [a dozen] and I am charged the same for 50 dozen." And so on. "Now what should be the reason for this," he continued, since "you tell me you have it in your power rather to furnish me cheaper than any other Person can, because of your great Property in Copies."[5] Strahan: "Probably Mr. Neave was put in Cash to buy the Cargo with Ready Money, and charges besides so much p[er] Ct. commission upon the whole Amount."[6] Alexander Donaldson, Hall informed Strahan, "proposes selling considerably lower than I can have from any other."[7] Strahan replied, "He is upon the Pyratical Scheme, and has printed a good Many Books in a cheap Manner, by reducing their Size from 4° to 8° and from 8° to 12mo but in general so wretchedly incorrect and on such indifferent Paper that Gentlemen are much disgusted at them when they see them; so that his Trade is dwindling fast. He is the Rivington of Scotland."[8]

This comparison totally discredited Donaldson with Hall, as Strahan well knew it would, for Hall detested and feared Rivington, who was equally unpopular in London where his ruthless tactics and unorthodox methods had turned the trade against him. Rivington's various schemes, which encompassed Great Britain and the American colonies, included book piracy, price undercutting, and misrepresentation.

Rivington went bankrupt in 1760 with debts amounting to £30,000. But his course was not run, for the following year he set up a shop in New York. His opening campaign for the American market was typical of his tactics: he announced that the book-sellers of the New World had been universally cheated by their English agents. Hall was made uncomfortable by Rivington's closer proximity. His discomfort was intensified when Rivington opened a second shop in Philadelphia. Occasionally, Hall found himself competing with Rivington in his own *Gazette*. In the October 22, 1761 issue, for example, companion advertisements of Hall and Rivington promise the lowest wholesale prices and the best terms for libraries.

Not until 1767 did Rivington's sharp practices catch up with him, and although by then he was generally discredited, he had caused more conventional provincial competitors much anxiety. But Hall knew that not all English dealers who offered bargain prices made reliable agents. Some of his own customers, temporarily lured by the promises of Rivington and his like, had also learned this lesson and returned to Hall. In 1763, Edward Shippen instructed his son to place his book orders with Hall "for I shall buy no more pigs in the poke as I did two years ago from Rivington."[9]

It was not only about prices that Hall complained. His letters to Strahan are peppered with criticism—about titles sent and not sent, superseded editions, missing volumes in sets and in periodical runs, and damaged items. For example, he complained to Strahan that:[10]

> "The spelling books you sent are too small."
>
> "Never send Volumes in Quarto when they may be had in Octavo."
>
> "You have sent too many Plays."
>
> "Why have you sent six Sets of Tillotson? They will be hard to sell in six Years."
>
> "Send no more Chapbooks of the religious Strain."
>
> "Send nothing relating to Scots Affairs."
>
> "Divinity is a most dull Article here. Send no more."
>
> "Make it a Rule, when Books are to be had in one Volume, not to send them in Two."
>
> "Send no more political Pamphlets; they are mere Trash and Pickpockets."
>
> "Locke, Tillotson, and Puffendorf [sic] are 'heavy' here."
>
> "Your not sending me the Remainder of Ruddiman's Rudiments, . . . is really not well done, as to be out of these School Books, which are continually wanted, may be of worse Con-

sequence than perhaps, you are aware of. It is dangerous . . . for our Customers to find the Way to other Shops."

And Strahan, for his part, would comment to Hall:[11]

> "There is no such Book as Pearson's Paraphrase on the Scripture, but Pearce's is a well-known good Book."
> "I believe you will find Abbé Batteau [sic] on *Taste* not on Trade, which you say is not sent."
> "What [the Union Library] seem most angry at my having omitted viz, the Fifth Volume of Lardner's Jewish and Heathen History was never printed, there being only Four."
> "You mention the History of the Devil, of which I sent you 25, tho' you had not ordered one. Here you will find you are mistaken; for in your Letter of Nov. 25, 1769, you order 6 and in your Letter Febry 6, 1770, you order 12 more. The Book was then out of print . . . when these Orders were sent. Now as you had wrote for 18 so long ago, I thought there could be no harm in sending 25 when it was reprinted. Indeed your repeatedly sending for them made me reprint the Book, having a considerable Share in it."

Hall's contradictory statement makes a nice conclusion to the series: "Don't you take Memorandums of some things that are not to be had when my Orders come to your Hands, and yet may be got, and sent some Time after?"[12]

In spite of his complaints, some of which seem unreasonable, Hall was well served by Strahan. On the average, Strahan's prices were competitive with those of other reputable dealers. His standing in the London trade insured the cooperation of other wholesalers when he could not himself supply Hall's orders. He was an invaluable negotiator in Hall's dealings with other merchants in London and Edinburgh. He acted as Hall's banker in arranging for the acceptance of bills of exchange and the conversion of payments in foreign currency into sterling. Strahan also had a good sense of the sort of books that could be sent to Hall without orders. Even during the years from 1765 to 1769, when a depression and general shortage of cash seriously affected the bookshop, Hall's standing order to Strahan to send "all new Books of Character" remained in effect. Strahan willingly complied—since he was usually involved in their publication.

These advantages—the association with the Franklin name, the availability of the *Gazette*, and the services of Strahan—must have given Hall the edge over his competitors. Exactly how successful Hall was we shall not know unless further documentation emerges. But the following points do suggest how considerable was his achievement. He was in the business for twenty-five years, a record equaled in Philadelphia only by his contemporary William Bradford. Competition in Philadelphia was keen. The volume of his importations was large. He paid his bills promptly. His bookselling business was not "carried" by his printing, since the profits from the latter, which are precisely known for the period 1748 to 1766, did not equal the sums paid out for imported books.

Hall's books came from disparate sources—some from as near as his own presses, others from as far away as Dublin, Belfast, Edinburgh, and London. The majority of Hall's titles were imported from abroad. The contributions of his own press stood next in number. The product of the other Pennsylvania presses and publications from other colonies followed. Together these books sampled the output of many presses scattered throughout the English-speaking world.

The most popular books in Hall's stock were some of the printing-partnership's own publications—the almanacs, particularly *Poor Richard Improved* which was issued in annual editions as large as 10,000 copies, a catechism, and a primer. Thousands of copies of these titles were sold in Hall's shop and elsewhere, and Hall counted heavily upon the income from their sale. Other books and pamphlets from Hall's presses must also have crossed over to the bookshop, but not in comparable numbers. Hall engaged in a modest reprint business. I use the word "reprint" because he did (i.e. "London Printed: Philadelphia, Reprinted"). Technically some of these publications could be termed piracies: for example, the 1749 edition of Lord Bolingbroke's *Letters on the Spirit of Patriotism*. Although an advertisement in the *Gazette* (9 January 1750) noted that "By all accounts from Great Britain, no Piece ever published has had so great a sale" there is no evidence that the London publishers of the original edition received compensation from the Philadelphia shop.

The problem of literary property did not vex the colonial trade as it did the trade in London, in part because the colonies fell outside of the jurisdiction of the Copyright Act of 1709 and also because there was little occasion there for controversy over literary property. Had the English booksellers felt threatened by their lack of control in the colonies they would certainly have complained and Strahan, their ardent spokesman, would have voiced their complaints in his letters to Hall. But only in the late 1760's did he protest the publication of American "reprints" of English works when Hall's competitor in Philadelphia, Robert Bell, began issuing inexpensive American editions of popular English publications. "I am sorry Charles Vth [William Robertson's best-selling history] is printing with you," he wrote to Hall in December 1770 in reference to Bell's reprint of this work, "as the Copy Money, which was no less than £4000 has not yet been repaid from the Sale."[13] Hall was not particularly interested in the reprinting of new works and provided no competition in this enterprise.

Hall sold books printed in other Pennsylvania shops, including those of William Bradford, William Dunlap, and James Chattin. These and other Philadelphia printer-publishers advertised in the *Gazette*, which may explain Hall's willingness to sell their books. On one occasion, Bradford and Hall published competing editions of the same work—John Dickinson's immensely popular *Letters from a Farmer in Pennsylvania to the Inhabitants of the British Colonies* (1768). While Dickinson regarded Hall's as the "only correct"[14] edition, he did not protest the appearance in Philadelphia of Bradford's edition and that of William Goddard and still other editions in other colonies, for he sought the widest distribution for his manifesto. Hall must have felt differently. But even with the competition from Bradford and Goddard, sales of his first edition of the *Farmer's Letters* warranted a second edition in only four months.

Advertisements in the *Gazette* show that Hall occasionally sold works produced by other colonial printers. Perhaps he did so on consignment, possibly as a courtesy.

The content of the publications of the American presses which Hall stocked tended towards the parochial and practical, but there was also a brisk market for a wider spectrum of subjects which the colonial presses, including Hall's, could not satisfy, even through subscription publication. This interest could only be met by importations, primarily from England. Furthermore, book buyers were probably prejudiced in favor of English imprints.

I have described briefly the nature of the colonial imprints which Hall sold. The corpus of Franklin-Hall imprints is now known with the publication of Professor C. William Miller's bibliography. The contributions from other colonial printers while not numerous are conspicuously advertised in the *Gazette*. I should like now to discuss the bulk of Hall's stock about which we know the least—his imported books.

"Imported in the last Vessel from London, to be sold by DAVID HALL, at the New Printing Office, in Market Street, Philadelphia. A very large and valuable Collection of Books." Thus, for twenty-five years Hall announced to readers of the *Gazette* the latest additions to his shop and left a partial record of the books he offered to retail and wholesale customers in Philadelphia and surrounding areas. These advertisements in the *Gazette* are a key to the imported stock of this important book shop.

Of the 1670 discrete titles which appear there, between 1748 and 1772, I have been able to verify 1439 in bibliographies and library catalogs. The percentage of verified titles is high. My explanation is that most of the works are standard enough to have found their way into published lists. I do not know if the figure of 1670 titles is higher or lower than or comparable to other booksellers' total advertisements. It does not represent all of the titles which Hall ordered, for there is another statistic: 712 titles ordered in Hall's letters to Strahan but not advertised in the *Gazette*. Some of these were orders for individual clients and would not, of course, have been advertised. Others may never have been sent by Strahan.

I could verify only about sixty percent of this category of ordered but unadvertised titles. I expect that my poor showing was also Strahan's because this group contains much misinformation originating with Hall's clients and himself. I omit this group from the following subject rankings based upon title counts in *Gazette* advertisements for the years 1748 to 1772. School texts and literature for children are also excluded.

It will probably surprise no one that religion (predominately theology), law, and medicine rank high and that history (including travel and biography) is a close competitor. However, the greatest number of titles (245) falls in the category of literature. Even more interesting is the largest division within this category: prose fiction (90). In the other subject categories this distribution occurs: religion (177), history (141), medicine (128), and law (121). Among the smaller categories are: philosophy (46), fine arts (34), agriculture and animal husbandry (15), navigation (14), and surveying (5). While this measurement provides an outline of the subject division of Hall's stock, it may also lead to distorted conclusions because titles are given equal weight—with no reference to their *comparative* demand. For example, Voltaire's *Complete Works* has the same weight as the Bible, although Hall only ordered one copy of the former and over 10,000 copies of the latter.

Professor Howard Mumford Jones made comparative use of advertisements in his illuminating article "The Importation of French Books in Philadelphia 1750–1800,"[15] to gauge the popularity of sixteenth-, seventeenth-, and eighteenth-century French authors by counting the number of advertisements of their works, including those in translation, in several Philadelphia newspapers. Fénelon is first among sixteenth- and seventeenth-century authors because his *Télémaque* is cited more frequently in advertisements than any other title. Molière's plays rank second. And so on. Professor Jones notes the weakness in his methodology: one must assume that books are advertised because they are popular. But while his "best seller" list is rather speculative, he does provide evidence that Philadelphia's booksellers offered a rich variety of

French authors. The *Gazette*, incidentally, was among the most frequently cited newspapers and was also often the first newspaper to advertise French works.

Much of the correspondence between Hall and Strahan, from which I have quoted extensively in this essay, was not available at the time Professor Jones published his article. If he had been able to use this material, he might have added another dimension to his comparative measurement, for Hall's letters to Strahan record for about half of the titles advertised in the *Gazette* the date and size of their orders. I believe that most of these orders were supplied in the quantities requested, unless Hall's complaints and Strahan's explanations noted otherwise. *Gazette* advertisements also confirm the arrival of many of these titles, after the lapse of from six months to one year from the time they were ordered.

From the body of information in the Hall-Strahan correspondence and in the *Gazette* advertisements, I should like to conclude with some observations about Hall's imported book stock. The books are distributed into three categories: First, those of mature readers; second, school texts; and third, literature for children. The school texts and children's books are represented by many titles which were ordered in large numbers, but they are special subjects which cannot be considered here. The group of books for adults which has the largest number of titles, comprises a wide variety of authors and subjects. But its breadth is superficial. At the heart of the collection are no more than one hundred titles which Hall ordered and advertised over a long period of time. The demand for these works, while sustained, was not large, except for the Bible, the New Testament, the Book of Common Prayer, and the Psalter, and not even this quartet could compete in sales with *Poor Richard Improved* and Hall's other popular publications.

Religion and theology, practical treatises, and a few literary classics predominate. There is so close a correlation between the weight of these subjects in the simple title count and in the more complex calculation of advertisements and orders that their importance to Hall's clients is undisputed. Titles by seventeenth-century authors are conspicuous among the standard theological works.

The most popular of these, even counting *Pilgrim's Progress*, was *Seven Sermons* by the Reverend Robert Russell (between 1760 and 1765, Hall ordered 450 copies). Only one eighteenth-century collection of sermons approached this figure, and its popularity was short-lived—I refer to the Reverend James Fordyce's *Sermons for Young Women* (61 copies in one year).

Law, medicine, and applied sciences dominate in the group of manuals and treatises. Edmund Burke stated in 1775 that Americans knew and would maintain their rights because they had been for so long a period avid consumers of treatises on law imported from England.[16] The number of law books in Hall's stock lends credence to Burke's assertion. Blackstone, Coke, Locke, various reports and cases, and the *Statutes at Large* are here. But the most popular treatises are the most practical: the *Compleat Constable*, the *Compleat Jury Man*, the *Compleat Sheriff*, the *Tradesman's Lawyer* and *Countryman's Friend* and, in greatest demand, Giles Jacob's *Every Man His Own Lawyer*. In medicine, or "Physik," too, Hall's orders were largely for practical handbooks and manuals. In other subjects, similar works were equally popular, for example, Henry Bracken's *Farriery Improved*, Philip Miller's *The Gardner's Dictionary*, and *The Compleat Housewife; or Accomplished Gentlewoman's Companion*.

In poetry *Paradise Lost* was ordered in the largest number of copies. Close rivals were Isaac Watts' *Horae Lyricae* and Edward Young's *Night Thoughts*. But next, before Pomfret, Pope, Thomson (whom Franklin so admired), and certainly Shakespeare, was Mary Mollineaux's *Fruits of Retirement*, which was almost as popular as *Night Thoughts*. Substantial orders were placed for classical literature, but many of these were destined for the classroom. Hall's orders reflect only a moderate interest in English translations of these works. Seneca's *Morals* was the most frequently ordered title in this group. More popular works in translation were *Don Quixote, Gil Blas,* and *The Devil on Two Sticks*. Among contemporary English novelists Richardson was more in demand than Fielding, Fielding than Sterne, and Sterne than Smollett, of whom Hall disapproved.

No one author or work dominates history, travel, and biography. In this group the largest orders were for Thomas Salmon's *Gazetter*. Of the travel books, Nathaniel Hooke's translation of Andrew Ramsay's imaginary *Travels of Cyrus* seems to have been the favorite. Among historians Charles Rollin ranks high. Hume's and Smollett's histories of England did not catch on, apparently, nor did William Robertson's *History of Scotland*. This, of course, is only a sampling of some of the more popular works in the important subject areas in Hall's shop.

The high proportion of imported books in Hall's entire stock and the contents of these works do not indicate evidence of a spirit of American independence, nor does the stock fully reflect the richness of English publications of the time. Hall's stock is certainly not provincial, but I cannot apply to it Helmut Lehmann-Haupt's general assertion about the stock of colonial shops, that it was "in all essentials, except that of size . . . [a replica] of the London establishments of the period."[17]

In surveying Hall's imported book stock I was impressed by how well it complemented the colonial imprints he sold and printed. In ordinary times, when neither wars nor non-importation movements disrupted the flow of supplies, Hall was content in his role as printer-publisher to issue his newspaper and almancs, to execute job work, to print the works commissioned by the government, and to publish a variety of books and pamphlets of primarily local interest. Perhaps the indifferent reception accorded to Franklin's *Pamela* and his even more ambitious *Cato Major* just at the time of Hall's arrival in Philadelphia explains Hall's own reluctance to compete with London imprints. Surely, Strahan's efficiency as a book agent re-enforced Hall's disposition to rely primarily upon imported books to meet most of the demands of his clientele. For these reasons he declined to invest capital, equipment, and time in the speculative printing and publishing of titles more readily and profitably obtained from abroad.

When the non-importation movement associated with colonial opposition to the Stamp Act forced Hall, reluctantly, to cut off the flow of books from England, he realized the full measure of his dependence upon imported books. The patriot party must also have recognized the limitations of colonial presses, for during the Townshend Acts crisis, when Philadelphia was known for its strict adherence to non-importation, first school books, then books for libraries and "private Gentlemen", and finally all books were exempted from the embargo. The populace might pledge to observe frugality and to forego the importation of all luxuries and even of such staples as paper, which was one of the taxed items. But they could not do without books, and these Hall continued to import from England.

NOTES

1 William Strahan to David Hall, 30 January 1764, Strahan MSS. American Philosophical Society (referred to hereafter as APS).

2 Ibid.

3 Strahan to Hall, 17 July 1759, Strahan MSS. APS.

4 Strahan to Hall, 26 August 1752, Strahan MSS. APS.

5 Hall to Strahan, 25 June 1764, David Hall MSS. APS.

6 Strahan to Hall, 9 September 1764, Strahan MSS. APS.

7 Hall to Strahan, 25 September 1764, Hall MSS. APS.

8 Strahan to Hall, 30 November 1764, Strahan MSS. APS.

9 Edward Shippen to Joseph Shippen, 3 September 1763, Shippen MSS. APS.

10 Hall to Strahan, 13 July 1750, 16 December 1765, 20 November 1750, 2 February 1751, 21 March 1752, 22 December 1760, 16 September 1766, 21 November 1764, 3 September 1764, 17 December 1763, 22 October 1764, Hall MSS. APS.

11 Strahan to Hall, 8 July 1765, 19 September 1764, 11 November 1768, 19 August 1771, Strahan MSS. APS.

12 Hall to Strahan, 3 September 1764, Hall MSS. APS.

13 Strahan to Hall, 8 December 1770, Strahan MSS. APS.

14 John Dickinson to James Otis, 6 January 1768, *Massachusetts Historical Society Collections*, 72 (1917), 5.

15 Howard Mumford Jones, "The Importation of French Books in Philadelphia 1750–1800," *Modern Philology*, 32 (1934–35), 157–77.

16 Cornelius B. Bradley, ed., *Orations and Arguments by English and American Statesmen* (Boston: Allyn and Bacon, 1896), p. 22.

17 Helmut Lehmann-Haupt, *The Book in America*, 2nd ed. (New York: R. R. Bowker Co., 1950), p. 50.

The Fortunes and Misfortunes of
a Leading French Bookseller-Printer:
André-François Le Breton,
Chief Publisher of the Encyclopédie

FRANK A. KAFKER

> The truth is that M. Le Breton, so clear-sighted in matters of
> profit, is one of the most narrow-minded men in France, . . . that
> he has never had any idea of literature, still less of philosophy;
> that he is as cowardly and fainthearted as he is narrow-minded.
>
> Frédéric-Melchior Grimm,
> *Correspondance littéraire,* January 1, 1771

André-François Le Breton is best remembered as Grimm described him and as one of the villains of the eighteenth century; for
he was the publisher of the great French *Encyclopédie* who took it
upon himself to censor its last ten volumes of letterpress, an act its
chief editor Denis Diderot regarded as one of the most infamous in
the history of printing. But Le Breton was much more than a
villain. He was also one of the century's very successful publishers
and one of its ablest businessmen. Yet his life, apart from the
Encyclopédie, has received scant attention from scholars. This

brief study of his career and of his two biggest publishing ventures has two main aims: to introduce a man who deserves thorough investigation as an entrepreneur and to illustrate the pressures and anguish endured even by the official and most favored publishers in eighteenth-century France as they attempted to become prosperous.

Le Breton's parents died while he was still a child, and he was brought up in Paris by his maternal uncle Charles-Maurice d'Houry, the son of the publisher Laurent d'Houry. When André-François reached adulthood, there was some question whether he should take over his late father's minor judicial office dealing with Parisian tax matters or become a publisher. His decision to enter the book trade was prompted in good part by the death of Laurent d'Houry in 1725 when Le Breton was seventeen years old. A family squabble followed over who would control the rights to his grandfather's major publishing venture, the *Almanach royal*, a semi-official who's who that annually listed the rulers of Europe and the leading noblemen and royal officials of France. Le Breton's uncle-stepfather Charles-Maurice claimed the exclusive rights to the publication, which Laurent's widow contested. The case went to court, and the decision left the widow in sole control. She disinherited her son and chose her grandson Le Breton as her heir apparent.[1]

The grandson's drive, determination, and resourcefulness in the pursuit of profit were quickly evident. Although his grandmother lived until 1750, he assumed many of the burdens of publishing the *Almanach royal*. While serving as an apprentice to the printer Claude-Louis Thiboust from 1727 to 1732, he redesigned the *Almanach*, greatly expanded its coverage, and helped make it even more of a financial success. To be mentioned in its pages became an important status symbol. As Louis-Sébastien Mercier satirically said later in the century: "Those who rush along the roads of ambition consult the *Almanach royal* with a studious attention. . . . Pity the person not included in that book! He has neither rank, nor public office, nor title, nor occupation."[2]

Like Laurent d'Houry earlier, Le Breton and his grandmother

protected their investment in the *Almanach* by striving to outdo its chief competitor, the *Calendrier de la cour*. In addition to printing a regular edition, they published an abridgement resembling in size and content the rival publication, which was edited by the Collombats. This family enlarged the *Calendrier* to cut into the *Almanach*'s market. Suits and countersuits followed, each side accusing the other of violating the law by printing a work different from the specifications stipulated in the royal publication licenses and in various governmental resolutions.[3]

While this dispute flared off and on inconclusively, Le Breton's career flourished. In 1733 he was received as one of the one hundred or more official master booksellers in the Paris Corporation of Booksellers and Printers; in 1740 he was appointed one of the Printers in Ordinary to the King; four years later he gained exclusive legal control over the *Almanach*, defeating his stepfather's attempt to wrest it from him; in 1746 the royal administration made an exception in his case and permitted his entrance into the exclusive circle of Parisian master printers even though all thirty-six authorized places were at the time occupied; and from 1747 to 1750 he was a deputy of the Corporation of Booksellers and Printers, one of the five main executive officers of this guild.[4] Le Breton clearly knew how to make his way among colleagues and government officials. Even the police, who distrusted publishers, described him in a report dated January 1, 1752 as "a very honorable man, and quite well-off, who skillfully conducts his business."[5]

Some years before, Le Breton had begun the most important enterprise of his career, the publication of the *Encyclopédie*. It started modestly in January 1745 as a venture with the German Gottfried Sellius and the Englishman John Mills to translate Ephraim Chambers's two-volume *Cyclopaedia* into French with some expansions and corrections. But Le Breton could not get along with the other two men. He suspected them of swindling him, and he literally came to blows with Mills. Various law suits followed, with the final result that the Chancellor of France d'Aguesseau dissolved the contract; and some months later Le

Breton was permitted to begin the project again with three new partners, Antoine-Claude Briasson, Michel-Antoine David, and Laurent Durand, all members of the Paris Corporation of Book-sellers and Printers. Le Breton was the senior partner, retaining a half interest in the enterprise. The others had one-sixth each, and the contract put him in sole charge of the printing. To launch the venture, the four men invested thousands of livres and borrowed thousands more.[6] They assembled a small staff, which included Diderot and Jean Le Rond d'Alembert; and they chose an editor, Abbé Gua de Malves, whose inefficiency and financial mismanage-ment caused the publishers much grief. He resigned in August 1747, thirteen months after he had taken charge.[7]

A month later, to replace the Abbé de Gua, the publishers selected Diderot and d'Alembert as editors. Though at the time the four partners did not know it, this was a fateful decision. They thought that the editorial work could be completed in three and a half years and that the result would be a non-controversial book of knowledge, but they discovered otherwise. The new editors greatly increased the number of collaborators and encouraged lengthy contributions. The manuscript grew and grew, while Diderot fur-ther delayed publication by his imprisonment of 102 days in 1749 for writing scandalous works. Until subscriptions started coming in after the appearance of the prospectus of the *Encyclopédie* in October 1750, Le Breton must have been very worried about whether his investment in the work would result in the loss of tens of thousands of livres.[8]

Then for the next seven years sales mounted. The plan at first was to print 1,625 copies per volume; by printing time for Volume I the number had been raised to 2,075 per volume; and it was raised again to its highest limit, 4,225 per volume in February 1754, when Volume IV was being printed and the first three volumes reprinted to reach at least that number. By the end of that year, receipts totaled more than a half million livres.[9]

But even this financial success had its disadvantages, since it encouraged pirated editions. In 1751 a Dutch publisher J. Néaulme announced that he was contemplating a reprint of the

Encyclopédie with additions; nothing came of this. The publishers took more seriously a proposal by some English booksellers to print an unauthorized edition. David and Briasson were sent to England near the end of that year to prevent it. They negotiated with their business rivals and seem to have ended the threat, though one volume of a pirated French-language edition did appear in London the next year. Also in 1752 an English-language translation of the *Encyclopédie* was launched by Sir Joseph Ayloffe, but it soon failed. Moreover, four years later they acted against another proposed new edition. This one was to be an abridged, expurgated, and corrected version by the Prussian academician and man of letters Samuel Formey. At their behest, d'Alembert successfully recommended that the Director of the Book Trade, Malesherbes, forbid such a work from being published or circulated in France; and Formey decided to discontinue the project.[10]

Le Breton was also made anxious by the fact that Diderot, d'Alembert, and other Encyclopedists offended powerful people by unorthodox religious and political remarks in articles; to get them passed through censorship required duplicity on the part of Le Breton and his editors. The work had been suspended briefly by the royal administration in 1752 for comments in the first two volumes allegedly undermining Church and State. The frightful prospect was that it would be permanently stopped, its publishers and editors severely punished.

The storm that Le Breton feared took five years to arrive. It was first set off late in 1757 by d'Alembert's impious article "Genève" in Volume VII, an article which caused an international incident and helped to convince d'Alembert that he should resign as an editor. Then the appearance of Helvétius's even more impious *De l'Esprit* the next year made matters worse, for some conservatives imagined a conspiracy against Catholicism. By 1759 both works had been condemned by the Parlement of Paris and the administration; the publishers lost their license to publish the *Encyclopédie*; and they were ordered to pay back 72 livres to each of its approximately 4,000 subscribers, a sum that would have amounted to more than 275,000 livres. It took the publishers' ingenuity, as well as the compliance of various royal officials, especially Malesherbes, for them to emerge from this debacle. But arrangements were made to avoid most of the reimbursement payments and to continue the publication. The volumes of letterpress were allowed to be printed secretly and published all at once, while the plates were to be published openly and delivered as they came ready.[11]

Le Breton's anxieties mounted: the *Encyclopédie*'s enemies charged it with plagiarizing engravings; a lot of his own money was again being spent to produce the volumes (he had fifty workmen preparing the manuscript for publication in his printing shop alone); and he was deeply involved in a conspiracy to evade the law. It is from this perspective that one can understand, if not sympathize with, the fact that he and his foreman Brullé tampered with at least forty articles in the proofs of the last ten volumes of letterpress, cutting out or modifying political and religious impieties. As Diderot's daughter said, Le Breton "feared the Bastille more than a thunderbolt";[12] and no doubt also he wanted to safeguard his investment. The pursuit of money was for him a grand passion. The extent of Le Breton's censorship is still uncertain. He clearly did not ruin this work, for it remains a storehouse of literary gems, erudition, and unorthodoxy. Diderot discovered the publisher's excisions and emendations in 1764, probably while checking the printed sheets of the article "Sarrasins ou Arabes." He flew into a justifiable rage, never forgave Le Breton, and afterward treated him with contempt. In a vitriolic letter the editor asked him "if one has ever heard before of ten folio volumes secretly mutilated, truncated, hacked up, and dishonored by a printer? ... You will be referred to in the future as a man guilty of such a breach of trust and of such brazenness that there will never be anything comparable."[13]

Earlier the two men had been on cordial terms, although Diderot had sometimes found him miserly,[14] touchy, and boring, and found his wife a bundle of contradictions—pious and risqué, generous and covetous, intelligent and dull. Now Le Breton felt uncomfortable in Diderot's presence. The editor told his mistress that he was aware of Le Breton's "heavy and clumsy body all about me. He sits down, he gets up; he sits down again. He would like to talk, he remains silent; I do not know what he wants from me."[15] Whatever embarrassment Le Breton was suffering, he persevered in the task at hand—to prepare for the distribution of the last ten volumes of letterpress. It was during his term of office as *Syndic*, the chief executive officer of the Paris Corporation of Booksellers and Printers, that he started sending them to subscribers in early 1766. But a difficulty arose. The police asked him to delay distribution in Paris and at Versailles; for there was to be an Assembly of the Clergy, and the royal government did not want to give it cause for offense. Le Breton, however, could not resist sending a few sets to influential men at court. The police retaliated. For a week, from April 23 to April 30, 1766, he was imprisoned, though in a style that indicated that the administration was only trying to serve appearances. He was not interrogated and he was allowed to have a servant, books, and writing materials.[16]

The next six or seven years were the least troubled in the history of the *Encyclopédie*. The last ten volumes of letterpress and the remaining seven volumes of plates were eventually distributed and became so sought after that they soon sold for more than the current subscription price of 980 livres, despite the fact that various other French-language editions were being published in such places as Geneva, Yverdun, Lucca, and Leghorn.[17] Each of the four publishers or their heirs made a profit of hundreds of thousands of livres; the total net profits of the entire edition may have amounted to more than two million livres; and in 1768 the plates and reprint rights were sold for another 200,000. In all this, Le Breton took even more than his usual half share after Durand's death in 1763.[18] The only serious difficulty confronting the publishers during this period from 1766 to 1772 was a drawn out legal battle begun in 1769 by the man of letters Luneau de Boisjermain, who sued for damages, claiming that he and the other subscribers to the *Encyclopédie* had been overcharged. Luneau's case was caught in a legal tangle by 1772, but not before involving Diderot, who reluctantly sided with the publishers in this instance.[19]

In 1773, at age sixty-five, Le Breton could look back at his career with a certain satisfaction. Chosen by the leading businessmen of Paris for a one-year term as *Consul* in 1767 and a one-year term as *Juge-consul* in 1770, he had thus been honored with appointment as judge and chief judge of commercial disputes in the city.[20] Moreover, he had seen the *Encyclopédie* through to its completion. He went into semi-retirement, selling his office of master printer, while retaining his bookstore, his post of Printer in Ordinary to the King, and his publication rights to the *Almanach royal*.[21] Peace seemed at hand. But it did not arrive. His continued publication of the *Almanach*, which according to a comment by Grimm in the *Correspondance littéraire* of January 1, 1771 brought him 30,000 livres a year,[22] also caused him anguish. Though almost surely Le Breton intended no malice, he was severely reprimanded and his printing house ordered closed for three months because of a few words in the 1774 edition: that year the *Almanach* listed for the first and only time the name, title, and address of Louis XV's purchasing agent for grain, while France was suffering severe grain shortages and some Frenchmen suspected the administration of speculating in that trade. By the next year Le Breton was restored to royal favor. The new king, Louis XVI, bore no grudge; Le Breton was permitted to present to him in person a copy of the 1775 edition of the *Almanach*. But two years later Le Breton was again in trouble, caught in the middle of a clash between powerful rivals. The Paris judiciary was angered when the *Almanach*'s 1777 edition listed as former members of the sovereign courts some of those officials whom the royal minister Maupeou had selected and whom the judges had never recognized. According to Bachaumont's journal, "The printer is all the more reprehensible because, instead of submitting his work to the censorship of monsieur de Mairobert to whom it had been directed, he has considered it appropriate to choose monsieur de Crébillon: that shows scheming and bad faith."[23] Le

Breton was able to quiet the commotion by reprinting the edition after having removed the offensive parts.[24] Meanwhile, Luneau had revived his law suit against the publishers in 1776; and this case was not dismissed until two years later,[25] a year before Le Breton died.

A distinguished historian of the continental book trade, Robert Darnton, has written that except for a few atypical members who "dabbled in underground publishing," the Parisian Corporation of Booksellers and Printers "produced a limited number of quality books according to official specifications. It turned out traditional books for a traditional market, which it controlled by virtue of an official monopoly. It ran no risks, because it owed its profits to its privileges; and its privileges were family treasures, handed down from father to son and husband to widow."[26]

Le Breton and the three other publishers of the *Encyclopédie* often do not fit this general pattern.[27] A study of their family connections does confirm the fact that official publishing in Paris was largely a family monopoly: Briasson, the son of a bookseller from Lyon, married the daughter of a Parisian bookseller; David's relatives had been Parisian booksellers for some two hundred years; Durand married the niece of a Parisian bookseller; and Le Breton was the grandson of a printer who published the *Almanach royal.*[28]

An inference that they published traditional books for a traditional audience perhaps best fits Briasson, who was caricatured in Diderot's *Neveu de Rameau* as "a good man, dedicated to his business, . . . breeding with his wife a legitimate child every year, a good father, a good uncle, a good neighbor, an honest merchant, but nothing more."[29] David too published many non-controversial works; and a police report spoke of him as an able and intelligent businessman, but it also continued with the following remark: "Despite this an imprudent man. He is a little suspect, since he printed l'Esprit Despinosa."[30] Another police report described Durand as "one of the most suspect and cunning in the book trade."[31] It was he who sold clandestinely three of Diderot's daring early works, *Pensées philosophiques, Les Bijoux indiscrets,* and *Lettre sur les aveugles*. In 1751 Durand's unauthorized edition of Maupertuis's *Essai de philosophie morale* was seized by the police; and in 1758–1759 his publication of Helvétius's *De l'Esprit* was banned by the King, the Parlement, the Pope, the Archbishop of Paris, and others. Hoping to profit from the uproar, Durand published a second edition without even tacit permission.[32] It is clear from the police report on Le Breton that he gave the authorities less trouble than Durand. Although Le Breton may have been asked to, he almost surely did not print Voltaire's pamphlets attacking the miscarriage of justice which resulted in the execution of Jean Calas. On the other hand, he did publish at least five legal reports calling for the reversal of the guilty verdict and donated part, perhaps all, of his profits to the widow Calas.[33]

Moreover, all four publishers ran risks. Like any French publisher, they had difficulty outwitting foreign and domestic business rivals who were adept at pirating the successful publications of others; and they had the problem of interpreting what the public would pay to read and what Church and State would tolerate, tasks often worthy of crystal gazers. Finally, as we have seen, the business career of the remarkable entrepreneur André-François Le Breton was financially hazardous and personally dangerous, if in the long run highly profitable.[34]

NOTES

1 Georges Lepreux, *Livre d'or des Imprimeurs du Roi*, in the *Gallia typographica*, 5 vols. (Paris: Champion, 1909–14), Parisian series, I, part 1, pp. 298, 302–3; and Jean Le Rond d'Alembert, "Almanach," *Encyclopédie*, 28 vols. (Paris: Briasson and others, 1751–72), I, 290.

2 Louis-Sébastien Mercier, *Tableau de Paris*, new ed., 8 vols. (Amsterdam: n.p., 1782–83), IV, 9. For the information on Le Breton and the *Almanach* contained in this paragraph, see also Lepreux, part 1, pp. 298–99, 303–4; part 2, pp. 167–68; and John Grand-Carteret, *Les Almanachs français* (Paris: Alisie, 1911), pp. 26–28. On the controversy over whether Le Breton became a Master Freemason in 1729, see Arthur

Wilson, *Diderot* (New York: Oxford University Press, 1972), pp. 75, 732 n. 11. A recent authority convincingly proves that there is no evidence to think Le Breton was a Freemason. Pierre Chevallier, *Les Ducs sous l'acacia ou les premiers pas de la Franc-Maçonnerie française, 1725–1743* (Paris: Vrin, 1964), pp. 23–24, 51–52. For an attempt, based on very little evidence, to link Le Breton to Minerval Masonry, see Dorothy B. Schlegel, "Freemasonry and the *Encyclopédie* Reconsidered," *Studies on Voltaire and the Eighteenth Century*, 90 (1972), 1434–36, 1460.

3 Lepreux, *Livre d'or*, part 1, pp. 140–43, 152–53, 301; Bibliothèque Nationale, MSS, Fonds Français 22077, fols. 193–94, 203–6; and Grand-Carteret, pp. 31–32.

4 For his various appointments, see Lepreux, *Livre d'or*, part 1, pp. 298–300, 304; part 2, pp. 170, 172, 202; and James Doolittle, "The Four Booksellers and the *Encyclopédie*," in Bernice Slote, ed., *Literature and Society* (Lincoln, Nebraska: University of Nebraska Press, 1964), esp. p. 24. On the organization of the Parisian book trade, see David T. Pottinger, *The French Book Trade in the Ancien Régime, 1500–1791* (Cambridge, Massachusetts: Harvard University Press, 1958).

5 Bibliothèque Nationale, MSS, Fonds Français 22107, fol. 91.

6 A French livre in 1760 was roughly equivalent to at least $1.50 in present-day currency, and it took more than 15,000 livres a year to live in Paris like a gentleman.

7 On this early history of the *Encyclopédie*, see esp. Wilson, *Diderot*, pp. 75–81. Also John Lough, "Le Breton, Mills et Sellius," *Dix-huitième siècle*, 1 (1969), 267–87; Ralph Brown, "The *Encyclopédie* as a Business Venture," in Charles K. Warner, ed., *From the Ancien Régime to the Popular Front* (New York: Columbia University Press, 1969), pp. 4–9; and my forthcoming article "Gua de Malves and the *Encyclopédie*" in *Diderot Studies*.

8 Wilson, *Diderot*, pp. 80–81, 103–16, 120; Bowen, pp. 8–11; Jacques Proust, *Diderot et l'Encyclopédie*, 2nd ed. (Paris: Colin, 1967), pp. 48–51; and Frank A. Kafker, "The Recruitment of the Encyclopedists," *Eighteenth-Century Studies*, 6 (1973), 453–56.

9 John Lough, "Luneau de Boisjermain *v.* the Publishers of the *Encyclopédie*," in *The Encyclopédie in Eighteenth-Century England and Other Studies* (Newcastle upon Tyne: Oriel Press, 1970), p. 105; and Proust, *Diderot*, p. 51.

10 G. L. Von Roosbroeck, "Who Originated the Plan of the Encyclopédie?" *Modern Philology*, 27 (1929–30), 383–84; Lough, "The *Encyclopédie* in Eighteenth-Century England," in *The Encyclopédie in Eighteenth-Century England and Other Studies*, pp. 3–8; and Georges Roth, "Samuel

Formey et son projet d'"Encyclopédie réduite'," *Revue d'histoire littéraire de la France*, 54 (1954), 371–74.

11 For the information in the last two paragraphs, see Wilson, *Diderot*, passim.

12 Marie-Angélique de Vandeul, "Mémoires pour servir à l'histoire de la vie et des ouvrages de Diderot," in *Oeuvres complètes de Diderot*, ed. J. Assézat and Maurice Tourneux, 20 vols. (Paris: Garnier, 1875–77), I, xlv.

13 Letter of Diderot to Le Breton [November 12, 1764], quoted in Denis Diderot, *Correspondance*, ed. Georges Roth and Jean Varloot, 16 vols. (Paris: Editions de Minuit, 1955–70), IV, 302. On the causes, extent, and consequences of the censorship, see Douglas H. Gordon and Norman L. Torrey, *The Censoring of Diderot's Encyclopédie and the Re-established Text* (New York: Columbia University Press, 1947); Wilson, *Diderot*, esp. pp. 360–65, 434–35, 471–79, 488; Lough, "Two Unsolved Problems," in *The Encyclopédie in Eighteenth-Century England and Other Studies*, pp. 76–89; and Frank A. Kafker, "The Effect of Censorship on Diderot's Encyclopedia," *The Library Chronicle*, 30 (1964), 41–46.

14 Grimm too regarded Le Breton as miserly or worse. In the *Correspondance littéraire* of May 15, 1766, he told the following story. The Chevalier Louis de Jaucourt labored on the *Encyclopédie* without receiving any salary, while paying out of his own pocket the secretaries he needed to help him compile articles. Short of money, he decided to sell one of his Parisian homes. "What is amusing is that it is the printer Le Breton who bought this house with the money that the work of the Chevalier de Jaucourt put him in a position to earn. . . . I hardly know a breed of men more obviously dishonest than that of the booksellers of Paris." Frédéric-Melchior Grimm and others, *Correspondance littéraire, philosophique et critique*, ed. Maurice Tourneux, 16 vols. (Paris: Garnier, 1877–82), VII, 45. Grimm exaggerated somewhat. Jaucourt did receive a modest amount of money and books for his enormous contribution. But Grimm is right about the purchase of the house. It is confirmed by the discovery of the bill of sale dated March 11, 1761 for the amount of 18,000 livres. Attached to it is Jaucourt's complaint about Le Breton's notary who negotiated the contract: "He has gone minutely over this matter with the same attention to your interests as if you were negotiating for an object worth a million livres with a foreigner from Germany who is leaving Paris, offering land for sale, and asking for one hundred thousand livres at the closing." Lough, "Louis, Chevalier de Jaucourt . . . ," *The Encyclopédie in Eighteenth-Century England and Other Studies*, pp. 52–53.

15 Letter of Diderot to Sophie Volland [August 18, 1765], quoted in Diderot, *Correspondance*, V, 92–93. On Diderot's view of the Le Bretons see ibid., esp. I, 196; II, 120; III, 322–24, 337–38, 343; IV, 82–83, 105–6, 154, 192–93, 300–306; V, 16, 64–65, 91–92; IX, 28–35, 239–44; XI, 115.

16 Lepreux, *Livre d'or*, part 1, p. 300; Wilson, *Diderot*, pp. 502–4; and Frank A. Kafker, "The Risks of Contributing to Diderot's *Encyclopedia*," *Diderot Studies*, 16 (1973), 137n.

17 On the French-language editions, see John Lough, "The Different Editions" and "The Panckoucke-Cramer Edition" in *Essays on the Encyclopédie of Diderot and d'Alembert* (London: Oxford University Press, 1968), pp. 1–110; and Robert Darnton, "The *Encyclopédie* Wars of Prerevolutionary France," *American Historical Review*, 78 (1973), 1332–45.

18 On the publishers' profits, see Lough, "Luneau de Boisjermain *v.* the Publishers of the *Encyclopédie*," in *The Encyclopédie in Eighteenth-Century England*, esp. pp. 105–14, 142–53; Lough, "The Panckoucke-Cramer Edition," in *Essays on the Encyclopédie*, pp. 59–61; Bowen (see note 7), pp. 18–21; Proust, *Diderot*, pp. 57–58; and Wilson, *Diderot*, p. 578.

19 John Lough, *The Encyclopédie* (London: Longman, 1971), pp. 29–30; Wilson, *Diderot*, pp. 579, 604–7; and Louis Petit de Bachaumont and others, *Mémoires secrets*, 36 vols. (London: Adamson, 1784–89), VI, 150–51, 153–58 (June 19 and 23 and July 1, 1772).

20 Lepreux, *Livre d'or*, part 1, p. 300; and Antoine-Gaspard Boucher d'Argis, "Consuls des marchands," *Encyclopédie*, IV, 103–5.

21 Lepreux, *Livre d'or*, part 1, pp. 300–301, 304.

22 Grimm and others, IX, 208. Another source lists his annual income from the *Almanach* as close to 40,000 livres; and a third source says 65,000. Mercier, IV, 12; and G. d'Avenel, *Les Revenus d'un intellectuel de 1200 à 1913* (Paris: Flammarion, 1922), p. 313. All these figures are guesses. Le Breton's business records for the *Almanach* were not open for public inspection.

23 Bachaumont and others, X, 4–5 (January 5, 1777).

24 Ibid., VII, 121, 123 (February 1 and 7, 1774); X, 3–4, 6 (January 5 and 10, 1777); Grand-Carteret, p. 28; and A.-L.-T.-M. de Granges de Surgères, *Répertoire historique et biographique de la "Gazette de France"* . . . (Paris: Leclerc, 1902–6), III, col. 302.

25 Lough, *The Encyclopédie*, p. 30; and Bachaumont and others, vols. IX–XII passim.

26 Robert Darnton, "Reading, Writing, and Publishing in Eighteenth-Century France: A Case Study in the Sociology of Literature," *Daedalus* (Winter, 1971), pp. 230, 237.

27 A detailed study of their lives and careers remains to be done. This could be based on the Bibliothèque Nationale's records of the Corporation of Booksellers and Printers and its Anisson Collection, the books the four men published, and their correspondence, including Briasson's fifty-nine letters to Formey in the Nachlass Formey of the Deutsche Staatsbibliothek in Berlin.

28 For Briasson, see Bibliothèque Nationale, MSS, Fonds Français 22107, fol. 242; for David, see Denis Diderot, *Le Neveu de Rameau*, ed. Jean Fabre (Geneva: Droz, 1950), p. 209 n.230; for Durand, see Bibliothèque Nationale, MSS, Fonds Français 22107, fol. 26; and for Le Breton, see Lepreux, *Livre d'or*, part 1, pp. 298–99.

29 Diderot, *Le Neveu de Rameau*, p. 12. One must point out, however, that in addition to publishing such safe works as a translation by Diderot of Temple Stanyan's *Grecian History* and Pierre Tarin's *Dictionnaire anatomique suivi d'une bibliothèque anatomique et physiologique*, Briasson also published the 1753 edition of d'Alembert's controversial *Mélanges de littérature, d'histoire et de philosophie* with a false place of publication (Berlin) and without the name of either the author or the publisher.

30 Bibliothèque Nationale, MSS, Fonds Français 22106, fol. 270. David published many of d'Alembert's scientific works.

31 Ibid., 22107, fol. 26.

32 Wilson, *Diderot*, pp. 55, 83, 96–97; Bibliothèque Nationale, MSS, Fonds Français 22107, fol. 26; and D. W. Smith, *Helvétius: A Study of Persecution* (Oxford: Clarendon Press, 1965), pp. 20–21, 26, 29, 36–37.

33 For the police report on Le Breton, see Bibliothèque Nationale, MSS, Fonds Français 22107, fol. 91. On him and the Calas case, see Athanase Coquerel, *Jean Calas et sa famille* (Paris: Cherbuliez, 1858), pp. 495–96; letter of Voltaire to Etienne-Noël Damilaville, October 10 [1762], quoted in F.-M. Arouet de Voltaire, *Correspondance,* ed. Theodore Besterman (107 vols.; Geneva: Institute et musée Voltaire, 1953–65), L, 81, 81n.; and letter of Diderot to Sophie Volland [September 16, 1762], quoted in Diderot, *Correspondance,* IV, 153–54. Diderot said that Madame Le Breton had intended to make a profit from the sale of publications calling for the rehabilitation of Calas, but he chided and dissuaded her.

34 One notes from the will he made out a few weeks before his death that his household staff in Paris included a cook, a coachman, a porter, a housemaid, and other servants, and that he had working for him at his country estate at Massy near Paris a gardener and several farmers. Préfec-

ture de Paris. Archives de Paris, MSS, DC⁶ 258, fols. 98–100, insinuation du testament d'André-François Le Breton, le 12 novembre 1779. See also ibid., DC⁶ 263, fols. 13 ff., insinuation du testament de Marguerite Vaux [his widow], le 17 décembre 1785; Archives Nationales, Minutier central, MSS, XXVII, 405, testament Le Breton, le 30 août 1779; XXVII, 406, codicille Le Breton, le 5 octobre 1779; ibid., inventaire Le Breton, le 11 octobre 1779; C 852, testament Mme Le Breton, le 10 août 1782.

Small Profits Do Great Things:
James Lackington and
Eighteenth-Century Bookselling

RICHARD G. LANDON

The annals of the history of the book trade are replete with many a remarkable character, and of those few who have left substantial accounts of themselves and their occupation none is more curious than the cobbler-turned-tycoon James Lackington. He has earned his minor niche in the pantheon of English letters and is chiefly remembered today as the author of two eccentric volumes of autobiographical reminiscence; the *Memoirs of the First Forty-Five Years of the Life of James Lackington* (first published in 1791) and *The Confessions of J. Lackington* (1804). The second work consists of an attempt to withdraw much of what he had stoutly maintained in the first, and there is some evidence that, late in life, Lackington attempted to suppress both books.

Lackington's life and career are of significant interest to the historian and analyst of the book trade because he was the first cheap, ready-money bookseller in Great Britain. He achieved this distinction in three principal ways: by working on a small profit margin and huge turnover; by handling remaindered books as real discount items; and by refusing the extension of credit to anyone. His financial ruin was forecast unanimously by his peers but his policies were ultimately vindicated and his fortune made. His tendency to openly display the obvious manifestations of new-found wealth was much ridiculed but is perhaps an understandable eccentricity in a man who had overcome severe disadvantages in his climb through the social and economic strata of his time.

Information regarding the early life of Lackington and his career as a bookseller is derived principally from his *Memoirs*, which he published himself.[1] It first appeared in 1791 and the reputation Lackington had gained for eccentricity, heightened by certain paranoid tendencies, was confirmed by the triple dedication. Firstly "to the public," where the author takes the opportunity of expressing "the respect and veneration I entertain for you, resulting from the very extensive and ample encouragement with which you have crowned my indefatigable exertions to obtain your patronage, by largely contributing to the diffusion of science and rational entertainment, on such moderate terms as were heretofor unknown." The second dedication is "to respectable booksellers," who are praised for candor and liberality, and the third is "to sordid booksellers," who are severely castigated "whether they resplendent dwell in stately mansions, or in wretched huts of dark and groveling obscurity" (*Memoirs*, p. [iii]).

In 1792 a "new edition," considerably revised and enlarged to bring the saga of Lackington's business triumphs up to date, was published, and yet another "new edition," again enlarged, appeared in 1794. Editions after this date seem to be straight reprints, as the final annual profit figure reported by Lackington is for 1793 (*Memoirs*, p. 261). Seventh, eighth and ninth editions were all published in 1794, the year in which the business reached its peak of success, and the tenth edition of 1795, despite the title-page claim that it too is "corrected and much enlarged," is a page-for-page reprint of the ninth edition. Another "new edition" was published in 1803, and the thirteenth edition in 1813. These are all the recorded editions within Lackington's lifetime, apart from a New York edition of 1796. There is no sign of fourth, fifth or sixth editions, and perhaps they were merely skipped in accordance with one of the time-honored promotional devices of eighteenth-century publishing. All editions after the first contain a "preface to the second and subsequent editions." where Lackington says that when he "put the first edition to the press, I really intended to print but a small number . . . and of course had not any intention of printing other editions. But the rapid sale of the work . . . encouraged me to read the whole over with more attention. . . ." (*Memoirs*, pp. xvii–xviii). He then justifies his decision to revise the whole work, instead of separately publishing an appendix (mainly on the grounds of the revised editions costing a mere sixpence more than the first) and speaks of the addition of an engraving of himself as a frontispiece.

The *Memoirs* appear to have enjoyed considerable contemporary popularity although all editions of the book are scarce today. Lackington typically provides the information (on the half-titles of the ninth and tenth editions) that both a large octavo edition (at 5s 6d in boards) and a smaller duodecimo edition (at 2s 6d in boards) were required to fulfill the demand, but unfortunately does not divulge any precise sales figures.

The *Confessions*, a much duller work, was not nearly so popular as the *Memoirs*.[2] The first edition of 1804 was followed by a "second edition" during the same year which is a straight reprint of the first and appears to be from the same setting of type. New York editions appeared in 1806 and 1808, and the book has never been reprinted since. In the preface Lackington mentions the 1803 edition of the *Memoirs*, regretting that his old partners had reprinted it and assuring his readers that he had no connection with the firm any longer.

Both works contain only Lackington's own testimony, and as he spends a considerable amount of the space justifying his actions both as a bookseller and as an on-again-off-again Methodist they must be viewed with a certain degree of scepticism.

James Lackington was born, the first of four children, in Wellington, Somerset, in 1746. His circumstances were humble indeed: his father an itinerant, drunken shoemaker and his mother forced to take in spinning to support the family. He seems to have received a couple of years of rudimentary instruction at a village "dame-school," but did not learn to read until he was fifteen and could not write before the age of twenty-three. The first steps in his career as a bookseller were taken at an early age, when he hawked almanacs in the streets as an adjunct to the apple pies which were his stock-in-trade. At the age of fourteen he was apprenticed to an Anabaptist shoemaker in Taunton and eventually became a journeyman in that trade. During this time he was converted to Methodism by one of Mr. Wesley's preachers and commenced the spiritual wrestling with his conscience which resulted in his being reconverted several times during his life.

After completing his apprenticeship, and experiencing his first loss of faith due to the general debauchery associated with the 1767–68 elections, Lackington moved to Bristol as a shoemaker. He and a friend had acquired some taste for general reading but experienced the difficulty of literally having no idea of what books to ask for in bookshops. His dismay and the impact it made upon him are expressed in the *Memoirs*: "As we could not tell what to enquire for, we were ashamed to go into the booksellers shops; and I assure you, my friend, that there are thousands now in England in the very same situation: many, very many have come to my shop, who have discovered an enquiring mind, but were totally at a loss what to ask for, and who had no friend to direct them" (*Memoirs*, p. 89). The two friends did purchase Hobbes' translation of Homer and Walker's poetical paraphrase of Epictetus. Hobbes proved a great disappointment, but Epictetus charmed Lackington to the extent that he attempted to adopt the principles of the Stoics, a difficult task even for a lapsed Methodist.

In 1770 Lackington married and three years later went up to London to try his fortune, with the traditional half-crown in his pocket. One day in June 1774, while working at his last, he was told of a vacant shop in Fetherstone Street, where he decided to set up as a master with a combination shoe and bookshop. His initial stock consisted of Fletcher's *Checks to Antinomianism*, Watts' *Improvement of the Mind*, Young's *Night Thoughts*, Wake's translation of the *Apostolical Epistles*, Fleetwood's *Life of Christ*, Wesley's *Journals* and a few other works of a religious cast. As Lackington had rejoined the Methodist fold he was able to borrow five pounds from one of Wesley's special funds, thus increasing his stock to a value of twenty-five pounds and necessitating a move to Chiswell Street.

At this time he bade farewell forever to shoemaking and re-married, his first wife having died of a fever. The new wife was an avid reader of novels and introduced Lackington to *The Life of John Buncle*, the perusal of which confirmed his decision to quit the Wesleyan sect. The bookshop now began to flourish, and Lackington introduced the first of the innovations that attracted the attention and, initially, the derision of his peers: his system of bookkeeping. Strict accounts of all transactions were kept, and each Saturday night the balance sheet was posted for public inspection and, inevitably, comment. The Lackingtons made it a general rule never to spend more than two-thirds of the profits on living expenses.

In 1778 John Dennis, a silent partner with two hundred pounds to invest, was acquired, and the following year a catalogue of twelve thousand volumes was published. Lackington's business was now expanding quickly, but he decided that the surest way to expand it even faster was to lower his prices. In 1780 he hit upon the simple but revolutionary expedient of selling only for cash, refusing credit even to the nobility and his closest friends. His posted sign proclaimed, "the lowest price is marked in every book, and no abatement on any article." The trade reacted with amused condescension, while the Methodists were, according to Lacking-ton, wont to exclaim, "Oh Brother Lackington! I am very sorry to find that you who began in the spirit are now like to end in the flesh. Pray Brother, do remember Lot's wife" (*Memoirs*, p. 160). Dennis withdrew from the partnership, the two hundred pounds was quickly repaid and the business flourished.

In 1784 a catalogue containing thirty thousand volumes ap-peared, and this reflected Lackington's activity at the large trade sales held by the most prominent members of the publishing and bookselling fraternity for the purpose of disposing of both new titles and accumulated remainders of those books which did not sell quickly. Lackington was shocked to discover, when first invited to attend the sales, that custom dictated that the purchaser of a remaindered title would destroy half or even three-quarters of the stock and sell the remaining volumes at their full published price. Undercutting of prices was controlled by the threat of exclusion from the sales. Lackington, however, "resolved not to destroy any books which were worth saving, but to sell them off at half or a quarter of the publication prices" (*Memoirs*, p. 217). Because there were many alternative methods of supplying him with remainders and because he bought so many books from many different sources, the pressure of the trade was ineffective and the business continued to expand. He was now able to purchase very large lots of books and claimed to have had ten thousand copies of Watts' *Hymns* on hand at one time. In a single afternoon he is reputed to have laid out as much as twelve thousand pounds on books. All the books were priced as cheaply as possible, usually at about half the price asked by other booksellers, and sold in vast numbers. Lackington's formula for success was expressed by him in bookman's parlance as "small profits, bound by industry and clasped by economy." When he was able to afford a carriage he had lettered on its door "small profits do great things."

In 1793 Lackington sold a quarter share of his business to Robert Allen, who had come into the firm some years before as an apprentice. Lackington, Allen and Company then moved to specially designed quarters in Finsbury Square and opened the Temple of the Muses, which ranked with St. Paul's Cathedral and the Tower of London as one of the great sights of London. Charles Knight, who was taken as a child 1801 to the great domed building, had lyrical recollections of the experience: "We enter the vast area, whose dimensions are to be measured by the assertion that a coach and six might be driven around it. In the centre is an enormous circular counter, within which stand the dispensers of knowledge, ready to wait upon the country clergyman in his wig and shovel-hat; upon the fine ladies in feathers and trains; or upon the booksellers collector, with his dirty bag. . . . We ascend a broad staircase, which leads to "The Lounging Rooms," and to the first of a series of circular galleries, lighted from the lantern of the dome, which also lights the ground floor. Hundreds, even thousands, of volumes are displayed on the shelves running round the walls. As we mount higher and higher, we find commoner books in shabbier bindings; but there is still the same order preserved, each book being numbered according to a printed catalogue. This is larger than that of any other bookseller's, and it comes out yearly."[3]

Lackington was now at the height of his bookselling career, with a stock of between five hundred thousand and one million volumes. He issued trade tokens, on one side of which was a three-quarter bust of himself. The reverse contained a figure of Fame blowing a trumpet and the inscription "halfpenny of Lackington Allen & Co. cheapest booksellers in the world; payable at the Temple of the Muses." It is calculated that over seven hundred thousand of these tokens were issued. His success, however, did not guarantee his popularity; an engraving, published by J. Herbert in 1795, shows Lackington boarding his coach with the Temple of the Muses in the background. He is standing on the Bible, Tillotson's *Works*, and the Book of Common Prayer, and from his pocket protrudes a paper labelled "puffs and lies for my book." A group of imbecilic looking passers-by surround the carriage, while on the ground lies a copy of the *Memoirs* with a dog defecating on it. This was the view of such as "Peregrine Pindar," whose *Ode to the Hero of Finsbury Square* was published in the same year. It commences:

> Oh! thou, whose Mind, unfetter'd, undisguis'd,
> Soars like the lark into—the empty air;
> Whose arch Exploits, by Subtlety devis'd,
> Have stamp'd Renown on Finsbury's new Square,—
> Great "HERO" list! whilst the sly Muse repeats
> Thy Nuptial Ode,—thy Prowess great, IN SHEETS:

The last reference is presumably to Lackington's third marriage for which he is said to have advertised for a wife with twenty thousand pounds.

In 1798 the whole of James' part in the business was made over to George Lackington, his cousin, and he retired to the country. He was also once again converted to Methodism and in 1804 published the *Confessions* to make amends for having "publicly ridiculed a very large and respectable body of Christians" (*Confessions*, p. [v]). He also appended to it *Two Letters on the Bad Consequences of Having Daughters Educated at Boarding Schools*, a curious preoccupation for one who had no children. Subsequently he became a Methodist preacher and erected three Wesleyan chapels at Alveston, Taunton and Budleigh Salterton. He died on November 22, 1815, and was buried at Budleigh Salterton.[4]

The Lackington book catalogues provide a rough index to the firm's success. The first of 1784 listed for sale some 30,000 volumes. By 1790 the two-volume catalogue contained 70,000 volumes and continued to increase until 200,000 volumes were reached in the year 1796–97. These figures are, however, indicative of total volumes for sale, so that in the 1796–97 catalogue there are actually 23,158 entries. The difference is accounted for by multi-volume sets, many copies of some titles and odd lots labelled "miscellaneous English books 1/ per dozen." (It is amusing, and heart-rending for the collector of today, to note the Second Folio of Shakespeare priced at three guineas.) By 1801, after Lackington had retired from the firm, a 516-page catalogue advertised 800,000 volumes in 21,868 entries; perhaps some of the unsold copies of the numerous editions of Lackington's *Memoirs* made up some of the bulk.

Lackington's own statement concerning the efficacy of selling books by catalogue is contained in the *Memoirs*: "I publish two catalogues for the public every year, and of each of those public catalogues I print above three thousand copies, most of those copies are lent about from one to another, so that supposing only four persons see each copy, twenty four thousand persons look over my catalogues annually; no other mode of advertising bears the least proportion to it" (*Memoirs*, p. 269).

Lackington did not have to create the demand for his cheap books. An expanding population and an improved educational system had done that for him and he was able to prove that public demand for books which were within the economic reach of the working classes was insatiable. His career coincided with a time of general social and political upheaval and in particular with some popular movements with a direct bearing on the book trade. For instance, his comment on the comparatively recent advent of the circulating library is perceptive and astute: "I have been informed, that when circulating libraries were first opened, the booksellers were much alarmed, and their rapid increase added to their fears, and led them to think that the sale of books would be much diminished by such libraries. But experience has proved that the sale of books, so far from being diminished by them, has been greatly promoted, as from those repositories many thousand families have been cheaply supplied with books, by which the taste for reading has become much more general, and thousands of books are purchased every year by such as have first borrowed them at those libraries, and after reading them, approving of them, have become purchasers" (*Memoirs*, pp. 247–48).

The late eighteenth century was an era of profound change in the book trade. The functions of publishing and bookselling became more clearly delineated as the large publishing houses became more independently powerful. Publication by syndicates, as in the case of Johnson's *Dictionary*, where the capital investment was spread out between several partners, was less common, and after 1800 the central figure in the whole trade was the specialist publisher who, at his own risk, organized the physical production, the advertising and the wholesaling of an edition of a book. Lackington, in fact, did very little original publishing although he did issue reprints over his name. George Lackington, however, expanded this aspect of the business considerably to the point where he paid five hundred pounds for the manuscript of Richard Cumberland's autobiography.

Several publishers had responded to the demand for cheap editions of popular works from the past. In 1774 Alexander Donaldson won his famous case in the House of Lords against the concept of perpetual copyright and Boswell was able to remark that "as Alexander the Great sat down and wept that he had no more worlds to conquer, he might now, after his victory on Literary Property, sit down and weep that he had no more booksellers to conquer."[5] John Bell, the "very Puck of booksellers," Cooke, and Harrison issued their series of cheap reprints in prodigious numbers and sold them successfully to the expanding literate public. At the same time the prices of new books from the established houses rose sharply, due partly to the increased cost of the popular large quarto format and to the large sums paid to authors for rights.

For authors the spirit of the trade was liberal indeed. Private patronage had been dealt its death blow by Johnson, and authors were able to survive, and, in many cases, flourish on the proceeds of their pens alone. It is remarkable that nearly all the well-known writers of the time mention their publishers in enthusiastic and complimentary terms. There were very few who would seriously repeat Wolcot's saying that "booksellers drank their wine in the manner of the heroes in the hall of Odin, out of authors' skulls." Wolcot himself managed to persuade his publisher Walker to grant him two hundred and fifty pounds a year for life in exchange for the copyright to his verse satires. He is said to have managed this by appearing to be in the terminal stages of consumption, but upon the signing of the agreement his cough miraculously disappeared and he lived prosperously for many years after. Lackington, speaking as a relatively impartial but expert observer, says that "were all things considered, publishers (at least many of them) would be allowed to possess more liberality than any other set of tradesmen." He then cites a few examples: Dr. Robertson receiving four thousand five hundred pounds for *Charles V*, Hawkesworth receiving six thousand pounds for his compilations of voyages, etc. He also reports the case of an author who agreed to pay the expenses of publication of a work which the publisher had refused to buy on his own account. Upon being asked how many copies he wanted printed, the author first replied, "one for each family in Great Britain." He then lowered his requirements to sixty thousand copies and finally settled for twelve hundred and fifty. Under one hundred were actually sold (*Memoirs*, pp. 22–23).

The old monopolist publisher/booksellers (the Cadells and the Dillys) left the sale of cheap books to the new wave of men who had defeated their claims to perpetuity of rights and concentrated on the production of new expensive publications. They still resisted strongly, however, any attempts to undermine their control of the major part of the trade, in particular the prices of new books and remainders. Near the end of the century open war broke out between the "Associated Booksellers," to which Lackington belonged, and the monopolists. Lackington was able to cut his profit on new books to less than half the normal trade price and rely on volume of turnover to make up the difference. His volume of trade in fact made up much more than the difference and established his fortune. In 1791 Lackington reported profits of four thousand pounds, in 1792 five thousand and the same for 1793 (*Memoirs*, p. 261). To the charge that he had materially injured other booksellers by selling books so cheaply he replied, "I now sell more than one hundred thousand books annually; many who purchase part of these, do so solely on account of their cheapness; many thousands of these books would have been destroyed, as I have before remarked, but for my selling them on those very moderate terms; now when thousands of these articles are sold, they become known by being handed about in various circles of acquaintances, many of whom wishing to be possessed of the same books without enquiring the price of their friends, step into the first booksellers shop, and give their orders for articles, which they never would have heard of, had not I, by selling them cheap, been the original cause of their being dispersed abroad" (*Memoirs*, pp. 268–69). Whether due to the causes described by Lackington or not there certainly was a great upsurge of book buying during this period.

One great difficulty encountered by the monopolists who opposed Lackington was the problem of deciding what a remainder was. There was no set time period at the end of which the left over copies of a book would be considered to be unsaleable in the normal way. When Lackington was offered two thousand copies of a work at a greatly reduced price it became a remainder, at least in his eyes, and in our modern sense of the word. Lackington claimed that often his disposing of and circulating a large number of copies of a book would resuscitate its popularity and a reprint would thus be necessitated.

Lackington made two tours of England and Scotland, during which he enquired after the state of the new and antiquarian book trade in all the principal towns through which he passed. He was surprised and disappointed to find that, with the exceptions of York and Leeds, there were virtually none of the most esteemed editions of popular authors offered for sale in the provinces. His first tour was made in 1787; in 1790 he repeated the journey, confirmed his previous observations and asserted that "London, as in all other articles of commerce, is likewise the grand emporium of Great Britain for books" (*Memoirs*, p. 276).

In a general sense Lackington's free trade principles in the book business were not upheld by posterity. The "net-book agreement" ratified the view that "books are different" and thus legally subject to price fixing. His notion of the handling of remainders as discount items was, however, generally adopted, although it is still sometimes difficult to determine exactly what a remainder is. His career is an example of the successful application of a principle, formulated by himself to satisfy his own ambitions and pursued with all the energies of his own peculiar talents. His epitaph, composed by himself, in part accurately assesses his career:

> Much pride he had, 'twas love of fame,
> And slighted gold, to get a name;
> But fame herself prov'd greatest gain,
> For riches follow'd in her train.
> Much had he read, and much had he thought,
> And yet, you see, he's come to naught;
> Or out of print, as he would say,
> To be revis'd some future day;
> Free from errata, with addition
> A new, and a complete edition.
>
> (*Memoirs,* p. 318)

NOTES

1 James Lackington, *Memoirs of the First Forty-five Years of the Life of James Lackington . . . ,* 9th ed. corr. and much enlarged (London: printed for the Author, 1794). All references to the *Memoirs* in the text are to the ninth edition, the specific page citations of which are given following each quotation. For a discussion of the significance of the various editions, see pp. 2–3.

2 James Lackington, *The Confessions of J. Lackington . . .* (London: Richard Edwards, 1804). All references to the *Confessions* in the text are to the first edition, the specific page citations of which are given following each quotation. The second edition of 1804 is a straight reprint of the first.

3 Charles Knight, *Shadows of the Old Booksellers* (New York: R. R. Bowker, 1927), pp. 251–52.

4 Although it is commonly assumed that Lackington was buried at Budleigh Salterton, and while it is certainly true that he spent his last years there, there is at the present time no trace of his grave.

5 James Boswell, *Boswell for the Defence: 1769–1774,* ed. William K. Wimsatt, Jr., and Frederick A. Pottle (London: William Heinemann, 1960), pp. 240–41.

The "World" between
Seigneur and Peasant

ROBERT FORSTER

It must have been a bright, cheerful summer day at the end of June, 1782, in this particular village of Lorraine.

> All of Faulquemont was full of joy and appreciation from the moment of arrival to the moment of departure of Madame La Comtesse de Choiseul. Cavalry with flags and drums, infantry in full uniform, music from the regimental band of Schomberg, illuminations, bonfires, fireworks, *arcs de triomphe*—everything possible to show Madame la Comtesse how happy the village was to receive her. . . .[1]

This was not the Lorraine of metallurgy, that lugubrious ambiance evoked by forges, soot, and pine trees, but one that at least approached the idealized pastoral Lorraine so dear to Maurice Barrès. In June, 1782, the village (or *ville*) of Faulquemont (650 inhabitants) was the center of a cluster of fourteen villages that made up the Marquisat of Faulquemont. It had belonged to a branch of the family Choiseul, one of the great families of France, since 1751. The Countess Choiseul-Beaupré, dowager of fifty, was visiting her estate for the first time in thirty years. Her local steward and land agent, Pierre Du Seuil, was full of enthusiasm for this *visite* which he had been urging for some time. His letter to the chief manager (*intendant*) of the countess's affairs in Paris (rue St. Augustin) went on to describe the virtuous generosity of this "respectable" and "Christian" lady during her all too brief sojourn at Faulquemont:

> Madame has reestablished the full pension of M. Robinet (the *procureur fiscal*), she has increased the wages of the forest guards, she has added a new guard at Dalem, she has established a pension for a Vatelotte Sister as school mistress of the new girls' school, she has given 150 livres to Dr. La Baume to care for the sick of Faulquemont and of five other neighboring villages (1600 inhabitants) belonging to her. *Voilà des charités* forever memorable, not to speak of the money distributed, the 65 quarters of grain in extra alms. In all truth, she has come to Faulquemont to rain blessings from the sky.[2]

A more touching picture of seigneurial paternalism (or rather maternalism) would be difficult to find. But before we look more closely at the administration and activities taking place in the countess's fourteen villages, among her 4,000 "vassals," who was there to greet the countess as she descended from her carriage and made her way on foot to the *hôtel de ville* of Faulquemont?

No doubt by their waistcoats and their sashes, the "countess's men" stood apart from the rough blouses and wooden shoes of the crowd, an assortment of artisans, *laboureurs*, sharecroppers, day-laborers, a sprinkling of forest guards, cabaret owners, and petty hucksters. Who made up this little "notability" officiating at the town hall steps for the presentation of the wreath and garland of flowers, reciting "a little prose and a little verse"? Who dined with the countess at the curate's house?

The château was unfortunately not appropriate for a reception. Over the years it had become an enormous granary, most of the parquet floors heaped with grain reaching up to the flamboyant *boiseries* like golden termites. Only three or four rooms had been reserved for lodging the family of the *procureur fiscal* and his rather numerous progeny as well as the eighty-year-old *prévôt*, the seigneurial judge, his wife, and two thirty-year-old daughters. Moreover, the curé had planted a kitchen garden very close to the main *grille*—with permission of course—but the effect was something less than regal. The curé's residence it had to be, then, for the reception. Who was there to receive Madame la Comtesse?

There were five "notables" present, three of them with their wives. First, there was Monsieur Nicolas Marizien, chief advisor of the countess in Lorraine, a lawyer, *Conseiller du Roi*, and former Treasurer of Her Royal Highness, the Princess of Lorraine. He had joined the countess at Nancy, where he no doubt handled the estate affairs of other absentee landlords like the Choiseul. From his letters, we know him to have been a diplomat and conciliator; disliked by certain people who found him presumptuous, he was considered generous and "flexible" by other members of the seigneurial staff. He had learned how to promote his family by using his connections in high places. His son was an advocate trained in Paris, attached to the Parlement of Metz and recently married to Mlle. Gallois de Luneville, "riche de 200,000 livres," so it was said. His brother-in-law was the curé of Faulquemont, a much less exalted position no doubt, but a helpful one to Marizien in his services to the Marquisat.

The second was the curé Lombert, of whom we know less except that he was among those curés considered by the agents of the countess as good examples to the villagers, men who preached the regular life, like curé Steiner at Dalem to the north, or the vicar Bettinger at Redlach. He had been nominated by the countess, no doubt with help from his brother-in-law, and he accepted his "share" of the *dîme*. He was, in any event, not like those "crude and stubborn" curés referred to by the steward who were "independent-minded" because they held benefices from some religious order.[3]

Third, Monsieur le Prévôt (almost never called Gissier, his surname), was the seigneurial judge for the fourteen villages. In 1782 he was near eighty, and according to his colleagues, very authoritarian, considering himself the "sovereign" of Faulquemont in the countess's absence. His violence must have been something to behold. One of his subordinates heard him in the other wing of the château when he beat up his daughters to the point where they were in bed for days. But the countess said that his temper should be balanced against his long service on the estate. He had been seigneurial judge for over forty-five years; he was there before the countess bought the Marquisat as part of her dowry in 1751. He was paid one hundred fifty livres per year, plus lodging in the château, which he obviously valued almost as much as his right to bear arms and shoot game.

Fourth was Olivier Robinet, the *Procureur fiscal*, seigneurial attorney, second "officer" to the *prévôt*. This was the problem. His letters reveal a man of complete literacy and very sensitive to his subordinate place beneath the *prévôt* as well as the new steward. It irked him that he had little latitude to procure some of the material amenities (housing, heating, hunting) or, more important, to exercise some local power. He appealed to the countess directly on one occasion about his subordinate role and told her that his "Christian humility" alone sustained him. He had been in his post for seventeen years and was paid fifty livres per year.

Finally, there was Pierre Du Seuil, the new steward or *régisseur* (new in 1775). He had been sent from Paris and was a professional estate manager. Like many *grands seigneurs* in Paris, the Choiseuls were well aware of the alternative to leasing land to *fermiers généraux*. In this connection, the word *régie* refers to direct administration of a large private estate by a salaried steward (Du Seuil received 1,200 livres *per annum*) who was supposed to combine ingenuity with economy, reduce the middle-man costs while increasing the income of the land.

Du Seuil seemed able to combine these rather incongruous virtues. An active and busy man, "full of projects," said Marizien not altogether approvingly, "hard and inflexible" when it came to holding down expenses, Du Seuil, as the "newcomer" in the local administration, felt a special need to prove himself and his method of administration. He was well aware of the imperatives expressed by the countess to Marizien in 1775. "Du Seuil is highly recommended, but the proof will be in the increase in the revenues of my land."[4]

Here then were the "countess's men," not an elaborate administration, to be sure, but part of the "world" between seigneur and peasant. We might call them the "Insiders" to distinguish them from other "social types" who do not fit neatly into either of the ominibus categories of "lord" and "peasant." In depicting the "Outsiders" (outside of the seigneurial-estate apparatus), we must necessarily view them through the special perspective of those mentioned above (Du Seuil, Marizien, or Robinet) who have left us the written record. In the future I hope to find other sources of a more neutral, less subjective sort, though such "neutral records"—the tax roll, the parish register, the notarized contract, or the subdelegate's report must forego the "flesh-and-blood" immediacy which is for some the very core of social history.

A few years back, before 1775, Sieur Guyon, the most prominent *gros fermier* in the region, would have dined with the countess. In many ways, he resembled Du Seuil, the new steward who had replaced him as the principal intermediary between the countess and the landed society of Faulquemont. Marizien had described Guyon twenty-five years before (in 1757) as "active, hardworking, enemy of all litigation (*procès*), yet zealous in his will to sustain the rights of the *seigneurie*".[5] He was ably seconded, it should be added, by his wife, who had a strong sense of economy and shared with him the management of the harvests.

Guyon had certainly not wasted the many years he had spent as the countess's "principal tenant" for the entire Marquisat. In addition to personal ties he had forged—not all of them sentimental, to be sure—he had gained control of the principal farm capital—the livestock. Du Seuil was not too pleased with this situation when he assumed management of the Marquisat in 1775. At that time he wrote to the countess:

> I have arrived six months too late for the interests of Madame la Comtesse [March 29, 1775]. . . . the time is too short to obtain all

the livestock and labor necessary for this land. Forty horses and thirty cows (at least) and a lot of pigs are not found quickly. . . . The leasehold at Galenhols owes Sr. Guyon more than 1,500 livres; all the livestock and the next harvest will not be enough to pay this debt. To replace this tenant is not practical. All the good tenants are taken and to buy the livestock from Guyon will mean that he will take a large profit from our difficulties (*embarras*).[6]

Even after he had left the employ of the countess, Guyon was a rural capitalist who knew his business. Du Seuil had many occasions to go to Guyon, not only for capital (when there was none to be had even at Metz), but also for commercial expertise. Guyon often told Du Seuil when to sell his grain. Wait until the "little *laboureurs*" have sold theirs, he advised in July, 1778, then the price will rise. Or on another occasion he suggested that neither he nor De Seuil sell the harvest at all, but wait for the following season. After all, the château and every available loft could be filled with the precious grain. By July of the second year, Du Seuil reported that there was no bed space left for even one extra person in the château. "These granaries are absolutely necessary, but even so there are not enough to hold two years' harvest." No wonder Du Seuil was worried about the proper storage of his grain and requested the chief manager at Paris to send him a book entitled: "The Harvest of Grain and How to Prevent Spoilage at Harvest Time."[7]

Du Seuil came to feel some begrudging admiration for his predecessor, Guyon, when he was faced with the task of managing the subtenants, the *sous-fermiers* and sharecroppers, especially when it came to the division of produce rents. This was a complicated matter at Faulquemont, for not only were there a number of different sharecroppers, but they worked 120 separate pieces of arable land between them. Du Seuil was frustrated: "I cannot be in three places at the same time when the harvest must be divided at half-fruits," he complained. And furthermore, he said,

. . . these three tenants trick me despite all my vigilance. Under the lease terms they must work 15 *journaux* of land in wheat and 15 in oats. I furnish all the seed because this land is exclusively for my profit. The rest of the land is leased at half-fruit and half-seed. But if I am not attentive, they do not plow the 15 *journaux* sufficiently, nor do they provide fertilizer, and they keep the seed for themselves, which narrows my profit to almost nothing.[8]

And again at harvest time when they were supposed to cart Du Seuil's share to his grange, "they take it to their own lofts 'by mistake' . . . . But I cannot be in town and in the fields at the same time. I must watch the loading of the carts and the transportation to the storage bins. Theft is common at Faulquemont." No wonder he took the precaution of hiding the money he sent to Paris in the sacks of grain. Du Seuil also complained of the "insolent" attitude of the sharecroppers. He suggested that if the countess did not want to pay for an added foreman (a *maître valet*), at least it might be possible to reduce the three leaseholds to two—fewer people to watch and less cheating. Du Seuil added that one of the sharecroppers was a "pillar" at the local cabaret and often unable to perform his work on the farm.[9]

Yet when it came to foreclosing on a bankrupt tenant, Du Seuil revealed a certain pang of conscience, though not enough to halt legal proceedings:

> I have been forced to seize the possessions of poor Dufer, lest his other creditors get to him first. He does not have much. I will get what I can, following your order in your letter of December 30 (1786?). He has five mangy horses and a few sticks of furniture. I hesitate to sell these effects because . . . it will reduce him to misery with his large family without a home or bread. Moreover, he has been a tenant of Madame la Comtesse for 21 years.[10]

There is no more mention of Dufer, the tenant, in the Du Seuil letters. But one letter written late in the same year suggests that he followed his directives from Paris. "Most of the tenants have been slow to pay their rents; I will pursue them with rigor, since you have such a need for money."[11]

That the countess preferred a firm hand in dealing with the tenants is indicated by her own reaction to one Demoiselle

Couturier, *fermière* at Dalem for twenty-seven years. This woman claimed that a rise in rent would create a special hardship for her since she was already paying all the royal taxes and, more important, since the community of Dalem refused to pay their seigneurial dues in kind or perform the *corvées* (free labor services at harvest time). The countess was unmoved: "Why should she [the tenant] alone benefit from the rise in grain prices? She may be competent and solvent, but she is not irreplacable."[12]

Marizien, at that time the land agent, tried to soften the countess's stand by reminding her of the tenant's many children and her "attachment to the service of Madame" for twenty-seven years. He suggested a rent of 7,800 livres instead of the 8,000 proposed by the countess in Paris.

But Madame was intractable. The leasehold of Dalem at the end of the nine-year term—a substantial one as the rent indicated—was put up for auction three months later (October, 1772). The bids of prospective tenants raised the rent by 2,662 livres. Damoiselle Couturier asked for Madame to be generous. The reply was curt: ". . . if she refuses to meet the highest bid, pass the lease to the new tenant." The rationale of the countess on this occasion is worth pondering. "Such a sacrifice [of rent] would be detrimental not only to her revenues; it also would place a blot [*imprimerait une tache*] on [all] her lands from which she wishes to increase the return."[13] In short, Dlle. Couturier must not provide a bad example to the other tenants on the estate.

The countess also possessed important woodlands in her other villages fifteen miles north of Faulquemont itself (Dalem, Volmerangue, and Hargarten). As their value increased, disputes with the villages over communal rights seemed more frequent, and the watchfulness of the forest guards became more important. Toward them, Du Seuil was even less sympathetic than toward the tenants and sub-tenants. The steward felt they were negligent, arbitrary, untrustworthy, and drunk most of the time. In winter they never left the fireside except to go hunting with their dogs. They took bribes from the villagers who wanted to enter the countess's forests in search of fuel and forage, and these bribes frequently took the form of bottles of wine.[14] Yet the forest guards were paid 120 livres a year and could wear the Choiseul livery. No doubt there is a special history of *mentalités* to be written about forest guards. What was this "world" of guns and axes, dogs and rabbits, cold nights in pine forests filled with poaching fellow villagers, knowing that to perform one's function was to incur the hostility of the local inhabitants? As Robinet, one of the judicial officers, once put it: "I was reluctant to believe the complaints about him, because I know that a forest guard who does his duty is generally hated."[15]

Studies in the judicial archives of France as a whole suggest an increase in the quantity of lawcases between village communities and seigneurs in the last third of the eighteenth century.[16] An ethnographic study of this kind can not contribute much to measuring the incidence of this kind of litigation. But *procès* the countess did have with "her vassals" and "her villages." They usually pertained either to communal or seigneurial claims to the wood or to other seigneurial rights newly enforced by the countess. This aspect of the "seigneurial reaction" need not detain us here.[17] What is more interesting for our present purpose is the reaction of the steward of an absentee *grand seigneur* to such legal action undertaken by villages supposedly under his control.

This brings us to still another category of "outsider" in this expanding "world" between seigneur and peasant. It is the rural lawyer or solicitor working for the village community. There seemed to be a large number of them in the villages of the Marquisat of Faulquemont. Perhaps they represented a certain surplus of graduates from the nearby law school at Pont-au-Mousson.[18]

No one seemed to like lawyers, but everyone needed them. Du Seuil, the steward, did not speak only for himself when he referred to one legal brief as "already costing 18 *louis*, very prettily written, and half of it repeated in order to make the parchment longer." Surely there were some reliable lawyers to be found who could work for the countess, but Marizien, the family's manager at Nancy, thought that these were a distinct minority.

> The *greffier* (clerk) of Faulquemont has just married his daughter to one Sieur Liebaut, advocate of the Sovereign Court [of Nancy]. He wants to resign and give his office to his new son-in-law. I think this is a good idea. This Liebaut is like Robinet, the *procureur fiscal*: good men, not like other advocates and attorneys who bring nothing but trouble to the poor and the ignorant.[19]

In November, 1778, seven "individuals" of Faulquemont protested payment of a seigneurial right claimed by the countess. It was called the *Bled de Bourgeois*, a produce rent paid by *laboureurs*, day laborers, and widows. The recalcitrants included the mayor, the syndic, and some *gens de justice*. Among the latter was one Sieur Cosserat. Cosserat *père* had been a *procureur* at Faulquemont for fifty years, and Marizien called him a "country practitioner very eager for litigation."[20] Now his son, a man of thirty-six, advocate from the law school of Pont-au-Mousson and syndic of Faulquemont, was launching a lawcase against the countess. Du Seuil:

> This man, dangerous in every way, obtained the office of syndic after having solicited the votes of the inhabitants [*habitants*, not *vassaux*] by promising to free them from this onerous charge. He asked each individual to sign a petition requesting permission from the [Royal] Intendant to plead in court for this purpose.[21]

Here was a man who knew how to use the law to reach outside of the Marquisat. No wonder the seigneurial estate agents called him a *fripon* (a rascal); apparently even his own father did!

Du Seuil took immediate action. He suggested that the countess approach the royal intendant at Metz via Marizien, her manager, "who has considerable influence (*crédit*) with the indendant." "Since this syndic [Cosserat] is not from the 'high class' of the inhabitants [under the Turgot reforms], M. l'Intendant could annul this election and, advised by M. Marizien, he might prohibit Cosserat from exercising the office of village solicitor (*procureur postulant*). This clever advocate has already cost Madame 250 livres."[22] In the battle for the intendant's ear, the countess surely had the "Big Battallions"—family name, excellent legal advice, a *Conseiller du Roi* like Marizien on the spot in Metz, and quite possibly the shared belief that "bon ordre" should keep trouble-makers like Cosserat within bounds. Three months later (February 25, 1779) Cosserat was no longer syndic.

But Cosserat *fils* was not easily put down. He knew his law, despite Marizien's assurances that Cosserat's case was not defensible at law and that "we have all the titles." Du Seuil could not shake him. "Today Cosserat refers to another precedent as a basis for refusal to pay this seigneurial due [*Bled de Bourgeois*]." Again, just before Christmas: "Our advocate continues to excite the inhabitants and frequently convenes the community assembly."[23]

Controversy over payment of seigneurial dues often focused on the drawing up of the rolls of *terriers*. Robinet, the seigneurial solicitor, obtained a judgment condemning the mayor to turn over the list of inhabitants of Faulquemont indicating those who had not yet paid. This time the whole community was up in arms because of this *misérable* Cosserat, and still another lawyer, named Aug.[24] In fact, Aug had replaced Cosserat as syndic and *greffier* of the village, and as Du Seuil put it, he already had six "cabalistes" as his clients. When a third lawyer appeared taking up the case of the villagers, Du Seuil lost his usual composure:

> Sieur Gerardy is an ex-Jesuit and advocate from Saint Avold [10 miles northeast]. This man of terrible memory is chicane itself with his *tours* and *detours*, his delays and subterfuges. He may have discarded the frock of the Society [of Jesus], but he has kept all of their pernicious *esprit*. I tell you, if we emerge intact from the hands of this man, no one will try to attack us again![25]

But the *procès* continued. If it wasn't the *Bled de Bourgeois* at

Faulquemont, it was communal rights to the wood or the right to vacant pasture. Other communities in the Marquisat assembled throughout the 1780s. They even petitioned the countess directly and complained about her agents, placing Du Seuil on the defensive vis-à-vis Madame.[26] During her visit in 1782, the countess herself had written: "The inhabitants have shown me a great deal of affection and they now repent of having undertaken this lawcase . . ."[27] But the countess was deluded. The lawcases continued. Other country lawyers kept appearing. In 1787 it was one Gouget who threatened that he would prolong the case so that his adversaries (the countess et al.) would not obtain permission from the intendant to take [one-third of] the fines [from communal property she claimed].[28] By this time, the lawyers were even making trips to Paris on behalf of the villagers.

Not that the country lawyers were idealists working for nothing. In fact, a formal meeting of the community of Faulquemont made up of fifty-eight notables (about ten percent of the population) was called in the spring of 1787 to pay for the various trips of the solicitors to Paris. The bill was over 3,000 livres in notes signed by Jean Aug (the syndic) to a merchant at Saarbruck.[29] Many a village assembly had to balance its legal costs against the financial relief attendant upon winning its case. So did the countess. But perhaps one should also make allowance for "face" and "dignity" on both sides.

That the countess was sensitive to "face" apart from her financial interest is indicated by her reply to the community of Val which was demanding rights of pasturage.

> My intention . . . is to pursue the most exact justice in the administration of my land. I have verified the claims and rights of pasture. I am right. . . . I have always been charitable toward the needy. [But] they will not find me less decided to sustain *mes droits* when they are incontestably established, and when they wish to contest unjustly my generosity.[30]

As for the dignity of the *habitants* in the villages, it is less clear to what it should be attached. But the very experience (increasing, it seems) of *procès*, petitions, assemblies, and even voting must have made many a villager think of himself less as a *vassal* (a personal dependent of the Choiseul family) and more as a *citizen* of a local community.

Rents, dues, rights, *procès*, petitions, seizures—such is the stuff of so much rural history, especially as revealed by estate papers. But occasionally another dimension peeps through. For example, how did the countess and others on her staff feel about education for the children in the Marquisat?

In the spring of 1779 the Countess considered the appointment of a school master for the children of the village of Redlach (113 inhabitants in 1756). How should the "country people" be educated? It was a question very much in debate at the end of the Old Regime.[31] The countess might easily find ready advice on the matter. The anonymous *mémoire* that guided her is worth quoting at length:

> It is essential of course to teach Religion to children in the countryside. But is it so necessary to teach them to read and write? There is good reason to doubt it, especially to the little boys, who once they have acquired some knowledge, leave the village and become ashamed of the *état* of their fathers! If they remain in the village these half-educated country people [*demi-savants campagnards*] often prefer chicane to hard work. On the other hand, one can not sufficiently encourage school mistresses for the education of little girls. There is no disadvantage in having them learn to read. When they become mothers, they can keep the accounts of the family or of their husband's trade, and they can teach Religion to their children. As for the boys, it is sufficient that they learn the Small Catechism of the Diocese to the extent that their feeble intellects [*faible conception*] permit. M. le Deservant [ambulatory priest] can teach them the principal mysteries, the Commandments of God and the Church, and especially their duties to their *état* [their station].[32]

The priest will teach them to avoid "superstitious practices," preserving the "simple faith" of these poor country people, and "God will do the rest." The *mémoire* concluded by suggesting that the countess find a school mistress who would have additional social value if she could also serve as a midwife, "so much needed in the countryside."

The reaction to this proposal by the local priest was somewhat "interested," but perhaps less narrow. The vicar of Redlach (Bettinger) objected to a school *mistress*. Not only would she be difficult to find; as a midwife she would attract every pregnant woman in the parish to the little village. Better to rely on the certified surgeon of the Marquisat, M. La Baume, who could handle the three or four "legitimate children" born each year at Redlach. (One wonders how the other births were handled.) Moreover, Bettinger said he could use a male teacher who could double as chanter and acolyte in the parish church.[33]

The vicar's views of education, however, seem less narrow than the *mémoire* cited above. Not only should the boys learn their catechism; they should learn to sign their names.

> Often we are obliged to draw up contracts and no one can sign them. Moreover, they will be able to learn more if they are called to a particular *état* or employ, and in the village community we always need some people for the local offices. The royal ordinances require it. Country children are sometimes very useful to the State, in the Army, where to be able to read and write, even a little, is an enormous advantage. . . .[34]

The vicar added in a later letter that, at the very least, a new school teacher could help with public administration, especially if he could read German as well as French. "The community needs a man who can interpret the royal ordinances which arrive almost every week, and he can draw up the tax rolls because no inhabitant can perform these tasks at present."[35] Here we have a clear indication of the impact of public administration (bureaucracy, if you will) on education. The State needed a certain number of literate people even at the village level. Could this education be confined to specific skills, or would the very act of "interpreting" royal ordinances lead beyond a literal translation?

Du Seuil, our steward, saw no ambiguity, no risks. The function of education at Faulquemont was simple:

> We must teach the children to do better than their fathers and
> inculcate in them at an early age the principles of gratitude
> toward their benefactors and their seigneurs, principles which are
> not easily lost when they are linked to the Religion in which they
> are born.[36]

Du Seuil regarded religion in the same way. Priest and school
teacher marched together in his hierarchical world.

> We have an excellent vicar at Redlach. He preaches a regular and
> edifying life and prevents the inhabitants of the village from
> stealing wood . . . from Madame la Comtesse, which they used to
> do habitually, despite the forest guards. Perhaps we should give
> him [the vicar] 100 livres more this year.[37]

Unfortunately, the local clergy did not always measure up to
Du Seuil's standards. In 1771 when Marizien ran the estate, he too
remarked on the "independence" of some of the village priests.
One had even refused to distribute the rice the countess had
imported for her needy villages. The curé said the charity was too
little! "He is a fool and an *extravagant*. But then he was not
nominated by Madame la Comtesse."[38]

Du Seuil did not have much patience or understanding of young
people or indeed for disorder or irregularity of any kind. If he
used the word *fripon* to apply to most country lawyers, he
employed the word *débauché* to summarize another category of
bothersome people.

> They say that the city youth is debauched. It is no less so at
> Faulquemont. They prowl at night. One can not go out without
> being assailed by a hail of stones. They cut down trees, tear down
> walls, break in doors, dig up potatoes, ... They smash the
> windows of our solicitor; he is not safe. The market place is the
> refuge and fortress of this *canaille* day and night.[39]

The line between popular frustration and youthful vandalism was
certainly too fine for a man of Du Seuil's mental equipment. Rock
throwing, in any case, was not new at Faulquemont, nor always
directed against "the authorities." In June, 1775, on their return
from the fair, twenty boys threw so many stones that two people

were almost killed.[40] Yet Du Seuil was not uninterested in unusual behavior. In the winter of 1783 he remarked in a postscript that he had read an article in the *Journal de Bouillon* on epilepsy. "Terrible effects," he commented.[41]

Fear of *émotions populaires* was of course widespread. Even in distant Paris, the Chargé d'Affaires, Féron, worried about popular *fêtes* in Faulquemont. He criticized Robinet for not limiting a popular festivity that summer of 1779. Robinet replied that he had no mounted police, and the *fête* was one "big comedy" anyway. But Robinet kept his gun by his side during the parade, a symbol of status no doubt.[42]

If recent studies of the French villages demonstrate an easy tolerance of the community toward violations of the sexual code, there was precious little of it at Faulquemont. De Seuil reported "a *fille* lost to debauchery" at Redlach, the poorest village in the jurisdiction. When she had her second child by a married man, Du Seuil and the seigneurial judge decided to call in the mounted police and lock her up in the *Maison de Force* at Nancy to be classified as a "beggar." "That makes 31 livres, 15 sous to get rid of that bad lot."[43] Marizien shared similar views toward *libertinage*. A few years before, he had discovered a child buried without the sacraments. He suspected that "the *fille* of Saint Avold," who was pregnant when last seen, had destroyed her child. At the very least, she was guilty of not declaring her pregnancy under an old law. "I suggest we handle this before the royal judges get to it."[44] The demographers can tell us a great deal about illegitimacy from the parish registers; but only more qualitative data like this can tell us how it was perceived and "handled" by contemporaries.

The madman, the *fou*, was not tolerated in the corner near the fire either. The following case confirms what Foucault has said about treatment of the insane in the late eighteenth century.[45]

> The son of our *maître-valet* at Bonhouse is mad. He is violent, has harmed both his parents, and could set fire to the farm. His parents are looking for a prison at Nancy, but it costs 400 livres pension. There is no question of these *domestiques* paying such a sum. Could Madame obtain an order to put him in Bicêtre [the asylum in Paris] which is free? I do not want to lose the father

who has been loyal for fifteen years and manages fourteen farm-
hands. The parents are both on their knees before Madame. We
can get him to Paris by pretending we are on a pilgrimage; he is
very religious.[46]

Theft seemed to be the most prevalent crime in this region,
especially theft of wood in the forest of the countess—what was
called "degrading" the wood. There was some difference among
the staff on how best to deter this kind of theft. Marizien cited a
proverb to the effect that the "peasant is effectively punished only
through his pocketbook,"[47] but Du Seuil thought otherwise. "If
they do not pay the fines, they can go to prison for one or two
months on bread and water. Then they will think twice before
degrading the wood. That is my view."[48] When Nicolas Koch, a
young boy from Dalem, struck one of the forest guards with an
ax, he was fined 129 livres, but his mother had nothing. The
countess commented: "These are lost expenses, but inevitable
because, by leaving crimes unpunished, one increases the number
of beggars. . . . Therefore we must have some examples of severity
to deter the undisciplined (mutins)."[49]

The countess had never been unresponsive to the needs of the
poor of her Marquisat; she gave away 750 livres annually and in
bad years doubled and tripled this sum. In 1777 she arranged for
the importation of rice from South Carolina, shipped by the
Rhine, Moselle, and Saar Rivers. It was a mammoth operation
for the time, and the countess was able to distribute about 6,000
pounds of rice to her needy villagers. The ration was two and a
half pounds per family of four for fifteen days.[50] But the countess had always distinguished between the "deserving" and "unde-
serving" poor. Her orders for distribution of charity were formal:
"Give preference to the poor without any resource, to the aged,
the sick, the incapacitated, and those with large families. Drunk-
ards and loafers must be excluded from any help whatsoever.
Write to the curés to this effect."[51]

From the very special perspective of a Du Seuil or a Marizien,
the society of Faulquemont evokes the pages of Balzac rather than

those of Michelet or Barrès. Words like *fripon, mutin, tracasserie, chicane*, and *débauché* are so many signposts throughout the letters and reports of these two men. For this was a threatened society, full of distrust, suspicion, and occasional violence, demanding constant vigilance on the part of the instruments of social control—school, church, police, and court. Rapacious *fermiers*, cheating sharecroppers, shiftless forest guards, recalcitrant "vassals," troublemaking country lawyers, rebellious village assemblies, undisciplined youth, and unworthy poor—a sorry image of theft and trickery, scheming and shirking, drunkenness and debauchery. Who indeed could be trusted? On all sides there was little place for an easy tolerance, open relations, and mutual confidence. It was a cramped world, crying for an ideal or cause that might transport its members outside of their self-enclosed psychological misery and give them a new sense of community. Villages like Faulquemont may not have "provoked" revolution, but certainly they welcomed it almost as an emotional release, however temporary, from their pervasive internal hostilities.[52]

It was also a world losing its older loyalties to aristocratic superiors. Countess de Choiseul was distant in affection as well as in space; her local representatives were afflictions rather than protectors. In their hands seigneurial charity was not only inadequate, but given begrudgingly; seigneurial "justice" meant seigneurial rights and the presence of more armed forest guards. The "Marquisat" of Faulquemont evoked rents, lawcases, and "vassalage," not borrowed honor, respect and pride of an extended Choiseul family. Tocqueville's principle of aristocracy was dying; the "ties" that bound upper and lower classes together were wearing thin. Here at Faulquemont their frayed remnants are exposed in the day-to-day human relations of this world between seigneur and peasant.

Surely there were times when everyone on the countryside must have felt a certain nostalgia for an idealized past, even though it is abundantly clear to us that the old values had served their day and were no longer viable. Who could be completely unmoved by that moment of goodwill—genuine if brief—when the Countess de Choiseul-Beaupré made her visit to Faulquemont in June of 1782.

NOTES

The principal source for this paper is a large collection of family papers found in the Archives Nationales, series T-153 (sequestered papers). This particular series of over one hundred cartons contains the papers of the family Choiseul-Gouffier, one of the wealthiest noble houses in France on the eve of the French Revolution. The cartons used here are only those concerned with the family lands in Lorraine. Most important among them is the correspondence between Madame de Choiseul Beaupré (née Lallemand de Betz) and her land agents in Lorraine from 1754 to 1788. Fortunately, the letters of the agents *and* the replies of the countess have survived.

1 A.N. T-153-113, July 8, 1782 (hereafter cited by the carton number and date only).

2 113, July 8, 1782. The "Vatellottes," non-cloistered nuns, were apparently well-trained teachers in the Lorraine countryside. Equipped with their own special teachers' manual (*Méthodes familières*, 1725, and *Réglement pour les Vatelottes*, 1750), they were clearly superior to the male *maîtres d'école* in the province. See René Taveneaux, "Les Écoles de campagne en Lorraine au XVIIIe siècle" *Annales de l'Est*, série 5, 22 (1970), 164–65. According to recent research on literacy, Lorraine was one of the most literate parts of France at the end of the eighteenth century. Cf. Louis Maggiolo, *Pouillé scolaire du diocèse de Metz* (Nancy, 1883).

3 114, May 18, 1771, July 13, 1771.

4 113, September 6, 1775.

5 107, June 29, 1757.

6 113, March 20, 1775.

7 113, May 19, 1778, July 21, 1778, October 14, 1778.

8 113, July 12, 1777, July 29, 1777.

9 113, January 18, 1777, July 29, 1777.

10 113, April 19, 1787.

11 113, November 14, 1787.

12 114, July 23, 1772.

13 114, October 18, 1772.

14 114, June 4, 1774; 113, June 3, 1778, October 24, 1781.

15 114, August 17, 1768.

16 Cf. P. de Saint-Jacob, *Les Paysans de la Bourgogne du Nord au dernier siècle de l'Ancien Régime* (Paris: Société d'Edition "Les Belles Lettres," 1960); T. Le Goff and D. Sutherland, "The Revolution and the Rural Community in Eighteenth-Century Brittany," *Past and Present*, no. 62 (February 1974), 96–119; and E. Le Roy Ladurie, "Révoltes et contestations rurales en France de 1675 à 1788," *Annales E. S. C.*, 29 (1974), 6–22 (reprinted in English, pp. 423–51 of this volume).

17 See R. Forster, *The House of Saulx-Tavanes* (Baltimore: The Johns Hopkins Press, 1971), ch. 2, and P. de Saint-Jacob, *Les Paysans de la Bourgogne du Nord*, passim.

18 My colleague Richard Kagan has investigated the matriculation records of the law school at Pont-au-Mousson in the eighteenth century; they indicate a sharp increase in the number of certified lawyers, not easily absorbed into traditional outlets like the *parlements*. See also Lenard Berlanstein, *The Barristers of Toulouse in the Eighteenth Century* (forthcoming at The Johns Hopkins Press).

19 114, October 6, 1773.

20 114, September 2, 1768.

21 113, November 4, 1778.

22 Ibid.

23 113, November 15, 1778, December 21, 1778.

24 113, February 3, 1779.

25 113, February 25, 1779.

26 113, March 15, 1779.

27 113, July 3, 1782.

28 113, November 14, 1787.

29 Ibid.

30 113, April 11, 1779, March 15, 1779.

31 See Harvey Chisick, *Attitudes toward the Education of the "Peuple" in the French Enlightenment, 1762–1789* (Diss. Johns Hopkins 1974). See also Colloque d'Aix, October 25–26, 1969, *Images du peuple* (Paris: Colin, 1973); M. Fleury and P. Valmary, "Les Progrès de l'instruction élémentaire de Louis XIV à Napoleon III d'après l'enquête de Louis Maggiolo," *Population*, 12 (1957), 71–92.

32 113, April 17, 1779.

33 113, July 19, 1779.

34 Ibid.

35 113, September 29, 1779. The village of Redlach does not seem to conform to the general conclusions of a recent work on rural schools in Lorraine by Alix de Rohan-Chabot, *Les Écoles de campagne en Lorraine au XVIIIᵉ siècle* (unpublished *thèse pour le 3ᵉ cycle*, 1967). Rohan-Chabot claims that Lorraine was "advanced" compared to other provinces in the kingdom.

36 113, February 23, 1780.

37 113, December 24, 1776.

38 114, July 13, 1771. On religious observance in Lorraine at the end of the seventeenth century, see Michel Pernot, *Etude sur la vie religieuse de la campagne Lorraine à la fin du XVIIᵉ siècle* (Nancy: Faculté des lettres et sciences humaines, 1971). Pernot writes: "Christian morality was neither

understood nor practiced" (108), at least among the 10,000 inhabitants of the Xaintois district in 1687. The Catholic Reformation had apparently been more successful in teaching country people to read and write. See Taveneaux, "Les Ecoles," pp. 170–71.

39 113, July 12, 1780.
40 113, June 20, 1775.
41 113, February 15, 1783.
42 113, August 16, 1779.
43 113, June 23, 1779.
44 113, July 24, 1773.
45 M. Foucault, *Madness and Civilization: A History of Insanity in the Age of Reason*, trans. R. Howard (New York: Pantheon, 1965), ch. 2.
46 113, January 16, 1782.
47 114, July 13, 1765.
48 113, May 28, 1777.
49 114, July 16, 1770.
50 114, May 8, 1771.
51 114, January 24, 1756.
52 Only a study of these villages during (and after) the Revolution can substantiate this, of course. It is possible too that the "paranoia" of the agents may have biased my view of the villagers in the direction of mutual distrust throughout the community. A greater pessimist than I might also argue that this is part of the "human condition" and that there is no need to suggest either "revolutions" or abstract models of "cohesive communities."

Rural Revolts and Protest Movements
In France from 1675 to 1788

EMMANUEL LE ROY LADURIE
Translated by Olive Classe

I

Numerous articles and well-known books have been written about the long series of anti-fiscal revolts and peasant wars that took place in the seventeenth century. In the forefront of these movements, in certain southern and western areas of hill country or wooded pasture-land (the Cotentin, Brittany, the Angoumois, Périgord, the Boulogne region, the Vivarais), there figured various groups of village communities. The uprisings were aimed essentially against the establishment and functioning of the taxation mechanism, the bureaucratic and military machinery which the royal administation had been continuously developing, expanding and making more onerous since 1624–25. The last of such revolts, those in the Boulogne region, in Béarn and in Brittany, between 1660 and 1675, though perhaps directed somewhat more markedly against seigneurial oppression or the tax privileges of the nobles, had nevertheless not been very different in character from the first rebellions, those that had started in 1624.

Although they were aimed mainly against certain cogs (especially fiscal ones) in the machinery of State, and not against the Supreme Cog, incarnated in the monarch, the revolts of the 1624–75 period *were* liable, in a spasmodic way, to challenge certain aspects of the seigneurial system or of the *dîme* (tithe).[1] They sometimes also attacked the tax exemption enjoyed by the privileged classes; such exemptions were all the more galling to those who did have to pay, since from the time of Richelieu the total tax burden had increased enormously. Seen from this point of view, though it is only a marginal one, the cycle of scattered and diverse revolts that occurred between 1625 and 1675 is a presage of the anti-seigneurial protest that would begin as a trickle, become more apparent in the eighteenth century, and then, from 1788 to 1789, turn into a raging torrent.[2] Here is another analogy: when the Fronde started in Paris, and the people tore up cobblestones to build barricades, the accompanying revolts did sometimes, in the provinces, halt for some months the functioning of the power apparatus. During the politically long hot summer of 1648, in the "liberated" regions of the Massif Central and the South-West, the tax-officials had the sense to lie low for a while, or else to decamp; and so the strike against payment of taxes became as effective then as it would be in 1789.

Nevertheless, as these rural revolts in the seventeenth century were directed specifically against the State, considered the summit of the overall socio-political structure, they did not represent much of a danger to the seigneury, who, in the peasants' eyes, still continued for a time to be part of the changeless order of rustic life. The spearhead of the rebellions was turned against the sharks of the military-financial complex. The rebels were therefore all the more naturally inclined to look for allies, and even for leaders, among the local lesser gentry and gentlemen-farmers, among the priests or curates, and among the advocates and minor men of law, embittered or prosperous as the case might be, who had been born into the Third Estate.

But after 1675, in the Catholic areas containing the immense majority of the rural population, we find no peasant war comparable to the practically endemic ones that occurred several times during the long period extending from 1548 to 1675. (The Huguenot rising in the Cévennes in 1703 presents specific problems which do not invalidate the preceding statement.) It is true that the Papist peasantry's new quiescence was nowhere near total: as late as 1707 armed mobs, in the best tradition of anti-fiscal and militarized action set by the *Croquants* (peasant revolutionaries) of 1593 and by the "new" *Croquants* of 1637, formed themselves in the Quercy-Périgord area, which of all the regions of France was the most productive of protest in the whole long seventeenth century. "The peasants all rose up . . . in armed bands, sacked the tax-offices, gained possession of a small town and several chateaux, and forced a few gentlemen to lead them," writes Saint-Simon. As always, the Duke's swift intuition takes him straight to the heart of the matter. "They declared for all to hear that they would pay the taille and the capitation tax, the tithe to their priests and the dues to their lord, but that they could pay no more, nor could they hear any more about the . . . [new] taxes and vexations . . . [contained in the] royal edict taxing baptisms." This edict was, in fact, according to Saint-Simon, scrubbed by Louis XIV, alarmed by this revolt, though he did put it down by sending regular troops.[3]

In spite of these last "little local difficulties," it is undeniable that the revolts that took place at the end of the seventeenth century were mild ones, and that those of the eighteenth century were even more so. For this there are many reasons, which, taken together, explain why there were no more peasant wars.

First, since Colbert's administration, the tax system had managed to rid itself to a certain extent of some of the large-scale thievery that had plagued it at the time of Richelieu and Mazarin; taxation had become more and more indirect, less and less direct.[4] Of course, this act of translating taxes into an indirect form was not a panacea against revolt; witness the numerous anti-*gabelle* (i.e., anti-salt-tax) risings in the seventeenth century. But since the tax farmers (*fermiers généraux*) contrived simultaneously to diversify their exactions (for example in the case of tobacco), improve their methods, and give their thefts a more civilized form, it is true that indirect taxes were more readily accepted by the French than direct taxation, always looked on as a kind of fleecing of the citizen. In the eighteenth century (as the wise old man Bras-dargent remarks, in the village of Rétif de la Bretonne's father), the State had become on the whole more wily and subtle in its ways of squeezing money out of the taxpayer.

Secondly, in the days of the Cardinal-Ministers the provincial Intendancies were hated by the rebels because they were rightly believed to be doing the Treasury's dirty work; but from Colbert's time onward the Intendancy made a move towards an alliance with the village, helping it escape the clutching talons of the members of the different *Parlements*, in their dual role of creditors and magistrates, whenever the great problem of the communal debt arose;[5] again, the Intendants defended the village against the food and provision profiteers.[6]

Thirdly, we must take account also of religious evolution: in 1685, at the summit of the irresistible rise of the Century of Saints, the State, thanks to the "miracle" of the Revocation of the Edict of Nantes, brought about, in spite of Jansenist grumbling, the union of Church and State. This Orwellian gesture did not transform the Huguenots into good Papists. But it did finally bring back into the bosom of the monarchy a Catholic Church that from 1560 to 1660, in round dates, had been a thorn in the flesh of the Valois, and later of the Bourbon kings. The monks of the League of 1590, the curates who in 1639 sided with the *Nu-pieds* (Norman peasant rebels led by some priest), and the priests (*curés*) who supported the Fronde in 1648 had left the Monarchy with some unpleasant memories, and Catholic protest in 1588, and again in 1610, had even gone as far as regicide, first in theory and then in practice. In 1685 Louis XIV, by repressing the Huguenots, since he could not suppress them altogether, gave a considerable sop to the Church, and thus integrated it completely in the national community. In exchange, the favor-crammed clergy gave their king a loyalty which, though not absolutely perfect or uncritical, was, nevertheless, preferable to the Papist eruptions of the good old days of the League. (Three years later, the Glorious Revolution of

1688 was to bring about a similar political recoupment, apparently in the contrary direction, on the other side of the Channel: the English monarchy, new model, would make an alliance with some segment of the former opposition, just as Louis XIV had done with the erstwhile pro-League, then pro-Fronde clergy.) At village level, there would henceforth be in France, a valid alliance between power and presbytery; in the second half of the seventeenth century those parish priests who had earlier been loose-living and insubordinate gradually turned into religious civil servants, "natural assistants to the Intendants," as one might say. Formerly, they had not been above turning themselves into the apostles of anti-State protest. Now here they had, in pulpit and confessional, become the mouthpiece of legality. When necessary, itinerant preachers came to the help of the parish priests; like the Breton Jesuits in 1675, they dowsed the flames of peasant and popular revolution with the tepid water of pastoral preaching. After 1685, Catholic loyalty became quite admirable. "We bleed ourselves dry paying taxes, but our great king, who has just revoked the so-called Reformed Religion, amply deserves all our efforts," writes a Papist of Languedoc at the end of the seventeenth century, before paying his share of that province's heavy taxes.[7] The total oppression of the Protestants—like that of the Jacobites in England—was the high price it was thought worth paying in order to give the Monarch a free hand outside and inside the Kingdom.

Fourthly, among a French peasantry that between 1680 and 1720 was becoming deeply permeated with a Catholicism more active than ever, the damping down of primitive violence and of criminality helped to diminish revolt and to eliminate the occurrence of civil wars.

Fifthly, during the post-1720 period, the Treasury drew in its horns considerably. The nightmare of the great levies of Louis XIV's era had been exorcised. At the same time, slowly but surely, the gross agricultural product was growing, as also was the amount of capital owned by taxpayers. Consequently, as the tax collectors' demands were becoming stable or even declining in *real* value, they were also tapping an expanding volume of taxable assets;

they were therefore felt much less acutely by the taxpayers than in the previous century. All these factors converged: recourse to violence no longer seemed a universal panacea against tax-collector or exciseman, now that rural society had become more docile, more orderly and less wretched.

II

However, these new circumstances, and they all made good sense, by no means imply that village protest movements had purely and simply faded out. To see the explosion of 1789 as coming like a bolt from the blue would be to misunderstand it completely. In the eighteenth century, law and order were not universally respected throughout the countryside—far from it. Protest still existed, but its objectives and causes had altered. It had gone through a change of heart, of tactics, and of strategy.

After those of Georges Lefebvre, the most conclusive analyses for a comprehension of rural unrest during the Enlightenment, in the part of France north and east of the Loire, have been provided by Pierre de Saint-Jacob. This Burgundian historian has not merely projected on to the mentality of country people during the Enlightenment conclusions drawn from the valuable but belated information available in great quantities from the *cahiers* (*de doléances*, memorials setting out local grievances) of 1789. More than that! Chapter by chapter, stroke by stroke, Saint-Jacob goes through the last century of the Ancien Régime drawing up a minute chronicle of "village disturbances." His careful interpretation of these allows us to understand in depth, on this century-long scale, the essentials about what changed and what remained the same.

We start, at the close of the seventeenth century and the beginning of the eighteenth, from a situation in Burgundy already very far removed from the great uprisings of the classic and "Borchnevian" type that had shaken the French provinces between the Catholic Holy League and the Fronde (among "these great uprisings" had been the insurrection, in the years 1589–

1594, of royalist peasants in the Beaune country against the League, against brigandage, and against taxation; and the drunken revels of the vine-growers or Lenturlus of Dijon in 1632, rebelling against a ministerial turn of the tax screw). Towards the period 1680 to 1720, in the large provincial area of east-central France, there was now hardly anything in the way of agitation except the small action of latent protest against the seigneur, and even that would be insignificant except that it might be seen as an omen of things to come. These actions, aimed against one or another local magnate, were sometimes planned at the traditional evening hemp-working sessions.[8] One may note among them refusals to pay the *champart* (levy in kind) called the *tierce*, raised on formerly common land that had been put under the plow by a tenant. The chapter of Autun, and various temporal lords as well, met with rebuffs of this kind at the end of the seventeenth century and in 1728. Other "rebuffs" were dealt, about 1717–24, to the seigneurial taille, when the seigneurs were asked, with a pointed regard for modern red-tape procedure, to produce their original title to it. There were also some small strikes against the tithe on wool and lambs (this was much contested at all times and in all places); in one village, in 1687, the tithe-collector went from pillar to post, finding no sheep-farmer who could bring himself to be the first to pay. In 1680 there were law-suits going on against the *corvée aux Saints* (labor-service due to the priest.)[9] Quarrels flared up easily over common grazing and reciprocal rights of usage, which made coexistence difficult for the village on the one hand and, on the other, the *métairie* or tenant farm, which had been formed from the edges of provincial lands by some seventeenth-century land-grabber, nobleman, bourgeois or *parlementaire*. These quarrels show the peasants challenging the shift of the seigneurial system towards a more modern, large-scale type of agriculture. In the same spirit the peasants objected when common lands were usurped to be turned into quite large individually held properties by urban land-grabbers coming from the so-called "pure" nobility, the *noblesse de robe* (new nobility of legal office holders), or the new nobility of tradesmen; or from all three directions at once! After 1660, in Burgundy, this "pro-communal" resistance received sympathetic help from Intendant Bouchu; and later, quite frequently, from his successors, right up to the end of the Ancien Régime. From this detailed example we can see how it came about that the rebels slipped from protest against the State and the Intendancies, which was characteristic of the early part of the seventeenth century, to anti-seigneurial protest, which on the other hand would be decidedly typical of the eighteenth. For those who lived on the land, the Intendant was no longer the bogy-man he had been taken for at first.

In the list of the other "various protests" during the period 1680–1725, those that this time did not involve the seigneury, I mention first, with Saint-Jacob, riots that fall into some particular category: those of the vine-growers of Sloutré, who rebelled in 1680, probably because of the low price of wine; those of the wheat-buyers, whose anger reached its peak at the time of the grain war, when, in 1709, armed bands representing country districts on one side and the towns on the other fought each other in the area round Beaune. We also see again the old anti-tax reflex, when in 1713, bands of robbers, perhaps acting partly out of a vague sense of justice, steal the tax-collectors' carts. Labor troubles, on the other hand, were relatively acute in Burgundy and in Languedoc during the seventeen-twenties: this decade of sparse population suffered the after-effect of earlier high mortality, so that labor became scarce, expensive, demanding and pugnacious. Thus, until about 1730, strikes by Burgundian harvest-workers managed to slow down for a time the movement towards very low wages which, in the second part of the eighteenth century, would continually oppress the rural proletariat.

On the whole, these different categories of revolt very rarely break the routine of the years 1680–1725; we must not overrate their importance just because they are arranged in a pattern in a historian's card-index, for really they stand out as exceptions against a general background of incredible resignation to dire poverty. In any case, around 1730 they tended to die down altogether in a climate of (very relative) "prosperity." When they begin again about 1735–40, they will change in depth and in intensity.

III

The new anti-seigneurial struggle, as it began to develop (for example in Burgundy) from 1735–40, as it flourished from 1750, to spread at last like wildfire from 1780, is in many ways a classic example of a battle against the old system of domination and exaction, and against the countless seigneurial rights, "these dues unworthy of the age we live in," as was written in 1789 in the *cahier de doléances* of Aigney.[10] This struggle was certainly evidence of how the seigneury was trailing behind cultural evolution: seigneurial tallage was contested as being arbitrarily imposed; and contested next were the *lods et ventes heriots* (taxes levied by the seigneur when land changed hands), the *banvin* (the lord's right to oblige his peasants to buy a certain quantity of his wine), the so-called "wheat for the bake-house, and the customary fowls," and the monopolies and various banal obligations (on the community, such as that to use the lord's mill, wine-press, etc.). As for the increase in poaching, a prime example of propaganda through action, what it amounted to was a demand for the democratization of the right to massacre the fauna; the Revolution was to accord it without discrimination, thereby helping to make present-day France an area of maximum wild-life extermination. The Burgundian peasants, just like those in the North, studied by Lefebvre and Trenard, protested, quite naturally, against tithes, especially when it was proposed to raise them from the agricultural lands that had been created or made fertile by clearances or modern farming developments. Lastly, the wave of enclosures of formerly common lands raised acutely the question of *tierces* or *champarts* (levies in kind on the harvest). These dues, which, as it happened, were very heavy in Burgundy, were exacted on pieces of common land only recently come under the plow: hence strikes against the *tierces*.

On the other hand, the *cens recognitif* (form of quit-rent established by precedent), though important to the seigneurs, since it supported and proved their title to the fief, was very light (thirty to forty liters of grain per hectare), and hardly ever contested; except when it was exacted in a lump sum, in the form of arrears, after not having been collected for twenty-nine years. Another phenomenon worthy of note is the relatively pacific atmosphere in Burgundy that surrounded mortmain and the surviving remnants of serfdom.

Was this docility on the part of those liable to mortmain due to the particular backwardness of their villages, and to a state of passive alienation that prevented them from rattling the chains encircling their fields? In fact, it would seem that the real reason for this attitude lay elsewhere. Coming down through the ages, mortmain had shown itself, through use and after constant wear, as one of the best possible shields against bourgeois or seigneurial-cum-bourgeois encroachments in Burgundy,[11] for it made the mortmain payer's little field a precarious possession, with the threat of a possible return to the traditional seigneur's estates always hanging over it. So, by the insecurity of tenure it carried with it, mortmain discouraged bourgeois imperialism, or the new look imperialism of the seigneur cum-bourgeois, as it was practiced, for example, by the members of the Dijon *parlement*, to the detriment of rural small farmers, as well as to that of the ancient nobility. On the whole (in this special case of mortmain), the more ancient the seigneury the less it was disputed. And the opposite was true, too. It was when the seigneury became the vanguard of rural modernization that it was most determinedly harassed by the peasants. In the eighteenth century, the Burgundian peasantry was anti-feudal because it was anti-capitalist.

Of course, the anti-seigneurial struggle as it developed in east-central France between 1730 and 1788 was also a protest against domination, and a demand for peasant power, a power that the peasants, now better educated and more self-confident, had become fit to exercise. "I am convinced that desperate ills need desperate remedies; moreover it does the peasants good to be ruled with an iron hand," writes the Chevalier de Caumartin, prior of Saint-Léger and seigneur of Binges, in 1765, when asking his officers to take severe measures. Under the shocking system that prevailed, the seigneur, as we know, was judge in his own cause; his agents meted out justice, enforcing labor at the wine-harvest, and defending the master's woods and pastures against excessive or permanent grazing. Let us imagine that, as often happened at the time, these judicial powers passed out of the hands of a local man in favor with his fellow-citizens (see the example of Edmé Rétif) and fell into those of bourgeois outsiders (who were another feature of a certain degree of urbanization that was a modernizing trend in its own way). Then justice was very likely, in the period of protest from 1750–89, to provoke strong resistance among the people. Particularly, it was often on the days manorial courts were held to judge cases on the domain that there were outbursts of popular feeling against the master and his creatures. So R. Robin stresses the frequent linking of lord and lawyer as targets for the frustrations expressed in the *cahiers*.[12]

Yet the aggravation of anti-seigneurial struggles in the eighteenth century was not simply the result of a revived hostility between two traditional enemies; enemies, moreover, who had previously become friends on many occasions, locked in a complex of inextricable relationships wherein hatred was mingled with what one can only call a sort of mutual affection. In fact, the increase in hostilities from 1740 onwards is due also to altered conditions. The two antagonists, each on his own side, were changing, drifting, each in his way, along irreconcilable channels, towards two different kinds of modernity. This drift put a distance between the two partners, gradually turning them more and more into strangers.

IV

The peasants of 1750–80 were becoming less and less like what they had been in the past. In this connection, their change of attitude toward the seigneury was inseparable from the changes in their behavior with regard to the towns, to culture and to religion. Not that the Catholicism of the good old days, which after 1750 relaxed a little of its formidable hold, had necessarily been a factor tending to social peace, and lending comfort to the mighty of the earth. The gradual Christianizing of the countryside that had been going on in depth since the Middle Ages had brought into confrontation on one side the principle of the old tripartite schemas, originating in the dark Indo-European past, that defined the hierarchy of priests, noble land-owning warriors, and land-workers; and on the other the principle of a scriptural, originally Semitic conception, distinctly more egalitarian than Dumézil's triad. Through this Biblical influence, the peasants, put wise by Franciscanism, had arrived at the famous and dangerous slogan: "When Adam delved and Eve span/Who was then the gentleman?"

Still, one can always come to some kind of arrangement with heaven, even the Old Testament heaven. And the Counter-Reformation, after some false starts, had managed since the seventeenth century to establish between the parish Church and the lord's chateau a *modus vivendi* not disagreeable to either party. This new compromise had its drawbacks, though: religion had now become the bulwark of the social order; but this bulwark had to be kept in good repair. And, though one cannot yet speak of dechristianization, certain phenomena occurred in Burgundy around 1760 that are reminiscent of those studied by Michel Vovelle in Provence.[13] On some important holy-days which the peasants of the east-central region had formerly kept assiduously, the churches were somewhat emptier, the drinking-houses fuller. The state of mind nurtured in taverns was not a good thing for the church seigneury, because of the sensitive question of tithes; nor, consequently, for the temporal lords (since they, in Burgundy, had their own little gold-mine of feudal tithes). The taverns were developing through the simultaneous increase in consumption and in sociability; a great rash of smoking habits spread, between the seventeenth and eighteenth centuries, from the coastal regions, first to become smoke-ridden, right to the nation's heart, which was slowly infected in its turn. So the new leaders—future local politicians, or the militants perhaps of later riots, or mere loud-mouths—got their training amidst clouds of smoke and jugs of wine. The leaders and their adherents were becoming more and more literate. They rarely drew their mental nourishment from Rousseau, but very often from the *livres bleus*, the blue-covered chapbooks that were spreading the relatively new theme of Old Man Poverty: this character preached the eminent dignity of the poor—here below, not only in the kingdom of heaven. Politiciza-tion of public opinion came also from the towns, which, as the result of the drift from the land, were a catchment area for massive numbers of rootless ex-peasants falling down the social ladder. In town, these peasants developed frustrations far greater than those they would have harbored had they stayed in the country with their family, to whom, since they remained in touch, they now described their feelings and passed them on. These frustrations were themselves inseparable from the "greater expec-tations" acquired through contact with more favored urban groups. As they had found in the town no substantial improve-ment in their standard of living, the rising expectations typical of the century made the ex-peasants demand all the more from rural life, even and especially if it did not change much, for, in compari-son with the new *dolce vita* of the urban elite, existence in the country seemed far more intolerable than it had done to the previous generation, although their standard of living had been even lower.

More prosaically, politicization of public opinion proceeding from the towns assisted the maturing (limited though this was) of public spirit in the village. Sometime around 1762–63 the strikes of the different *Parlements* were followed or accompanied by strikes, demonstrating solidarity or airing the same kind of griev-ances, staged by some seigneurial local officials. So more than one hot-headed peasant must have thought: "Well, if the local judge goes on strike himself, why shouldn't I demonstrate, too?" The overall development of the new popular culture, based on literacy and chapbooks and on private person-to-person contacts, was helped by an increasing volume of population exchanges and migrations and by people's general mobility. This culture, then, nurtured the so-called "wrong spirit" and created growing numbers of "recalcitrants." As examples of the "wrong spirit": it was known for peasants to address their seigneur as "tu," a familiarity which of course was by no means a sign of affection! On the days when the lord's courts were held, the local law was no longer treated with the old respect. As for recalcitrants, they sprang up all over the place, in different rural milieux, like toadstools deadly to the rustic order. The local leader—and there might be more than one in a village—who spread reckless excitement among the country people might be a lawyer, a merchant, a priest, or a notary; but also a cartwright, a weaver, or one or more manual workers with plenty to say for themselves. As up-to-date interpreters of the new civilization of reading and writing, which as far as they were concerned was barely a few hundred years old, the protesters in the small country areas, sometimes only a handful of them, would ask to see the original document showing title to a feudal due; and this in places where hitherto there had simply been an easy-going tradition of spoliation, where for ages the seigneur had been able to declare, without fear of contradiction: "Possession is title." Yet after all, demanding this documentary proof, even if it might have been lost or non-existent, and laying a profane hand on the most sacred dues, be they onerous or ultra-light, amounted merely to imitating Colbert without knowing it. A good century earlier the minister had set a bad example to the administration, and, through the administration, to the nation. In his famous *Reforms of the Nobility,* he had required the production of a written title to blue blood, whereas up till then nothing had been needed but the quiet enjoyment of rights and an age-long usurpation. A hundred years after Colbert's initiative, it was the turn of a few resolute rustics to make use, against the interests of their lord, of the power conferred on them by their very recent entry into the Gutenberg Galaxy.

All this exploded, or at least began to smolder, at the time of the great politicization of the Burgundian village, evident during the seventeen-eighties. One or two procurators were retained by the peasants to fight methodically, inch by inch, through the juridical *maquis,* against real or sometimes supposed encroachments by the seigneur. But we must not imagine, just because the country people were fighting against a master who, now that his concerns lay mainly in the towns, was becoming more and more a part of the dominant urban society, that this led within the village itself to a plastering over of the cracks of internal conflicts, so as to present a united peasant front to the world. Far from it! It is true that antagonism between village and village became less active, and this lessening of discord between territorial communities is an undoubted sign of modernity. But politicization stirred up divisions in the seventeen-eighties within the village itself: between rich and poor, between farmers and day laborers, between young and old, and even between men and women! Of course, this electric atmosphere prevailed only in villages where there was unrest or militancy, and the historian must not forget, at the provincial or national level, the tautologically silent majority of peaceful villages. Still, the air was sufficiently stormy during the seventeen-eighties for the villages of Burgundy to draw up in 1789 *cahiers* that were often very harsh; stormy enough to explain why, during the summer of fear, peasant insurrections broke out in the Mâconnais region; and, in general, why there were revolts in Eastern and East-Central France, where the feudal system still reigned.

V

So we see that there had been a modernization—ideological, cultural and social—of the peasant; or at least of certain groups of peasants numerous enough to form a critical mass of humanity which, at a certain moment, refused to go on living as it had lived in the past. In a country where, at the rural level, repression by police or military was, as the case might be, non-existent, inefficient or out of the question, this kind of evolution could lead in no time at all to revolutionary consequences.

But modernization did not affect the peasants only. In a very different way it affected the landed nobility. And the course of rejuvenation undergone by the seigneuries helped increase the distance between them and the men they still looked on as their subjects.

Pierre de Saint-Jacob has perspicaciously attributed the transformations that were taking place in the seigneurial organism to the effects of physiocracy. There is no question, of course, of exaggerating in this connection the weight carried by the writings of Quesnay, or of even imagining a direct influence: in this case, they were symptomatic, not determining. Physiocracy is simply the name Saint-Jacob finds it convenient to give to attempts at agriculture by ground-rent and tenant-farmers on a large or medium scale. These attempts, whether in Burgundy or elsewhere, depended upon the seigneurial land-estates, seen as a starting-point and as a growth objective. From selfish and even highly disreputable motives, these nobles tried to ensure their own benefit by limiting the number of "lame ducks," in other words, of scattered small-holdings, yielding a low rent, that characterized the old-style seigneurial empire. When "physiocracy" was put into practice thus, it worked toward the advantage of large or relatively large farms. It aimed at a better response to market stimuli (aimed, that is, when it came down to brass tacks, at feeding the hunger of the townspeople), as well as at a better response to the growing demands created by urbanization and increased consumption. Verenne de Lonvoy, for example, acquired seigneurial rights over two villages at the end of the reign of Louis XV.[14] This man's behavior was, moreover, so brutal as to provoke a backlash of revolutionary feeling in these districts at the end of the century. Now Varenne de Lonvoy was the very type of important personage who took shelter behind the label of "seigneur" and the particle "de" in his surname in order to propagate a kind of capitalism in the countryside. For Monsieur de Lonvoy would do anything to increase the extent of his property, tacking on to his domain the peasants' little plots and former hempfields, creating artificial meadows, enclosing his pastures, taking over common lands and "making them part of his estate." To water his meadows he used the stream of the former public mill, that disused symbol of a feudal entity, or of a communal group, to which this land-grabber now preferred the profits of large-scale real estate, in the bare modern sense of the term. Lastly, Varenne also made energetic use, for the benefit of his business affairs, of the tax privilege attached to his title and status. In eighteenth-century England, where economic progress and increased production of subsistence commodities had a high priority over the social well-being of the country-people, Varenne de Lonvoy, regrouper of land, irrigator and encloser, would have been praised to the skies by Arthur Young, who would have seen him as a determined modernizer of agriculture and a creator of food surpluses that could be sold at good prices in accordance with the theories of laissez-faire. In France, where agricultural revolution in the English style, involving enclosures and regrouping of land, met with terrific resistance from the peasant masses and their ideological allies or exploiters, Varenne de Lonvoy, if he had lived, would probably have ended his career by being sent to the guillotine by the Popular Societies of his district.

It was exactly against men of this type, of whom Varenne was a particularly odious specimen, that revolutionary anti-seigneurial-ism (or perhaps one should call it anti-capitalist reaction) was aimed in the last decades and years of the Ancien Régime. Saint-Jacob, whose files register with complete objectivity all peasant disturbances recorded in Burgundy between 1740 and 1789, notes in the list of anti-seigneurial acts, dozens of riots during this period precisely against enclosures, i.e., against one of the essential forms taken by modernization in stock-breeding areas. He mentions numerous collective acts of violence against the *triage* (transferring of one-third of common land, especially woods, to seigneurial ownership), against the buying up of common land as it was carried out by privileged landowners aiming to create larger estates, against the draining of ponds, and against the fencing off of woodlands to permit the creation of that typically modernist phenomenon, the regulated forest. All this popular action, then, was directed against an evolution which was seigneurial in form and capitalist in content.

Lastly, Pierre de Saint-Jacob stresses the importance in the pre-revolutionary period of the pro-seigneurial and anti-protest stance of the rich farmer, a prosperous peasant in clogs and a black *blaude* (smock). He might go round in clogs but, just the same, in the farming world this wealthy type was the essential instrument of seigneurial oppression and capitalist modernization, rolled paradoxically into one.[15] There were some seigneurs, like Saulx-Tavannes, who left their lands looking like a meaningless jig-saw puzzle, fragmented into little scraps rented out as farms. But still, there was in Burgundy a stratum of well-to-do farmers who took on the entire leases of sizeable bourgeois farms of from twenty to thirty hectares or of seigneurial lands of from fifty to a hundred hectares.[16] These men had their own quarrels with their lessors, but, as potentially hateful or hated agents of the large or medium-sized "capitalist-cum-seigneurial" estate, they were a direct provocation for bitter protests from village democrats; typical examples of this are the well-heeled farmers or *matadors* (bosses, bigwigs) described by Georges Lefebvre. Also typical was the farmer of Planay, in Burgundy, a big stock-breeder and employer of labor: "The farmer of Planay has a prodigious number of pigeons that foul the water-tanks so essential in this dry region; with his numerous laborers he gets in his grain harvest a fortnight before everyone else, then turns his two hundred sheep loose on the stubble, where they take the opportunity to go off and eat his neighbors' standing crops."[17] Once the events of 1789 had started, and their noble landlords had emigrated, a lot of these rich farmers would turn their coat, or rather their smock, buy some of the *Bien National* (lands confiscated from nobles and clergy), and become the village leaders of a peasant revolution. But Georges Lefebvre and Pierre de Saint-Jacob have shown that one is not entitled to project backwards on to the last decades of the Ancien Régime the a posteriori attitude adopted by the group of big farmers in and after 1789. Before the Revolution, a rich farmer might possibly oppose a neighboring seigneur, but as for his own seigneur, who rented him his land, the prosperous lessee, even if he complained, saw their two interests as coinciding rather than conflicting. As a farmer's son, and a friend of the big *laboureurs* (peasants renting enough land to live in well-off conditions), François Quesnay had already realized that there was a complicity linking his farmers' physiocracy with the land-owning class of nobles and clergy; to leave this modernizing complicity out of account would be to see the seigneurial domain as the pure parasite it was made out to be in the diatribes contained in some of the *cahiers de doléances*. This would be the same mistake a historian of the twenty-first century would make if he viewed the chainstores of the nineteen-fifties through the distorting lens of the slogans or invective of Pierre Poujade. Our own century, though people are now so much better informed, has produced too many large-scale examples of the bad judgment of the *homo demens* for us to assume that the peasant masses of the eighteenth century, systematically under-informed as they were, always had a clear knowledge of where their own best interests lay, even in the short term. Did the peasants of Burgundy realize, when they objected to the laying out of a *bocage* (pasture land with hedges or woodlands), that it was by such methods that their brothers in Lower Normandy and in Brittany and Britain had solved for centuries the problem of supplying milk for their young children? It is unlikely.

So, when we try to understand rural disputes at the end of the eighteenth century, let us resist making implicit value judgments arising from the hindsight of teleological historiography. The struggle of the peasant against his seigneur, under Louis XV and Louis XVI, is not simply a clash between the democratic, the progressist, or the bourgeois future, whichever one prefers to call it, and the reactionary and feudal past. It also reflects the antagonism between two forms of production, both of them very much alive and remarkably *present*, both of which have already fired many shots into the future: on the one hand, there is the peasant economy, with its fragmentation of the land (Chayanov); and, on the other, the system of big seigneurial estates. This latter, with its unfair advantages of judicial powers and tax privileges, often leads the way to large- or medium-scale agriculture carried out by farmers.

This antagonism is seen clearly in Burgundy, although it is

considered to have been a very backward province. It is even more easily visible in the Paris region. There, the most serious peasant, or rather peasant and artisan, revolts that took place at the end of the Ancien Régime brought about no longer, or perhaps one could say not even, a confrontation between peasants and nobles, but a direct conflict over the grain shortage between manual or agricultural workers, together with their artisan allies, and the big capitalist farmers. These latter were theoretically agents of the seigneur, but in daily life, as the masses knew, they were the real possessors of agricultural wealth, of power, and of wheat, at village and small-town level. That is why in 1775 the flour war waged round about Paris by the lower classes against the land- and grain-potentates was so bitter. Under these circumstances it is not surprising that anti-seigneurial protest movements at the time of the Enlightenment should have moved away a little, simultaneously, from both patterns based on the past or oriented toward the future.

As regards past-based patterns: though it did not disappear completely, the struggle against fisc and State, the preferred form of protest in the seventeenth century, now faded into the background; henceforth, protest was aimed no longer against the very *existence* of some hated tax, but against inequity in the collection of it, symbolized by the fiscal privileges of the nobles; or against ways of extorting it judged to be barbarous, like, for example, the road-construction *corvée* (labor-service) imposed on the peasant by the State.

Futurist patterns: not many of our rural protesters had these in mind either. Farm- and land-redistribution, given a concrete form by "agrarian laws," was not envisaged as a possibility until the eve of the Revolution, save exceptionally in the *cahiers* of some extremist villages. So it seems that the possession of land by legal right, even when it took the form of seigneurial estates, continued to be a much respected taboo. Only certain peripheral aspects of the seigneurial system were challenged vigorously: judicial powers, payments of dues, etc., or its ambitions toward and attempts at aggrandizement (*triage,* enclosures). Land-hunger, made more acute by population growth, certainly existed at the end of the eighteenth century. But it did not express itself, as it would in the twentieth century, in demands for agrarian laws and land-reform. It would really find proper relief only after the outbreak of the Revolution; then some of the peasants would push themselves to the front when the *Biens Nationaux* (confiscated lands) were auctioned. In come regions, they would manage to force the rich bourgeoisie out of the bidding, leaving them to look on in impotent rage while they, the peasants, acquired the priests' former lands (see G. Lefebvre for the case of the department of the Nord, not necessarily typical of France as a whole). As for other even more futuristic schemes, which would one day find expression in Socialism and Communism, it is no good looking for these in the revolutionary projects of the peasants we are studying, though we must make one of several very rare exceptions for the patriarchal and communalistic Utopia innocently proposed, in a work that was known only to a few, by the ex-peasant Nicolas Rétif de la Bretonne.[18]

VI

In spite of a few blank spaces, Saint-Jacob, thanks to the "feudal" backwardness of his native Burgundy, has been able to depict anti-seigneurial protest there in bright colors and clear outlines. The pattern discerned by this historian can be applied, with a few corrections and attenuations, to the relatively feudalized regions of Northern France; and also, perhaps even more aptly, to the large areas of eastern and east-central France;[19] the places where in 1789 will flare up the major revolts, against seigneurial institutions and against society as a whole, whether noble or bourgeois. But in the Massif Central, which stands apart geographically, and also in the most southerly parts of France, from the Rhone to the Atlantic, Saint-Jacob's analysis loses much of its relevance and its bite. The Auvergne and Languedoc peasantries, illiterate and non-French-speaking, had not attained a point of cultural development where they could be reached by the main currents of popular thought circulating in French in northern and Franco-Provençal regions, thanks to the *livres bleus* (chapbooks) and many other vehicles. In addition, the agrarian systems of the *pays d'oc* (i.e., southern regions of France speaking their own dialects) and of the mountains of central France were not the same as those of the northern and east-central areas; seigneurialism and the capitalist dynamic were less aggressive there. That is why peasant protest in Auvergne and Languedoc has some unusual aspects and at times less fire than in Burgundy or in Artois.

In Basse-Auvergne, for example, according to Poitrineau, the very backward but well-off peasantry possessed sixty-one per cent of the land. Consequently, rural discontent was less acute than in Burgundy. Poitrineau's important monograph,[20] as exhaustive as that of Saint-Jacob, records only *one single* case of rioting, between 1730 and 1789, against the buying up of communal lands by a wealthy citizen; on that occasion a cowshed was set fire to and a hundred cows and a quantity of hay were destroyed. This relatively rare occurrence of riots against the *triage* in Basse-Auvergne, in comparison with the much more troubled situation in Burgundy, is easily explained: in the large province of the Massif Central the buying up of communal territories was not (as it was near Beaune or Dijon) carried out only by the powerful landowners, even if these did play a part in the process. The *rôtisses* (land subjected to slash-and-burn agriculture), *rompues* (pastures being put under the plough), and other kinds of temporary turning over to cultivation of common lands in the hills of Auvergne were carried out not by seigneurs but by commoners or even by manual workers, using this means to nibble bits out of the grazing rights possessed by the great noble estates and by the towns and villages. So these unimportant Auvergnats, putting a scrap of land under cultivation, had no reason to provoke a pro-communalist riot in the Burgundian style against what they were doing themselves.

Again, in his section on rural unrest, Poitrineau does not record much more, from about 1734 to 1747, than a few small-scale popular disturbances directed against the tax privileges of the nobles, to which must be added a petition from the Auvergnats who had become temporary migrants in Paris, asking for the setting up of an equitable *cadastre* (register of land-values for taxation purposes) in their home province. The same section also records a few rare protests against the seigneurs' dispensation of justice; several gunshots fired at a terrorized seigneurial judge;[21] two brief subsistence riots in 1748–50; and some trifling collective breaking of new enclosures, after 1750.

In fact, during the part of the eighteenth century before the storm, Basse-Auvergne acted as a breakwater to the social order: anti-fiscal disturbances died away there completely after 1756 and the capture of Mandrin and his robber bands. As for the Auvergne nobility, in spite of or perhaps because of its increasing absenteeism, it too meets no serious opposition until 1788. The time of the *grands jours (d'Auvergne)* (special inquiries into misuse of seigneurial rights), directed against the robber barons so hated by the countryfolk in the seventeenth century, seemed to have been forgotten. Probably, the local nobility had become somewhat more urbanized and civilized. However, in 1789, Auvergne in its turn, waking up belatedly to what was going on, would follow the example that had already been set for some decades by other more northerly provinces, and throw itself into the protest movement. The village *cahiers* of Limagne and of the mountainous areas would then raise objections "to the seigneurial ovens, the *lods et ventes* (taxes levied when land changed hands), the *percières* (*champarts*–payments in kind–exacted on *rôtisses*), and the feudal tithes." As for the Auvergne farmers, before the Revolution they were most submissive to their good masters, but once it had broken out they became anti-feudalists overnight. At least, a certain number of them did.

So, until 1788, Basse-Auvergne, whose peasant population was, up to 1789, neither rebellious nor deeply divided, reacted, we see, much less harshly to the seigneurial system and role by magnates than did the Mâconnais or Artois. Perhaps the Auvergnats did "grumble away in secret," but they did not rebel openly at the seigneurial court. One day they would throw themselves into the struggle against the rulers, but after the fashion of those people who joined the Resistance at the eleventh hour, on the fifteenth of August 1944.

In Languedoc, peasant unrest manifested itself, once more, in ways very different from those observed in Burgundy. It is true that the people of Languedoc did not exhibit the out-of-date quiescence of the Auvergne peasantry. Several times between 1680 and 1789 we see them engaging in social battles on a considerable scale. At the end of the seventeenth century, the farmers of large church domains put up strong opposition, during the crises, to their ecclesiastical landlords, and in the seventeen-twenties, during a period of labor shortage, strikes of hired farmworkers are recorded in the Lauragais region. More generally, action against the southern French forms of the *dîme* went on almost non-stop during the sixteenth, seventeenth, and eighteenth centuries. After fluctuating over the centuries, they became more marked again after 1750–60. Practically everywhere in Languedoc, after that date, the peasants refused to pay the *carneaux* or *carnencs* (tithes on cattle), and the tithes on millet, flax, and vegetables; they forced down the rate of the tithes on wheat and rye grain, which indeed were excessively high in this southern part of France. On the other side of the balance, we have the members of the *Parlement* of Toulouse, not content with having had Calas broken on the wheel in the name of the true faith, rushing to the aid of the tithe-owning clergy and proceeding to nourish and succor them with a shower of *Parlement* decrees in their favor. Nevertheless, in spite of this acute agitation against tithes, Languedoc was free, or nearly free, from the great battles waged so often, farther north or farther east, against the physiocrat seigneurs.

How may we account for the relative abstention of Languedoc at the time the "anti-feudal" struggle was going on elsewhere? In addition to the general reasons mentioned earlier in connection with the whole area made up of the Massif Central and the southernmost parts of France, there were other more local factors.

In Languedoc the tailles were *réelles* (that is, levied not on income but on the amount of land owned), so that the tax-exemption enjoyed by nobles, seigneurs, and big landowners was insignificant in practice, and could not be used as a weapon for the benefit of large estates. So protest against tax-privilege never got started— there was little or nothing to fight against. As for the great capitalist and seigneurial land-grouping offensive, it was certainly important round cities like Toulouse and Montpellier. But in Languedoc as a whole it was on a much smaller scale and far less violent than in the north.[22] So that in this southerly province we do not find the explosive mixture of feudalistic survivances and the drive towards large-scale farming which evoked such bitter protest from the Burgundian peasants. Against the much more relaxed background of Languedoc, acrimony in the villages was focussed essentially on tithes: out of 1122 complaints in the *cahiers* concerning seigneurial rights in the region of Alès, Uzès and Nîmes, 562 attack the tithe.[23] Far behind, as causes of anti-seigneurial wrath, came tolls (notably at Pont-Saint-Esprit); and the judicial functions of the seigneurs, which, here as else- where, were a key to power. (But this seigneurial right to dispense private justice was much more restricted in Languedoc than in Burgundy, because of the vigilance of the law-officers of Crown and community, which by-passed, from above and below respec- tively, the seigneurial tribunals). Lastly, the *cens* (quit-rents) were very small in Languedoc and hardly disputed at all; this was even truer of the *tasques* or *champarts* (payments in kind levied on harvests), the *corvées* (labor-service or payment in lieu), the *colombiers* (vexatious regulations relating to pigeon-keeping), and the *francs-fiefs* (payments for freeholds), which were all rarer or less intolerable than in northern France.

Far distant from the southern provinces, among the *bocages* of western France, there remains a last area of (relative) social peace for us to describe. This region saw far fewer disturbances before 1789 than the zones of rural turbulence situated in Burgundy and the eastern provinces. This specific behavior of the *bocages*, quite evident when we read Jean Meyer's important thesis on Brittany, is attributable to many causes not all of which are very clear. In Brittany, the passivity of the peasants may perhaps be explained by the marked absence of great social changes during the eighteenth century: Armorica in the years of the Enlightenment did not undergo a demographic revolution, nor a large-scale spread of literacy, nor a *deep* penetration by the capitalism that was on the other hand so dynamic in the coastal regions, at Nantes, Lorient, and Saint-Malo. No one in Armorica was traumatized between 1750 and 1789 by the Enclosure Revolution, for the simple reason that it had already taken place there centuries ago. The Breton seigneury's position rested securely on the pauperism of the *métayers* (share-croppers), of the other farmers, and of the *domaniers congéables* (tenants with specific leases). All of these were firmly in the seigneur's power; they took off their hat when they addressed "the master"; they drowned their sorrows in cider and they enjoyed their lord's complicity when they went in for tobacco-smuggling. There came no large-scale social change, such as might have infused a capitalist spirit into the seigneurial farm or the *domaine congéable*, and social relations in Arcoat, the inland part of Brittany, pursued their monotonous, wretched, humdrum way undisturbed. There were hardly any peasant uprisings in Brittany between 1676 and 1789. Quaint and pious Papists, they stagnated instead of protesting, though in 1789 they did set fire belatedly to a few chateaux.

The real drama, then, was played out far from the *bocages* and far from the *pays d'oc*—in the northeast, the east, and in the east-central parts of the kingdom. On the one side there was a landed nobility slowly moving towards physiocratic and capitalistic views and gradually becoming urbanized, and on the other peasant minorities becoming more and more educated and refusing to sacrifice their increased expectations on the seigneur's altar of English-style capitalist evolution. Between these advance-guard antagonists there took place in the eighteenth century preliminary skirmishes, which were minor or abortive until 1789, but which revolutionary events would throw into unexpected importance.

NOTES

This essay has also appeared, in French, in *Annales*, 29 (1974), 6–22.

1 The history of revolt has been particularly affected by "teleological" views of it produced retrospectively by the French Revolution and, later, by bourgeois, then socialist, historiography of the Revolution. Because of this, people have been led to place in the forefront of their consideration, lavishly illuminated by the events of 1789, a few revolts which, on the basis of unfortunately vague, dubious, or inadequate documentation (such as the problematical Peasant Code of 1675 in Brittany), may, it is true, be reasonably supposed to have had a violently or spasmodically anti-seigneurial and/or anti-noble character. The great bulk of revolts, those that were both fundamental and typical, which until the end of the seventeenth century were directed in the main against the state, paying little or no attention to the seigneurial system and the nobility (except insofar as they looked to them for leaders), have either suffered long neglect or, more recently, have been seen distorted by the false light inevitably thrown on them as the result of the aforementioned teleological approaches.

2 In this connection, the revolt in the Boulogne region in 1662 seems to me very important; it took place, for a change, not in the south or the west of the kingdom, but close to the regions that would be the classic terrain for the northern peasant risings of 1789. Coinciding with the subsistence crises of 1661–62, led by a member of the lesser nobility "given to drink and debauchery" who was taken on as leader rather late in the day by the peasant rebels, this revolt was a protest, in State lands, against an avalanche of new taxes. In this respect it is very typical of the age. But it protested too, and in no uncertain fashion, against "the farmers of land belonging to the nobles who claimed they were exempt" from taxes old and new. Here, in a region that is much more interesting (from the very long-term pre-revolutionary point of view) than Brittany, or the Périgord of the *Croquants*, or the Cotentin of the *Nu-pieds*, we get a vivid picture of how a classical type of agitation against taxes could turn into a protest against fiscal privilege and then, as would be the case in the eighteenth century, slip finally toward attack on the seigneurial system and the nobility. In this sense, these *Lustucrus* rebels in the Boulonnais in 1662 are to the insurgent "Peasants of the North" in 1789 what *Australopithecus* is to *Homo sapiens*: they are true precursors, in the real sense for once, of a term too lightly bandied about (cf. Léon Bernard, "French Society and Popular Uprisings under Louis XIV," *French Historical Studies*, 3 [1964], 458).

3 Pléiade edition (Paris: Gallimard, 1953–61), II, 766.

4 According to Yves Durand, *Les Fermiers généraux au XVIIIe siècle* (Paris: Presses universitaires de France, 1971), the proportion of revenue raised from indirect taxes rose from 24.2 percent in 1643, 23.7 percent in 1648, and 16.6 percent in 1656, to 46.7 percent in 1662 and to 53 percent (average figure) from 1685 to 1695, when the *traitants* (tax-farmers) were at the (relative) height of their power. In the eighteenth century, the proportion of revenue raised from indirect taxation varied between 42 and 47 percent.

5 Cf. Saint-Jacob, *Les Paysans de la Bourgogne du Nord au dernier siècle de l'Ancien Régime* (Paris: Société d'Edition "Les Belles Lettres," 1960).

6 G. Frêche, unpublished thesis, p. 949 (for western Languedoc).

7 Quoted at the end of my *Paysans de Languedoc* (Paris: S.E.V.P.E.N., 1966).

8 *Écraignes*: evening sessions of hemp workers. For this kind of disturbance in 1728, see Saint-Jacob, *Paysans de la Bourgogne*, p. 328.

9 Ibid., p. 135.

10 Ibid., p. 520.

11 Ibid., pp. 48, 462, and passim.

12 Régine Robin, *La Société française en 1789: Semur-en-Auxois* (Paris: Plon, 1970), p. 235.

13 M. Vovelle, *Piété baroque et déchristianisation en Provence au XVIIIe siècle* (Paris: Plon, 1973).

14 Saint-Jacob, *Paysans de la Bourgogne*, pp. 427–28.

15 Robin, *Semur-en-Auxois*, p. 173.

16 Saint-Jacob, *Paysans de la Bourgogne*, pp. 52–53.

17 Ibid., p. 529.

18 This "Utopia" has been printed in the recent edition of Rétif de la Bretonne's *La Vie de mon père* (Paris: Garnier, 1970).

19 In Provence, according to M. Pillorget, a third of the "revolts" that took place in the eighteenth century were directed against the seigneurs.

20 Abel Poitrineau, *La Vie rurale en Basse-Auvergne au XVIIIe siècle* (Paris: Presses universitaires de France, 1965).

21 This tiny shooting incident gives me the opportunity to insert a parenthesis: now, it was a better-educated peasantry, with raised hopes (or "expectations"), but also better armed physically, with shotguns instead of arquebuses and crossbows, who would stand up to the seigneurs. This spread of a greatly improved firearms technology also helps to explain the general aggravation in the seventeenth century of quarrels over the seigneurial hunting monopoly.

22 See the map showing land ownership in France according to broad social

groups, published by M. Vovelle in his *Histoire de la Révolution française* (Paris: Editions du Seuil, 1973).

23 Abbé Brancolini, in an unpublished study. In Upper Languedoc, which exported grain, one must also add the subsistence riots. See G. Frêche, unpublished dissertation, p. 937.

The Irish on the Continent
in the Eighteenth Century

WILLIAM D. GRIFFIN

For most students of the eighteenth century, Irish history is merely an appendage to that of England. When it receives any notice at all, the images customarily evoked are those of an Anglican gentry idling in splendid Georgian mansions and a Catholic peasantry brooding over immemorial grievances in picturesque squalor. But there is another dimension—the Irish on the Continent. The research upon which this paper is based was undertaken to explore that missing dimension. Presented here is a report on what became a very extensive exploration, offering an overview of the Continental Irish, their characteristics and their way of life. Within the necessary limitations of space, it examines a singularly neglected topic—one that deserves the attention not only of those concerned with the complexities of the Irish experience, but also of scholars investigating the interaction of social groups and the process of cultural transmission.

Lecky, author of the classic *History of Ireland in the Eighteenth Century*, was alluding to France, Spain, Italy and Austria when he wrote: "... it is in these quarters that the real history of the Irish Catholics during the ... eighteenth century is to be traced. At home they had sunk into torpid and degraded pariahs. Abroad, there was scarcely a Catholic country where the Irish exiles or their children might not be found in posts of dignity and power."[1] A pamphleteer of 1792 put it more succinctly: ". . . the mind of Ireland is to be found in a colony of refugees."[2]

The Irish have always been an inquisitive and venturesome race—witness the ninth-century German chronicler who wrote of "the Irish nation, with whom the custom of travelling into foreign parts is now become almost second nature,"[3] and it is undoubtedly true that the flow of Irish refugees to the Continent began in the late sixteenth century and increased significantly in the seventeenth. Yet it was in the hundred years between the Treaty of Limerick and the collapse of the Old Regime that the great exodus took place, and it was in the eighteenth century that the Irish emigrés emerged as a distinct element in European society. During this span of three generations, the greater part of Ireland's natural leadership class lived in exile. The origin and structure of this "colony of refugees" demand analysis.

Why did Irishmen and women leave their homeland in the eighteenth century? Loyalty to the Jacobite cause was the principal motive of the first wave of emigrés. In the conviction that they had lost several battles but not the war, the partisans of James II rallied on the Continent, constituting His Britannic Majesty's army in exile, preserving the red coat and English as the language of command even while passing temporarily into the service of their King's Bourbon allies. Down to mid-century the hope of a Stuart restoration continued to animate the Irish Catholic aristocracy and to attract fresh recruits—the so-called "Wild Geese"—who flew away to join those Irish Brigades abroad from which the Jacobite invasion army would be formed. To this motivation, the imposition of "anti-Popery" legislation at the turn of the century added a longing for religious freedom and individual opportunity. The Penal Laws imposed what Edmund Burke called "penalties and modes of inquisition not fit to be mentioned to ears that are organized to the chaste sounds of equity and justice"[4] upon the vast majority of the Irish population. Catholics were forbidden to acquire land, vote, hold office, seek an education, engage in the professions (including that of arms), keep weapons, or even own a horse. Hence the clergy and the gentry were obliged to go abroad for schooling, and while many of the priests returned to risk imprisonment or martyrdom in the "Irish mission," there was little inducement for others to go home when they might fulfill their aspirations in another land. On the other hand, the Catholics of the towns who prospered in trade and industry—the only sphere left open to ambition at home—often did so through overseas contacts, and sent younger sons to promote the family's business interests on the Continent. These upper and middle class elements in the emigration were reinforced by the large number of discharged Jacobite soldiers and sailors who found humbler occupations in civilian life abroad.

Where did these exiles settle? The Irish Colleges on the Continent, founded during the sixteenth and seventeenth centuries for the training of priests, provided the nuclei for the initial colonies. They included some thirty institutions, the most important being those at Douai, Alcalá, Salamanca, Lisbon, Bordeaux, Paris, Santiago, Louvain, Lille, Rome, Madrid, Antwerp, Toulouse, Poitiers and Nantes. In addition, the Irish Francisan seminaries at Prague, Capranica, and Boulay in the Duchy of Lorraine were significant rallying points for the Irish abroad. Most of these, while essentially clerical in character, welcomed lay students for secondary or even advanced schooling. Although there were no specifically Irish religious houses for women overseas, there were numerous convents in France, Spain and Belgium where a contingent of Irish nuns or the presence of an Irish abbess led them to welcome Irish girls, either as novices or pupils.[5] Irishmen seeking medical training congregated at the universities of Prague, Rouen and Montpellier. The influx of Irish soldiers and sailors made the capitals and the principal garrison towns and seaports important rendezvous, and a "Street of the Irish" dating from this period can be found in Paris, Madrid, Prague, and several other cities. Certain commercial centers, especially those serving the seaborne trade, attracted large numbers of Irish merchants. Nantes and Bordeaux had the largest Irish communities, though Rouen and St. Malo received their share of settlers. In Spain, Seville and Cadiz were thronged with Irish exiles, while in Italy Naples and Parma drew Irish swordsmen and their families. The Belgian provinces, newly transferred from Spanish to Austrian rule, had their Irish colonies at Brussels and Antwerp. France was undoubtedly the favorite "new land" of Irish emigrants—"the asylum of our poor fugitives," an Irish scholar wrote near the end of the century, "for seventy years past."[6] But the establishment of a common dynasty in both France and Spain had put an end to the dilemma of earlier Irish refugees, who had been obliged to choose irrevocably between one or the other of the hostile Catholic powers. Now Spain, and the later Bourbon acquisitions of Naples and Parma, were linked to France in a "Family Compact," and the Irish moved freely and frequently among the civil and military services of the allied states. The Habsburgs still claimed the allegiance of many Irishmen who were prepared to travel farther afield, while even in non-Catholic countries occasional Irish families were to be met with, such as the Lacys and O'Rourkes in Russia, the O'Reillys in Hessen-Kassel, and the O'Briens (O'Breens) in Holland.[7]

What careers did the Irish on the Continent pursue? Lecky provides some notable examples:

> Lord Clare became Marshal of France. Browne, who as one of the very ablest Austrian generals, and who took a leading part in the first period of the Seven Years' War, was the son of Irish parents; and Maguire, Lacy, Nugent, and O'Donnell were all prominent generals in the Austrian service during the same war. Another Browne, a cousin of the Austrian commander, was Field Marshal in the Russian service and Governor of Riga. Peter Lacy, who also became a Russian Field Marshal and who earned the reputation of one of the first soldiers of his time, was of Irish birth . . . He sprang from an Irish family which had the rare fortune of counting generals in the services . . . of Austria, Russia and Spain. Of the Dillons, more than one attained high rank in the French army, and one became Archbishop of Toulouse. The brave, the impetuous Lally of Tollendal, who served with such distinction at Dettingen and Fontenoy, and who for a time seriously threatened

the English power in Hinustan, was the son of a Galway gentleman. Among Spanish generals, the names of O'Mahony, O'Donnell, O'Gara, O'Reilly and O'Neil sufficiently attest their nationality. . . . Wall, who directed the government of Spain with singular ability from 1754 to 1763, was an Irishman . . . by parentage. MacGeoghegan, the first considerable historian of Ireland, was chaplain to the Irish Brigade in the service of France. The physician of Sobieski, King of Poland, and the physician of Philip V of Spain were both Irish; an Irish naturalist named Bowles was active in reviving the mining industry of Spain in 1752. . . . In the diplomacy of the Continent Irish names are not unknown. Tyrconnel was French Ambassador at the Court of Berlin. Wall, before he became chief minister of Spain, had represented that country at the Court of London. Lacy was Spanish Ambassador at Stockholm, and O'Mahony at Vienna.[8]

Service in the armed forces of the Continental princes was undoubtedly the route by which the majority of Irishmen made the transition from the old country to the new. Even after the massive reduction in troop strength following the Treaty of Utrecht, France retained five regiments in its Irish Brigade and Spain three, with a fourth Spanish regiment transferring to the Neapolitan establishment in 1740. Although there were no Irish units as such in the Austrian forces, hundreds of Irish officers held commissions under the Emperor. In all of these realms, the profession of arms, to which the Irish gentry turned almost instinctively, was the avenue to the titles and rewards, civil as well as military, that their religion denied them at home. Of the fifty-four patents of nobility conferred upon Irishmen in France down to the Revolution, the majority were earned by military or naval prowess, and the record is comparable elsewhere.[9] Count Taaffe, Chancellor to the Duke of Lorraine, Count Wall, Foreign Minister to the King of Spain, and Baron O'Connell, Chamberlain to the Holy Roman Emperor, among other statesmen, all started out as fighting men. For "other ranks," the evidence is less abundant. Many enlisted men seem to have spent their entire working lives in the army or navy and to have raised their sons to follow in their footsteps. Others, procuring their discharge, turned to a variety of trades, though two commoners who emerge from historical obscurity were both shoemakers: Joseph Kavanagh, a leader of the attack on the Bastille (where two of the seven prisoners were Irishmen) and later a police inspector under the Terror, and Daniel Murphy, whose daughter, Marie Louise, became mistress of Louis XV and mother of an Irish-Bourbon daughter.[10]

The merchants and bankers of the great Continental seaports also formed an important component of the Irish abroad. "From the time of the early confiscations . . . many of the dispossessed Catholic landowners drifted into the cities and towns" of Ireland and "there applied themselves to trade."[11] The mercantile element in Ireland was thus in part composed of families having ties to the Catholic landed gentry and to the émigré families abroad. These merchants, in turn, often found it expedient to send younger sons to the Continent, not to be soldiers but to be businessmen. The Blakes of Seville, the Coppingers of Bordeaux, and the Fitzgibbons, Kellys and Moores who settled at Lisbon, Bilbao and Alicante were all branches of this Irish mercantile elite. Certain fields of business in particular seem to have attracted the Irish: in Spain the Wisemans of Seville, the O'Neales of Jerez, and the Lynchs of Cadiz were wine merchants, and in France the Byrnes and O'Quinns of Bordeaux followed a similar trade, while Richard Hennessy founded the distillery in Cognac that still bears his name. Both Anthony Walsh of Nantes and Walter Rutledge of Dunkirk became wealthy from West Indies privateering, and the Clarkes and Shiels of Nantes were great shipowners as well, operating half the vessels of that port engaged in the lucrative slave trade.[12] As early as 1718, Irish shipowners in the Low Countries took a leading part in planning the Ostend East India Company, and the advice of men like Count O'Gara of Brussels and General Plunkett, Governor of Antwerp, was eagerly welcomed by the Habsburgs. Throughout the eighteenth century many Irish families were involved in banking in France, including the Quains, Woulfes, Darcys, and Arthurs; George Waters of Paris was the confidential agent and banker of the Stuarts and the chief financial supporter of the Jacobite Rising of 1745.[13]

During the Penal Era, and in defiance of the prohibitions against seeking education abroad, the Catholic clergy of Ireland received its training on the Continent. Each year, graduates of the Irish Colleges would return to their native land via the same clandestine route by which they had left it. Fully half the priests of eighteenth-century Ireland were educated in France, with Spain, Portugal, and the Low Countries providing most of the rest; even the College in far-away Prague produced 115 alumni (including two future bishops) in the last three decades before the anti-clerical Joseph II closed it in 1783.[14] A considerable number of Irish students, however, did not return to Ireland—at least, immediately—finding positions as chaplains in noble households or in the armed forces. Others settled down to parish or monastic life, or found a niche in the Continental hierarchy. Most notable among these prelates was the Franco-Irish ecclesiastical magnate Arthur Richard Dillon, who became, successively, Bishop of Evreux, Archbishop of Toulouse and of Narbonne, and President of the States of Languedoc, France's largest province. Irishmen in the influential office of Vicar-General, as Abbé Kearney at Tarbes and Abbé Walsh at Clermont, were not uncommon. Perhaps the most remarkable ecclesiastical career was that of Patrick Curtis, educated in Spain, and a chaplain in her navy during the American Revolutionary War, then rector of the Irish College at Salamanca and Royal Professor of Philosophy and Astronomy at the University there, a friend and helper of the Duke of Wellington (a fellow Dubliner) during the Peninsular War, and then, after an absence of nearly sixty years, appointed Archbishop of Armaagh and Primate of Ireland in time to take an active role in the Catholic Emancipation campaign of the 1820's.[15]

Irishmen distinguished themselves in a variety of professions, particularly medicine: Philip V of Spain and his successors had Irish physicians, as did Louis XIV, XV, and XVI. Dr. John Mac-Mahon, a native of Limerick and graduate of the faculty of medicine at Rouen, acquired the title of Marquis d'Eguilly and founded a line which included a son who served as Ambassador to the United States and a grandson who became President of France.

Irish scholars in France and Spain attained distinction in the more controversial aspects of philosophy and theology, both as university professors and writers. While Dr. Brady of Lisbon and Dr. Birmingham of Salamanca were credited with reviving Greek studies in Iberia, Richard Cantillon, the Paris banker from Ballyheigue, author of the "Essai sur la nature du commerce en général" has been called "the father of political economy," and Bernard Ward, economic reformer and minister of commerce, was one of the outstanding figures of the Spanish Enlightenment.[16] The economist Ward belonged to a dazzling constellation of Irishmen who strove to achieve administrative and fiscal modernization in Spain. It included William Bowles, geologist, naturalist and royal counselor, Alfonso O'Crouley, geographer and historian, Bernardo O'Connor, governor of Barcelona and initiator of social reform, Count Lacy, diplomat and patron of scientists, and the indefatigable Dr. Timoteo O'Scanlan, who introduced vaccination into the country.[17]

To what degree did the Irish on the Continent retain their distinctive identity? Although there was no bar to Irish integration into the host nationalities, and despite the fact that a sizeable minority married outside their own community, the majority of eighteenth-century Irish émigrés seem to have remained firmly committed to a distinctive identity. Congregating in certain cities, marrying their compatriots, and attending by preference their own churches and schools, they remained a breed apart. Even when travelling on the Continent, the Irish liked to break their journeys at the homes of kinsmen, or at least fellow-Irishmen. Some comfortably-situated exiles, such as the abbé Griffin, Canon of the Cathedral of Cambrai, provided what amounted to a hotel and mail-forwarding service for their wandering brethren.[18] The affluent followed the practice of providing burses, or scholarships, at the Continental colleges for Irish students, sometimes limiting them to particular clans or particular native counties. In many families it was customary to send expectant mothers back to Ireland so that children might be born in the old country though they would be brought up in the new home.[19] Some families preserved distinctively Irish given names through the generations, as did the Kindelans in Spain, who have honored their patron, St. Ultan, by christening the eldest son Ultano down to the present. The Continental Irish customarily used English within their own community, and were regularly employed as interpreters, intelligence officers, and envoys during the wars and negotiations of the era. Major O'Reilly of the Hessian army, for instance, acted as Provost Marshal of New York during the British occupation, because he could communicate with equal facility with British and German troops; General O'Donojú served as Spanish liaison officer with Wellington during the Peninsular War. Most families also passed on a knowledge of Gaelic to the younger generation: the six O'Donnell brothers, who won distinction in the Napoleonic struggle, though born in Spain were all fluent Gaelic-speakers. The ancestral tongue was used in everyday conversation by the rank and file of the Irish Brigades, at least through mid-century.[20]

The most striking manifestation of Irish identity and solidarity on the Continent is their invariable determination to look after their own. Irish officers made frequent trips to the homeland to reinforce the depleted ranks of their regiments. (Those in the service of the Bourbon princes, who were usually at war with Britain, did so secretly, and at peril of their lives; neutral and friendly states, like Austria, were generally given tacit permission to seek volunteers.) In seeking out and sponsoring cadets of Catholic gentry stock, some senior officers, like Count Daniel O'Connell of the French army, were virtual one-man recruiting bureaus, and his concern for the advancement of his kinsman and fellow-Kerrymen was characteristic of the Irish abroad. Well-placed Irishmen in the military, government, and business were ever alert to procure places and opportunities for their brethren. Ambrose O'Higgins, for instance, who came to Spain originally as an apprentice in a banking house, procured a commission in the royal engineers through the influence of Colonel John Garland, who also got him started on a career in South America that culminated in his becoming Viceroy of Peru, the highest-ranking position in the colonial service. O'Higgins, in turn, brought his nephews over from Ireland and appointed them to provincial governorships and military commands; his son, Bernardo, became, of course, the founder of the Chilean Republic.[21]

Florida was another happy-hunting-ground for Irishmen in search of advancement: the Hibernia Regiment captured Pensacola in 1782, its colonel, Arturo O'Neill was appointed governor, and four other "Wild Geese" ruled East and West Florida in succession. American frontier provinces were usually placed under the direction of army officers, and the Irish in Madrid proved adept at securing these governorships for kinsmen such as Hugh O'Connor in Texas, Philip Barry in Nueva Vizcaya, and Charles Murphy in Paraguay. The Irish were able to win special residential privileges in Puerto Rico in 1775, and they rapidly engrossed a large share of the island's commerce. Julio and Enrique O'Neill, brothers of the Governor of Florida, and Miguel Conboy became leading businessmen, while John Kennedy controlled the slave trade. They acknowledged the primacy, however, of the O'Dalys. Colonel Thomas O'Daly had been named chief engineer of the insular fortifications by Inspector-General Alexander O'Reilly, and his brother James created Puerto Rico's first export company in 1786, shipping tobacco to Holland from his plantation, which he named San Patricio. James O'Daly's son, Demetrio, gained the rank of general in the Napoleonic campaigns and later represented Puerto Rico in the Spanish Parliament.[22] The Irish, for all their demonstrated loyalty to their adopted countries, clearly preferred to have their own kind about them, and to fill up the jobs at their disposal with their relatives. Nepotism was deemed a virtue. Colonel Henry O'Shea, for example, military secretary to the Duke of Orléans, procured a commission for his nephew, Henry Clarke, from the Duke and the latter acted as the young man's patron until the Revolution, during which Clarke became successively a general, Minister of War, and Duke of Feltre in the Imperial nobility; Clarke, in his turn, obtained for *his* nephew, Andrew Elliott, a colonelcy and the post of aide-de-camp to Bonaparte. [23] Regimental commands in the Irish Brigades were handed down from father to son, and choice commissions were reserved for the colonel's clansmen—whence the numerous generals and colonels bearing the surnames of such powerful houses as Dillon and Walsh. The large number of admirals and naval bureaucrats named MacNamara in France and MacDonnell in Spain testifies to the prevalence of similar practices in the sister service.[24] The existence of virtual dynasties like the Comyns and O'Reillys in medicine and the houses of Cantillon and Waters in banking confirms that the system was followed in civilian circles as well.[25] Nor were national boundaries a consideration: the influence of Wall and O'Reilly in Spain secured the importation of the Irish economists Ward and Bowles from France. John Vincent Dillon, of the Neapolitan branch of that family, transferred to the French army as chief engineer for the construction of the Seine bridges.[26] Many officers moved through three or four different countries in search of advancement, usually following the summons of some relative or friend who had paved the way for them. A network of communication and collaboration extended across the Continent— one almost expects to find complaints about an "international Irish conspiracy."

The Irish abroad, then, preserved a vigorous social self-consciousness. But what was their attitude towards Ireland itself? Among the exiles as a whole, the preservation of tradition was supplemented by correspondence and visits, often clandestine, through which they maintained their ties with those left behind and with the scenes of their youth. Not infrequently youngsters born abroad were sent for a brief sojourn with kinsfolk in Ireland, and there are many instances of foreign-born Irish who had reached maturity without making such a trip seeking the opportunity "as the Muslim yearns for Mecca."[27] News from Ireland was closely followed through the press and through private informants. Erin's past, present, and future were matters of interest and concern. Literary men among the overseas Irish demonstrated their preoccupation with such volumes as the *History of Ireland, Ancient and Modern* by the *abbé* MacGeoghegan, the *Elements of the Irish Language* by Hugh MacCurtin (who also published an Irish-English dictionary and a book on the antiquities of Ireland),

Nomenclatura Hibernica by Hervy Morres, and the Marquis de Lally-Tollendal's *Tuathal-Teamar, or the Restoration of the Monarchy in Ireland*.[28] On a different level, there were gatherings of the sort described in the *Annual Register* under the heading for March 1767:

> On the 17th of this month his Excellency, Count Mahony, Ambassador from Spain to the Court of Vienna, gave a grand entertainment in honour of St. Patrick, to which were invited persons of condition, that were of Irish descent; being himself a descendant of an illustrious family of that kingdom. Among many others were present Count Lacy, President of the Council of War, the Generals O'Donnel, McGuire, O'Kelly, Browne, Plunket and McEligot, 4 Chiefs of the Grand Cross, 2 Governors, several Knights Military, 6 staff officers, 4 Privy Councillors, with the principal officers of state; who, to show their respect for the Irish nation, wore crosses in honour of the day, as did the whole Court.[29]

For some exiles there was a lasting bitterness, a desire for revenge: General O'Reilly longed to lead a Spanish invasion army to Ireland and strike down the Protestant cousins who had usurped his patrimony; exiles in France produced invasion plans each time during the century that France went to war with England.[30] For others, there was the hope that an enlightened toleration might prevail, and that one day they or their children might be accorded the full rights of free men, so that they could return to Ireland and live as contented and loyal subjects. In 1778 Count Daniel O'Connell wrote from Paris to his brother in Ireland, commenting on recent partial measures of "Catholic Relief":

> Your publick Papers have transmitted here the pleasing account of the New Laws in favour of the Roman Catholicks. A Revolution so unexpected and so long wished for must needs procure, in course of some years, an accession to the power and prosperity of the Kingdom of Ireland, and unite in one common sentiment of loyalty the hearts of that long-oppress'd and long unfortunate Nation. One step more still remains to be made—I mean the Liberty of spilling their blood in defence of their King and Country. I doubt not 'twill soon be granted, tho' no motive

could ever induce me to bear arms against France, where I early found an Asylum when refused one at home. I still wish the prosperity of the country, and at the same time that I pursue with inviolable fidelity that of my adopted King, Nature, stronger than reason or principle, still attaches my heart to Ireland.[31]

The second half of the eighteenth century was a time of change for the Irish communities abroad. Following the Jacobite disaster at Culloden (where a contingent of the Franco-Irish Brigade stood and died covering the retreat of Prince Charles Edward), the prospects of a Stuart restoration languished, and the unifying force which the dynasty represented faded away. On the death of James III in 1766, the Pope refused to recognize his son as king, and the appointments to Irish episcopal sees, which had hitherto been made on the nomination of the Pretender, became a purely papal concern.[32] The frustrated and increasingly dissolute Prince Charlie ceased to extend the patronage that his father had always granted the Irish exiles, and gradually lost their loyalty and even their interest. The decline of Jacobitism was paralleled by a falling-off of recruiting in Ireland. The unjust condemnation and execution of the Irish hero Count Lally, after his defeat in India, was a further blow to morale, and even his posthumous rehabilitation—won by his son with Voltaire's crusading aid—did not cancel out the impression of royal ingratitude, or restore the flow of recruits. The Irish Brigades of France and Spain were presently filled up by a rank and file who were predominantly non-Irish, though the officers, to the last, remained Irish-born or descended.[33] During these years the growing disinclination of the Irish peasantry to enlist for foreign service, and a tendency of the lower social class to integrate more readily and more thoroughly into the host population, served to emphasize the elite character of the Irish communities abroad. Irishmen continued to seek their fortunes on the Continent, but they were usually young gentlemen who expected direct commissions or "junior executive" status.

The year 1793 brought two developments which proved decisive for the fate of the Irish on the Continent—the downfall of the French monarchy and the passage of the Catholic Relief Bill. The former led to a general European war and two decades of political anarchy. The latter opened a wide range of civil and military offices to the Irish Catholic gentry and permitted them to carve out careers in their own country.

Most of the Irish in France remained loyal to the unfortunate Louis XVI—indeed, it was the *abbé* Henry Edgeworth who gave him the last consolations of religion on the scaffold—and they frequently paid the supreme penalty for their identification with the Bourbons. The abolition of the Irish Brigade as "the mercenary instrument of monarchical tyranny" drove many Franco-Irish officers into a new exile. Some, like Count Daniel O'Connell or Colonel Edward Stack, who had fought against George III in the American War, now received commissions from a belatedly tolerant British Government and raised regiments among the Catholics of Ireland to fight for that same king. Others, like Colonel Brian O'Toole, who commanded successively Germans, Corsicans, and Portugese, drifted from one country to another.[34] Those Irish generals who tried to survive the transition to a French Republic were regarded with suspicion: "He is an Irishman," wrote a police official about one victim of the Terror, "and they can't get Republicanism into their skulls." Ward, O'Moran, and Arthur Dillon all died under the guillotine's blade, Theobald Dillon was murdered by his own troops, and Admiral Henry MacNamara was lynched by a mob. But some younger men, like Harty, Kilmaine, Blackwell, and the O'Meara brothers, flourished with the New Order. Robert Arthur, Jacobin and member of the Commune, won the nickname of "Little Robespierre" by his revolutionary zeal, and Jean Baptiste O'Sullivan conscientiously inflicted his own Reign of Terror upon Nantes.[35]

Spain, too, was divided by the spreading Revolution, with General O'Donojú heading the loyalist War Ministry at Cadiz while General O'Farril served King Joseph Bonaparte as War Minister at Madrid—the one supported by Irishmen like Generals Blake and Sarsfield, the other by men like General Vincent Kindelan. Some, like General Luis de Lacy, fought in turn on both sides. Similar dislocation and confusion beset the Irish in Italy and the Low

Countries. Like many other European institutions, the Irish "nation in exile" was shattered by the earthquake of Revolution.[36]

For the Continental Irish, a way of life had come to an end. The abolition of "foreign" regiments in one country after another ended their distinctive military role, and while many families continued to follow the profession of arms during the nineteenth century, they did so as individuals, without the old esprit de corps. The Irish radicals who fled to France after the collapse of the French-sponsored Irish rebellion in 1798 were never really accepted by the surviving old regime families, and for the most part did not mingle with them. The growth of opportunities for the Catholic gentry at home, especially after Emancipation in 1829 removed the remaining disabilities, made emigration unnecessary, while for the poorer classes the gold-paved streets of the United States and the dominions proved more enticing. Maynooth now provided the priests for the Irish Catholic Church. Mercantile ties with the Continent were not renewed after the war. Without the stimulus of new arrivals and the inspiration of unfulfilled dreams, the Irish on the Continent gradually lost their identity, marrying outside their nationality group, spreading beyond their traditional centers, abandoning their cultural heritage and both their languages. In time they became merely Frenchmen, Spaniards, or Austrians with incongruous last names, having only the vaguest notion of what brought their ancestors to alien shores and sustained them in their adversity.

The history of the Irish people in the eighteenth century can be fully understood only in a European context. To talk about Ireland solely in terms of its relationship with England is no more profitable than to discuss the so-called "Irish Question" of the nineteenth century as if it were purely a British constitutional problem. In both centuries the Irish overseas constitute a dimension essential for a complete picture. Within the past few years scholars have begun to recognize that nineteenth-century Irish history must be interpreted within a broader framework.[37] But recent historians of Ireland's eighteenth century have not heeded Lecky's suggestion as to where the "real history of the Irish

Catholics" is to be found. Sir Herbert Butterfield's 1970 essay on the historiography of eighteenth-century Ireland relegates the Continental Irish to a brief footnote.[38] The two latest aspirants to Lecky's crown devote a bare two pages of familiar generalizations apiece to the topic.[39] Aside from a few monographs already cited and a handful of articles (mostly on military matters), there has been no serious work in the field; seekers of dissertation topics have apparently sought elsewhere.[41] This neglect may be attributable to the complexity of the subject and to the wide dispersal of the sources; certainly those historians who acknowledge the importance of research in this area seem to regard it as a task for someone else.[42]

The fact remains that the Irish on the Continent were not a separate race, but a part of the Irish people and Irish history; they are, to reiterate, the missing dimension in that history. Furthermore, they are a part of Europe's history, integrating Ireland into Europe indepently of the British connection. As a European phenomenon, the Continental Irish offer much of interest to students of eighteenth-century social, cultural, and religious history. Here we have a network of communications and kinship spreading over Europe, linking the Irish in France, Spain, Austria, and beyond with one another and with Ireland. Here we have emigrés forming their own interlocking system of schools, churches, businesses, military units and professional ties, based on family bonds and a common national origin. Here we have, in each of the major countries, a body of resident aliens, guarding its distinctive language and traditions, reinforcing its numbers by recruitment from a homeland with which they retain the most intimate ties, and yet winning a notable degree of social and political power in the host countries. Here we have an intricate pattern of nepotism and patronage transcending frontiers and even oceans to encompass the colonial as well as the metropolitan positions of authority. Here we have generational and ideological conflict, developing as Jacobite loyalties die, the intellectual currents of a new era exert their appeal, and committments based on national allegiance rather than monarchical largesse divide the Irish communities. No other European ethnic group (except, perhaps, the Jews) underwent a comparable experience in the eighteenth century.

The "Wild Geese" readily captured the fancy of their contemporaries. Writers as varied as Lesage and Montesquieu alluded to the distinctive traits of "les Irlandais"; Boswell noted that "the Irish have ever been, and still continue to be, highly regarded upon the Continent," and Swift declared: "I cannot but esteem those gentlemen of Ireland who, with all the disadvantages of being exiles and strangers, have been able to distinguish themselves by their valour and conduct in so many parts of Europe above all other nations."[43] It is ironic that few of those who today talk knowingly of the eighteenth century seem to be aware of their having ever existed.

NOTES

1 W. E. H. Lecky, *A History of Ireland in the Eighteenth Century*, new edition (London: Longmans, Green, 1902), I, 248.

2 Anon., *A Review of the Strictures on the Declaration of the Catholic Society* (Dublin: Walker, 1792), p. 8.

3 Quoted in Tomas O Fiaich, *Irish Cultural Influence in Europe, Sixth to Twelfth Century* (Cork: Mercier, 1971), p. 3.

4 Edmund Burke, "Letter to a Peer of Ireland," in *Writings and Speeches of Edmund Burke* . . . (Boston: Little, Brown, 1901), IV, 233–34; John Brady and Patrick J. Corish, "The Church under the Penal Code," in *A History of Irish Catholicism*, ed. Patrick J. Corish (Dublin: Gill, 1971), vol. IV, pt. 2, pp. 2–6.

5 Cathaldus Giblin, "Irish Exiles in Catholic Europe," ibid., vol. IV, pt. 3, pp. 3, 54.

6 C. O'Conor to E. Curry, Dec. 25, 17____[sic], in Historical Manuscripts Commission, *Eighth Report: Appendix, Part 1 (O'Conor Manuscripts)* (London: Stationery Office, 1881), p. 464.

7 The manuscript sources for the history of the Irish on the Continent are widely scattered. The principal collections to which reference will be made in this paper are the Archives Nationales (AN), Archives de la Guerre (AG), Archives de la Marine (AM), and Bibliothèque National

(BN) in France, the Archivo Historico Nacional (AHN) and Archivo General de Simancas (SAG), in Spain, the Archivio di Stato of the Kingdom of Naples (NAS) in Italy, and the Royal Irish Academy (RIA) and National Library of Ireland (NLI). For the Irish in France, see Richard Hayes, *Biographical Dictionary of Irishmen in France* (Dublin: Gill, 1949) (hereafter cited as Hayes), and Canice Mooney, *Irish Franciscans and France* (Dublin: Clonmore and Reynolds, 1964). For those in other lands, see Maurice Hennessy, *The Wild Geese: The Irish Soldier in Exile* (London: Sidgwick and Jackson, 1973), and Christopher Duffy, *The Wild Goose and the Eagle: A Life of Marshal von Browne, 1705–1757* (London: Chatto and Windus, 1964).

8 Lecky, *History of Ireland*, I, 250–51.

9 AG: historiques/anciennes: t. 3084, 3090; BN: Collection d'Hozier: Dossiers bleus-1, 3, 4, 7; SAG: Guerra moderna, leg. 2588, 2590; NAS: Sezione militare: Guerra e marina (Lib. di Vita e Cost.) 792; RIA: McSwiney Papers, Box 6 (papers relating to Irishmen in the service of the Dukes of Parma); M. de Woelmont de Brumagne, *La Noblesse française subsistante* (Paris: Lagrange, 1928), passim. For Spain, see Micheline Walsh, ed., *Spanish Knights of Irish Origin*, 3 vols. (Dublin: Irish Manuscripts Commission, 1960–70).

10 AN: sér. F. 7, car. 4775; Hayes, pp. 132–33, 206–7.

11 Maureen Wall, "The Rise of a Catholic Middle Class in Eighteenth-Century Ireland," *Irish Historical Studies*, 11 (1958), 104.

12 Richard Hayes, *Old Irish Links with France* (Dublin: Gill, 1946), pp. 12–21: Marquis McSwiney, *An Irish Trade Venture in the Eighteenth Century* (Cork: Browne and Nolan, 1932), pp. 9–11; NLI: MS 826 (Bellew Papers) contains many references to Irish mercantile enterprises on the Continent.

13 Hayes, *Old Irish Links*, p. 315; Charles Petrie, *The Jacobite Movement: The Last Phase, 1716–1807* (London: Eyre and Spottiswoode, 1950), pp. 59–66. For earlier Irish activities in Belgium, see Brendan Jennings, *Wild Geese in Spanish Flanders, 1582–1700* (Dublin: Irish Manuscripts Commission, 1964).

14 Historical Manuscripts Commission, *Report on Stuart Manuscripts* (London: Stationery Office, 1902), I, 351; Patrick Boyle, "Glimpses of Irish Collegiate Life in Paris in the Seventeenth and Eighteenth Century," *Irish Ecclesiastical Record*, 11 (1902), 482; Brendan Jennings, "The Irish Franciscans in Prague," *Studies*, 28 (1939), 221–22.

15 AN: sér. H. 5, M. 147; William McDonald, "Irish Colleges Since the Reformation," *Irish Ecclesiastical Record*, 9 (1872–73), 139–41; A. Mathorez, "Notes sur les prêtres irlandais refugiés à Nantes aux XVIIe et XVIIIe siècles," *Revue d'histoire de l'église de France*, 3 (1912), 169–72.

16 Hayes, *Old Irish Links*, pp. 25, 185; P. Lopez, "Notas de bibliografia franciscana," *Archivo Ibero-Americano*, 2 (1942), 455–62; Jean Sarrailh, *La España ilustrada de la segunda mitad del siglo XVIII* (Mexico City: Fondo de Cultura Economica, 1957), pp. 40–42.

17 Sarrailh, *España ilustrada*, pp. 46–48, 53, 82, 127, 362. See also A. O'Crouley, *The Kingdom of New Spain*, trans. and ed. Sean Galvin (Dublin: Allen Figgis, 1972); B. Ward, *Proyecto economico . . .* (Madrid: Ramirez, 1762); W. Bowles, *Introducion a la historia natural . . .* (Madrid: Alvarez, 1792); T. O'Scanlan, *Ensayo apologetico de inocculacion . . .* (Madrid: Alvarez, 1792).

18 Edward MacLysaght, ed., *The Kenmare Manuscripts* (Dublin: Irish Manuscripts Commission, 1942), pp. 87–91.

19 RIA: MS 12N, 13–14 and MS 24D.9, 1039; J. C. O'Callaghan, *The History of the Irish Brigades in the Service of France* (Glasgow: Cameron and Ferguson, 1885), pp. 27, 58.

20 SAG: Guerra moderna, leg.2565,2568; R. R. O'Cochlain, "Leopold O'Donnell . . . ," *The Irish Sword*, 7 (1966), 183; Wiliam D. Griffin, "A Hessian O'Reilly," *The Irish Sword*, 9 (1970), 244. There are numerous articles on eighteenth-century Irish military and naval service on the Continent scattered throughout the volumes of *The Irish Sword*—the journal of the Military History Society of Ireland.

21 John Brady, *Catholics and Catholicism in the Eighteenth-Century Press* (Maynooth: Catholic Record Society of Ireland, 1965), pp. 32, 35, 311–13; M. O'Connell, *The Last Colonel of the Irish Brigade: Count O'Connell and Old Irish Life at Home and Abroad, 1754–1833*, 2 vols. (London: Kegan Paul, 1892), passim; Brian de Breffny, "Ambrose O'Higgins: An Enquiry into His Origins and Ancestry," *The Irish Ancestor*, 1 (1970), 82–89.

22 W. S. Murphy, "An Irish Regiment in Mexico," *The Irish Sword*, 2 (1956), 258–63; T. J. Mullen, "The Hibernia Regiment of the Spanish Army," *The Irish Sword*, 8 (1868), 218–23; Arturo Morales-Carrión, *Puerto Rico and the Non-Hispanic Caribbean: A Study in the Decline of Spanish Exclusivism* (Rio Piedras, P.R.: University of Puerto Rico, 1971), pp. 126, 128; Albert Mauncy and Ricardo Torres-Reyes, *Puerto Rico and the Forts of Old San Juan* (Chatham, Conn.: Chatham Press, 1973), pp. 63–72.

23 M. de Gonnerville, *Souvenirs militaires* (Paris: Plon, 1895), p. 125.

24 Hayes, *Old Irish Links*, pp. 59–70, 88–89, 305–9; Micheline Walsh, *The MacDonnells of Antrim on the Continent* (Dublin: National University of Ireland, 1960), pp. 3, 24; Micheline Walsh, *The O'Neills in Spain* (Dublin: National University of Ireland, 1957), p. 39.

25 The "dynastic history" of these Irish medical families may be traced in

the Comyn Manuscripts (24B4) and the O'Reilly Manuscripts (24D7) in the RIA.

26 NAS: Sezione militare: Guerra e marina: Reviste antiche, t.340; Sarrailh, p. 293. On the movement across national frontiers, see the collection of documents compiled by Philippe Jean-Baptiste O'Kelly, the Empress Maria Theresa's Chief Herald for the Low Countries, c. 1770, in the John Rylands Library, Manchester (Irish MS 119).

27 O'Connell, *The Last Colonel*, I, 66; Brady, "The Church under the Penal Code," pp. 309, 314. See also the letters relating to the Irish in France in NLI: MS 2552.

28 Giblin, "Irish Exiles," pp. 31–36.

29 *Annual Register . . . 1767* (London: Dodsley, 1768), p. 93.

30 AN: Fonds Guerre, ser.A.1, car.3535 (contains proposals for an invasion of Ireland, including letters from Viscount Clare, 1759). Count O'Hegarty favored setting up Ireland as a separate kingdom under Prince Charles Edward (AM: ser.B 4.82); another plan envisioned selecting a king from among the old Irish nobility (AG: ser. M 1414). See also E. Desbrière, *Projets et tentatives de débarquement aux îles britanniques* (Paris: Plon, 1902), pp. 29, 47–48.

31 Daniel O'Connell to Maurice O'Connell, October 5, 1778, in M. O'Connell, I, 207.

32 Giblin, "Irish Exiles," pp. 50–52.

33 SAG: Guerra moderna, leg.2670; Arthur Dillon, *Historical Notes on the Services of the Irish Officers of the French Army* (Dublin: James Duffy, 1880).

34 O'Connell, *The Last Colonel*, II, 138ff.; Hayes, *Old Irish Links*, pp. 265, 290.

35 For a general view of the Irish involvement in the Revolution, see Richard Hayes, *Ireland and Irishmen in the French Revolution* (London: Ernest Benn, 1932).

36 William D. Griffin, "Irish Generals and Spanish Politics under Fernando VII," *The Irish Sword*, 10 (1971), 1–9.

37 See, for example, Arnold Schrier, *Ireland and the American Emigration, 1850–1900* (Minneapolis: University of Minnesota Press, 1958); Thomas N. Brown, *Irish-American Nationalism, 1870–1890* (Philadelphia: Lippincott, 1966); Alan J. Ward, *Ireland and Anglo-American Relations, 1899–1921* (London: Weidenfeld and Nicolson, 1969).

38 Herbert Butterfield, "Eighteenth-Century Ireland, 1702–1800," in T. W. Moody, ed., *Irish Historiography, 1936–1970* (Dublin: Irish Committee of Historical Sciences, 1971), p. 55.

39 Francis G. James, *Ireland and the Empire, 1699–1770* (Cambridge, Mass: Harvard University Press, 1973), pp. 297–98; Edith M. Johnston, *Ireland*

in the Eighteenth Century (Dublin: Gill and Macmillan, 1974), pp.
22–23. J. C. Beckett, whose *The Making of Modern Ireland, 1603–1923*
(London: Faber and Faber, 1966) has been hailed widely as the best
general history of modern Ireland, has nothing at all to say on the
Continental Irish. The long-talked-about *New History of Ireland*—a massive collaborative enterprise that has experienced the delays usual to such
projects—has allotted a section on the Irish abroad to J. G. Simms, an
historian best known for his work on late seventeenth-century Ireland.

40 Articles of more than limited interest include R. J. Hayes, "Irish Historical Sources in Foreign Archives," *Archivalische Zeitschrift*, 5 (1955),
235–45, and Dorothy Molloy, "In Search of the Wild Geese," *Eire-
Ireland*, 5, no. 3 (1970), 3–14.

41 The annual lists of "Research on Irish History in Irish Universities"
published in *Irish Historical Studies* reveal no dissertations in this field
during the past two decades. Comparable guides to research in the
United States, Britain, and Western Europe confirm this neglect.

42 Within the past decade a beginning has at least been made in locating,
identifying, and copying the manuscript remains of this lost dimension of
eighteenth-century Irish life. The National Library of Ireland, the Irish
Manuscripts Commission, and the National University of Ireland have all
taken a hand in producing guides to Continental sources—the most
important being R. J. Hayes, ed., *Sources for the History of Irish
Civilization*, 11 vols. (Boston: G. K. Hall, 1965). University College,
Dublin, has assembled at its Belgrove Archives a collection of microfilms
and transcripts (mostly from Spain) that promises to facilitate preliminary research. The volumes by Jennings and Walsh, previously cited,
though on circumscribed topics, are notable fruits of this new activity.
The author of the present paper is gathering materials for a comprehensive history of the Irish on the Continent in the eighteenth century.

43 Lesage, *Gil Blas*, ed. C. de Chateauneuf (Paris: Dupont, 1825), I, 7;
Montesquieu, *Lettres persanes*, ed. A. Adam (Geneva: Droz, 1965), p. 95;
J. Boswell, *An Account of Corsica* (London: Dilly, 1769), p. 18; Swift is
quoted in R. Hayes, *Ireland and Irishmen*, p. 4.

Daniel O'Connell
and the Irish Eighteenth
Century

MAURICE R. O'CONNELL

Much has been written on Daniel O'Connell, but no historian has tried to set him against his background in eighteenth-century Ireland. A serious examination has been made of his views on the Gaelic language as he found it in his early years, and some attention, however inadequate, has been paid to the origins of his attitude to violence. But other aspects of his relationship to the Ireland of his youth have scarcely been studied at all. These include his loyalty to the British crown, his veneration for Grattan and "Grattan's Parliament," his early associations in the legal profession, his attitude to the Irish Protestant Ascendancy and his views on separation of church and state.

The present writer has edited O'Connell's correspondence, which is in the process of publication.[1] This project has brought new sources to light and has made it necessary to investigate much old and half-forgotten material. The information obtained has made it appropriate to attempt this study of O'Connell against his environment in eighteenth-century Ireland.

On his attitude to the Gaelic language it is not necessary to dwell for long, because the subject has been dealt with very effectively by the late Professor Gerard Murphy in his article "The Gaelic Background."[2] Murphy sees O'Connell allowing the Irish language to pass out of use partly because of his utilitarianism and partly because the Gaelic culture was in decay: the language had come to be regarded by the Catholic gentry as little more than a patois. The culture belonged to a former aristocratic world and was now politically archaic. It had little in any direct way to offer a subject people seeking to better themselves and forced to compete in the economically and politically advanced English-speaking world. Murphy considers the choice before O'Connell a difficult one: whether to make a herculean effort to re-Gaelicize the country and achieve, perhaps, only some form of bilingualism, or to accept the supremacy of the English language and all that that acceptance would involve. He regrets that O'Connell chose the latter course but concludes that, given the utilitarian bent of his mind and the current state of the Gaelic language and culture, the choice was a natural one.

There is one qualification which might be made of Murphy's appraisal. It arises from the fact that O'Connell was deeply influenced by the Enlightenment and shared its concentration on the universal at the expense of the local and the particular. He did not have that lively interest in the cultural tradition of his own people which the Romantic movement was to give to most European nationalists in the nineteenth century. This negative factor must be added to the two considerations already described—his utilitarianism and the backward state of the Gaelic culture—which induced O'Connell to prefer English as the medium of communication for the new Ireland.

The aspect of O'Connell that is perhaps the most relevant to Ireland today is his espousal of moral force and constitutional methods and his hostility to violence. Nearly all his biographers have pointed to his schoolboy experience of the French Revolution as a major determining factor in the development of his views on violence. Yet there is little evidence to support so definite a conclusion. Were it true, one would have to explain why he was so soon—by 1796—to abandon his Catholicism in favor of rationalism, to read much radical literature and to express the most decided approval of Paine's *Age of Reason* and Godwin's *Political Justice*.[3] This was strange behavior for a young man who, it is alleged, had suffered a traumatic experience in France only four years earlier. In later life he was to express his disgust with the violence of the French Revolution, but such statements were merely what one would expect from any man who disliked violence intensely. There is far greater reason for holding that O'Connell owed his life-long aversion to violence to his experience of conditions in Ireland and to what he saw of the Rebellion of 1798. The evidence for this will now be considered.

The first recorded statement of O'Connell's concern with violence is an entry in his journal for December, 1796. In the previous week a French invasion fleet had moored off Bantry Bay on the south-west coast, and though it was to sail away without effecting a landing, its appearance alarmed the whole country. O'Connell set down his reaction to these events in a very significant passage:

> Liberty is in my bosom less a principle than a passion; but I know that the victories of the French would be attended with bad consequences. The Irish are not yet sufficiently enlightened to bear the Sun of Freedom. Freedom would soon dwindle into licentiousness, they would rob, they would murder. The altar of liberty totters when it is cemented only with blood, when it is supported with carcasses.[4]

This comment was all the more significant in that he had been expressing the strongest admiration for Godwin's *Political Justice*, which exhibited a highly optimistic confidence in almost unrestricted individual freedom. Clearly, O'Connell was extremely apprehensive of the likely effects of violence in Ireland. Two years later, shortly after the brutal suppression of the Rebellion of 1798, he wrote:

> I dined this day with [Richard Newton] Bennett. We talked much of the late unhappy rebellion. A great deal of innocent blood was shed. Good God, what a brute man becomes when

ignorant and oppressed. O Liberty, what horrors are committed in thy name! May every virtuous revolutionist remember the horrors of Wexford![5]

Again, O'Connell's tendency to link the evils of violence to the Irish scene is illustrated by an "Address to the People" which he drafted for a Catholic meeting in Dublin in 1813. In this document he called on the people to abstain from membership of illegal secret societies, and he went on to say,

> Reflect, also, upon the inutility of these associations. What utility—what advantage of any description has ever been derived from them? None—none whatsoever! No redress has ever been obtained by their means. They have been quite useless! Nay, worse, they have always produced crimes!—robbery, outrage, murder!!![6]

All this does not mean that O'Connell's experience of the French Revolution left him indifferent to its violence. It is merely contended that that experience did not have the traumatic effect that historians have too readily seen; and it is further contended that his aversion to violence owed much more to his appraisal of the Irish environment than to what he witnessed in France.

There is another aspect of O'Connell which historians have neglected to deal with. It is his unequivocal loyalty to the British Crown. Many in the twentieth century have been puzzled by such a loyalty on the part of this quintessential Irishman. They have felt that he must have lacked a full sense of independence or that he was servile in some curious way. There is no great mystery about the matter to anyone versed in Irish history—O'Connell was the product of his age and social background—but historians have not attempted to give any explanation. They have just stated the fact and left it at that. In order to appreciate O'Connell's attitude one must first consider the historical background to the political loyalty of Irish Catholics of the propertied classes towards the end of the eighteenth century.

Through the centuries after the Norman invasion the people of Ireland, whether of the Pale, the Norman-Irish areas or the Gaelic parts of the country, accepted the English kings as lords of Ireland. No doubt that acceptance in some areas was informed by a spirit of loyalty while in others was based on a passive recognition of the status quo. The Reformation and the complete conquest of the whole country by the Tudors introduced new complications, but the bulk of the Catholic population continued to recognize the sovereignty of the English crown. There were rebellions against English rule—that of Hugh O'Neill at the end of the sixteenth century being the most serious—but these never had the support of the majority of Catholic leaders, clerical or lay. Such rebellions, even when enjoying Spanish or Papal support, could scarcely be regarded as "national movements" in any modern sense.[7]

In the seventeenth century Irish Catholics supported Charles I in the struggle between king and parliament: in the (Catholic) Confederation of Kilkenny they took as their motto, "Pro Deo et Rege."[8] At the time of the Glorious Revolution Catholics fought in large numbers in the army of James II and continued to give their loyalty to the exiled Stuarts into the eighteenth century. The Penal Laws, deriving ultimately from the sixteenth century though mainly enacted in the late seventeenth and early eighteenth centuries, made it difficult for Irish Catholics to recognize the accession of the Hanoverians to the British throne. Debarred from entry to parliament, government service and the professions, and suffering other serious disabilities, they went abroad to take service in Continental armies.

The position of Catholics was complicated and rendered more vulnerable by the fact that the Papacy continued to acknowledge the Stuarts as the legitimate sovereigns until the death of James III in 1766. This recognition involved allowing the Stuarts the right of nominating to Irish bishoprics. It bore heavily on Catholics, since it laid them open to the charge of political disloyalty and served as an argument in favor of the retention of the Penal Laws. By the death of James III, however, it was clear that all hope of a Stuart restoration to the British throne was gone, and the Papacy refrained from acknowledging the claims of his son, Charles III

(Bonnie Prince Charlie). The way now lay open for Irish Catholics to come to terms with the House of Hanover, that is, to give their explicit loyalty to George III and seek relief from the Penal Laws.

Realizing that there could be no hope of having these laws repealed until Catholics formally declared their loyalty to the British sovereign, the Catholic Committee—a body of landowners and merchants of a loosely representative character—were most anxious that the Irish Parliament should pass an act providing an oath of political allegiance which would enable Catholics to qualify as loyal subjects. In 1774 such an oath was enacted but it contained several phrases—most of them implicitly insulting to the Pope—which many Catholics found unpalatable. A number of prominent laymen and some of the bishops took the oath, but other bishops refused and sought a formal condemnation from Rome. Though expressing strong disapproval of the oath Rome refrained from condemning it. For a time the Committee was deeply divided on the matter, but by 1778 virtually all opposition to the oath was abandoned.[9]

Daniel O'Connell's forebears were among the limited number of Gaelic and Catholic landowning families who survived the turmoil and confiscations of the sixteenth and seventeenth centuries and emerged into the late eighteenth century still in possession of some of their ancestral property. It is almost certain that many of O'Connell's relatives took the 1774 oath, as did the bulk of propertied Catholics. His uncle, the head of the family, Maurice ("Hunting-Cap") O'Connell, must have done so, since he was made a Justice of the Peace on the passing of the Catholic Relief Act of 1793 (the measure which made it possible for Catholics to hold this appointment), and the taking of the oath would have been a prerequisite for this (unpaid) position. One can take it as certain also that the O'Connells, as members of the Catholic propertied classes, saw no difficulty in recognizing George III as King of Ireland as well as Great Britain. O'Connell's great-grandfather, John O'Connell, and many of his other relatives, had fought in the army of James II. On the passing of the first Catholic relief act, that of 1778, O'Connell's uncle, Lt.Col. Daniel Charles O'Connell, showed that he fully recognized the sovereignty of the British Crown over Ireland when he wrote home from France:

> A Revolution so unexpected and so long wished for must needs procure, in course of some years, an accesssion to the power and prosperity of the Kingdom of Ireland, and unite in one common Sentiment of loyalty the hearts of that long-oppressed and long unfortunate Nation. One step more still remains to be made—I mean the Liberty of spilling their blood in defence of their King and Country. I doubt not 'twill soon be granted tho' no motive cu'd ever induce me to bear arms against France, where I early found an Asylum when refused one at home.[10]

Thus it was perfectly natural for a man of O'Connell's family and social background to recognize the sovereignty over Ireland of the English Crown.

But Irishmen in the twentieth century are puzzled not merely because O'Connell recognized the Crown but also because he did it so exuberantly. Again, there is no mystery. Throughout his public life he was constantly accused of being disloyal to the British connection, so that he was obliged to proclaim his loyalty to the Crown frequently and loudly. Then there was the fact that he was committed to leading his people away from lawlessness and into constitutional paths. It would help that purpose considerably if he could awaken in his followers a lively sentiment of veneration for the Crown. His enthusiasm for Queen Victoria, his "darlin' little Queen," has attracted special attention, some of his biographers attributing it to his sense of chivalry. But there was a more substantial reason for it. In the early years of her reign Victoria was a Whig and thereby, whether she realized it or not, a friend to what Irish historians call the Drummond Administration. O'Connell labelled that administration the best that Ireland had ever known and he was determined to keep it in office. When the Whig Government resigned in 1839 the Queen had to ask the Tory leader, Sir Robert Peel, to form a cabinet. Before taking office Peel insisted that she must replace her Whig Ladies of the Bedchamber with Tories, thus precipitating what is known in British history as the Bedchamber Crisis. She obstinately rejected his demand, whereupon he declined to form a government, and the Whigs came back to power for a further two years. Meetings in both Britain and Ireland congratulated the Queen for so bravely standing up to a Tory "despotism," and one English gathering applauded her for refusing to let "her Belles be Peeled." O'Connell's affection owed as much to political considerations as to chivalry.

In appraising his attitude to the political institutions of his time it is vital to remember that he was born into a family that not only had lineage but—and this was more important—had achieved economic success. His uncle, Hunting-Cap, had added enormously to his patrimony by farming, smuggling, lending money, thrift and hard bargaining. By the end of the century he was a rich man. O'Connell's father followed Hunting-Cap's example, though on a more modest scale and more humanely. He ran a general store, reared ten children and died prosperous. This combination of lineage and economic success meant that O'Connell grew up without that inferiority complex and consequent envy and bitterness so frequent among Irish Catholics. He could look the British Government and the Irish Protestant Ascendancy straight in the face and not feel it necessary to hate them.

But O'Connell's attitude to the political establishment towards the end of the eighteenth century, to the institution known as "Grattan's Parliament," went beyond mere loyal acceptance: it was one of enthusiasm. This can best be shown by comparing his outlook with that of Hunting-Cap. The first evidence of this enthusiasm can be found in the alarm created at the end of 1796 by the danger of a French invasion.

This alarm was sounded by the appearance of a French fleet in Bantry Bay on the south-west coast, not far from Derrynane where Hunting-Cap resided, in December, 1796. Wolfe Tone, the founder of the United Irishmen, was on board, the project owing much to his persuasive powers with the French Government. But a large part of the fleet had been dispersed by a storm, and when it did not arrive, the ships in Bantry Bay weighed anchor and returned to France. Hunting-Cap was informed of the arrival of the French fleet, and immediately sent word to the authorities in Tralee, the county town of Kerry.

As a law student in Dublin O'Connell shared in the general excitement and was full of eagerness to join one of the lawyers' yeomanry corps. However, as Hunting-Cap's heir, he had first to obtain his uncle's permission. Two of three letters in January, 1797, from the young man to Hunting-Cap on this issue are extant.[11] It appears from this correspondence that O'Connell had earlier been refused permission, but with the news from Bantry Bay he renewed his plea. He pointed out that the present alarm had induced nearly all members of the legal profession in Dublin to take up arms. Should he be the only one not to do so he would come under the unfavorable notice of the Government (a point likely to influence Hunting-Cap). He added that he was "young, active, healthy and single," and attributed his eagerness to being "surrounded as I am with young men whom the moment has inspired with enthusiasm; with the blood of youth boiling in my veins, you will not be surprised that I should be more than usually animated."

In the second of these letters O'Connell tactfully expressed concern lest he might have pressed his uncle too warmly for the permission, and he attributed his ardor to "the danger I was in of being looked upon by the men who are to be my companions and fellow labourers through life, as a coward or a scoundrel, or as both." He ended this letter by giving a more self-interested reason why he was opposed to a French invasion:

> That invasion which if successful should have shook the founda-
> tion of all property, would have destroyed our profession root
> and branch. All that I have read, all that I have thought, all that I
> have combined was about to be rendered nugatory at once. It was
> little. But this little was my all.

The requested permission was apparently given but obviously with reluctance. In future years Hunting-Cap was to advise his nephew repeatedly to apply himself to his profession and not become too deeply involved in the struggle for Catholic Emancipation. He was no doubt advising him now to concentrate on legal studies rather than indulge in semi-military activities.

It is generally agreed by historians that the bulk of propertied Catholics in Ireland supported the passing of the Act of Union between Great Britain and Ireland in 1800, and were encouraged to do so by the virtual promise that Emancipation would follow. O'Connell was the only member of the Catholic community [12] who is known to have stood out prominently against Catholics generally on this issue. He did so by addressing a Catholic meeting in Dublin in January, 1800. It appears from the press reports that he was the only speaker, and he proposed five anti-Union resolutions which were adopted unanimously.[13]

In his address he explained that the Catholics of Dublin had earlier decided to stand aloof, as a sect, from political discussion, but it had now become necessary for them to come forward, as a sect, to contradict the false and scandalous charge that "the Roman Catholics of Ireland were friends to the measure of Union." He described the Union as "the political murder of our country," and ended his speech with the words:

> I know that although exclusive advantages may be ambiguously held forth to the Irish Catholic to seduce him from the sacred duty which he owes his country. I know that the Catholics of Ireland still remember that they have a country, and that they will never accept of any advantages as a *sect*, which would debase and destroy them as a *people*.

This address provoked a stern rebuke from his uncle. In a long letter[14] Hunting-Cap declared he had for some years disapproved of the "unwise and intemperate" conduct of the Catholics, "whether they assumed the character of the Catholic Convention or of the aggregate or select meeting of the Catholics of Dublin." They seemed to him to have completely lost sight of the fact that they owed the favors they had received not to the Irish Parliament but to the British Government, and that it was to that government that they must look for future favors. This consideration was all the more important now that "the Orange Lodges are rapidly spreading through the Kingdom and that the hostile and rancorous spirit that forms and pervades them is so generally known." He regretted to observe that these Catholics had

> all along been the dupes of designing and insidious men, who under a mask of fellowfeeling and liberal friendship were slyly and assiduously and treacherously urging them on to their ruin, subtly depreciating the favors they received, and artfully holding out objects not attainable at the moment, to excite their impatience and involve them in ill-timed and intemperate measures and demands.

He ended his strictures with the warning:

> I know you have a facility of disposition which exposes you to rather an incautious compliance with those you live in habits of friendship with, and I am also aware that professional young men are in general disposed to accede to measures that place them in a conspicuous point of view. In some instances it may be useful, very frequently not. The little temporary attentions it produces soon expire. Popular applause is always short-lived but the inconveniences may be serious and lasting. In the present case I must earnestly recommend that you keep clear of all farther interference, the part you have taken must have rendered you unacceptable to Government, and it is therefore necessary you should be particularly circumspect and correct with respect to your words and conduct.

In this passage Hunting-Cap was no doubt referring to the United Irishmen, and more definitely, to anti-Union Protestants whom he saw as exerting an undesirable influence over his nephew.[15]

Hunting-Cap's hostility to the Irish Parliament because of its attitude to Catholics was not new. In 1780 the Knight of Kerry, one of the M.P.'s for Co. Kerry, asked him if the Catholics of his neighborhood, Iveragh, would combine with the Protestants to form a corps of Volunteers (the voluntary yeomanry of that time).[16] Hunting-Cap rejected the request on the ground that it was illegal for Catholics to bear arms, and he took the opportunity to express his very unfavorable opinion of the Irish Parliament:

> I am fully convinced that the Roman Catholic gentlemen of Iveragh would readily unite with their Protestant neighbours . . . to form a corps did they think such a measure would meet the approbation of the Legislature. They would, in common with every Catholic of standing in Ireland, be exceedingly happy by every means in their power to give additional weight and strength and security to the kingdom; but what can they do while the laws of their country forbid them the use of arms? Under such circumstances I look upon it to be their duty to confine themselves to that line of conduct marked out for them by the Legislature, and with humility and resignation wait for a further relaxation of the laws, which a more enlightened and liberal way of thinking, added to a clearer and more deliberate attention to the real interests and prosperity of the country, will, I hope, soon bring about.[17]

O'Connell's opposition to the Union no doubt owed much to the fact that he was a member of the Irish Bar. Quite early in the great debate on that measure an indignant meeting of barristers in Dublin condemned the Union by a vote of 166 to 32.[18] But the opposition of the Bar could be predicted. Barristers are traditionally associated with law-making as members of parliament and as drafters of legislation. The loss of a legislature would mean a loss of business for the profession and a decline in status since many barristers were in the House of Commons and the chief judges sat in the Lords.

There is an entirely different consideration but one which also arises from the fact that O'Connell was a fledgling barrister in these last years of the eighteenth century. His nearest friends would have been law students and newly qualified barristers, and he was of a gregarious disposition who made friends and acquaintances readily. One can safely assume that fully eighty per cent of his young companions in the legal profession were Protestants,[19] and his association with them would help to explain why he adopted an attitude to the Union very different from that held by the bulk of propertied Catholics. There is the further consideration that he had abandoned the faith in which he was reared and was now a rationalist. This would make it all the easier for him to be influenced by those not Catholic.

At the Dublin Catholic meeting in 1800, which has been described, O'Connell proposed five anti-Union resolutions which included the statements,

> The proposed incorporate Union of the legislatures of Great Britain and Ireland is, in fact, an extinction of the liberty of this country. . . . The improvement of Ireland for the last twenty years, so rapid beyond example, is to be ascribed wholly to the independency of our legislature, so gloriously asserted in the year 1782 by virtue of our parliament co-operating with the generous recommendation of our most gracious and benevolent sovereign and backed by the spirit of our people. . . . If that independency should ever be surrendered, we must as rapidly relapse into our former depression and misery; and . . . Ireland must inevitably lose with her liberty all that she has acquired in wealth and industry and civilization.

Though modern historians would find this evaluation of "Grattan's Parliament" much too rose-tinted, it remained part of O'Connell's political *dicta* throughout his life. He repeatedly praised that parliament and never ceased to express veneration for Grattan. In 1810, for example, he addressed a Dublin meeting in favor of the repeal of the Act of Union, and ended a long speech with the plea,

> Let that spirit which heretofore emanating from Dungannon [the great meeting of the Volunteers in 1782] spread all over the island, and gave light and liberty to the land, be again cherished amongst us. Let us rally round the standard of Old Ireland, and we shall easily procure that greatest of political blessings, an Irish King, an Irish House of Lords, and an Irish House of Commons.[20]

When Grattan died in 1820 O'Connell proposed his son, Henry Grattan, Jr., to be his father's successor as M.P. for Dublin City. He commenced his speech on this occasion with the words:

> We are met on this melancholy occasion to celebrate the obsequies of the greatest man Ireland ever knew. . . . In 1778, when Ireland was shackled, he reared the standard of independence; and in 1782 he stood forward as the champion of his

country, achieving gloriously her independence!... After the disastrous act of Union, which met his most resolute and most determined opposition, he did not suffer despair to creep over his heart and induce him to abandon her, as was the case with too many others.... His life, to the very period of his latest breath, has been spent in her service—and he died, I may even say, a martyr in her cause.[21]

His veneration for Grattan survived the bitterness of the Veto controversy. This issue arose from the proposal in 1813 and subsequent years to procure Catholic Emancipation by granting to the British government a right of veto in the nomination of bishops. Grattan gave the most decided support to this proposal but O'Connell rejected it utterly and treated many of its protagonists to no small amount of invective. But his censure of Grattan was mild, and qualified by praise of his past labors. Probably the harshest comment he ever made on Grattan formed part of a speech on the Veto in 1815:

> I see with regret that, except his services in our Cause, he has since the Union made no exertions worthy of his name and of his strength. Since he has inhaled the foul and corrupt atmosphere that fills some of the avenues to Westminster, there have not been the same health and vigour about him.... I feel for him unfeigned respect; but he has refused to accept the Petition [to the House of Commons for Emancipation] upon our terms.[22]

O'Connell's restraint was all the more significant because, in an address to the Catholics of Ireland, Grattan described him as a shallow and cowardly opportunist.[23]

An indication that his veneration for Grattan did not diminish with the years can be seen in an incident that occurred in 1843. In that year the *Dublin Review*, of which O'Connell was a founder, published a review of the *Grattan Memoirs*[24] that amounted to a scurrilous attack on Grattan's public character and reputation. O'Connell must have expressed indignation because the magazine's temporary editor, Rev. Nicholas (later Cardinal) Wiseman, wrote him an apologetic explanation of "some circumstances connected with the article on Grattan in the last number, which I find gave you pain."[25]

It is of course true that O'Connell had good reason to remain on friendly terms with Grattan. The old man had done his life's work, but he was a revered figure in the British Parliament and enjoyed the respect of a great many Irishmen, Protestant and Catholic. He could still be a useful ally. It was good politics to try to quiet Protestant fears by portraying the Repeal of the Act of Union as merely a return to a happy constitutional position rather than a leap into the future. Nevertheless, O'Connell's praise of Grattan and "Grattan's Parliament" went far beyond what was necessary for these aims, and was clearly inspired by a positive enthusiasm. That sentiment was not shared by Hunting-Cap, whose disdain for the Irish Parliament has been shown, nor by the bulk of propertied Catholics, since they supported the Union which involved the destruction of that late eighteenth-century constitution.

O'Connell saw the historic Irish nation as the Catholic population in existence before the Reformation. Paradoxically, he regarded Grattan and the Protestant Ascendancy as Irish, and their Parliament, even though it excluded Catholics, as a great and traditional Irish institution. In neither speech nor writing did he ever suggest that they were *colons* or that their parliament was a colonial institution. It is true that later generations of Irish Catholic nationalists came to see the Protestant Ascendancy and the eighteenth-century parliament as colonial, but that development owed more to Thomas Davis[26] and Romantic nationalism than to O'Connell. Though a Protestant, Davis was hostile to the landlord classes who were the backbone of that ascendancy. In many articles in the *Nation* he denounced the landlords as tyrannical, anti-Irish and alien in race and religion to the people of Ireland. He was scarcely conscious of the extent to which these widely read articles were identifying the nation with Catholicism and cutting off the Protestants. By a curious contradiction he also claimed that the nation comprised men of all religions and of different racial stocks—Gael, Norman and English. It was only the landlords he denounced as alien, but a later generation could find it easy to conclude that if landlord Protestants were alien in race and religion then all Protestants must be alien. The struggle over the land and Home Rule encouraged Catholics to pay more attention to Davis's denunciation of Irish landlords as alien than to his more modestly expressed definition of an Irish nation as inclusive of all religious and racial stocks.

In order to understand how O'Connell could identify with both the historic nation, which he saw as Catholic, and the eighteenth-century nation, whose constitutional leadership was exclusively Protestant, one must remember that he was a child of the Enlightenment. A rationalist in early manhood and having the utilitarian and universal outlook of the Enlightenment he had no difficulty in seeing the whole community as the nation. It was Romanticism which encouraged an interest in racial origins and traditions, a potentially disruptive development in Ireland where religious difference marked off the Protestants, mostly descended from seventeenth-century immigrants, from the older, Catholic, stocks. [27] Furthermore, Romanticism gave to nationalism a sacredness and vigor which quickly led to intransigence. Where O'Connell saw self-government as vital to good government, the Young Irelanders saw self-government as an end in itself, a spiritual necessity. Thus support for Repeal became an essential part of Irish nationality, a way of separating nationalist from alien. By the mid-1840's O'Connell's old-fashioned all-inclusive eighteenth-century nationalism was giving way to the new Romantic nationalism which would exclude those—in effect, the Protestants—refusing to support Repeal.

Before concluding one must point to another sphere—relations between church and state—in which O'Connell must have been deeply influenced by the experience of eighteenth-century Ireland. He was the first Catholic political leader in Europe to espouse religious freedom and separation of church and state, not merely for Ireland, where the established church was Protestant, but for France and Spain and even the Papal States. [28] As already explained, Irish Catholics had suffered from the union of church and state as expressed in the Papal recognition of the exiled Stuarts. Paradoxically, Catholic Ireland enjoyed virtual separation of church and state, since the exiled Stuarts had no political power: they could nominate to vacant sees, but they had no means of enforcing their will on the bishops when they had been appointed or on any other part of the ecclesiastical structure. O'Connell was born into an Ireland in which this unhappy problem of Pope-King relations had just been resolved. Consequently he was "conditioned" to be sceptical of the value of the traditional union of church and state and to be prejudiced in favor of their separation.

O'Connell emerges from this study a man more closely tied to his eighteenth-century environment than historians have usually thought. His espousal of the cause of separation of church and state undoubtedly owed much to the unhappy effects of the continued Papal recognition of the exiled Stuarts and also to the surprising amount of freedom from state interference in its internal ecclesiastical structure which the Catholic Church enjoyed in eighteenth-century Ireland. His adoption of constitutional methods and his aversion to violence can be ascribed much more to his Irish experience than to his sojourn in revolutionary France. O'Connell's loyalty to the British crown, which has puzzled much Irish popular and even educated opinion, was natural and reasonable for a man of his religious and political traditions. He accepted the political institutions of late eighteenth-century Ireland, including the exclusively Protestant Parliament, as Irish; and he accepted them with a certain enthusiasm. It seems clear that this enthusiasm owed much to the influence exerted on him as a young man by his Protestant colleagues at the Irish Bar. Seeking justice and equality for Catholics and attempting to obtain the repeal of the Act of Union he had to spend most of his public life attacking the Protestant Ascendancy, yet he always regarded its members as Irishmen. In this he differed from later generations of Catholic nationalists who frequently tended to see those Protestants, and indeed all Irish Protestants, as alien.

NOTES

1 *The Correspondence of Daniel O'Connell*, which is being published by the Irish University Press in Dublin and Barnes and Noble in New York City. The work comprises eight volumes, of which vols. I and II appeared in 1973 and vol. III in 1974.

2 Michael Tierney, ed., *Daniel O'Connell: Nine Centenary Essays* (Dublin: Browne and Nolan, 1949), pp. 1–24.

3 O'Connell kept a journal intermittently as a young man (Arthur Houston, ed., *Daniel O'Connell: His Early Life and Journal 1795 to 1802* [London: Sir Isaac Pitmand and Sons, 1906]). In it he frequently lists the books he is reading and sometimes expresses his opinion of them. Many statements in the journal as well as its general tone are proof of his rationalism. In 1803 he was still a rationalist, since he wrote to his wife who was ill: "If I were a religionist I should spend every moment in praying for you; and this miserable philosophy which I have taken up and been proud of in the room of religion, affords me now no consolation in my misery" (O'Connell to Mary O'Connell, Feb. 1, 1803, Maurice R. O'Connell, ed., *The Correspondence of Daniel O'Connell* [New York: Barnes and Noble, 1973], I, letter 85). By 1809 he had recovered his religious belief and was a practicing Catholic, since his wife informed him: "I can't tell you what real happiness it gives me to have you this sometime back say your prayers and attend Mass so regularly, not to say anything of your observance of the days of abstinence" (Mary O'Connell to O'Connell, Mar. 21, 1809, ibid., I, letter 237).

4 Houston, *O'Connell*, p. 155.

5 Ibid., p. 236.

6 John O'Connell, ed., *The Select Speeches of Daniel O'Connell, M.P.* (Dublin: James Duffy, 1854), I, 404–5.

7 Some interesting comments on the political attitudes of Gaelic Ireland have been made by the late Rev. Francis Shaw, S.J., Professor of Early and Medieval Irish, University College, Dublin, in his article "The Canon of Irish History—A Challenge," *Studies*, 61, no. 242 (Summer 1972), 113–53.

8 The celebrated seventeenth-century Gaelic history of Ireland known as the *Annals of the Four Masters* recognized Charles I in its preamble as King of Ireland.

9 Maureen Wall, "Catholic Loyalty to King and Pope in Eighteenth-Century Ireland," *Proceedings of the Irish Catholic Historical Committee, 1960* (Dublin, 1961), pp. 17–24.

10 Mrs. M. J. O'Connell, *The Last Colonel of the Irish Brigade* (London: Kegan Paul, Trench, Trübner & Co., 1892), I, 207–8.

11 O'Connell, *Correspondence of O'Connell*, I, letters 24a and 25.

12 Since O'Connell was a rationalist at this time it seems more appropriate to describe him as a "member of the Catholic community" than as a Catholic. He never broke openly with the Church (until his journal was published in 1906 historians did not know that he had ever lost his religious belief); and his attendance and speech at the Catholic meeting in Dublin in 1800 indicate that he was publicly identifying himself as a Catholic.

13 This report is taken from the *Dublin Evening Post* of January 14, 1800.

14 Hunting-Cap to O'Connell, Jan. 30, 1800, MS 15473, National Library of Ireland.

15 Hunting-Cap did not come forward as an early advocate of the Union. On June 28, 1799, Robert Day, a Justice of the King's Bench in Ireland, wrote to the Earl of Glandore, a North Kerry landlord and the Governor of the county. His epistle included the advice: "Do not fail to address a flattering letter to Maurice O'Connell, the King of the Romans, who is one of the few of any respectability in our county who have not to my knowledge declared in favour of the measure" (Talbot-Crosbie Papers, National Library of Ireland). The advice must have been taken, since Glandore later informed Castlereagh, the Chief Secretary in Dublin Castle, that Hunting-Cap's name had been added to the Kerry declaration in favor of the Union. He described Hunting-Cap as "a very sensible man, of considerable property both landed and personal and of great influence amongst the Roman Catholics, by whom he is considered as the head of the independent part of their communion—I mean such as do not derive immediately under my lord Kenmare." He added that Hunting-Cap attributed his conversion to Unionism to his (Glandore's) arguments (Glandore to Castlereagh, Aug. 16, 1799, Talbot-Crosbie Papers). For bringing my attention to these letters in the Talbot-Crosbie Papers I am indebted to Dr. Anthony P. W. Malcomson.

Hunting-Cap was to return to the subject of how easily his nephew was influenced by undesirable persons even when a mature man though, on this latter occasion, it was in reference to business affairs: "I can scarcely express to you the uneasiness I feel since this matter has occurred to me, well knowing as I before mentioned the softness and facility of your disposition and with what ease designing men may draw you into their measures" (Hunting-Cap to O'Connell, May 16, 1811, O'Connell, *Correspondence of O'Connell*, I, letter 337).

16 O'Connell, *Last Colonel*, I, 264.

17 Ibid., I, 265–66.

18 G. C. Bolton, *The Passing of the Irish Act of Union* (Oxford: Oxford University Press, 1966), pp. 77–81.

19 According to Watson's *Dublin Almanack* for 1800 some 160 men were called to the Irish Bar during the five-year period 1795–99. A large majority of the names are English-sounding, while many of those with distinctively Irish names can be taken as Protestant. Only 3 besides O'Connell had the Gaelic prefix "O" whereas there are 20 with that prefix listed in the almanach for 1840 as being called to the Bar in the five-year period 1835–39 (one would have to allow for the fact that some men restored that prefix in the early nineteenth century under the influence of Romanticism, but the comparison is still impressive). In an article, "The Catholic Bar," in the *Nation* of March 2, 1844, Charles Gavan Duffy says that less than one-fourth of the Irish Bar are Catholics. That is only an impressionistic estimate but it does indicate that the number of Catholics becoming barristers forty years earlier must have been slight. O'Connell's closest friend in the legal profession in those years was Richard Newton Bennett, a Protestant from Co. Wexford. Bennett is repeatedly mentioned in O'Connell's journal, and their friendship was to endure for a generation.

20 O'Connell, *Select Speeches of O'Connell*, I, 24. When the chairman of the meeting observed that the reference to "an Irish King" could give rise to "calumny and misrepresentation" O'Connell assured the audience that he was referring to George III, who was "abounding in every great and good qualification calculated to make his people happy" (ibid.).

21 Ibid., II, 72.

22 *Dublin Evening Post*, Feb. 18, 1815.

23 In 1847 William Fagan published a long excerpt from this address in his *The Life and Times of Daniel O'Connell* (Cork: J. O'Brien, 1847), I, 524–26. Fagan's accompanying remarks and the excerpt itself show that the address belongs to the period September 1815–July 1817, but it does not appear to have been published. It was so venemous that Grattan's friends may well have dissuaded him from publishing, or possibly even delivering it. The omission of any mention of it in contemporary newspapers could raise a doubt as to the veracity of Fagan's excerpt but that doubt cannot be sustained. Grattan's sons, James and Henry, Jr., were adults at the time of the Veto controversy, and Henry, Jr., had written his father's *Memoirs* before the appearance of Fagan's biography of O'Connell. They would surely have protested against the publication of a report so damaging to the popularity of their father's reputation if that report were untrue. Lecky and the editor of O'Connell's correspondence in 1888, William J. FitzPatrick, treated the excerpt as genuine (W. E. H. Lecky, *Leaders of Public Opinion in Ireland* [London: Longmans, Green, and Co., 1903], II, 24; W. J. FitzPatrick, *Correspondence of Daniel O'Connell* [London: John Murray, 1888], I, 60, note 3).

24 Henry Grattan, Jr., *Memoirs of the Life and Times of the Rt. Hon. Henry Grattan* (London: H. Colburn, 1839 et. seq.). The first four volumes were reviewed in this article in the *Dublin Review* of September, 1843 (vol. 15, no. 29, pp. 200–52).

25 Wiseman to O'Connell, Dec. 15, 1843, *Irish Monthly*, 11 (1883), 340–41.

26 Alf MacLochlainn, "Thomas Davis and Irish Racialism," *Irish Times*, Nov. 20, 1973; Maurice R. O'Connell, "Thomas Davis: A Destructive Conciliator," *Irish Times*, Aug. 6, 1974. Davis's ambiguity on the origin and composition of the Irish nation may well have arisen from the fact that he was descended not only from the Cromwellian Protestant family of Atkins but also from the ancient and much more interesting Gaelic Catholic family of O'Sullivan-Bere.

27 A perusal of any edition of Burke's *Landed Gentry of Ireland* indicates that the Protestant Ascendancy had a larger share of Gaelic and Norman-Irish blood than is allowed them by popular opinion or even by historians.

28 My article "Daniel O'Connell and Religious Freedom" in the *Irish Times* of March 4 and 8, 1971, depicts O'Connell's role in this context. The subject has been dealt with comprehensively by Sister Helen Coldrick, R.D.C., in her "Daniel O'Connell and Religious Freedom" (Diss. Fordham University 1974).

Executive Board, 1975-76

President: VICTOR LANGE, John N. Woodhull Professor of German, Princeton University

Past President: GEORGES MAY, Sterling Professor of French, Yale University

First Vice-President: ELIZABETH L. EISENSTEIN, Alice Freeman Palmer Professor of History, University of Michigan

Second Vice-President: GWIN J. KOLB, Professor of English, University of Chicago

Executive Secretary: PAUL J. KORSHIN, Associate Professor of English, University of Pennsylvania

Treasurer: JEAN A. PERKINS, Professor of Modern Languages, Swarthmore College

SHIRLEY A. BILL (1978), Professor of History, University of Illinois, Chicago Circle

ROBERT HALSBAND (1978), Professor of English, University of Illinois, Urbana

DONALD J. OLSEN (1976), Professor of History, Vassar College

JULES D. PROWN (1976), Director, The Yale Center for British Art and British Studies

LEONARD G. RATNER (1977), Professor of Music, Stanford University

MADELEINE B. THERRIEN (1977), Professor of French, Emory University

497

Institutional Members

of the American Society

for Eighteenth Century Studies

Alfred University
Bryn Mawr College
Butler University
University of Calgary
University of California, Berkeley
University of California, Davis
University of California, Irvine
University of California, Los Angeles
University of California, Riverside
University of California, San Diego
Case Western Reserve University
Catholic University of America
University of Cincinnati
City College, CUNY
Claremont Graduate School
Cleveland State University
University of Colorado, Denver Center
University of Connecticut
Dalhousie University
University of Delaware
University of Denver
Detroit Institute of Arts, Founders' Society
Emory University
Fordham University
University of Georgia
Georgia Institute of Technology
Georgia State University
University of Hawaii
University of Illinois, Chicago Circle
University of Illinois, Urbana
University of Iowa
The Johns Hopkins University
University of Kentucky
Lehigh University

Lehman College, CUNY
The Lewis Walpole Library
University of Maryland
University of Massachusetts, Boston
McMaster University/Association for 18th Century Studies
The Metropolitan Museum of Art
University of Michigan, Ann Arbor
Michigan State University
Middle Tennessee State University
The Minneapolis Institute of Fine Arts
University of Minnesota
Université de Montréal
Mount Saint Vincent University
University of New Brunswick
State University of New York, Binghamton
State University of New York, Fredonia
State University of New York, Oswego
University of North Carolina, Chapel Hill
North Georgia College
Northern Illinois University
Northwestern University
Ohio State University
University of Pennsylvania
University of Pittsburgh
Princeton University
Purdue University
Rice University
Rockford College
Rollins College
Smith College
University of South Carolina
University of Southern California
Southern Illinois University

Stanford University
Swarthmore College
Sweet Briar College
Temple University
University of Tennessee
Texas Tech University
Tulane University
University of Tulsa
University of Victoria
University of Virginia
Virginia Commonwealth University
Washington University

Washington and Lee University
Washington State University
Wayne State University
West Chester State College, Pennsylvania
West Virginia University
University of Western Ontario
The Henry Francis du Pont Winterthur
   Museum
University of Wisconsin, Madison
The Yale Center for British Art and British
   Studies
Yale University

Index

Absalom and Achitophel (Dryden), 69, 71, 77
Accomplished Gentlewoman's Companion, 367
Addison, Joseph, 98, 296, 337
"Address to the People" (O'Connell), 478
Adolph, Robert, 252n27
"Adultère" (Voltaire), 162n4
Aeneis (Dryden), 74
Age of Reason (Paine), 477
Agricola, Rudolph, 262
Aickin, Joseph, 233
Aldrich, Henry, Dean, 346
Alembert, Jean Le Rond d', 169, 374, 375
Alexander's Feast (Dryden), 74
Alfieri, Vittorio, Count, 282
Algarotti, Francesco, 32
Allen, Robert, 392
Almanach Royal, L', 372, 373, 378, 379
Altamirano, Calderón, 188
Alzire (Voltaire), 162n4
Amphitryon (Dryden), 73
Analysis of Beauty, The (Hogarth), 13, 18, 19
Ancient Constitution, The, 90, 94
Anderson, David, 204
Andioc, René, 174
Anne, Queen of England, 141, 297, 308
Annual Register, The, 464
Annus Mirabilis (Dryden), 71, 74, 76
Antal, Frederick, 14
Anti-Gothicism, 93
Anti-Normanism, 93
Aranaz y Vives, Pedro, 196

Armstrong, George, 299, 302
Arroyal, Léon de, 165–68, 176–80
Arteaga, P. Esteban, 191
Arthur, Robert, 466
Arthur family, 458
Art of Stenographie, The (John Willis), 237
Astell, Mary, 121–36
Audin-Rouvière, 309
Aug, Jean, 412
Augustan Reprint Society, 149
Augustine, Saint, 68n4
Autobiographical Notes, The (Hogarth), 13

Bacon, Francis, 262, 264
Bails, Benito, 196
Baker, Timothy, 249n4
Balfour, John, 358
Barry, Philip, 462
Barthes, Roland, 208
Bartholomew Fair, 17, 18, 19
Baudelaire, Charles, 185, 186
Beccaria, Cesare, 293
Bécquer, Gustavo Adolfo, 187
"Beggar's Opera, The" (Hogarth), 14
Behrend, J. A., 301
Bell, John, 396
Bellori, Giovanni Pietro, 320, 321, 322
Benlowes, Edward, 263–70
Bennett, Richard Newton, 494n19
Bentham, Jeremy, 101
Bentley, Richard, 347
Bermúdez, Ceán, 175

Bernabeu, Francisco, 180
Bernascone, Ignacio, 180
Bible, The, 365, 366
Bijoux indiscrets, Les (Diderot), 379
Bird, John, 233
Birmingham, Doctor, 460
Blake, William, 55–68
Blake family, 458
Boehme, Jacob, 264
Boileau-Despréaux, Nicolas, 285
Boisjermain, Luneau de, 377
Bolingbroke, Henry St. John, Lord, 362
Bolton, A. T., 338
Book of Common Prayer, The, 366
Book of Urizen, The (Blake), 60, 62
Bosarte, Isidro, 193
Bosch, Jerome, 197, 200n16
Boswell, James, 11, 21, 24n1, 396
Botello, Francisco, 187, 189
Bowles, William, 460
Boyle, Robert, 43, 254, 259, 271
Bracken, Henry, 367
Bradford, William, 362, 363
Brady, Doctor, 460
Bramston, James, 338
Bretonne, Nicolas Rétif de la, 426, 443
Brettingham, Matthew, the Elder, 346
Briasson, Antoine-Claude, 374, 375, 379
British Journal, The, 144
Brownlee, John, 298
Brückner, Johann, 293
Buffon, George-Louis Leclerc, comte de, 176
Bunyan, John, 307
Bürger, G. A., 304
Burke, Edmund, 91, 92, 100, 133, 155, 454
Burke, Joseph T. A., 22, 25n9
Burlington, Richard Boyle, Earl of, 341, 342, 345, 350
Burroughs, James, Sir, 346
Butler, Samuel, 71, 72, 73, 266
Byrne family, 458
Byron, George Noel Gordon, Lord, 284

Cabanilles, Antonio José de, 169
Cabarrús, Francisco de, 174, 178
Cadalso y Vasquez, José de, 185
Cadell, Thomas, 357
Cadogan, William, 297

Cahen, L., 163n12
Calas, Jean, 380
Calendrier de la cour, Le, 373
Cantillon, Richard, 460
Cañuelo, Luis Maria García, 171, 172, 177
Capmany, Antonio, 196
Carlos III, King of Spain, 166, 168, 178
Carlos IV, King of Spain, 166
Caroline, Princess of Wales, 306
Cassirer, Ernst, 261
Castro, Francisco de, 195
Catherine I, Empress of Russia, 155
Catherine II, Empress of Russia, 155, 296
Catholic Holy League, The, 428
Caumartin, chevalier de, 433
Century of the Names and Scantlings of . . . Inventions . . . , A (Edward Somerset), 247
Cervantes, Miguel de, 185
Chamberlayne, William, 69
Chambers, Ephraim, 373
Chambers, William, Sir, 347, 348
Chapuis, Alfred, 51
Charles I, King of England, 479
Charles III ("Bonnie Prince Charlie"), 480
Chattin, James, 363
Chaucer, Geoffrey, 77, 80
Chesterfield, Philip Dormer Stanhope, Earl of, 342
Choiseul-Beaupré, comtesse de, 401, 402, 403, 407, 408, 410, 412, 413, 415, 417, 418
Chute, John, 343, 344, 347
Cibber, Theophilus, 18
Cipolla, Carlo, 43
Civil War, The (Cowley), 69
Clarke, George, 346
Clayborough, Arthur, 186
Cleveland, John, 265, 267, 269
Cobban, Alfred, 178
Cock and the Fox, The (Dryden), 78
Coffey, Charles, 14
Cohen, Jonathan, 257
Colbert, Jean-Baptiste, 425, 436
Coleridge, Samuel T., 100
Coles, Elisha, 235, 242
Col. Jacque (Defoe), 110, 118
Colquhoun, Patrick, 141
Colvin, Howard, 340
Comenius, Johannes Amos, 240–42, 244
Compleat Constable, The, 367

Compleat English Schoolmaster, The
 (Elisha Coles), 235
Compleat Housewife, The (Philip Miller),
 367
Compleat Jury Man, The, 367
Compleat Sheriff, The, 367
Complete English Gentleman, The (De-
 foe), 108
Conboy, Miguel, 462
Condorcet, Marie Jean Antoine Nicolas
 Caritat, marquis de, 151–56, 158–62
Congreve, William, 104
Conjugal Lewdness (Defoe), 104, 110, 114
Cooke, John, 396
Cooper, Christopher, 235, 236
Coppinger family, 458
Correspondance littéraire, La, 378
Counter-Reformation, The, 434
Countryman's Friend, The, 367
Covarrubias, Sebastian de, 192
Cowper, Thomas, 63
Cromwell, Oliver, 161
Croquants, 425, 449n2
Curtis, F. B., 68n1
Cyclopaedia, The (Ephraim Chambers),
 373
Cymon and Iphigenia (Dryden), 78

D'Aguesseau, Henri-François, 373
Dalgarno, George, 238, 272
Dante Alighieri, 50
Darcy family, 458
Darnton, Robert, 379
Davenant, William, Sir, 69
David, Jacques-Louis, 331, 332
David, Jean-Pierre, 308
David, Michel-Antoine, 374, 375, 379
Davideis (Cowley), 69
Davis, Thomas, 489–90, 495n26
Defoe, Daniel, 43, 46, 98, 103–19
Delacroix, Ferdinand Victor Eugène, 185
Delécluze, Etienne Jean, 332
De l'Esprit (Helvétius), 375, 380
Deleuze, Gilles, 203, 208, 210
De Morbis acutis infantum (Walter Harris),
 299
Denham, John, 260
Denina, Carlos, 169, 170
Dennis, John, 391
Descartes, René, 43, 171
Desessartz, Jean Charles, 301

Devil on Two Sticks (Lesage), 367
Devil to Pay, The (Charles Coffey), 14
Dialogue on Painting (Francisco Alga-
 rotti), 32
Dickinson, John, 363
Dictionnaire philosophique, Le (Voltaire),
 162n4
*Didascalocophus, or the Deaf and Dumb
 Man's Tutor* (George Dalgarno), 238
Diderot, Denis, 152, 153, 169, 283, 285,
 287, 326, 327, 328, 329, 333, 371,
 374, 375, 376, 378, 379
Dillon, Arthur Richard, 459, 466
Dillon, John Vincent, 463
Dillon, Theobald, 466
Donaldson, Alexander, 359
Donne, John, 69, 73
Don Quixote (Cervantes), 367
Don Sebastian (Dryden), 73
Douglass, William, 305
Drottningholm Royal Court Theater, 16
Dryden, John, 68, 69, 73, 137n6, 229,
 246, 260, 261, 263, 273
Dublin Review (O'Connell), 489
Du Bos, Jean-Baptiste, *abbé,* 324
Ducrot, Oswald, 203
Dufresnoy, Charles Alphonse, 317
Duke and No Duke (Nahum Tate), 14
Dunlap, William, 363
Durand, Laurent, 374, 377, 379
Dürer, Albrecht, 45, 46, 48
Durham, Thomas, 357
Du Seuil, Pierre, 401–408

Edgeworth, Henry, *abbé,* 466
Edict of Nantes, 426
*Elements of Speech: An Essay of In-
 quiry . . .* (John Wallis), 239
Elements of the Irish Language, The
 (Hugh MacCurtin), 463
Eleonora (Dryden), 73
Elizabeth I, Queen of England, 155
Elliott, Andrew, 462
Elvira (David Mallet), 11
Encyclopédie, L', 371, 375–77, 378, 379
English Grammar (Joseph Aickin), 233
English Grammatical Categories (Ian
 Michael), 230
English Teacher, The (Christopher
 Cooper), 235, 236

Espronceda, José de, 187
Essai sur les moeurs (Voltaire), 162n4
Essay of Dramatick Poesie, An (Dryden), 70
Essay towards a Real Character and a Philosophical Language (John Wilkins), 235
Essay upon Nursing and the Management of Children (William Cadogan), 297
Essay upon Projects (Defoe), 105
Estala, Pedro, 165–68, 173, 176, 180
Evening Post, The (London), 143
Examen Poeticum (Dryden), 73

Fable of the Bees, The (Mandeville), 142, 143
Fables Ancient and Modern (Dryden), 74, 75, 76, 77, 78, 81, 83
Family Instructor, The (Defoe), 119n1
Farriery Improved (Henry Bracken), 367
Faust (Goethe), 185
Félibien, André, 319, 330
Feltre, Duke of, 462
"Femme" (Voltaire), 162n4
Fénelon, François de Salignac de la Mothe de, 365
Fernández de Navarette, Martín, 180n1
Fernando VI, King of Spain, 168
Fielding, Henry, 14, 46, 116, 188
Fitzgerald, Maurice, Knight of Kerry, 485
Fitzgibbon family, 458
Flexner, Eleanor, 138n32
Floridablanca, José Moñino, Count of, 169, 170, 171, 179
Fludd, Robert, 263, 264
Fonvizin, Denis I., 282
Fordyce, James, Reverend, 367
Formey, Ludwig, 304, 309, 310
Formey, Samuel, 375
Forner, Juan Pablo, 165–80
Fortunate Mistress, The (Defoe), 112
Fothergill, John, 307
Foucault, Michel, 261
"Four Zoas, The" (Blake), 61
Fragment on Government, A (Bentham), 101
Frank, Johann Peter, 304
Frank, Joseph, 265
Franklin, Benjamin, 355, 356, 367
Fronde, The, 424, 428

Fruits of Retirement (Mary Mollineaux), 367
Frye, Northrop, 59
Fuseli, Henry, 319, 325, 326, 330, 333

Galiani, Ferdinando, 282
Gardner's Dictionary, The (Philip Miller), 367
Garland, John, 461
Gascoigne, Bamber, 26n13
Gautier, Théophile, 185
Genette, Gérard, 217, 222
"Genève" (Jean d'Alembert), 375
George, Margaret, 138n32
George I, King of England, 141
George III, King of England, 342, 347, 466, 480
Gibbon, Edward, 296, 297
Gibbs, James, 340, 343, 344
Gil Blas (Lesage), 367
Gillray, James, 44, 51
Glanvill, Joseph, 254, 257, 275
Goddard, William, 363
Godolphin, Sidney, Earl of, 101
Godoy, Luis, Don, 180
Godoy, Manuel, Duke of Alcudia, 166, 172, 180
Godwin, William, 300, 477
Goethe, Johann Wolfgang von, 310
Goldoni, Carlo, 282
Gondibert (Davenant), 69
Goya y Lucientas, Francisco José de, 166, 185, 186, 187, 191, 198
Grammatica Linguae Anglicanae (Christopher Cooper), 236
Grattan, Henry, 475, 487–89
Grattan, Henry, Jr., 487, 494n23
Grattan Memoirs, 488
Grattan's Parliament, 475, 482, 487, 489
Gray, Thomas, 347
Grenville, George, 348
Grimes, Ronald L., 66n1
Grimm, Frédéric-Melchior, 382n14
Grounds for Grammar (John Bird), 233
Gruner, Christian Gottfried, 298
Gua de Malves, abbé, 374
Guardi, Francesco, 29–35, 38n20
Guardi, Gianantonio, 38n20
Guiborry, Achsah, 83n1
Gwynn, John, 339, 342, 345, 347

Hagstrum, Jean, 14
Hale, Matthew, Sir, 91
Halfpenny, William, 340
Hall, David, 355–69
Hamilton, Gavin, 358
Harlequin Doctor Faustus (Rich), 13
"Harlot's Progress, A" (Hogarth), 14
Harrington, James, 93, 94
Harris, Eileen, 347
Harris, Walter, 299, 300
Harrison, James, 396
Hartley, David, 43
Havránek, Bohuslav, 256
Hawkesworth, John, 396
Heberden, William, 308
Heideigger, Johann Jacob, 47
Hennessy, Richard, 458
Herbert, George, 78
Herm'aelogium, or an Essay at the Rationality of the Art of Speaking (Bassett Jones), 242
Hind and the Panther, The (Dryden), 70, 76
History of Ireland, Ancient and Modern (*abbé* MacGeoghegan), 463
History of Scotland (William Robertson), 368
Hobbes, Thomas, 43, 93, 267
Hoffman, Ernst Theodor Amadeus, 185
Hogarth, William, 11–27, 41–52, 303
Holbach, Paul Henri Thiry, baron d', 152
Holder, William, 239
Hooke, Nathaniel, 368
Hooke, Robert, 272
Horae Lyricae (Isaac Watts), 367
Houry, Charles-Maurice d', 372
Houry, Laurent d', 372
Hudibras (Butler), 69, 76, 81
Huerta, Vicente García de la, 168
Huguenots, The, 425, 426
Hume, David, 99, 100

"Industry and Idleness" (Hogarth), 15
Inquiry into the Origin of Moral Virtues, An (Mandeville), 142
Iriarte, Tomàs de, 168, 195
Isla, José Francisco de, 185, 188

Jackson, Allan, 26*n13*
Jacob, Giles, 367

Jacobites, 427
Jago, Richard, 344
Jakobson, Roman, 208
James II, King of England, 454, 479, 480
James III (James Francis Edward Stuart, "The Old Pretender"), 465, 479
Jaucourt, Louis de, 382*n14*
Jenner, Edward, 307
Jerusalem (Blake), 58, 61, 63, 64, 65
Johnson, Samuel, 308, 395, 396
Jones, Bassett, 242
Jones, Howard Mumford, 363, 366
Jones, Inigo, 340, 341
Jonson, Ben, 263, 270
Journal de Bouillon, Le, 416
Jovellanos, Gaspar Melchor de, 174, 175, 176, 179, 194, 200*n15*
Junius, Franciscus, 317
Jurin, James, 305
Juvenal, 121

Karamzin, Nikolay Mikhaylovich, 282
Kavanagh, Joseph, 458
Kayser, William, 186
Kearney, *abbé,* 459
Kelly family, 458
Kennedy, John, 462
Kent, William, 339
Kindelan, Vincent, General, 466
Kinds-mörderin, Die, (F. Schiller, H. L. Wagner), 304
Kirby, John Joshua, 348
Klingender, Francis, 44, 50, 51
Knight, Charles, 392
Konishi, Jin'ichi, 80
Kristeva, Julia, 203
Kynaston, Francis, Sir, 69

Lackington, George, 394, 395
Lackington, James, 387–98
Lacy, Count, 460
Lacy, Luis de, 466
Lacy family, 456
Lally, Count, 465
Lally-Tollendal, marquis de, 464
Langley, Batty, 340, 341, 342, 344
Laporte, Joseph de, 176
La Pucelle (Voltaire), 218
"Laughing Audience, The" (Hogarth), 14, 15

Laugier, Marc Antoine, *abbé*, 330
Le Breton, André-François, 371–80
Lecky, W. E. H., 453
Lefebvre, Georges, 428, 431, 440, 443
Leibniz, Gottfried Wilhelm von, 43
Lema, Francisco Pérez de, 170
Leoline and Sydanis (Francis Kynaston), 69
Lépicié, Nicolas Bernard, 327, 328
Lessing, Gotthold Ephraim, 319, 332
Letters from a Farmer in Pennsylvania to the Inhabitants of the British Colonies (John Dickinson), 363
Letters on the Spirit of Patriotism (Bolingbroke), 362
Lettre sur les aveugles (Diderot), 380
Lewis, Mark, 242, 243, 250*n9*
Licensing Act, 16
Lichtenberg, Georg C., 18
Llaguno y Amírola, Eugenio, Don, 170
Lobo, Gerardo, 187
Locke, John, 43, 367
Lodowyck, Francis, 250*n12*
"Loi salique" (Voltaire), 162*n4*
London and Westminster Improved (J. Gwynn), 338
London Stage, 1660–1800, The (G. W. Stone, Jr., ed.), 12, 20, 21
López, François, 177, 178
López, Pedro de Lerena, 178
Lorenzana, Francisco Antonio de, 177
Lorenzi, Francesco, 34, 36*n3*
Lorraine, Duke of, 457
Louis XIV, King of France, 425–27, 459
Louis XV, King of France, 438, 441, 458, 459
Louis XVI, King of France, 459
Louvoy, Varenne de, 438, 439
Lovell, James, 339
Luzán, Ignacio de, 174, 189
Lynch family, 458
Lyttleton, Charles, Dean, 348
Lyttleton, George, 349
Lyttleton, Richard, Sir, 346

MacCurtin, Hugh, 463
MacFlecknoe (Dryden), 69, 74, 76
MacGeoghegan, *abbé*, 463
Machiavelli, Niccolò, 95, 99
Mack, Maynard, 41

MacMahon, John, Doctor, 459
MacNamara, Henry, 466
Mallet, David, 11
Malthus, Thomas Robert, 304, 314*n38*
Mandeville, Bernard, 98, 141–50
Maratti, Carlo, 320–23
María Luisa, Consort to Carlos IV, 166, 179, 180
Marías, Julián, 170, 172
Maria Theresa, Queen of Hungary and Bohemia, 155
Marivaux, Pierre Carlet de, 295
Marizien, Nicolas, 403, 408, 410, 411, 415, 417
Marks, Mollyanne, 102*n19*
Marlborough, John Churchill, Duke of, 101
Martin, John, 50
Marvell, Andrew, 254, 265
Matteis, Paolo de, 334*n14*
Mayans, Gregorio, 197, 198, 201*n16*
Mazarin, Jules, Cardinal, 425
Meléndez Valdés, Juan, 168, 189
Melón, Juan Antonio, 165–68, 173, 176, 180
Mémoire pour les femmes (Voltaire), 162*n4*
Memoirs of a Cavalier (Defoe), 110
Menéndez Pelayo, Marcelino, 175
Menescardi, Giustino, 30, 33
Mengs, Antonio, 190, 191, 195
Mercier, Louis Sébastien, 281, 303, 304
Metamorphoses (Ovid), 80
Meyer, Jean, 448
Michael, Ian, 230
Mill, John Stuart, 154
Miller, C. William, 364
Miller, Philip, 367
Miller, Sanderson, 339, 344, 346, 348, 349
Mills, John, 373
Milton, John, 63, 68*n4*, 69, 71, 72, 73, 74, 82, 129, 137*n6*, 337
Milton (Blake), 61, 62, 63, 68*n5*
Mirabeau, Honoré Gabriel Victor Riqueti, comte de, 178
Miravel, José, 192
Modest Defence of Publick Stews: or, An Essay upon Whoring (Mandeville), 144, 145, 148, 149, 150

Moll Flanders (Defoe), 106, 110, 114, 116, 118
Mollineaux, Mary, 367
Monbron, Fougeret de, 282–90
Montagu, Mary Wortley, Lady, 127, 306
Montesquieu, Charles Louis de Secondat, baron de, 98, 152
Moore family, 458
Morals (Seneca), 367
Moratín, Leandro Fernández de, 165–80
Moreri, Luis, 192
Morvilliers, Nicolas Masson de, 169
Moseley, Humphrey, 253
Mouhy, Charles de Fieux, chevalier de, 282
Mukařovský, Jan, 255, 256, 259, 260, 268, 274
Müller, Günther, 77
Mumford, Lewis, 43
Murphy, Daniel, 458
Murphy, Gerard, 476
Murphy, Marie Louise, 458

Napoleon I, Emperor of France, 101
Néaulme, J., 374
Neave, Richard, 359
Neveu de Rameau, Le (Diderot), 379
Newdigate, Roger, Sir, 346, 349
New Testament, The, 366
Newton, Isaac, 43
Nicolson, Marjorie, 262
Nifo, Francisco Mariano, 176
Night Thoughts (Young), 367
Nolens Volens: or, You Shall Make Latin whether You Will or No . . . (Elisha Coles), 235
Nomenclatura Hibernica (Hervy Morres), 464
Nu-pieds, 426, 449n2

O'Brien family, 456
Observations on the Dropsy in the Brain (Robert Whytt), 307
O'Connell, Baron, 457
O'Connell, Daniel, 464, 466, 475–91
O'Connell, Daniel, Count, 461
O'Connell, Daniel Charles, Lieutenant-Colonel, 480–81
O'Connell, John, 480

O'Connell, Maurice ("Hunting-Cap"), 480, 482–86, 489
O'Connor, Bernardo, 460
O'Connor, Hugh, 462
O'Crouley, Alfonso, 460
O'Daly, Demetrio, 462
O'Daly, James, 462
O'Daly, Thomas, 462
O'Donnell family, 461
O'Donoju, General, 461, 466
O'Farrill, General, 466
O'Gara, Count, 458
O'Higgins, Ambrose, 461
Old Testament, The, 434
O'Moran, 466
O'Neale family, 458
O'Neill, Arturo, 462
O'Neill, Enrique, 462
O'Neill, Hugh, 479
O'Neill, Julio, 462
Ong, Walter J., 249n6
Oppé, A. P., 22
O'Quinn family, 458
Orbis Sensualium Pictus (Comenius), 240–41, 244
O'Reilly, Alexander, 462
O'Reilly, James, 462
O'Reilly family, 456
Orléans, Duke of, 462
O'Rourke family, 456
O'Scanlan, Timoteo, 460
O'Shea, Henry, 462
O'Sullivan, Jean-Baptiste, 460
O'Toole, Brian, Colonel, 466
Ovid, 74, 77, 81

Paine, James, 350
Paine, Thomas, 275
Palamon and Arcite (Dryden), 75, 77, 78
Palladio, Andrea, 340, 341
Palomino, Antonio, 195, 197
Terreros y Pando, P. Esteban, 193
Paradise Lost (Milton), 67, 68, 69, 71, 82, 83, 367
Paradise Regained (Milton), 69, 82
Paris Corporation of Booksellers and Printers, 373, 374, 377, 379
Parker, Edmund, 143
Paulson, Ronald, 12, 14, 15, 16, 18, 20, 25n8, n12, 47, 49, 53n14

Peel, Robert, Sir, 481–82
Pennsylvania Gazette, 356, 357, 362–66
Pensées philosophiques (Diderot), 379
Philip V, King of Spain, 168, 459
Phil-Porney (Defoe, *A Modest Defence . . .*), 145–48
Physiocrats, 287
Piazzetta, Giambattista, 29
Picornell, Juan Antonio, Don, 182*n24*
Pilgrim's Progress (Bunyan), 367
Piquer, Rita, 167, 176
Pitt, Thomas, 346
Pitt, William, 101
Platner, Johann Zacharias, 308
Plunkett, General, 458
Political Justice (William Godwin), 477
Pope, Alexander, 17, 50, 123, 137*n6,* 267, 367
Pott, Percival, 308
Poujade, Pierre, 441
Poussin, Nicolas, 324–27, 330, 331
Praz, Mario, 228*n45*
Preciado de la Vega, Francisco, 195
Prévost d'Exiles, Antoine François, *abbé,* 286
Protectorate, The English, 93
Protestant Ascendancy, The, 475, 489, 495*n27*
Prowse, Thomas, 339
Psalter, The, 366
Puglia, Santiago Felipe, 177, 182*n26*

Quain family, 458
Quesnay, François, 438, 441

Raggi, Giovanni, 30, 33, 34
"Rake's Progress, A" (Hogarth), 18, 20
Ramsay, Andrew, 368
Ramus, Petrus, 252*n22*
Redlach, vicar of (Bettinger), 414
Reforms of the Nobility (Colbert), 436
Rejón de Silva, Diego Antonio, 191, 193
Religious Courtship (Defoe), 107, 110, 111, 113, 114, 116
Rétif de la Bretonne, Nicolas Edmé, 285, 433
Reynolds, Henry, 263
Richardson, Jonathan, the Elder, 324, 325, 326
Richardson, Samuel, 116

Richelieu, Armand Jean du Plessis, duc de, Cardinal, 424, 425
Riffaterre, Michael, 203, 226*n1*
Riou, Stephen, 341
Robertson, William, 368
Robespierre, Maximilien François Marie Isidore de, 173
Robin, R., 433
Robinet, Olivier, 404, 411, 416
Robinson, Francis, 347
Robinson, Thomas, Sir, 345, 349
Robinson Crusoe (Defoe), 91, 118
Rose, E. J., 66*n6*
Rose, Henry, 250*n8*
Rosenstein, Rosen von, 306
Rousseau, Jean-Jacques, 152, 203–12, 287, 310, 435
Rowlandson, Thomas, 44, 51
Rubens, Peter Paul, 328, 329, 335*n39*
Russell, Robert, Reverend, 367
Rutledge, Walter, 458

Sade, Donatien Alphonse François, comte de, 159, 215–26
Saint-Jacob, Pierre de, 428, 438, 439, 440, 443, 444
Saint-Pierre, Jacques Henri Bernardin de, 281
Saint-Simon, Louis de Rouvroy, duc de, 425
Salazar y Castro, Luis, 187
Salmon, Thomas, 368
Salmon, W., Jr., 340
Sareil, Jean, 227*n19*
Satires of Juvenal and Persius (Dryden), 73
Saulx-Tavannes family, 440
Saussure, Ferdinand de, 261
Scammozzi, Vincenzo, 344
Scheherazade (*A Thousand and One Nights*), 222
Schiller, Friedrich, 304
Sebold, Russell, 174
Second Defence of the English People, The (Milton), 71
Sellius, Gottfried, 373
Sermons for Young Women (Reverend James Fordyce), 367
Seven Sermons (Reverend Robert Russell), 367

Sex Libri Plantarum (Cowley), 69
Shaftesbury, Ashley Cooper, Earl of, 43, 321–33, 334*n16*
Shaw, Samuel, 244, 245
Shenstone, William, 343, 344
Sheppard, Samuel, 254
Shippen, Edward, 360
Shrimpton, John, 339, 340
Sidney, Philip, Sir, 70, 253
Simmons, Merle, 183*n26*
Sloman, Judith, 75, 84*n4*
Smith, Adam, 99, 101
Sobrino, Francisco, 192
Society for the Reformation of Manners, The, 142
Solís, Antonio de, 189
Somerset, Edward, 247
Song for Saint Cecelia's Day (Dryden), 69, 72
Song of the Soul, The (Henry More), 69
Southern, Richard, 24*n3*, 26*n13*
"Southwark Fair, The," (Hogarth), 18, 19
Spectator, The, 337
Sprat, Thomas, 254, 257, 258, 270, 274
Stack, Edward, Colonel, 466
Staiger, Emil, 83
Steele, Richard, 98
Sterne, Lawrence, 49, 367
Steuart, James, Sir, 293
Stone, George Winchester, Jr., 12
Strahan, William, 355–69
Strickland, William, Sir, 345
"Strolling Actresses Dressing in a Barn" (Hogarth), 16
Summerson, John, Sir, 340
Sussman, Herbert L., 44
Süssmilch, Johann Peter, 294, 297
Swift, Jonathan, 137*n14,* 198*n2,* 469

Talleyrand, Charles Maurice de, 133
Tamerlane (Rowe), 18
Tate, Nahum, 14
Tavira, Antonio, Bishop, 176
Télémaque (Fénelon), 365
Temple, The (George Herbert), 78
Temple of the Muses, The, 392
Testelin, Henri, 318, 330
Thiboust, Claude-Louis, 372
Tiepolo, Domenico, 29, 30, 34, 38*n20*
Tiepolo, Giambattista, 29–35

Tiepolo, Lorenzo, 29, 30, 34
Timoni, Emanuel, 306
Tochter des Pfarrherrn von Taubenheim (G. A. Bürger), 304
Tocqueville, Alexis de, 418
Todorov, Tzvetan, 203, 226
Tomalin, Claire, 381*n32*
Tom Jones, The History of (Fielding), 302, 303
Tompion, Thomas, 42, 44
Tom Thumb (Johnson, R), 13
To My Honour'd Kinsman (Dryden), 75, 76, 80
Tone, Theobald Wolfe, 482
Tories, 92, 93
To the Dutchess of Ormond (Dryden), 80
Tradesman's Lawyer, 367
Tragedy of Tragedies, The (Fielding), 14
Traité de l'éducation corporelle des enfants en bas-âge (Desessartz), 301
Travels of Cyrus (Andrew Ramsay), 368
Tuathal-Teamar, or the Restoration of the Monarchy in Ireland (Lally-Tollendal), 464
Tucker, Josiah, 100
Turner, Edward, Sir, 346
Tuveson, E. R., 90
Twells, John, 249*n3*

Unitarians, 90
Urquhart, Thomas, 249*n7*
Utopias, 90

Vatelotte Sisters, 402
Vertue, George, 45
Vestibulum Technicum (Mark Lewis), 242
Victoria, Queen of England, 481
Villarroel, Diego de Torres, 176, 187, 194
Vindication of the Book . . . (Mandeville), 144
Virgil, 191
"Vision of Mirza, The" (Addison), 296
Vodička, Felix, 268, 269, 272
Voltaire, François Marie Arouet de, 152, 160, 162*n4,* 284, 288, 306, 310
Vovelle, Michel, 434

Wagner, Heinrich Leopold, 304
Wallis, John, 234, 236, 238, 239
Walpole, Horace, 341, 345, 347, 350

Walsh, *abbé*, 459
Walsh, Anthony, 458
Ward, Bernard, 460, 466
Ward, F. A. B., 42
Ward, Seth, 251*n15*
Wardle, Ralph M., 138*n32*
Wark, Robert, 12
Waters, George, 458
Watts, Isaac, 367
Wealth of Nations, The (Smith), 101
Webster, John, 251*n15*, 267
Wellington, Arthur Wellesley, Duke of, 459
Wesley, John, 390, 391
Wharton, Joseph, 347
Whytt, Robert, 307
Wichmann, Johann Ernst, 309
Wilkins, John, 235, 238, 239, 254, 272, 273
William III, King of England, 142
Willis, John, 237

Wiseman, Nicholas, Reverend, later Cardinal, 488
Wiseman family, 458
Wittkower, Rudolf, 338, 341
Wolcot, John, 396
Wollstonecraft, Mary, 121–36, 300
Wood, Gordon S., 100
Words Made Visible: or, Grammar and Rhetorick Accomodated to the Lives and Manners of Men (Samuel Shaw), 244–45
Woulfe family, 458
Wright, Joseph, 44
Wycherley, William, 42

Yates, Frances, 250*n11*
Yenn, John, 348
Young, Arthur, 439
Young, Edward, 367

Zavala, Iris, 182*n24*